Charles Olson and Frances Boldereff

CHARLES OLSON
AND
FRANCES BOLDEREFF

A Modern Correspondence

❧

Edited by

Ralph Maud and Sharon Thesen
and with an introduction by
Sharon Thesen

WESLEYAN UNIVERSITY PRESS

Published by University Press of New England / Hanover and London

Wesleyan University Press
Published by University Press of New England, Hanover, NH 03755
© 1999 by Wesleyan University Press
All rights reserved
Printed in the United States of America   5 4 3 2 1
CIP data appear at the end of the book

This publication is supported, in part, by The Charles Olson Fund, Archives & Special Collections, Thomas J. Dodd Research Center, University of Connecticut Libraries.

Contents

❧

Acknowledgments

The editors are grateful to Frances Boldereff Phipps and Thomas E. Phipps Jr., for their generous hospitality and permission to publish the letters of Frances Boldereff to Charles Olson. We gratefully acknowledge the assistance of Lucy Wilner in making available books and papers belonging to her mother, Frances Boldereff. Some clerical and financial support for the project came from Capilano College and Simon Fraser University. For providing photocopies of the letters we thank George Butterick, the late curator of the Olson Archive, and Rutherford Witthus, curator of Literary Collections, Archives and Special Collections, Dodd Research Center, University of Connecticut, Storrs. Charles Olson's previously unpublished works are copyrighted 1999 by the University of Connecticut Libraries.

R.M. and S.T.

Introduction

༺༻

SHARON THESEN

Most readers of American poetry will be familiar with Charles Olson; few, however, will have heard of Frances Boldereff, the woman with whom Olson corresponded during the years of his formative work as a poet—the late 1940s and early 1950s. Their correspondence reveals the depth, passion, and significance of Olson's relationship with Boldereff, so far unknown except for references in Tom Clark's biography of Olson, *The Allegory of a Poet's Life* (New York: W. W. Norton, 1991), and the publication of some of the early letters in *Sulfur* magazine.

A central figure in post–World War II American literature, Charles Olson helped shape the direction of midcentury thought toward a postmodernist concern with the business of language in the world and with the transformation of consciousness. Out of the depths of the historical past and the personal unconscious, through the work of cultural and political reckoning and with the empowerment of love, Olson believed that a renewal of the human spirit could be articulated. Olson's own articulations, his opus of poetry, prose, lectures, and letters, are valued in part for their range of feeling and subject matter. Many correspondents encouraged Olson on this path, but the one who seems to have set his compass was Frances Boldereff. Her correspondence with Olson provides fresh insights into many of Olson's important works, including *Maximus Poems*, "The Kingfishers," and his essay "Projective Verse."

These are also love letters poignantly revealing of Olson's emotional complexity. For any number of reasons, Olson chose never to acknowledge publicly his relationship with and dependence on Boldereff; but as readers of these letters will see, her significance to his development as a poet is undeniable.

Boldereff's letters to Olson and his to her are part of the Olson archive at the University of Connecticut. What follows is an overview of the development of the relationship between these two extraordinary people. But first it is necessary to give some introduction to Frances Boldereff.

Frances Motz Boldereff was a typographic designer by trade; by vocation, an independent scholar and exegete. After graduating in 1926 from the University of Michigan at Ann Arbor with an honors degree in philosophy and English, Boldereff worked at the New York Public Library as a children's librarian, at the same time taking advantage of its extensive collection of rare Irish books to study Irish literature and history. Boldereff's passion for James Joyce and her research into his sources began there. Frances was also a lover of all things Russian (she said they had a wildness that "pursed-mouth Americans" couldn't possibly understand). She studied the Russian language and later maintained a private imprimatur called The Russian Non-Classic Fiction Library. At age 25 she married Sergei Boldereff, a Russian-born lawyer many years her senior.

In 1929 she landed a typesetting job at the Jersey Printing business, handling everything from time, costs, and personnel needed to complete an order to layout and the mechanics of printing itself—photogravure, offset, letterpress, and web printing. From 1934 to 1939, she worked in the production department of *The New Yorker* but left New York City for Iowa with an idea of opening a small progressive school. The school never opened, but for the next four years, Boldereff produced *Parnassus* magazine at the State University of Iowa. After returning to New York and unsuccessfully attempting to make a decent living as a freelance book designer, in 1944 Boldereff became publications production manager at Pennsylvania State College and took her small daughter with her to live in Woodward, Pennsylvania.

A divorced working mother living in a refurbished grocery store was probably an uncommon sight in rural Pennsylvania in the mid-1940s. The village of Woodward, situated in the midst of Amish and Mennonite farming communities, had been founded by Boldereff's paternal forebears, German immigrants named Motz (pronounced "moats"). Despite her local pedigree, however, there were times when Frances Motz Boldereff's nonconformity excited suspicions that she was a Communist agent. Having been married to a Russian seemed proof enough. One of the more florid rumors was that she was transmitting information by radio to Russian spies from a red wagon she used to collect firewood.

One November afternoon in 1947, Frances Boldereff was standing "longingly in front of the Melville shelves" in the Pennsylvania State College library. What she found there was Charles Olson's newly published book on Melville's *Moby-Dick*, entitled *Call Me Ishmael*. Amazed and delighted by this book, Boldereff wrote an enthusiastic note to Olson at his publishers. In his reply, Olson informed her of the publication of "In Praise of the Fool" in *Harper's Bazaar*. Boldereff dashed off at once to find the magazine and immediately wrote to Olson to tell him that she was "so surprised to find a poem." She also said, charmingly, "I would wear the poem around my neck to make a speech for me" (19 March 1948). Later that month she wrote to ask Olson to send her "other things" he had been working on. And soon after that she sent him a design she had made, with the inscription: "for Olson, with whom I would like to get drunk" (20 June 1948).

When their correspondence began, Charles Olson was largely unknown as a poet. Wesleyan University, where he had received an M.A. degree; Harvard, where he almost had completed a Ph.D.; and the Guggenheim Foundation, which had granted him a fellowship (1939–1940), knew him as a Melville scholar. After the war years in government service in Washington, D.C., Olson concentrated all his thinking on Melville and America into that short but seminal book, *Call Me Ishmael*, published by Reynal and Hitchcock in 1947.

With this book, Olson launched, among other things, a writing career disposed toward allonyms, "Maximus" being its most developed figure. Frances Boldereff also admitted to "stumbling all over with new names" (20 January 1949). Born Frances Brubacker Motz in 1905, she used her married name, Boldereff, for most of the nearly twenty years (though the bulk of it was concentrated into the 1949–1950 period) of her correspondence with Olson, with brief reversions to Motz (often used as a nickname, as in "the Motz") and a short spell as Ward.

But it was in her own books that Boldereff most publicly addressed identity and authority, constantly reinventing, revising, and refusing attribution. Most of these names are attached to those of men with whom she was involved.[1] Two of her books on James Joyce, *Reading Finnegans Wake* (1959) and *Hermes to His Son Thoth* (1967), list Frances Boldereff as the author. Her first book, *A Primer of Morals for Medea* (1949), named no author, and *A Blakean Translation of Joyce's Circe* (1965) listed Anonymous as its author. *Verbi Voco Visual* (1981) is by Thomasine Rose; *Let Me Be Los* (1985), by Frances Phipps (after her marriage to Thomas Phipps Jr.). *Time as Joyce Tells It* has no publication date and its author is Reighard Motz, whose date of birth is listed as 1945; the date of birth listed for Frances Phipps in *Let Me Be Los* is 1924. This elasticity of identity, if not self-effacement (Boldereff declared to Olson she was "not a writer"), can be understood as integral to Boldereff's idiosyncratic writings—a statement about the writer's exact biographical and psychological relationship to the text at hand.

James Joyce was not the only subject of Boldereff's impassioned reading. As an independent researcher, Boldereff had for years been formulating "a critique of my time, for myself," a critique that drew on the poetry of William Blake, Arthur Rimbaud, and then (1947), with the appearance of *Call Me Ishmael*, Charles Olson. In her own work, Boldereff had been contending that modern women were in an impossible sexual and spiritual bind and that Americans of both sexes had "gone dead." When she came upon Olson's work, Boldereff had been thinking through an alternative, one she was extrapolating from her study of art forms and traditions that were "western" yet not part of the Hebrew-Greek-Roman vortex. James Joyce, as far as Boldereff was concerned, fought in his writing against the pull of this vortex. The new-

---

1. Frances had a twin brother, and I have often wondered if her need to be linked to men with whom she identified (and she sees these links as passionate, familial, and connected by "blood") was related to this fact. Olson sometimes referred to Frances as his "twin," his "sib" (as in both "sibling" and "sybil"). Frances early on called Olson her "closest of kin" (8 January 1949) and declared herself his "actual flesh sister" on 27 May 1950.

ness of James Joyce was his oldness, an archaic voice steeped in the tradition of the Irish bardic practitioner. And he wanted Ireland, as Frances wanted America, to "stop being a fool" (6 July 1968).

When she began her correspondence with Olson, Boldereff had just written, designed, and published her first feminist manifesto, *A Primer of Morals for Medea*. The text consists of plates of certain works by Michelangelo captioned with admonitions concerning the realities of female existence: The sequence "You are a slave, Medea"; "That which enslaves you was not created by man"; and "Nature enslaves you" comprises the first three in a set of thirty (4 March 1949). Women can achieve freedom and joy (and *must* achieve it), Boldereff states, but only through acknowledgment of nature's imperial demand and through the authority of the experience of joy. Frances admitted later, however, that in her relationship with Olson she had been "misled by joy," a self-judgment she seemed quietly to accept.

Ishmael and Medea: two investigations into the American unconscious—Olson's trope, the whalehunt; Boldereff's, the insulted feminine spirit. In her first letter to Olson, Boldereff described him as "one of the ones we so urgently need." Under her influence Olson would theorize poetic form as a force of nature, rejecting expressionism and idealizing an artless formality. Models for such a poetics lay in ancient dance-drama, shipbuilding, second-millennium B.C. mythology and iconography, the cosmologies of indigenous American peoples, and some instances of contemporary music, painting, architecture, and engineering. For her part, Boldereff gained impetus and support from Olson for her own studies, her writings on Joyce, Blake, and Rimbaud—and for her ideas about what was wrong with the American sensibility. In Olson, Boldereff believed she had found not only a kindred spirit but a lifeline, a persona, a twin. And to Olson, Frances became muse, sibling, and sybil.

Early in their correspondence (9 April 1949), Boldereff had responded to Olson's quotation of a line by the Greek philosopher Maximus of Tyre by using the words "Re Maximus" in the position of her usual salutation, "Charles," thus seeming to address him as "Maximus." Olson may or may not have filed this form of address. In any case, that so many of the Maximus poems are titled or numbered as "letters" perhaps owes its provenance to the context of the correspondence with Frances Boldereff and a working out of ideas and images toward the idea of Maximus, an eros-charge, and Maximus, America's interlocutor.[2] It was Frances Boldereff who requested of Olson, after she had read and responded enthusiastically to *Call Me Ishmael*, "tell me about America—tell me how it is for you" (26 June 1948).

2. Olson began his first "Maximus" poem in the course of a letter to Boldereff (17 May 1950). As was sometimes the case throughout the correspondence, Olson's sentences would shift into cadences, as they did in this letter, the cadenced lines then being repeated in the letter's postscript as the first stanzas of a poem entitled "I, Maximus." Thus is born an alias, an eye, a source.

Which is, more or less, what Olson proceeded to do, working toward his first long poem, "The Kingfishers" (1949). But Boldereff was no mere sounding board. She too was engaged in trying to express a new vision to stand against what both she and Olson felt had gone wrong. Boldereff saw Olson at times as America's savior. And between them there was much mutual congratulation for belonging among "the few" who were truly alive—or, as Boldereff had it in her first letter, the few "who could read." In Boldereff, Olson had an admiring yet merciless reader who never failed to express disappointment, even scorn, at what she thought was not worthy of him. For instance, a poem ("Lady Mimosa") written to praise Frances and to display compassion for the lot of womankind was energetically repudiated. This was the voltage that charged Olson's writing at that time. Olson came to depend on Boldereff's responses and challenges, and the scrupulous integrity of that work was also hers. What this correspondence demonstrates is that an intimacy of two strong minds helped to engender Maximus.

In her letter of 8 January 1949, Boldereff names as her "particular trio" Rimbaud, Joyce, and Blake. Boldereff unabashedly claimed kinship with the writers she loved; she believed they literally spoke *for* her, in her place, and that their work therefore "belonged" to her. "My sentences—his art," she said of Michelangelo. Of Rimbaud: "he . . . the poet, I the words" (30 August 1950). Of Olson: "my blood is his ink" (17 February 1950). This ventriloquism arose from Boldereff's insistence that she was not a writer and that it was her fate to "obey" the requirements of genius. Far from being unaware of the position this put her in, she tended to embrace it. "No woman has ever more completely given herself to man's ideas, or felt less antagonism towards him than I," she declared (9 April 1949). And to Olson, on 21 March 1950, she said, "any thought or word or thing I ever put in a letter is for you to use if you wish to so honor it," evidently in reply to his suggestion that she write a "reinterpretation" of the Bible. "I *am* not and am never going to be a writer so never again urge me," she told Olson. He did urge her, though. In July 1950 he suggested she write a book about women that he thought could reconfigure history by reclaiming the pre-Christian intelligence of the "Pistis-Sophia," the indwelling goddess of wisdom whom Olson referred to as "our SUMER GIRL" who would help realize "the absolute dynamiting of, the PATRIARCHY" (13 July 1950). Boldereff lost her initial enthusiasm, claiming that there was "nothing in Matriarchy" (25 July 1950). Olson quickly agreed.

"[A]s far as I can remember there are no books in the world which are concerned with the fate of a woman's soul, but only concerned with woman as a tool, whereby man destroys or saves his own soul," Boldereff wrote in her 1935 notebook essay on female experience (16 April 1949). At times she suffered precisely because of this lack of "books" or precedents. Repeatedly, Olson asked Boldereff to sacrifice her desire to have him physically present in

her life. He appealed on behalf of a higher good—his writing—not only for
what it was in itself but even more for what he knew Boldereff believed to be
its cultural and spiritual necessity. From the beginning, this necessity was
what Boldereff called "America." Olson's avowal of "this green republic now
renewed" (23 June 1948) became a code for the project Olson and Boldereff
had embarked on together in full agreement—sexually, emotionally, and intellectually. The altruistic hope for a greener republic was Boldereff's accepted
portion—when she was able to accept it. There were times, she said, that she felt
that she was "just some damned note-taker" for Olson (3 March 1950).

The question naturally arises why Olson never publicly acknowledged
Boldereff's existence, let alone her influence on his life and art, especially since
it was clear that their relationship was vitally important to both of them.

   One answer is that during the fevered years of the correspondence Olson
was living with his common-law wife, Constance Olson. Boldereff's letters,
along with the rest of Olson's mail were delivered in the morning while Connie was at work, but some packages were delivered in Connie's presence, pro-
voking crises, panics, and temporary solutions such as post office boxes. Another problem was that Frances was also married during the early years of the
correspondence, although she seems mostly to have lived apart from her husband, Duke Ward, whom she later told Olson she had married "to bring
Olson near" in an effort to make herself less sexually threatening, "like covering up the snake" (14 July 1950). Boldereff had outgrown, or exhausted, her
sexual interest in Olson by the time he attempted seriously to reconnect with
her after the death of his second wife, Betty, in 1964. In the end, we may read
what is said in the letters and take it at face value: Olson chose to maintain his
domestic circumstances with Constance and then with Betty, believing himself to have been in the best situation for his writing. Part of that situation was
the ongoing dialogue with Frances—who not only treasured her independence but was trying to live out her belief that a man "is free and therefore
better than she is, and it is this freedom which she worships." The most important thing to a woman in the man she loves, says Boldereff, "is exactly his
freedom from the need of her."[3]

   Despite her heroic claims for herself, Boldereff was not spared the indig-
nities and sufferings of her situation with Olson. One reads with astonishment Boldereff's expressions of disappointment that Constance Olson was
unable to "love" her, since she, Frances, "loved" Connie.

   Olson's vehement proposition in many of his letters to Boldereff that

   3. Boldereff had addressed the issue of female sexuality in a notebook essay she wrote in 1935, which
she subsequently mailed to Olson in March 1949. Olson typed a transcript and mailed the original back to
her. This notebook and the *Primer*, she told Olson, go with each other. The premise of both texts is that because of her subjection to nature, a woman suffers from "fundamental inequality." Yet even though a
woman (unlike a man, who is perpetually dissatisfied) is capable of creation, this same "belongingness"
with nature means that "she cannot be free." The original notebook is owned by Lucinda Boldereff Wilner.

"words are acts" and that all he could offer her were the images she invoked (18 April 1950) sometimes did and sometimes did not find a sympathetic ear. Whenever Boldereff threatened to withdraw from the relationship, Olson would counter with reasons she should continue. In addition to desiring her sexually, he desired her insight, acumen, scholarship, curiosity, and canny knowledge of the direction of the underground stream of his thought.

It was Boldereff who introduced Olson to the work of Samuel Kramer on the Sumerian sources of the Gilgamesh myth; Boldereff whose letters often provided words and images for Olson's poems; Boldereff who helped formulate the notion of what he came to call the postmodern, a way of reclaiming the vitality and "directness" (13 January 1950) of a worldview Boldereff called the "unHebraic" (14 March 1950); Boldereff who led Olson to Edith Porada's work on cylinder seals, to the notion of form as "obedience" to the laws of nature, to an impatience with the "whole inherited puff ball" (2 January 1950); Boldereff who posited the "core idea" of form as an activity that "can only be done by line, not by story" (26 December 1949); Boldereff's training as a book designer that inspired Olson to consider the role of typographical spacing as units of meaning, of "breath" as constituting meaning much more immediately than the rhetoric of debate.

It was Boldereff who encouraged Olson in the notion of a poem as a construct of energy and therefore Boldereff who stands behind the ideas in "Projective Verse." When Olson sent Boldereff a copy of "Projective Verse," Boldereff replied that "the essay is terrific. . . . The main points have points lying behind them which are all Motz points. . . . my critique of my time for myself" (13 February 1950). Olson admitted even to imitating Boldereff's speech patterns and gestures: "now four months since you saw me under that mask which almost drove you off . . . olson continues . . . to warm his face and body, to loosen the visored grip on his flesh, by way of the very gestures, the very bottomed speech, the beautiful *release* of MOTZ!" (17 March 1950).

Many of Boldereff's enthusiasms and bibliographical leads were exact. She sent not only suggestions but pamphlets, books, offprints, photographs, and posters to Olson. In a May 1949 letter, for example, she refers Olson to Franz Cumont's volume of plates of the frescoes found at the archaeological site Dura-Europos. She writes, referring to a plate depicting a priest in the midst of a ceremony, that "the look in the eyes the Christian world has not so far touched—the unworld brought to view." She continues, "the whole Byzantine world—Sumerian world and Dura-Europos absolutely drives me crazy. . . . I have a pamphlet on Gilgamesh I will also send you" (10 May 1949).

"What a terrific aristocrat you are," Boldereff wrote early in mid-January 1949. "Your poems are the purest, hardest most perfect diamonds that any poet has written since Villon—they have the same kind of dispelling surface and they are so hard one can use them for cutting any rock that gets in one's way." It was this "hardness" and dispelling surface that Boldereff was to praise, again and again, in Olson's work. What was most inimical to the progress of Olson's thought, Boldereff seemed to think, was his Catholicism. Once, when Olson mentioned reading Wallace Fowlie's "Clowns and Angels," she shot back: "something makes me furious at this great Catholic procession—the womb path—back to warmth, authority—no—" (25 January 1949). A large part of Boldereff's objection to Catholicism and to Judeo-Christianity in general was what she referred to as the "depraved sex morality" at the root not only of female (and by extension, male) oppression, but of bad art—including that of Shakespeare, whom Boldereff considered the inferior of both Rabelais and Blake.

Boldereff encouraged Olson to look to the Gothic ("northern") abstraction she saw as resonating more naturally with a pre-Christian aesthetic and worldview. This aesthetic Boldereff found described in the book by Stryzgowski, *Origin of Christian Church Art*, which became an important document for Olson as well, though Olson objected to Stryzgowski's "petulances." Styrzgowski's research traces Gothic religious architecture out of Middle and Near Eastern abstract patterning and Norse boatbuilding, bypassing (or rejecting) the Mediterranean habit of representation. Boldereff compares the "Southern—your 'slayers'—the boys who gave us representation" to the "Northern—the rhythm to speak direct—no copy of nature" (29 January 1950). Strygowski's research helped both Olson and Boldereff to articulate a worldview Olson was later to explore in essays such as "Human Universe." Central to his theory was the notion of a "stance toward reality" concomitant to the projective speech-act, "the habits of thought" being also "the habits of action."

Boldereff had already introduced the notion that it was necessary for "man . . . to have the humilitas to know the secrets objects share" (2 March 1950), as well as the idea that "humanism" was full of "errors" (26 July 1950). This stance was turned away from the habit of "clinging to the white thing," which Boldereff said Melville "by his suffering" had tried to "get us clear" of. In an earlier context Boldereff had written, "the turn, the arch—the beak are so exquisite because they represent really represent, as not even poems do—the God speech, which over and over is—keep it clean, direct, open, proud and detached. . . . no God business, just man enlarging the use of his senses and not substituting mental images for real objects" (10 January 1950). About Olson's poem "Upon a Moebus Strip," Boldereff states that "the lines do for me what has never been done heretofore by anything but nature direct—as Dostoevsky pointed out about Christ, the involved respect in making each man do his own job" (13 January 1950). And Christ, Boldereff was convinced after reading Stryzgowski, was "a man on a horse" (28 February 1950).

This edition of the correspondence ends on the Labor Day weekend of 1950, when Boldereff, after several weeks of Olson's making then reneging on plans to visit her, wrote to tell him she had met a young man on the subway. The young man "rode home" with her, and Frances made it clear to Olson that they intended to see one another again. Olson arrived at Frances's door within hours of receiving her letter. It was too late, however—Frances would never again be as responsive as she once was.

After a two-year hiatus the correspondence resumed, and apart from a long break between 1959 and 1964 (during Olson's marriage to Betty), letters continued to go back and forth between Brooklyn, Black Mountain College, Trenton, Gloucester, New York, Lawrenceville, and Buffalo. There were flurries of passion, times in which Olson would declare undying love or Boldereff would hint that a relationship might be resumed or, longing to renew their intimacy, Olson would venture a plan and Boldereff would politely refuse.

In August 1954, Boldereff sent Olson a copy of her "Credo in Unam," a series of feminist maxims interspersed with stanzas from her translation of Rimbaud's poem of the same name—her first and only "literary" work, as she described it, and also one that she believed could function as "a vast program for the education of young modern woman." "Credo in Unam," Frances wrote, "means to me, 'I believe in wholeness.'" Olson responded with the poem, "I Believe in You." In 1956, he sent *Maximus 11–22*, Frances responding that she thought he had published the poems too soon.

This filial and at times nostalgic exchange was violently interrupted, however, when in September 1964, a few months after Betty Olson's death, Boldereff informed Olson that she had met someone "more Maximus than yourself" and that they were buying a house together. At this, Olson blew up. Not only was he personally heartbroken, he was furious that Frances had appropriated the word "Maximus" to use against him. In his long, emphatic letter Olson criticized Boldereff for "devoting yourself to men of language" and for her habit of "use[ing] the cry of men's lives, and work, as though *theirs* were *yours*." Of course she did; she had said so on many occasions (as recently as 1953 she had written that it was "as though I am literally Rimbaud in female form—the identity of our natures in all its bad as well as good points is so close"), but Olson's "use" also protests the burden of vicariousness that Frances had charged him with from the beginning. This blast was followed by a calmer, more affectionate note a few days later, in which Olson declared once again both his love for Frances and his anger at her misappropriation of his persona, his struggles, his work. Even so, "your friend," he said, "is a lucky guy."[4]

Olson and Boldereff corresponded sporadically in the years between 1965 and 1968. Boldereff informed Olson of the progress of her books, the

---

4. Frances did not marry this "more Maximus" man. She is now married to Thomas E. Phipps Jr., a physicist, and lives in Urbana, Illinois.

enormous printing costs they entailed, her shaky finances, and her disappointment in the Masters of Library Services program she had enrolled in at Rutgers: "School is so boring and meaningless. Marshall McLuhan strikes me as being a most consummate knave. . . . He misinterprets everything, but is giving sly warnings to us all," she complains. Olson's letters are brief; he complains of health problems and domestic chaos and sends Frances poems and lends her money to help finance the publication of *Hermes to his Son Thoth*.

Their last few letters are brief, tender, solicitous—the letters of old people. Frances Boldereff read of Charles Olson's death in the newspaper. On 28 May 1969, a few months before he died, Olson had written to Boldereff what would be the final letter of the correspondence, an affectionate note whose last words are "p.s. I adore you."

A Note on the Text

❧❧❧

As to editorial procedures, we have taken it as our responsibility to correct silently the correspondence's misspellings and unintentional punctuation lapses. The paragraphing and spacing of the letters have been faithfully reproduced. Especially in Olson's letters, idiosyncrasies have been retained when they were judged to be deliberate. For example Olson sometimes opened a parenthesis without closing it, a mimicking of the way the active mind interrupts a flow of thought and does not always tie up loose ends. Occasionally, however, very occasionally, it was felt that adjustments in parentheses and syntax should be made when Olson had obviously not gone back over his writing to safeguard the reader. The editors could see no point in reproducing odd carelessnesses or making them more conspicuous with a "sic." But readers should be assured that they are not being deprived by these editorial procedures of anything that contributes to the meaning of these communications.

Charles Olson and Frances Boldereff

PART I

22 November 1947–26 May 1949

As she writes her letter of appreciation to the relatively unknown author of Call Me
Ishmael, *Frances Boldereff is a forty-two-year-old divorced professional woman
with a young daughter. The correspondence begins slowly, for she catches Olson on
one of his rare trips away from his Washington, D.C., home base. In July 1947 he
had gone across the continent with his wife, Connie, to give a lecture at the North-
west Writers' Conference, University of Washington, Seattle, and had stayed on
alone in California to pursue a research project on the gold rush. As he writes his be-
lated reply to Boldereff on 29 December 1947, he is two days past his thirty-seventh
birthday and has published six poems.*

◄ 1 ►

Woodward to New York c/o Reynal & Hitchcock[1]
22 November 1947 (postmark 23 November 1947)

[letterhead: Frances Boldereff BOOK DESIGN Woodward, Penna.]

November 22—

Dear Mr. Olson—
    Yesterday, standing longingly in front of the Melville shelves, I found your
Call me Ishmael. Every lover of Melville must feel deep gratitude towards
you—for the understanding
    for the clear and so intensely personal style of the language
    for the perfect taste in the acknowledgements
    for the hints about us, now
    and in general for betraying yourself as one of the ones we so urgently need.
A perfect book which I intend to see that all the people I know who can read
receive a copy of. (I'm not saying it's so many.)

In very great gratitude,
Frances Boldereff

1. Olson's study of Melville, *Call Me Ishmael*, was published in New York on 17 March 1947 by Reynal
& Hitchcock. The letter was forwarded first to the Olsons' home, 217 Randolph Place NE, Washington 2,
D.C., and then to the West Coast.

᪥ 2 ᪥

Sacramento to Woodward
29 December 1947 (postmark 30 December 1947)

Sacramento, California
December 29, 1947

My dear Frances Boldereff—
   It is generous of you.
   I am very curious to know what yr own work is—BOOK DESIGN.
   You'd have had my pleasure in your letter earlier—but for the forwarding involved. I am out here running out the lines of search which a new book—on archetype creatures of our past—pushes me along on. It's a wretched, thin stage of the method: journals, maps, letters.[2]
   You might find some interest in one of the tarot pieces in December Harper's Bazaar.[3]
   You see what you've done.

Thanks,
Charles Olson

Permanent address:
217 Randolph Place NE
Washington 2, D.C.

᪥ 3 ᪥

Woodward to Washington
[probably 4 January 1948]

   Whenever I ride on a train, which is fairly seldom these days and someone asks me "What do you do"—I know beforehand I am wasting my breath—"I am a typographic designer." Oh!
   And the "Oh" is always followed by the silence of a complete lack of reciprocity. Same as when I used to answer "A curator of art at the University of Iowa"—
   I know, Charles Olson—that you *know* what I do—only—how do I do it in Woodward—and live? Harry Sternberg, the etcher, said, "And Motz,

2. Olson was writing a book on American history tentatively titled "Red, White and Black," which was never finished. The publication that ultimately resulted from this research was Olson's introduction to *The Sutter-Marshall Lease*, a Book Club of California pamphlet (1948); see *Collected Prose*, pp. 295–96.
   3. The poem "In Praise of the Fool" appeared in *Harper's Bazaar*, December 1947, p. 194. (See *Collected Poems*, p. 57.)

what kind of plague do they have in Woodward, that you pay $10 rent?"—
Funny, but it's true.

Only free lance at this distance from NYC proved difficult so I commute 32
miles to State College where I have charge of the printing. No one but a New
Yorker would think that was close, but I love all the minutes I waste riding
back and forth—the only ones that are absolutely mine.

I shall most surely look up the Harper's.

I wrote to Norman Foerster at Chapel Hill—about you and I have been
making myself fairly obnoxious to a number of other people all of whom I could
knock over because they act as though someone tells them about a book like that
often—whereas I consider it in a group of maybe three in twenty-five years.

Once I said to Philip Guston[4] that people are always wanting to know details about artists, musicians—and God! all the details are so *given* in their
work—sometimes the spirit coming through so naked and uncovered that
one walks very quietly for fear of intruding.

In a way I believe I have never seen—you kept yourself out and yet are so *in*
your book.

I cannot pretend I do not know you.

And I am so damned grateful you've no idea.

I am surrounded in the daytime by the bourgeosie complete in the only
German word I know—ohne[5]

Frances Boldereff

※ 4 ※

State College, Pennsylvania, to Washington
19 March 1948 (postmark)

State College.

Mr Olson—

In a recent story of Vladimir Nabokov's in *Directions* he said he was at
times in a quiet way fairly fond of his inefficiency—that could be my statement too. But when it keeps me from finding something I really need—a *In
Praise of the Fool*—then I grow furious—imagine anyone getting so excited as
to read quite plainly "Harper's Bazaar" and then to tear off in the completely
wrong direction asking for a Harper's! I like your writing because I can not
read every word—I was so surprised to find a poem—some day you can say
what the word is—I liked *your* "is" too, in the letter.

I would wear the poem around my neck to make a speech for me—but it

4. American Abstract Impressionist painter of Russian émigré parents.
5. German adjective meaning "without."

wouldn't help because I don't know anyone here who could read it—Wonderful to have a speech made *for* you—especially when your heart is burning with fury.

In Woodward, a remote village once belonging to my grand pa-pa—they have several expressions I have not heard elsewhere—they always ask—"Shall I go with?" leaving the pronoun unsaid.

The poem "goes with" so terrifically—hard for me to believe you are living anywhere within the U.S. borders. All the elegant people are dead and the other kind alive or dead I wouldn't know. (I know you know some—I spoke only for myself.) Elegant carries its dictionary meaning. And you aren't and that's what I keep saying to myself can not be true.

Frances Boldereff

◄§ 5 §►

Washington to Woodward (postcard)
11 May 1948 (postmark 11 May 1948)

May 11

Dear Frances Boldereff:

Nonsense.[6] Truth is, was in California longer than expected. And, with return here, had spurt of work in all directions: prose, play, verse. (Psychotic!)

Still running, like herring in spring.

(Back on Dante yesterday myself: de vulgare eloquentia.[7] As of what is Am. vulgare: the present oppose to Whitman and son Pound. The oppose, of course, is continuum. But what?

You are right, and they are wrong, on "Fool" (which is on Black Sun Press, Paris, with 4 better ones, now, and is called THE GREEN MAN.[8] Better?)

Cordially,

Olson

P.S. I shall be curious to have your judgment on type of "y & x." Proofs came this week—& it looks to my untrained eye as perfect type: like revolutionary broadside.

6. This retort must refer to a comment in a missing letter from Boldereff, probably of early May 1948.

7. Olson wrote to Monroe Engel at Viking Publishers the same day requesting their *Portable Dante*: "What I was after was DE VULGARE ELOQUENTIA, in English, now that my Latin has dwindled."

8. "In Praise of the Fool" appeared with slight alteration as "The Green Man" in *Y&X* (Black Sun Press, 1948).

◆❧ 6 ❧◆

Woodward to Washington
[around 20 June 1948]

I have written something like thirty-five inscriptions[9] and cast them all aside—the final one is—

For Olson—with whom I should love to get drunk.
                                                        the Motz

When will it be possible to see any of the other things you have been working on?

◆❧ 7 ❧◆

Washington to Woodward (postcard)
23 June 1948 (postmark 25 June 1948)

                                                      June 23 xlviii

Thank you for the delightful design—and invitation. Fact is, the fishing is still good. I have finished one dance-play and am off into another,[10] and it very much looks like I'll tolerate this Afric place/

y & x has also wilted with the summer and I reckon it'll be fall before any more is done on it. It appears there's no press other than newspaper to take the 54" sheet the design involves, and that it must be spliced. Which may be just as well. For the middle hinge was a weak point in the design and Bayler, Union Square, sez, it's like a bone, better after broken.

                                        My greetings to you
                                        Olson

            A crowd in a forest of the city make
            attention turned as heads which hear demand
            the green republic now renewed.[11]

9. Presumably, the inscription was to go with the "design" referred to in Olson's next postcard, a design no longer extant.

10. Olson had finished "The Fiery Hunt" and was soon to finish "Troilus"—see *The Fiery Hunt and Other Plays.*

11. Olson wrote these lines in a New York art gallery in April 1948; see *A Nation of Nothing but Poetry*, p. 58.

≈ 8 ≈

Woodward to Washington
26 June 1948 (postmark)

Saturday—

Olson my friend—

I take off my hat—I have been wondering how a person like you could cope with an invitation like mine—never saw my face—never had a letter which was me—and yet a polite person—I decided several times to help you out—but an imp prevented me.

I finished several days ago, *Walden*—am so grateful I never read Thoreau before because this was exactly the right week of my life to read it—he tells how the conversations in the winter nights demanded room—a whole roomful of space between himself and his guest and as I read I thought—"Olson doesn't know this is why and I am not going to explain—that is it—he is a man with whom you can have a conversation which requires a whole big roomful of space between the speakers—I am not going to tell him that I am above the bourgeois explanation—that in a sense the invitation was not an invitation—it was a recognition—and I disdain to change its form because God has placed me in the female sex. In my house he can be free—and I will hear him"—and it seemed to me very proper in a deep sense that I had expected so much comprehension from you, of unknowns, and felt so sure because your book proves so amply how wide is your interior.

The month has been marvelous—a Hungarian friend left a few days ago after spending several weeks and they were a marvelous two weeks—next year I plan to go to Italy with her if I can save the money—she knows it so intimately and I not at all.

I have magnificent plans of work for the coming six months—I am so sure that the circle of our lives will bring us face to face some day (sounds like a Sunday school class but you know the important thing is that you are alive in my place and time).—I laugh as I write this—because God knows you could never have a guarantee that I am what I am—it is very good to me that you are full and flowing—I am wondering how can you say "the green republic now renewed"—oh! Olson please say if you mean that—I am sure the whole shell has to be sloughed off and of men alive I know maybe of four.

When you get time write me a letter—no matter how many months it is and tell me about America—tell me how it is for you—for I expect nothing and then your book comes along and upsets my calculations—and so I do not know what she has in her bosom—

Frances M.B.

❦ 9 ❧

Washington to Woodward[12]
14 November 1948

   for FB

      Olson

          November 14 '48

And something unique for her—1/2 of *y & x*, which I usurped from the printer. (The other 1/2 joins to the right of "the shields." The whole is now in NY to be spliced and boxed

❦ 10 ❧

State College to Washington[13]
23 November 1948 (postmark)

To—
   Charles Olson

   Is your green man the Green Man of Blake's *Jerusalem*?
                        FB

❦ 11 ❧

State College to Washington
1 December 1948 (postmark)
[letterhead: The Pennsylvania State College, Dept. of Public Information]

Olson—
   I believe it will please your soul as it has surely pleased mine that the en-

12. The following note was written on a typescript of the poem "Trinacria" (see *Collected Poems*, p. 45). Olson also enclosed the printed sheet which comprises half of the published *Y&X* (Black Sun Press, 1948) and includes the poems "The K" and "The Green Man" (see *Collected Poems*, pp. 14 and 57). "The shields" refers to one of the five drawings by Corrado Cagli that accompanied Olson's five poems in that volume. This material is in the possession of the recipient.

13. The envelope was wrongly addressed to "17 Randolph Place" and was returned by the post office on 29 November 1948. Boldereff enclosed the envelope and note in her next letter.

closed note was sent off *before* I had gotten home to Woodward and received your envelope. I will write at length when your book comes—in the meantime I wish you to know that in my opinion your poem *The K* is definitely the greatest poem which has been written in any country in this century (excluding the drama of Garcia Lorca, of course)—I am agin modern poetry in general on account it has all gone up into the head—

If I could write poetry your poem would have come out of me as an *exact* statement of my position as of December, 1948.

I am publishing a book of my own and will, and have been planning to, send you a copy as soon as I receive them—4 to 6 weeks.[14]

With love for you for what you do—

FB

⊰ 12 ⊱

Washington to Woodward (postcard)
2 December 1948 (postmark 3 December 1948)

dec 2

FB:

I am looking into JERUSALEM for the 1st time & find this wondrous line: The Male is a Furnace of beryll; the Female is a golden Loom.[15]

Thank You. "of great hardness, occurring in hexagonal prisms, commonly green or bluish green"

No. My Man comes out of tarot card numero zero by way of babylonians tzigane italian-magi (short for farmers) cagli[16] & olson. "Druids", I'm afraid WB wld call 'em! Big & black and covered with hair! Beautiful!

Yr book I'll lk fr'd to

O

O numero O

⊰ 13 ⊱

Washington to Woodward
22 December 1948 (postmark)

---

14. Boldereff's *A Primer of Morals for Medea* was privately printed in March 1949.

15. William Blake, *Jerusalem*, plate 5, l.34.

16. Corrado Cagli, the Italian artist, Olson's friend and collaborator on *Y&X*, taught Olson the procedures of the tarot.

Olson, his greetings[17]

SIENA 1948

Awkwardness, the grace
the absence of the suave

At once/ a boy walks out of his father's house
a field planted to angles & infinity goes off
/and above/ the boy enters the desert to meet
the Christ
          He meets the Christ

Lazarus is raised by a glance

Two men cast a net / a third stands on the shore.
The sea is grass, and the fish
as large as the boat, are
flowers. The boat is
as a child carves
wood. He on the shore is
the Christ
          The Christ is a fish

Nicholas hovers over the city walls

Wolves came in close in those days
or tore the farmer's child. But shall we say
miracles are not necessary now
to stop marauders?
Clare, Francis be
our protection
          at sea/ before the sultan/ death.

From the trough of the wave where only our heads show
(the ship a postcard sunk in hillocks thru which swim
a man wrenched round to point at him who like a haloed stump
raises his hand above us)
          we who are awkward ask

from THE WESTERN REVIEW 1949

17. This greeting is added in ink to a typed copy of the poem. The text is as published in *Western Review* 13 (winter 1949): 100 and in *Collected Poems*, pp. 78–79.

❦ 14 ❧

State College to Washington
8 January 1949 (postmark 8 January 1949)

January 8.

Olson—

What happened the first time I read *Trinacria*[18] I do not know—at any rate
I most surely was somewhere else—for on a second reading it suddenly
opened for me and I think it is magnificent. I can not see that you know less
than the bravest and best—my particular trio—Rimbaud, Joyce and Blake—
if you live with the verve, depth of understanding and courage you show in
your writing—America is a blessed land indeed. ("There is a sword"—how
right oh yes. It occurs to me that Blake has directly willed his to you.)

There are several things in the other poems I do not understand—and the
titles?—were you in Italy and Sicily recently—the only connection I could figure for the Christmas poem was Duccio—so masterfully a Christian painter—
I received it precisely Christmas morning and considered it a very fine present.

I am so glad to touch at this moment, via the U.S. mails, a human who has
nothing to do with my private life—I am trying to prepare a show of my
stuff—my adorable daughter suddenly came down with the measles the
morning after her birthday party at which she achieved the pride of six—you
would much approve—silken and white and black—I am trying, after being
very polite, detached and unhurried, to gouge my book—complete—by February first out of a printer who has not yet submitted a color proof!

Olson—in a way not meant to be intrusive and making no comment on
whomsoever's feet are parked on top of your best recordings—I consider you
alive on the earth today as my closest of kin.

                                        Frances was Motz
                                        had been Boldereff

                                                please use Motz—
                                                inside and out

❦ 15 ❧

State College to Washington
[mid-January 1949]

18. One of the five poems in *Y&X*. Boldereff received the book via the publisher of Black Sun Press,
Caresse Crosby, who had telegraphed Boldereff from Washington on 31 December 1948 to announce that
it was being sent special delivery.

Every night the faces of William Blake and James Joyce lean out of heaven and repeat to me the stupid sentence I wrote to you "If your life is lived"—the punishment is that I have to look at them. And I think—"What if Olson were to send that sentence back to me when he receives my book!"

It is not the first time I have wanted to bite my arm off at the shoulder—

At any rate I found a copy of Blake's plates for *Visions of the Daughters of Albion* and I simply could not believe my eyes—I had not read it before and when you receive a copy of my book you will see why I consider his poem my personal property.

In the morning I walk along the street saying over to myself the first two stanzas beginning "Upon a Moebus strip"[19]—

The music sings itself—and it reconciles me as only Michelangelo and Beethoven have—I keep saying "Thank you God"—

I think your poems are the purest, hardest most perfect diamonds that any poet has written since Villon—they have the same kind of dispelling surface and they are so hard one can use them for cutting any rock that gets in one's way.

"Itself a leopard"

Olson, I am so pleased it has taken me so long to be able to *read* your poems—if a man distils the conquest of years into such concentrated lines the reader definitely should be admitted only by his own purchased ticket.

I thank you and I hope when you receive in two weeks my book that you will feel the same.

The cover had a very slight error and has to be reprinted—the inside is not perfect but I am refraining from asking the printer to do it again as probably no one will feel as badly about it as I do.

Frances Boldereff

It is driving me crazy to wait.

❦ 16 ❦

State College to Washington
20 January 1949 (postmark)

Just came back from New York where I showed your poems to several discriminating persons—the one whose opinion I value most said, about *Trinacria*
"It's the most aristocratic thing I've ever seen."

The comment in my other note was not meant to imply that your writing was

---

19. The first line of one of the poems in Olson's *Y&X*, published later with "Moebus" changed to "Moebius" (*Collected Poems*, pp. 54–55). The poem includes the phrase "itself a leopard," quoted later in this letter.

not your life—as it so obviously most surely is—the comment was only in brief passing to remember Melville—whose years alone cause a burning fierce pain.

I am stumbling all over with new names—

F.B.

∗⧼ 17 ⧽∗

State College to Washington
25 January 1949 (postmark)

I gave your poems to a young Englishman who has just turned up here—he was very grateful—last night I read Wallace Fowlie *Clowns and Angels*—I do not know, but something makes me furious at this great Catholic procession—the womb path—back to warmth, authority—no—

Blake Underground,[20] so very.

I am shouting all of them—the Moebus Strip—each of them to myself—And I am saying—

"Where and how did we get this?"—oh Olson! What a terrific aristocrat you are.

Apropos of "So came to apogee and earned and wore himself as amulet."[21] the only one I know who can repeat those lines or at least is looking forward to being able to—said—

"What do I care if he is my brother? What good is that to me?"

And that is the fierce modern truth—to each man his own single honor, unmatched, attained and looked at coldly.

∗⧼ 18 ⧽∗

Woodward to Washington
[4 March 1949][22]

Dear Charles Olson—

All of us have hundreds of levels—you of all of us would know that best and so you would understand the swift passage from sorrow to levity.

Tonight alone in my house (I have just said goodbye to a guest whom I have not seen since college—nor heard from, never intimate and it was a per-

20. A phrase from "La Préface" in *Y&X*, *Collected Poems*, pp. 46–47.
21. From "The Moebus Strip" in *Y&X*.
22. In the Storrs file, this undated letter has an envelope addressed but not stamped. It was presumably enclosed in the larger envelope that also contained Boldereff's *A Primer of Morals for Medea*.

fect thing, the most effortless absolute harmony I have ever experienced) I am reading about Blake and very suddenly your poem starts to say itself aloud—again and then once more and oh! Olson—Meister Eckhart put in his appearance and said "Can't you see how perfect and beautiful a connect is now existent? Why would you press to something which can never be perfect?" And I understand and I want you to know there is no voice quiet enough for me to say how much I thank you.

For these brief hours I have been able as Boehme so long ago taught me "Desire God."

For some time past I have said "the only prayer possible is 'Hallelujah.'" Lovely Ninette said out of her French Catholicism—"But of course you pray—you are a prayer." And in my sense, so I am, tonight.

[Enclosed:]

A Primer of Morals for Medea[23]

(Russian Classic Non-Fiction Library)

To Michelangelo
*who has seen deeper and has
stated with a more rigorous candor
than any artist who has lived,
woman's knowledge
of life*

1 *The greatest good which can be done to any being, greater than any end to which it can be created, is to make it free.*
                                                   The Journals of Soren Kierkegaard. 616.

2 You are a slave, Medea.

3 That which enslaves you was not created by man.

4 Nature enslaves you.

5 Nature is therefore your enemy.

6 Man discovered this for himself thousands of years ago, but you, Medea, are only discovering it now.

7 This places upon you a burden.

8 You, Medea, can not ignore nature—you will get your nose broken if you try.

23. This privately printed volume was sent to Olson on publication, 4 March 1949. The numbered passages correspond to photographic plates of Michelangelo's sculptures.

9   Do you remember the fable about the water wearing away the stone?

10   The water is a new kind of vision.

11   The vision is not a man vision: it is not a Blake vision—it is a vehement desire without form.

12   You can not escape nature, therefore all known methods of combat are ruled out as useless. You can do as she asks. During the years when you are paying her hundred-share your vision must be so vehement as to burn without fuel—you will have no fuel to give. All of your fuel will be thrust into a Rimbaudian hell where with the greatest will you will seek to destroy yourself.

13   During these years the net of your vision will drag illness, despair, loss of identity, revilement, torture.

14   You will not sleep, nor let sleep.

15   No man will put out his hand to you because the form of what you are doing will be your own and invisible.

16   All traps which nature has placed at your disposal for the enslavement of man you will come to despise as the enemies of your being.

17   You can not exist if you plot.

18   All plotting is of the animal world and is to be discarded.

19   When the demons depart, having learned that your self-torture is greater than any of their devising, you will be left standing with either foot straddled across a bottomless pit—you will have warning that the line of its curve may change at any moment—demanding your readiness to jump, to change the foothold at any second.

20   And then one day it will be whispered to you—"Now you are free."

21   That will not be the end, Medea. That will be the beginning.

22   Then Medea you must journey into the world—a mother—some Time in fact, always in deed.

23   You will then, Medea, have become a mother who spurns security for herself and for her offspring. You will have learned, Medea, that security is a mirage, that man rightfully has despised you because you have never once up to now forsaken it.

24   You will give to each who needs—without regard to his beauty, power, or achievement—whomsoever God places before you—devotion—generosity—warmth—passion and above all—joyicity.

25 You will give, as you have always given, but with this difference—not to possess, but to let go free.

26 Then thou wilt perceive, Medea, that God has placed over thy shoulders a most able cloak.

27 And while that cloak will cover thee, thou wilt come to understand that thy relation to the moon is an allegory of thy indirect relation to all things. For thee will everything take place but thy name will be everywhere unknown except to him alone in whose heart it burns. The direct tasks belong to a man. Thine are the indirect.

28 For what reason shalt thou thus belabor thy soul? In steadfast, bitter aridity?

29 That thou mayst walk the earth an adult.

30 *And in like manner, many things have heretofore been despised, because they have not been put to the proper use.*

Loosely quoted from New Essays
Concerning Human Understanding
Leibnitz

Copyright 1949 by
Frances Ward

❧ 19 ☙

Woodward to Washington
[26 March 1949]

Saturday

Olson my friend—

Let me say first you manage always to present yourself on the right day— today is my birthday and when I received your letter[24] this morning and opened it and saw it was a letter I could not believe my eyes—something I was very far from ever expecting to receive. I consider your letter quite literally the only birthday present I have ever received in my life.—

In general I agree about everything.

So happens there is a notebook written 14 years ago—I have been saving it

---

24. Olson's letter in response to *A Primer of Morals for Medea* is missing. We learn from a subsequent letter that it was removed by Duke Ward, whose name Frances had taken at the time (the book is copyrighted by "Frances Ward").

until after my death because it has never seemed appropriate to do anything about publishing it while I was walking around. The thing came out all at one sitting, fast as I could write and scalding hot. I remember I wanted to be sure to do it before I forgot—before the pain cooled down. I know it has several sentences in it which are necessary and right. I will send it to you. I will ask you not to make any detailed comment because it has nothing to do with writing or books or achievement. It was something I was born to do and I did it. There are thousands of young woman errors in it—so very many I blush inside—but the point I am sure you will feel is—it has the other thing the thing no man anywhere has stated in words—the young woman terror—and I did not say fear. And a program—harsh as you could wish even though it is clothed in Moses language—the result of passionate Bible reading and doing—anyway Olson—after you have seen it we can talk. In the notebook it states definitely that I am not the one to *write* it—I am the one to live it—it states that there is a man—a writer—who will come after—you can judge yourself if it is you—certainly if it is not you, it is no one else. I have been waiting for this man, into whose hands to place it.

I resent that I sound so damned biblical—but it is the result of a chosen thing in adolescence, which permanently affected my whole speech every day. The reason the primer has the form it has is because I am not a writer and could never write a book and someone who loved me said I should do something—so I did the primer. The notebook is what should have gone with—to you.

The whole thing is very feminine—I mean all the reasons—I love Michelangelo and I love to have those beautiful things somewhere where I can see them and also I felt that it was good to make public my love. I looked at proofs in black and three shades of brown and chose the pink brown for a very good reason—I also love 14 and 15 and they looked so beautiful that way—then the one across from the dedication which I also am very devoted to has a Latin clarity of simple statement printed in the light color—as soon as you make it dark, it becomes ominous and brooding which I do not believe Michelangelo intended.

You said exactly the right thing about 14—I was searching everywhere and when I saw the thing I stole it—not a print, a page from an old edition of Symonds *Life of MB*.[25]

I also very much love 15.

The first one and the last one are the same woman—from two angles—

I happen also to love (in the slang sense) I believe it is 4 (I have no copy here) the woman staring her head off at herself in the hand mirror with the brief statement.

And purely as a woman having nothing to do with a book the figure of the pregnant woman is the best summary of that whole deal in existence and the

25. John A. Symonds, *Life of Michelangelo*.

one with the head on her lap is the best summary of that particular little moment when you give up the ghost. I am just very grateful to him—like I said.

And the word "joyicity" Olson I put in on purpose for this reason—I had mentioned Blake and Rimbaud and I did not want to leave Joyce out so I put his word—anyway I thought it was his word—from the marvelous section in *Finnegans Wake* where the Gracehopper is entertaining Vespetilla and Flori and the other lovely ladies—"happy in his joyicity"

It was merely a passing salute of deep affection to a man whose arrogance I have always thought so good.

And as in the case of Michelangelo I wanted to state my love in public.

Like wonderful old Stendhal who had carved on his gravestone—"He loved Cimarosa, Mozart and Shakespeare."

I have been planning to start a publishing company for some time of some of the marvelous Byzantine studies and some of the very Russian philosophic religious questions not as yet translated from the Russian[26] and I thought it was silly to have *two* publishing companies for a very great total of at a maximum 5 books—and besides as long as I was being anonymous—what the hell—

Also I hoped to advertise the thing in *The New Yorker* and to intrigue old Vladimir Nabokov into sending for one—I used to work there and he writes some things for them now—not that it matters. If you think the thing doesn't say enough to advertise—just tell me—about money or any of the other allurements I care as little as you guess.

I enclose a picture of myself which I believe you will like it as much as I do—it says something the book doesn't say—it is my old man, who is now somewhere else off this planet, whom needless to say, I adored. Return—please.

It will take several weeks to dig up the notebook—I will send registered—if it is yours—you may keep it.

Frances Motz

◄≼ 20 ≽►

State College to Washington
[27 March 1949]

You will see how nutty I am because I was in bed when it occurred to me after re-reading your letter[27] that you thought the notes are comments on the pic-

---

26. Olson presumably had been curious as to why *A Primer of Morals for Medea* had been published under the imprint of "Russian Classic Non-Fiction Library."

27. Olson's missing letter in response to *A Primer of Morals for Medea*.

tures—so I have come up to my office to tell you how the thing came about.

In August 1948 I wrote the sentences exactly as they are—wording, order and the numbers attached. A very literal autobiography—may be the shortest on record.

I used to be a curator of art—I knew in a fairly accurate way that Michelangelo was the boy that for my money knew about women—he keeps saying over and over again the thing which you will find in my notebook. I own a few of the prints in the book. I have absolutely no money and damned little free time—so I did not have all or even a fraction of Michelangelo at my disposal. I had precisely what I could take from the books in the possession of the College Library. I had copies made of all the ones that said anything about women.

When I made up page proofs for the book I came up to my office at night to work alone—here I sat and watched my sentences—his art. It was one of the most intensely exciting nights I have ever spent. Perhaps you can find in your tarot pack the answer as to why they fit so uncannily. There is special reason behind each choice—Some day I will tell you what each one means to me. It took 2 weeks to decide to put the picture and wording of No. 2 together. Number 14 I was up a tree about. Nothing would do. So one day I got desperate I went to the office of a man who has a lot of stuff on Michelangelo—he fortunately was in Mexico—I pulled my prestige to be allowed to enter alone and I looked through that pile of stuff until that magnificent answer fell into my hands. I promptly and quietly stole it for the meantime. It took courage for me to print it—it was very hard to send it to the printer—but I realized that the world is dumb—if something is labeled "Art" you would never catch them getting it confused with life.

You are probably the only human being who will see it who will understand how terrific the solution is—both on Mike's part and on mine.

There are places where the thing is so naked I deliberately chose a picture to lead astray.

But Olson—perhaps as I am towards you you are towards me—silent on things you have said which are too terrific—it took me twenty-five years to learn to do the one marked No. 25 which you passed in silence.

If what the dumb bastard wants to do is to get himself crucified then your part is to throw in everything you've got—and when the dead body lies in your lap—not to shudder—not to cry—not to turn down the lip—but to raise the hand in silent question—"Whose obedience has cost him the most—mine to endure his fate or his to endure his fate?" Anyhow—at the end of 25 years I bow my head in acquiescence—you do the one that gets handed to you.

I love you Olson as you goddamned well already know.

◆§ 21 §◆

Washington to Woodward
29 March 1949 (postmark)

Immediately, this, as you ask[28]—with my delight, & thanks. You are quite as I might have imagined you to be.

   And yr father, the kind of head almost gone away in this dirty time.

                                                           Yrs, Olson

Maximus of Tyre *Dissertations*

(If you happen to look on this side, & are curious of the above, the reference is 24(18), particularly

[quotation in Greek])[29]

◆§ 22 §◆

Washington to Woodward (postcard)
30 March 1949 (postmark)

A propos joy-i-city (the personal meaning of which you convince me of, which in no way diminishes the nix I put on it in the public print) cf. the current Herper's Boozoomzar (April, in other words, spring, & only & exclusively spring by permission of MODESS)

                                        p. 129
                                        2nd column
                                        28th line fr top
                                        to end of para[30]

or Bra-zar
or Bubsie-zar
or Boob-zar

                              yrs for shame
                              or any equally brazen offence.
                              ♀

---

28. Olson presumably is returning the photograph sent by Boldereff in her letter of 26 March 1949.

29. Olson wrote a line in Greek from the bilingual Loeb Classical Library *Lyra Graeca*, ed. J. M. Edmonds (1922) vol. 1, p. 154, which gives the English translation: "both declaring that their beloved were many in number and that they were captivated by all beautiful persons."

30. Desmond Harmsworth "James Joyce: A Sketch" *Harper's Bazaar* (April 1949), p. 129. The two sentences Olson directs attention to are "He seemed to tap a private source of Panic laughter. It was a separate art of Joyce's, and it did not deserve to perish."

⊰ 23 ⊱

State College to Washington
[early April 1949]

I am not at all the type given to vulgar statements but page 150 of the same issue—re the first half of the last line of part 2 of your poem[31]—always arouses in me the desire to lift one out, and with the serious face of a Saks Fifth Avenue shopper—courteously inquire, "And what would be the price per pound?"

I am sure Joyce could not laugh at one of his own, better than I—over your postcard—after the shock.
And again I thank you
    reread Melville business[32] two nights ago—that is one magnificent statement—
    the definition of a great portraitist is 1\2 sitter 1\2 artist—no one knowing which half is where—
Thus you.

⊰ 24 ⊱

Woodward to Washington
[early April 1949]

Your poem[33] is so open, so naked, so full of the exquisite and modest tenderness of a man who is forced to repeat the request for everything, that it makes me terribly shy. I feel as though an aristocrat has entered the door and laid aside his armor there—to be (away from butlers and servant girls) quickly transferred to his interior, where it becomes fire. See *Trinacria*.

There is a way in which I am extremely pleased that it should make a public appearance among the servant girls—those few readers who shall see it will have gratitude and the others will not even know to stare at you—on account you leave your robes at home.

(And worse than servant girls I take it we both dislike professors)
I take "the good tree" to mean the "tree of the knowledge of good and evil" condemned by Blake—if other, and more—and you care to someday enlighten me—o.k.

                                                                Frances

31. Olson's poem is "In the Hills South of Capernaum, Port," in *Harper's Bazaar*, April 1949, p. 193; the last line of part 2 begins "The life is more than meat." See *Collected Poems*, p. 61.
32. Presumably *Call Me Ishmael*.
33. Again, "In the Hills South of Capernaum, Port," from which the phrase "the good tree" is quoted below.

⊷ 25 ⊷

State College to Washington
9 April 1949 (postmark)

Re Maximus:[34]

After you have seen the notebook—going forward to you next week—you will understand about the photo. It represents to me the proof of the achievement of laughter, which is innocence—the prize.

Along with Christopher Morley, I have always considered Whitman's *Preface to the 1855 Edition* as the most beautiful essay in the English language. When Whitman's poet suddenly stretches across the whole new wide horizon—I could not help giving a female squeal of joy—the throated midnight statement of love—but I never have once intruded upon your privacy which to all aristocrats comes as the No. 1 prerogative.

I hate careful—I hate the golden mean—I love the way Pantagruel looked at Panurge and said "I will love you all my life and we will never part." It is my connect with the Russians—the wild ones—whose knowledge you include.

The very von Motz-Motz

⊷ 26 ⊷

Woodward to Washington
[about 16 April 1949]

May 1936[35]

If only Otto Weininger had not written that sentence, "If only one woman could be shown to have existed in relationship to the moral idea, then my entire theory would be blown to bits" *(Sex and Character)*

Let it be said at the beginning, that no woman has ever more completely given herself to man's ideas, or felt less antagonism towards him than I (so little antagonism that when I read in a German book that this feeling was universal, except in cases where a woman was born a courtesan type, I decided that I must be a courtesan type, and then, on different days, when I objected in my

34. Boldereff is responding to the Greek quotation from Maximus of Tyre in Olson's postcard of 29 March 1949.

35. When Olson received her May 1936 notebook from Boldereff he typed these extracts for his own use before returning it. In parentheses are his own added comments, sometimes in the form of question marks or exclamation marks. The original notebook has not been available.

soul to this explanation, I decided that I felt an antagonism) and for this reason I have for many, many years suffered under the conviction that women
possessed no souls, that I, myself, had none and in support of this belief, there
is certainly abundance of evidence. How embarrassed I felt with myself when
I happened to read in the notes in *Desert Islands* the story from the Bible of
Ammon and Tamar. Much as I cherish the beauty of the prose, the simplicity
and life justice of the remainder, what it reveals of a father's heart, no one can
erase the memory of. "And I, whither shall I cause my shame to go?" The fact
that even in the Bible the woman's shame is not important enough to dwell
on, but only so, causes me to blush inwardly, for it is so apparent that as to the
fate of her soul, no one is concerned, but only as to how she will be the instrument of her brothers' evil the one in doing, the other in atoneing. And as far as
I can remember there are no books in the world which are concerned with the
fate of a woman's soul, but only concerned with woman as a tool, whereby
man destroys or saves his own soul. Let no one suppose that I object to this on
foolish grounds of "It ought to have been otherwise"—the *fact* that it has not
been otherwise burns a deep hole in me, that is all.

And so, I say, when I had read Weininger and followed closely all he had to
say and knew in my soul it was far more true than untrue and came to his outline of the distinction between talent and genius and then to his question,
taken by me seriously, "Is woman, then, a plant, or an animal or a human
being?" I realized, all of a sudden, that it is foolish and wrong for me to deny
to myself that I possess a soul—the facts are all definitely shouting that I do
possess one and that perhaps I was born on this earth to *be* a soul and to show
how it is possible.

..... (on sense of vocation).... and expressing it.... it has actually occurred
that a woman has lived on this earth who has taken upon her own soul all the
burden of being a woman, all the shame, all the sorrow, all the inward dis-
grace, all the longing, all the lack of freedom and has felt guilty before life of
the sins, the pettiness, of all women. (HERE IS THE CHRIST COMPLEX,
almost wholly stated)

.... (she hopes she may, in the far-off ages, become the heritage of each
woman, hope it is a secret plan of God's)

.... what I struggled for with almost super-human courage and it is another
of God's miracles that a body could be sustained on this earth in comparative
health which has fed on nothing but intense agony for so many important
years. But remember Dostoevsky, who was a greater miracle, and be silent.
(!!!

Can I speak in this place of how flowingly, how reaching to the sides to touch, stream-like, I love every human being on this earth? Even my mother, whom I have disliked more intensely than any other person I have met? Who stands to me for the qualities in life which I abjure.

Let me go back and begin now, where I first remember. I remember my father, seated beside my mother in the upper sitting room handing to me the wet diaper of my tiny sister and asking me to carry it to the bathroom; the intense dislike with which I touched it and how carefully I held the very smallest edge I possibly could in order to convey it, the satisfaction with which I laid it down and ran away. Just now it occurs to me that this may have been one of the causes why I always disliked my sister, until I had reached the age of 16. It also is clear to me now why my father hounded me so—to be rid of this quality of fastidiousness, which was one of my chief inheritances.

. . . . loneliness . . . . deep opposition of father

To illustrate, and I would never put this on paper if I did not know that I will be out of this life before these words are read, when I was perhaps ten, I went one Sunday morning into his room without rapping, to reach from a lower dresser something I needed for Sunday School and he jumped from his bed as though touched by bolt of lightning and rushed across the room to strike at me and missed my head by perhaps the smallest part of an inch and left in a plaster wall so deep an indentation that plaster fell down inside (it was covered by wallpaper) and left a deep place for many months, until the room was repapered. I hurried out, said nothing—mother found it out, of course, but in my breast I will always remember the silence which struck in on me at that moment, the open-eyed, quiet child knowledge that life was composed of dark things

. . . . then, or later . . . . the deep antagonism lying between a man and a woman . . . At least I learned one good lesson, which none of the dead intellectuals know, and that is that passion is in no sense a thing to be played with, it strikes out of anywhere and all you can do is to scatter or succumb, you can not say it isn't so.

At what age, then, did I begin to promise myself that I would never tease a man, that I would never play with his feelings, that I would never by word or a look imply something which I did not mean and that if I did give, by accident, such a word or a look that I would live up to it honorably and give as much as I promised

. . . . the years had so quick an eye for beauty and when I also embraced the

Christian ideal wholly . . . . and came to know the soul of Russia through her books and through the faces of the children in my Soho library ((???))

    Outwardly and inwardly I was a clean human being . . . . and would not allow my little finger to betray my weakness and prayed ardent prayers to God that I might regard my body as a temple . . . . sadness, but i did not *feel* innocent, and the feeling of guilt mounted and mounted in me—not then, but later, and became the undertone of my whole life.

> (obviously, the guilt, of masturbation, or repression, and so, when, as it goes on, it comes out, the quote, fr Zossima, "We are all guilty of one another's sins and each must bear on his own soul the guilt of all men," and she yeas, and says, I knew it at 18, only then I had no proof I knew it.

the young man who laughed, when she said, I am as guilty as you, and she goes on, "I know what it was, it was the ardent, ardent wish that I had committed sins, more than he, and that in the knowledge of my sins and the love of my heart, I could say, in his sense, truly, "I am as guilty as you are." Every man longs to be forgiven—but he can not believe that an innocent human being can be guilty or can forgive. Christ did it, but he knew the sins, because He is God. And this is the reason why I praise God that he gave me *the burden of the sin of my body* (!) to bear for so long a time—because, now, when I say to my husband "You are not guilty", quietly, quietly in his soul he feels joy—for I, who have known sin consider his sin to have been of no moment(!). I never wish to imply that I can forgive in God's sense, only that for a fellow human being to forgive in the human sense, being very conscious of the full meaning of the crime, is very comforting to the human soul.

    (2p passage on May, how beautiful life is, on Christ and his doubting his mission, and how divine that makes him to her, and Goethe, that nature has proceeded, not by wild eruptions but by slow, or maybe quick, but quite quiet, change . . .

I am not sure that what was in Him is not in me—I feel so entirely close to what He was that it seems as though no time has elapsed, and though I shall never die for man, nor be divine, I feel that my life is for man and is a gift, smaller and gentler, but made of a little piece of what made Him. . . . . The quality of love felt towards man is of like kind.

. . . . My soul was given back to me by a miracle

. . . From whence came the sudden knowledge that each man desired to save his soul—that the pain of his body was nothing to him? There were twenty odd years I did not know this, and one day, sitting in my nice green chair, I looked at the title page of a book in which was written a quotation from Byron, and I knew it. And since then it has been the purpose of my life to help each human being on this earth *to gain the possession of his own soul and to gain it in joy.*

I have not acted outwardly as though this were my purpose—outwardly I have worried about my appearance and about jobs and about parties I was giving and about how to cover up the enormous
(!)   difference between myself and the people with whom I was; I have said mean things, not because I felt them but to hide from another person the embarrassing sight of how mean his meanness was; I have
(!)   pretended to a hundred weaknesses I do not possess, to take away my feeling of strangeness between me and whatever woman I was with; I have talked empty platitudes, to cover my silence and I have feigned helpessness, for another to understand that I needed him. I have done worse, I have acted with love, real love, towards a human being whom I hated and desired to see dead because he caused me such terrible suffering, praying to God to forgive me for showing love towards one whom I did not love and underneath both the love and the hate, which were of actual life and were in themselves the process of growing, as plants stick out new leaves, I know that the love was the real part, because I felt the pain of my husband's soul, but in order to protect myself, in order to be able to live and to endure the suffering of the terrible accusations he put on me and that I deserved, but for which I had already paid so deep a penalty, my body and heart, me, in this life, not my eternal self, put out all over me a thick covering of intense hatred and in that hatred I lived until strength for top love, as well as bottom love, came to me. This hatred was not only to protect my inner life from the terrible sorrow of absolutely not being believed, but also was to protect me from the terrible misery of seeing how deep was his suffering, how much greater to endure than mine, for he had the earthly and also soul shame of having married a woman who seemed for that time to have been without shame and without honour, and also the terrible frightening necessity to depend on her for aid, to be unable to leave her because of love and to have no chance to work in life in a fine way which would be great enough to cause forgetfulness, or great enough to prove his worth or even great enough to prove his love and to have almost no hope. Later there was

no hope at all, but in the beginning, there *was* hope of fine work ahead, otherwise he would not have lived at all. As it was, his terrible hallucinations are as great a suffering as Ivan had in BK which only a Russian soul could endure.

. . . what to tell . . . . so many cheap confessions. . . . Every strength which I have possessed has come to me directly from the courageous life of someone in the past—Let the one reader, then, who will have a great soul, interpret

How clearly stands out each detail of the night which separated me from my past. It was June 4, 1923, clear, with stars and dark trees. The place where we were was surrounded by beauty, but the unevenness and coarseness of the grass and stubble immediately around was ugly, as so often happens in nature's scenes. Everyone knows the rise and fall of the heart when two are young, the hope and disappearance of hope at any rate, I asked a question, forgotten now, and for reply there came, slowly, "You know how it is". For me they were filled with such an unanswerable pain; it was commanded that I should assuage it. I remember the brief second of the feeling of doom and the impossibility of with-staying it. But what I want to speak of are the few moments between which I arose and made my way to the car and placed myself in it—no foot ever felt so heavy, the extreme slowness with which I walked, the complete unimportance of my physical pain, the tender quiet way in which I opened the door and folded my skirts and closed it again. I was as completely sad as only the earth itself can be; (!) I had no anger, no surprise, no worry, no thought of what I had lost or if it could have been otherwise. Only the gentlest, gentlest penetrating sadness from which I could not escape. What I have never been able to find out is, *why* is the soul sad when the body comes to maturity? I believe to every other problem of life of which I am aware I have found an answer for myself—but this question neither I, nor anyone I could or have discovered has so far been able to answer. Weininger says that coitus in itself is not a sin—it is only because man's soul is completely submerged that it is sinful. (!). And I remember now that many years later I came to the conclusion that it is to give the soul a brief reprieve from its endless search that we are so blind, so altogether lost—that his blindness is the only kind in the world which will cover up the soul's pain for a moment. Not that this is in any way an answer to the question of why man grieves at the loss of his innocence.—I think if we knew the answer we would know for sure whether or not man possesses an immortal soul.

> (the days following—sorrow, refusing to see the boy, sorrow, conviction she had gone against her beloved Christ—finally sat down and wrote, confessed to a girl thousand miles away

. . . . no desire to write this, but somewhere I *must* say how strongly I protest the accepted version of woman's character. Let the genius who will come after me write a great book—I only desire to drop a hint as to how the life was lived, the life wherein God set one woman free.

All of a woman's troubles proceed from the fact that she never admits to herself her fundamental inequality. When I used to torment myself daily with the question, "Why can a woman not create something of the first rate, why are all her works not great, but full of immense talent only?", I finally was, in a brief moment, brought face to face with the idea that in woman there is no necessity. Every woman is an actual or a potential mother—that satisfaction which penetrates to the last corpuscle in her body, to her subconscious life, to her blood, as well as to her mind and nerves, when she brings forth a child, is complete. It is the only complete satisfaction known on this earth, and it is complete because it is filled with all possibilities, each time. Life is magic, none of us are aware of what it is—neither Plato, nor Gogol, nor Rameses. But we all know it contains wonderful possibilities—and a woman has that deep, unspoken knowledge in herself when her child is brought forth. Now a man is never granted to create in this life any one thing, any painting, any book, any piece of music which will satisfy him—he and all others will be able to find in it some fault. It can not grow—it is finished. And this fact that it is not perfect is what tears his vitals and causes him to go crazy and demands that he shall try again—every time he hopes that he shall have a whole thing—some times he approaches almighty God in the beauty of what he has done, but never really. So he lies awake and in his soul—through thousands of years, dissatisfaction has been his daily bread. Out of that pain comes his intense mastery, his freedom, his glory and his bitterness. For life he never will be able to grasp. Now a woman cannot grasp life either, but she is it—she partakes. Once—for a brief second, I felt in all its joy this superb possession which a woman has, of life—and I felt in my heart the terrible loneliness which crushes down a man, because he can only attempt to revisualize it, he can not be it. In this one moment, I felt sorry for man (here, here, lady, who wants it, who.) I have never forgotten that sorrow, but I have never been able before or since to glory in a woman's belongingness.

This belongingness is what I want to speak of—this is a woman's enemy, her terror, the cause of every sin, of every weakness, of all mystery. She can not be free. And she does not know it, except, rarely. Weininger points out, in bitterness, how deeply a woman craves coitus, how every moment is towards or away from, centered on, fruition. Has he, or any man, any man, including Christ, ever once expressed what a terrifying burden this is—did woman make herself bound, or was she born bound—does she not belong all days, in all moods, to the earth—and is this not the cause of her great sadness, her slavery, her pettiness, her vengeance, her intense pursuit and glory in a man's soul's betrayal, her triumph in a child, her never ending convergence on her own tangent? Let him who has a great soul weigh this in silence—*who* is responsible for the profound inequality of a man and a woman—for the absolute impossibility of her escape from earth. Who? No one. Then let his soul stand up and recognize that injustice is inherent in the nature of our earth—that only God can conceive of an answer and it does not lie here. Weininger says, "Let a woman give up the desire for coitus and she will become free." I realize the beauty and longing (SHIT) with which Weininger wrote, but he is wrong, nevertheless. A woman cannot give up coitus—it would result only in that she would cease to be—not in her freedom. This 20th century affords many examples of women who have tried—other generations also—the result is so pathetic, so unfree—so miserable, that no great man could possibly think of this as the answer. What I say is,—let a woman admit in her soul her burden—let her say to herself—I am a lesser creature, from me no great thing will ever proceed ((THIS IS THE RUB, for FB,))—let her realize that each soul on this earth stands in complete, imperishable, not-for-one-second-ending solitude—let her say to herself "The earth is complete sorrow—I will never, at any moment, believe in or seek my own happiness, and though it be logically an absurdity, let me live for the sake of other human beings, for their happiness." This is a task the strength for which must proceed from God—few shall attain, but she who does, shall emerge, miraculously, free.

Paul I Timothy 2:11–15 quoted. . . . she protests . . . on woman as transgressor . . .why has no religion, since the beginning of time, been great enough to perceive that woman is precisely not deceived, that therein lies her tremendous tragedy, but that she is *forced* to obey the rule of the earth which lies deeply within her?

(more paul)

It has been a facile explanation—Eve's guilt—how profound an injustice

The necessity to endure—the will to life—*it is* the cause of her hypocrisy. Could a woman face life—and *live*? ((WELL?)) Could a woman say to herself where she stands and what she is and go on? What has man to offer her that is of the slightest value, once she realizes the place in which she is—can any *thing* of this earth, jewels, house, children, comfort, security leisure answer to her for her essential inequality ((SHIT))—they can not.

(then Jesus, go, and sin no more . . . . . she says, not enough.) For to a woman it is not a sin, *neither is it a good thing*—it is a law from which she has not the power to escape. And since this law is part of the earth's rhythm, since therefore it moves in the immense body rhythm of the universe—it shall some day, by God, be reconciled. We do not know how.

The body of a woman is an instrument—the only one she has completely at her command . . . . and how ever hard a woman has stuggled to despise her body, she has never been successful. It is herself.

Can the great man, therefore, when he has bowed himself down to the earth, for the refreshment of which he stands in need in proportion as his greatness takes him off this earth O can he, when having received that refreshing blindness, have pity on the blindness that gave him succour? The greater the man is the more highly resentful is he of his earthly attachment, of his human frailty (!)—he would love to be of God—Godlike (!), and so when he returns to the earth and restores the earthly man, after he is refreshed, in his new strength he is apt to strike out against the necessity and the nearest and most obvious "cause" is woman. The hatred which man has in the moments when he has arisen from his trappedness I do not despise—all that I say is, Let a man beat his own breast, not the woman, for neither he nor she is to blame and in addition *she bears the humility of having to want his weakness.*

Let no man, great or small, take unto himself glory because a woman has so great a need for him—let no man, either great or small, think to himself that he perceives the whole woman, perceiving her need. For the need of woman is a great covering which she must penetrate, and I see no other way open to her to come through that covering, but *by wearing it* out. . . This is why Thais . . . Sonia . . . excessive use and there, shining through the worn places, was the most pure soul(!)

(This is not what she is, this covering, but only what she must come through in order to be herself.

And when she has, she has emerged, sometimes, well nigh a direct child of God—witness Gorki's grandmother.

. . . . However it may be, this is true, that if a woman were permitted to use her body at the age when it is pressing most closely about her, to whatever full extent that body required, when the moment of sufficient use had passed, she would be ready to take her place in life with all sincerity

. . . . completely selfless

. . . obvious reason why not, is, a woman can not drip seeds nor does she care to—the law of nature's waste.

. . .that body a sounding board from which she would *like* to hear every note—

she usually hears one or two . . .wakes up, man's rules, strikes out blindly—to grasp when it is too late—How wise must be the woman who knows her own need at her own hour.

Marriage. This almost every woman is wise enough to seek. But fulfillment according to her own need is why DHL—he knew a woman *must* find according to her own need, or her life will add further impotency. . . . but not enuf—another necessity: the desire to win respect. Now follows a law: when the body is indulged in without restraint, it chokes the soul.

If by some honest fallacy such as I myself struggled under (that a man's bodily pain is as great as a woman's . . . so never flirt). . . . but this error, and have no idea where answer lies

It is this desire for respect which has led woman to confuse her own issues—It is because man *can* be free from his body, can possess his own soul in strength, that a woman so passionately believes in him. It is also why she hates him. A woman who loves a man finds in him this freedom. If ever she suspects that he has lost it, have he every other good thing & be he ever so kind to her, to the woman he is a useless, pitiable object & she despises him. This is why a woman will follow . . . rain . . . sleet . . . devotion—what man stands in need of. A woman, on the other hand, can, by and large, never gain the respect due her, except rarely, rarely, in the eyes of one man who will glimpse what she is. . .

What she wants much much more than love, no matter what she says. . .

So, conundrum: if a woman loves a man, she will contentedly offer him devotion and he will *not* respect her—for respect from either sex can be based upon one thing only—the freedom of soul, but love from a woman obliterates her distance, makes her literally belong to him, because he is free and therefore better than she is and it is this freedom which she worships. This is how a woman can be nurture in the physical sense to a man whom she loves—her body is separate from her desire for freedom—because her body works . . . because the important thing in her eyes in the man she loves is exactly his freedom from the need of her. And she knows no *man* gives his body without tenderness.

Why the law which has allowed sexual license to man and forbids it to woman is so cruel.

She stands in terrific need of license—despising her need but nevertheless feeling it—whereas a man is in no need whatsoever—his body, if taken care of by a passionate woman, is answered and he can go on about his life. The reason he does so frequently betray his beloved, sexually, is that he seeks separateness, and, continually, in a new person, has the illusion of finding it. It is for this deep cause that I believe men and women should not marry because of love, but this on mutual respect. And the only way a woman can gain a man's respect is to be more free of him.

◄§ 27 §►

State College to Washington
8 May 1949 (postmark 9 May 1949)

Sunday night

Olson—

Just dropped into my office on a hunch—just came up this minute from Woodward—which is so very subtly penetrating—a marvelous place to come to write.

There are several facts I should love to tell you so that you can think of them in making plans for your coming year—I am moving to Albuquerque New Mexico around June 15–22—my place in Woodward I am absolutely sure you would love and if you are not tied up in a job or in the fall or Christmas vacation or all year would like to live there I am sure you would find it very perfect and of course you would be free to invite a friend if you so cared. It has three bedrooms a marvelous old pot-belly stove which does a terrific job—beautiful view—it is an old barber shop reconverted—anyhow I am sure you would love it—I went through real sacrifices to pay for the damm thing and just as I get the last check mailed I have to give it up—I would never rent it—I am not the type—so if you care to make use of it at any time I will mail you my keys of which I have a duplicate set. I hope you will not think there is any subterfuge lurking in all this—there is not—I can not be there—I love it dearly and I believe you will too and it is all paid for and since I tore the insides out and designed it myself it is very much me and we would know each other better—I do not care how long is required for you to know if my notebook can be employed by you—if it can I shall be very happy, but I in a deep sense consider it someone else's business—like God.

Do you know Bryon Rice's *Birth of Western Painting*[36] about terrific Byzantine stuff from which El Greco directly stems? A magnificent book—get at library very out of print—Routledge & Sons.

Stuff I want to work on I am sorry to say I will have to dig up again when I have leisure—was in Russian and my Russian contacts have disappeared here—anyway I am very in it (Byzantine) too.

36. Robert Bryon and Talbot Rice, *The Birth of Western Painting* (New York: Knopf, 1931).

I wanted like hell to design one of these posters announcing Olson—we got a terrific report on you from Black Mountain—I knew before it came—but I was glad to have the people here have proof[37]—now I have to go away and if you get invited next year, because I have so deeply believed in you, please accept if you can to show them you are just as up there as I say.

Your friend
Frances now Ward

◄§ 28 §►

State College to Washington
10 May 1949 (postmark)

Addenda—

    1. No. 14—the reason you have never seen this anywhere is because the art historians in their great majesty have decided Michelangelo probably did not draw it—it is a drawing in preparation for an allegorical painting which he never completed—believe he sent it as a gift to his Tommasino but of that I am not sure—it is in the private possession of a man in Paris—

    2. If you are connected with a college ask the librarian to borrow for you from the Library of Congress Franz Cumont's volume of plates in color on the frescoes found at Dura-Europos.[38] (This fresco was destroyed by the Arabs and now exists nowhere in the world except in these colored reproductions.) There is a particular plate which I wish to talk with you about which will drive you wild—a priest in a ceremony—the look in the eyes the Christian world has not so far touched—the unworld brought to view—Rostovtzeff[39] says this fresco is the long sought link between the Western and Eastern worlds—I can get you lots of dope—accurate—in case I have not given enough to locate the book which is probably in the reference room—

37. On 30 March 1949, Philip A. Shelley, head of the German Department, Pennsylvania State College, had written to Black Mountain College (undoubtedly at Boldereff's instigation): "Word has reached me that Mr. Charles Olsen, a young poet and writer, has recently delivered a lecture or lectures at Black Mountain College. Would you be so good as to inform me confidentially concerning Mr. Olsen's accomplishments as a lecturer? He is under consideration to deliver a lecture at the Pennsylvania State College." The current registrar of Black Mountain College, David Corkran, replied on 4 April 1949: "We have found Mr. Charles Olson a popular and effective speaker. He is at his best in talking about Herman Melville. He is animated, imaginative and bold, having the capacity to stir up considerable discussion." (Both letters are in the Black Mountain College archives at Raleigh, N.C.) No invitation was, in the end, extended.

38. Presumably the second part of Franz Cumont, *Fouilles de Doura-Europos* (Paris, 1926). Olson wrote "DURA EUROPOS" as a note to himself on the front of the envelope of this letter.

39. Michael I. Rostovtzeff excavated the Turkish site with Franz Cumont and wrote *Dura-Europos and Its Art* (Oxford, 1938).

The whole Byzantine world—Sumerian world and Dura-Europos absolutely drive me crazy—I had to get excited all by myself—since no one else seems to care—I have a pamphlet on Gilgamesh I will also send to you—

Anyway I believe the salutation used by that young Roman patrician whose name I always forget—whom Michelangelo loved—to be the most beautiful in history—

"Unique, my lord"—

3. Also a very marvelous Byzantine history by a great Russian historian Vasiliev—vols No.14–15 of Wisconsin Social Studies translated by Ragozin[40]—he lives in Washington—I can get his address if you would desire it. (In this history there is a gal who is more like me than any female I have ever met—perhaps she could suggest a form—I forget the details.)

≪ 29 ≫

Woodward to Washington
16 May 1949 (postmark)

Olson—

I am sorry, but since Rimbaud the only person's poetry I can take is yours (you know Francis Thompson & Garcia Lorca are excluded from this comment)—I am no Yeats lover—I get ill and unhappy when I look at literary reviews—I hate the first article and I hate the review on Starkie's book on Rimbaud because I loathe that book—I am glad Rimbaud can not see it[41]—

When I was digging through some of that old Byzantine stuff I came across a sentence from a Second Crusader—so man—so man and so loved I purposely forget it to find afresh—the idea that the beauty of Constantinople causes the heart to tremble of the most valiant who has won his way there. Shaken to its inmost existence—like the letter of Michelangelo who refused the dinner invitation because "You must know that of men living I am the most given to loving and when I see something to command respect in another—I love him so completely and give myself so entirely that from your banquet I would come home not refreshed but exhausted"—(very loosely). *Anyhow* the tremble Starkie aint got.

All of which is to say I feel dirty in literary reviews—I save myself by remembering the beginning of *Jerusalem* where Blake so quietly and unironically attaches pity to Palamabron(?) to the spirit of Evil.

40. A. A. Vasiliev, *History of the Byzantine Empire*, trans. S. Ragozin, 2 vols. (Madison: University of Wisconsin, 1928–29).

41. Enid Starkie, *Arthur Rimbaud* (New York: W. W. Norton, 1949). Apparently Boldereff enclosed a review and another pertinent article, both now lost.

It doesn't matter if you can't read my writing—I am getting so I hate almost everything but silence and your poems are so ardently aware of silence—until the new harsh form shall flower—oh Olson—harsh—(in a bloom so sternly and so unexotically alive)

I am sending Northrop Frye who deserves them—a copy of your poems.[42]

◅ 30 ▻

Woodward to Washington
[about 20 May 1949]

Olson—

This was given me by Kramer—whom I just walked in on one day at the Un. of Pa. Museum and started to talk to—There is a very nice translation by William Ellery Leonard—*Gilgamesh*. Eventually—I would wish to have it returned—

The mysterious note inside the first page seems to have come there by itself—I do not remember seeing it before and have no remote notion whose handwriting it is!—anyhow I am pleased.

Factual world intrusion: Life is in enormous flux—until you hear to the contrary I am to be found in Woodward under my good father's name.

I love very deeply—the lines at the opening of *Call me Ishmael*. Are they early Swedish?

Hope to go to New York in June for a hunt for some Byzantine art Russian original manuscripts.

[*Enclosure: offprint of S. N. Kramer, "The Epic of Gilgameš and Its Sumerian Sources," reprinted from* Journal of the American Oriental Society *64 (1944): 7–23. Boldereff wrote the following note inside the front cover of the offprint:*]

I thank you for the *Western Review*[43]—which I was unable to buy or borrow in State College. I approve of its typography—will look at the articles—I have been grateful and many many times have used the prayer

42. It is not known if Frye responded.
43. The winter 1949 issue of *Western Review* contained Olson's poem "Siena," from which Boldereff quotes the last line below. On the cover of the magazine (in the recipient's possession) Olson wrote "for the Motz."

We   who are awkward   ask

I notice the novel by Herbert Read—I found in *Graphis* 24 a very fine article by him—was quite amazed because I did not expect any official Unesco's
to come up with something I could respect and value.

❧ 31 ❧

Washington to Woodward
23 May 1949 (postmark 23 May 1949)

Mond May 23 xlix

FM:
    I have started K's Gilgam over coffee, but break off to write you & send one
of my earliest verses, unpublished, on G, for you.[44]

You will excuse me, you have not heard before, but I only returned from
another Black Mt fatigue-duty yesterday. By the way, does Albuquerque
mean the Univ of NM? if so, my present, (and only disciple?), a Jack Rice
down there at BM, I learned this past week, goes to NM in the fall to take up
the career the two of us have shaped for him this winter, kultur-morphologie
(to steal a description from Frobenius). Rice is in danger of rigidities due to a
sense of himself as temple-builder, but he has gone farther than anyone in taking such same cues as ISHMAEL presents. I have the feeling that field work
(& further translation & acquaintance with Frobenius) plus the discipline of
americanist study (which seems to me more fixed than more ancient research)
may keep him in line and cause him to be of use.
                                                        You may meet him.

And it is fine, to have from you yr house in Woodward to light on, comes
the event. I have no present way to know what the next year brings. If I could
manage to acquire this house here (it costs 20,000, is bank priced 7500), such
acquisition patently to be gift of one or more non-existent, or not yet dreamed
up sponsors, then I would have BASE; and would, I'm sure, start moving
around like mad. It looks now that, by fall, I shall either have to have it or get
the hell out. So things are water.

Or does yr last notes indicate your New Mexico move is postponed?
The Michelangelo quote is impeccable: oi how true

44. This early Gilgamesh poem, "Tomorrow," is dated 1941 on the copy enclosed with this letter (see
Collected Poems, pp. 9 and 645).

& harsh, is it?

ooooooooooooo☿

They are Early olson

Do you know V Bérard on the Ody-
ssey?[45]   is the frobenius of same

      TOMORROW

I am Gilgamesh,
an Ur world is in me
to inhabit.

Race of waters run
in the blood
red with the fathers.

They told me of flood,
of the earth dissolved,
of drowned mountains.

I live in the land
and know people,
see love recur.

They said the heart
knows no evolution:
it is as it was when it is.

They called me Gilgamesh
and gave me Ur
where I dwell.

for FM
for what it is
Olson

written 1941   xlix

---

45. Olson, in exchange for Kramer, offers Boldereff the name of a commentator on Homer he had discovered via Edward Dahlberg. He later owned Victor Bérard's *Did Homer Live?* (New York: Dutton,
1931).

Washington to Woodward
25 May 1949 (postmark 26 May 1949)

LA CHUTE

O my drum, hollowed out thru the thin slit,
carved from the cedar wood, the base I took
when the tree was felled
                                        o my lute

wrought from the tree's crown

my drum whose lustiness
was not to be resisted

my lute from whose pulsations
not one could turn away

                                        They
are where the dead are
                        my drum
fell where the dead are, who
will bring it up, my lute
who will bring it up
where it fell in the face of them
where they are, where my lute and drum

        have fallen?

fm:
recognize it?[46] my
thanks

                                        olson
                                        may 25
                                        xlix

[*on back of envelope:*][47]

46. Olson has adapted lines from Gilgamesh translated by S. N. Kramer on p. 20 of the article Boldereff had sent him.
47. These lines are indebted to Boldereff's comments on a fresco of Dura-Europos in her letter of 10
May 1949.

to come to the look in the sacrificer's eyes
archaism sought, the harshness
unsought
          where blood is
is form

⤙ 33 ⤚

Washington to Woodward (postcard)
26 May 1949 (postmark)

Cancel blood

Fr unsought, add

          And the eyes
                    which should burst
     do not.[48]

48. This emendation to the draft of the previous day appears in the poem as sent to Edward Dahlberg a few days later (see "Dura" in *Collected Poems*, p. 85.)

PART II

❦

25 May 1949–31 October 1949

With Kramer's article on Gilgamesh, Boldereff has not only supplied Olson with what he might otherwise have missed but, in doing so, has given him the impetus to a new poem. She has put him onto Dura-Europos, and another piece of verse has resulted. An intellectual relationship is in rapid bloom. Shall they risk meeting? With Boldereff's ending of her brief marriage to Duke Ward and the consequent abandoning of her move to Albuquerque, it seems inevitable that she and Olson will get together. The first attempt was in June 1949, when Olson was to visit his aging mother in Gloucester. Telegrams were sent, but connection failed. The next opportunity was not until a similar errand at the beginning of November 1949.

Meanwhile, Olson is engrossed in giving a course, "Verse and Drama," at the summer session at Black Mountain College and is working on his first major poem, "The Kingfishers."

❦ 34 ❦

State College to Washington
25 May 1949 (postmark)

Olson—

This is one of those weekends when the whole past is sharply brought into focus—I wish to God it were over—

I have to tell a man again that I have to go my own way—I have been married so briefly and I hate, Olson, so terribly to see weak people suffer—

I am and have been a racing flow of Woodward mountain stream—I will be so glad when the deed whatever it turns out to be will be over.

I look with my flesh not on but towards your face—I know no single fact about you—but out of one brief line in *Ishmael* I somehow have a very definite though unoutlined picture and I know that for me this weekend it will have that impassive and outwardly motionless aspect of deep response—what I need I can take for free—I will take and thank you—

Woodward to Washington
30 May 1949 (postmark)

Olson baby—

I was going to send you a wire—but Woodward telephone service is skittish—

At last,—I can not tell you any more than the wire would have said—

Olson baby—you shut up—you are too damned good—

It is so original[1]—so you—and yet such a complete restatement of the whole works—done as usual with the iron of the countenance of that great Verrocchio equestrian statue named—

Must say I am well pleased

Why are you always using french I never knew the meaning of? not to mention greek

That rhythm gets me—

I cannot understand why, but I do not recognize it, though it rings as familiar in my blood as the rhythm of motherhood—it is very very satisfying—I do not know why—also I do not know for what or why I am being thanked—nor do I know the meaning of the postcard—I only understand the lines which have been erased[2] (I think it was so very kind of you to send me that—as knowing I would not look in too familiarly, but would see with a deep blush of pleasure to imagine for an instant the exquisite pleasure to sign to you "mother")

And I am not too sure about the outside of the envelope—

I only know I needed you and you were here.

A patrician—

god watch over me this night.

~⟫ 36 ⟪~

New York to Woodward (telegram)[3]
18 June 1949

1. The following comments are on Olson's letter of 25 May 1949, which contained "La Chute," and on the postcard of 26 May 1949.

2. Olson had reused a postcard, deleting the former message, which read: "Dear Charles thought you would like the clippings—love mother."

3. Olson was on his way to visit his mother in Gloucester. Presumably some missing letter or telegram would explain what arrangements Olson had tried to make for a rendezvous in New York City.

HAVE LEFT WASHINGTON REGRET MISSING YOU HERE WRITE ME STAGE FORT AVE
GLOUCESTER MASSACHUSETTS

OLSON

⋙ 37 ⋘

Cambridge to Woodward (special delivery)
27 June 1949 (postmark)

Monday
june 27

fm
    i write to you   i am in the basement of fogg,[4] under a photo mural
of piero's arezzo

                  to say i have left gloucester, that i shall be in new york again,
& that the very 1st thing i shall do on arrival there wednesday evening is to call
the Fifth Ave hotel on the second try to coincide with you   i should be in
around 7 & shall act as tho you and i will have dinner together

i have a couple
of days business & appointments before i go off to north carolina friday

look,
why don't I call at the 5th Avenue myself both wednesday & thursday, so that,
if you care to, i can find there any kind of message, including yourself?

this is
olson

⋙ 38 ⋘

Woodward to Black Mountain
[probably 2 July 1949][5]

    I am simply not able to believe that I was talking to you[6] and that because I
was so excited the brain could not reach to the so simple solution to spend two
beautiful days with you and to accompany you as far as Baltimore, where, as
it turned out, I was, all day on Friday. Oh Olson—from Baltimore I was going

---

4. The Fogg Art Museum of Harvard University.
    5. Boldereff addressed the envelope to Mr. Charles Olson, Visiting Poet, Black Mountain College, N.
Carolina, and added a note, "N.C. Postmaster Please locate." However, she evidently changed her mind
about sending the letter. According to a note in the Storrs collection, it was "not sent."
    6. Olson presumably telephoned Woodward from New York City on 29 June 1949.

to wire your train to ask you to detrain for an hour or so—but I decided that it was not curiosity which is compelling us—I don't care at all what the shape of your nose is—and I already know all the important things that matter to me—about your fingers—and the back of your neck and all that—it would be ridiculous for us to stand and look at each other for an hour—and that is why I did not ask you.

Olson, I forgot to listen to your voice I was so terribly anxious to hear what you said—and it is simply driving me crazy to have touched so close and yet not to have exchanged our so very like rhythms. In Robert Graves' *Watch the North Wind Rise* they ask the poet "Do you like us?" and he says "Why?" and they say "Because no important conversation can take place between two people who do not like each other's selves."—And we would so immediately exchange and so immediately know.

And now I understand why you wanted it to be in New York—where you could so politely find so many reasons—in case we didn't—but now I want to ask you—please to think to a place and to name it—even if it is all wrong—I simply detest waiting Olson. If you ask me I will come.

Frances

🕸 39 🕸

Black Mountain to Woodward
10 July 1949 (postmark 11 July 1949)

july 10 xlix

for fm, greetings

LA CHUTE[7]

II

If you would go down to the dead
to retrieve my drum and lute
a word for you, take my word,
I offer you directions

do not wear a clean garment
they below will dirty you
they will mark you
as if you were a stranger

7. This is a typescript with some holograph corrections. See "La Chute II" in *Collected Poems*, pp. 83–84.

nor rub yourself with oil
the finest oil from the cruse
the smell of it will provoke them
they will walk round and round
alongside you

carry no stick, at least
do not raise it
or the shades of men will tremble,
hover before you

Pick up nothing to throw, no matter the urging.
They against whom you hurl it
will crowd you, will fly thick on you.

Go barefoot, make no sound,
and when you meet the wife you loved
do not kiss her nor strike the wife you hated.
Likewise your sons. Give the beloved one no kiss,
do not spit on his brother.

Behave, lest the outcry shall seize you
seize you for what you have done
for her who, there lies naked, the mother
whose body in that place is not covered
whose breasts lie open to you and the judges

in that place
where my drum and lute are

                                        olson

≈ 40 ≈

Woodward to Black Mountain[8]
[10 July 1949]

                                        Sunday

Olson, Charles—
   My daughter has a fairy of the feminine sex whose name she insists is Angelo—Angelo is good at riding atop soap bubbles and other feats difficult for

---

8. This letter was addressed exactly as Boldereff's previous letter. Again, the Storrs note says "not sent."

humans to perform—when we go swimming she sometimes grows tired because the flowers she likes to rest on are so few beside the way.

At this moment you also have the abilities of Angelo and have been sitting so close beside me that twice I have begged your pardon for brushing you with my hand as I leafed my Blake—Finnegans Wake—Frye—Bible orgy so compelling I forget to eat—I am ordering Robert Graves book *The White Goddess* not because I am so attracted by moon lore as because I have always thought he was an O.K. human.

Olson, Charles, I recognize the footfall in the pattern of your actions—since the beat is so well known to you—please place in the mail for me some physical object you daily touch—I shall give back in due time—you know what I would prefer, but if your New England blood objects—send a handkerchief.

Frances

❧ 41 ☙

Woodward to Black Mountain
15 July 1949 (postmark)

I count upon you to know—five minutes after I had done it—how amazed I was about the letter I sent you—I want you to know that in that picture was only you, not I—that I was dreaming of walking around looking at those lovely shells and pebbles and I suddenly saw you and I felt how quiet it would be to sit on my knees and *feel* the fine beautiful thing that comes out of every pore of you—

The letter[9] is fairy tale ending—Ninette was in college with me—she had already been married and in the war and was a woman and I do not remember ever saying a personal word outside of class—I never saw her—but I remember terribly liking her—I never saw or heard from her after school—all these enormous years and in February—a hand made Christmas card—Frances Motz—University of Michigan—finally turned up at State College—Saying precisely nothing—I answered at once—she came to Woodward for a week and it was the most perfect week I have ever spent in my life—absolutely effortless—and a spirit so kin—
Blake keeps saying over and over—"And he became what he beheld"

And please know without my telling beforehand how I loathe phrases "for my sake"—I can make such bitter fun of such phrases—please do not do it to me

---

9. Boldereff enclosed the letter from the friend described in this paragraph.

I think it is so marvelous how you understand so well *how* and where to keep silence—I am trying to learn from you

◄ 42 ►

Woodward to Black Mountain
21 July 1949 (postmark)

Found this—which forms one picture in my mind—the Olson picture.

Tha mon o'micht, he rade o'nicht
Wi' neider swerd ne ferd ne licht.
He socht tha Mare, he find tha mare,
He bond tha Mare wi' her ain hare,
Ond gared her swar by midder-micht
She wolde nai mair rid o'nicht
Whar aince he rade, that mon o'micht[10]

And in the course of one day I am the flower which bends towards you, the light which polishes your nails and the no-sound which informs you.

◄ 43 ►

Black Mountain to Woodward (postcard)
12 August 1949 (postmark 13 August 1949)

fri aug twelve xlix

i have been so distrait i had forgotten, until this moment, i could at least send you a penny pc! you know what base means to me, & here i am only the tail of a kite

    you'll judge my condition when I tell you that only yesterday, after two months, did i do a piece of verse worth speaking of!

& i feel bad, for yr three lovely letters & my book, ask this plus

            but it will soon be over, and i'll be back where my hive is (leave here sept 1, back wash abt sept 15)

i am grim

                yrs   o

---

10. Boldereff found this fourteenth-century "charm" in Robert Graves's *The White Goddess* (1948), chapter 1.

❧ 44 ❧

Woodward to Black Mountain
17 August 1949 (postmark)

Olson—

Two years ago when the grimness had gone on for me so long that I began to feel that despite the fact of my baby that the amount of time I could continue to hold on was numbered in days—I went to the library and my hand found by itself *Call me Ishmael*.

I brought it home and I read it and I got up and walked around and said "It isn't possible—in this barren landscape"—

I tried to make my letter sober, out of respect—I do not believe I mentioned to you then or later that you had saved my life—absolutely literally.

There is no way in which I can make a direct return, but at whatever time it is returned to you Olson, in whatever form, you will know that one of the sources is me.

Frances

Nietzsche   Will to Power

#163   Jesus bids us: not to resist, either by deeds or in our heart, him who ill-treats us;

He bids us admit of no grounds for separating ourselves from our wives;

He bids us make no distinction between foreigners and fellow-citizens, strangers and familiars;

He bids us show anger to no one, and treat no one with contempt;—give alms secretly; not to desire to become rich; not to swear; not to stand in judgment; become reconciled with our enemies and forgive offences; not to worship in public.

"Blessedness" is nothing promised: it is here, with us, if we only wish to live and act in a particular way.

#405   We do not yet know the "whither" towards which we are urging our steps, now that we have departed from the soil of our forebears. But it was on this very soil that we acquired the strength which is now driving us from our homes in search of adventure, and it is thanks to that strength that we are now in mid-sea, surrounded by untried possibilities and things undiscovered—we can no longer choose, we must be conquerors, now that we have no land in which we feel at home and in which we would fain survive. A concealed "yea" is driving us forward, and it is stronger than all our "nays". Even our strength no longer bears with us in the old swampy land: we venture out into the open, we attempt the task. The world is still rich and undiscovered, and even to perish were better than to be half-men or poisonous men. Our very strength itself urges us to take to the sea; there where all suns have hitherto sunk we know of a new world . . .

My guess is that you and Nietzsche are in no way specially close—I enclose because I found it a day or so after seeing the Easter Poem[11] and it seemed amazing that two men otherwise so far apart—should have chosen so like—The list in Nietzsche remains cold and unhelpful while yours is a hand.

I have a young cousin who has won four summers in a row (Saunderstown RI) over the Gloucester star boat class sailors—I remember the first night I ever went out in one and when we came back he said "Well—Cousin Frances—you pass the test—you didn't ask us any silly questions." I was proud.

And when I rock myself to sleep in the sound of these hemlocks—I think of all the places in which to wait—when the inner world is water—a boat is best . . .

I once saw Vanderbilt's boat in a private bay at Newport and all of my life I have thought it the cleanest and most magnificent thing there is to own—I never can imagine Olson owning anything else.

D.H. Lawrence in Studies in Classic American Literature spoke so eloquently of the daemon of this land which we have so ruthlessly destroyed having to be assuaged before we could begin with our gift and I somehow always see Olson as the clean thing that strides from side to side—without base—cleaning and clearing for all of us!

⊷ 45 ⊶

Woodward to Gloucester[12]
13 October 1949 (postmark)

Olson—

11. "In the Hills South of Capernaum, Port" was published in *Harper's Bazaar* (April 1949) under the heading "An Easter Poem." It paraphrases the Sermon on the Mount. Boldereff draws a line up to connect these remarks with the phrase "reconciled with our enemies," in the first part of the quotation from Nietzsche.

12. In a missing letter or telephone call, Olson must have said that he would be in Gloucester in October, but by 6 October 1949 he had returned from his New England trip. This letter was forwarded to Washington from Gloucester on 15 October 1949.

I know you can not write—this has nothing to do with letters—I am living every minute of your thing and it becomes unendurable. I want to ask a few questions—I have thought of someone who has or could have $7000.—he might conceivably be persuaded to buy 217 and rent it to you for a lifetime—would that be of any use to you. I doubt that he is alive enough just to do the thing and present it to you—but anyway I shall try if you say that 217 or any other suitable place is there to be worked on—

Or if you think of any plan which could be useful to you—despite all the facts of my own life—it seems absolutely unbelievable that the thing has become so relentlessly hacking—so avid of death.

Do not expect any communication from you but if there is a scheme which I could take to someone for persuasion—outcome absolutely unpredictable as you know—please let me know at once.

Frances

⊰ 46 ⊱

Washington to Woodward (special delivery)
17 October 1949 (postmark 18 October 1949)

washington

217

october 17 xlix

frances:

i shall not be able to say it all, if i say anything i am too stirred up,
jumpy

in place of "pertinent" the wire was to read "karmic" but for my fear of those bunglers, WU:[13] i do not see how you could have known that I am here at the moment just to see if i could not, some way, manage to stake out this base, 217, for good, that this is my present concern, has been since june

and that i have been forced to approach the problem in the most goetic terms, wildly to imagine that i could, this month, by making a call on my landlady (she has just returned from europe), somehow manage to talk her into a position, even though i have never been able to endure her greed (she is wealthy) nor her self (she is five feet, red, and 95, all pepper, all iron, came out with Henry Adams & John Hay, has had, & buried, four husbands, among them Ogden Jones who owned most of Chicago downtown!) and

---

13. The Western Union telegram is not extant.

would come to her with nothing but letters from my publisher and from Duncan Philips (of the museum) vouching for me   she has no sense of the artist as poet, but only as sculptor (her last husband was the state whore of bronze and stone, Paul Bartlett, for whom this studio, 217, was built) or painter—& painter only as hireling of the Navy or Marine Corps, to celebrate Guam or Iwo Jima or General George Washington

the reason why, after seven years, the present crisis, is that the place is up for sale, & that the sculptor who has the other half of the compound may any moment be in a position to buy both!

but to hell with all this   it is not what i want to tell you   you ask me a question: my answer is yes   but i want to ask you a question: what, yourself, is your explanation of your insight, & your act? it is so very beautiful and astonishing that i am moved to the center and the root of life by it

i am the more disturbed, that i had decided last night to write you today and argue you out of your assumption that my cold controls were valuable to any one else, specifically you, to tell you that i wanted you to speak out to me without regard to my necessary total position as a worker of "Charles the Cold"   (i have been full of you the past week; i found my soul back where it was the end of june; i tried to write a third La Chute, which came acropper; but in the process i rewrote L.C.II, and was to send you today the shred it has shrunk to) at which point, before i have got up, comes your letter, and the passage about yourself;[14] look, frances: if my vision once was enough to ward off the enemy, it shall be, anytime, and it will be; ask me, and i'll write it again; or spell it out for you direct, for that, too, is often necessary, as i damned well know: we are all forever lost even though we are equally redeemed

well, this is what i can say now   it is nothing
Olson

⋇ 47 ⋇

Woodward to Washington
18 October 1949 (postmark 19 October 1949)

Olson—

14. Boldereff's letter is apparently not extant.

I am trembling because there are facts I have to get down and beyond that—the part of your letter that refers to me and to you—I am not sure I understand but my guess is that I do—anyway—to try to tell you an explanation is not possible because in the very most real sense I do not know—ever since I have been a very young child it has kept happening that I sometimes just "know" things and I absolutely do not know why—I can only tell you now that since the same early childhood I have actually lived in a world of vision and if there are not any others alive who do then it is not possible for me to remain alive—you are important to me in that you exist—I do hope to meet you—but that is not it—the fact that you exist is to me America's No. 1 fact—and I am not one to go around acclaiming authors—I can not stand it—if we have no way to make provision for 1 Olson—and although I am helpless it is necessary for me to try.

I will tell you later maybe about myself—but it is so lousy for me now—that the only good thing is that you would be able to work—if not that—then I must go into the desert—thinking very seriously of trying to leave for Russia—I prefer the tyranny to be outward and visible—anyway Olson I do not know one word what to say to you—I am a touch embarrassed because I think you are trying to tell me that in a personal way you can be of no use to me—but I think we should not even think of such things—I want some day to see you but I can not say how important it is that you go on being alive—that you do not stop writing—(I am trembling so terribly I just can't hold the pen) I mean there is nothing if you can not write America can not *be*—

Anyway, Olson—I would not have written before I knew what I could do had I known for sure the house was available—I have not the most remote idea if I can be successful—there is a chance—there is also a chance the man and his wife I am going to see may be willing to let you have their very very nice place in Highland Mills (not the furniture, etc.) for not too much rent—(I mean very little, since it stands empty most of the year now)—it is about 1 1/2 hours outside of New York—they are there a part of the summer only—anyway if they can not help on the other and some sort of permanent occupancy of their other place could be arranged (they live in a large house they own in Brooklyn Heights-Monroe Place)—would you be the least interested—it has a very large library—did not examine too carefully—my general impression—interesting, not scholarly.

Wire me these facts on 217:

How much time is there? (If enough for several more weekends do not wire, but I must either go this weekend to see them in New York or not for several weeks—at least two.)

How much money is required—now and total amount

Would they, if they became owners rent to two people—in other stupid words—income to be derived?—loathe to ask you—but they will surely ask me—since they are rich also—I already tried one place and I had to go through a routine—

Is the house in decent condition—roof, etc?

Frances

Saw Henry Miller's essay "When do angels cease to resemble themselves?"[15] and wept for hours because he is so right about Rimbaud—I have placed Rimbaud for years as the West's No. 1 saint.

◄ 48 ►

State College to Washington
24 October 1949 (postmark)

[letterhead:] Nittany Printing & Publishing Company, State College, Pa.

Realize that my letter is probably embarrassing hell out of you—If I pull something off will wire you—if a man is willing for the right reasons he can investigate the data himself, n'est-ce pas?

You realize how I despise fumblers.

Frances

Spent yesterday on a hillside listening to the enclosed great glorification of hypocrisy[16]–Cannot say my spirits were raised.

Also realize I did not read the part of your letter correctly—I am sure you know that there are times when nothing done in words has any usefulness—I once rejected all books for over a year—the pain too deep—none of the books bit in—either you are treated to the sound of a footfall or not—

An artist I know said of the Russian officers he met during the war and he is to-the-limit American "In comparison with them, our officers seemed frivolous." You probably do not share in the slightest degree my feeling—I love them—all their passion and as you have discovered long ere this, a female would rather be slit through the throat than exist in a world where men are shadows. T.S.E. shadows.

◄ 49 ►

Washington to Woodward
26 October 1949 (postmark 26 October 1949)

217
Wednesday

15. Henry Miller's essay, subtitled "A Study of Rimbaud," appeared in *New Directions* 9 (1946): 39–76.
16. What was enclosed is not at present known.

                                        October 26
                                            xlix

frances

  no. just complicated

  look: there is no rush (I dread so to come to grips with the old bitch I put it
off easily)

  wait until you hear from me: i have been checking, & found out Monday
there are no other buyers (the price is almost 3x the value the bank puts on
it)   And my sculptor neighbor has decided to let it ride until such time as
she is deceased, & her executors face reality

  & the present situation, so far as rent goes (the exigencies), is better than any
other owner could be—the very vices of the lady in question are here a virtue
(it takes some time for her to catch up with velleities. In addition she loses
m.o.'s, & cashiers' checks!)

  i am enclosing a piece from that which, at the moment, I am trying to finish
off

  the whole is as long as any thing I've done, except for the dance-play for the
Graham company (& that was most prose—((& flat, god 'elp me)))[17]

  what i send you is part II, after a longer I (in I is the catch of the "light in
east" proposition: Mao's report to CP of

China, December 1947–48, in which he sd

                        la lumiere de l'aurore est devant nous,
                        nous devons nous lever et agir![18]

                                affection plus
                                       o

i am trying to get   (p.s.: the enclosed is in answer
rid of *The King-Fishers*   to a question you asked
in order to get at,   me one year & five
what may come out as   months ago).[19]
The She-Bear, with
a less harassed
mind

                        "under the ego, under the wanton-
                             ness, under the She-Bear"[20]

---

  17. "The Fiery Hunt" (a dance in four parts, based on *Moby-Dick*) was written in April 1948 for Erick
Hawkins of the Martha Graham Company but was never performed (see *The Fiery Hunt*, p. xiii).

  18. These lines appear in section 2 of part 1 of "The Kingfishers." Enclosed with this letter is the remainder of the poem (parts 2 and 3 as published), inscribed "from THE KINGFISHERS for fm."

  19. Possibly Olson is referring to the letter of 26 June 1948, which asked him to "tell me about America."

  20. These lines were not contained in the final version of "The She-Bear," finished March 1950 (see
Collected Poems, pp. 129–34.

❧ 50 ❧

Woodward to Washington
31 October 1949 (postmark)

"Know ye now, Bulkington? Glimpses do ye seem to see of that mortally intolerable truth; that all deep, earnest thinking is but the intrepid effort of the
soul to keep the open independence of her sea; while the wildest winds of
heaven and earth conspire to cast her on the treacherous, slavish shore?"[21]

I thank you the sohne—
And now I am going into a deep sleep

On the horizon are the faintest glimmerings of an answer—it will be four
months or so before any development—and if by God's grace something were
to be concluded, I think it would need not be avoided because it would not
come about because of the slightest understanding, or because of greed—not
because I have asked, who have long since earned.

If like Queequeg, I sometimes occupy more than my half—it will be for his
reasons.

Charles the sohne.

21. From chapter 23 of *Moby-Dick*.

PART III

❦

10 November 1949–6 December 1949

It seems that in his lifetime Olson did not tell anyone (beyond Connie) about his liaison with Frances. Since Olson's and Connie's deaths, Frances has been interviewed by some researchers, including Tom Clark, whose Charles Olson: The Allegory of a Poet's Life *(New York: Norton, 1991), pp. 154–56, recounts her story of the first rendezvous, in early November 1949, in the New York Public Library entrance, and the lengths to which Olson went the next day to get on the same train as Frances, who was visiting friends in Tarrytown, New York. The poem "Epigon," sent by Olson on his return to Washington, celebrates an event that was magical to both of them, taking place in a "faery circle" of trees near the Hudson River (see* Collected Poems, *p. 93).*

⋅⋅❧ 51 ❧⋅⋅

Woodward to Washington
10 November 1949 (postmark)

A brief list.

1. The negro who had taken such loving care of us on the way to Baltimore, walked up to us in the dining car and leaning towards Lucinda asked, "Do you know I have been saying over and over again, 'How's your little girl?'" And he surrounded us with his thoughtful beautiful service.

2. The taxi ride was passed between dream and reality—

3. When I stepped into my home I had forgotten that I had left fresh daisies —and they were so fresh, so speaking—so alive—cannot tell you how that "hold" pressed its tiny fingers against my consciousness.

4. Since arrogance is my metier—decided *not* to work this week—but to do it all in one fell swoop next week.

5. Received, after I had gone to Pittsburgh and seen how unready the plant was for my layout and instructions and had surrendered all claim to any

job done—a check for the complete business which Roney says they decided afterwards they could use. The complete surrender and then the
win.

The circle completed.
And with this morning, a terrific sense of the muscles of the foot pressing
firmly, by very strong feel—the eyes not for the present of use, either closed or
open. First the foot muscle bespeaking the silent orders to all the gradations of
life in the universe.

◄ 52 ►

Washington to Woodward (special delivery)
11 November 1949 (postmark 11 November 1949)

EPIGON

in whose heart it
burns

Beauty hath
two forms

in the hidden wood, in
the room, sleep

Lady, who
art

birth is as green and rock
as magic ring and hummock by
wearing water. Birth
is a euphemism, two eyes
is more accurate: it is the mortal which matters,
from which I now spring

intent,
the measure

Nature,
is proved again

I am
of use

blood has to be spent, this boreal heath warmed
out from this faery circle (in the November sun
creatures present, including the angelic orders, ordering)
to take on the demons, to regain
first principles, crying
redeem, redeem
the dead

you,
who art awake!

olson, motz
11 11 xlix

✥ 53 ✥

Washington to Woodward (postcard)
12 November 1949 (postmark)

dein Brust
ist Ruh

mein Herz
stark

✥ 54 ✥

Woodward to Washington
12 November 1949 (postmark)

Saturday

Meant to say this to you while we were in that last big conversation, but the thing flowed so rapidly and I didn't get it in there. This is not a final statement, but just the impression I had immediately upon reading it and an impression which deepens after a reading of Gorki's *Barbarians* (a clear call for you and me to come into the ring) and after some more Blake—

The Kingfishers is new Olson—direct speech—the beginning of the form—

not law, and not dance pattern, but the dance rhythm of the most potent establishing the free moving pattern of all participants. I request that once when it is printed it say in parenthesis or somewhere to L.F.M. (my father) whose name was also Francis—because this morning it strikes me with what anxiety he awaited you and how he would have opened his passionate eyes and shut them again and spoken to you so sternly "Give me a kiss".—

I am too excited to speak of the lines in detail but the thing seems so separate from whatever has gone before—I feel that the form will press itself through the great wide crack more and more firmly—not in the head, but in the snake-head via the hand.

Frances

⋅⋗ 55 ⋖⋅

Woodward to Washington
13 November 1949 (postmark 14 November 1949)

Sunday—Lucinda in church

Woodward now the way I love it—gray and hidden into itself—in my stove the odor of hemlock which Lucinda and I in the bright grass gathered—she scolding, I obeying!

For some years my brain has been lazing away from one or two problems—I am too easy now to express them accurately—but this is public notice that they are passed on, that the blood has to be spent twice, once to flare, to illumine and a second time to rhythm-hammer a new out.

I read Melville as an adult for the first time.

"I'd strike the sun if it insulted me. For could the sun do that, then could I do the other; since there is ever a sort of fair play herein, jealousy presiding over all creations. But not my master, man, is even that fair play. Who's over me? Truth hath no confines."[1]

EVEN THAT FAIR PLAY. WHO'S OVER ME?

Meister Eckhart has a sermon on *Disinterest*—which I have always considered his best and my best. But in the unexamined residue of my spirit, where I have not had the passion to follow (having employed my passion to follow out the other question—"what is a man and what is a woman"—) I have more than once suspected that this was a *very* fancy card sharpers' trick—to win.

WHO'S OVER ME?

1. from chapter 36 of *Moby-Dick*.

Why should I not strike the sun? Why does any vaguest suggestion of humility enter *at all*? Why should man not raise the top of his crown and *push—hard*—suppose the Pequod does go down—are there no more boats to follow? Suppose he does get beaten, not through one life but through five lives—is the question less a question?

WHO'S OVER ME? Nothing at all to do with the Christian problem relation to fellow man—only to do with how? the manner. You know that Gilgamesh *found* the herb of life, but when he lay down to sleep—a serpent stole up and ate it. To require first principles indeed—let us go back to the beginning—not to fake any of the glossed over ones—if we never get over the first one—O.K.—we will not have glossed it. Why shouldn't the sun be beaten to a pulp if necessary—why should man have pity, humility, gratitude—any of it?

Why should he not stand with his terrific hammer and turn with such a fierce turn that that serpent-head—his spoke—will send clarity through all the surrounding movement and in that immense clarity the beloved instrument, the insight, the brain serviced to the beat—will press, press—for the out.

And gracious indeed the hand there extended—thou God callest on me—thou art indeed welcome—shall we drink?

Problem 2, which is different, some other time
  "   3, which is related,   ditto

Most perfect and silence-surrounded gift I have ever received. I make no sound because in the morning—I remembered "And if you never hear from me"—and my soul—aghast—answered—"You know I can do it, I can and I will—but oh! please do not demand this of me"—and in the evening, the gift and I so shy to receive.

✥ 56 ✥

State College to Washington (special delivery)
15 November 1949 (postmark)

By virtue of its essence or "idea" the personality is both immortal and eternal; but our world is especially fatal to everything immortal and eternal. For that reason, the personality is most in danger of death when nearest to self-realization.

                                                                Berdyaev

✥ 57 ✥

Woodward to Washington
16 November 1949 (postmark)

Wednesday 3:30pm
alone in my house

I am proud, Olson, that I have put the niggers in their places so that no one acted as though he had even noticed that I had been away and now I have made my escape again for this week.

It is not possible to exaggerate what mountains of time have reared in front of me since receiving your postcard—Monday a.m.—each minute of the day Tuesday existed as a solid entity with which I had to cope—this letter is not to be a letter—I am strung somewhere between myself and the solution of pain—it is only to say—to repeat You are to stay alive—that is all that matters—to stay alive so that you will again be able to work—you have given yourself so many jobs and I have several such beauties waiting to thrust at you.

I expect absolutely nothing from you—except what the special requested —that however long it takes—when at last there is some peace—some road, bought at whatever price and no matter paved with what—nod to me—because until you can go down—I can not live.

And I am absolutely completely at your service—if the house thing comes up or anything else—I feel such terrific strength—transferred from you to me—you must have felt it in the Sunday letter.

I read *Genius and the Mobocracy*[2] and it seems to me that even the architect has to wait until Olson has laid a landing plot. This is a wild love letter filled with all the wildest expressions—I greet to all in your new name.

I would appreciate one thing—I have no copy of The K—if you get time, would you type it out for me.

I hope to God these my letters are not intrusions.

Frances

✧ 58 ✧

Washington to Woodward
[17 November 1949]

thursday

If I have time! Time
is a shell love breaks

I send you the K[3]

---

2. Frank Lloyd Wright, *Genius and Mobocracy* (New York: Duell, Sloan & Pearce, 1949).

3. This letter exists in the Special Collections Library of the Pennsylvania State University, laid in #1 copy of Olson's *Y&X* (1948). To supply her with the poem "The K," Olson apparently sent her a copy of the whole volume that contained it.

My hands are ready to grab new life, new work, but I am still so full of blood my energy merely thrives on itself.

I am a lion, & it is all too clear. I have no talent to dissemble.

About your letters. I have to have them. On top of that you must be as free to write them as I am (if you are not, I am not). So, to be practical: right now, when the thing must be hardest for Con, write me whenever you want, but send 3 to General Delivery to 1 here, regular mail.

Your letter today gave me tremendous joy, and amazement that I understood exactly what you mean by mountains to time reared in front of you. Me, too—and with the strength, God save me, to confront the solidity. In fact, if I could get down from the delightful, painful particulars, I could write, crave to write for you, an EPOS (better, an EPOPÉE). And I mean right now, today. After I mail this we shall find out whether it will get born or merely swim in my blood. (I shall never again refer to "tide": it is an image too dispersed in time, belongs to nature not to man, whose blood is instant to act. There's his difference, & his tragedy, sez this new-born child.)

love, motz

o

❧ 59 ❧

Washington to Woodward
18 November 1949 (postmark)

      for your amusement   friday
      copied off from a letter to
      guess who[4]

they
are the light-hearted races,
therefore
enjoy nothing so much, obviously,
as the cracking of skulls

Troy's fields
were covered with 'em

4. Olson has here typed in verse form a postscript to a letter to Edward Dahlberg dated 18 November 1949 (see "The Laughing Ones," *Collected Poems*, pp. 95–96).

Their mortality
is altogether pervasive, these
chillun
of the sun

The earth
(the others
call it darkling)
they flee. Persephone
is never of their making, nor
Demeter. So
women are delights, things
to run with, play, equals,
deers they slay

It is true. The sun breeds slayers,
makers of spring, & slayers. There it is:
Celts   light, light, thin with it,
& only in love with
the dark, which they never know. How can they?

Their blood does not go down, races out.
And they like to see it,
out
    They only remember what space has had her arms around

You dark men root in woman as the cave. They,
the splinters, want to dance,
only to dance,
& slay. They,
are without suspicion, stupid,
gay, think the world is a banquet leading not to conversation but
a scrap
       O
what shall men do with these empty-heads, before they destroy us? you,
who favor the beat, not the color of,
blood?

what shall we do to bring them down, the laughing ones
who do not have beautiful teeth?
                      one of 'em
                          o

    p.s. hot off—do drop it back: maybe there's a line in it. Tell me, my wizardess.

⇥ 60 ⇤

Millheim, Pa. to Washington (postcard)
19 November 1949 (postmark)

Saturday

Report on offspring—
      I was begged to read La Chute II
      Verdict: "It's a beautiful poem, MaMe"—
         BUT I STILL HATE OLSON!

      Prophecy: Victory
         and may it extend to all the 2nd generation
         once said to my wailing child, opening an
         enclosing arm "You want to come into the
         magic circle too?" end of wails

      Am overwhelmed with your generosity—heaviest volume of poetry in existence—and that includes EURIPIDES.

⇥ 61 ⇤

Washington to Woodward
21 November 1949 (postmark)

monday evening

darling
      for reasons you & i know the cause of, i have been smashing, the last two days, & sending out, pieces done last winter i was then reluctant to release   i wish i'd made a copy of yesterday's, which went to England,[5] for it is was much better, but this, today,[6] i send you, not in pride but merely to be present to you, (merely, says he!)
      i am going down now to the P.O., in fondest hope
((in the mails today came
the news the melville piece (on hawthorne, homosexuality & hebraism) is to

---

   5. With a letter of 17 November 1949, Olson sent to Peter Russell, of *Nine* magazine in England, two Pound-related items he had in his desk: (1) "This Is Yeats Speaking," already published in *Partisan Review*; and (2) "GrandPa, GoodBye," the latter typed up from notes of his last visit to Pound (see *Collected Prose*, pp. 145–51).
   6. This is the seven-page essay "The Dryness, of 'The Tempest'" in the Olson Archives at Storrs. Boldereff returned her copy.

appear in the current Western Review,[7] & when my two copies come—that's
the pay—you'll have one))

> it is a thing i thank life for, you stay so alive inside me
> the O

p.s.: send the enclosed back some time

[*Enclosure:*]

THE DRYNESS, OF "THE TEMPEST"

Prospero, and the verse, are an odd mark of Shakespeare's play, and for a
common reason: they back and halt as though they bridle at what life is, and
spring their act, or burden, out, in despite of it, that is, in despite of life. Prospero's dry answer, "'Tis new to thee" to Miranda's giddy exclamations on her
first look at the brave, new world, is the mainspring of the machine which creates both Prospero and the lines, the intent phrase and the removed man.

For Prospero is distant from himself by a distance so great as to distinguish
him from any other "hero", at least in Shakespeare. Or not so distant as, dis-
junct: he does all things but sees all things suspect. Prospero is the opposite of
both the enthusiast and the cynic, yet each of these is the pole of his behaviour
and his statement. Prospero accomplishes both a righting of justice and a
wished-for marriage (these are the plot), looks on both with a sort of pleasure,
yet, like the verse, his color is all cool. (A production of the play, admitting the
noise and raiment, the baroque of the dukes, Caliban, the storm, Ariel, the
masque, must disclose this other aspect, or fail. It is the mark of the play's intensity.)

It is easy to put a hand on the passage which reveals this Prospero, but not so
easy to make it do it. It is so well known for its rhetoric its dramatic purpose
is hard to see. On the surface of it, it seems what it has been taken for, the fa-
talism of the ideal:

> And, like the baseless fabric of this vision,
> The cloud-capp'd towers, the gorgeous palaces,
> The solemn temples, the great globe itself,
> Yea, all which it inherit, shall dissolve,
> And, like this insubstantial pageant faded,
> Leave not a rack behind.

It is the burden of Prospero's sense of life, but, phrased so (the passage does not
yield the same secret of the verse), it is too philosophic to give Prospero up in

---

7. Olson's review of F. Barron Freeman's *Melville's Billy Budd* appeared in *Western Review* 14 (fall
1949): 63–66. See *Collected Prose*, pp. 109–12.

his proper density. For Prospero's nerves are more interesting than what he calls later in the same passage his "beating mind." (I suppose one has to lay the large flaw of the play to his nerves—the sudden decision, a hundred lines later, at the beginning of Act V, to forgive Antonio, Sebastian and Alonso, a mechanical ending of conflict too lax even for the convention the TEMPEST is cast in, however best that can be defined. It is a sudden sway of his system, after a Faust-like exercise of power a philosophic slack or shrug, "it's not worth, the baseless fabric, the effort.")

This polarity of Prospero is why Gonzalo matters, both in the play and in Prospero's mind. Gonzalo is the good, but the good with no fight in it, a Gloucester who sees that Prospero and Miranda have food and clothes and books when they are treacherously put to sea by orders of Antonio, but who goes on serving the man who aided Antonio in his deed. Gonzalo is also philosphic, the man who knows the ideal and labors for it, that is, approximately. It is Gonzalo, it needs to be remembered, who proposes:

> I'th' commonwealth I would by contraries
> Execute all things . . .

a passage, by the way, I have seen somewhere so misunderstood, recently, as to be said to have been uttered with the tongue in the cheek. Nothing could be more base in error, nor more mistake Shakespeare's intention in this play.

That intention is, to pitch the matter precisely in between two poles, between enthusiasm and dismay. The TEMPEST is, by this irony, the least a tempest of any Shakespeare play. By contrary to its pother, storm, enter mariners wet, great dukedoms stolen, married into, voices, music in the air, magic, drunkenness, the TEMPEST is a wry thing, not even a play, a drama. It defies formal definition because it purposely sets convention outside its business, most obviously uses the conventions only to arrive at a position of life quite beside them, and I can think of an equivalent only in another tradition than the whole of Western drama, from the Greeks to now. So far as its form, and Prospero's position in that form go, the TEMPEST carries more of a suggestion of the Noh of Japan, though it needs immediately to be said that the TEMPEST's form is too personal to its creator to have any of the force or arrive at any of the drama that the Noh, with Zen Buddhism behind it, accomplishes.

Which leads me to the verse, its creator's cloth, and, through the verse, to that which is the complexity of Prospero. Others among the modern poets have observed how feminine and dry the metric and the syntax is, how much the effect lies in a precision of language quite fresh and new to blank verse as it had been handled up to the TEMPEST's day. In this play it is almost as though Shakespeare was as done with the conventions of language as he is with those of life. Take him in the masque itself, where he is, as in the play proper, using these conventions to the hilt. Lines come out most clean:

> Of wheat, rye, barley, fetches, oats, and pease

> Which spongy April at thy hest betrims
> To make cold nymphs chaste crowns

And phrases: the bachelor "lasslorn," Ferdinand's, the "bed-right". But it is in the intricate satisfaction of the full idea made to enunciate itself without any elevation that the new power shows itself:

> Her waspish-headed son has broke his arrows,
> Swears he will shoot no more, but play with sparrows
> And be a boy right out

or

> You nymphs, called Naiades, of the wand'ring brooks,
> With your sedg'd crowns and ever-harmless looks,
> Leave your crisp channels, and on this green land
> Answer your summons

What is true of the verse of the masque is true of the verse of the play as a whole, from the opening care with the seaman's idiom (the curious rimes: cheer, stir, yare), the quick, caustic scrap that follows between the bo'sun and the lords, into and throughout the play, even to such use of the old image as this:

> And think'st it much to tread the ooze
> Of the salt deep,
> To run upon the sharp wind of the North,
> To do me business in the veins o' th'earth
> When it is bak'd with frost

This is a poet who knows verse shall be as sharp and sweet as wood is made, of its grain, and use. And when there is a rise in it, it is in a phrase, not a sounding line:

> "thou earth", says Caliban

or

To name the bigger light.

There is even, in a remark of Sebastian's (I,i,185), such an obvious allusion to Lyly's "To go a bat-fowling for stars," as to suggest that Shakespeare felt himself starting all over again, at the point where he went off with the lyric, with the false sweet, to do it again, now, and right. At this other extreme, Prospero's, from VENUS AND ADONIS or THE RAPE OF LUCRECE, the verse and the matter must declare one answer, and that the same answer that Ariel gives to Antonio, Sebastian and Alonso, when he has rehearsed their crimes to them and warns them there is but one way out:

> nothing but heart's sorrow
> And a clear life ensuing

For the verse and the matter are one, are of Prospero's, and his creator's place, one step off from man, from his vulgarities, and his obscenities. The play is loaded with deprecations of man:

> When they will not give a doit to relieve a lame beggar
> They will lay out ten to see a dead Indian

or Antonio's

> All idle—whores and knaves

against which Prospero, Gonzalo and Ariel raise up not so much half-hearted but fully-dismayed objections. Gonzalo:

> If in Naples
> I should report this now, would they believe me?
> If I should say, I saw such islanders
> (For certes these are people of the island),
> Who, though they are of monstrous shape, yet, note,
> Their manners are more gentle, kind, than of
> Our human generation you shall find
> Many—nay, almost any

to which Prospero, in an aside, says

> Honest lord,
> Thou hast said well; for some of you there present
> Are worse than devils.

To the quandary, what is the essence of man, in the dirtiness where is the humanness (which Ariel, in conversation with Prospero, suggests is the capacity of the affections to become tender), the TEMPEST has no answer. Between Caliban and Ariel, Prospero cannot put out his finger or his rod and say, this is it. What Prospero does is what characterizes him, the verse and the play: he merely suggests a methodology by which to get through life. It may best be called, the method of, by the coldness of chess and snow.

It all comes to bear by one obsession, Prospero's obsession: innocence. This is all he—or Gonzalo—can oppose. It makes the plot. Prospero wants one thing, the marriage of his daughter, but he wants it high, wants it in a way he has not found life, wants it with the high control of the puppet-maker he is because he has found out no other thing than that he, too, is a puppet, and that life, if it is to be a clear life ensuing, must be by a method of control. Its declaration, and the upshot of the whole TEMPEST, verse et al—is in these lines:

Prospero (to Ferdinand)*:*
    Look thou be true. Do not give dalliance
    Too much rein. The strongest oaths are straw
    To th' fire i' th' blood. Be more abstemious,
    Or else good night your vow

Ferdinand:
                                 I warrant you, sir.
    The white cold virgin snow upon my heart
    Abates the ardor of my liver.

It is only on such terms that Prospero will allow the transfer of his potency, and it is only when he believes that he has effected it, that he breaks his rod.

⇥ 62 ⇤

New York to Woodward
22 November 1949 (postmark)

aboard "Montrealer" New York[8]
Tuesday

A bad ceth, Babe, to those gods of ours who were, up to now, propitious. (I am confusing myself, these days, with one, Julius Caesar)
       I hope I flushed no sitting ducks. I took ultimate care. The idea was, to come to Woodward for the night. (Dahlberg suddenly called me early this

---

8. This letter was written on board the train to New Rochelle, New York.

morning to ask me to appear in court, New Rochelle, tomorrow morning, 10:10 AM, in his fight to have some custody of his two boys.) I'd hoped to turn a duty into a joy. But, anyway, it would have had to be Harrisburg, in order for me to have got N Rochelle. And does lightning strike twice etc. (Those planes you talked of, are no help.) Back Washington tomorrow. Let's drop the General Delivery. (It was the Special Delivery caused trouble) Let 'em come, straight.

Signed, at the moment,

Catullus "Odi et amo,

etc"

⤞ 63 ⤝

Woodward to Washington
23 November 1949 (postmark)

Wednesday

at last by myself

Olson you lovely baby—

I have a feeling that this letter will also arrive at the wrong time—I purposely went out late at night with the special trying to schedule the thing right—but missed—sorry on that one—but I am going to do as daddy says.

Don't you know that although your gods were out, mine were here? I spent literally most of the night hours in so ardent communication with your vibrant spearhead—couldn't it be that you didn't know you really were here, since I woke up all beautiful and "shone with ardor" as Blake tells.

I am so excited about the poem and "the dryness"—about that in a minute—

hear my boy Blake

"Luvah and Vala, henceforth you are Servants : obey and live!
You shall forget your former state. Return, O Love, in peace
Into your place, the place of Seed, not in the brain or heart.
If Gods combine against Man, Setting their dominion above
The Human form Divine, Thrown down from their high station
In the eternal heavens of Human Imagination, buried beneath
In dark Oblivion with incessant pangs ages on ages
In enmity and war first weakened; then in stern repentance
They must renew their brightness, and their disorganized functions
Again reorganize, till they resume the image of the human,
Cooperating in the bliss of man, obeying his Will,
Servants to the infinite and Eternal of the Human form."

Four Zoas—Night IX

"Visions of these eternal principles or characters of human life appear to poets, in all ages; the Grecian gods were the ancient Cherubim of Phoenicia; but the Greeks, and since them, the Moderns, have neglected to subdue the gods of Priam. These gods are visions of the eternal attributes or divine names, which, when erected into gods, became destructive to humanity. They ought to be the servants and not the masters of man, or of society. They ought to be made to sacrifice to man, and not man compelled to sacrifice to them; for when separated from man, or humanity, who is Jesus the Saviour, the vine of eternity, they are thieves and rebels, they are destroyers."

Descriptive Catalogue iii, p. 21

I am very well pleased Mr. Charles the sone with your poem, which does not amuse[9] but very much impresses me. There is one thing that makes me unhappy—I dare to mention it, not because you are wrong, but just to have my say—to rid of a small pain left from the past.

"You dark men root in woman."—could it not be left so? A very beautiful sentence. I will copy you out from a very tiny notebook of a young 18-year old Ganny in a minute—But want to add this—among one or two of my brightest young men—the ones who know—"cave" due to Plato and his others has come to stand among us, as all that entangles life and prevents young men from moving—"cave" has come to be all the part you can't move which destroys you and has such a deep weighted overtone of sorrow to me personally—

So could it not be please—"You dark men root in woman". I hope you are not playing—I hope you mean the toes grasping with such Michelangelo joy into the warmth of the living bowel of woman—because that is the image I get—nothing but that lovely sensitive arch and the finding toes sending living sprouts of freedom up into the spearhead and beyond, into your well loved instrument and the male arching neck.

From a tiny hand-made book given to me by Ruthie 1923—the Mrs. Bodycombe I visited with Elizabeth—the entry reads October 16—with no year—my guess is 1924—I wish, (you will please understand this) it could be read to Connie in a dream.

"If I have failed to keep my inward poise, must I be sad? I feel that I am the blossom, and he, all the sustaining plant. He is firm leaves and roots that are strong to find. He, the substance, and I the enjoyment of it and the purpose. We are the meaning of each other, each separate and yet one together. This is sorrow; it is also joy, and if it hurts a little that the seed must burst open in the

9. The poem discussed here is "The Laughing Ones," sent 18 November 1949.

dark earth, so does it hurt that my understanding opens in the darkness of a wound he had to give, much as a farmer needs to plant."

I think I mentioned that I never read Shakespeare because of the barbaric antiquity of his sex morality—*so* your piece comes as a very great thrill—to meet Shakespeare through Olson who is so very right—I can never tell you what a thrill— I want to keep and copy and will then return. Your mind and your language are the personal—therefore in my language the most profoundly religious of anyone's I have ever found.

Your loving appreciative daughter.

⋘ 64 ⋙

Woodward to Washington
26 November 1949 (postmark)

Saturday afternoon

Olson dear—
   I walk around fearful that in my enthusiasm for a new life I have pulled another grade A boner. And please say I most surely do not expect any sort of acknowledgement.[10]

I love your poem without title very much ("Otvechai" means the imperative tense of "answer"—it is the title I have given it)[11]—it has several very powerful things in it perhaps best of all I love

"light, light, thin with it,
only in love with
the dark, which they never know."

Among other things what a fine passionate speech on the subject of what love can not do—I found in my 18-year-old notebook last night (January 18 of the following year I presume)

"How often has it come into me that love is not enough—"

You would love Woodward and I beg you to come—if possible alone, but I will know how and could with genuine pleasure receive both of you. I am, as

---

10. She had apparently sent a package to Connie Olson—the one referred to in Olson's letter of 28 November 1949.
11. This is again "The Laughing Ones," sent (without title) 18 November 1949.

I am sure you are—a person devoted to secrecy—if I am married 14 years I do not want the light in my eyes to show in front of anyone—even my brother and I want never even myself to know—what is the hour to come in to me—

I return your article which I am too lazy to copy, but carry around in my head for reference in future study.

But let me remind you that Jesus is the one who said—

> And one came to the master and said, "Lord, I would follow thee.
> But first let me go bid farewell to my family—"

And Jesus said—(may eternal glory shine on his mouth)

> "No *man*, having put his hand to the plow, and looking backward
> is fit for the kingdom of God."
> "Get down family—where you belong!"

On the subject of no "sitting ducks" Lucinda said very aloud in the diner to the waiter (the one we knew from before), did I tell you?—

"Yes, and I can tell you who she's going to marry. She slept with him last night."   !

The Motz

Boldereff the I "No man can ever say I have ever slept with a woman."

almost forgot—

Sunday morning—in bed with Lucinda the light pouring in—she told me she was disappointed in Martha this time—so I entered into a long serious discussion of what is happening to people in This Country—how she must be prepared to pull her heart in and expect almost nothing from people in the way of being able to really communicate—told her about your saying that she and I must start a new race, what you meant—and she said, "Who else belongs?" and I told her you and the Brookhaven Laboratory Don and F.L.W and Mrs. Davis (who is a mother) and much later she asked, "Does grandmother understand about this new race?" and I said "Definitely not." She declared, "That's what I thought." Oh thou maker who has created understanding in the hearts of children—

And you know she will come through with god's grace.

The big big thing I want you to work on darling is the pattern of innocence—no one I have discovered, not Blake, not Joyce, not Kierkegaard, not Dostoevsky—has been willing to throw overboard completely the sin business—the necessary guilt—the thing born with Adam—and I *feel* although my head is not strong enough to figure out how, that original sin in any degree whatsoever is nonsense—also the existence of a previous golden or good anything. I would like in other words to take the whole Sumerian-Semitic myth and cast it out. I think man has to strive for innocence not because he is sinful but because innocence is the real home of the creative being—the milieu in which he can alone *make*. And let us by all means cast sharp, hurtful stones, as you suggested in La Chute II on the lazy, the uncomplaining, the good-natured—who have ruled this earth so god-damned long. Gorki has a marvelous burst of pain in his "My university days" on how we should burst the bonds of the weak who have been trampling on the strong for centuries. This is why you have hated the Christian so much—

✦ 65 ✦

Washington to Woodward
28 November 1949 (postmark)

monday

daddy to the Motz, communication:
   if i had them, it would be necessary to transplant my iron nerves to you but i do not have any such caesarian things   mine are purchased at human life's cost

   it is also true, and this has to be reckoned with, that i am not so caesarian as to take action swiftly, where vital things are concerned   a poet of my stamp is as conservative on one side, the side of the mechanics of living, as he may be the opposite on line and form (i reckon the cost here too, but the method, where work is concerned, has its advantages)

   you quote me men whose wisdom, over there, i can respect—the difference is, over here, i have my work to do, and it is of a vastly different order, or, rather, of method, again, because, among other causes, i am, as man is, omni-vore

   darling, you have had a taste of the man, but you know the poet better (better, i can tell you, than he knows himself; thus he can learn)   always imagine his exigencies, and their effect upon the man

****

olson, to you, for love's sake:
   i have been off beat for some days, exhausted from that fast trip (it turned out to be a tremendous act for Dahlberg, and, thus, the turning of an arc in, for me), and from a 24 hr visit from Ragsdale which, because it came before I could pick up rest, knocked me out

your package came plump in the middle, and goes back to you unopened by the lady to whom it was sent and who thus disposes of it

i read Blake the afternoon after your letter came, and, for the first time, was inside him   the letters, though, & the catalogue prose on Chaucer, not the verse (it still balks me, he did not give the language the care it, because it is an organism, like the rest of us, demands) one image that delighted me i give you back for the joy: "doubt not yet to make a figure in the great dance of life that shall amuse the spectators in the sky" (to Hayley, 1/27/1804)

otherwise it is my big man Sauer who turns my attention back to work by sending me his paper on "Environment and Culture During the Last Deglacia-tion,"[12] read before the American Philosophical Society, two years ago   it is on the fresh-water fisher folk of Mesolithic time, and sends this child

who is an awe-

ful lot

yrs

◄ 66 ►

Woodward to Washington
29 November 1949 (postmark)

I loathe this paper and this pen!

"Below the surface of our present age, psychic forces have been released, and are obscurely stirring and heaving, that cry out for a new Pantagruel to interpret them. With some of these forces Rabelais would have profoundly sympathized, confronted by others he would have been completely at sea. One by one the wild-eyed heads of these new-born Ideas emerge, and emerge from queer directions and unexpected quarters. But one thing we are already permitted by destiny to note; namely that the impulsion behind them is from below, and *yet not from hell* (italics his)
    "Their movement is spiral; but it is on and up and out; not round and down and back."

John Cowper Powys in *Rabelais*

And he names names—his enemies—Reinhold Niebuhr, T. S. Eliot, Berdyaev in some respects—the whole Catholic and/or reactionary world. And you can see—who have already received your orders which you so

12. Carl O. Sauer, "Environment and Culture in the Last Deglaciation," *Proceedings of the American Philosophical Society* 92 (1948) 65–77. An offprint inscribed to Olson was retained in his papers.

deeply obey—that all of us, Northrop Frye-Powys-Rimbaud—me—are aware that we need you—

My step on the earth is a beseeching that your strength and beauty will readjust any confusion which my unwarranted poking in of my presence has caused. And a further silent beseeching that I may not cause you any more confusion

My light-stepping, elegant Potemkin.

Brubaker Motz

◃ 67 ▹

Woodward to Washington
30 November 1949 (postmark)

Wednesday morning in
haṣte before my bus
comes your Monday
letter just received

So many letters from me are because you once said you loved mail, but if receiving them takes out from you something you need—the quantity can instantly reduce—and thereby the quality will rise—this is no childish nonsense—just in case the above is true just a p.c. to say "slow down, Motz" will do the trick.

do not know for sure at the moment what the first several paragraphs exactly mean but hasten to tell you, dear, that I feel that a person like you should move slow as mountains—why should *any* details of life have to be paid attention to by you—as far as I am concerned the only reason you have to do anything about eating, sleeping—forms of life is because as you say you are an organism. Whatever phrase of mine could have made you feel I expect anything—if it was "enthusiasm for the new life"—that meant the picture I dream of to come into being 10000 years from now. I get into trouble (like sending the present) because I slip identity so damned easily—I sit inside other people and love and feel their language and I forget they don't do it and then I am simply awkward.

this letter is only to say again I expect nothing—I trust you absolutely about everything—if it doesn't suit you to write me for 6 months do not do it—I am strong, I love you with every particle of my being—you have given me such courage and joy that at the moment I balance this globe on my ring finger and don't even have to look—I am doing beautiful stuff in my printing plant[13] and I try in every way to make my position strong so that some day I can be of real use to you as I dream.

Your devoted daughter

◅ 68 ▻

Washington to Woodward (postcard)
1 December 1949 (postmark)

keep emcomin, lady mine

◅ 69 ▻

Woodward to Washington
3 December 1949 (postmark 5 December 1949)

Saturday

Olson dear—

I do not know what is the tiniest, shyest creature you have ever stared at, but my guess is it is the one now standing in your hand. It is taking all the love and all the adulthood at command to open that door, the entrance to your home, this small fraction to slip inside and to stand there and speak loud enough for you to hear. Soon I am going for a walk in my white Woodward where very small and shy things come close and the terrible shyness in my breast bones subsides. Since earliest childhood a raised eyebrow has put me to torture and to be exposed three nights running when I am asleep and defenceless to the presence of Olson scolding me almost parts the thin skin over those breast bones—never more than covered at best.

Whatever the world does or has done, my Charles the son, let you and I have this: I have given you my trust, you give me yours. My hold will endure to the end of the world—the only thing that could make it disappear would be a suspicion that I was in the way—so I will accept as an agreement between us—since I really am so trembling in the presence of something I respect—that if for any reason the thing alters between us that you will state this aloud—not in silence—and with this understanding I can go on without words from you for a very long time.

13. Boldereff had been working for over a month at Nittany Printing & Publishing Company, State College, Pennsylvania.

I despise hints—no quotation I ever sent you was ever any kind of suggestion or comment or hint—the Blake was only a proud mother holding up her baby to say "see how handsome." I happened to mention the nose, but equally could have called attention to the fingers.

Please my darling with that exquisite tenderness you have—do not speak to me but put out that large finger and stroke it down my whole very very minute self so shyly present.

> That daughter who once almost
> lost her life for entering
> unbidden

⊸< 70 >⊷

Washington to Woodward (special delivery)
3 December 1949 (postmark)

saturday

i know, sweet   i have taken up the same kind of power, swell out until people can't stand it, and run away   it happened hugely one night this week (it has been a peculiar week, for tho i have yet to lick that cold fatigue brought on, i have had the goddamndest social week, out every night to dinner, lecture, theatre, party, and days to gallery, funeral, a political chore, making arrangements and keeping appointments to mount a Cagli show December 15 I dreamed up and acted on out of our power)   and it has been like a 1st olympian game, testing, testing who this new man olson is   of course the characters don't know he's testing himself, all they see is altogether too much pressure coming in at them   the incident was at a studio after Jose Limon danced (the performance was my 2nd in life of the mud'n dance, and led to final conclusions, & embarrassment the Graham Co owns that piece of my property, ahabadance, alias the fiery 'unt)   i was wild, and successively the best dopes i know hereabouts including old rock rudd fleming and a new one that night from new orleans, the photographer laughlin, and couple of ladies, managed to go away! drift off to the turkey, or for coffee, or excuse themselves, their 'escorts (rime:horsecarts) were ready to take 'em home

you don't
know, perhaps, but i don't much go out   the people's poor banquet society is too thin a table, mostwise   and this will end tonight   but it has been one of those things like politics where i see what happens with my energy

which is

all beside the point, for the real power, what you are talking about, stays home, though i am such a sensualist that i have not yet put it to work, have only allowed myself to feel it like a goddamnwonderful bull (haven't done a piece of words since that trip broke me off a week ago monday with the dryness, o tempest potatoe)[14]

by the way, i was most excited by yr remark about mr will shax barbarity womanwise   when i am with you i am going to lead you out on that one   now that i am a wiser man i am sharpened on like feelings about him, and, as i hope was clear, au fond to the piece on THE T, the settlement for in-no-sense on prospero & gonzalo's part was meant to indicate i thought such idealism sought from unappeased violence was short of solid sight   tell me, does the piece give this hint, or no?

no sign yet of DAVID YOUNG, DAVID OLD, the W.R. melville piece,[15] but in the mails this morning from tokio came la preface[16] standing up well off the page in eng-lish, in friend kitasono's CENDRE-VOU 33   the poem still catches some of my attention, for certain severities, & for the projection of present necessity, but i no longer like (did i ever) such a pun as vita nuova (in the way, i accept), such extra push as cunnus in the crotch and, generally (& this I object to in THE K, certainly in the Green Man, least, now, strangely enuf, in Moebus) a posing of the self on the surface of the poem, instead of most presently if anonymously inside it (this posing came, comes from the eyes too directly out on social reality . . . . . .)

so, there, darling, is olson on olson just for a token of telling to the motz how what she has had to say about the motz on olson has sharpened daddy up—eh?

it is cold as a bitch here today   i can't get the furnace to make steam   i am wrapped in my joseph robe, a high colored afghan mother mary made for the son some years ago

this is also to tell you I'll be along soon to you   you must confirm my impression you are home in woodward from wednesday afternoon through monday morning? and that monday-tuesday are not so good? i have boxed myself in a little by suggesting & getting this Cagli show at the Watkins Gallery, for, in the package, they have asked me to make a spiel the night of

14. Olson is referring to the short essay "The Dryness, of 'The Tempest,'" which he had sent to Bolder-eff on 21 November 1949.

15. Olson's copies of the fall 1949 issue of the *Western Review* had gone astray. He learned this in January 1950.

16. "La Préface" had previously been published in *Y&X*, as had the other poems mentioned: "The K," "The Green Man," and "The Moebius Strip."

the opening (the 15th) on cagli and my experiments with non-euclidian space

how would it be if i came on the 16th? (i wish that it were not in the way & i could come on a wednesday, or thursday: just in case, in yr answer, let me know how this coming thursday (the 8th) would sit with you   i think now the 16th is the more likely, but, if you can, say how both are

i better go & get some heat up, even tho i don't need it with the heart pouring out what it is pouring out

love,

O

◄ 71 ►

Woodward to Washington
5 December 1949 (postmark)

Monday morning

It is money thrown away to send me specials—Woodward is such a tiny place that modern contraptions have no meaning—a telegram is liable to reach me in three days and I get a special when the mail comes in—the same time I would get it anyway—

My big serious brother supervising engineer of T.V.A. whom I have not seen for maybe 4-5 years and then only for a few hours and previous to that not for 5–6—who has always loved me very dearly—a kind of sex deal which he ignores and maintains towards me a distant admiration and absolute silence—is coming on the *16th* to Woodward—only person in the family he has called on in 25 years—big honor and all that—the old lady will be here and I am expected and will enjoy to kill the fatted calf—shine up the silver and make him welcome—you would have approved of him in his youth—his nickname "The Prince"—tres elegant—red cheeks—black hair—white skin—tall willowy—dancer—now a heavy serious army man not in the army except Reserve but very the type—expert in concrete—the old Brubaker brain

So, darling if you *can* make the 8th I will love it—my old lady leaves on Wednesday night on the bus I come home on—7:30 p.m. if it is not late—Monday through Wednesday *out*

I have four things to scream with you about

1. That Blake's language was not given care—opposite is true

2. Melville's relation to sex—found a sentence that as an old female expert on a hot man practically knocked me out—now think he was a very passionate guy who was nuts about women—too damned involved in that 19th century and his idea of honor especially in relation to marriage—Christ if I only could have been with him once—much of the gravity of his de profundis chapters is that terrible loss of no hot cunt to pour it into and of course it would have had to go with eyes and the 19th century just didn't furnish such an animal

3. The old man Shakespeare who has been for years since 16—to be precise—one of the No. 1 Motz enemies. "Frailty—thy name is woman"

4. That James the Joyce had no message.

Will also discuss freely La Préface etc.—my objection to it has always been what you mention   eye on social reality—
Otvechai
The King Fishers
Epigon (only fine love poem in existence) not necessarily for publication
The She Bear

that's the list

Wish to God you had been on a party with Brubaker Motz when she was pouring out the wit so goddamned hot and fast—we are perhaps the only two equals alive in the world today and we are better than the Medici—the golden age of Pericles or what have you—

⊷ 72 ⊶

Washington to Woodward
6 December 1949 (postmark)

                                                                tuesday

Lover I: In my breast bones
           I am shy

Lover II: The struggle is
           this simple: where
           we are weakest, there
           strength
           is to be won

Lover I: When you scold
           you almost part
           that thinnest skin
           over them

Lover II: Your breast
           is strong

baby, i shall come this thursday   the only way turns out to be bus all the
way, arriving on that same evening bus you take home from work
           even olson can't say any more: what was it
           you used to put it, about trembling?
                    o

PART IV

❧❧❧

14 December 1949–4 May 1950

A second meeting, this time in Frances's home in Woodward, takes place 8–12 December 1949. There is not to be another for several months. The long absence takes its toll on both parties: Frances rails against the deprivation, while Olson sticks to his typewriter, but not without guilt. These are, however, months of great creativity, of which the writing of letters is not a small part.

❧ 73 ❧

Washington to Woodward
14 December 1949 (postmark 15 December 1949)

wednesday afternoon

my darling: i have stayed in bed to do the Cagli lecture, & (shout The Praises!) it is DONE—in a little over 3 hrs! (On arrival Monday, 5 characters from Black Mt on our doorstep, who bunked in the studio overnight, only left at 2:30 yesterday afternoon; & otherwise occupied with details of show—catalogue, etc.:—all this, too, is pretty much set) So, like you, I spin the ball of reality with the little finger

Forgive paper, & pencil, but if I get up, it is very cold, & I want, after this putting of myself in CONNECT with you, to give myself my 1st chance to catch up on a little sleep.

The POWER stays. It was all even more beautiful. I dream. Nothing is impossible. Hold, sweet one, hold. Your pains are known, & shared. We can look forward, all three of us. The sense we are creating acts for men & women to come is very alive in me at the moment—and that, surely, is of your birth, for, much as I might have imagined such things, I had, pretty much, isolated my sense of such accomplishment to the creative life. You cause me again to think it possible in life unmodified, and it is very beautiful, you are very beautiful.

A letter has just come from Cagli, with his prices,—& this cryptic graph, following on these words: "Suppose: if these drawings (from geometry to paint-ing) will succeed in provocation and cause of another sudden link between you and I—than

answer you answer—

y   x

—the conclusion (for the time being, there is no conclusion, the conclusion
     Poesia orfica   or let me try to be clear

                                        Amaro
                                        stil
graphic automatism   novo
            (geometry)   so long Elliot
subconscio individuale   goodbye Pound
            AULA Della Memoria
            secondo Sant Agostino and Yung
subconscio atavico
            rest to be digged out from xooooo years ago
        to come to coscienza primordiale
                                    LOVE,
                                    Corrado

I am vexed about one thing. I had got very happy & excited when I thought, "Wonderful, I shall send Lucinda my boy Indian stories (Tocamoc Edition), with inscription, "Big Tree to Little Branch," but, for the life of me, I can't find them, & I must have left them in Gloucester. I shall get it in June. Mean-while, somehow, secretly, get over to her, that the old man loves the daughter, too, for her beauty. (If you will please keep L's drawing, my part of the enve-lope, for me, of you dancing on the road, MEMENTO AMARE, & the lovely flying angel, please)

This is a lighted-headed love letter, frances, to tell you DELIGHT, to give you DELIGHT, from him whom you delight[1]

1. This letter was written on the back of a sheet which contained the following notes:
            OLSON
                    HOW ARE YOU?
                    Donald Alter
            Ho Kee-Klop!
            —Flea— P.S.
                        I SHALL WRITE
Olson adds at foot of page "[Black Mt characters]." "Flea" is Fielding Dawson.

Woodward to Washington
15 December 1949 (postmark)

My bedroom streams full of light—it is very Woodward quiet and I am absolutely alone except for the very soft falling of the coal into ash
I send you from an Egyptian legend of Creation—[2]

"I lifted myself up from the watery mass, out of inertness.
I did not find a place where I could stand.
I was alone.
I took courage in my heart.
I laid a foundation.
I made every form.
Many were the forms coming forth my mouth."

FROM EARLY EMPIRE

"There are saamu-flowers in my wreath.
One is uplifted in their presence.
I am thy first sister.
I am unto thee like the acre
Which I have planted with flowers
And all manner of sweet-smelling herbs;
And in it is a pool which thy hand has digged.
In the cool of the North Wind,
It is a lovely place where I walk.
Thine hand upon mine, and my body satisfied,
And my heart glad at our going together.
It is mead to me to hear thy voice,
And I live because I hear it.
If I but see thee
It is better to me than eating or drinking."

Woodward to Washington
16 December 1949 (postmark 17 December 1949)

2. The source of the following lines is at present unknown.

Friday evening

Charles, our pulse—

I was amazed that your letter came so rapidly—but only this moment I realize it is Friday, that the timing is the same—but wish to thank you for it because my guess is that you, like me, move indistinctly everywhere outwordly until a crested thing—a talk before others of something one respects—has been spat out. So I do thank you for thinking of me here and understanding how precious a piece of paper from you would be.

It is a prayer I carry inside me that your Connie—the beauty of whose spirit and being are so clear to me, will one day accept me with love—I need that, in order not to be parted from you when you are moving about elsewhere.

In the unpretentious quiet of Woodward the gift of enlightenment Christ left as his legacy to each of us descends very closely about my spirit and I have absolute trust in us three, each of whom contributes everything that he has.

In the Russian church on Easter all men greet one another with the statement "Vaeestanu voscreci!"[3] and salute one another with three kisses—I am happy that Corrado signs love to you, our pulse.

One day I will take you to the service on Thursday night before Good Friday—the greatest music that has ever been written to express the depth and naked passion with which man moves forward alone through this visible earth.

I can never tell you what beauty it was for me to hear and feel and see you, moving within my physical horizon. It is so beautiful for me that I press silently in my imagination for some pattern which will permit moving in each other's orbit. I also believe slow and easy does it. Lucinda contributes her all— a child can not be won by knowing of your love—she can only be won by your worth—by the sense of your spiritual value—and I am doing I believe a quiet nice job of very slowly letting her perceive why I love you and that I do.

May God in his wisdom and grace watch over all of us—that we may create a noble pattern indestructible and without armor of any fashioning.

Pognod cectpa

(rodenaya sestra)[4]

⊰ 76 ⊱

Washington to Woodward[5]
16 December 1949 (postmark)

3. "Truly He is risen!"
4. Boldereff signs this letter with her Russian equivalent of "your own sister."
5. This letter was written on the back of a flyer for "Drawings in the 4th Dimension & An Introductory

friday

dearest baby, i did the chore, & tho i was praised, my mouth & spirit was, i
don't know why, full of ashes (the 1st time i have heard the song of the worms
since tarrytown)   i have the feeling it was, because you were not there   even
The Kingfishers did not raise me up   what did, was the only piece i read
which is still in the works, the opening of THE PRAISES, which, because it
did, and despite it is, in my eyes, still mss., i shall now send it to you to make
as tho you were there

i miss you, high, beautiful spirit   ilya came, & the Bot-
tle, & because i am a squirrel, i have put them, as I put the Crock of gold, in a

---

Note by Corrado Cagli, Watkins Gallery, The American University, Dec. 15–Jan. l, Opening at 8:30,
Thursday evening, December Fifteenth, with lecture and readings by Charles Olson."

Drawings in the 4th Dimension
by
Corrado Cagli

Two Tempera Drawings
Four Cado Pen Compositions
Seven Lithograph Illustrations
Eleven Hypercube Drawings

When I speak of drawings in the 4th dimension, I am referring to those of my own which obey the
optic spirit and taste, which the mathemetician Donchian has expressed in his projections of solids in the
4th dimension.

To be elementary, that which appears as a cube in three-dimensional space, will in the space of four dimensions, take the form of a hypercube. Once the antithetic space significance of these two solids is understood, it becomes possible to see them as measures of two different pictorial systems—the cube as the rule
and the measure of all painting in three dimensions, the hypercube as the rule and the measure of painting
in the 4th dimension.

Naturally, as the painter makes use of two dimensions to represent a third, so Donchian has had re-
course to three dimensions to represent the 4th. In his house in Hartford, his entire series of solids in the 4th
dimension (excepting the sphere and the cylinder) present to the eye of a painter, a new optic order, and a
principle for the penetration of space here made manifest for the first time.

The painter, however, who is enriched by these new principles of projection, and who seeks to carry
them over into his own field of activity as new laws and new functions, will find himself confronted by a
new fact, that it is impossible to "draw" in the 4th dimension without abandoning line in favor of metal
wire and without abandoning paper in favor of three dimensional space itself.

On a page of two-dimensions, a drawing in the 4th only takes an allusive, not representational, force,
and I strongly suspect that we will not be able to adventure into the slightly explored field of the n-dimen-
sions until we are prepared to give up both the frame and canvas. We must take the step away from the
two-dimensional frame and come to prefer a frame quite differently conceived, one which remains a continuous plane, to be sure, but one which exists in three dimensions.

I have, within the limits of my research, made some experiments with the Moebus strip (it is obtained
from a rectangle whose sides are in a proportion of one:five or one:six) and it offers a pure shape and a continuous surface no less suggestive than the circle, no less impressive than the sphere.

The solution of the problem, after all, rests at that point where the two spheres, architecrure and painting, meet. Should the present-day architects achieve the pure and abstract forms which call for the painters
integration, it will then be clear to all—and above all to our sense of first principles—what the function was
which, in the past, rational architecture achieved than the functional, and more recently the organic.

It will be necessary to discuss these problems with the architects and with the other painters, for it is a
collective work—like that of a dark-yard, which the new style proposes.

hole, while I pleasure myself that they are mine   or, to shift to an image i used in ISH, i seem always to take a step back before i come forward to make the thrust

it may be, that why i felt futile last night was my utter lack of interest in discussing things publicly   what do i care to argue or to explain that which moves me   all i wish to do is to use it   and if i expose something, like Kaggli's drawings before others, let them use them, find out   people are lazy, that's why they take personality as a pill of force   i feel nothing but contempt, and it is an emotion which i do not like, for it assaults my faith, & drains me

frances, dear, i hope you are all right   poor chest, i hope i did take the pain out, for good— you did look so well & handsome when i left you   i hope it held

i walk around your little town   it is strange, we were so inside, but the greys of the houses, stone, pines, highway, air are in me sharp pressed up against your Hines cheeks, my sib

i shall now make you your copy of the verse

this is merely hello
today   love
o

[*enclosed:*]

THE PRAISES[6]

She who was burned more than half her body
skipped out of death

1

Comes the E, comes the five, and after
the rage of song

comes the E, comes the five, and, after, on the 6th day of the new moon,
at the 1st casting of the three lots, neither deuce nor tre is thrown.
And the reason

---

6. There are a number of differences between this draft and the poem published (see *Collected Poems*, pp. 96–101).

has not been divulged.

Thus we begin, with the arithmetical, the mathematical
praises

2

Observing that there are five solid figures, the Master
(or so Aetius reports, in the *Placita*) concluded
that the Sphere of the Universe arose from
the dodecahedron

          Whence Alexander,
appearing in a dream to Antiochus, showed him
and on the morrow, the enemy (the Galates)
ran before it,
before the sign, that is

By Filius Bonacci, his series, rediscovered Pisa 1202, we shall attack,
for it, too, proceeds asymptotically toward the graphic & tangible,
the law now determined to be
phi

   its capital role in the distribution
   of branches leaves seeds (ex.,
   the ripe sun-flower

   the ratios 5/8, 8/13
   in the seed-cones of fir-trees,
   the ratio 21/34
   in normal daisies

   Pendactylism is general in the animal kingdom, but crystals . . .
there, pentagonal forms or lattices do not, can not appear

   So we have it: star and jelly fish, the sea-urchin,
   whose mouth is a five-point maw, is Aristotle's lantern.
   For marine animals, like man. And fruit blossoms,
   the briar-rose, the passion-flower.
   There is an ideal, and constant angle,
   for leaves and branches on a stem,
   which produces the maximum exposition to light,
   that light vertical, but lilies,

tulips, the hyacinth, like crystals

here we must stop, and ponder, for Nature,
though she is, as you will know
(so far, that is, as it is allowed to a mortal to know)
from all points of view similar to herself, yet
minerals . . .
                o, that's not fair, let
                woman keep her jewels, odd man
                his pleasure of her glow, let
                your lady Nephritite
                pumice her malachite, paint
                her lids green against the light!

Sd he:
        to dream takes no effort
            to think is easy
                to act is more difficult
        but for a man to act after he has taken thought,
        this is the most difficult thing of all!

⋅⋖ 77 ⋗⋅

Woodward to Washington
[19 December 1949]

                                    Monday evening
Charles dear—
    First to tell you that I sat alone last night reading (guests dropped in to in-
terrupt and I was in my p.j.'s with my hair pinned up above my head and they
very elegant—they brought an angel for Lucinda they say 'tis antique and
fragile and I am excited—she has a penchant for angels) your present[7]—it is
so very very fine a job you have no idea how thrilling it is to me and how this
country can sit quietly and ignore such a terribly exciting deed as that book I
am hard put to it to figure out except that it does require a little awareness
which means previous unsloth—Nietzsche summed it all up perfectly in a
sentence—I was embarrassed, *very* that I had been so gauche as to let you
know I had never owned one—again I caught myself in my dreams explaining to you how my stockings had holes and I had been in and out several times
buying beautiful things for my family and never even remembered that I need
them and how my coal scuttles both have holes—and that I have needed a

7. Olson sent *Call Me Ishmael* (1947) with the inscription "And for Frances   Charles" (in possession of recipient).

hairbrush for four years—all to prove that the fact that I need something and really want it has so little to do with my buying it. I am ashamed but I do so love to have a copy from you and I do so very appreciate your sending it.

It is strange to me so many times it happens between us—your note after the Cagli show with its mood so exactly matching my mood today when I was longing so deeply for dissolution. I guess, dear Charles when I look at every minute, that you and I pour out so very very much and people give back so very very little—we press ourselves so hard and they never press about any-thing—to me the final stile one steps over into maturity is the bearing of the pain of utter disdain—of expecting nothing from them—of knowing that they will never arise and walk—they will always expect Jesus to do it for them—

I have had time to read the poem only once and that is never even a begin-ning for me—it makes me happy at once and I expect to push through to un-derstanding—there are places where I will need help—but the first impres-sion is a great deep spread of happiness—how satisfying to be in the presence of the bearers.

I am extremely pleased with the Cagli translation[8]—will analyze later my reaction—but there is a full swooping flow to it something weighted and male and full of mind—I would be so very very thrilled if you were to translate the Michelangelo sonnets.

Lucinda and I were showing each other last night how Olson stood up and pointed his leg forward and said "O la! la!"—she was practising saying it with the Olson accent and we were howling with laughter—we are working very very close behind you—you are getting all the adoration sans the messiness of sentimentality of being a father—we approve of Olson and he causes in our house a big passage of radiance—you should have seen my brother open his eyes when he saw me—I was more beautiful than I have been for years—and I served such a magnificent dinner—and I was so furious that all this went to him and to Olson the worst, the worst—the worst food and then no food—and me so unsparkling and all very far from what I usually give to a guest—but I was so terribly excited I simply had not the ease to do it the right way—

Your flowers stayed fresh and I arranged them so very much better for my brother—they were there—a hand held out to me and making me so gay—my brother put his arm around me and said—"It is so good to see you so on top of life"—(and I did not tell him who I was atop of)

And smallest squirrel that ever ever ran briskly—if you want to add to your pile of hoard the really beautiful book from which the Egyptian poems came—that is yours too.[9]

8. Olson's translation of a letter he received from Corrado Cagli. See letter of 14 December 1949.
9. It is not at present known which volume is referred to here. No such volume existed in Olson's library.

Washington to Woodward
19 December 1949 (postmark 20 December 1949)

12/19/xlix

There is in your hair the flowering of your body.

To it, I rise, I am

your sib. Your cheek

is musk, and my lips

are planted there, grow

by essence of you,

who are woman, all manner of

sweet-smelling herbs. I dwell

in you, walk

in that lovely place we have made

together, my heart

full.

frances

I came up out of the water, out of the inert.
I did not find a place where I could stand.
I was alone.
I took courage in my heart.
I laid a foundation.
I made every form.
Multiple were the forms
which came out from my mouth.

i attest:[10]
charles

---

10. Olson has, in the two parts of this verse letter, repeated in a modified form lines from the Egyptian "Legend of Creation" sent him by Boldereff on 15 December 1949.

≼ 79 ≽

Washington to Woodward
22 December 1949 (postmark 22 December 1949)

thursday december 22 xlix

frances: yr beautiful letter of friday came yesterday (a measure of what to expect of washington delivery in this dirtying of childermass)   it is so beautiful

i am actually too weak, i think, to tell you (i have been in bed three days
with some virus—and with dreams which net the ugliest bottom, both now
passed)

o sweet we may, we may press, as you say, in our imagination for that
pattern, for that pattern without armor of any fashioning. For that is what is
going on these terrible, wondrous days. And I am so proud of life. You need
not feel parted from me, need not, indeed, because we are not, nor, in deed,
because of Constanza, who, as you have prayed, speaks your name now,
speaks Frances, almost as i might, and struggles with every ounce of her
strength, to deal with this thing, and to move ahead with it

all my soul cries
out against life's defamers, is, at this moment of low physical energy, full of
rage i am not there somewhere with a huge sword to point out and kill the de-
ceivers (at the moment it is again kierkegaard and all users of his word—the
absurd—Malraux, at the moment, and his dirty, evil subject, T.E. (The Evil)
Lawrence ((that two men should have lived at the same time with that name,
so that we have to distinguish LAWRENCE (da hai) from that filthy mechanic!)):listen to his own obituary which he wrote just before he was killed
on his little onanistic motorcycle

Being a mechanic cuts one off from all communication with women. No
woman, I believe, can understand a mechanic's happiness in serving his bits
and pieces

o, god, to cleanse them all away, where they are, in high places, thrown up
from their own grease, to make the Flood again!

i despair. Only by stories can
one do what Lawrence did. And I, line-maker, am hid in Japanese and Italian
books!

but of course i do not despair, for the deed, the act now, is yr man Murametz (how do you spell his beautiful name), to *be* the strength you are, to use
it, use it, give it out, even as you sleep, because you don't sleep, you sit, and
pour, pour, pour it into every instant, every person, every thought, spending it

as you sit, which is prayer and use, and the one communication now when time is making, and act, act is already born

those⎫
only god, to be rid of their⎭ wrongs, not for ourselves, but for the others who are not able to struggle to be clear, who do not spend their time and pain so, who thus look to leaders, and, in their simplicity, are apt to trust

    (no, i know they do not, ultimately, but power arrogates to itself words and actions which bedung even the things we are able to see and hold as precious, your tiniest of flowers, darling, your delicate weeds, your little red eyes which you see there in the woodward forest when you turn those immaculate eyes of yr own, yr eyes which bear as no other eyes can have the fought-for belief, BELIFE

        o darling i say now quietly i love them

                        i wanted to begin to tell you about an illumination which has been stirred up in me as a leafing of this love which has been born and of the struggle we are involved in to give it exact life   i am only beginning to part it, but i should like to share to you some sense of it   it has to do with a face i see behind both beauty and truth, and i think it is, for me at least, the Babe, my Howling babe   it is driven home to me, that what we seek, that what Beauty and Truth are only the Angels of, that what our job now is, that what we mean when we speak of use, of dedication, that what is our responsibility, to each other in the sense of your phrasing, "to free",

        (o, lord, i am so hot and breathless, from this fired-up room, i have lost my language: excuse me, darling i'll lie down, and try it there)

    (I'm down, and i'll do it, but not today   i am wondering if it doesn't deserve to be verse to go to you   maybe, tho it is equally uncertain that today i could make it verse   and it may be merely this: that light has been thrown on my own root position, which i have never known, clearly   and that it is not so much verse, but law   and that i better merely acquaint myself with it, as a weather has to be known

    there is no question i see a face, and it is of God, and its meaning is a clarification, a clearing away of much that has been lyric in a long past from a false deification of Beauty and of much that has been absolute from an equally wrong dedication to Truth and from both of these 2-dimensions there has been made a false 3-dimension of man, which has left him

                            to bear his own anguish intolerably alone

o sweet my eyes are on you, i am near, to give you whatever sleep or wake you want

≼ 80 ≽

Woodward to Washington
22 December 1949 (postmark)

Thursday morning

Charles, my heard,

It indeed should be reported to the rent control board that of this reconverted dwelling there are now three inhabitants, Charles, Lucinda and Frances. Because now you never leave—you are present.

I have just reread all of Y & X—(staring at your note from Corrado I finally for the first time understood "Y" and understood "X"—oh! dull Motz whose brain laggeth so far behind!) I love that great Charles that poet who is the only poet alive today on this earth—for the first time also I understand certain lines of La Préface oh! Motz come awake, hurry up—I miss so much—no wonder the lazy amoebas do not pursue Olson—

I have brought home Dunne's *An Experiment with Time* and am pleased to notice that he and I are formerly acquainted, that he wrote *The Serial Universe* which I carried home two years ago and am now in a position to cope with better. Coxeter seems to know the right people. (One for Connie—very sotto voce—I had yesterday to layout a job for one—Cockshutt)

Spengler speaks in the *Hour of Decision* about those moments in a culture when events follow one another at a rapid pace—when literal moments and hours are of vital consequence and the parts click off in a passionate speed where every move has the integration and rapidity of a dance—I am of the impression that at this moment this is true for man on this earth—I brought home another thing my guess is is also new—has the earmark of a contribution—will tell you about it after I examine it—and this morning I feel so conscious that doors are being opened—that you and I in the swift organic movement of events of accomplishment personal and impersonal—are there such things?—are matching and also forming part of this swift change of phase that our personal as well as our positional events are ourselves with the finger on top, obeying—that all around us are the eager waiters and those who unbeknownst to us are pushing through the veil in another circled area. I love for this reason *The Praises* it fits in so perfectly—is a clarion—has a title which for graciousness of hauteur in recognition has *never* been matched—oh thou my king—I have to work at it—as I have still work to do on every other one you have ever written except La Chute I which is absolutely now mine—known to me.

The library presented me day before yesterday with the two volumes of Blake—would rather own those than a house on the ocean front in Yucatan— and I save for your great pleasure—they had been searching since February and were purchased in London and came across this ocean to spell—Motz is in love.

I restrain myself from wild raving out of respect.

Pognod

And I wish to report to you that last night, reading Dunne—a great joy pervaded me of recognition and I now *have no pain*   I am consumed with gratitude to the deity that I should be honored to be put to the proof that what I said I searched for, I wanted and am able—the most terrific joy presses from inside against the nipples of my breast.

◄§ 81 ◄§

Woodward to Washington
[23 December 1949]

Friday morning

Dearest—

Up until now, this moment, I have had absolutely no idea whether I was right or wrong—I have been totally blind, with no light anywhere—and I could see D. H. Lawrence staring at me and saying "How could it be right to go so violently against nature and to deny the living flame between you?"

But now darling—like Donchian's pre-visionary plastic?,[11] I see that you and I have outlined for several years to come the whole plastic form of man-woman. I feel it is done, now, dear, and if you will permit me, baby, Ma-Me will now lie down to rest.

◄§ 82 ◄§

Washington to Woodward (special delivery)[12]
23 December 1949 (postmark)

Lucinda:

Jesus is the Largest Angel, and I wanted you to know, this Christmas, what the Real Knowers say He did, to commemorate Himself:

11. Boldereff is referring to "Drawings in the 4th Dimension"; see note 2 to Olson's letter of 16 December 1949.
12. This letter is addressed to "Frances & Lucinda Boldereff."

Jesus: To be delivered is my desire
                                    and I desire to deliver
Disciples: Amen
Jesus: To be blessed is my desire
                                    and I wish to bless
Disciples: Amen
Jesus: To be born is my desire
                                    and I wish to engender
Disciples: Amen
Jesus: To be nourished is my desire
                                    and I wish to nourish
Disciples: Amen
Jesus: To sing is my desire
                              let us dance together
Disciples: Amen
Jesus: Those who do not dance
                        will not comprehend
                                    what shall befall!

Disciples: AMEN

                              x   Blessings! Dance!
                        x   x   Olson
                        x   x
                              x   Xmas xlix

[*enclosed:*]

THE BABE[13]

Who it is who sits
behind the face,
who it is looks out by both,
by beauty and by truth,
those cheeks, mere Angels side by side
the greater one

Who it is whose eyes
what it is to look where eyes are
where eyes are form, not by lyric, not by absolute
whose eyes at one are maculate and innocent, by
mastery won

---

13. This poem grew out of the latter part of Olson's letter of 22 December 1949; it was not published until *Collected Poems* (pp. 101–2).

Who it is looks, can look
into the smallest thing, and says,
it was made for us both, we are committed
to be just, who says, to the very largest,
none is over us
when we have earned it

Look, in that face,
and read an answer, you
who are alone, what you ask,
that you be justly done by,
that what price you pay be more
than beauty or than truth, be
the recognition that you are
of use

one to another separate, but
the form we make by search, by error, pain
be seen by eyes other than our own

dedicate, thus, one to another, aid:
to offer, able to offer the just act, the act
crying to be born!

> for frances for christmas
>   xlix
>   olson

❧ 83 ☙

Woodward to Washington
26 December 1949 (postmark)

> December 26th in bed
>
> strong rain—5:00 p.m.

Charles strider and balancer

1. To tell you my sister worships you from afar and has joy because you live

2. To tell you that both of us in an unmental direct way realize how man you
    are—how you are holding with what silence of sweetness of man—the

tensional curve between the flowers that side you. That the silence and devotion with which you do this is appreciated not only by me but by my sister in some unspoken way

3. and to say that while I have been deeply disturbed by your physical condition which is greatly unsatisfactory to me that at this moment I perceive
that perhaps it is useful for the great strong balancer to need help, to
slacken—that this releases strength and in deep unconscious ways produces
joy—I say no more—I want never again to speak of your physical machine—I despise people who rob God of the responsiblity—he is so able to
carry—but I will be *glad* when you are in the sun at Yucatan, where neither your heart nor your lungs nor your blood are disturbing you—I want
for you to be a snake uncoiled and baking your vitals.

The Thursday letter and poems arrived together the day before Christmas—it was once a special did help—as always they are my only gift—and I
can not say now how utterly I love them, both—but to tell you quickly that
The Babe conveys the immediate conviction of a necessary truth—that you
have brought up to man for his use the reality the mind of man has been struggling for for the last seventy-five years. The idea you have seems to me original and inevitable—now is the time when we must hear what you are saying
when we have gone to the ultimate last proof of the wrongness of the two absolutes you mention—an extremely original and absolutely core idea—I am
wanting to tell you that in my feeling today it can only be done by line—not by
story—there is a hint of why in the pages I enclose—I found them just now
when I opened my Italian writing case—they were done in Iowa ten years
ago—and show you how your Motz has really been awaiting you—I enclose
them for one or two lines which are for you and it seemed to me they would
carry their meaning better if I left them in the otherwise unimportant context.

I will copy off all of your poems I possess in manuscript very soon—one
copy for you and one for Helen—she loves *the K* and got the idea immediately
of Otvechai as I am sure all of America that counts would. I dandle all three of
us (C.C. & F.) in my arms with strong sexual laughter and kisses.

That Motz who has been
yours since
the hour of her birth—[14]

❦ 84 ❧

State College to Washington
27 December 1949 (postmark)

14. With this letter, Boldereff enclosed her essay entitled "Walt Whitman and the Millenial Re-
Union," which Olson annotated and returned. See his letter #132 of 15 February 1950.

When I came to look over the others[15] my guess was you had a copy of each—if you do not please let me know.

I want a copy of the section you recited to me in front of my stove—the thing you did aloud at Black Mountain. I can remember the cadences perfectly but have no idea what the words are—was it part of the *Kingfishers?* anyway I do want

Today is your birthday—Dunne's *Experiment with Time* gives me such a detached feeling towards what appear to be events in time—I am so convinced you were always there—and that I have always at all times been wholly in love with you—

I now want to spend the next ten years moving towards a quiet power—so comes my baby's birthday I can phone you a perfect villa on the shore of the Azov sea.

What miles we have paced since Tarrytown. I want to be a beautiful slave girl and I want to dress you exquisitely, starting with the fine oil rubbed to your legs and back and done so absolutely perfectly that the Persians would appoint me and the Byzantines at their most elegant would not withhold praise. In folded things of so quiet and daring color combines you could carry heavy gems without ever having them show before the glitter—the so hard, male glitter of your king countenance. I begin at once—

⊰ 85 ⊱

Washington to Woodward
29 December 1949 (postmark)

thursday

this has just locked itself up—after 8 months!—and it goes off to my only tender public characters, the Western R[16]

it's what i have been busy about, plus a fast trip to take my mother out for xmas dinner

and today is one crossed rightly in the stars, for your two letters, which i have anxiously awaited, came, and i have yet to read them as i want, in that mood i cherish, a step back   o, darling, your sensuality meets mine at that other cross-roads, down below

---

15. Boldereff apparently enclosed typed copies of several of Olson's poems.
16. A typed carbon copy of the finished poem "The Praises" was enclosed. It was not published in the *Western Review* but in *New Directions* 12 (1950). See *Collected Poems*, p. 96.

by the way, did you get a yellow sheet (posted Monday, a week), with a rewrite of the Egyptian piece (the lst), and will you make a copy of that, too

> love, and to Lucinda, and,
> for the new year, these
> that I speed to you
> charles   φ

& i need no bait but you, lady!

now, maybe, the ways are
cleared for,
the She-Bear!

But who can say,
        what will come?

Am reading Lawrence, & though he knew,
says, impersonality, i wonder how
far it went in his beauty, how
much he possessed it, he who was
so much in awe of it?

no question he had it, but he goes dreamy over, injuns,
he wished to punish the white so, back (lawrence SPARAGMOS)

-·§ 86 §·-

Washington to Woodward
30 December 1949 (postmark)

                    friday

frances, i want to tell you right away what i owe you, right now that i owe it
        i had not, when i wrote last night, as i said, read your letters as i wanted
to, i had been so busy finishing the Praises, and getting copy off   then,
after i had posted the P to you, i did read, and read yr Whitman piece   (i
am going right now and read it again, because of what it sent me into)

                                                            you
say that Dunne confirms your knowledge that time is not the truth   i tell
you YOU confirm mine   again, as when i read your Notebook, i, even i,

am amazed how early and surely you put yr truth down, for this Whitman piece is of like grip, is in there at the entrails   i am deeply moved, love, and tell you so this plainly, though it is not my wont, because it is beautiful, makes me beautiful, AND HAS FOR THE FIRST TIME IN MY LIFE GIVEN ME WHITMAN

       god, am i grateful   it started when i went to my copy to look up the passage you indicate only by the pages 107–8   i haven't found it yet, but it doesn't matter, for i have, last night, and this morning, read the Children of Adam and the Calamus, and am covered by yr cloak of joy

                    YOU

have broken me thru his iambs and anapests, and i have read all those poems without gagging except at one point, his use of the verb "flits"! Lawd, lawd: when i think how love can set aside a fin oreille! how it simplifies me, this Whitman, Lawrence, YOU

> (it is curious, how i have fought to
> leave the rough down stairs: i am but the
> bottle of a genii, and i have, because of
> these States and how they have denied and
> lost the hand-to-hand he cried for,
> stoppered and stoppered my presence . . .
> well, as that old sweet man says "Yet out
> of that, I have written these songs"!)

The struggle has been to be direct. You say America sleeps, the daughter. This son, this Murametz, has also been asleep! Or, rather, has been sitting by the fire, altogether, maybe, too carefully!

              ((Hi! Watcher! look: the eyes are on you!))

    It interests me, because i have been so slow, have believed in my slowness, that this burst of WW's ("my resurrection, after slumber", he even uses yr imagery!) appears to have come in his 40th year

     "life that is only life after love"

    (who has done better than that?

     i send it to you as our calamus,
       the sweet flag,

     a banner for yr heart
          Charles

❧ 87 ❧

Woodward to Washington
31 December 1949 (postmark 31 December 1949)

December 31, 1949

Charles dear—

This hurried, because Lucinda waits for me.

I enclose a picture which just fell out of my Whitman which I send to show you I seem always to have been detached, examining, separate—they are Ruthie who phoned to Elizabeth whom we visted in Whitestone and a dear little J.J. O'Neill who used to follow me around the streets saying, coaxing, "Ginny, will you give me a pinny?", and my beautiful sister and me, the non-beautiful.

This cannot be the letter I planned, but I want to say I am happy about the Whitman—you are the only person who has seen those pages, which I wrote for myself and forgot.

I want to tell you something nice—a win for Olson. Lucinda received the poem on Christmas Eve with absolutely no comment. It dropped into silence. After Christmas she said, "I thought Olson liked me." And I said "He does," and she asked "Why didn't he send me a gift?" and I explained to her about how you despise to move in patterns other people have made, that you looked, found nothing right and refused to be forced into giving an ugly gift—she seemed to understand but no comment. Yesterday out of the blue she said, "Ma-Me—Jesus didn't *dance*". And I said "Oh! but yes, and if you do not dance you can not understand him" again silence. Last night for the first time since your visit we went to the restaurant and as we walked up—the sky cold with stars "I wish Olson were with us" and then she burst into laughter and commented "I never said that before."

And at night when undressing—"Ma-Me, did you say Olson sent me a poem for a Christmas present?" And I told as carefully as I could what a *gift* a poem is, how a man does not buy a poem, but makes it out of his guts—and I am sure I conveyed what a poem making really is and she said "It was a good present."

Verdict—and delivered with that straight clear unforced thing of a child's mind left to itself.

I shout for joy because I as the mother know for the first time you are taken in—and in a child's world—you only have to be taken in once—it is for keeps.

I will copy the Egyptian poem too precious for comment and will later tell you how Olson writes poems the way he makes love—with a great Beethoven thump which cleaves apart everything that is not absolutely alive.

Frances

≈ 88 ≈

Woodward to Washington
2 January 1950

January 2nd

Before the Praises—I am rereading *Ishmael*—10 or 12 pages at a time, because
I get so excited I can not read more—a few days ago I came to "and thus creates the Moby-Dick universe in which the Ahab-world is, by the necessity of
life—or the Declaration of Independence—included." Oh! Olson beloved
Irish hind (in its 2nd meaning)—why don't these bastards get down on their
knees—! I have never laughed more fully—I can never ever *say* how *everything* one feels about America is there wryly strung up by Olson nailed by his
suffering and identified by his wit for our large consolation. Did I say I press
gems on your fingers? I will say more—and this in reality—Melville is himself reconciled—one Olson has repaid him—oh! all that polishing you did has
created such a full box of treasure—

And now to the Praises—
    The title is I believe the best title I have ever read. *The Praises* which con-
tains a Motz pere quietness—praises as the male gives off praises—in silence
of exhortation.
    I walk around saying over and over and over to myself—some damned in-
cantation which restores my aged bones "By Filius Bonacci, his series"
    I remember seeing in the horrible Readers Digest an anecdote from
Charles Schwab—very good—in which the idea was—you have to make
people want to do something if you expect to get it done—you have to supply
the motive.
    I am reading Trigant Burrow's *The Neurosis of Man* for reasons—he seems
to be trying to develop a method whereby man can reach the error of the "I-
persona" and root it out and while I am for anything which can bring this
about—science—psychology—medicine—I keep thinking "what about the
motive—who will supply that?"
    When these science boys so gayly dispose of the hero and poet I think—
"Who do you think is going to make us *want* to?"—one page of Dostoyevsky
one page of Stavrogin's passionate irrational language and one *wants* to understand one *wants* to enter his world and see it from Stavrogin's eyes—and
why—because Dostoyevsky has made it attractive and what has he made it attractive with—with his spoke—translated through that lockment in his pea
of bone.
    And as I read the book—*Neurosis of Man* I think God—it has taken him
his whole life and hard work and here he is—just saying how to find it, the

wrong and Olson has stated the whole thing in *Trinacria* much more accurately and then has made you (the reader) proud, strong, able to imitate—and on top of all this—an increment—for free—a poem—a proud separate lovely new thing in the universe which can be placed in the house like furniture.

To proceed—No. 2 is a perfect gradation of ascendance and then comes ()[17] and that is perfect, because that is what Olson does—what no one else is doing today—Olson takes all the inherited puff ball (I have a beauty in my house Lucinda and I found in the woods to show you) and with his mind like a powerful hand splits it open and the spores to beget new life fly out and the deadness falls off and you are left face to face with the stern newness, the unfilled space and to make it absolutely clear he says

> "What belongs to art and reason is
>   the knowledge of
>   consequences."

and all the slothful think they know that Olson is telling us something he has heard

but

Olson is taking that powerful mind hand and turning us about to face outward and pushing us violently (though everywhere and always without hurt) into the starkness, the examination of consequences. There has never been a more ruthless tearing away of meaningless accretions, a placing them in the light for what they are, than

> "You would have a sign etc."

Olson, with every poem, you introduce

I am beginning to believe that there is a possibility that the Michelangelo deed may one day be paralleled by Charles Olson. I say this never to be mentioned to ourselves or to anyone aloud because I walk with such attentive lightness over the arrangements of the facts seeking not to disturb by any breath the possibility and I tell it to you in silence to be known in silence between us—the tremulous possibility.

The designated to
The Designate

❧ 89 ❧

Woodward to Washington
5 January 1950(postmark 5 January 1950)

January 5

---

17. The typescript of "The Praises" that Boldereff was looking at had a set of parentheses before the part of the poem beginning "Avert, avert." These do not appear in printed versions.

Trigant Burrow—chapter *The Genesis of Man's Dissociation*

"Through this handy process man was no longer subservient to the fixed nomen governing all dependable experience. The power that makes for harmony and order in the universe of matter and energy had now become something quite alien to him. The basic organism of man was no longer an expression of this universal motivation, but a thing apart and subject to the private will of each and every man. Now that a whimsical numen or false image of authority had replaced the authority that resides in the consistent correspondence between man's senses and the external world, his interrelational continuity was interrupted and his organism was no longer bound by a consistent law of behaviour. The omniscient and omnipotent principle or nomen that resides within man and that governs his relationship to the environment lacked the organismic support of conscious correlation. Henceforward man could believe as his fancy dictated, not as his senses ordained. Such is the autopathic dictatorship of the numen over the social processes of man.

"Here was impediment, with its inevitable repercussion and introversion. Here was first incurred man's compensatory neurosis—the obsessive compulsion of labour and toil, the relentless dichotomy of 'right' and 'wrong'. Here was exacted of man the awful toll of self-division, of the ulterior aim, of partitive retroflection. This divisive element has played havoc with the folk mind. Throughout the chronological descent of our various cultures theologians and metaphysicians have called it by different names—the Devil, the Bad Angel, the Evil Genius or the Unconscious. Through this impediment in the basic feeling of man, man unwittingly tricked himself into a mere charade of behaviour. Henceforth there was only pretence of feeling, or an affective replacement of the organism's motivation and interest. Man had succumbed to the lure of the social image, with its *self* reflections, its *amour propre*, its false personal identity. In the introversion of his sick empathy—in his *auto* empathy, man saw only the falsely begotten *image* of himself—an image in which his whole world was transmuted into mere affect or into autopathic thinking.

"This psychic transformation, this sleight-of-head magic, man wrought within himself through his false use of the symbol. But this device of man's symbolic ingenuity recoiled upon man himself and henceforward he could only seek to explain with more symbols his own disordered state of mentation. In the semiotic systematizations of pseudo-religion, philosophy and metaphysics, man could only employ further elaborations of the symbol in attempting to explain himself to himself.

"This was man's fall. This was his entrance into sin and transgression—into *original* sin and the numen. For man had sullied the original springs, the organismic principle of his very own identity. But it is not true, as the pseudo-religionists would have us believe, that man's trespass is irretrievable, that the earth is cursed in his name. If, repudiating the false Gods born of autopathic images, man returns to the primary source of his defection; if, regardless of his own habitual wishes, man applies to man a scientific principle of behaviour, the secret of his own secretive infoldment and introversion will appear to him in as clear and objective perspective as the once mysterious sources of infective disorders appeared to the bacteriologists only a few decades ago.

"With the interruption of man's organic fidelity to external stimuli, with the accession of the partitive, autopathic persona and the intrusion of private affects upon the organism's symbolic function, man sustained a biological trauma of incalculable severity. Through this phylic trauma his primary behaviour in relation to the environment—his orthopathic feeling and thinking—was artificially shifted to a level of response that was purely autopathic and fictitious. Substituting for the world of objective reality a superstitious, numinal interpretation of the phenomenal world, man unconsciously abrogated the law or nomen that governs his primary interrelational behaviour. Under the sponsorship of a whimsical social image, or numen, there was no longer the consistent correlation of man's senses with external phenomena. There was no longer the external constant. From now on man's world came to be tinged with fanciful attributes of his own making, with affective intimations and discolourings wholly alien to the objective circumstance, so that henceforth man's behaviour was exempt from the inexorable control of organismic law."

I want very much to have you read *Neurosis of Man* if you have time—Burrow and Gesell, following the suggestion of D'Arcy Thompson *On Growth and Form* (the chapter "On Leaf-Arrangement" being all that I learned from *The Praises*, including Philolaos, and Olson's sign φ which I was hard put to it to explain to my daughter) each in their separate fields are doing what Olson preaches and I might add with Olson's tenderness and dignity. I also am proud of life that it could contain in a dance Gesell, Burrow, Olson and Lucinda whose magnificent *feeling* for the law of rhythm is such a proof of Burrow's thesis.

He has a paper *The Origin of the Incest-Awe* in the Psychoanalytic Review Vol V which might interest you and in the same Review Vol. 30—an article of Dr. Galt "Our Mother Tongue—Etymolgical Implications of the Social Neurosis"—read yesterday "our mother tongue" does not mean native language, rather Mother is used as matrix, the tongue as the thing out of which man was formed. Good stuff.

I am terribly excited by these studies—Olson's instinct about himself and his job seems proven so deep and correct and necessary—like I said, the only poet alive today.

Where is David Young, David Old?

Woodward to Washington
9 January 1950 (postmark)

> Sunday morning alone
> downstairs—three children
> & Warner & Elizabeth
> upstairs

Charles dear—

I have been so very disturbed because it has occurred to me that in the Lucinda story you may possibly have thought that what I gave her as an explanation was my understanding of you. Not at all—it is that a child asks questions out of the blue—you have no time to think, you have to say something that to them makes some kind of sense—and in this one instance it could not be the real explanation as Lucinda believes and does not know the ugly thing the world has done with Christmas, so all of the *real* reason and your so right reaction to it I had to leave out—which left me hard put to it. I also could not *insist* that a poem was a gift—this is most parents' technique, but a human being has to come at his own hour to his own understanding, something very few adults are willing to wait for—so what I said Olson while slightly dopey nevertheless is the breach *served* and I was so thrilled at the enormous distance her understanding both of the meaning of the poem and of its meaning as a gift had travelled in such a short space of time absolutely unforced by me and in order to get this you had to know what happened at the beginning.

Oh darling—letters are hard for me—but I want you to know I love your generosity which has delicacy and perception and I consider you the most magnificently generous of persons—and I would die if I thought for one second you ever believed I could feel a *thing* could have value in comparision with a poem of your making.

The trouble is opposite—having read Olson—I can now only read stuff like D'Arcy Thompson who seems to be such a lovely human being because the so called creative writing today of any kind, after reading you, just has no taste to it at all—I just have to ignore it because after tasting Olson the stuff just won't cause any juices to flow.

I am wondering if there is not some technique whereby the only men in this country who would appreciate you, like Burrow and Gesell and some of the fine scientists could know that you are there—they don't know that there is an Olson who has their absolutely clean ruthless relentless brain ticking ticking ticking and that he is fashioning stuff they would not have to be ashamed to use—I am thinking that perhaps a review in *The American Scientist*, where I know of three readers whose minds could cope.

Please Charles wherever you are, write me a p.c. to say there is no wall between us.

Frances

⋅ℰ 91 ℛ⋅

Washington to Woodward
10 January 1950 (postmark)

tuesday

the news, my lady, is good, this morning, for a change   i have a letter from
Ray West, saying, he does indeed like "The Praises", and thinks the Western
Review will use it   he explains, too, why you have not seen "David Young,
David Old", because I haven't, that my two copies went astray, and he cannot
yet replace them due to a sell-out of the issue (not, I think, because I, yet, !, am
that effective!), and we must wait until some return from booksellers   (i
tried to see it at the lib. of cong. last week, and they too have no copy

in fact, the news is a little bursting, and i share it with you: yesterday i was
asked to submit "The Kingfishers" to the Hudson Review (ever see it?) if for
no other reason than, that, in their current issue, their attention has been
called to the work of one, olson, by some two unusual references to his ishmael
in an article or review by Stanley Edgar Hyman, linking him to one to whom,
at this moment, he would rather be linked than any other known man, David
Herbert Lawrence[18] (the editor of the HR is supposed to come call on me this
week)

so, sweet believer, shall we see, in all this, extensions of force outward? or shall
we be as before, and think it is another winter flurry? In any case, it recreates
my old problem: if these two chillun get into public, I shall be scared, for there
is not their equal done and ready to push after them, to crowd the scene

I play a little, in saying that, for, by now, I am used to this mood of falling back,
and pay it little mind   As a matter of fact I have been reading wildly
(widely), and it is the usual step (falling back) before some further thrust, for
good or bad   Mostly Lawrence, and if I had the patience, I crave to do a narrative, which, of course, I suppose I won't, born without patience as I am

I did

18. Olson "is the biggest thing in Lawrence disciples since Edward Dahlberg"—Stanley Edgar
Hyman, review of *Call Me Ishmael* in *Accent* 8 (spring 1948): 188.

one thing, to be abreast of you; picked up the same lead, and have looked into Dunne. But so far he adds nothing to me, in fact irritates me some, he is a sal-vationist. There is a wrong (and a peculiarly important wrong right now) in such men's overt apocalypsisms. (I suppose that is why I protest, this is a time when only the creative man can be the proper leader, can deliver the clues properly to the folk)

((I should be telling you this! after the lovely things you have sd, about olson, and this dance, darling. But I am only saying it back, to make it clear to myself. In fact, if I can keep at it, this morning, I should like to unwrap before you several positional principles which have come tumbling out in the last few days.))

To get back to Dunne, Whitman, Burrow, Ghyka (my "Praises" source), Freud (less), or (least), Berdyaev, perhaps, all but the very exact scientists and—He-who-offends-least-of-all—DHL   Of course these men have come into existence. They had to. It is always that story of Bolyai Farkas and Bolyai Janos, the geometer son to his Euclidian father, when the son came up with his non-Euclidian universe, and cried to his dad: "I have created a world out of nothing", and the father replies, "Yes, but, when men need it, men spring up, on all sides, like violets in the spring."

It is that damned business of containment, that 'oomin meestarey. When Dunne comes to talk about the Symphony of All Creation, I reach for a line to slay him with. (Immortality, Bah!). (It was the same when Fjelde kept press-ing me to read Sullivan on Beethoven.) These creatures, because they cannot create, suddenly slide, after their excellent research, into images of the past—and it seems always to be art—to give the emotional fillip to their Revelations. And why I say it is deep wrong, is, that each time has a rhythm and images proper to itself, and any perception, arrived at from research, must be deliv-ered up by that rhythm and in that image or it does more harm than good. For if it depends upon the images and rhythms of the creators of the past, it be-comes a road block in front of the passage of the creator of this time straight, by his magic, to the very people for whom the message is intended.

Or some-thing like that.

It outrages that thing I cannot put another word on, than pudor. I call it mys-terious. For it is, that resistance in us to good when it is exposed before us without its proper cloak, the cloak which returns it to us as object, for use, not for aspiration—or worship. It is this damned religious overtone that I despise, the "ideal", "noble", "Truth". Shit.

Why I cry, "Lawrence," is—o god he is beautiful—he knew. I have read "The

Man Who Died" or "The Escaped Cock", and there is one perception in it
which I do not think any other man before him had made, and one so essential
that his making of it is straight miracle, and is a proof that men should come
on getting born and live for ever because there is so much work to be done. It
is the "he" of his story's recognition, when he is confronted again by
Madeleine, that the depth of his human disillusion lies in the double edged
thing that humans do, they both give and they take too much. O frances, what
a thing it is! And how I know what Lawrence is talking about! And how it
does, what he says, put a man off. God, god, what an incredible perceiver he
was. It is beyond belief (except that he proves it) that a man should have gotten
in there so far—by his own little means, bless him, and all separate humans
like him.

The clue *is* impersonality. I have been slashing away now for some time at
personality. (I think I wrote you how struck down I was by being fed on for it
in that Cagli spiel.) It has been in back of a year's talking, this uproar in me at
"lyricism". But it is only now that it suddenly comes to me that the opposite,
what I have for so long hammered away at with the word "object", is IM-
PERSONALITY.

Which is the human equivalent of what Dunne and all the others are mis-
taken in whoring after in other than human terms: four-dimension. I know
now why I have felt no surprise in modern discoveries, and why I have
protested that the poet has preceded these others in space SPACE. All that
modern discovery is, is an application of imagination to the non-human. And
thus, its results are of little use, except as they may furnish us images to make a
bridge again to our people. For dimensions only matter as they enable man
and woman to enter a life their own life contains. The only path to the universe is through yourself. (I think the last half of "The Man Who D" is
wronged by Lawrence, not in the lady of Isis or in her dedication to which she
is led by the words of the old man, the philospher, but by the trumpery of the
temple itself—after he has cleared crist of the religious, to leave woman in religion (as he did not do, by the way, in Lady Chat) is to do a wrong—; but is
there anywhere the equal of the "he's" realization, now that he has been dead,
that the dimension of life to hew to lies in life itself, and is that extra dimension which is separateness, the bronze separateness of the clanging COCK?
(I got started into all this *from* Whitman, and if you have not read recently
Lawrence on him in "Studies", do it again, for Lawrence is here, too, impeccable. I may not stomach his vocabulary, "the Open Road", and even his use
of "sympathy", but his distinction of "sympathy" from "love", at least as Whitman uses it, (except in that banner line I sent you),

 YOUR LETTER JUST CAME AND no, no, baby, there is no wall. I have to wander in time as well as space, and I shall always give you the willies with that god damned olson silence, which is not that, but he speaks so much when he does speak, that when he is gathering his forces, it is as tho he were off the planet, which is something true, because he is way down where your smallest of little things (that I, by the way, do not perceive as you do) begin to have their roots.

It is roots I wanted to come back to, was going to talk about, when I mentioned pudor.

> ((Before I forget it: somewhere last week, reading, I ran into—I think it was a propos Einstein—a terrific confirmation of that polar experience of yrs which I got into THE BABE, of the smallest and the largest, and how that tension is what has blown the old concepts sky-high!))

Pudor, and containment; the secret of secrecy *is* some law of life, and it has to do with how the things we put into ourselves (of emotion as well as of experience, knowledge) *do* grow roots, stick their little feet down into the soil of the soul, and quickly, and that it abrogates this human knowledge (the instinctive knowledge of the secret) to have others expose in public something where the roots and the dirt around them have been shaken off. It is what happens to all apocalypses other than the works of art. A man must somehow leave that connect, as you'd say, that bunch of roots and dirt hanging down into himself, or the thing is DEAD the moment you come on it.

> (And it is that that Lawrence knew beyond all men, beyond a willem shaxper maybe, tho the gentlest formulation of it is the latter's, even tho it does refer to the old easiest business, of the affections—wait, wait, I better say that better for god knows the affections is still the greatest struggle, to have clarities here; what i mean to say, what the renaissance, and xtianty as a whole, put the stress on, as of the human thing, was the affections. And, because it got too easy, (the formulation), they pissed the whole thing out. Now, we have to get back to the affections, and their mysteries, by coming on them in a sense without them, by protesting a whole series of other outrages (against the destruction of the species, for example, biologically; against economic outrages; against the State; against "Culture"; etc.)

Anyway, it is Cordelia's answer to Lear: "I cannot heave my heart into my mouth."

Darling, I want to get this into the early afternoon mail so you will have it tomorrow. So, tho I feel as tho I could run paper over this machine to you for the rest of this day, I'll ship this off as an installment I may continue afterwards. To send you

> his love, he
> who causes such hell,
> god help him
> Olson

❧ 92 ❧

Washington to Woodward (postcard)
10 January 1950 (postmark 10 January 1950)

THESE DAYS

Whatever you say, leave
the roots on, let them
dangle
     And the dirt

        just to make clear
        where they come from
           o   1/10/L

❧ 93 ❧

Woodward to Washington
[10 January 1950]

                     Tuesday night

Because I am excited—

    I could dance around my house out there in that cold light *because* my dear Olson it appears to me at this moment that the reason Woodward means so much to me, the reason I have to live here now is because it represents above all others things Motz impersonality (I am saying thank you)—creating one's own stasis—all the excitement of the balance *within* where it belongs—where it is in snakes—lions—grasses and what others of beauty there are—everything that has elegance in life gets the balance from the adjusted polarity, the adjustment always being made and won and established—that the turn, the arch—the beak are so exquisite because they *represent* really represent, as not even poems do—the God speech, which over and over is—keep it clean, direct, open, proud and detached. Keep the balance—and I am proud because when there has been no one at all to understand and my own perception was deeper than mental—I have sought and clung to this thing which I have always felt everyone will rub against when I am dead like the beautiful sheen on marble—I so much love your mentioning "give too much and take too much"—God, what screaming from various females who have been in love with me I have listened to because I will not allow them to give too much—how heavy the toll collected—because eventually of course they always make you pay (life forces them to balance).

I told you Lawrence has it in several stories—I would say it was his main theme—though I never could have expressed it as you have nor fastened so clearly on it—but I guess you know already that mentally I operate 100% within the gift of my sex—that is, I get things in a way no scientist would credit and reach it up to my head last—when it is all assimilated into my blood and actions.

Anyway this past week has represented a terrific Motz balance. I did a magnificent job of entertaining the three children and the two adults—Monday morning came and each separately said "I don't want to go—I can't"—and I was pleased because inwardly I was terribly worried about being pregnant my body is gamboling around in the nuttiest ways conceivable—and I am waiting for a job I want to do to come in momentarily—but it doesn't come and Olson silence, mountains of it, is absolutely O.K. when I am certain I have caused no smallest hurt—because any slightest cruelty is not Motz's cue—and anyway I straddled all this plus my mother against whom I have to do the iron act—she pulls every trick any female ever had in the bag—tears, physical pain, gratitude, sarcasm etc etc—and I hold the whole damned thing in line and force the air of gayety (which she is *the* enemy of) in *my* house because Motz is gay, because she is in love with the law—which as she said years ago does not speak itself aloud and will break your spine in two—if you do not catch on quick.

I ditto on Dunne—only point I seemed to have skipped the part in Symphony of All Creation because it all began to look like goo—I used only for what I told you—to keep time in its place.

I am going to try to hang on to D'Arcy Thompson until I see you because he is a clean boy—stays in his own track completely and contains 2000000 beautiful facts all unknown to Motz—

picked up a lovely little essay last night on Bagdad mathematicians and the book includes another on Greek, Moslem and Chinese design in Mongol scientific instruments—I can see those old darlings pacing it off—

Anyway just a word about Burrow—I think he is not for me and you in the sense of our in any way needing it—but I am pretty sure he is on a path which is going to be useful—he wants man to get rid of all his images—and get down to rock bottom and start responding to his surroundings not "at it, but with it" the whole in a circle ⊚ if I may say so—anyway no God business, just man enlarging the use of his senses and not substituting mental images for real objects. It sounds nutty as I describe it, but I am reading carefully and will try to digest for you—because I suspect man will pick up anything faster from a laboratory than he will from a poet and for as far as he goes he is O.K.—he is a doctor—and it is mostly like a knife scraping.

Could never see this Freud—as Burrow says—sex is just one of the outward symptoms of how man is basically off center and I add that the real job man needs to do Freud never got to—he is a sort of medicine man a la mode for the decadent.

All of my studies prove to me that my Blake is the great man and he would, Olson, so believe in you—

I was sitting in the bus station reading and reading all of the poems I have from you now typed and how they are in there doing a job for us. Do not know what pudor means—

Bumped into Ammonius last night in the essay—and said Hi! Ammonius.

Read Sauer who also seems to be a nice man—one can feel through the subject matter, just sounds OK—essay interesting to me for different reasons than the ones you picked up—I was terribly interested to see *how* Olson mind works and to note how different it is—I felt confidence in Sauer's accuracy but should like to know more about how they know—exactly what methods etc.

Found a thing in the Book of Revelations which is perfect for me to use in a new straight deal on women—if I were not lazy and primarily a receiver. And Christ I should like to make my own drawings—imagine if Motz could lightly draw the terrific images which flash Christ, woman, and an angel—in a fast conversation.

Have not read Lawrence on Whitman for years but remember very well and loved him that he specifically included anger in sympathy as Olson and Motz so well illustrated that perfect weekend. Christ—nice clean passage "flow" between of anything "each to the other separate"—oh you Olson poet beloved

Thought of a guy up in Boston who might be perfect if you get in a jam about your joint.

Please return photos.

[Boldereff retyped the sections from "The Kingfishers," which Olson had sent to her on 26 October 1949, and added some questions and commentary, notably re "cad" in Part III:]

I think what you would be if you didn't commit yourself is the new courageous unknown—man now is investigating, beginning to try to know & since he has no slightest notion of what purpose, if any, he serves, he is scarcely in a position as yet to make any judgment concerning his Act.

Didn't get this—who can give freedom—I thought the law was that it can neither be given nor taken away. Does it mean "given my freedom *not* to commit myself, I do." It seems cleaner to me to say he has a strong compulsion to commit himself—the poet to pick up out of the void the fruit passed on to him—which may or may not be justified—he obeys blindly which is his honor—sole adornment—that he stalks through his commitment with *no* assurances & absolutely no knowledge—moral, religious, scientific or intuitional as to what should or should not be his cue—he obeys his blood as I feel it—which he trusts.

Which is where you love DHL
And I am so happy about that.

⊰ 94 ⊱

Washington to Woodward
11 January 1950 (postmark)

THE ADVANTAGE

I

Where do these
   invisible seeds
      settle from?

      And how are men able
         to spore them
            into air?

            For the gains are
            thus communicated.

      Shall you say there are not Powers
         when men spring up

    (like violets, said Bolyai Farkas)
        on all sides,
                to the need?

Men have their proper season, and that season
its act and image,
    image more than act,
        a rhythm more than image or than act,
proper to them

II

So if we now again shall call
    the sun a male
        And give him back the moon
            for mate

                        who'll say we're wrong, we
                        who have endured to rotting
                        the old device, the making
                        domestic abstract gods
                        of paled-out humans,
                        father mother son?

Will you say
    the root of universe is not
        the root of man?
deny
    the edge of mystery is
        the edge of life?
cry down
    the act of touch,
                the dumb thing knocking, knocking
at that door?

                        for Gan,
                            what followed,
                            yesterday
                            O

(It's off, to Accent,[19]
I don't know why)

19. The poem was not published until *Collected Poems* (pp. 105–6); see also *A Nation of Nothing but Poetry*, pp. 67–68.

₃ᴇ 95 ᴇ₃

Woodward to Washington
13 January 1950 (postmark)

Because I am shy I love to picture the "dumb thing" as a tiny adorable spider
staring at me through its infinitesimal eye to live please, Miss Motz, with you
in your house—as happened last night late, when a tiny one wove so beautifully a web on quietly breathing Frances who sent out so much love

Friday morning

Charles dear—
    I must to household things—want to say darling 1.—to thank you because
you operate so whole—you can not conceive what a profound rest (although
at the moment I am in a most fierce mood because those who surround me at
work have no passion at all—no belief, no hold, no nothing, just emptiness
which they pretend to fill and are vaguely curious to wonder why the feeling
of hunger—and other things—anyway I dig very deeply within my own
rocks to be able to make jokes with that lovely black head that sometimes
sleeps beside me) to know a human being who really relates, who having done
the act of casting off self, moves around free from taint and pursues man's
work.
    2. It often occurs to me but I just haven't bothered to say that I would ap-
preciate so much if I go off in reading a poem that you would take the trouble
to set me right—because they all require from me deep work and the strange
thing is all the places that I am sure I am right the explanation or illumination
as to their meaning always comes to me unpressed for—in the midst of living—and I pick up one tiny section after another and I always note how right
they are—how genuinely simple and unaffected and accurate—so full of integrity—but anyway I often feel a touch uneasy as I write to you about any of
them because our interiors start from such a great distance and I start off with
nothing in my hand but an intentional sense of their direction.
    3. Last night *again* such deep soothe for the absence of your physical hand
present, those hands I have looked at so hard which speak so aloud of Olson—
in Upon a Moebius Strip
                    materials and the weights of pain
                        their harmony.
    I wonder what seems wrong to you about "pain"—you cannot imagine to a
woman how amazingly weighted with rhythmic palliation the physical sound
and feel of that word is—the lines do for me what has never been done heretofore by anything but nature direct—the inclusion in her living breathing
which is sometimes sound and sometimes a quieter pulsation like the tiny
grasses to one another. Anyway, for a woman it is the only word consolation

that has ever been made—to my knowledge—and that, because it enters direct, not like speech, like thought, but like the quiet living warmth of male hand—not asking—but being. And it is a very great great thing to say to you—I could not have made it up and Christ the gulf—it has never been passed over in speech before—and very seldom elsewhere by an art of man—

I did not mention about Hudson Review—because I take for granted that the thing will be slow, also unescapable. Since you are, not made up by me, but actually, the only artist of any kind I know today man will dig his hand in and find and he will not do it hurriedly because you make a mutual thing, demanding—which is the great love—as Dostoyevsky pointed out about Christ, the involved respect in making each man do his own job.

Love you Olson—who are so beautiful an achievement.

In my physicist who was writing about the mathematicians I found "the tense and superb arrogance of Michelangelo"—remember beautiful Olson those words your Frances wrote to you and apply. Man is a very old animal who comes up with amazing perceptions as I remember writing once before

◄ 96 ►

Woodward to Washington
15 January 1950 (postmark 16 January 1949)

Sunday

I have been thinking about Lawrence and about how Lawrence was an ill man whose illness caused him to hate things and how Olson is not ill and gives off a perfume of sweetness.

I have been reading for several days in Meister Eckhart and over and over again it appears to me that the chief idea you love in Lawrence is to be found clearer in Eckhart—whose mind has seemed to me one of the very finest that has ever existed—I feel that in Lawrence the deep driving power behind his not wanting to mingle, to be untouched physically—impersonal—was the cringing in flesh that carries pain. In Eckhart the drive towards Impersonality is knowledge—knowledge of unity, of the being of God—

although I have sworn never to send you a quote again you, the poet, would love this (Legend on page following)

I interpolate names of two sermons to show you something of how fresh, real and un-middle ages was Eckhart

Sermon I—This is Meister Eckhart from whom God hid nothing

Sermon 10—God laughs and plays

Fragment 27

Speaking of knowledge and love—knowledge is better than love but the two together are better than one of them, for knowledge really contains love. Love may be fooled by goodness, depending on it, so that when I love I hang on the gate, blind to the truth about my acquaintance. Even a stone has love—for the ground! If I depend on goodness, which is God's first proffer and accept God only as he is good to me, I am content with the gate but I do not get to God. Thus knowledge is better, for it leads love. Love has to do with desire and purpose, whereas knowledge is no particular thought, but rather, it peels off all and is disinterested and runs naked to God until it touches him and grasps him.

Legend of Meister Eckhart

Meister Eckhart met a beautiful naked boy.
He asked him where he came from.
He said, "I come from God."
Where did you leave him?
"In virtuous hearts."
Where are you going?
"To God"
Where do you find him?
"Where I part with all creatures."
Who are you?
"A king."
Where is your kingdom?
"In my heart."
Take care that no one divide it with you!
"I shall."
Then he led him to his cell.
Take whichever coat you will.
"Then I should be no king!" (One of the deepest sentences, out of the bowels
    of reality, I ever found.)
And he disappeared.
For it was God himself—
Who was having a bit of fun.

Does it give the Middle Ages as they are given to us? Or does it toss one high in the air with joy?

The Pope John XXII in a bull published after his death spoke of him as having been deceived "by the father of his who often appears as an angel of light" into "sowing thorns and thistles amongst the faithful and even the simple folk." The legend plus the Church's action is the whole picture of what we are fighting.

◄§ 97 §►

Washington to Woodward
16 January 1950

monday jan 16 L

i have to make that copy of the K'S to go off to try to make its way in the world
of the small realities, but before i set to it (i do not like to fill my ears and work
into my throat again rhythms which i am done with) i want you to have me as
i come fresh from sleep and from your delicate beautiful letter of friday,
which came shortly ago, and which is my motz voming (not a bad verb) (also,
how about *w*oming) across straight (god knows i know what you mean about
letters, and how difficult you sometimes find them; and if i forever tell you
how wonderful language is because it can be made to give us up, and that
there is peace in making it carry our rhythm and meaning by way of a form
we make it give up, you will listen to this old animal who sometimes comes up
with perceptions)

Composition (straight fr the Motz) by musical phrase, reads:

> man
> is a very old animal
> who comes up
> with
> amazing perceptions

why not, was to be the lst words of the letter you would have had today, in
answer to yr letter-&-package of friday arrival, had it come without this new
letter   why not   why not   in answer to yr cry, if motz would draw-
paint-cry

> christ woman an angel talking
> split fast, walking
> not like Tobias
> but like his fish uncaught, talking
> like fish gleam,
> like humans caught
> in love

why not?

Another version:

Christ, woman, and an angel
in a fast
conversation
(not like Tobias
with a fish and an angel
by his side.
Then, walking,
not like Tobias
but like Tobias when
the fish was uncaught, when
the angel had not come, when
Tobias was quite alone
as each is
talking, talking
like fish gleam, like humans
caught
by love

my motz, again your old man makes his push, knowing
what his lady has in her, sounding
her vitality, admitting
what she has drawn / from the seas
of the body / joining
her urge to make form of life, life, that discontinuous bitch

this is a recognition, motz
has done it (thus her elegance
the inexhaustible gayety on which all
feed,
the possible only
to those who throw their own life in, who risk
(each separate instant syllable)
their breath

but now the involved respect says,
motz, you earn yourself, the pleasures
of your own creations, the spaces, the lines
you put down, the intervals
of grass-blades
you who have trusted your mind & body, trust
the legs of an angel of your own making, the eyes
you'll put in the head of christ—i know those eyes—

the vocables
in that swimming silence

  baby, Pushkin sd,
the natural stupidity of the poet,
which is whot
nature hath

     do not question her, you
    who know how to obey

When you say there are things more than poems you are not right, my darling, simply because they come from the same place nature, as you so finely
know, (and forget?) (forget? hell, you do not, you
          go under, as who does not, balked
       by the discontinuous
               (the Devil is a bitch, the spawn
           of a dam)
nature
    does not have
        hierarchies
           They
are of man's making
            She
flows

((Is it not a clue of immense importance to you that nature is, that the image
of her is, woman?
       which you are,
And anything that you tell yourself that you want to do, who is speaking?))

Try this on for size, frances: the only true elegance / is art

                      (I, too, hate what
has happened to the word. And it is the false great who have done it, by arro-
gating to themselves, because they sense a difference, something which does
not belong to them. Men have lost, in the slackening of the tensions in the
West, the necessary humilitas. The fools! How patently they are no more than
instrument.)

                      At the same time,

of course, I deplore anonymity. It is a lie. Tense and arrogant. Of course. How else get the work done. How does nature maintain her self?)

Extend your discipline
to the grass-blade in you,
to the syllable you hear,   Only form slayeth
(which is also the discontinuous)   the discontinuous
and slay it
by form, which is our only
weapon, (as you know who made that amazingly beautiful Penn State Catalog

((Darling, you know where this comes from, or I'd shut up. I will in a minute, but, I am suddenly reminded of something which, a propos yr formulation Godspeech VS a poem—this:

the problem of a poem (that which explains the coming into existence of form) is, that it stay within itself. Not spill out, and, likewise, that it contain all that it has to contain. This is the struggle. And it is permanently difficult, is new each time, & defies any law other than the new one each new one creates. And the only clue is rhythm, which is only to be described as the force & use of, the discipline of, the individual who has listened, & wants, at the moment he or she writes draws hammers shapes, to speak

Which leaves unsd much: how beautiful Lucinda is (even the wrist is a Fatima!); & if yr dear body is okay; and how happy i am when you can feel the olson hand present; and when you tell me (you so rarely do) how your work goes; yr triumphs (which I always see as that terrific laugh and down, down, derry derry down throatspeech, sex-all-over-the-place, of the Motz)—arrrH you LaDy, YoU!

for a quick present, two more little ones like the p.c. i sent you, two pieces which flew off that work last week:

A CONDENSATION

to be given too much, or,
to take too much, both
outrage the soul

OBSERVATION

of one cloth, if of two colors, nature
made man & universe

love, up & down
o
Chollie

We go under
(each interval)
down   downed by
the discontinuous
(is a bitch
the Devil is a bitch, the spawn
of a dam)

p.s.
Are you going to keep the name of your physicist secret from me?

p.s. The Egyptian poem is a lover—change:
"Your hair is the flowering of your body (no period)
To it I rise (no comma) (space) I am
Your sib (no period) (space) your cheek

.   .   .   .

herbs (no period)

.   .   .   .

full (And no PERIOD!)"[20]

-δς 98 яɞ

Woodward to Washington
17 January 1950 (postmark 18 January 1950)

Tuesday night

Charles dear—
    I remember that I planned all my life and at last victoriously found myself
with a leave of absence of three months which had been—had to be scheduled
a year ahead and this was to work on a book—and in exactly those three
months motz was pregnant as it came about and the mind shut down as
though it had never been there and here I was all supplied with paper, solitude, freedom, will, everything—and the mind absolutely shut off.
    I said "OK nature you win—I see you are wise, but don't expect me ever to
forget this insult."

20. Olson is here making emendations to the poem he sent on 19 December 1949. Neither this nor the
other verse in this letter has been previously published.

I am so very far down under that only the repetition of Olson's quiet "hold, Motz" keeps me from death. I am stretched tight to the absolute limit of my capacity. I understand in a certain indirect way your letter but can not read it really—

It is rolling waves of despair—the dryness and the terrible coldness of everything that surrounds me and under it all my body pressing me to the wall in a way that makes the Germans look innocent.

And I don't even have privacy because my mother sees the tears I so violently despise and resent (how nature insults you Charles dear you can not really imagine)

And those people in my office—darling—don't you understand they even hide things from me—because if I get my hands on a job it will take an extra ten minutes and I am no longer the customer I am an employee.

I am ashamed to tell you but I want you to understand if I can not write.

This is that beautiful Michelangelo woman with her hand dragging on the ground—that no man except Michelangelo ever saw, the quintessence of things unhoped for.

Frances

A pure animal man would be as lovely as a deer or a leopard—burning like a flame fed straight from underneath. And he'd never cease to wonder, he'd breathe silence and unseen wonder, as the partridges do, running in the stubble.

From St Mawr—DHL
Copied today   Tuesday

❧ 99 ❧

Washington to Woodward (postcard)
18 January 1950 (postmark 18 January 1950)

THE DAY'S ORDERS, BOYS[21]

See that you keep
yr passion dry

Carry yr guns
high

---

21. This poem has not been previously published, except by Fielding Dawson, in a slightly different version, in *The Black Mountain Book* (New York: Croton Press, 1970), p. 106.

And fire only
when you see light
in an eye

o

1.18.L

❧ 100 ❧

Washington to Woodward
18 January 1950 (postmark)

wednesday

i am beginning to prowl again around the edges of james joyce but that's not the
point   it isn't yr argument for joyce, it's more such as the Eckhart   or the
Dura-E of last spring   or the egyptian

you see, you sld know what you do, delivering to me up clean out
of the delicate sure fingers of yr mind, such things, & Blake, &, for as much as
i can take, crist

you wouldn't know how much that i
might value & use has been cut off for me by educators (i wish I could name
them as small as they are)
for years i was imposed on, because i
am stupid and naive, by the knowledgeable bastards   (if for no other reason than, that he sprung me, i shall bat for dahlberg)   they so left their
slime tracks over such magnificent things, that it was traumatic, the way some
men's works were closed to me

i just wanted to tell you, my funny thing, how beautiful it is, to have things
passed to me clean for a change   for even the others, my respected friends,
have a way of being unclean about those they have enthusiasm for   i need
not tell you that what we have been saying abt love between persons—to keep
it dry while hot—goes for knowledge, in this sense, too

baby, this is a quick
kiss
o

Washington to Woodward
18 January 1950

SUMMUM BONUM[22]

We should, said meister Eckhart,
despite the church & pejerocracy,
speak of knowledge and love

> Knowledge
> is better than love,
> but the two together
> is better than either

> Love
> can be fooled by goodness, come
> to depend on it. When I love thus,
> I hang on the gate. I am blind
> to the truth about my acquaintance.
> (Even the stone has love
> —for the ground.)

> If I depend on goodness
> —it is God's first proffer—
> accept God only
> as he is good to me,
> I am content with the gate.
> And I do not get to him.

> Thus knowledge is better,
> for it leads love.
> Love has to do with desire & purpose, knowledge
> is no particular thought. It peels off all,
> is disinterested,
> and runs naked to God
> until it touches him,
> grasps him.

22. Based on Boldereff's letter of 15 January 1960 (#96), this previously unpublished poem, missing from the correspondence manuscripts, is taken from the "Unpublished Poems" file at Storrs.

I met a boy.
He was naked.
I said to him,
"Who are you?"
He replied,
"A king."
I asked him,
 "Where?"
He answered,
"In my heart"

I offered him a coat.
He refused it.
I questioned him, why.
"Then," he said,
"I'd be no king!"

And he disappeared.
For it was God himself,
having fun.

for frances 1/18/50

what do you think?
does it work?
tell me
i don't know
i think it does, has
a hidden form, maybe
the middle ages' exemption
but give me your
impression,
collaborator!

Charles

❧ 102 ❧

Washington to Woodward
19 January 1950 (postmark 19 January 1950)

babe, for holding,
(in place of God-speech)
a little thing

              'CENTO[23]

Man is a very old animal

who comes up with

amazing perceptions

ex.: Christ, woman and an angel in

a fast conversation

(not like Tobias
fish & angel by his side,
not like Tobias then, walking

but like Tobias when
the fish was uncaught, when
the angel had not come, when
Tobias was quite alone, as each is,

              talking, talking

like fish gleam, like humans

caught by love

                              olson   1/19/L
                                  from a man

                    ◅ 103 ▻

Woodward to Washington
19 January 1950 (postmark)

Charles dear—
    I am holding in the only way I have ever understood—the instinctual thing
of an animal—searching to stay alive—
    I have come up with a plot for the defeat of my enemies—to take the Motz
out of their power—if it works you will hear later.

23. This previously unpublished poem is made from material in Olson's letter of 16 January 1950.

My mind is still far away from sharpness—my response to *Summum Bonum* is an immediate very very good

Please send it off to be published—if nowhere else than to Harper's Bazaar.

Thank you for returning the pictures.

Neither you nor I have ever made the mistake of saying "We can be the same thing—one thing" have we?—we know how terribly difficult the problem is and how sharp is the line of demarcation between man-woman. I take this to be the meaning of

"from a man"

meaning to say—a man, which means immediate blood ignorance of the problem involved. I am sure it was not intended as superiority.

I tell you this so you understand how I feel—

I am the most alive giant Sequoia which has been torn out ruthlessly roots and all by a hurricane—turned upside down and made to brush top down against the dirt of the world and then thrown so powerfully as, alive though it is and hard as living wood fibre is to shatter, to be utterly absolutely broken into small fragments.

In the night, when the mice talk and I love their talking—to crawl alone out over this earth (so me, myself, a female) and collect without sight those pieces which without mind I somewhere know in the daylight I can some time once again put together into living form.

Frances

⤳ 104 ⤶

Woodward to Washington
[21 January 1950]

1950   21 Ganuary[24]

[*first drawing*]

I had a little moppet,
I put it in my pocket,
And fed it corn and hay;
Then came a proud beggar,
And swore he would have her,
And stole my moppet away.

24. Lucinda's date on her drawing. The rest of the written text is by Frances.

Lucinda hanging from Olson's pocket—looking bright and happy if I may comment. Mother complete with breast pin and barrette in her hair.

[*second drawing*]

Hill Steep La Chuta

At the bottom the Guardian Angel of Hill Steep La Chuta.
The tree of Hill Steep La Chuta with the fairy of Hill Steep La Chuta with the house "High Mountain" of Hill Steep La Chuta.

[on the cardboard protecting these drawings:]

I forgot to tell you
          Lucinda explained to me
     "Roots dangle, so the lines dangle!"

❦ 105 ❧

Washington to Woodward
25 January 1950 (postmark)

Wednesday

lady, i'm grim, again   will you say why, who'll say i'm wrong? it's spring this morning, and i can't see it, my nerves are in a knot

too goddamn much
work maybe, rather, wrong work maybe   anyway, for two days i've been try-ing to get ready for press a prose piece   (i hate prose, rather, hate my own prose   i can't get a prose which allows the irrational in   it ain't the prose, as language   it's the form in which the prose is put (would like to edit a mag in which all the god damn inherited deductive forms and organizations were kicked to hell   and the thing composed as a whole, the mag   so one moved openly from one ope biz to another   i'm all right when i'm writing straight from olson, abt anything, but when, as in this one, I'm trying (wrongly?) to write abt something and someone else (the King James Version as the putting into existence of the only common body of events and images which both the pippul & the ritters had for 250 yrs,—and what HM did with it, the only one who did   if it don't come round today i'm dishing it   (the idea was to get it ready for the 1st no of a friend's new mag, Payne, the MON-TEVALLO REVIEW

my jaws are like a cat on a bird, that's what i mean by grim   so this is going to be a just a note, a p.c., to tell you i'm in the land of the unliving, for what good that is......

and it's a shame, for i've got from you such things! from you & luce: & both, pure motz and pure luce

ain't it awful, the way we go tumbling off where we think (that bitch, illusion) we're gonna stay

profane, profane, i am, i have to be   who can be holy in a shit-pile   we are, this fucking culture, so ill-prepared for life god damn them all, fr conception on down

at the same time i feel a sonofabitch to take you like this   but there it is, daily livin, correspondence ain't daily living, but if it ain't used staggered as is, it dies   so here's olson, with a bird a bird in his mouth

& ready to kill,

the other olson

& not even a good new line to send you,
just a word, and ain't it a beautiful word
    profane
            profane
    profanation   prof-a-nation
        fuck-a-nation
    to be clean

◄ 106 ►

Woodward to Washington
[26 January 1950]

Thursday night

Look Charles—
    You can not exaggerate or put into ugly wild enough language the way I feel at the moment about this whole business we are in—I had already decided regardless of what you told me about how they will follow out the same thing—to ask your help and if I didn't get it to do it without your help about really kicking the whole thing apart for myself and go to Russia and wait on tables and speak nothing—the grimness I feel is as great as any you could feel—in my office Tuesday—I didn't go Wednesday because I am so boiling

with fury—they told me I can't touch any job from the college "so as not to insult the customer"—I will not bore you darling with all my furies.

Anyway this is the Motz decision—I am going out to Albuquerque and try
to get a job in the Univ Press which does some good things—if the thing
doesn't work—then I am selling every damned thing I own—borrowing
money on the legacy Lucinda received and leaving for Russia—I enclose two
separate things which are perfect—just to let you see how well I know where
we are—am reading Spengler—

Would it occur to you in your wildest dreams to take a shot at that wild
Murometz land?

I send you one quote from Spengler:
"Here we have beginning and end clashing together. Dostoyevski is a saint,
Tolstoi only a revolutionary. From Tolstoi, the true successor of Peter, and
from him only, proceeds Bolshevism, which is not the contrary, but the final
issue of Petrinism, the last dishonouring of the metaphysical by the social, and
ipso facto a new form of the Pseudomorphosis. If the building of Petersburg
was the first act of Antichrist, the self-destruction of the society formed of that
Petersburg is the second and so the peasant soul must feel it. For the Bolshevists are not the nation, or even a part of it, but the lowest stratum of this
Petrine society, alien and western like the other strata. It is all megalopolitan
and "Civilized"—the social politics, the Intelligentsia, the literature that first
in the romantic and then in the economic jargon champions freedoms and re-
forms, before an audience that itself belongs to the society. The real Russian is
a disciple of Dostoevski. If the Bolshevists, who see in Christ a mere social revolutionist like themselves, were not intellectually so narrowed, it would be in
Dostoyevski that they would recognize their prime enemy." (Motz NOTE: in
a book just published by American Council of Learned Societies from Russia
last year Russia lists publications, some of them in 42 dialects—everyone, but
no Dostoevski listed not one page—they read Spengler as I have had proof elsewhere and are smart enough to pick up hints.) "What gave this revolution its
momentum was not the intelligentsia's hatred. It was the people itself, which,
without hatred, (testified to by many exiled Russians) urged only by the need of
throwing off a disease, destroyed the old Westernism in one effort of upheaval
and will send the new after it in another." (I think this will not be done by revolution but by the people's forcing their own pattern—such as getting back
their worship—over time, at the moment they see with their own eyes they
must have our stuff, our guns, etc. in order to defeat us—)
"For what this townless people yearns for is its own life-form, its own religion, its own history. Tolstoi's Christianity was a misunderstanding. He spoke
of Christ and he meant Marx. But to Dostoyevki's Christianity the next thousand years will belong." (And Motz believes this absolutely.)

Reading Strzygowski—*Origin of Christian Church Art*[25]—finding deep explanations about Olson—why he hates lyricism—why he hates Christ—Christianity—why he loves red and yellow—very very fertile deep research—great stimulating stuff.

Baby darling—shall we pull the Japanese stunt and hand each other the dagger with which to slit our throats?

Sold 2 copies of my book this week.

Your loving
Cecḿpa[26]

[*enclosed: hand-drawn valentine by Lucinda*]

❈ 107 ❈

Woodward to Washington
29 January 1950 (postmark 30 January 1950)

Sunday morning

Charles dear—

Your voice darling[27]—some great well from which everything comes to me—Charles beloved it occurs to me this morning that perhaps it is necessary to stand in a sandpit where absolutely nothing grows in order to have a magic love like ours. I do not stand off and look at it I tremble every second in regard to us—but I know in my soul that you have to search far and far and know very much to be able to find anything so beautiful so full of integrity so unasking—better than any of the ones I know about—far more—in a whole different realm more beautiful than any of the Tristan and Iseults I know about. The desert which surrounds us right up to our mouths which fills our ears and our eyes and our nostrils and our lungs and our stomachs and our legs and our nails with sand—the absolutely arid from which we can make nothing—only stands there as backdrop to expose the rich teeming flow that is our only life—the Egyptian poem this morning comes true—I see it is really so—not words—we exist absolutely within one another. The miracle which it all is—I tremble every second and you know that I am not looking at it—Built out of absolute obedience.

25. Josef Strzygowski, *Origin of Christian Church Art*, translated by O.M. Dalton and H. J. Braunhollz (Oxford: Clarendon Press, 1923). Olson later obtained his own copy.
26. Russian: "sister."
27. Olson presumably telephoned to propose he make another visit to Woodward.

I am very very excited about the Strzygowski because something I never knew before which he has absolutely proven—that "Gothic" came out of Iran and Armenia—the spacing as he says in some of those 5th Century churches has never been surpassed—oh! Christ darling and maybe Christ was not a "Christian" but a Manichee—anyway darling the thing I have always wanted to know—what happened in the dark ages I have searched and searched and here—1st century—2nd century right up to 6th and 7th those silent passionate people creating *all* the forms out of which that damned Europe took everything it has—we have never heard of any of them and very few names are known—but all done out of intense religious belief—Rome contributing *nothing* only borrowed—"Romanesque" did not grow out of the timber covered Basilica says Strzygowski—anyway Strzygowski can name you right off 6–7 of the deepest characteristics of Gothic which came directly from Iran and Armenia and the other contributing force was Scandinavian wooden mast columns—the ship transplanted to the church out of four masts gradually twelve—and on and on with aisles and stuff—but darling oh! you must read how he hates Southern "your slayers"—the boys who gave us representation—and he shows so clearly that "northern" spirit—and he uses northern in a way I adore—ignoring geography—Armenia Iran Russia Sweden—the sweep—all passion and non-representational decoration—the rhythm to speak direct—no copy of nature—no Tintorettos if I may so say—explains Olson all so clearly—

still haven't said what I am *so* excited about that is that in the places no common person has ever dreamed of in the unheralded and uncredited was *all* the fountain. Europe took about all of it out of their passion and Motz, darling, sees that there is no substitute and that where there is passion there is creation and these filthy bastards have to use it because they have none—you see where I am driving—that if it must be alone—just Olson and Motz then that's what it will be—we have to expect nothing and to eat our suffering out of which we churn their butter—dearest I have two ideas—Baby beloved walk with a light step do not look to right or left—speak silently—I will press to bring both of them about. Not that either one of them can be of the slightest personal use to either of us—neither of us dear has any "personal" life at all—from morning to night we pace that treadmill and make grain out of our anguish—

If you can come Wednesday on that 6 something bus from Sunbury—please dearest get off at that little restaurant where we ate and wait there until 7:30—because I have to go to work Wednesday a man is bringing the manuscript of a book I am designing for him which means I cannot be home until 7:22 p.m. and mother will get on that bus—

The complete interpenetration of all our cells and life makes it impossible to tell where is Olson—where is Motz—

You can tell Con—Constanza—if she would like to hear—that the dream was all reverence—she was dancing—like Nijinsky—alone—her absolutely lovely shoulders and the dear padded lovely look of her almost unbreasted body and the hips rising like a calyx and all so beautiful I did not step near nor touch nor desire to touch—I only remember smiling and the man who stood beside me smiling also—and neither of us speaking—it was absolutely satisfying—the dance was so marvelous—such interlaced movement so quiet and gracious and the body the most exquisite ever seen and I kept thinking, "This is what he means by 'fine'."

⊰ 108 ⊱

Washington to Woodward
30 January 1950 (postmark)

monday

darling motz:

     yr letter (& enclosures)[28] just came   i waited to get this note off, and now i must get it in the early collection to make sure you have it tuesday

     i'm going to try to come this wednesday   i've checked the god damn connections, and it is not true the sunbury way is any help   so i shall have to arrive as before, thru state c, on the evening bus   and leave thursday evening on that bus back thru the sunbury way, due to the same godmn connections

     why don't i have the driver drop me up the road a piece, where that country road goes off just before the bridge? in that way you won't have to fuss with ma, and she can go off on that bus without me dropping in her lap?

     i wish that i might send you a long rage & demonstrandum written at one sitting thursday (5000 words) a critique of the whole wrongs & necessities of the dirty world, with the characters present being Lawrence, Shakes, Dostoe, Melvile, Blake, Dante, Homer, Pound, Joyce, & olson crying out, secular secular but i had to quit it to get off a piece on Pound to the Hudson, and it is in no shape, just wild prose as it came, which you only would follow, but i have to keep it to work on it today (it is a part of the article which had me stymied last week for the Montevallo R, and may or may not (the new passage I mean) make or break the piece[29]   I shall have to find out the next two days   it is suppose to be a deadline of the 1st

28. Presumably referring to Lucinda's valentine. Other enclosures are not known.
29. The manuscript, "The Mystery of What Happens When It Happens," remained unpublished. The Pound piece referred to here was "GrandPa, GoodBye," later rejected by the *Hudson Review*.

instead, just for a little peace, my baby, I send you (& maybe it is
nice enuf for lucinda to take it too, as a howdedo, for her valentine:

SO GENTLE[30]

so gentle
nobody seems to have paid him personally much mind,
as they did Ben

so gentle,
when he slipped off to Stratford he left no ripple behind,
the Swan

love

charles

❧ 109 ❧

[*letter not sent*][31]

Woodward to Washington
[31 January 1950]

Tuesday night

Charles
    I really was angry—

    Why do you have to rob me of sleep all the time?
    When I handled my thing with Duke I did it without involving you in any
way. Why the hell, since you have made me wait so long—didn't you just
keep quiet and then come? Two weeks is one eternity and I was just beginning to get some rest.
    It begins to bother me because even in the letter you announce your inten-
tion to voice the possibility you *might* not keep your word.
    What's the matter with you Olson—
    If I make up my mind, unless I die, I keep my word.
    Why can't you make up your mind—after all—
    You are driving me plain nuts so nuts I am beginning to hate you—

30. Published posthumously in *A Nation of Nothing but Poetry*, p. 78.
31. This letter is in the possession of Sharon Thesen.

⊰ 110 ⊱

Washington to Woodward
31 January 1950 (postmark)

> There are practicals, of course (such as
> the two which, in any case, bracketed
> the trip in 24 hrs)   but you & i know
> how much deference they deserve
> from the likes of us—no, this letter is
> *below*

tuesday

frances, frances, frances
            i was a fool to think i could come, yet am still so deter-
mined to try i am not ready to say i cannot   instead will call you if i cannot
                                                                                    but
i must, (because i am from somewhere directed to), write you now, out of the
deepest conviction that a false move now on either of our parts is crucial   i
am trying to walk like an angel in order to keep this thing which is so very
beautiful alive, and a going concern
                        i may be a writer but if so i am one of such
a nature as to believe that it can all be got down in words, that words are
health because they are capable of the exactitude it is customary to attach more
to action than to words
                        and at this juncture i feel the pressure of words more
than action
                    what i am doing is what i shall always try to get my flaming motz
to do, what i keep trying to get her to do, to write out the particulars   the
illuminations rise out of the documentation (at least now, when fragmentation is the LAW

                                    ((if i could give you the whole story of
fragmentation, then you would not suffer as you palpably do from the bastards you work for, from an isbrandsen ad, ideal marriage crap, from an illusion of russia, from all the the terrible things which invade and rush over
you, and from which i would save you

                                    spengler, nobody, knows in precisely
what way THIS is *our* state,—and not because i am wiser, but because i have
the advantage of living at this later stage of the decay, and the madness

i abhor "news"   all public event is a lie, in the face of yr private horror, my private task   but good god, sweet nature, one must who lives in washington or new york these days be just like a goldsmith scale & gauge that moment of time to a hair when from then on the risk of physical fragmentation is 100%, in other words, the very image of our actual mortality is, fragmentation, or, that peculiar sister of it which is the irony of the whole horrible thing, vaporization

how i should be talking about this, when all i am concerned with, is our separate and joint necessities, peculiarly, at this juncture, yours   and i am terribly terribly rocked   (in addition to all else, i had, last night, one of those dreams which tease you out of thought, they seem so revelatory of your root nature, and this morning i am able to see in a way i have not been, yet the only clue i hold on to is my identity with John Keats, who said one thing once which makes more sense to me about myself than any other thing i have ever come to know   he sd that even when he entered a room full of children, their identities so entered on himself that he was they, and not himself   ((you probably recall the formulation this seems to me to have led him to, the notion of "negative capability" as the mark of the Shakespearean poet as against the others, the false sublime, the Wordsworthian, the Egotistical Sublime, was his phrase!))   it causes me such despair, especially this past ten days, and, pointedly, this morning, for i am so
                                        i do not have, men like keats and i do not have that resistance, that necessity, that beautiful, beautiful pugnacity of one's own life and necessities, not the least of which advantages is, that it leaves the existence of another person, their mortal reality, theirs   ((you, i imagine unknowingly, gave me a terrific clue recently when you sd, a propos my health and/or otherwise, that's god's business, and must be left to him::::: o the lord have mercy on me, if i only had such realism   but it is not permitted the likes of us who are born to be mere instruments of the writing of verse

Or so it seems to me in the face of my obvious inaction in the face of your troubles   ((you see there is a thing which accompanies the negative capability which is hidden to most people, in fact was, i think, hidden from me until you so wonderfully gave me the sight of it by believing in it—i was going to call it another egotism, an egotism completely different from that which creates mortal, individual resistance and fight for one's life; but your word about me "cold, cold," is much much more accurate   it is that terrible, terrible thing which will sacrifice all, everything, everyone, for the one thing, to get the words, the words, mind you, not the acts, down, to make the god damn poem, not get the acts called for done, if the words are in the soul
                                        jesus, jesus, what *is*
the answer to the existence on this earth of such, such creatures

Let me tell you something. Let me see, let me be exact in time, so that you can fix it on your own events and see if I caught a smell across space, or it was, what i suppose it was, that other horrible thing, the normal and expectable arc in which time works itself out where our flesh feeds:

i suddenly felt you could not stand this situation any longer   i dare say i may have caught it from your letters, but my impression is no, for you had not, a week ago, spelled it out, on the contrary even that incredible (I still dare not speak of it) vision,[32] the olson Cocking, was forward, as we have gone forward, AND I MIGHT ASK, if I ever asked anything, THAT WE MAY BE ABLE TO GO FORWARD, o motz, motz, this dreamer, this fool, who patently knows nothing of that other reality, that reality which someone meant, i imagine, when he wrote of "the whole catastrophic problem of sorrow"

((follow me, babe, hold: i am quite, quite naive, and am so puzzled, so ignorant before this riddle, i am prepared that you, or anyone else, find me wrong or stupid or fantastically unawares   i also have the horrible thought that this letter will not involve that kind of attention which you, beyond anyone else, have given my verse, and that it will not yield up to you the usable truth you have taken from the verse, and that would destroy me BECAUSE THIS LETTER IS MY KIND OF ACTION, at least my kind of action at this moment when i am in the iron grip of one necessity, that cold, murderous necessity, to do nothing, absolutely NOTHING but THAT WHICH CAN BE DONE WITH WORDS

there it is, that's what i have been fighting awake night after night for now one week, that all ALL i can do is //// //// //// yr letter posted monday has just come, & i shall not open it until i have finished this pitiful attempt to speak it all out to you

all i can do is precisely what i have been doing, and am doing right now, my work

((it came to an unbearable and ironic climax i did not tell you about on the phone by wednesday night, last week, i had decided to go against this deep resistance to displace myself—it is, by the way, not a resistance to move to you alone, it is a resistance to any kind of displacement of any sort, even to the act of eating, or saying a word to anyone so, thursday, i was going to come   and do you know what happened thursday?   i think i told you, i sat like some manacled mad thing, some punished creature at this desk for 9 hrs straight and wrote that 5000 words on the secular, a passage which, when it is done,

32. The allusion is to a special delivery letter (also referred to in Boldereff's next letter) that is no longer extant.

should be the fullest statement of the way i see things that i have ever managed))

look, i'm sure to anyone but you and me this must seem a simple proposition, that olson is in a mood   but that's the very devil of what i am talking about, that if one's job is this crazy thing, language, then a mood   (and girl, is this provable!)   is the very conduit, the only conduit, greater than action, greater than anything else, yourself or any person, the only connect, to use a motz, which is in there, to use another francesism

(((one of my secret delights is to find myself suddenly not just using the motz vocabulary, but the twisting of the mouth, the exact same heat and pressure of breath, the gestures, the works!   and finding that it makes people jump   and i mean jump!   what a wonderful wonderful thing you are, what a power and beauty))

I'm willing to settle for the fact that it is a mood   But that don't do you one good god damn good (say that very slow)   AND THAT'S THE WHOLE TROUBLE, for that other side of me, that son of a bitch bastard swede or new englander or god damn stupid american or whatever it is, that craving to make life have the shape one can only give a piece of work, that's what kills me, has wracked me for seven days, and will wrack me to the end of my time, i fear

that i have nothing to offer motz but this that i do

((I am astonished to discover that this seems to be what i had to say Good god, darling, nothing, nothing,   merely an explanation of my nature   What in Christ's name is this   what good is this to you

I'm exhausted   You see, I am not well, have not been   I have no more strength than what i am giving daily to this machine   For every night i am wasting what i am, plotting to come to you, and then, when morning comes, staying, instead, here   It has to come to an end
     I thought sure I'd end it by the act of coming   But obviously what I am forced to at this moment is, this day at least, instead of spending my strength on the work in hand, to merely spell out my defeat straight to you

I'll read your letter

It is beautiful, beautiful, & I thank you for it, I thank you, Frances. And don't, please, if it is humanly possible, let the above knock you one jot off the hold yr letter shows. I am not much use, but believe me, baby, there is no carelessness here. Write me, write me as much as you can possibly tell me, regular mail, & I shall telephone you.

(I wish I could draw, as Lucinda, or Cagli—*and as I think you might.* For I should like, now that the tension is going out of my throat, to make with the hand things to make you happy, kisses to make you gay. For I want to be gay. I do not know what is what I have sd today. You must tell me, please. For it is my work for today. And it is yours, yours, baby, whatever pain it causeth.

Love, love
Charles

◄< 111 >►

Woodward to Washington
2 February 1950 (postmark)

Thursday
your letter just received

Charles belovéd—

Dearest Charles—no—it is not because I can't stand the situation any longer—in fact—the breaking point was that vision, that is why I had, that once, to send you a special and I so deeply appreciated your not commenting or scolding because it was absolutely necessary that once—you see, dear, I had been enduring a physical necessity so strong that it could never be described and I can not remember even in my early twenties enduring anything which was so unspeakable the physical need so powerful that the two days it lasted I mean a whole 48 hours, I thought each moment I could not possibly hang on until the next one—I do not understand it—I have never heard of it in another woman—but I suppose for a woman as alive as I am—when the body signs off its power to reproduce it makes a last violent attempt to continue—anyway dearest, I can tell you now that I know I have endured the worst, it can never never be that way again—I told you yesterday over the phone a dream because I didn't want to say over the phone how it was—that I was unable to sleep at all—I was afraid literally to have Lucinda beside me because I am sure I would have tried to take her whole small beautiful little body and cram it into my womb—dearest—it is past and I am embarrassed into the roots of my being and would not tell you if I did not so deeply want you to understand and know how it has nothing to do with my living faith in us—which did not enter in at all—but can you understand now what that vision represents something I believe which never took place in this world before—a woman at for her the very bottom pit who arose out of her bed and made out of that pit a vision—and I do not believe that the vision is in any way sensuous—is it darling—I mean it is clean—it doesn't give off any odor of uncleanness does it dear—I transmuted—out of the hell of that want which I have always been powerless to change—this once, Charles, I transmuted it into beauty—and I think the thing is absolutely genuine—real—I think it represents truth—and of course you know I am a believer—but maybe that is the great crowning thing in all my life—that God grasped up my pain and enabled me to do that eternal thing—that real one—with one—with one—with that Reality whose name I do not know but with which Motz is so deeply in rapport. And I also want to tell you how God watches over me that in the middle of that 48 hours there rapped on my door a coal dealer who used to be a professional automobile racer who has a body I am absolutely nuts about and a good face too and he stops in here once every 4–5–6 months just to see if there is a possible screw—all done politely with male technique—no overt words or actions—and Motz stood at that door and with so much dignity and politeness and quietness bowed him out—and about a half hour later, I said "Christ there was something to use, why didn't I use that?" and I realized how my deep subconscious watches over me—because of course I would wound myself with a deep permanent wound—but the notebook tells how you have to accept that—anyway darling—my interpretation of that is that I love you because under any other circumstances I feel certain I would not have closed the door—

Darling my vitals just plain ache—I mean the entrails, not what I have just been speaking of, because of the terrible emotion of these last some weeks. I would like to write you about a 100 pages because your long letter does not knock me off at all—it only arouses a desire to tell you in minute detail so many things about both of us—anyway I love you in a way that doesn't seem to me to be human—I believe absolutely and it is not possible for me to conceive anything else.

And I wish to tell you my beloved that your understanding of your orders is my understanding also—I believe also that that is what Charles is supposed to do—Everyone and above all, the creator, is bound to obedience and to nothing else. That is the only gift within our power to give—our absolute obedience—then each man is in reality his brother's Keeper and watcher over and consoler. And believe me only your obedience can console me—nothing else. You know darling I am a woman of faith—I move literally in the universe created by God and I suffer so terribly exactly because this world is not real to others—and I feel such immense suffering for their blindness—it seems literally sacrilege to me to buy life insurance it seems literally sacrilege to concern myself over my health or your health and while I did not in any sense intend it as a clue for you because I had no idea you needed such a thing,

for me, dear—in the way it must have been for Jesus—I walk with my hand literally held by God—and any kind of worry appears to me interference and unbelief—I realize that such belief is the same thing as being alive—it cannot be transferred—the reality is just present to me—I get so *torn* not because I do not believe but because I am a woman—and a woman exists only in immediate reciprocity and I am surrounded by death lovers and if I find one little little sign of life love I am so elated—(You know I don't mean that stupid Catholic business about God watching over and providing—I mean the opposite—the clean joy in both destruction and fulfilment, the disinterest.)

You see from this how what you are doing is for me the only possible thing you could be doing—

The mundane details are that I no longer have a job—and the reason for my unhappiness is not worry—I don't care whether I eat or whether my daughter eats or any other thing about clothes or houses or anything it is simply that I have this terrible vitality and I must create with those spaces and lines or I go mad and I am desperate in the fear that such an opportunity will be very hard to find—I move forward blindly obeying instincts (it is hard to believe but people do not even acknowledge my serious and obviously not worthless letters). I am working on several jobs at Nittany which I have just begun so I will be there same schedule perhaps for a month, two months, I don't know exactly—As regards money darling for the immediate present I can take care of myself—so please do not mention it to me or try to help me.

Yesterday I was told that Eisenhower (Ike's brother who comes to Penn State as the new president) had sent the library a letter saying he had examined the two library handbooks I showed you carefully, found them very beautiful and was passing them on to the library in college in which he now is, for their possible use and guidance.

Please dearest angel do not come when mother is here—but if you want to make it Wednesday and can OK, but above all do not please worry—I do not wish you to worry—the hard part is over—

Your very absolutely loving
sister and this
in closest bond of Christ.
Frances

DHL has a paragraph you will love in the bibliography New Mexico published.

◄§ 112 §►

Washington to Woodward
2 February 1950 (postmark)

thursday

girl, they're giving it to the old man these days! "THE K'S"[33] came back this morning! Two days in a row, and on those two days the two pieces I'm fool enuf to look on as my warrants, year 1949! Plus the little darling, the dry temp! Plus O, (the slayers) last week. Plus rejection for a 3rd Guggenheim which i was chump anuf to put in for privately to Moe, to mister no-mo! Plus what-else

AND ALL when this child, this horse, this nigger is all the way in there, cocking, cocking. When he's cracking open a prose he's been after all his much too long it took life to get   (a prose which is oral, which suspends its clauses as thought does, which goes ahead with image without the old long care which is not literate, literary, or even as "managed" as ISH, which is just the boy presenting himself as he ticks—jeezus, & just then every god damn sheet is closing itself down on 'im!   Just when love has dried out the last watery places of birth   (he was born, by the way, with a caul, & had to be shook, & so, i suppose, these were the reasons why only now he may have arrived at the heraclitean wisdom, the dry soul, keep it dry, sd the boss)

(See, sis, how troubles twin us!)

It's in the stars (no, brutus, not in yrs, nor are you right, edmund, not in old stars, or as they were conceived)   In stars as a sun is a star, and in stars as our fellow shitizens are abt to convert the earth   In stars, are we, as stars are energy, the burning of substance, organized light the result, my love. In stars, baby. Twin stars. God damn them.

Quote: the artist is capable of myth when men are capable of reverence. it is simply a question of the dimension that men are prepared to give to their lives.[34] UnQ

Rewrite: when men are capable of destruction   a question of the shit-pile   Close

Open (as f. says, the legs) open, you bastards, i'm open, i'm staying open
     And not to fuck you, brothers   You do a wonderful job for yrselves

---

33. The pieces mentioned in this paragraph are (l) "The Kingfishers," returned from *Hudson Review*; (2) "The Praises," returned from *Western Review*; (3) "The Dryness, of 'The Tempest'"; (4) "The Laughing Ones" (entitled "O!" in one Storrs typescript).

34. The source of this quotation has not yet been ascertained.

somewhere there's a thousand lines for you, for you, lady, this moment
only they ain't on paper   and i can't send   'em   but they're going
to be there, 'cause they are there, lady whose hair is strong!

the Old Man

o

⋙ 113 ⋘

Washington to Woodward
3 February 1950 (postmark)

friday, friday

thank you darling thank you
     beautiful thing[35]

O

⋙ 114 ⋘

Woodward to Washington
4 February 1950 (postmark)

Dearest Old Man—
    Mother is screaming with laughter—they have left us absolutely noth-
ing—except the fact that we both know they are scared to death of us—this is
why my former boss secretly gives orders to the Nittany Printing that I am not
to be allowed to touch in any way any college job (while I learned a week or
so ago the man who took my place didn't know that the spacing between lines
is leading—that that is what makes type readable, beautiful, etc—never heard
of leading and so far not one single design—only bad copies of Motz.)
    Baby darling last night I came up with a magnificent idea—Motz is going
to take a little trip right straight into the enemies camp and do an Admiral
Halsey—while the Japanese are busy shooting hell out of each other—skip
down the middle—if it works it will be one of the great steals of all time and if
it fails it still will kill them dead when they find it out—I am waiting for you
to come and as soon as you go I will go—I wish you could come with me—
Christ we would have a marvelous time—since neither of us has any money
what the hell—my guess is will cost $100. I can get this for myself if you could

35. Olson has received Boldereff's letter of 2 February 1950.

swing it for yourself. Could you or would you care to—if you are too busy just skip my mentioning it—I am not sure yet where—have to find out—but all that is easy—Anyway baby dear—tread the earth lightly.

I adore you—you know that—this is the moment when God wants to see if we mean it—and of course we do—no fancy words necessary—

I am going to try two good things in my own field and if they don't work I am going to put a ritzy ad in the NY paper to be a servant to take for children—and I will save some money and do at last that magnificent Russian stuff I have been pressing towards for over 10 years now. American Council of Learned Societies is spending millions reproducing Russian books—all out dated encyclopedias and stuff no alive man science or otherwise can use—but that Rozanov I want to do is the straight stuff about sex and Christianity and it would be terrific at this moment to bring a translation to America.

I have been a servant and can do the thing very fancy and the idea intrigues me—two years could have enough to do four books—and a beautiful copy of my baby slipped in for free!

Dearest angel—of course I am furious at them and I hope to God you are able to sustain yourself—because it does hurt like hell—as I know so well—but I am always your servant to bring you whatever you need—and I have never been so sure that the vision is the ABC truth.

I love you—I kiss your beautiful self all over and am ready to go on your errands to the end of the earth.

Frances

◄§ 115 §►

Woodward to Washington
6 February 1950 (postmark)

Sunday night I have been
alone in the house for hours

I have just finished *Call Me Ishmael*—last time for awhile—greatest and most fruitful study ever made—(how I would like to *design* this book the relationships are all fouled up because they didn't want to spend any money—Christ I can see it someday I'll do it.)

I have just read aloud all Caresse Crosby's published poems[36] (I hate Caresse Crosby—may I?)—aloud—oh! God I see them standing in their iron

---

36. Presumbly *Y&X* is meant.

identity straight up in the world of space—clanging aloud their magnificent rhythm and sound to tell men as far (in time) as there are men that here stood Charles—a man—gifted and proud and the sound of them is so magnificent and so proclaiming the hour of birth of a land.

If all the reverence of earth is gathered into one small focus, Frances—then so be it—who are we to see how eternity shall measure itself in space and that I stand for all men in that moment when they too shall be "shook" (I the mother—funny funny funny little me-eye I cover you with nonsensical kisses—) is something absolutely known to me.

The boss, Motz suspects, didn't "sd" nothing—
the bastard is just stubborn
if men want to kill him off he prefers today as he says to stay open
and the opening and the closing shall not be controlled
by anyone's police—in any form they know how to
shape police
the twin says "I carry a club and on occasion I wield it"

and right now I have decided that my baby is encased in impenetrable aura of my worship and let venture to come near him he who dares.

⋯ 116 ⋯

Washington to Woodward
6 February 1950 (postmark)

monday

PROJECTIVE
          (projectile
                    (prospective
                              VS.
                    non-projective, or, closed
                                        VERSE

which is what i am going to try to set down the limits & advantages of, this day
          (it is, i think a better way to talk abt verse than to use such a distinction as the "aural" or "dramatic" or non-lyric: for any verse is, in a real sense, any of these, even the closed as against the open verse   BUT the real difference

is the amount of projection involved (which is a measure of the necessary ob-jectism now)

well, well, listen to all Pope O!

just a note to catch the early afternoon catch, that I shall come thursday, on the one which i came before, and i shall try to come wednesday ahead of myself; plan on thursday, but if you do not hear from me by phone wednesday by 3:30, 4:00, expect me wednesday—i put it that way because there is no stop fr here to there, and, knowing myself, i'll skid into the station, flag the bus, get aboard and be in state college before i can catch a breath! So, to make myself clear: thursday, but if i can come wednesday, i shall come on the same bus (meeting you, i hope, at s.c., but if you do not happen to work wednesday, i'll have the driver drop me as i suggested last week, at the corners up the road so that i shall miss mdme, mere)   to do it wednesday may be a push, so don't be dis-appointed if i should put a person call thru, which will find you either at work or at home

'bye, baby
O

◦§ 117 §◦

Washington to Woodward
8 February 1950 (postmark)

wednesday

frances, baby, i'm going to be calling you in a short while, but i want to begin to see-say some of the things i want to try to say   they are, at heart, extensions of what i said last week   for the fact is, the same god damned necessities hold me in their grasp

what seems now to be the thing to be faced is, how can you tolerate this olson system, with its crazy slow time, its intolerably long faiths, this space-system which is capable, i guess, of 40 days in a desert but which carries out such dis-ciplines precisely not in deserts but in the gardens of its own delights

for it is
the delights of what we have made together that i am convinced i am serving in this fantastic resistance to come to see you   and tho you have been equally fantastic in the beauty with which you have so far endured, & believed, i must raise another cry to you, to hold, darling, to hold

i'm terribly, terribly stub-
born   i sd, two years ago, in the beginnings of a book on my father, that it

was his stubbornness that killed him,   and it was, and i watched it, and i
know what's in my blood, and i weigh and weigh it, out of fear   yet, when i
have thrown it over, i have been wrong   when i have obeyed it, i have
found my holy ghost
                              i obeyed those days in brooklyn and tarrytown, obeyed
like i never have before   i obeyed when i came to you with such joy in december   and if now, against all sense, practical sense, and against my
heart's knowledge that you are back against a wall, i obey, believe me, it is
no nonsense, no diminution of you, it is the way this thing we have made
seems to go
                      the terror is, it can only go forward like a huge archaic dance if
you go with me, and that i want, want it like my blood, of which you are a part
    and that is, as well as our vision, a matter of practicals, alas
                                                              it is the practi-
cals which wrack me, yrs & mine: mine, at the moment, are gone wild again,
house, work, con, assurance, all suddenly in a boil   it's crazy   but there they
are, they have to be faced

    And i can do it (that's one thing, at least, that one acquires)   It does not
make it easier that you, too, are in a whirlwind   And i know i play a part
in it, in sowing it   And I equally know i cannot help, that is, by my presence   But—my argument is, that i can help in one terrible way, by holding
to that which can be shaped (what we have so far shaped), and not giving in to
anything less, god help us

these are practicals of the order i am best made to serve   but the thing is, i
have a present advantage (in addition to that which you spoke of, of having
my dailies taken care of)   it is the advantage which you discovered in the act
of setting down the olson cocking   And it is one i try to enlarge in you, because i believe you are capable of anything, motz, my terrific motz
                                                              i know i
am a fool, in the old sense   (these days when everything is kicking me back
in the face, i am made peculiarly aware of how right i have been to dub myself so—
        ((it is amazing to me, this is: to come to the realization that only the
fools can give birth to souls   i begin to discover that there are human beings
who cannot be helped simply because they do not have souls!   a couple of
them, writers, have showed me it clearly the last ten days   and man as mob
has, as crowd   As a matter of fact I begin to see that quantity is simply the
running away from the agony of finding out how to be born as a soul   It
looms on me, that it is the lost secret, the secret that the soul is not born in each,
that each has to give birth to it—and that the process has got to be given back
to people
        Here, my sybil, you seem to me to be ahead of the o.m.!

o god, it is a matter of what chagrins!   all this business

And, as I sd to you on the phone, the o.m. is in a state he does not like, for it is most difficult to write verse in that state, the state of CONFUSIO   (I called it a vertu, I suddenly realise, only last week, in a piece which I don't think I'll publish, but which is now in the "Hudson Review's" hands.[37] And ended with this quote—which also, at this moment, seems to have been prophetic! And I thinking all the time it was old cold O!

> But al so siker as *In principio,*
> *mulier est hominus confusio,*
> Madame, the sentynce of this latyn is,
> Womman is mannes joy & al his blisse!

(It is Chaucer's Cock to his dame Pertelote in the middle of the night, after he has waked, and waked her, with his dreams. And the two of 'em are talking it out on their perch!)

But that's our trouble: you can rise to a plan, and swing that motz laughter, that wonderful Celt high-tone that comes into yr voice when the worst is on you

And i can rise to a word
                                    jeezus,
shall we trust forever this vitality that no one else has? !

baby, this little child is going it blind, and makes no excuses
                                    what he does
make is, more love, more love for (the Russians used to have this birthday greeting: "more life, more life!")   for the motz, that is, love, but jeezus, i'd like also to have some more life, more life for you and for me
                                    this is mighty little o

⋅⋙ 118 ⋘⋅

Woodward to Washington
9 February 1950 (postmark)

Thursday morning early

---

37. "GrandPa, GoodBye," first published in *Charles Olson and Ezra Pound,* pp. 97–105.

Charles darling—

No idea if the early morning mail reaches you any sooner than the evening or not—was tied up with appointments all day at work and when I reached home the mail had already gone—dearest—I am rushing just to tell you that I spent most of the night feeling how I had added yesterday to your burden—by seeming to be unreasonable[38]—dearest angel—everything I accept which is necessary between us—and I realize what a very great thing you carry—being responsible for another person and it isn't the same as Lucinda because that has an obvious necessity in the obvious inability of childhood—but yours is a moral thing—plus the great weight of trying to create against the whole immoral weight of your day and then all the terrible practical realities—I will ask the man on Monday if he would consider to buy your place—please let me know at once what the score is about 217—

I am sending Lucinda away for the weekend—anyway—if I do not have you—I can have myself alone with no interference which will mean having Olson to myself.

Darling—

Frances

≼ 119 ≽

Washington to Woodward
9 February 1950 (postmark)

thursday

i wld like to phone you, just to take off yr heart, that crazy word "ever"—o baby you are dramatick. Look: i have kept telling you the character is in a mood, pronounced mud. i keep telling you he goes by his nose. if i am stiff and tough, its the issuance he's after, not the being stiff and tough. & just because this is a bad time, why make it forever, my sweet scared thing, my white-doe (remember what the Master identified doe with)   You are, darling, not dramatick, just god damned nervous abt all other hyoomins, as who is not who has rested any weight on 'em. Bro. Tortoise knows. Only look, sis: we gotta go it differunt. See. You damn well know the scale this thing is on.   It got born big.   crist, you stood 2 yrs of the brewin of it. & once it got born, you didn't have to do without a sight of the character. so why blow yr top after 2 months?

and when you say i don't know what you are going thru, please, baby, of course not, yet yes, the blood's the same   i tell ya, the blood's the same

38. Presumably a reference to the telephone conversation in which Olson said he was not coming to Woodward.

i can't figure out how the mails are screwed up, but if they were ever good, i wish they'd be good with this note

things look really bad abt the house, worse than ever but we've been thru some crises, and maybe   only this time they plan to "convert", put in dough, make 3 rents where now there are one, my shaky one but i'm in a reckless mood, and somehow don't care there isn't any way to solve it, that i can see
    and in any case i must say it is foolish to stay permanently in any such city with that little c.s. man sticking his finger up nature's business as he is, these days

i say reckless   jeezes, you can't imagine what a run of rejection I've been in the last two weeks! (And I'm not a kid, any longer.   It's tougher, the later it is. EVERY damn thing. Not an exception. Not one god damned little bird has yet settled into print. Well, maybe THE KINGFS. Only they want changes.[39] And if that doesn't burn me. Editors have the c.s. complaint too. And at a time when . . .

                       at a time when i feel that winding up which comes along every so often before a launch into something
                                                      (WHICH IS WHAT, i think, YOU HAVE BEEN PUTTING UP WITH, just for a real guess)

i feel very much as tho, if i could get settled down for abt a week or ten days, i'd break out a new long baby

    FOR I KNOW WHAT I'M UP TO: suddenly i see what verse it is I'm after. In fact I've been blocking out a tricky prose definition of

PROJECTIVE   VERSE

          (projectile   (prospective   (percussive
                              vs.
the non-projective (the "closed" as some french guy puts it, the lyric, poysonal, OMeliot)

    but i don't get time to finish a god damn thing: the hot stuff of two weeks ago (is it today?) is still sittin as it came, untouched, and me fucked up with it

39. Robert Payne asked for one small change in accepting "The Kingfishers" for *Montevallo Review*, summer 1950 issue. Payne didn't like the Italian quotation from Marco Polo.

o baby, this is jes news over the fence, & love

o

P.S. Suddenly occurs to me: these discrepancies in the mail—maybe i'm on the list in this scared city, of those whose outgoing mail is gone over?! What a thought! (All they have to do is read through these new envelopes!)

❦ 120 ❦

Woodward to Washington
9 February 1950 (postmark)

Thursday 1:10

Charles darling—

This is for lightness—for easing of your burden—I am now light—I do not know why—everything about a woman is so irrational—the sorrow which weighs with the weight of rain and then the lightness which skips in like cloud—all so beyond direction—oneself so an instrument played upon— now dearest I feel terribly strong and very light and terribly in love with you—if the studio should be bought now to protect you—send me the name of the bank and if you have any idea of the price—that too—I know a wonderful rich doctor up in Providence who might be willing and able—he would understand what I am talking about anyway—old Doc Halsey deWolf—does Connie know him—he and his wife both rich and he understands about suffering also about creating I will write to him at once as soon as I hear from you where he can find out the particulars—

I wonder if you have any idea how much I love you

I want to show you Robert Maillart when you come—for this time he is the one who has raised me from despair—he is another reason that I beg you darling to go on—not to die (although I am sure you are burdened to your utmost capacity) because I feel in him your closest and nearest of kin—he died 1940—not heralded—a bridge builder in Switzerland—who was often defeated and made many magnificent bridges which exist only on paper and sometimes had his living elegance destroyed by forced changes from the authorities who were living in the roman era but despite all this who has built bridges more light more loving of earth than anything here—I am sitting with a picture before me of a number of engineers and himself photo'd above a beam during construction[40]—talk about innocent, immaculate eyes—all the

40. Boldereff is looking at the photograph on p. 112 of Max Bill's biography *Robert Maillart* (Zurich, 1949; New York: Praeger, 1949), and later quotes are from p. 33.

others look like nice men—men whom some woman loves—but he—he sits there very ungoodlooking with the immaculate innocent look of a baby chipmunk—impossible to describe—just a man who absolutely obeyed—who for our time was doing it the Olson way—projection so absolute

"Matter certainly conforms with its own particular laws, but within that conformity various possibilities remain open for creative imagination, producing the greatest variety of form. Because Maillart's medium has particularly severe laws and because its nature leans towards the constructive and not the decorative, his merit is all the greater, as he had to shape it in a severe struggle with its limited possibilities." All an exact description of my baby's situation today—so little is left to you to choose because of the incrustations both in material and form and everything you do is so very new—I hate to use the word but nothing from you ever sounds as though it were written in the language of any of the old boys—always sounds like a language Olson created—as of course he does—

May I *please* see at least part of that 5000 word scream which is warranted by my blood also?

> Your dipper-in and
> benourished
> I love you—

Forgot to tell you—I am going to stay in Woodward all the time for the present not going into State College—at all any more, old lady not here—any day OK.

❦ 121 ❦

Washington to Woodward
10 February 1950 (postmark)

friday afternoon

darling, yr two letters just came   i wrote a thing yesterday i am going to try to shape up and send off to a mag, and i was just about to set to it, after a morning of pain & disruption from this character moving in (he & his gang woke us at 9—when i go to bed 2, 3!, and am always exhausted fr a day of writing like yestiddy! Lah!)(the real trouble is, he has to use our toilet! ugh)
     but before so, let me wrap down the house details:

the last i heard the Old Bitch was asking 20,000 for my half of the quadrangle (40,000 for the whole piece which includes the huge sculptor studio now renting to de Weldon at 100 smackers a month) the bank values my half at more than de Weldon's (& they are right, in the sense that, converted, the three elements of this house, studio and L, could turn out an income of 225)   up to last month it was turning out only my 50 bucks; now, today, with the arrival of this 2nd "sculptor" in the compound, this side is turning out 100   if, as i learned wednesday, the old lady puts toilets in the other two parts, and outlays plenty to make the L (which is now a mere, but handsome, shell, dirt, little else, was originally a coach-house, and has three pieces which have flooring, two upstairs, one down) she plans to up us (I'd guess to 75), ditto the other two parts   ((& by jesus if the agent did-n't have the gall to suggest we move into the L, which is on a bad alley, tho it could, if they opened it north, be quite charming))

to get back: the bank values my half at 7500, the other at 6800, that is, they'd be willing to put up that much, regarding it as its assess value   you there-fore see the discrepancy of the asking price!   but the bank told de Weldon to be willing to go to 12,500 for his piece, just because, as studios, such places are impossible to duplicate in Washington   (and my little two room joint has charmismic values, if utterly impractical for the average citizen's livin': no bath at all, only a shower in a stinking cellar; and the small room useless in the winter, it is so cold: brick plus plaster, no insulation)

those are the details as i know them   i should be full of doubt that the O.B. will go thru with her plans to remodel everything; she gets like spasms every so often, tho never such a thoro one as this; and when she finds out costs, i sort of think she will back off; yet, financially, she'd be a fool not to go ahead, for her total income a year, on both pieces, which has been, up to now, 1800— that is, when she has been able to collect fr me!—could jump to 4000 a yr!

so: now, to yr plot, of deWolf   it is a terrific idea baby   god knows what the effect, if it worked, wld be on Con   my suggestion is this: i imagine the deWolf's would operate thru an agent or lawyer   if he acted on their behalf, with no mention of me, it could go ahead for the present in either of two directions, to the O.B. herself direct, or to her agent, who is the A.D. Torre Realty Company, 1625 North Capitol Street, Wash.   (Mrs Paul W. Bartlett, 1561 35th St. NW, Wash.)   and the negotiations should begin with an offer of 10,000 looking towards a compromise of 12,500

which is one slew of dough! wow!

((((It occurs to me: the problem, for Con, would be, of course, that it is you who would be behind it   There is this thought i toss up to you: i have had one patron in my life, and, though he was ready, i think, is ready, at any time to give a lift where there is an utter emergency, I have myself only called on him twice, and the total about 350 in ten years   I should be reluctant to call on him now, as a matter of fact he just wouldn't act where such sums are involved   (he likes to be a small patron to several)

What I have in mind is, he just might be yr stand-in, even unbeknownst to himself, though, if the deWolfs wanted to, there is no reason why they should not, so far as he was concerned, say that "a person interested in my work had interested them in buying sd house, and would he vouch for me" I just damn well believe he would, and the terrific part of it is, he is non-pareil in their world, is one of that Boston-NY mixture of which the deWolfs are a part (do not forget that Hoiman Melville was one such, and *of the deWolf* family by god!)

Anyhow, here he is, for what he is worth: Dr Henry A. Murray Jr., 37 Brimmer Street, Boston (son of a Morgan partner, married to a Rantoul, former head of the Harvard Psychological Clinic—its founder, and he is, by the way, the brother of the Mrs. Robert Bacon who is the chief Republican hostess of this hyar capital of the woild!) (& thus, I should imagine, a budd of Mrs Bartlett) (He is Melville's chief biographer now alive. And that is both how I know him, and why, because of a certain rivalry he feels towards me, that I go gingerly with him. For he is more than a patron. He is our friend, both con's and mine.)

What I mean by stand-in, in this direction, is, of course, that it could be he who put the deWolfs on the trail. And so the deWolfs might, at yr direction, say, & act, if you should choose.))))

o baby pay not one jot of blood or any cost for this business, understand? And go slow. There is no haste. Let me know if you should think it advantageous to use Harry, in case the cat shld get out of the bag. So far these crises have come & gone, and the guerilla situation, tough as it is when the crisis is on, has been to our advantage (up to the time, a yr ago, when Mrs B finally put our house in the agent's hands, for rent collection, as well as for sale, i was able, as i had been instructed by my predecessor, to drop a rent here and there. And I don't think I'll have to pay the piper! Tho the old lady's plenty sharp: Torre told me Wednesday, she claims i owe her *one year and a half!* That's over seven yrs, but it ain't quite that bad, I assure you!)

well, I'll get this off pronto, & send the piece, if I can polish it, later: love,
charles

A sum of facts: 217 & 219 Randolph Place NE Washington (1/4 a city block) (one compound)

asking price	$20,000	$20,000 = $40,000
bank's estimate value	7500	6800 = $14,300
bank's suggested top offer	$12,500	12,000 = $24,500
present income (unimproved)	$ 100	$100 = $200 a month
possible income	$ 225	$100 = $325 a month

I'm pretty sure Mrs. B's bank is THE RIGGS NATIONAL, Farmers & Mechanics Branch.

≼ 122 ≽

Woodward to Washington
10 February 1950 (postmark)

Charles dear—
     Everything is breaking up inside me—
     I pray you if you can not come to allow me to come for a few hours—
                                                                Frances

≼ 123 ≽

Woodward to Washington
10 February 1950 (postmark 11 February 1950)

                                                        Friday night

I am alone—Lucinda has gone—
     If I could hang my body out over a fence somewhere there would be no problem—I am not scared—
     This is the fifth letter I have begun
     I am afraid to say anything
     I quote you D.H. Lawrence—I do not remember the white doe—
     "The soul itself is the source of all authority, and the man of the purest, strongest soul-flame is the highest authority in the world. But even he must discipline his senses, his spirit, his mind and body, all the time, to the fulfilment of the soul. And every man's life, in so far as it is truly lived, is a long self-discipline."
     I am always willing without question to have Olson obey in whatever way

is necessary to him. Darling—you are generous and loving and kind and thoughtful and as you said in the letter about Keats—you get into trouble that way because then when you are not able to give you get angry and strike out and wound and all because your heart is warm. I remember Eckhart and I darling am really giving every ounce I have as you I am sure, feel.

I believe in you and in you alone of all men I am able to see—I trust you absolutely and I am able to wait as long as you need me to. I did not understand and you who have Connie must please kindly realize how it is to walk around untouched, when touch is the answer one craves.

❧ 124 ❧

Woodward to Washington
11 February 1950 (postmark)

Saturday morning

Charles dear—
When I think of my notebook and my primer I think "how could I ever have restrained myself so much in saying the wild agony of it?" Only Rabelais—in the third book—that man—doctor—wrote a paragraph—I am going to incorporate it into a new thing I hope some day to start—if I ever get my body satisfied—
The New Testament (meaning exactly that, the Bible New Testament) for Aristocratic Women—there are two things in it (the existing one) I hope to shove forward into new space—
It is morning—sunny—I look on the two of us with infinite compassion.
Frances

I wish to god some kind hearted male would be great enough to open a house of call—as Buck Mulligan once said he was going to do on an Island—

❧ 125 ❧

Woodward to Washington
11 February 1950 (postmark)

Saturday afternoon in my
bedroom working on the
layout for the first big freelance job Motz ever got—a
Walt Whitman book of pre-

viously unpublished stuff—
written at 22 years one or
two things I want you to
see—when made will give
you a copy ready by July 1 I
hope.[41]

Charles—

How many hours in a Motz day—? "More than you can count."

I went this morning for a walk through the iced sunred earth, very damp and soft—back to the place where the act of "Sun" took place—and sat on some rocks and felt that damp rich sexy earth-cold—coming up into me and plowed all around with passionate pressing footsteps and *made* that earth so bursting ready to give as soon as sun comes out, yield to me. Olson says poems can do it but that is not true—nothing but the physical earth—the ocean—and the earth they are the only two agents woman has for stilling.

I hope to Christ my three letters will not appear to be demands on you—in the name of Jesus, literally dearest—I do not wish to intrude myself upon your labors—nor to interrupt you—I will pick up two or three loose screws where I know where to find them and that will take the worst off this longing for Olson which is just expressed through flesh but actually is a passionate yearning of the spirit.

I will send all the powerful sends I have in my blood and spirit to be with your blood to make fight against all the "practicals" and *for* the new long baby to come.

I quote you one more D H Lawrence—

"To have an ideal for the individual which regards only his individual self and ignores his collective self is in the long run fatal. To have a creed of love which denies the reality of power makes at last for mere anarchy. Man lives by cohesion and resistance. The greater the resistance the greater the cohesion. Absence of resistance is the breaking down of life itself, for all life depends upon the limits of form, and power sets the limits of form, power and resistance."

There darling beloved Olson—go tack it up where you shave each morning or afternoon or not at all—and remember to Motz's credit that she sent it to you—

Isn't it a sheer honey?

Like the old man says—me and him—we got the vitality and we are the only ones who do.

41. *Walt Whitman of the New York Aurora, Editor at Twenty-Two: A Collection of Recently Discovered Writings*, edited by Joseph Jay Rubin and Charles H. Brown (State College, Penna.: Bald Eagle Press, 1950). "Designed by Frances Boldereff."

❧ 126 ❧

Washington to Woodward
11 February 1950 (postmark 12 February 1950)

sat.

f.: i'm putting the original off to you: i did (!) get it rewritten in all that pother yesterday and, as a result, my skull aches tidday   i'm shipping it off to IMAGI (near you by the way: Allentown) right now—there are several changes, but they are mostly to take the bristles out, to formalize the treatment. So you must just regard the meat of it, and take it, as it is in the mss., much as a letter. For it is just as it came off the machine, 1st run.

add. thot. on dewolfes: that there could be one advantage of some size in their creating themselves the patrons of a writer on a house—i could get my architects from Black Mt (and they're plenty able) to come camp here this summer, and do a *real* conversion on all three parts of the property, especially on the L, which I can see them turning into a dazzy joint!   i could feed & house 'em (one of em, & one of the best was ready to follow me & Woellfer to Yucatan last October jes to be around this character and draw up thereby!)   and for the cost of the materials, the dews. could have startling improvements

as a matter of fact this could work without b.m.c.: if i owned this place, i intended to rent the L to a potter, for pennies so long as he would put floor in, insulate, add a studio window to the north, plumbing etc. Then, after a yr or so, one would have a rentable place.

new step: YOU
                 look: olson is some pumpkin if he can't help his baby in that ancillary art to language, print   you must tell me what your attitude is toward those presses which do "fine" work   i'm thinking of those around new york tho my ties are strongest with those in S.F., tho that far away is the last place i'll permit you to go!
                       Seriously, darling, you speak up the moment you want to move on any job i might conceivably know the bosses or assistants of: there is, for example, Laughlin, and his ties   there is Gerry Gross who designs for Harcourt (and Giroux there, the boss editor, is a friend ISH-MAEL made me, a good friend)   and Harry Ford, who did ISH, god help him, and is just that no good, but he is beholden to me, and is still in the game   And the Cummington   And NW Ayer, Philly

I had this in my noggin to talk over with you when I came this weekend. But

I don't want you worryin', if you are worryin', about economics, and if you
want me to move, just flash the signal.

You know the way of jobs: one lead
leads to another. And goddamn any of 'em, if they have eyes to see, all I have
to do is send them my precious PENN STATE CAT (alogue)!

I must quit. Anderson's the guy who moved in yestiddy.   He's an idiot, an
old idiot.   Helpless.   He must have interrupted me a dozen times yesterday!   To pea, to help him light a fire, to ask where wood is, to put on lights,
etc: and of course the whole thing is only because he is so old and so lonely he
makes excuses to talk to a hoomin bean.   Poor creature.   I'll have him in
hand. It'll only take a couple of days.   But o god, it takes it out of you.
    (Where are the strong, where are they?)

I know one.   She's you.   Love: charles

[*enclosed typescript:*][42]

you keep this   this is for you
o

PROJECTIVE   VERSE
        (projectile (prospective (percussive
                vs.

the NON-projective, what we have had, pretty much (outside Pound &
Williams), what a French critic calls the "closed", the visual verse, the lyric, if
you like, the "personal" over against objectivism, the "private soul", print.

Advantages of PROJECTIVE as tag: (1) "aural" won't do, because any verse
worth the name is aural; (2) "dramatic" is no good, it describes a literary form,
does not go inside to the poetics, (there is no question, for example, that Eliot's
line, from "Prufrock" on down, is a dramatic line, doth stem from Browning
(?), certainly hath obvious relation back to the Elizs., especially to the solilo-
quoth; yet OMeliot is *not* projective, goeth by his personeth instead of by object and by passion; as a matter of fact, this is precisely why he fails (and i say
this carefully) as a dramatist: his root is the mind, and a scholastic mind as
well, not even an intelleto, and he has not succeeded in getting back and down
to where drama comes from, where both the conception and the language of
drama comes from, which is where? which is where the breath hath its locus,
doth begin where the breath comes from.

42. This early draft of "Projective Verse" may be compared with the revised version in *Collected Prose*,
pp. 239–49.

(All these "eths" are out of the revised)

Verse now has become a matter of its instrument, the VOICE. And I am not necessarily referring to recititation, not at all to performance, though this is certainly going to be a matter of some importance. What I am deliberately talking about still is composition, composing verse by voice, by, if you like, musical phrase, but specifically by the rhythms as well as the images personal to the composer. Which sounds like what we have heard before. Only it ain't. And for one straight reason: that it must be faced, that we have lost secrets of both the physiology of the human voice, and its usage. I quote:

"It is highly probable that all modern singing would strike a classical Greek ear as an out-cry; and in any case *such variations of pitch as are inconsiderable in modern singing are extremely emphatic in the speaking voice*, so that they might well make all the difference to an ear unaccustomed to organized sound beyond the speaking compass."

" . . . the lim-ited compass of Greek musical sounds, corresponding as it does to *the evident sensitiveness of the Greek ear to differences in vocal effort*. We have only to ob-serve the compass of the Greek scale to see that in the most esteemed modes it is much more the compass of speaking than of singing voices."

"the enhar-monic tetrachord, the most ancient, gathered the lower three notes very closely to the bottom *C, A flat, G prime, G*." C, A♭, G', G

"Greek mu-sic represents an organization of *the rise and fall of the voice* as elaborate and artistic as the organization of the verse, powerful in heightening the emo-tional and dramatic effect of words and action, and essential to the under-standing and organization of the works which it adorned."

"Thus the rhythm of classical Greek music seems to have been entirely identical with that of verse, and its beauty and expression appreciated in virtue of that identity. From the modern musical point of view the rhythm of words is limited to a merely monotonous uniformity of flow, with minute undulations which are musically chaotic." This we are putting an end to.

Or, if I could, I would present you Michael Lekakis sounding piercingly Hip-polytus's prayer to Artemis, or Rudd Fleming reading, beating, modally, Odysseus' conversations with Kalypso.

Or tell you what men existed in India before the Moslems put them out of business by bringing the tri-art of song-drum dance in from the outside, those "bulls" of men who could use the human voice in such a manner as to cause it (without any loss of the subtleties which we have unhappily got into the habit of associating with silently read verse) to reach 100,000 listeners.

I know myself only one current example you may refer to: the priest, in Eisenstein's "Ivan", who, at the very beginning of the movie, in blessing Ivan at his coronation, fills the cathedral one by one noun after another breasting out and up from his drum of a body.

All of which is performance, yes, all of which is what will be, the mounting of productions, in the theatre sense, yes, yet in each case, and in each case to be, there must be something which is produced—and that is made-verse, which comes first, but which itself is made in the light of its registration, and the means for such registration.

What we have suffered from is, manuscript, press, the removal of verse from its producer, voice, the removal by once, twice remove from its place of origin. (When breath goes, spiritus goes.)

II

The irony is, from the machine now comes deliverance. For the advantage of the typewriter in composition is precisely its capacity to indicate exactly what breath, what pauses, what precisions the maker wants to give his work. For the first time the poet has the stave and bar a musician had. And can indicate, the moment the convention is recognized, how he would want any reader to voice his work.

It is time we picked the fruit of the experiments of Cummings, Pound and Williams, each of whom has, after his own fashion, already used the machine as a clue to his composing, to its vocalization. (Let the doubter know, how the poet works with his throat!) If a contemporary poet leaves a space as long as the phrase before it, he means that space to be held an equal length of time. If he suspends a word or a syllable at the end of a line (the syllable is most Cummings') he means the time it takes the eye, that hair of time suspended, to pick up the next line. If he wishes a pause so light it hardly separates, yet he does not want a comma which is an interruption of the meaning rather than the sounding of the line, follow him:
"What does not change / is the will to change"

And so it is with the juxtaposition of lines:
"Where do these
        invisible seeds
            settle from?"

which is both a progressing of the

meaning and the breathing forward without a progress outside the unit of time local to the idea.

(This is put simpler—& more verse added)

There is more to be sd in order that this convention be recognized, in order that the revolution out of which it came may offset the counterrevolution now afoot to return verse to inherited "English" forms of cadence & rime. But what I want to emphasize by it, is the already PROJECTIVE nature of verse as the sons of Pound and Williams are practicing it. Already they are composing as though verse was to have the reading its writing involved, as though not the eye, but the ear was to be its measure, the measure both of its meaning and its registration.

          And the ear presupposes the voice.

III

Which gets us to what distinguishes the content of Homer, or of Aeschylus, or of Seami from the "literary" tradition. For the content does, will change the moment the projective purpose of the act of verse is recognized. If the sound and the rhythm both come from the projective as it is the composer, and by the projector as he is public and projector, then the material of verse shifts. It starts with the composer. The dimension of his line alone,—not to speak of his conception, of the matter he turns to, of the scale in which he imagines its use,—changes. I myself would put it in a physical image. It is no accident that both Pound and Williams were involved in a movement which got called "objectivism". But that word was then used in some sort of necessary quarrel, I take it, with "subjectivism". It is now too late to be bothered with the latter. It has excellently done itself to death, even though we are caught in its dying. What seems to me a more valid formulation for present use, is "objectism", a word to be taken to stand for the kind of relation of man to experience which a poet might state as the necessity of a line or a work to be as wood is, to be as clean as wood is as it issues from the hand of nature, to be as shaped as wood is when a man has had his hand to it. It is the getting rid of the lyrical interference of the individual, of the subject and his soul, that peculiar presumption by which western man has interposed himself between what he is as a creature of nature with certain instructions to carry out and the other creations of nature which we may, with no derogation, call objects. For a man is himself an object, the moment he achieves a humilitas sufficient to make him of use.

It comes to this, to get back to where we started from: the moment a man and his work are PROJECTIVE, he has to have a dimension larger than himself.

Or be foolish. Neither a dry technique or a dry self will make it, the moment a man has to do more than slide his work over in print. Sound itself is a dimension. Breath is the life in us, what nature put there. And a man's problem, the moment he takes up speech, is to give it seriousness enough to stand alongside the things of nature. That is not easy. Nature works from reverence, even in her destructions (species go down with a crash). And the dimension of art at any given time is the amount of reverence man is ready to give his own living. Projective size is what one might acknowledge that the play "Agamemnon" possesseth: it is able, I judge, to stand beside the Aegean. Or, in a wholly less "heroic" dimension, but equally of nature's cut, the Fisherman and the Angel in "Hagaromo". Homer is such an unexamined cliche, I need not press home Nausicaa's girls washing their clothes.

Conclusion

Anyhow, if you want to forget all this, don't forget what lies behind it: a voice, a machine to record the uses of words, & the necessary steps we must take to give projective verse PROJECTION!

olson

feb 9 '50

the most changes are here

"It comes to this: the use of a man, by himself and thus by others, lies in how he conceives his relation to nature, that force to which he owes his somewhat small existence. If he sprawl, he shall find little to sing but himself, and shall sing, nature has such paradoxical ways, by way of such forms as rime & meter outside himself. But if he stays in himself, if he is contained within his nature as he is participant in the larger force, he will be able to listen, and his hearing through himself will give him secrets objects share. And by an inverse law his shapes will make a way. It is in this sense that the projective act, which is the artist's act in the larger field of objects, leads to dimensions larger than the man. For a man's problem, the moment he takes speech up in all its fullness, is to give his work his seriousness, a seriousness sufficient to cause the thing he makes to take its place alongside the things of nature. This is not easy. Nature ... reveres ... crash. But breath is man's special qualification as animal. Sound is a dimension he has extended. Language is one of his proudest acts. And when he rests in these as they are in himself . . . if he chooses to speak from these roots, he works in that area where nature has given his size. It is projective size . . .

[letter not sent][43]

Woodward to Washington
[12 February 1950]

4:00 A M Sunday
morning

Charles—

Every night I hope when I go to bed that I will be granted a night's rest but every night I awake and I am tortured. I am writing all of this to you in the spirit of the worship of God. I do not know whether it is right or whether it is wrong for a person to force themselves to what I force myself. I will move forward with you—no fear of that. I want you Charles to try to help me know what is right.

I am trembling very violently and I go on to write you because it is a question which one day you and I must solve.

The existence of Connie tortures me as mine so obviously tortures her. She has not moved towards me at all. You know dear that whatever God requires that will I do. There is no pattern to follow. I am tortured by two things—is it right for us to deny the living flame between us? I feel in my soul that I am wedded to you through all life. If the pattern we are following now is the right one I am willing to go on with it. I believe that you serve God and that both of us try insofar as God gives us the strength to be as perfect in our conduct as we are able to conceive. I am also afraid for the thing to be out of balance—we should give and receive equally because if I give out of proportion I will earn your hatred, which is one of the things D. H. Lawrence was saying in the quote I sent (I sent it to you to show how I believe you are right to obey your Holy Ghost).

If Connie is a living real necessity to you then perhaps we should give up our physical closeness. You should never fear that I will cease to give every ounce of my attention to what you do—I believe in you as the servant of God and I believe in the presence of God that it is right and a privilege He grants to me to be able to be of use to you. Your physical presence is very precious to me—I have wondered several times if the three of us could live together if I were willing to renounce inwardly all physical connection with you. I love you in a way that makes anything possible to me. I am searching for a path. I can find guidance neither in the Bible, nor in Blake nor in Lawrence. You and I have to create the pattern.

43. This letter and the following letter are in the possession of Sharon Thesen.

If you are too pressed upon to be able to give thought to this—I can wait until your next breathing spell—

And I want you to know Charles that if the way it is at present is the best then that is the way we will do.

You know without my telling that physically there is no substitute for you—our oneness in spirit creates a oneness in the flesh—if I live without physical closeness to you then I will shut myself off from my body.

There is nothing wild about me now—I am quiet and I never pray—but I hope some guidance will come to me.

Thy blood and my blood are indeed one.

Frances

◄ 128 ►

[*letter not sent*]

Woodward to Washington
[12 February 1950]

Sunday

Olson dear—

I have been in a really heroic struggle all day long to try to bring into clear vision to myself how I should act—I have been having serious Connie trouble for some time—it would make everything so easy for me if she would love me—but enough of that—I have darling been stretching my power as hard as I can—I believe I know several things—one is that you are God's chosen and it is my business to go with you all the way—I wish I could see if this terrible struggle I make is of use—I mean of use as pattern—I, like you, am blind—I do not know whether I ask something of myself which is wrong—that is, I am not sure a beautiful thing like ours should not be lived out in actual daily practice—but in the meantime dear I want this message to go to you—because I have been fighting over and over with myself to try to get clear of my own need and my own physical jealousy and to project forward to you the pure essence of my belief and faith. I hope God looks down on my suffering (I realize of course that all the God there is is what we bring into being) because I do not believe any woman has more body to discard, or a clearer vision of in what way it is the enemy than I (that is that it looms any larger on her own horizon)—I feel like taking a knife to myself—but living—the forcing of the will into the service of the real imaginative concept of human relations is the problem I am too much of an aristocrat to walk off from—

I hope to God darling you regard me with tenderness for I am truly being flayed alive for my effort to reach God.

Frances

❧ 129 ☙

Washington to Woodward
13 February 1950 (postmark)

Monday

frances
    yr 4 notes today are like 4 fingers

    o my lady

    look: i cannot permit you to come here (i thought of it myself—remember, *always*, i am of inexhaustible energy & mind, & i go over *all* things, because i am an objectist, and where my acts are i am total) because i cannot dissemble & because i cannot, where the crisis is as intense here as there with you, add one straw more

baby, believe me, believe me, i am doing the very maximum in all directions
    the pitch is unbelievable, & inscrutable   i never knew i could do so much
    (for what it may be worth, i should *never* have been so strong had i not, originally, moved to you, motz extraordinary)

    i know that maximum is clearly, so far as you are enduring at this moment, a minimum by any ordinary measure   i know god, you couldn't say what you have said about this man's imagination, and now deny he is capable of being over there, & know, know what he is exacting of you   i equally know
    (and though it alleviates nothing for you, it should drive any doubts from your mind that there are things you might do which are not done: believe me, you are putting it all out, baby, and this tough bird gets it)

            i equally know (and this makes me full of the terror of life) that what is being done is right, god help us all—you say, compassion, i say, pride, yes, in the beauty we the weak are capable of

    this i promise: i shall continue to hold, and shall seek to stay right right through every thing   And only because & *only* thus can any of us inherit what is in this *ahead*

& frances, if i am harsh, have been, i have not meant to be, do not ever mean to be: i may not put every word straight down the alley, though that is my intent & my life, but the *acts*, the central stem, that's straight

believe that
charles

❧ 130 ☙

Woodward to Washington
13 February 1950 (postmark)

Monday

Charles Frobenius Potemkin—

I have written you so many letters and even mailed some of them only to snatch them all back—*no* one has ever changed more violently more times faster than I during the last few weeks—there is one constant—the "God thou knowest I thank thee for Olson."

Please return the sheets I sent on Whitman—I found two different ones (about Santayana's criticism of WW) yesterday you will love—I am going to ask Jay to let me print them in the back of his book in great big 14 pt type—under Whitman's lines "My pay is sure." OK? If not, tell me, cause I don't care—fun to design big type. I love it.

Am filled as you can guess this A.M. with a new form of attack—may work. The darling Mrs. Davis in State College returned my daughter 1. with a beautiful new pair of shoes 2. two new books 3. more money than she had when she left 4. candy chewing gum and cookies 5. a note which got lost

Sometimes I realize that in this dumb world there are dumb inarticulate citizens who don't know what the hell it's all about—do not understand me and have no way to help me—but Christ do they love me—sometimes I feel the damned stuff coming up out of the pavements at me—my hair dresser told me I reminded her of Greta Garbo and the laundress said—When I go to the movies I am always seeing you on the screen—

My agony has passed for the moment

I raise you dearest poet with care from under the armpits straight up above my head and hug you hard and kiss you and laugh.

Was just this second interrupted to go to the phone—another free lance job—series of posters which I *love* to do—you have never seen any of my good ones.

And darling I can swing getting Jay to publish your stuff but I would like to see it better places if at all possible. Am going to try to scratch my head about that. How about a bunch of essays which he would like better than the poetry which is way way beyond him? Send me copies of the one you sent to England David Young David Old (we can get reprint permission?) the Tempest your long scream—anything you want. If you would like it I will press hard to do a book of your stuff, but you might not think it worthwhile. And Christ would Motz love to do an introduction telling the boys what have we here?

Motz

⟪ 131 ⟫

Woodward to Washington
13 February 1950 (postmark 14 February 1950)

Monday night

Olson—

Think the essay is terrific—makes marvelous points very clearly—I think "goeth by his personeth" is one of the neatest slayings (less blood showing) than anything I remember seeing—hope you didn't remove that one![44]

This is not a serious critical statement. I have read only once and have many points which especially excite me—but I wanted to get off at once how happy I am about it because 1. it helps me to understand Olson's typing better! 2. the main points have points lying behind them which are all Motz points (I mean, never stated by me but my critique of my time for myself)

I am anxious to step up and say for my Russians that even today there are saloons in Russia where a poet can arise spontaneously, speak out verse (this is a fact I have proof for), be listened to with pleasure by all and without his being or anyone else's being self conscious, sit down again and get drunk—and I am sure if another Russian got a good correction he would stand up and speak it off—they are the only drums left alive in the world today outside of you and you—face and hair notwithstanding are Potemkin Murametz Rasin—which is why Motz loves to be in bed with you—

The whole thing is provocative as hell—I am very happy about it—the part you marked as most changed is the part I think is said best except for the penned part which is superb.

Want to talk over with you my whole immediate plan for the future—next six months—Motz is going on secrets not hunches—or instincts—I mean secret in the way you have used it in your essay—a sense of the possible if no

---

44. The phrase was not in the published version of "Projective Verse."

man brain wilfully disturbs—want to discuss the whole thing with you when we can be together. Proposed a scheme to a printer this afternoon—he seemed interested—is going to let me know—for the present I am staying here—I am tempted as hell to go to one of the people you mention but instinct warns me off—I am a hot little babe in this territory and I am working out from there—and my methods are unorthodox as all hell because I can't draw—and would throw those N.Y. boys off though as far as feeling with fingers what things should be—I would match my feel against anyone's.

The printer turned up with one of the bindery help and when he was putting on his hat to go home he said he would like to throw a party in my place and I said OK—it will probably be a real brawl—and probably everyone here will go to bed with someone before the night is over. They are young and it will be straight Gorki stuff—I mean clean and hot—do you—would you like to be here—I like all of them.

⋙ 132 ⋘

Washington to Woodward
15 February 1950 (postmark)

wednesday

you sound boomin and bloomin, and i love it, despite the fact i am not the cause, or am an inversion of same, and am of course wildly chagrinned i am not at the brawl, at which i am sure, i would sit in the corner like little tom horner and enjoy, and enjoy, and make no outcry!

and of course you are live-right to let the motz wave ripple out from where she is, where she is so root and pow'ful strong   before i got yr letter just now, i was going to tell you that for i was happy beyond the telling abt the WHIT-MAN, abt free-wheeling-motz-jobs anyhow   you see, sez he, it has to be that way with a temperament which is really free   every time, in the last three weeks, that you have chafed and been spittin-sore on the 'ittany prass, i was so full of understanding   christ; i was never able to work with anyone when it came to taste (only ben,[45] come to think of it, and that was due to some sort of common thing more of the balls than the fingers, and because we are chillun of the same alleys of this pejerocracy)   or maybe because we are fellow semites! Lekakis saw ezra one-ounce[46] when he opened his show here recently,

---

45. Ben Shahn was Olson's co-worker at the Office of War Information in 1943.

46. The sculptor Michael Lekakis's conversation with Ezra Pound is also mentioned in *Charles Olson & Robert Creeley: The Complete Correspondence* (Santa Barbara: Black Sparrow Press, 1980) 1:51. The zigzag verse enclosed in this letter was also sent to Lekakis the same day and likely refers to Pound. Previously unpublished.

and came back to tell me the old bastard's attempt to turn the sword of my presence here aside—he has the unhappiness that those who see him see me— is now to call me "semitic", and a save-the-world character!   ((O for the day when 'ittle man shall break the mirror in which he sees himself!))

no, baby, you are absolutely right   i was so full of pain i was of no use to you, i couldn't, when you were thrashing around to go to new mex or to new russ, repeat what i had urged on you at t-town, and believe, that you are much too precious right here to remove yrself   i must say i'm a bit of an expert at stick- ing to this ground myself (22 yrs now straight, come june) stubbornly stick- ing—and stuck with the shit of it—and know you know that and can hear me; it is the price, it is the price, on us exorcisers, to love, to love where there is nothing apparent to be loved   nor does it matter that in the end (i begin to sense i am coming to it) you were wrong, wrong, that is, to think there was something to love   and that, in the hugest possible rage, you will damn them out of existence, this bloody empty people

do you know how excited i am that motz is on her own with type & text! god, it's wonderful, and apt, apt, that some, whoever "jay", is it, is, should come along now for you to do little walt worth-a-whit!   (and this horse is grateful, mistress motz, that before it happened she let him have her piece and opened up for this h. that po-et which is there and whom i had not seen, the blade of the grass was so small—(you see, baby, how olson can acquire a skill the motz eyes have, to look so sharp a blade is clear!) i'm sure, 2 months ago, i'd have sd, why whit, & whit's work at 22, what use?   now he is pleased as hell

AND GOES FOR MOTZ ON WHIT IN THE BACK, if that's where it has to go (should be front)   (I remind you Bolyai Farkas was appendix to papa, & we remember papa only coz . . .)   Questions only 14-pt, yet, by the very ar- gument of the critique i passed to you the weekend, on the typewriter, have a whole series of things to take up with your knowledge abt the shifting of type face, and will want to talk abt this when we are together   Look: am now con- vinced type, so far as verse goes anyhow, should shift according as the raga of the poem is different

RAGA	RHYTHM	TIME	SENTIMENT
	(the 4 determinants the Hindu		
	song-dance-drum art declares)		
ex.VILASA[47]	bhairo	a bar of	morn- calm &
	4 & 8 beats	ing	erotic

47. A word denoting the function of Hindu music to display exuberantly tone and rhythm. Olson pre- sumably learned of this from Nataraj Vashi, dance instructor at Black Mountain College.

(ain't that beeyootiful?
even to my anti-O?)

Anyhow, I learned something from the printing of *y & x*: master printer Lescaret was right in setting *preface*—and wrong for all the rest, altogether wrong   Why?   astre italic gets a broadside quality in p., and for the rest is altogether too lush, too decorative   (there should be tensions, most of the time, between type and tone, not symmetries)

If I am right in the argument abt what the typewriter has offered the poet in composition, then it seems to me to follow that, in the printing of language which is projective, there ought to be another convention accepted by the reader—that type-face may change page to page

Now I don't much think that's going to be easy (lekakis, by the way, told me of a little known but fine greek contemporary whose poems were set in type as he wrote them, and then, after his death, were issued fr alexandria, with his type retained page by page, and color and design attempted with each page in the spirit of the type)   but for such a convention to come into existence here, the audience has to be signalled, to slow themselves   the eye runs away with all reading now, no?   and the eye is altogether too fast   too much change of type is like Hindu mime, distracting, and irritating

The trick, (excuse the old man, he's thinking out loud to you, mistress printer, and not making statements but asking his baby questions for his own furtherance) is the subtlest kind of changes, the sort of narrow range of change you surely made a triumph of in the P.S. Catalogue   & LEADING   (pun: leading on, the dance!
                    my motto for the lovely lady, today:
                    LEAD ON, THE DANCE!

I'll shut up. And give you instead of jaw, the 1st verse in some little time:

O
  h !

    h
      O
        W
(o w)

e
  e

```
    r e -
PEE
    t
      s
            ( k )
( t s k )


e
e!
```

[enclosed: typescript of Boldereff's essay entitled "Walt Whitman and the Millen-nial Re-Union" with Olson's handwritten marginalia]

Baby: suggestions, most merely:

In studying Whitman, it is necessary to separate, as one separates in a new ac-quaintance, the many layers of influences from without, to find the essential core of his own nature. He can be understood only in the light of faith and be-cause he possessed a gentleness and tenderness known only to true saints, whose life is passed in loving acceptance, it is wellnigh impossible for our gen-eration to come to an understanding of him. It is my opinion that in this man America produced a soul which had the essential simplicity and profound faith of those saints and heroes who stand as figureheads at the opening of every new culture.[48]

"By the term 'historical pseudomorphosis' I propose to designate those cases in which an older alien Culture lies so massively over the land that a young Culture, born in this land, cannot get its breath and fails not only to achieve pure and specific expression-forms, but even to develop fully its own self-con-sciousness. All that wells up from the depths of the young soul is cast in the old molds, young feelings stiffen in senile works, and instead of rearing itself up in its own creative power, it can only hate the distant power with a hate that grows to be monstrous."

This is Spengler's analysis of what has happened in the cases of several cul-tures, notably the Arabian and the Russian. He has not analyzed the case of America in relationship to this idea and although the situation is far from identical, the idea is fruitful with relation to the present condition. It is evident to all modern thinkers on the subject that America has carried out to its ulti-mate conclusion the basic European cultural idea—the will to infinity—that we have represented in our architecture, our technique, our speed and our

48. Olson's comment: "I'd cut this & open with Spengler quote & introduce Whitman as you do so movingly on p. 2."

frenzy for work, all of the last stages of the working out of the Faustian ideal. All the signs we watch and tabulate so carefully of our own separateness and individuality have so far been either marks of our physical difference, such as speech, way of walking, reaction at public performances, manner of wearing clothes, and attitude on meeting, or historical records of actual happenings which have necessarily been separate, our nation having occupied a new part of the globe and thereby having inevitably had a separate history. It occurs to me that all of these signs are interesting, but not vital. They make interesting conversation, are undoubtedly facts, but to the one who looks deeply, are utterly irrelevant to the portrayal of this country's soul, or at least serve merely as the field of enterprise on which we may have developed that soul.

The situation is analogous to nothing that has ever occurred before—the only part of Spengler's idea which applies is the obvious fact that the psychology of our nation is the result of an idea begun long ago in Europe and that this idea is *not* native, but has overspread our country so completely as to be inseparable from any thoughts about her. We suffer at once from old age and from lack of experience. We suffer more deeply, however, from lack of identity, or soul. Every living American somewhere deeply inside himself envies that man who belongs to a nation, the impression of which in his own heart is clear, though undefinable. This is not to say that he wishes to belong to any other nation, mostly, he does not. He wishes only that there were in this land an underlying spirit so real as to greet him when he returned home and to comfort him in his deepest hour of sorrow. This we sadly admit to ourselves we have not. We will have it only as silently accrues to us the interest of any valid lives we may have produced. Such living develops out of a courageous, unconsciously native answer to the reality of the day in which a man may exist—it can not be produced purposely and can not be hurried and is in the most true sense the nation's fate. Out of the suffering of the Civil War came one such moment—a time which produced all of the unmistakably native soul that we have.

It would be a good thing if there could be a deep and meaningful silence poured into these pages on the subject of our country—America is so in need of silence and reflection. If I could stand beside her and watch over, I would cover her with a coverlet and smile—for I know that she is sleeping.

While a myriad life tears across her dreaming, many, seeing the variety and intensity of that life, take it to be her own, but it is only the reflection of another's life, brought with her when she came. Up until now, she has grown beautiful in the sun, is unconscious of any direction and is not grown enough even to experience the pain of saying to herself, "I am unformed." For how long a time she will continue to lie asleep—to be unaware of her morning, I can not guess. Some of us who have stood by her bedside have several times been in despair—the dream is so violent that we tremble lest she end her life unknowingly, in a dream, without ever having awakened.

It is certain, however, that thus far she has not begun to live her own life. Whatever has happened, no matter how true, or meaningful, has happened within her dream and this dream came into her life through her mother. All, all that happens, pertains to that mother—railroads, ships, canals, factories, tools, even words, none came out of herself, to be herself, and to be grown into a future self. And because in her dream she went further and faster than her mother, many think the dream important. It seems to me dangerous and sad. It is dangerous, not because it was not stimulating, but because it has been taken by her watchers to be her own life. And maybe this does not matter, for it is not the watchers who will make her life, but she herself.

There is one who seems to me to be the proof that she will awake and step down from her violent dream into a rich and meaningful morning. That one is Walt Whitman. He it is who knew his country as only a watchful parent can. And for that country he had inside himself a calm and patient sureness—he understood that she must become and he waited with love in his heart for her to become a real, existing soul. I can not say he too did not accept the dream, but he saw deeper and knew that she must create herself, must find her own way, never before announced, and must labor to make it loving, clean and full.

Today the country is crowded with those who have no faith—and to tell them that in spite of all appearances, a clean and true way must be found to deliver her life out of the dream into a morning where good things will grow, is to repeat words for one's own ears. This in no way alters the case and it is a joyous thing to have had a poet who, with all his faults, contained so deep a love as to be in himself a beginning of his country's creation. Every line Whitman writes bespeaks his deep love and it is out of the wellspring of his affection, undeviating, that America will cast off her dream and painfully, with much striving, accept, create the day.[49]

To think of all her activity as representing nothing of value to herself is hard, but it is harder yet to conceive that she should have no life of her own.

She was born so beautiful and so many endearing movements has she made in her sleep that despite the mad pace of her dream we must believe her capable of a beautiful existence. Listen then, in your dream, America, to the voice of your watcher and hear what you will be and do not fear to awaken to so hard a task, for that is the most glorious of the fates—to have the task set high—[50]

Your poet has said of you that you must contain love.[51] All day and unceasingly you must search out the need of your brother, you must hunt up his hurt and his emptiness and heal and fill them, and you must be joyous in your task.

49. Olson struck out the last sentence of the paragraph. By the phrase "for one's own ears" he wrote "(I love it!)."

50. Olson's comment: "I like the content at this point, but I, for one, would like you get the apostrophe out."

51. Olson's comment: "Would you accept DHL's attack on W's use of this word & accept his preferring 'sympathy' (Open Road)?"

For not only are you to give, but also to receive, to accept back into yourself the sacrifice and courage of your children[52] and to go on to ask more of them. This will be expected and in doing this will your heart grow as beautiful as your physique.[53]

Let the love be pure, let it be constant and never grow afraid. Think all things worthy and they shall all have a meaning. Embrace your children and they will embrace one another.

Whitman was certain that we would develop a new race. And he could be sure, because he was, within himself, the forecast of its future. Every nation has grown out of its vitals a man who is in the beginning, alone and unafraid, what they will later become. This interchange between a man and his country's identity is the most profound spiritual interplay of forces which the earth knows. He *is,* because it *will be* and it becomes, because he *was.* Every word one reads of Whitman convinces one more and more deeply that in his soul he knew the future and his own relationship to it. Out of this sureness came the leisure he was capable of—that great, quiet, waiting, confident leisure, which so inspires the reader with belief. And he knew that time, great time, was required to bring about our future. He may not have foreseen the details of the extreme sorrow of our situation today—our life without belief, without inner greatness—shaken in its pride and not strong enough for humility. But he knew that whatever the road, in the end we must come to ourselves. And his existence is one of the proofs that the potential desire is buried within us, and being buried, it is a matter of time until it come forth.

"You unseen moral essence of all the vast materials of America (age upon age working in death the same as life)
You that, sometimes known, oftener unknown, really shape and mould the New World, adjusting it to Time and Space,
You hidden national will lying in your abysms, concealed but ever alert,
You past and present purposes tenaciously pursued, may-be unconsciousness of yourselves,
Unswerved by all the passing errors, perturbations of the surface,
You vital universal deathless germs, beneath all creeds, arts, statutes, literatures,
Here build your homes for good...
For man of you, your characteristic race
Here may be hardy, sweet, gigantic grow ..."

Walt Whitman is America's saint, her religious voice[54] that may not be

52. Olson's comment: "The more you shrink the parent image, the better you avoid the old State-game: 'beloved,' isn't it truer, & cleaner?"

53. Olson's comment: "This has a pure Motz cadence & could be rewritten from 'the primer'!" Olson is referring to Boldereff's *A Primer of Morals for Medea.*

54. Olson altered this to read: "America's secret identity, the voice."

echoed by the people for a millennium. He has a gentle, loving perceptive appreciation of life which is given direct, in completeness and without need of stimulation. Only a pure and great spirit can receive so deeply, in affection, and know all the sorrows without succumbing to them. He's our St. Francis and that which he understands and loves is ourselves. Some poets have not liked him and some have criticized his ideas and the formation of them. Both are unimportant—his thoughts, regarding man's achievement were all borrowed and his opinions were all those of his century. He is important not for what he thought, but for the purity of his affection. He is not received now by those to whom he wrote; it may be long, long years before he is set in his proper place[55]—but the fact of his undeviating love and searching to release the wounded is vital now and will be—one can feel his deep, thrown-forward-into-my-life affection—it was unclouded and really saintlike.[56] Whatever we will become, his breadth of affection will inspire us and tenderness be ours.

In many, many ways he speaks a language which is Russian in character.[57] They, too, suffer for the lost and are anxious to embrace their brethren. Ours is somehow more casual, more humorous, less religious. But both would immediately comprehend one another, for both are filled with love and need to give it out. Russia has already been cast in a mould—she but waits to exhibit it more fully. America may not be cast for hundreds of years. I do not know nor guess the hour of her visible existence, but I believe she came into being with Walt Whitman: "I also sent out *Leaves of Grass* to arouse and set flowing in men's and women's hearts, young and old, endless streams of living, pulsating love and friendship, directly from them to myself, now and ever. In my opinion, it is by a fervent accepted development of comradeship, the beautiful and sane affection of man for man, latent in all young fellows, north and south, east and west, that the United States of the future are to be most effectually welded together, intercalated, annealed into a living union."

One could devote time to analyzing the defects of Whitman's mental equipment, but for the present it seems to me undesirable to examine them further than to point out that his appreciation of his country's position and of the world's was extremely nineteenth century—all the over-confidence, all the belief to have accomplished miracles, all the flush of hope for the greatest country in the world, without self-examination or proper estimation of the past. But what he did see clearly was that if his country were to become great it would have to develop men and women who were strong in life, accepters of its conditions and affectionate partakers of its sorrows. He spoke with the clear, direct imperiousness of the prophets—if you are to have reality you

55. At this point Olson wrote "over," directing Boldereff to the poem "A Pact" by Ezra Pound, which he typed on the back of the sheet. Olson added the note: "NOT olson, i want to make clear, tho olson thinks it very fine!"

56. Olson deleted "and really saintlike."

57. Olson's comment: "Spengler *was* referring to Russia."

must cast off the exterior bonds—the correctnesses which hamper, and live in truth towards one another.

As the saint receives complete communion with God in his action towards any of His creatures, so the poet, Walt Whitman, received the divine out of all forms and it is for this reason and for this reason alone that he values all things. He never meant to say that all things are of like worth—merely that to him whose soul contemplates the vast design of the universe, the individual parts are all of importance and therefore deserving of attention and of love, for the possibility which they contain of forwarding the good. The saint does not stupidly accept evil, he understands its necessity. Now, so far no one has succeeded in explaining its relationship to life and because no one has explained it, the savants consider that it cannot be understood. But to a pure soul, it is immediately apparent, whether explainable or no, and to Whitman all things were, in God's time. He therefore loved all things, but this is not to say he did not choose or that he did not value what had already been permitted to stand as an expression of God. It is perhaps a fault, but a fault which all saints share, not to differentiate more deeply. In the preoccupation with giving, they overlook relative worth and have their eyes set only on the possible perfection. It is this seeing of the possible perfection in his fellow being which is Whitman's constant refrain. This is why he urges again and again that a man believe in himself, and it is the nearness to that fellow being which identifies him also with each bird, tree and water-form. He knew all of these in his soul, and being in real love, waited for them to come to their full expression of God's identity.[58]

◦⊰ 133 ⊱◦

Woodward to Washington
16 February 1950 (postmark)

Thursday night

Charles dear—

I always believe—everything—long before you ask—your eyes as they were that day lying beside me that first Saturday when you left to go to Gloucester suddenly presented themselves to me full force—that is it—I am bound, as in cast rings, to all of my understanding—I am not able to strike out one smallest fraction at Connie whose lack of affection *hurts*—I have compassion—I remember what Alyosha said that the saint now has to move out into

---

58. Olson's comment: "This last sentence is what I mean by dry, clean statement—as Eckhart!" Pertaining to the paragraph as a whole, Olson adds, "I'd squeeze this paragraph hard, write it most carefully, to clear the vocabulary of all old words."

the world—I am beaten with an iron thong until I am absolutely empty—
Do you remember Frances once wrote to you

"Whose obedience has cost him the most, mine to his fate or his to his fate?—anyway—at the end of twenty-five years I bow my head in acquiescence—you do the one that gets handed to you"—

I know you do all—I understand perfectly how every fibre is pressed—and I am very proud—because I know those feet press in the blood of my being and are able to be separate because so at one with me—the knowledge is very proud that I do as I am commanded.

Whether any of our deed will issue in a day when man exists in spirit I am not able to know—I know you and I are obedient, that we are sacrificing our first born, and that the nature we thus despise with arrogance *is* wrong, however, blind and possibly purposeless our effort to move over into the eternal may be.

Yesterday nature—the earth—delivered a drama which made me smile so wryly—"Thou sayest it." I spoke to her—enormous 50 ft trees came crashing—ice and great wind and driving wild rain and literally hundreds of great branches and whole tall trees cracking and breaking and falling in piercing screams—all the lights and telephone gone and the Narrows wild confusion and I walked out in it all feeling "Oh Christ, move up a little more—just a little more to match that tearing ruthless pain in my entrails."

I add only one word—the reason I despise nature—the whole wild thing is so rhythmic—some day—probably when I am with you—I shall awake as serene as a baby and wonder "I wonder what that was." You can imagine how wryly Motz smiled at that question you ask in your essay "and where does the breath come from?" and I said "Answer me that, you humanists!"

> I save Strzygowski whose last chapters are terrific with your essay—should be published alongside.

[enclosed: drawings by Lucinda, with comments by Boldereff]

a portrait of Woodward I send for
lightness—
a book design for love
Please save and bring back

Washington to Woodward
17 February 1950 (postmark)

friday

ma-ma—dotter: the BIG WORLD is bee-yootifull!   & the BIG BOOK! o
how handsome the titles look! i am sufficiently published therein! i dwell on it
as one does when a book is come home to roost   and am in love with oneself
for that hair of a second which god permits his anonymous workers! and such
a discrimination in the selection of the verse:[59] lucinda, you are not only excellent in the hand but also in the matters which go about the ear! i am wholly
charmed, and full of the delight of thanks   (mama-tell-daughter, convert
these adults woids, convey, from him who is in awe of what hidden capacities
to see, draw, dance her light in its feminine hath!)

it is all topsy-turby, things: another day yesterday rejections blew in like snow
   i was supposed to go to baltimore to meet bill williams to talk over the pa-
terson-reading we are to do in april, but i was again so aroused and spittin
wild with fight, i stayed here and poured mss. back to mags, and wrote bill a
long cover-letter to a piece on pound which bounced[60] & on which i want his
advice whether to bury for the present or to push out once more this time it
was the HUDSON REVIEW, which dumped everything back!

but the joker i wanted to tell you of, is, that at this moment when my work,
which i am now most stubborn about, is being refused on all sides, i am suddenly being sought after on all the other planes! that's for laughs: next week i
am to meet with the potter Leach because it is assumed only he and i are fit for
each other (!), and this is by "important" invitation; i am (2) to appear on tele-
vision to argue the case for the return of american education to classical studies; and (3) i have been invited to do a 3 hr lecture and discussion on herman
melville the great! what do you say to that, for irony! olson the anonymous,
who has lived seven years in this tent pitched on the edge of a capital of doom,
and has quietly gone about his business, is now, when his business has produced some certain things in words, is, on the one hand, rejected for the
words, and on the other, accepted and drawn out from his tent, for his person!
   motz, make a motz wry laugh to go with an olson one!

59. The titles drawn by Lucinda illustrating her "Big World" book are titles of Olson's poems:
"Epigon," "The Babe," "Otvechi," "The Kingfishers," "La Chute I," and "La Chute II."
   60. "GrandPa, GoodBye," which Olson sent to William Carlos Williams on 16 February 1950, asking
his advice.

it is mean cold here today   i slept until 2, needed to, from the exhaustion of these weeks   and now must turn around myself to see if there is any words in me today which need to come out but i wanted to tell you & lucinda how good the mail was to me today, because it came from you, and to hope this may give you back a weekend of some small delight, my own delight we are all alive!

which is most certainly love's doing

Charles

❧ 135 ❧

Woodward to Washington
17 February 1950 (postmark)

I can see exactly why Ezra would hate your guts—all that he knows you know—and then Olson has something to say.

All of your notes on the Whitman are right—but the total result is I feel shy and have decided to keep it where it has been—the important thing about Frances and she has always known it, is that she keeps alive the secret so that "his hearing through himself will give him secrets objects share."[61]

As you say, I taking a further meaning—Lead on, the dance—which requires of me the kind of movement I have always made—what Kierkegaard calls the movement of faith—This last two months and especially these last several weeks are a proof to me that I do truly exist in faith—I could not describe to you the feeling—as a boat knows it will go forward through water if handled properly no matter what sky and ocean may be raising—that is how I know—I have no thoughts no worries—no ecstasy and no sinking—simply know I will go forward to arrive—when and where, another's job.

For the coming six months I have decided to pay out the line as far as she will go—I am working on a deep run—which is intimately connected with you—your work—I will not speak aloud nor turn to look—I am always safe—because I am indifferent—I am fucked of Olson every minute of every hour of every day and every night—I belong to him as god has never before envisioned in flesh—forever it will never be possible to separate an Olson from a Motz because my blood is his ink.

❧ 136 ❧

Woodward to Washington
20 February 1950 (postmark)

Olson—

61. The "Projective Verse" essay is being quoted.

Monday morning

The mood this cold morning is ferocity—

You said on Wednesday "nor does it matter that in the end (I begin to sense i am coming to it) you were wrong, that is, to think there was something to love—and that, in the hugest possible rage, you will damn them out of existence, this bloody empty people."

This is to tell you that I have not at all decided finally—I put so much suffering into getting this place to live that out of sheer stubbornness I refuse now to move away—just when I can begin to collect on my suffering and live here practically free.

I have written to a friend in Budapest to see if she could dig me up a job— I give myself the next year and a half to look around this American with ice cold eyes for the last time and see whether or not I can take its smugness its love of death its swinish lolling while everything alive is being tortured.

DeWolf sent me the most perfect New England letter you have ever read— a flat refusal from both him and his wife—and he dares to speak of the "fascinating life of Herman Melville"—he stated the truth for of course the horrible sufferings of the alive are lovely to watch from the other side of the cage.

I am already working on another angle—but that is not the point—

Included among the New Englanders this morning is Connie—whom I now classify as an enemy.

Olson I would like to get out with some ax—some great ax and literally hew them all down—I can not believe that your magnificent speech is refused—Christ when I think of those three—Kingfishers—The Spoilers (my new name for Otvechai) and The Praises not to mention my poems—

God and you say no one publishes poetry pick up Publishers Weekly— Christ there is book after book of it I know it isn't poetry but those bastards don't know what poetry is so why by accident can't they let yours through—

You know I am a fierce beast—if I am faced with a desert then I want the thing to look like a desert—I am afraid of nothing—neither physical nor mental and I am this morning only a body containing hatred (towards everything but Olson)

Motz

Monday night

Charles—

I remember now a banker I knew as a young woman who was sent to Wall Street for a few years from Austria? Hungary? can not remember which— anyway once—in a difficulty I have now forgotten, complained of to him—he looked at me with his very powerful, penetrating, detached and so knowing face and said "To sit still and to do nothing is sometimes one of the greatest actions one can accomplish" and proceeded to describe a time when as a quite young man he had been sent to London and his whole duty, for almost a year, was just simply "holding"—showing no strain—ease—doing nothing—waiting for the pot to boil.

I have a wise plan in reference to myself—but for the moment am forced to idleness and in order to pull the thing off must have ease—when I look at my daughter and count how many existent dollars I have it is not easy, Charles.— (The man I referred to, to finish that story, dropped me because I was too serious—he felt very drawn—very close—but he was full of sorrow and said he wanted a "kitten" and of course he was wrong—a man can not really escape—"Who fights behind a shield."[62]

Tonight I am finishing the *Origin of Christian Church Art*[63]—how deeply and straight you go back to your pre-Christian and very very early Christian ancestors—North Swedes and Celts—they both were against the personal in sculpture—both used line and took terrific joy in what they did—representation—the human figure used realistically, came from the south—you will accept Strzygowski as a brother—the whole book is wonderful—last two chapters very strong and illuminating.

I love Charles.

Frances

I spent the day reading aloud all the great poems of the great poet Olson—they have to be read aloud—(hug yourself)

Am I in love with the Kingfishers? It never came out as it did today and brother that is really putting them straight down the alley.

Oh Charles darling Christ—someday people will recite them on the street—it is really really in there and will cause joy once they learn how—the young Henderson Forsythes of America.

And I hate all my friends and I don't give a damn how foolish they consider me—and I love my house in Woodward where the rhythm of each article, in relation, sings—to me the Motz who loves beauty. And I love your face and your way you walk and the terrific dignity of my baby's demeanor—and I now absolutely all of a sudden don't give a damn about Connie—I don't care *why* you want so much to hold her—I don't care how much you love her and in what ways—how much you give to her—or anything else—I only care about my Charles—for him to be undismayed—"he is the greatest best good little giant in the world"—I kiss you every inch from head to foot—I am an Irish maid—I bring hot towels warm clean water beautiful soap—I wash you—bring you food—skip dance and sing—waiting on my baby—whom god gave to the world soon enough for me to see and behold.

62. Boldereff is quoting the first line of "Trinacria."
63. Josef Strzygowski, *Origin of Christian Church Art* (Oxford: Clarendon Press, 1923).

-☙ 137 ☙-

Washington to Woodward
21 February 1950 (postmark)

tuesday

frances:

it turns out, this potter, bernard leach, was good to meet, and we would
have had the kind of talk which breeds things had not the host, my silly friend
& so-called poet, richman, who heads the institute of contemptible arts,[64]
found it necessary to protest my premises (i am rove these days by the fantastic
presence in our culture & behaviour of "argument", that filthy whore-daugh-
ter of logic, of aristotle, of the medieval; the more i think of it the more it is my
impression that the renaissance was a superficial invasion which actually did
not disturb the feudal base; the joke in it all, so far as i am confronted by it, is
that i was, from age 14 to 21, turned out as a master of argument, and i learned
to abhor its human consequences—thus i also know its devices, the reasons
for its use, and am ahead of any use of it before me; it becomes increasingly
impossible for me to find that kind of conversation which reading is only a
substitute for; so i read more!

leach was that kind of man (painters or craftsmen are often so) who knows
that each man, as Frederick of Prussia put it, has to save himself in his own
way, and recognizes that a man's premises, if they are his own, is the man, &
you don't engage a man as you do a syllogism—you listen, warmly, (it is the
act of touch as touch is also a part of the intellect's life), you add your differences (which are actually your own delineations), you listen, as he has, (which
is the exchange of experiences), and, in it and after it all, there is the fragrance
of wood or violet's odor (Kitasono's use)

leach just happened to have learned to be a potter in japan under a master
who was in direct descent of discipline from the Sung of the 12th century (it
is marked, how japan was the switch-point of Chinese culture to the west—
leach repeats, on his level of pots, fenollosa on language, and i, on the noh
plays)   leach and i could have added sums to each other (as we walked to
lunch i advanced a notion which must have come to flower from your protest
against asia which i took seriously: it was, that it is in such particulars as pots, a
Noh play, the structure of the ideogram, the Anatolian plain, that a westerner
may learn, NOT in the philosophies or religions or architectures or state-
systems of asia   an idea which carries with it the premise that culture is the

64. Robert Richmond was the director of the Institute of Contemporary Arts in Washington. Bernard
Leach, the well-known potter, later came to Black Mountain College at Olson's invitation.

actionable acts, and that any place is source, given the severe application of a man's own interest)   i was developing the notion, that western culture has become, like western sport, mere spectator stuff, that the provocation to action, to like action, is no longer implicit in either its enjoyment or its presentation, and that this condition must be struck at

and leach was following, for he saw that this was a frame in which the sort of William Morris revival that he represents, that so much of this whole recrudescence of the crafts represents, could fit, in fact fits better than all the guild-or-progressive-or-people's-doing-instead-of-thinking sort of crap that is usually argued for the coming back into existence of the acts of the hands

when piss-pot-robert started to take me on! and of course i am a fighter, and when my neural system is rasped, as it is rasped by the verbal-minded, i throw a rage more now than ever (paranoia, isn't it the word that the rationalists are using to offset the likes of me these days?) ((i learned last night that poor sweet lawrence got a persecution time in mexico, that he was sure some killer was coming out of those terrible hills to get him, and that he hired a body-guard, who was later known to one of my friends in Patzcuaro, to sleep across his door at night!))

in a way i am disturbed by this shrinking of my human environment, by this raging which takes such toll of my strength, if for no other reason than it is in such contrast to the olson who wrote ishmael, who was a sharp, tough, cool character who stepped straight from the Democratic National Committee into that prose & form

you will understand, because you are frances, that i feel as in an envelope of your love today, of your wisdom and gentelnesse, and am talking to you as one might, most close   i am, if you like, unhappy, but that is such a silly word, & only relates to upper surfaces which don't really interest you or me; my base, which seems now secure in precisely the degree to which my rage increases, is not unhappy; on the contrary, vitality creates unhappiness of this sort

what is the pity of it, is, that environment *does* shrink, that the price one pays for going out to one's fellow men gets greater and greater, and one is more and more thrown back on oneself, is isolated   it is not apparent to those who cannot see; as a matter of fact one *looks* tougher, more hide-like, when actually my skin is more sensitive today than ever before!   and one has even stronger hungers for environment!   but there it is, and i imagine it is each one's paradox (i am thinking of yr own delicacy and consequent tortures, my motz)

and i'm sure one little thing i am doing as i write you is to gird myself for another engagement this night before which i am sick to the bones! for there i'll be at 8:30 as in a torture chamber of steel points, surrounded by eight academic minds, and alone to argue classical studies! becoz i believe the artist today must be a culture-carrier, i welcome the spot, yet the battle is so huge, most of the time i'll trade it for a line!

of which lines there are few these days, and i always chafe when i am in one of these prosy periods   i have had to get used to them as preparing times, but i hate them, they are such fall-backs (i still like that image of the bull-fighter i took from Ortega and used in ISH)   it is like going up (& i am some way lazy!) a height to look yr country over, to see where you've got to, in order to go on
        and perhaps it is just at such times that i feel most embattled (you could not imagine how much your tremendous letters ease me, darling, our images!)   i am pushing off, i sense, pushing off at last on my own (i whisper that! asking of god his aid)   and it is not easy (let those who argue with me find out!) and lord, is it hardest of all for the combination of, traditionalist & rebel   (the stinging word, the word which makes me shamed of my fellow men, is egotist, which is thrown at me like hot rivets of which i am the pail they're caught in! Egotist!
                        ((I also learned last night of a title i treasure, of yr friend stendhal, "Memoirs of an Egotist!"—that's the way to give it back to 'em))

I'll quit now, go back to bed, and see what i can do to prepare some notes for this goddamned business tonight.

But let me tell you the only words yesterday came up with. Williams (WC) had written me asking whether i wanted him to join my pound piece to one of his own, and some others perhaps, to be published in a broadside by some booton, new jersey, printer, or whether i wanted still to try to sell it to "Poetry" or PNY. (Of course i decided to put in with the broadside!) I was thinking out loud, deciding which way to throw it, and getting off that new rag of mine i wrote to you about, about the deductive in the mags, and how it kills, when the alternative kind of structure came out this way, that is, the advantage of such a new conception of a mag came out this way:

. . . . of presenting men with their hot as it is, as it comes, stem on, head after
. . . . .

Maybe these words from Bill may interest you:
        "Something's got to bust around here soon. I wish I knew how to
        bring it about. Something's got to out-step the big army smash-up

or it really *will* get us. Always this approach to a break through in the arts coming JUST before our presence becomes intolerable to the money boys and the blood has to spill.

(this is accurate: the decision to go to war was made about 10 days ago)

"I've been noticing myself recently, how repulsive the faces about me on the street have become—and numerous. Not the poor. They at least have a beauty. But the money guys, the little money guys. They are getting dominant again and they are ugly, ugly as hell. And they're everywhere." (and ain't this true!) I like this guy's way of taking things in

which is his way of putting them out

Good day, baby, in everything

       Murametz,
       waking up

WHAT GOES, OR, NURSERY TIME[65]

rub, rub, dub
& find out who
you are!
y'are

❧ 138 ☙

Woodward to Washington
23 February 1950 (postmark)

Olson dear—

It is slightly fantastic how we parallel—again and again and again—me too on the debate business only it didn't take me until 21 to catch on—once I arrived in college I said no more thanks—Christ I could be the most crooked lawyer in the US as far as my mind goes—did I ever tell you the letter that Frances wrote—alone—at 23—for the Jersey City Printing Company—to get them out of the biggest legal jam they were ever in and their lawyers worked on it and the Pres worked on it and the Vice Pres and Gen Mgr (my

---

65. Previously unpublished poem.

boy Black) worked on it and my boss worked on it and in absolute derision my boss threw the letter at me one day and said with the inevitable laugh—here, motz, you answer this—and answer it I did and to this day nobody sort of believes it—it stopped the law suit cold—one letter. Told you before?

This is to say darling that I am excited about your renaissance comments—does this boy Strzygowski hate these humanists and has he got a story—backed by terrific research—you are so right it did not disturb the feudal base—and darling here is my idea now about us—over there in places you can not pronounce every idea almost that we have had in art in 2000 years (not painting) architecture sculpture, was originated—the only other places were pagan Sweden and Northumbria and Ireland—all that Renaissance death business—is as Strzygowski says just a sponge absorbing. I am writing badly I am not in the mood at all—only want to get this one thing off my chest—that the impulse, the living impulse and creative act is actually god damned rare—I am amazed out of how small an area in time and space came such growth—that today a new age actually has begun—that it is picking up contact around the globe small point to small point that we are more alone than has ever occurred before for reasons I am too lazy to say and that it is my impression it is a whole change in pace—
there has been as described by Spengler
Culture—⌒ that pattern
now man cannot quite with a long face pull off any more of these god inventions
he is stuck with the knowledge that whatever gets done he has to do—that we are as big as we are—(to sound like Olson) that there is now not all that tarum tarum and then fanfaronade and then death—there is now like eating every day man has to consume himself and every day is the day of judgment and every nightfall he has to give birth and it is all very undramatic and unspectacular and adult as all hell—the new Olson Motz whoever else there is pattern.
You said when were riding on the bus together "What economy there is in this thing"—referring to our anger
Dearest—how about moving up a mountain right into the 20th century's greatest climax (in this field of creative effort (male-female)) in the first half of the first act—as we have done these last 2½ months—no wonder we both ache and are unhappy and neural and all that—no breathing allowed—just a goddamned Mozart flute concerto!

Today Motz is relaxed—happy-confident-dreamy—dancy and hummy—feminine—soft-easy—everything—
God just came last night and said, "Honey, this is enough"—and raised the whole trap right off me and I am free as man has dreamed since man began.

I love Olson.

apropos Bill's paragraphs—I am chuckling to myself—the money boys never hunt me out of the pile because I look so terrifically OK—just what robber baron ordered for his hideaway—and so I pump my blood to Olson—Olson pumps his to live etc and so on and the poor devils never catch up.

⪥ 139 ⪤

Washington to Woodward
23 February 1950 (postmark)

thurs.

this is that notation, that yr anchor is here, and haulin', sweet line

I'm getting it off as I leave to go to the 1st of the 2 three hr sessions on HM, because I question that I'll get back in time to make a letter today

I feel swell, and excited to be sitting down with some people around to talk about HM just now. (The funny thing is, this is actually, so far as I remember, the 1st time I shall have talked about him formally since a dinner in Pittsfield as long ago as 1935!).

And the reason is the upshot of all this work of the past month or so: i am prepared to speak & act, 100 years after the very days he was poking his way into M-D, as though i were his inheritor! (You have given me the privilege of so characterizing myself!)

I shall moo, and gnaw, and be very quiet, very severe. For this is big business, whether those who will be listening know it or not! (Read Richard Chase's book on him yesterday, as a freshener and self-provoker, and tho Chase is right wrong, yet I like his knowing that he is walking around a rock as big as the Caucasus)[66]

So, babe, keep the fires burning. And I am your coal.

Love   O

⪥ 140 ⪤

Woodward to Washington
24 February 1950 (postmark)

66. Richard Chase, *Herman Melville* (New York: Macmillan, 1949).

Friday morning

Charles—

By accident I pick up and read again the end of *Women in Love*—I thought I knew all of it—but at this moment the speaking father of Lawrence is quiet within me—forgive me angel—it is not personal—not triumphant in that sense—but I *feel* that the chains I have hacked through in the last two months because you on your part are the necessary designated—*is* the open gate that Lawrence so passionately was searching for was pleading with us to set up— I feel elated, because I feel that the dark creative not-known Lawrence stood so in reverence of is at least for our time empatterned in my Olson. I speak this in silence as you are aware.

I love my vision—every word is the right word—it is all exactly how it is—

I enclose a drawing which very deeply thrills me—I feel again in silence of reverence that *somehow* I have gotten over to Lucinda the truth—without words—look at the worldly aristocratic grown-upness of the face of Washington out of her mind and look at the full lips the round cheeks and eyes— the rose quality of Jesus saying "Yes"—all Lucinda's idea. (She put in the two erased "yes's" on purpose to spoil it (please cover up when looking at it) because she wanted to give it to her teacher and I made so passionate a plea she could not resist but thought I would give it back were it spoiled—oh! dark lovely child!

[*enclosed: drawings by Lucinda of George Washington and the Stars and Stripes and Christ and the Cross.*]

◄§ 141 §►

Woodward to Washington
[25 February 1950]

Olson dear—

This program on Dreiser is one of the few great radio programs that has ever been given in this country. Henderson Forsythe, the wonderful young man I told you about, read this with a slow rise in intensity a cold controlled rise that was the greatest stage thing I have ever heard. Everyone who heard the program was stunned into silence—it was absolutely magnificent—the thing was handled this way—Hank asked me the questions which I answered—two answers enclosed and the reading (herewith)[67] was thus introduced—I wish to God Dreiser could have heard it—I am positive no greater real tribute has ever been paid to him than that boy's reading of this thing—

67. The reading was the murder scene from Theodore Dreiser's *An American Tragedy* (here omitted).

at the end his face was dead white and just pouring perspiration and he never allowed his voice to get away from him once—the whole thing so subdued— so tense and the rise in tightness in passional inescapement *the greatest*. I wish to God we could dig up some other kind of performance and I could locate Henderson through the Alumni office at Iowa University.

I am squeezed in my own heart to my capacity to pass breath—Remembering Henderson and the America he longs for—I hold for today—I love my Olson.

Charles dear—this was for Iowa radio audience and is expressed as unsubtly as possible—because they are dumb—but I wanted to win their respect for Dreiser.

[*typescript enclosed:*]

I feel that Dreiser has one great quality which I have never heard mentioned in connection with him. It is a quality which I call "the subdued tone"—there are no hysterics in *The American Tragedy* although the characters are mainly noticeable for their weakness. You know that they suffer very painfully and that their joy is youthful and captivating, yet in the whole two volumes there occur not as many as five lines of emotional writing. This lack of comment, of the swelling emotional phrase, has been taken by many people as due to Dreiser's essential coldness, his lack of concern for the implications of his drama, but I am wondering if the opportunity to point our own moral, to tear, as it were, our own hair is not doing something a great artist is compelled to do? Does it not force us to draw conclusions for ourselves rather than to absorb today and tomorrow and forget sentiments the artist has worked out for us? In contrast with a novelist like Thomas Wolfe, who evokes so well his feeling about America—has a novelist like Dreiser achieved less and felt less, because he forces us to feel more? I remember reading once a page of Dostoyevsky's which I tore right out as I turned it over, so hard was I involved in the outcome of the hero's fate—well—the same thing happened with Dreiser—he makes those tense quiet scenes between Clyde and Roberta so dramatic you feel they must explode—but they do not and in this subdued understatement they penetrate in a lasting way into your memory.

It is true that I am excited and it is because I feel *American Tragedy* to be one of the few great books America has produced in our century. To me its best quality is a characteristic I have never heard anyone speak of—as though it were not there or were not attributable to Dreiser's genius, but I feel it to be intimately bound up with Dreiser's method—this quality is his power of evocation. How he managed to do it I do not know, but in the silence surrounding each major scene are a host of questions, dynamic, powerful and crying to be answered. Take for instance the very first scene in the book—Clyde standing in the street with his parents, who conduct a street mission, watching them preach and being forced to join in their hymn-singing. Clyde rebels, not knowing that he rebels; he feels uncomfortable and ashamed—this feeling he never expresses—but it constitutes his rebellion—and that dumbness speaks so eloquently of all the things in his life which will act as his enemies. Is not Clyde's discomfort directly related to the most fundamental attacks on Christianity—its lack of joie de vivre which has been lamented not only by Nietzsche, but by an ardent Catholic poet like Francis Thompson? If you were to pursue the implications of only this one scene, you would come bang up against problems it would take a life-time to settle.

When an author is able to tell a scene directly, simply and without comment and to do it in such a way that the thoughtful reader has meat for a year's reflection, it seems to me he deserves being excited about.

◄§ 142 ▓►

Woodward to Washington
26 February 1950 (postmark 27 February 1950)

                                        Sunday

Charles—

I am very excited by the contents of your note—so very excited I say no word. I told Lucinda in a way for her to understand about moo and gnaw—we each laughed our own.

Baby, how about this page out of *Bend Sinister* of Vladimir Nabokov (the boy for whom I inserted the $50. ad about my book in *The New Yorker*, which brought me not one sale.)?!

"His name is protean. He begets doubles at every corner. His penmanship is unconsciously faked by lawyers who happen to write a similar hand. On the wet morning of November 27th, 1582, his is Shaxpere and she is a Wately of Temple Grafton. A couple of days later he is Shagspere and she is a Hathaway of Stratford-on-Avon. Who is he? William X, cunningly composed of two left arms and a mask. Who else? The person who said (not for the first time) that the glory of God is to hide a thing, and the glory of man is to find it. However, the fact that the Warwickshire fellow wrote the plays is most satisfactorily proved on the strength of an applejohn and a pale primrose.

"There are two themes here: the Shakespearian one rendered in the present tense, with Ember presiding in his ruelle; and another theme altogether, a complex mixture of past, present and future, with Olga's monstrous absence causing dreadful embarrassment. This was, this is, their first meeting since she died. Krug will not speak of her, will not even inquire about her ashes; and Ember, who feels the shame of death too, does not know what to say. Had he been able to move about freely, he might have embraced his fat friend in silence (a miserable defeat in the case of philosophers and poets accustomed to believe that words are superior to deeds), but this is not feasible when one of the two lies in bed."

Nabokov is the only man alive on this earth who could dispel the Russian dream and this afternoon he is doing it (I can understand why America has ignored this novel so that I bought a new copy ordered from N.Y. for 75 cents.) He does it on the only level where I am absolutely vulnerable—with Nabokov's own sleight-of-hand he convinces me they are the enemies of quality in itself. I should never have believed this from another living soul on this earth.

So read the first paragraph again Olson—and *add why* this little beaten Motz is No.2 why—excited.

⋙ 143 ⋘

Washington to Woodward
27 February 1950 (postmark 27 February 1950)

monday feb 27 50

it was more of a week, last week, than i had predicted to you ahead of it; it was a week, one of those times by which one measures oneself   ((i dislike the abstract pronoun, hate it, but i am going to have to be as careful in my use of the self-addressing "you" with you as i demand of its use to me, for you are like quick and self-involved, and mistook, as i guess i might have, my use of it in the passage on the "empty people", and the leaving of 'em—i was talking to myself, the you was me, but this damned but beautiful language, because it is undeclined, has such holes in it: i do not forget your telling me of a Russian noun!)

one miracle was included   i was pouring it out the 1st of the 2 days of the Melville spiel   (you were there, for the pitch of it, the positivity, the wonderful way in which it stayed, not 100 ago, but right straight with the hand on this prick of now) And as i went along i was aware that there was one other person present who was not just following me but was anticipating me, had worked himself through to premises which were (at least in this instance) identical   It was, in fact, a new myth, of a less order just because lawrence is right, the 1st relation is man to woman, and man to man is of a second order, but it was another epigon, darling: suddenly my blood was re-iterated outside me   I can best describe this one as not *our woodhenge*, but as a new inverse tale of narcissus and echo This sculptor and potter, Alexander Gianpietro, was Unecho to my Unnarcissus!

The issue, over the night, and on the second day, was so strange i do not yet know its outcome, but i should imagine that one of my gravest wounds has now been, not healed but erased, removed as my beloved Cabeza is said to have removed from the Indians the gashes and their scars left by the mysteri-ous mouth of the Bad Thing   After the lecture a pseudo-poet named Dona-hoe, who has, for all his cowardice, a swift mind and a quick sympathy, (he had comprehended, as no one else had, what Gianpietro had shown), told me, without any further development, that G was a formal and severe Catholic!

I thought of it later, and said to myself as i was going off to sleep, "Then, Olson, perhaps the base of you is more Catholic than you have been willing to admit, after the 25 years of rejection". Just that, no more, merely a brushing of the thought

Came Friday. I walk in. One boy is present, who had borrowed my copy of Ishmael over night. Says he, I should like, today, if you would talk about your "Christ" section! Then, says he, I am going to tell you something you will not like. Well, says I, maybe you might be wrong, maybe I might fool you   Any-how, says he, yr book is a litany! So that was that, and others including Gian-pietro, came in   (The boy's name, by the way, you will cherish too: Lebherz!)

So the lecture went off, with only one reference to Catholicism   In describ-ing the nature of the amor between Melville and Hawthorne, I took occasion to point up the curious interest of both of them (in Pierre and in the Marble Faun) to the same double Italian theme: incest and the Confession. Otherwise, nothing.

Came the end, all had drifted out but Alex and Lebherz! So Alex fixes his fine eye (no so much mediterranean as high-minded, "aristokratein", to use a motz), and says, "I'm going to say something you won't like!" "O", says I, "Gian, you are going to say my thought is Catholic, my boy!" bro., i might have sd, but in that one split instance I, for the first time, *jumped* him! for that split second my Unecho was Echo!

It was then we went on to what may forever heal me. For it came to this. A Catholic, for the 1st time in my life, listened to yr old man say, sure, i suppose you are right, that my conceptions are of the natural man, and if you find that the Mass is the precise image of the same content—Eckhart: God is interested in *me*; the Mass is his participation in me; it happens because i am reverent, i am Stephen—then, will you accept this proposition

(parenthesis: sd A, if the Mass one day isn't the most necessary image of man's participation, then Catholicism is wrong, and deserves to be finished)

We came together on this ground. Sd I, But may we not look to this possibility—that the Mass be lost like a manuscript (I was thinking of the total disappearance from history of the playwright who defeated Euripides the day "The Trojan Women" was his chief piece of 4), still man will invent another image, some other supper to replace and recreate a commemoration.

To which Alex, because he is a man, agreed. And thereby gave me a sort of peace.

((I don't think we ever got around to it, but what made me able to dance on all this point was, that Stephen has seemed to me for long the most important resurrectable figure in Xty. And the other amazing fact of the week, was, that on Monday last, I had picked up for 2 bucks Eusebius' History of Xty from Augustus to Constantine,[68] and I had picked it up to find more facts of Stephen, but had, up to now, still not read anything but the murder of James, which I read in the streetcar bringing the book home!))

There are so many other things to say, especially to respond to yr letters, and to yr sense of Dreiser (which is another coincidence of major order)   But I have spent so long telling you, blocking out only, this lovely business, that I must quit, and go down town. For today, if a shrewd trader will give in, I shall be buying a flock of Lawrence I discovered Friday. It was another flower of the week. And what breaks my heart is, amongst the collection is a water-color by DH, the original, which I should wish that I might own: it is a man pissing against a wall, standing in narcissi and daffodils!

Frances, under the muzzle of the gun, man is still reborn!

Love, love
Charles

p.s. curious thing is (it must be a law of the other order) i am and have been completely uninterested in Unecho as, i imagine, he is, in me—that is, in any daily way

68. *The Ecclesiastical History of Eusebius Pamphilius* (Bohn Edition, 1903) was in Olson's library.

Woodward to Washington
28 February 1950 (postmark 1 March 1950)

Tuesday night

Charles dear—

For the very first time I do not understand what you are saying to me—
whether it is because you crowded too much flow (Alex-Olson) into too few
paragraphs or whether because I have been for some time in a violent Anti-
Catholic humor, or whether because I am after all deeply a protestant—or
whether because I have yearned for you so much until now I am no longer
rapport—or whether because of the to me very exciting discovery that in the
very early days of Christianity in the first and second centuries the Christ was
conceived by those nomads in Altai-Iran to be a man on a horse—and have so
shown him in one bas-relief remaining from Egypt where the concept pene-
trated—for what or all of these reasons—I do not follow the paragraphs
about the catholic thing—they are not clear to me—wish to god I could *see*
you to talk—it finally gets impossible to talk in letters (for instance the first
paragraph mentioning "empty people" and a mis-reading of "you"—do not
remember your paragraph nor my answer—do not even know what letter to
look in.)

I am sad not in a surface way—opposite of what you were talking of last
week—on the surface in my mind I am OK but deep down underneath I feel
as though the well has dried somewhere. I am very thrilled about your
epigon—a terribly necessary thing for you—

I feel shut up and dry—it is so long since you have actually answered a letter that there seems to be no flow.

Your last sentence I too believe with all my soul—and was trying to tell you
in my letter you received today that I am now convinced that here with you
and those around you, Olson, lies the rebirth.

But for me—I am like a woman who has just given birth, before the milk
comes—I am absolutely drained—

One more Charles—last week I found an old *Publisher's Weekly* very old
was about to throw it away wondered why I had saved it—looked through it
to make sure and found—what I intended to do something about, but you can
now lend me—either a new edition or anyway one I had not the number of—
of Eusebius—which I had marked to buy—!

Please mail your Christopher Smart—will return—if not too much trouble to wrap and send.

One note more the phrase "poor beaten little Motz" was with a grin—anticipatory of my friends' delight when they learn Motz's Russian phobia has waned by a hair.

Do I have to Keep on writing?

I am with Blake—I want no more suppers invented. I want no part of Christianity except Christ and today I do not want any brothers—I feel a great love bull whale—with one fin gone and eyes blind.

◄ 145 ►

Washington to Woodward
28 February 1950 (postmark)

tuesday

it is true, i have a stinking cold, the second worst of the winter, which is my misery time   it is true my wits are not sharp these days (i found out last night, trying to read lawrence's rainbow, that when irritation supervenes my intelligence declines)   it is true also that my rhythm is off (yesterday's humpy letter to you showed it)   it is true all this is the price i pay for the way i poured it out last week, especially as of one, herman melville (which is long for c. olson)

so, if these things are true, should we be surprised your letter, which just came, with the nabokov quote, is an untangible riddle? (untangleble, only untang-able sounds better

please, baby, because such defeats prey on my mind, tell me when you write again: (1) how does the passage "dispel the Russian dream"?

(2) explain: "read 1st Para, and add why this motz is No. 2 why—excited"?

I can say this: one sentence alone of N's is precious, William X, cunningly composed of two left arms and a mask. That's beautiful, as is, the proof that the Warwickshire fellow wrote the plays—is most satisfactorily proved on the strength of an applejohn and a pale primrose.

Today I should dawdle,[69] look my world over, piss and sing, be robert burns. Or throw an arm up into the eye of the wind, swing sail with my balls, and head down ward. Look up, hear the curlew, right straight up the ass of a

---

69. Olson rearranged this letter (from this point on, to the end) to produce the poem "A Po-sy, A Po-sy" (*Collected Poems*, pp. 107–12).

daisy, from below, definitely from below, "There is no more time, no more, bro., no more

   tea is for tiffins, the likes of u—o, y-ooooooo" Ah, Gassire! Watch out! citizens They got you where it hurts, citizen! Those brothers in harlem who lived with everything. And shat in the paper cartons   (One of 'ems my neighbor now)   My neighbor, now (with the vocal by Ophelia, high and o—so ephe-drine   Jelly is the gas we're trebled by Down, derry o kiekorro you lie Listen to the partridge SING (ophelia-high still) s-i-n-g like thistles   Ojai   where all tha fakirs be   O lyrik souls   the Oooooooo

                              RIENT   Let's go west, boys there's no rest except with one's legs twisted round one's

                                   yes, my friends, this is a discussion as free as paper bags, and comes to you—oh, no permissions granted leaves cancelled   Ariadne's silk is mulberrys GO BACK TO WORK (5 minutes is all the research necessary to get a fact straight   Can you read a maze when you see one?   Look, you sucker   I tell you a nose is, a nose is, sure it is; just what you think it is   Wipe it, citizen   Get on with it

   the trace, the dogs with the fine limbs are on the hounds   Here, bro., try to bring an interval down at any pace   See, where the blood streams   It is not in the firmament   My thumb hurts   "What are all those snakes in her hair?"   My god, man, don't you know your robert when your fat burns?

   Where have you been all these unwhole years? Try again to bring her head around   The buoy is just off yr starry plough   Make yourself booo-oi   Make yrself period   Who does not fight will remain unhealed, no matter how many rains he holds in his outright palms   pansies was a translation   dazies, they call 'em, in the high-brown section of

                              medusahatta   (and he didn't know it, nor did his bigger brother, but with his brother it din't so much matta, except for the surface of his

                   prow   Sd Mrs Henry Adams about Mr. Henry James "He didn't bite off more than he could chew. . . .

                              and there's the one about time wounds all heels

                        it is brooks that make the proper current, yr predeces-sor, little running water   start right now, if you are a twig, settle right down where you are in order to stop being inextinguishable from the element

                                                  he chews and chews and chews more than he has bitten off

                                        ah, gas! HERE! HERE! HERE-and-now:

IN ORDER TO BE A ROCK,
one of those things they make their walls of . . .   And that tired robert so he
started to make the ladies

balls, or the image 3 sure, it's all over his work
(mine too) And why not? What direction do you go in, who's lead, where is
the fin, the stump the vessel walked right off the course and up on the land
with

BY?

piss-and-vinegar he called them, suffering as he was from a sacroeleac, and
Akademos' no-garden

o, brothers, who, after a thousand toils, have gained
this point of vantage, smell   the ground!

soil is of the matter, and the smallest king of an eye is the largest thing on a
dollar bill   SPEND IT, you fools   And she sd, make me a mysterious
statue

And we did this, incommmerotionofhim, walking as the wind went,
with only blood for a thread

So we have it—Alkinoos, and three blind lice (In
whose chamber?) (You want to know? Honest-to-gawd? Well, rustle that
ivory drapery   And put your hand on that stucco   Let your eye be as light
is, westering, on brick   Only hold on tight to your mast   musk is a fragrance which earth hath

make yr Lady a posy   she's sweet

⊷ 146 ⊶

Washington to Woodward
2 March 1950 (postmark)

thursday—yr letter just
come

frances:
        the truth is, you do have a whale on yr hands, with one fin gone, and
all blind   trouble is, he can't put his flukes down on you, and pin
you   For a whale knows what it is not to be a whale: that's what nature gave
him that hell of a hard wall of a head for   After all, even in their screwin'
whales are long, and their seasons on the line are yearly, reiterative

o frances
baby, i'm not playin   images are my business   And i believe in holding   Otherwise there ain't any   Funny thing is, I must have anticipated
this letter of yours, for I got up to write you today one fact, got up to try to impress on you a piece of information i should be surprised if you would include
in your calculations (I forget it myself)   It is this: it was just five years ago
january 1st, that i took up my business   I was already 34 yrs old when I put
aside all the monkey business i had been busy with   I believe in the way I
did it, but one does not learn a craft except in the practice of it   And it takes
time, time   And I need not add the pressure of death, when one practices
a trade of the breath like verse   Only in these months since tarrytown have i
had the necessary boldness, the thing one earns   SO, if I am as stubborn as
a bull whale to stick my ass to a chair, and moo, gnaw, dig with my ears where
the sounds are, it is because I *have* to get on with that which is—so far—a 5
years old baby   (Curious: Lucinda, identical, no?)

And when you write
that you found no reception in you to my tale of Unecho—my lawd, frances,
do you think i do not know what I ask of you? Baby, you are a very great lady,
and I'll go down acting precisely in the dream   But I also know not one of us
is, split second forward, a dream (1) why should you tolerate another epigon?
(2) with yr vision, which is protestant, why should you include the catholic in
me? (3) how can letters, which are as crucial to me as poems, be so fertile to
you as act? (4) who but a totally aware god damned fool like olson should ask
you to extend such a precious concept as 18th dynasty sib to include a bro.?
Etc. Etc. For there was layer on layer of exaction in that letter monday, and i
felt it, but i believe in you, believe in the size of this thing, will, in the fact of
all coming events, so believe, and shall act (this is the hardest belief of all). But
you *must*, frances, never, never forget, one thing: I know what the hell i am
asking you to put up with.

These are the kind of weeks like I imagine those weeks of Rimbaud were
when he was there in the family barn muttering out the season in hell.
Words—my god, when I think of the presumption of the notion that action is
more ultimate than words! I know action. I know what it means to take the
body and throw it (for let no one be fooled, action is motor, is, at heart, dance,
when it is high, when it steps off from merely pushing other people around,
when it is more than the mere expression of power). But this other thing, this
desperate job, this business of words, words, words, this hammering of oneself out on the anvil of oneself, this taking up of faith in exclusion and privacy,
with no other human being but oneself, this stopping before the acts of personality, flesh, action, and keeping them all in there, in that receptacle, language—well, it's not simple; and what *is* the answer to Rimbaud's becoming
a gun-runner for Menelik?

I've got a poem I want to try to re-write. And there is no coal to be had in this city—and I with no more than 3 shovelfuls left! But I do not like to leave you, even tho you felt as you do as long ago as Tuesday, even tho that wild letter of mine has intervened, & you are too rich to dwell in pain. For I should like (1) to woo you to trust letters now. And I should like (2) to engage this catholic question you raise.

Of 1, what more can I say? I can only ask you.

Of 2, that's big, also. (It is strange, that both the protestant and the semite want Christ alone. The catholic *is* another way.) But I think the truth lies elsewhere—(i don't mean the truth which Dostoevsky sd, if it were proven Christ and it were different, he'd stay with Christ!)

What I mean is, the shift which makes possible new culture, new history, new life, is a shift of the point of vantage. (You have me on: objectism!) This Stryzgowski, for example. I have not yet read yr book. I can feed on what you give me. But wow! darling, what you do give me in his concepts! Jointed to the economics my pal Brooks Adams offers in "The New Empire", it is straight beautiful sculpture!

Darling, this is a note, just to tell you, just to tell you
love,
Charles

≪ 147 ≫

Woodward to Washington
[2 March 1950]

early Thursday—A.M.

Charles dear—
My violently unhappy reaction to your letter about Gianpietro is something I am afraid to touch because it is very explosive—I do and can say this:
I *hate* all sense of participation in the crucifixion—my reaction to man's gloating over the crucifixion is Nietzsche's. I believe man can be joined to man not in an onanistic ceremony like the communion service (is the Mass the part of the Catholic service where you are offered the bread and wine in remembrance of the Last Supper—what I call "Communion"?) but in what Olson is and stands for—in battling to free his imagination forward into new cleaner more exact formulations. I have loved you because you have seemed to me the most courageous, spiritual, clean man alive whom I could see—I believe all

men should come up out of *past* pictures into future ones and to hear Olson saying he had a beautiful sense of understanding over a ceremony any kind of ceremony just plunges a dagger into me—I am sure I have somewhere misunderstood the whole point—I am sure the wound was erased and that is something precious to me—but Olson when you use words like commemoration—I want man to do exactly as you described in your essay you sent to *Imagi*—to have the humilitas to know the secrets objects share.

I am against Melville's Hebraism when he echoes Ecclesiastes—I do not believe all is vanity—it is not vanity for a woman to dedicate her life to trying to break the frightful bonds of her flesh and to love a man not for what he gives to her but for what he is—with no self—no possessiveness—I believe that is a very great step forward and I believe with Blake that every *eternal* action of man constitutes a brick whereby he builds a vision that will at last *break* the flesh apart—and allow man to *live* in the spirit daily—every day—

"Who does not fight will remain unhealed" how many fighters are there, Olson? Do you know beyond yourself and myself other real fighters? I hope you do—I do not.

Beloved Charles perhaps I am making myself unhappy for no reason—I surely have gone off somewhere wrong—because my Olson could never turn T.S. Eliot on me—

◄§ 148 §►

Woodward to Washington
[3 March 1950]

Dearest dearest Charles—the suffering that is involved in trying to live alive, to perceive and act according to perception, that is burning the flesh off my bones—

And dear darling man who is exhausted from having given out so greatly—your intellect is not suddenly weakening[70]—the Nabokov quote in its full meaning could not come across out of context—I put it in for the thing about Shakespeare and the sentence about God hiding and man finding and the next paragraph which makes sense in the book and not out of it I included because of the phrase about the two men being unable to kiss one another, one a poet and the other a philosopher because "p. and p. are accustomed to think of words as being superior to deeds"—and I had a childish glee in this—since I remembered your letter "what *is* the answer to the existence of creatures like

---

70. Boldereff is replying to Olson's letter of 28 February 1950, in which he expresses puzzlement about the Nabokov quotations in her letter of 26 February 1950.

us—who would sacrifice anything, anybody, to get the words down, not the acts, the words."

And I said that Nabokov was that afternoon dispelling the Russian dream—by his *whole* book—and what it proved, namely, that quality in and of itself is something the present regime is the enemy of—because if you can prove to me that a man or a nation hates quality, then I become an enemy at once, since that word comprises my whole faith. What D. H. L. means when he speaks of "resistance-power."

And so—in the first paragraph as I had been thrilled because my big beautiful Olson was giving of his beautiful beautiful self *out* in public, where someone could perhaps grasp and take in to pass on—I was in addition, excited "No. 2 why"—because as well as being important here—he is now possibly the only such giver out of beauty on this small globe—i.e., if the Russians are not pursuing a real valid dream, then there is nowhere to look but in America, the place I so am ill of, and quite possibly the whole thing centers in my baby—*now* can you understand why I got violently sick and wept for one whole day when I thought my baby was turning catholic on me?

≈§ 149 ≈

Woodward to Washington
3 March 1950 (postmark 4 March 1950)

                                          Friday

Charles dear—

A fine human is a complicated affair—each part of a sentence one writes has so many ancestors—known to myself only—I will jot down most briefly several notations because I love you and because I believe that in addition to being useful to one another we also wish to be known to one another. For my part anyway, I wish to know about you and for you to know about me and then swiftly I hope to come to the part I want to say which is important.

These are little things—just to tell you—on the night I wrote I was throwing in Christ out of courtesy—out of courtesy to my past, man's past, you, etc. When I said I want no brothers—I was not thinking of Gianpietro and not even of Olson—I meant—in general—for man—I do not want to think of him with brothers—I said on purpose—(I could see you smiling and you low down dog—stole it from me 'hath the advantage'—in this case and how can I prove?) that I was a great lone bull whale—for that night I was adrift in the great chaos alone—and I could not entertain the thought of *anyone's* having a brother or a savior or an opposite sex or an anything—just alone—in the primeval void—this is a very fierce deep necessity in me—and personally I do not understand it because maybe you have but I have never known in a woman other than myself such a recurrent passionate demand for starkness for the separate alone, pitted and grim and precisely whole—maybe there are other women who have it but I have never known any myself—all the women I ever knew who liked to tramp around in woods and stuff alone or spider-hunt or that kind of thing were defaulted somewhere in their sex—it was a minus thing—but mine seems to be without reference—I remember in Iowa when I was literally suffering a form of insanity because of that whole school episode I have told you so little about—I kept wondering and wondering—how did it ever come about that man invented houses—who can live in a house and every night as I lay in my bed I suffered physical agonies from having the great high 14 ft brick ceilings and walls close down slowly and crush me—and it kept happening night and night—anyway that eagle thing in me which wants no mate, no companion, no babies, no prey, no nothing—just the blue and Motz wheeling the great slow grim wheel of beauty—I am sure you have a deep enough soul to imagine what anguish and suffering I have paid because of that need. I feel certain it is spiritual—some section of the spiritual *is* where I share with Melville et al. N'est-ce pas? If you have another explanation—it is O.K.—you can state it.

The part of your letter which knocked hell out of me, still does—I really do want to wait until I see you because for this once I feel sure it really is a matter of a misunderstanding and of semantics—your quote of Eckhart[71]—you see I feel Eckhart is my boy—I am German—old—with all their *very* faults but the same cold, ice-cold *form* and I feel Eckhart is *known* to me—I could be absolutely wrong but my *feeling* is he is mine—so I *feel* I understand what he is saying. Now if I believe anything I believe Olson knows how to read—so, Eckhart is his—so, when you quote Eckhart and put a meaning in the words I feel to be crazy—to be just plain insane—then the ground begins to give way and I start to sink and end up by being swallowed. So sometime I will want to know—what *did* those words mean.

Too lazy to look up the quote just now—to proceed—I have been studying medieval catholic thought with love since I have been 20 years old Olson—I mean exactly 20. I know Anselm, Ambrose, Bernard of Clairvaux, St. Francis, Duns Scotus, Eregina, those boys—have read many others, also studied the Scholastics. I probably know them better than you do—because I have of my own volition and without ever speaking of it, studied them very hard for many years—with love—I *am* Bernard—I myself know the 12 steps of humility—I have faith—I do not know whether what you give me to drink is thick oil for the lamp or water—I also sleep on bed of need and order about

71. In Olson's letter of 27 February 1950.

Kings to my faith—I have more than once received from a Catholic eye such a deep look of love and respect and heard—"What a great Catholic you would make—what faith you have—how Catholic is your thought"—and I know in my soul there is walking on the earth today no Catholic whose faith is more grounded—more absolute than mine—mine comes out of "the core of my being"—

But I Olson darling am on a new tack—I see the image created by that first poem I read "Follow fool—" I can not *find* it now Olson when I need it—found it two days ago, but can not now—I never remember lines on purpose anyway one of the images in your first poem you sent me to and it is that feeling—the man who goes quietly through the unspectacular landscape—unspectacularly looking for a new image—*I want that new image.* And I suppose again this is just that old German high blood stuff—the *love* of the unhewn out—the pleasure—and as you say you believe in me baby—so do I, you are the great Kingly stuff—and believe me dear Olson poet, I know somewhere in my blood—by female osmosis—that the word thing *takes* blood as no action can—that is what Motz Knows—why she holds. I also *know* really Know how god damned long it takes to learn how to do one tiny tiny tiny perfect thing. *Know* that. Want to say in parenthesis that my special personal difficulty is—I *believe* in the man's anguish—in the honour of it—but due to my upbringing I am crazed with suffering over my unfaith in the greatness of my part—I believe it is very necessary, I just wish to god I could *feel* it was glorious, because god knows I feel it deserves to be glorious—Christ knows I pay as high a price to stay in there with you as any man has ever paid for any line that has ever been written.

And you are right dear that I am far from dreams—that I am weak of the flesh—that I said (but not the night of the letter—the next day and the next night I said) Connie has his body—and this man has his spirit—where do I fit in—I'm just some damned note-taker—to hell with that—But long before I met you beloved I worked my way up out of the ego routine—so that is one I know how to handle—

I am tired darling—I also am god damned frightened about this future (daily bread) I have taken on—I want to go to bed and rest—but shall we drink darling tonight beloved out of one cup to my Stryzgowski—who has really laid his stuff on the line (I am trying to buy some of the others despite the fact I own precisely 63.43 to my name) and if I find some and can afford will lend you.

And will you look at me with those great Olson eyes and say over again—Always always always trust me—and hear me darling look—I always always do.

Pulse

I never did get to the important part

Washington to Woodward
3 March 1950 (postmark 6 March 1950)[72]

friday

darling—

i just came on this as I was looking for some unpublished verse to ship out

it is notes on Graham Greene's *Heart of the Matter*, which Viking had sent me ahead of publication (was it 2 yrs ago?)

do send it back—but i wanted you to have a kiss, more, an embrace, to ease yr worries abt the old man ever fooling around with that old deck!

P.S.S last lines of recent poem
pss!

And we did this incommemorationofhim,
going as the sea went.
With only blood for a thread.

YES, MAM!   the cassock is
                the cock
                              the OLD MASTER,
                                  he knew!
    just abt everything!

(A reviewer of *y & x* sd recently "olson's myth derives from Jung!"[73]   will ya pay that off!   with his obvious papa written all over him!   god, how ignorant the americans are!   no hope   have to make a new race   no hope, but *Hopis galore*! (damn pen)   AND DON'T WORRY *SO*! my little one!

o

p.s. both the BATTLE BOOK *AND* the Smart[74] will go to you, say, Monday: I have not been able to get out for some days.

[The following notes on Graham Greene's Heart of the Matter *enclosed with this letter were written around 9 June 1948, to be sent to Monroe Engel. The page reference is to the Viking edition, 1948.]*

72. The back of the envelope has a note: "Monday: okay, again. Only regret delay."
73. Kenneth O. Hanson's review of Y&X in *Interim* 3–4 (1949–50) mentions (p. 52) "the influence of Jungian theory."
74. The books reached Boldereff on 22 March 1950. It is not known what is meant by "Battle Book," but the Christopher Smart was presumably the copy of *Rejoice in the Lamb* that Dahlberg had given Olson.

Greene's book has stirred up so many things, and I am, as I think you know, a precise specialist in his matter: "Nul n'est aussi competent que le pecheur (the accent left off is purposeful, here) en matiere de chretiente"! Besides, I was raised in the filthy faith, which is an incubus by day and a succubus by night

but p. 228

G's perceptive sentences of today's fallen experience

Let me put it another way: at 228 Scobie ceases to be interesting just because any Catholic of his range has passed the point which buggers him the rest of the book at aetat 14! To tell the truth, Greene must have missed a crisis with his mother such as Joyce or I had, or he'd never have pitched his book on the problem of Louise-and-Communion. I very much suspect this is true: a further proof is his handling of suicide. (meninger)

G is somewhere arrested psychologically

Scobie's devil of responsibility   S. deeply bred

Ask yourself what is Helen; even though she is as accurate and purely made as Scobie? With that question answered ((there seems to be only two women men can make any more, Candida and Mildred)) it is nonsense to talk of love and its tragedy

((It does not seem to occur to anyone simply to put it, love is not present, and for the same reasons nothing else is present. And to let that be where we stand. It is much more honest, actually is where Scobie and Helen stand until Greene goes wishy on us, as we will, thinking love at least must live. Why should it, when all that should enforce it, reinforce it, all the frames of purpose to existence, are shot to hell?))

((For Greene to raise up that tacky machinery of the Church to measure love is quite, quite horrible, and puts us back, by his sad wish (boy's wish) a thousand years))

EVEN A CATHOLIC WOULD KICK LOUISE SQUARE ON HER PRAT OUT OF BED!
Museyroomofmudandart

Or perhaps I should declare the premise, that any handling of a subject lower than the most intense experience of the same subject the writer knows or can imagine is bound to fail, cf. tragedy. Which, I should say, is the reason why the average, as person, by democratic or proletarian dictation, is not fit vessel for tragedy. I do not mean, of course, that what the world might take to be the meanest, commonest person might not well be made a tragic hero. (Take *Notes from the Underground*, or, for that matter, Bloom). It is only the degree to which he can, in the hands of his maker, be made to exhaust his problem. Scobie is, in the sense that he is a policeman, say, unexceptional. In fact, what gives Greene an unusual power, is, in the other stories, his intimacy with what might be called the common person, and her & his problems. It is precisely because Scobie, I think, is superseded, at the Communion rail, by Greene himself, that Scobie is faulted.

And isn't it a better way of putting the principle of tragedy that, rather than the fall of a prince, it is the fall of a man extraordinary enough to be capable of the proper intensity of his hubris—and that, certainly, does not require trappings but only the aristocracy of spirit which can be born in any man.

⊷ 151 ⊷

Woodward to Washington
4 March 1950 (postmark)

Saturday late afternoon

Olson, sacred to my soul—
    I have spent the afternoon in a healing way you also would love—gathering beautiful firewood left from the storm I described, walking over those meadows beside the stream once all belonging to my grandfather and somehow in a deep way mine—clear beautiful air—so clean and oh! you cannot imagine how lovely is the smell of my Woodward where many people burn wood all winter to keep warm—oh! sweet sweet earth so full of beautiful smells that man has almost destroyed—Woodward that has healed me so many times in the past—the only mother I have ever had.
    I send you a direct quote from Strzygowski

"The Hvarenah Landscape
    "At the very heart of Aryan piety on Iranian soil lay the idea of Hvarenah. Soderblom has shown in his work, *Das Werden des Gottesglaubens*, that it represents the crowning glory of Iran. A comprehensive description of its nature is given in a long hymn in the Aresta. It is connected with the cult of the dead, representing the might and majesty of departed spirits. Hvarenah is the power that makes running waters gush from springs, plants sprout from the soil, winds blow the clouds, *and men come to birth*. It governs the courses of sun, moon and stars. Hvarenah therefore is that which permeates the whole

countryside and particularly the land of Seistara through which the river Helmand flows. To this country, alternately frozen and parched by drought, water forms the very pulse of life and is full of a mysterious beneficent potency. 'O water, to him who sacrifices to thee vouchsafe thy glory!' Hvarenah, created by Mazda, is the power that makes the waters rise from the world-ocean. From Hvarenah the sun derives his strength. If the 'mighty immortal Sun with swift steeds illuminates and warms' if it purifies earth and water and banishes the evil demons of darkness, it is from Hvarenah that such magic influence comes. Even so are moon and stars endowed with power and fulfilled with majesty.

"Were such ideas expressed in art, we should expect to see a barren landscape, above it the sun with his swift steeds, below it the world-ocean etc.

"Are there such landscapes? If so, they would not be representations in the strict sense, but compositions pieced together out of the elements enumerated above, mere symbols of nature, devoid of realism. Other artistic treatment could hardly be looked for in Iran. I thus find myself on the track of a kind of Asiatic landscape, originating in religion, or rather in a philosophy of the universe, and based upon significance and form, not, like the landscapes of the Southern peoples, upon actual objects exactly reproduced."

I add one fact, Olson, which I state quietly—in such landscapes Jesus was given standing on red clouds. You will recall my vision—the redness—and the barrenness of the landscape. I reproduced exactly what I saw—although in my natural life I do not remember ever to have seen a red nightfall (pink clouds, rosy air—that is different—this was not at all like rosy—I wish I could paint). And you know I had not read this at the time of writing the vision. I mention this as a fact which quietly overwhelms me.

I might also say if you go to Italy where one of these mosaics remains I hope you will see the Jesus—the clouds do not represent rising into heaven in glory or anything like that—they are precisely stage stuff—to point up the vast distance between Him and the other figures. He looks so *man*—stern— Lawrence would have loved him—male although like all that Byzantine stuff, no sex nor naturalism.

Frances

◄§ 152 §►

Washington to Woodward
7 March 1950 (postmark)

tuesday

frances:

i should like to be extremely gay to you today, to make like a trovador   for it is the only answer i know to trrobb-les

for i am, i suppose, a Cino, a scamp (what are poets but valves, crockery-breakers, "slayers"—full of loud laughter, men of bad teeth!)   i have to bear down so hard on all that passes through me, language is all one earns, and language has to run—cockatrice, o cockolly!

alas, the light-hearted!   i am no hero, nor no saint   is it not one of nature's ironies, that these carriers, these bearers, are not what their words are? (or are they?)

i give you, play, lady!   i give you, dance, lady: WOIDS! O, the SUN![75]

So i'm sure i misuse yr Eckhart, (yr echt-heart) And i'm sure you're pure catholique (which i am not, who am nothing but hermetique!) (O! Strzygowski, stir-this-coff-ski, my little Afghan hound)   O brothers, he cried, who, after a thousand toils, have reached this point of vantage, smile, bro., smile ((Wipe that grin off youse face, sd the Pope, P—on the Pope, Pach-elli, Pace-jelly, Pox-Pope, Vox-Pop))

"He-Who-Runs-Away-To-Play-Another-Day was one of the names of that Omaha chief who is also known in history as Great Jump Puss   He was one of the founders of that curious Indian society known as the Backward Boys   It was a special Plains society, of which the members did everything including the carrying of a lance and the riding of their horses, backwards."

"It was rumored that, and it is now thought that, there were hidden sexual motivations to this strange behaviour. It is true, all Indian life, particularly that of the Plains Indians of North America, exhibits a violence which the modern mind cannot, now it has acquired the proper tools, avoid seeing as repressive in origin. It is only now beginning to be clear, for example, that the war-whoop, which seemed, to the early settlers to be only a device of what we would now call "psychological warfare" was, in truth, nothing but an obvious sign of Indian arrestment at a pre-Oedipean level. We are beginning now to do adequate research into this interesting orality."

I remember that day, it was so many, many years ago, when spring was on me so—it was a Sunday afternoon, April, perhaps, and I had persisted in sitting alone on the grass, when my two friends had insisted I come in and be

---

75. From this point on, this letter was recast to become the poem "The Morning News" (see *Collected Poems*, pp. 118–25).

present when they entertained their girls at cocktails. But here is the point: when I did come in, I was so caught in the afflatus of Aprilis with her arrowes sweete, that I sat plump down between the two ladies and took them both in my arms! At which point—and since that day—those two buddies have been consistently but hiddenly, mine enemies!

   ((God damn this flu. During that last para, I suddenly have got sick to my stomach.   (And who shall say,
it is not possibly, like that old Indian chief,
p-sy-kick   who'll
deny

to this brief vigil of our senses, knowledge

of the unpeopled world

inside us—or behind the sun—O!

Armourer of the Hold?)

I, too, wear,

the Visored Face

                                   (Look! look! where the blood

has ceased to run

in the collapsed veins.

                                   O Doctor, Doctor!

do not, do not pour in

more air!)

We are such trembling vapors as

trains are run on. Do not count

the telegraph poles.

                                   (Hold! Hold!

O Amoreur!

This is the day of no light, this is the day, the gray day. When she passes, re-member, to tip yr hat.

Wear yr hat,

with a difference.

If you can bounce high, bounce for her,

too, until she cry, "Lover,

gold-hatted, high-bouncing lover,

I must have you

        you who have stayed—at the oar-locks

Ore-
looks! O'erlooks, what
desolation!
        "I cannot stand
yr new
civilization!"   (What a shot
                            that
                            was!)

If you would look, look now.
Or you'll never see its like again.
For the rails are layed down,
and even the engine
has got its steam up.
Don't, Pearl,
lay yrself across the tracks.

And he shot across the sea
put a belt round the earth
before the Supreme Court sd,
Dred Scott!

The sun sat there like a great squash,
the two of them squshed me
with their spread fat asses: who the hell are they to say

this is going to be a great

DAY!

        And we used to do it,
        at dawn on the deck,
        and toss the bucket overboard,

dawdle-ing it a couple of times (the bucket)
to be sure it was clean

What I remember most,
is the smell of Shea's
tobacco, and his talking,
before breakfast, of
"Kunrudd", as he prounounced it,
"Kunrudd".

It was Red Flaming who sd,

desolation. (He was, with all his strength,

one of the Boys.)

But

CAN YOU TELL A DAWN WHEN YOU SEE ONE?

"Aw, a pox a lips! Gimme no more of yr

JAW!

Put a tackle on it! It's
hangin', son

What he meant was, the chin. And it is already clear, to Fenichel and others, that when the chin is large, there's been too much eating going on, even though it can just as well be self-satisfying as actual cannibalism.

"This is now so apparent that there is no longer any need to study any further the institution, among the tribes, of what can be called Saint Stephen's rite. Stephen is interesting as the founder, as the first one to see how necessary it was to a hunting society that there be a masticatory image that the people might understand what they were doing with their daily lives. But like so much else of the late Metastatic culture . . .

We break off the musical part of the program to bring you a

special news bulletin:

"CIBOLA

has

FALLEN!

The Anthropophagi

ARE IN COMPLETE RETREAT!"

And now the poet has a word for you,

to ease yr minds:

THE POET: "O! seven cities,

        that made this country great,

        whose skies, *profumo*, blotted out the sun!

        o, Smog

        who once so poisoned all our children that

        they opened out, *colombo*, every West!

        deny not now, as you lie down,

        (o, Cain!)

        your glorious

        wrongs!

We bring you now, before we settle down, before we cease,

the HANDSOME SAILOR!

(*Crowd noises:*

   "sesquepedalian   sesquepedalian   sesquepedalian"

"HE stutters!

    EAT 'm!

EAT 'm!

no, citizens,

no

(*musical bridge*:

"This is, this is,

the NEW Da-Y!"

And they cuffed him.

And our tears

were as gold.

"It is cold, here.

You must go out and bring in

some old wood.

There is much to be done"

And we obeyed her,

because she was

our mother.

hi! motz: i cured my stomach   but now i must eat   it's been all afternoon   i guess one can only sing songs in the evening, to charm a proper
lady!

love

pssst: remember, you sd yu'd yell if and when you needed dough—63.63 don't
sound like much to me! Wot in 'ell you gonna do, ba-bee?

Woodward to Washington
[7 March 1950]

[*letterhead:*] THE CARROLLTOWN NEWS

> Carrolltown, Pa.
> Frances Boldereff
> Book Design Layouts

Now you little Olson—don't you go getting excited—I don't know any more
about what this means than you do—Frank just wrote to me and asked me to
design him a letterhead which could be used two ways—with and without
my name and gave me the copy as he wanted it to read!! (love the design without my name and I am not going to use them myself—embarrasses me). This
is as you say darling a funny funny country—you would love as I have always
loved the nutty Carrolltown News—who never remember to send bills—
who did any favor asked no matter how enormous—who buy any beautiful
type face or any expensive paper no matter how small the job and who drive
around the country despite all their ungrasping ways in beautiful sleek con-
vertibles and the elder of whom (died suddenly four months ago) once drove
to my house in State College one evening—unloaded gifts for 1/2 hour—
handed me a huge paper bag full of sourballs and said "Here, here's something for your kid!" and then with a funny face said "I want to give this to
you—I grew it myself"—a lovely rose—and when it quietly became clear
that I was not in the market for a lover said quietly "You are a wonderful
woman, Frances," and sat out in my kitchen until almost dawn drinking
whiskey and talking to me about Rembrandt and never resented at all that I
gave him no response. Nutty nutty family and I love them dearly. All terrific
Russian drunks who work like demons in their plant. One more story which I
love (told you before?) one summer in the late afternoon Dennis Hammond
was sitting in the bay where I eat, typing, shirt sleeves—Georgie drew up in
his automobile as long as my house front and steps out and into my house (do
not think he had ever been here before uninvited) and stepping inside the
door looks at Dennis and asks "Where's Frances?" and Dennis said "She's off
at a dinner party in the country side somewhere" (true) and Georgie said
"Who are you?" and Dennis said, "I'm her brother" and Georgie said, "So am
I" and jammed on his hat and went home.

This started out to be a very serious letter but first—want to say I picked up
the beautiful lines the first time darling—when they were written out like

prose in that wild wild letter[76]—didn't mention them not because I didn't jump out of my chair, but because I did—like *La Chute I*, these lines are mine, whatever and however much they may ever mean to anyone else—they are my procedure stated to me in Olson's terrific original beauty accurate as all hell as usual.

Dearest here begins a summary—

Ahab and the Carpenter

"Cursed be that mortal sister—indebtedness which will not do away with ledgers. I would be free as air; and I'm down in the whole world's books. I am so rich, I could have given bid for bid with the wealthiest Praetorians at the auction of the Roman empire (which was the world's); and yet love for the flesh in the tongue I bring with."

Ahab and Starbuck

Let the owners stand on Nantucket beach and outyell the typhoons. What cares Ahab? Owners, owners? Thou art always prating to me, Starbuck, about those miserly owners, as if the owners were my conscience. But look yet, the only real owner of anything is its commander;"

The Quadrant

"and cursed be all the things that cast man's eyes aloft to that heaven. . . . Level by nature to this earth's horizon are the glances of man's eyes; not shot from the crown of his head, as if God had meant him to gaze on his firmament."

The Candles

"Oh! thou clear spirit of clear fire, when on these seas I as Persian once did worship, till in the sacramental act so burned by thee, that to this hour I bear the scar; I now know thee, thou clear spirit, and I now know that thy right worship is defiance. To neither love nor reverence wilt thou be kind; and e'en for hate thou canst but kill; and all are killed. No fearless fool now fronts thee. I own thy speechless, placeless power; but to the last gasp of my earthquake life will dispute unconditional, unintegral mastery in me. In the midst of the personified impersonal, a personality stands here. Thou but a point at best; whenceso'er I came; whereso'er I go; yet while I earthly live, the queenly personality lives in me, and feels her royal rights. But war is pain and hate is woe. Come in thy lowest form of love, and I will kneel and kiss thee; but at thy highest, come as mere supernal power; and though thou launchest navies of full-freighted worlds, there's that in here that still remains indifferent. Oh,

___

76. Boldereff is referring to the three lines quoted in Olson's letter of 3 March 1950, previously found in his letter of 28 February 1950.

thou clear spirit, of thy fire thou madest me, and like a true child of fire, I breathe it back to thee.

"There burn the flames! Oh, thou magnanimous! now I do glory in my genealogy. But thou art but my fiery father; my sweet mother, I know not. Oh, cruel! What has thou done with her? There lies my puzzle;" . . .

"What hast thou done with her?"

That mother country for whom the unborn are searching.

Olson, beloved,—here in Melville I find as in graded steps, the clear outlines of the credo by which these new people must come to birth,

1. All men are part and parcel of each other.

2. So the flesh cannot be owner; owner is the commander—the one who descries material for his tongue in the mouth of another.

3. The flesh was wrapped about us precisely so that we should observe here—so that we are forced to act in the here—to see the action only here—where I admit and see and act the fact that my tongue is formed from Connie's breast.

4. That whatever lies behind, whatever it may be, is one thing for sure—an aristocrat who expects proud separate strong defiance—of the pain, of the unknowledge, of the moving. That the existence of a separate, recognizable form is the goal—for each—

The dance as thy lady moves to it.

❧ 154 ❧

Woodward to Washington
8 March 1950 (postmark 9 March 1950)

Wednesday night

Charles darling—

I remember when Lucinda was a tiny baby I noticed that babies always look at you to see if you meant to hurt them before they start to cry! If they discover no look of insult then they bear their troubles without notice and smile at you. Like a baby, I now look at you, darling, to see, does your letter mean to hurt me—are you some way making fun of me because I have been wrong or not adequate? I only hope not darling because in a world where you have everything else to carry I should hate to have added one smallest fraction of unpleasant or unhappy.

Your letter bothers me terribly darling it sounds so very unhappy and oh! my darling for you to be ill and unhappy is something I cannot bear. I try not ever to think of your health because I have noticed several things that frighten hell out of me—I simply can not imagine existing without you darling—and when you're so vulnerable I can not stand it. I don't see why you have to live in the terrible climate of Washington when you so need sun—whatever you do darling—I will come as near as you want me—is there no other place with a great library where you could work?

I mentioned the money business only to show you that when I say feeling my way in the dark—trusting my instinct—that is really so—and that I do not jump when the devil says jump—

I love Ahab—and now for me—the whole thing assumes this meaning— he does not lose because he is wrong—or evil—or desiring vengeance—he loses only because Nature—the world created—its I am—has a head of white whale hardness and it is going to take many boats and many lives before man breaks through fact—before he can wrench his life into the shape he dreams—when Blake says "Oh Son! how unlike the Father" that is part of it. I now conceive *Moby Dick* to be my personal banner—every word seems written to us now—

Oh! darling your letter causes such pain in me—I remember Ahab saying to himself how he wished he could argue his own soul into belief as he has argued those of his men.

Dear Charles—please write to me at once—it is so very long before letters get answered and tell me angel you are alive and that the terrible unbearable pain has a little passed over.

Frances

You know dearest I can not stand prayer—the idea of it—and I have no way at all to take care of you—please my angel try to find some answer about your heart and throat and all that that is so hard for you—

And I beg of you to write to me as soon as you receive this—do not make me wait until Monday.

And you beautiful Charles with the warmest kindest smile ever seen that you so freely give to many—with so much love—you are so much more

❧ 155 ☙

Woodward to Washington
9 March 1950 (postmark)

Thursday 1:10 pm

Charles darling—

I do not know what is the matter with me—why do I love Woodward so much? I can see there isn't anything specially beautiful and all the houses are ugly and the people are almost animals—but still remains that I love it with every fibre—the wind blows harder today than I have ever felt it—the way it must be on the ocean sometimes—no beast or man is out—only dear little birds trying to find food—

why also do I love Charles so much? how have you stolen into all my blood and being until I can claim nothing but my mistakes as my own—everything else is Charles.

The plan darling for the next few months is this way—I am going to stay here until Lucinda finishes school for this year—May some time—if I get paid for the two jobs I am doing I will be able to live (there are two others pending which would make me rich!) if I do not get paid I will do something about it when the time comes. I have proposed a plan to Frank Hipps at Carrolltown—do not know whether he accepts or rejects, but if he accepts I think I shall be doing something I love—if not, I will take a job in the library at State College and do free lance stuff of which there is always a certain amount there to pick up—*because* I want to buy a little house in Woodward—cannot explain it to anyone—but all the winds of the world could blow over me if I lived in a house built by my grandparents for one of their millers—I want Lucinda to be in a Quaker school—the only decent ones existing today and I am quite willing to eat bread and water to see that she gets there.

Dearest beautiful Charles—you have no idea with what hunger I would like to be a poet just for this once—to write you a love poem—I am so enamoured of the beauty of these lines

And we did this incommemorationofhim
going as the sea went.
With only blood for a thread.

God I love them.
I am sure Christ loves you as deeply as I do.

Frances   xxxxxxx

⤞ 156 ⤝

Washington to Woodward
9 March 1950 (postmark)

thursday

that's another beautiful letter i have just read,[77] my little motz-potz: beautiful from the paper its written on, from the proud commander's flag it flies, all the way thru to its last, & leading words, frances moves to the dance: it is another nobilisime visione, 2nd only to the o-cock,—and the moving thing is, to me, that "dat Old Man" is yr text, that Old Man whose words you have again opened my eyes to and

I *am* happy that my violent little poem was a letter to you (it is out now (IN-TERIM) under a title I like: "A Po-sy, A Po-sy"

(Add 2nd: "The Morning News", which is out, to GLASS HILL)

Shall we both clench the lightning chains, and pray up to that papa, that they won't come back before lead has been melted for them in—what's the name of that pot you people use?

(The bouncing back, by the way, has a little bit ceased, except for the PRO-verse, which little tom cole (cold, tom's a-cold) just couldn't understand—it made me capable of shaking my fist in his puss, that he had the gall to say he liked part 3!—and thot the section of the typewriter was good, only, olson, don't forget punctuation, and how important that is to sound-effects! jeezus, the little dung-heaps, as Dahlberg used to say, on which editors put their god damned pipe-stem legs, and talk me down as I stand on the ground!)

it's out again—I have discovered the only thing to do with rejections is to fire them right back out there the day they come in. Or one gets covered with one's own pigeon dust; this time, hopelessly, to Poetry (haha) New York—my "friend" fjelde, who has, to this writing, never taken a goddamned thing, including Kingfishers, and, I suppose, the Spoilers, which he now also has)

(but what I thot you'd be interested to know—only, of course, as i am, for print's sake—Laughlin has, for the 1st time, taken an olson: The Praises will appear in New Directions Xii, out next december. And I think you know The K's will be in the 1st no. of Montevallo Review. And that Williams so liked the Pound piece he wants to publish it with a piece of his own on he whom he calls, part womrat, part skunk. To be printed as a pamphlet by some guy in Boonton, N.J. Truth is, if Po-sy and the News also didn't lay an egg, the next months would be a little 5 yr celebration of the writing of mr ishmael

his sire, mr melville, has been much in his mind these days   actually just floats, that peculiar unconscious way in which i follow my nose for no apparent good but i have read all the recent works on him, and a miss wright on his use of the

---

77. Olson refers to Boldereff's letter of 7 March 1950, in which she quotes Melville.

bible, and mister chase on him generally, are worth a run thru   Chase, as a matter of fact, has moved me most of any one who ever wrote on melville, including mister olson, who, by the way, as a result of reading chase, reread ishmael (or, as Sam Rosenberg put it, "Call Me Schlemiehl")   it was instructive, 1st time i was ever able to sort of look out of the corner of my eye at it, and say, aw, come on, o, where are you   exceptions: Essex narrative, the economics of whaling, Fact 2, and the Pacific conc. ((the Moses and the Christ, which had been, up to now, heart and head of her, left me unsatisfied: the big moments spread like a dum-dum, don't go in for the kill, clean   and the reason, i think, is because the job they do is the job of verse))

o, well, but chase has put a skylight in, and layed open for all to see, the fine quarter acre of brains which lies below

((yr tale of the Hammond Boys, and yr bay, is pure lovely francesism and sends me, gives me that old rise to the lady who carries her life like a flower, as gay as nature—and who earns her flower by the same turmoil as does. . . . . did the "News" letter carry this turning at the end:

And they cuffed him.

And our tears were as gold.

"It is cold here.

You must go out and bring in some wood.

For there is much to be done."

And we obeyed her,
because she was old,
and our mother.

END
broadcast

(p.s.: i just notice these rimes! didn't know they were there!)

Went out last night for the first time in 12 days! It was risky, maybe, but I wanted to hear Dylan Thomas read his work. He is not, by the way, the Byronic po-et Augustus John made him, but rather a wretched rabbit, fat and seedy on the outside. Quite frightened, I imagine, actually: to have written what he did at 18, and to be still obsessed with one moment of life, age 4½–5, I'd guess, when the world was as fresh and round as his mother (precise, in this case); and with language still all apple and honey, and the only articulation known to him terror & incest, so that his verse is full of burning, of green fire, and of curds and cream—he is Poet in the oldest Child sense, straight from God, with no interposition of man-act. The only chance for him would be if he were a dramatist, for he needs narrative at every point, as a sort of substitute for Ahab's boiled down vertebra. I proposed, like the chump I am, to Karl Shapiro, that Thomas has to be unstable just because he is all language, there is no man there—and, of course, got back only the look i am so well acquainted with, what in Christ's name is Olson talking about. Funny thing is, he is, thomas, an important measure of myself (and Rimbaud is also a fix): I am in love with God, when God makes such genius. I love it like Stendhal loved Mozart (as you told me). And I am so in love with it, and language, that I ask myself, what service are the rest of us. But of course I do like more the thing when the act of man has been necessary as well as the act of God.

(Rimbaud is, of course, different: in a minute I'll set down for you a draft of why. I should never in my life be able to take Rimbaud in my arms. But Thomas— oh! all my old impulse, if I were still that other man who lived in me for so long, would be to take him in my arms! (((Which causes me to say, that here is another of the grandnesses of nature's making of woman: that she can, without that bifurcation which the male is presented with because he is not God, take unto her *any* of nature's creatures   And is it not why man is, at heart, so knowing of coldness and isolation, why he is, god help him, the creator of space?   Is it not because he cannot, with the flesh at least, embrace all things, must fight every instant to keep that vertebra (you call it "maleness") poor Ahab would, in his agony, make a fat out of, to keep that vertebra bone all the way down to the tip of his erect cock?

frances, these are questions, honest questions And it just may be that what I am talking about is quite local to the struggle of a man these days, when the gravest dangers are a pock-a-lips, & yet when it is all pure beginning again, and the place is as raw as rocks, and there is a heave asked which is so austere that only a man slimmed down to the bareness of an integral, to the raw bone of male,

xxxxxx that nausea again, god damn it   jeezus, the toll   i must stop for a minute xxxxxxx

    (and he drank a glass of water)

((((Question: is it possible troubadour meant to find:gold?)))

((trovar-dor))

o frances thank you for
the beauty of yr letter

> i better quit and eat something, &
> tackle the rimbaud, which i'll
> enclose, if it comes off

> charles

'over)
better send this
off: it ain't
shapin, the R,[78]
fast enough   ♀

o, f., o

⇥⇥ 157 ⇤⇤

Washington to Woodward
10 March 1950 (postmark)

friday

frances, tho i can hope my letter to you yesterday will ease your concern, yet yr letter which came today is so full and, in another way, beautiful, that i am going to do what a note can do, tell you that there is one tremendous fact which delivers me from all evil (sort of):   if i can get it down, keep language moving ahead of me, i get over the stiles   And that is a thing you offer me which is so huge that i shall only mention it this once, for fear it will blow away!   You see, frances, you must never in this love again speak disparagingly of yourself as note-taker, as you put it   Good heavens, my lady! *Example*: as you must have gathered from my letter yesterday, that very letter which caused you such concern, issued as something called "The Morning News"   (O frances, to give another person SPEECH! can you imagine anything *more* than that?

the reason i didn't get the rimbaud done for you yesterday was because i came off your letter into something else, and just now, when my eye caught it over the cup of coffee, i kicked myself i didn't value the lines i had already done before i mailed yr letter to include them: so now i do, even tho i am nervous to do

78. Olson's letters of 14 March and 28 March 1950 contain further notes on Rimbaud. No formal essay was completed.

it before the thing is finished   But i want to send you quick some little token, for your letter and your travail. So here they are. Maybe they'll go on today, or another day:

These days
only the telephone men are spurred,
look, at their hips, prepared

There was a time
when singers issued from the hand of God holster and gun,
began their business properly age four,
drew up their language while the world was round
(and sweet as any mother), turned things on their tongue
as milk and honey, and then went out along their growing
full of incest and green fire![79]

i was supposed, this afternoon, to join Thomas in a session at the Institute, to talk about verse   but i decided not to go   i should like to have, but he is shy, and the characters who would be present (the same who heard me on melville) are—as the world is—forward   and i should surely have got my-self into the kind of argument which is too criss-cross to be of use   for thomas, now that i've caught him two nights, and added that to my reading of some years ago, is, for our time, the false poet   i learned last night that the academs. have him pegged as the leader of the "apocalyptic" school   and it ain't far wrong   and you know how i have to clear the situation from these very a-pock-a-lips they are so close to me, and yet they are so wrong (i now think that is why i expressed the amorousness toward him that i did to you yesterday)

it is a terrific problem, this walking a silk thread across canyons (i had a sharp training on the like situation in politics: so much of my vision can be confused, by the lazy and the slobberers, with fascism—Lawrence had a like fate, tho, on the apocalyptic side, he seems to me to have become a fallen angel ((Malraux, by the way, is the devil in this picture, the very devil of the in-tellect, and a very present danger))

so i stay home and take my joy in writing to you

(I have always been in love with that phrase of tennis, foot-fault. To serve these days, and not fault, is a job beyond Job: to give it to man straight and hard (cannon-ball), and get it in, right in the corner, so that he has to be quick, be nimble, to stay in the game himself, wow! what a game (love-forty!)

79. This poem that began as thoughts on Dylan Thomas in the letter of the previous day was expanded and given the title "Gloss" in another typescript (see *Collected Poems*, p. 125).

My quarrel with the Apocks, that blood-tribe neighbor me, is, they dream too easily, they dip themselves too readily in the sensuous. The bones are not there.

when the place is as raw as rock
a man must fight every instant
to keep himself vertebra, bone
from the neck to the tip of his cock

(Ahab
knew)

Man has to acquire his dominion precisely in that environment in which he finds himself. Or he'll not make possible a change. To dream up a change is one thing. But to take the now-steps to move on toward it, that's the under-job the romantics skip. And that's where you put your life in. Right there, spang where you are (one is). (It is a short definition of bone, what structures flesh. My senses love to race too, as does my spirit, to take this mortality and to throw it, ahead. But the fable requires two: the tortoise as well as the hare.

((this, by the way, is a more pertinent fable than that powdered one, of the angel and the beast sowed in man's hide, that Renaissance notion. Or, for that matter, the formulation, life is a protest raised up against death. Bah.: man is a protest raised up against himself. For he is, as swiftly changing as his cells are, constantly moving in and out of death, shuffling off, am i, this instant, like a snake, skins and skins of death, to offer you—my life!

(It is why I fight for speech, for others. ART-iculation. ACT-ivate.   two: the hair and the porpoise, what is on our heads and pelvis, and what moves like light on the sea. These are man's speeds, for him to calibrate, while he can. It is much more interesting than, self-expression. Ahab was full stop. The advantage: a hair is sufficient bridge across to another. I can be a porpoise, and still communicate. (There are electric eels!)

((It suddenly occurs to me: Lawrence! That impeccable thing, the last thing, called "The Flying Fish". He must have understood. How separate he leaves 'em where they are, doing their job in their environment.

Trouble is, the sweet man had to make up a mystique, for some reason, out of the light in us & in nature. My impression is, the sex struggle kept him cranky. And made him want a quick dream, for balm. (This develops,

by the way, from yr observation, he was sick,
and it led death more in than the power of his
protests lets most people see. His verse, if you
look at it, discloses this, poignantly.)

Yes, these Thomases, John Thomases, put me to it to keep myself clear of them. And it is just as much of a struggle for clarity where the values and problems of verse are concerned. For they also know the voice is the clue. Only the dream and the flesh of 'em softens the voice, uses it too slackly for the likes of me. The give-away, to my ears, is their need for narrative. It is a ballad that always makes them look best ((Lawrence's best poem, i think, is a thing called "Whether or Not", is written in that Mellors dialect, "tha be coont", and is story; Thomas Dillon the same: "The Burning Boy" is better than the verse)). Narrative is an outside structure. (It is like a mystique—or a Revelation, serves the same function in art that the mechanics of description of the City of God does in morality.) It is, in some subtle way, a substitution for the act by a man of the making of himself as the form of his own objectification. ((I am hammering here at the same idea the piece on PRO-verse was after: to stay in the struggle for open verse as against closed, in order to arrive at forms which come not from the outside, inherited or—the better—the narrative, but from the inside, from the working along with the self and the stuff in the open until some form comes out of it which is fresh and implicit to the-thing-needed-done itself.))

Forgive me, darling, for this turgid passage. I am still fumbling my way forward in it. (I share a bachelor-button with you: K. O. Hanson, in his review of *y & x*, says: "Mr. O is interested in the poem rather than the figure, the pattern rather than 'the pretty speech'".) (It is the next sentence I was after: ". . . (he is) concerned with the unique experience of each poem."))))

I'm going to move over now. This is a note. And you understand, don't you, frances, that these words and these letters are only possible because they are kisses, signs of love?

                                                                    charles

~ 158 ~

Woodward to Washington
10 March 1950 (postmark)

                                                                    Friday morning

Raduga moiya—[80]

There are moments in this house in Woodward when you are here so tangibly that upstairs would be much further away than you are—I put out my hand to touch your knee—I wish to tell you now as my man—as a burden I have, to make it better by telling—do you know in this day of thug behavior how difficult it is to rear a child?

There is no help from anywhere—the school—companions—air—all breathe off something so cheap—the child learns only impudence—impoliteness—disobedience—unappreciativeness—has terrible physical energy—and all turned against you—the only one who is making an attempt to shape something. There are days when I could dump my daughter in a rain barrel—this is the only time when I see how impossible it is to rear a child without a father (not that there are any real fathers around) she should be beaten or coerced or something very hard for the next several years—please do not believe I allow her to act like a barbarian but oh Charles what terrible terrible uphill work to act like a man—to bring that form alive—(without a man's emotional physical detachment.) When you speak of new race I think oh! I wonder if he has any idea how hard it is—how alone one is today when one tries. That is, in the flesh.

See a terrible terrible deep parallel between my Blake and your Melville— I think their speech is the same—and I now am sure that out of this worthless mess we have here we must somehow bring what they asked of us. And I believe the coming engine with its steam up is desirable—let the whole rottenness fall—let there be nothing at all but ruins—it will be cleaner and then perhaps ten will be persuaded that *all* of it should have been cast aside—and in the emptiness it will be clear there was only one living voice—the voice of my man Olson.

Darling I am simply terrible—I get book lists from New York—I passionately look through each time—if there is no Olson—I get sick, I throw it away, I think—there's nothing interesting there—I now only only can eat my Olson—anything else is of any flavor.

You who have stayed at the oarlocks. Today I am in that mood that Olson could ask four times as hard as anything up to here and all I would do is nod—and nod and say Yes yes yes to you whatever you ask I would rip my flesh straight down through the middle again and again for my baby who deserves everything not only from me but from all.

And I do not write not knowing—I remember over and over the passionate thing in the Bible

"And I John saw these things, and heard them. And when I had heard and

80. Russian: "rainbow mine."

seen, I fell down to worship before the feet of the angel which showed me these things.

"Then saith he unto me, See thou do it not. For I am thy fellow servant, and of thy brethren the prophets, and of them which keep the sayings of this book. Worship God."

and in the quietness I the Motz know that if you were taken from me I would have to go on alone—so I walk

Frances

❦ 159 ❧

Woodward to Washington
11 March 1950 (postmark 13 March 1950)

Saturday night

Charles dear—

Your Thursday Friday letters seem to me to ask a question which goes deeper even than poetry—it is fundamental to life—do you plot a dream—or do you wear the skin off your flesh finding one new peg with which to aerate the furnace?

I love Jesus precisely because in himself he seems to me to have been an actual bridge—you could ride up the past, come to the gorge, hop off, walk over Jesus' acts (words) and get on, now in the future. Big stuff—done with as few words as *Season in Hell*. Want you to spell out for me in very prose simple thought your whole response to Rimbaud—every smallest shade of your emotion or thought is important to me because I so love Rimbaud.

On Thursday when you were talking of Dylan Thomas I listened to you out of respect for Olson—and I thought, well, a man has to be generous, he can't live absolutely alone and if Olson is generous to Williams—Thomas—Yeats etc etc let him be—but *I* am not obliged to love them.

I love the wording of the question in the Thursday letter "Is it not because he can not with the flesh at least embrace all things, must fight every instant to keep that vertebra bone all the way down to the tip of his erect cock?" You know Olson you had my answer long ago in my notebook—stated very definitely—a man is useless if he doesn't do this—anywhere—on any level—and the idea of a poet without it is just 20th century mush. I was thinking in bed last night (just because you said "quite local to the struggle of a man these days . . . . when it is all pure beginning again and the place is as raw as rocks—") that even at culture summit, Mozart, Leibnitz—man as male has always always had to do this, *only* in an age more in form it was taken for granted—the aristocratic form was assumed and prizes passed out accordingly and women of use accordingly because the primacy of man's cock as the spiritual image par excellence, because it is outside him and irrevocably bound up with his welfare (a perfect image of the life paradox—the "each is part and parcel of all" with the absolute aloneness), was known and acted on without comment or discussion—that is what made the rich *flow*. Read *Sir Patrick Spens* the terrific impact of those genuine old ballads is not the narrative—it is exactly what you say—keeping the bone down to the very tip of the cock all the way from the back of the neck. And it was all communicated again and again by a nod—a gesture even smaller—an eyelid—

In bed on Monday morning in Tarrytown I remember saying that I did not think my life act from the standpoint of eternity specially noteworthy—I remember saying—"it is the next half-step up." and oh! Charles you know what I have endured to bring into actual being that outline—the actual outline of the look of the step to place the foot on next. All men and woman have been dreaming for 10000 years of the day when the sexes shall be no more—but for myself I have struggled to find that way that *with* the very present sex we now have to remove the thorn of it—and I am sure in your great soul that you realized that the 1-2-3-4 steps in the Melville comment letter represented for me at last that open ground—where I can honestly say to myself the sting is now removed—not only for me—but for any who care to get rid of it.

So my answer to you about you—about the poet—*has* to be what you do, what you are—10000 years—10000.[81] Indeed so—I am only ashamed that you should be surrounded with no man your equal—it is a very painful business and darling do not laugh at your little Motz who is trying so very hard to act like a man to be there for you.

I also thought last night that in a way your job is harder than Rimbaud's (not more painful) *because* he had to position us and he did it, like no one else—but Charles has to pull down from the loft the actual stair-steps for us to get to the floor directly above—he has to imagine what they look like and then figure out a way to unfasten them and then when they are loose and hanging how to peg them securely enough for men to use with confidence. Oh! dearest—no one said when you stepped out of that Democratic National Committee that you were "too lazy—just wanted to go and sit in the sun" that is, no *existent* person—for you thus took on yourself one of the biggest jobs that has ever been taken on—and it seems harder to me than the more obvious glorious ones because there is almost nothing to use—almost everything you use has to be dug out by Olson and I do not believe this was true for my boy Michelangelo in this sense—not to mention Shakespeare—etc. The reason the reviews of *Y & X* are so paltry (I am not at all satisfied even with the

---

81. Olson wrote on the envelope of this letter: "10,000 years."

Hanson boutonniere because he would not rest on this point (meaningless to one who has not read the poems, which should not be, of real criticism) if he really knew what the poems were saying) is because the spiritual size of men today is so reduced they actually have no idea of what you speak. *Trinacria* which I have found again and again to be an absolute—a thing *beyond* which it is impossible to go, I have not read one word on anywhere—*Moebus Strip* same—my friends know what they mean—why don't the critics?

Another reason your job is harder and in this respect I feel Blake and Melville shared with you—man in general has not yet an awareness of his de-spair—he knows he's tired—that's where *all* the Apocalypse gang-up en-ters—he knows he wants comfort—but that he despairs—and what of—he has not the most remote notion—I know—you know—but there is no Knowledge in the phylum and this a poet needs—*so* if you tell him it is an-other *alone.* Chalk off: language alone
                              definition alone
                              indication alone

That's why I love that dear Joyce
"And was there one in a thousand of nights who understood me?"
You would weep real tears to see how Joyce has studied Blake—it is the ab-solute Key to *Finnegans Wake*.

I am afraid to say aloud, dear Charles, *how* large I feel the job you have bit-ten off is and how absolutely alone I am afraid you are—but in that flash you once said the anonymous worker was permitted, I see Motz and Olson smil-ing to each other so foot sure across a great very great tennis court where they keep flying to one another that ball—that reality—the game as 2050 shall play it with all the Motz-Olson rules—so help my arrogant soul—thy arrogant soul.

You should Charles some day do the ten new commandments. I under-stand Yeats did a story which Joyce took as his staff—the artist in rejection, in reverso, on the Moses ten.

I love the business of the skins constantly sloughed off—indeed you are correct—the *life* in this vehicle is harder to hold than a soap bubble—did you understand my long pondered word in the Melville summary—the defiance of pain, the unknowable, and the moving meant everything by that all the ter-rific dexterity—the *work* of a Nijinsky to keep from breaking it—to hold it and not just lie down and weep at its shifting. Love you.

                                                            Frances

[*With this letter was enclosed a snapshot of Frances with her husband, Sergei Boldereff, referred to by Olson in his letter of 14 March 1950.*]

Woodward to Washington
[12 March 1950][82]

Sunday morning

Charles dear—

I can only say I am aghast at what a master I am of the unfelicitous phrase. The letter I sent you last night, to correct any wrong impression my first answer may have created was even worse—

But I always count on your understanding because it has always been so miraculous—the decision you have made is the most active one imaginable—but since I am *very* deep in Blake I am moving around in a place where the action of the "*Eternals*" is so present that I can use a word like "rescued" meaning something very different from anyone would mean—the great power of a lovely boat to come through a storm eighteen times its size (just in its immediate surrounding area) and vast beyond that.

And this is only to say Charles that I am thrilled beyond all measure—the phrase of "a bit of exercise" in my first letter was the wry face I am making over my own memories over the past few years of the agony it costs just to keep bread in one's mouth—if one intends not to sell any gifts to the devil.

This house is so lovely on Sunday mornings—we now have a new bedroom—you can have the big bed for your own comfort.

I am really reading Blake these days—and coming across many things I have not seen before—if you want to make another wonderful book—I have a long list—starting with "Portrait of the Artist as a Young Man"—of places where Joyce has quoted Blake or made immediate direct references to him—and I am sure the key to *Finnegan's Wake* is in the organization and form and basic symbolism of Blake's *Four Zoas* and *Jerusalem*—I wish I had the kind of mind to trace this out—but having once jumped at it, I am practically through—However, I am deeply convinced that Blake was the brother or father of Joyce in the sense you described of Lorca to Whitman. And much much more—because all of Blake's basic concept of how this world was formed has been taken over by Joyce—and literary devices even to beginning with a sentence which was the last sentence of a previous poem.

Please come as soon as you possibly can. Lucinda wants you, too.

Frances

82. This date is conjectural. The first paragraph refers to no extant letter.

Washington to Woodward
13 March 1950

Monday again. I have no idea whether this works or not. But it just might amuse you, and I send it along.

o

A VISITATION[83]

"So", sez he, "there are two:

hero,

and anti-hero,

the 'Andsome One,

and the likes, say, of me!

"And whether you know it or not", he throws it at me,

"you can have neither without the other. So cease!

cease immediately

yr name-callin'!"

> And he kept shaking his head,
>
> and backin' off,
>
> as though to avoid
>
> a bee

"Or so it has been," he put in

on the sly,

"since Moyses invented sin!"

He started again: "There was a time,

there was, when evil, that thing, stayed

(stook, you might say)

---

83. This typescript draft has not previously been published.

where nature put it,

where she intended it.

Famine and ill, the Old People called it,

famine and ill. And the contagion of it!

The contagion, mind you!"

He looked thin himself.

"And in those days, I may tell you,

it was a man's job

to avert it, to be rid of it!"

"And it will be so again!", sd he,

as an after-thought.

He was steady now,

from the pain.

"The trouble has been, the moment you have a single god"

he was off,

"you get the Doublet I spoke of.

And a lot of hate."

He coughed,

and went on.

"I know an old song.

I'll sing it for you:

'The Scape-goat stood
all skin and bone,
while moral business not his own
was bound about his head'

He looked at me, hard.

"Contagions, I said.

And we suffer from them!"

And off he went,

with this remark

tossed over his shoulder:

"There are those

who prefer to be clean

than to be handsome!"

And I could hear him muttering,

"Begin again,

oh, begin

again . . . .

O

March 13
50

⋙ 162 ⋘

Woodward to Washington
14 March 1950 (postmark 15 March 1950)

Tuesday night

Charles—

I am more excited than you can imagine at the content of your letter (the poem does not quite come over to me. May be unfamiliarity, but seems very bent in the right direction—reminds me of Dostoevsky who identified the devil as a man, little, whose clothes did not fit and the tip of whose nose needed wiping!) Milton's notion of evil as the shining Lucifer is so erroneous.

There is so much to comment I am stuttering!

First—I want more than anything in the world to come off with a NEW— an unhebraic notion of life—that is why I mentioned the cock as the *spiritual* symbol and the angle I want is so very unGreek too—*not* as nature, but as symbol of man's snare and glory (a kind of Lion and Mouse fable with the balls the net, the cock the Lion and the reason plus spirit the Mouse and God! to live to the day when I hear little One-eye open and say thank you to the spirit as the Lion once was *forced* to do!) snare *not* as sin but as net (all you do is lift it up but the claws do not permit as little Motz could write chapters and chapters to say (on her own claws)

Blake is old in that he conceived it once had been perfect—he is wrong

Melville is old in that he wants to return to a heaven which is not (egotistical) and implies a return to the forces which for some reason I believe he wanted to return to or accepted on the blind. (*love* him for using that word to refer to what we now have!)

I want to combine Melville's sense of the power of the out there—the immensity of what man does not and cannot know (stay on the problems you *can* solve, man) with Blake's fiery belief in energy—in man's necessary mental fight to draw out of the unknown the imaginative solution to man's spiritual relation to man.

Here is where Stryzgowski comes in—*he* proves that all that stuff *around* the Mediterranean, architecture, fresco and mosaic with figures is decadent Greek and hebraic and that everything which *made* Gothic, came from two sources only—your Scandinavian north very north and the triangle in Iran, Armenia, that the running fresco, the barrel vault, the dome, and Gothic use of the pilaster, etc. etc all originated in that intensely religious area where Jesus as I told you was a *man* on a horse all the time (God how I love that, what a new concept, how unhebraic—Christ—with that old Cossack discipline and the knees tight to guide a horse as they are hot to pump a woman) the thing about riding horseback is so accurate—a fine horseman has what they call "a light hand" he does it all with his knees and his voice and some general distillation out of the blood—black negroes are the finest riders in the world—saw one once in a hot real rodeo show in the open on a horse farm 100 years old out at Montauk, very tip of—they have to have that power through tenderness that DHL is speaking of in that bibliography I have mentioned—the only power that counts (kind Olson has)

And you know Blake believed in the strength of the pre-Greek stuff, that the greatest art visions are before Greece and Greece took the best of her art as her myth from something older and I am beginning to believe he was right—as man digs out more and more of that old stuff. And the fresco I sent you to Dura-Europa I do not know which book—maybe Morey at Princeton is the *one* reproduction of that priest with that terrific look in his eye as he dips a plant into a vase of water—sounds to me as though that too were a Hvarenah symbol (Rostovtzeff says he calls it all Mesopotamian because he doesn't know what the hell it really is) Hope that boy in New York can dig up more Stryzgowski soon on Mshatta—Armenia—Altai—Iran want to read them all.

And while I am being excited let us not forget my old friend Roger II of Sicily—the *only* boy to kiss Bernard of Clairvaux but to answer hu-uh (no— my phonetics lousy) on account of that unGreek and unJudaic background of his'n! Aramaic with splendor! "I ain't scared of your God, baby" says Roger II. I am for ousting all of everything except those passionate speeches of Jesus—the Timothy quote I sent you long ago—"No man looking backward is fit for the Kingdom of God"—how accurate and the others of like verve.

Let's get a new Jesus—let us have done once and for all with all the Hebraic notions—(I am *proud* proud that Motz's great slaughter of the idea of security (woman as its great believer-in!) has met in *all* Jewish breasts without exception in *absolute* silence—no answer to that one—and how they hate to surrender that mundane hell—that dear old Blake says help and pity are devices of the devil—oh! Blake how new is thy voice.

quote from *Finnegans Wake*
"The silent cock shall crow at last. The west shall shake the east awake."
That's us, honey!

and on Blake
"he vows him to be of the sir Blake tribes bleak while through life's unblest he rodes backs of bannars." p. 563 (speaking of himself) Please love him. Honorable my Joyce.

Is a Hot Shoppe a restaurant.
Who am I?
Poem gets better as one re-reads—let me not say just now my verdict

[*back of envelope:*]

Woodward
Where the Motz's hide
Pennsylvania

Hope you will approve the beautiful title page for Walt I made today.

≼ 163 ≽

Washington to Woodward
14 March 1950 (postmark)

Please read enclosed billet[84] AFTER letter

tuesday

---

84. Presumably Olson is referring to the enclosed poem, "Of Lady, of Beauty, of Stream," which grew from the phraseology of the first paragraph of the letter.

lady spence, it is wonderful, you, the eyes. and that hand, that hand! (and serge is so very serious, the mouth)   i thank you, frances, for it: i looked into those eyes, and again came that wonderful rising of the first which you cause, so very much as though you were bent over the clearest kind of water, clear because you have bent over it, and i were the goldenest trout way at the bottom in the shining sand, and i saw you, and came from a very long distance down, up, up through all that very clear water, with sun the only stain in it, light, light, right straight up into your eyes or your mouth, and you caught me in that most capable hand, that hand with such reverence to it, the delicacy, that beautiful strength!   lady of beauty

look, baby: you know you have two ways of remaining silent over something i have passed you—one when a thing goes in there and stays, deep, buried; the other when you do not like, or reject, something   i wish, a propos what i sent you yesterday, A VISITATION, that you would tell me whether it works or not (i have made one change, taking out "pain", which was not accurate, and that part of the gloss now reads:

he was steady now,
from the passion
of what he had to say.

Yr letter is so fat and heady, so rich I shall take it into myself, as I do, and let it grow there, as you do   But I do tell you now, how beautiful it is, and how, at this moment, your words on Jesus come home   I venture to think you do what Dostoevsky did, and what poor Melville wanted to, but couldn't, which is to distinguish Jesus from Christ (it angered me so, in Chase's book, to see him make one direct misinterpretation of me, on this point: I think I said so clearly it was Christianity, not Jesus, that stole Melville's strength away—he was right to make Jesus a lover, but Jesus became hermaphroditical to him because he could not clear Jesus of Christianity (I should, undoubtedly, have left that remark of Dostoevsky's in, that if truth & Christ proved different Etc..... it was in the original mss.)   But this is porcelain ground, and I should not walk on it unless I am prepared to go all around the edenic place!   All I meant to do now, was to preface an attempt to answer your request on Rimbaud, for your joining of Jesus as you take him, and Saison D'enfer, is most exciting: it is not something I had ever done.

But before Rimbaud too I stop. Though the first long poem I ever did was called "The True Life of Arthur Rimbaud"[85] (it

85. This poem, in MS at Storrs, remains unpublished.

was almost the 1st poem! done Key West five year agone, and sent out under a pseudonym I then fancied, "John Hines") I have no right to say yet anything of him. For I must read him, and have been creeping out on that act for years. I even for some months practiced my French by translating Baudelaire—and all as preparation to read Rimbaud! But then my own work intervened, and I have not got back. I despair of knowing him at all, without reading him in his own language. So all I better do is to try to get ready for you those lines on him which you must take as only a tentative gesture, no more solid, really, than the John Hines piece, which no one will ever see! It is solely intuitive and general, done, as you might say, like a quavering zither, under the window of the heaven he now sits in! to someone whom I love but do not know, whom I saw once passing, and wanted to court!

My god, is it true, what you say, that, for 10,000 years, men and women have been dreaming of the day when the sexes shall be no more? my god, that's enough to stop me right in my tracks and you better tell me about that   i can't get over it   good god, no, you mean that?   i thought that god damned fool melville in those lines i quoted about the Anarch blunder had said it, and that Plato had caused Aristophanes to bring up that image of the double-backed beast in the "Symposium"   but you now shake the life out of me, when you calmly say, that's the way it has been all the time!   I thought only the sick-of-life wished sex away

DO SPELL THAT OUT A LITTLE   (Of course I did realize what your 4 steps constituted, that's why I sd, beauty, beauty ("beauty is difficult, Mr Yeats")   But this other opposite thing, this neuter wish, good god, Frances, it is terrible!

I am afraid I think that idea is definitely one of the chief by-products (like slag, cinders, dust) of Moses and sin, that damnable Genesis, and those Two Trees; but 10,000 years? And NOW? The bracket I'd make is, (Plato to Melville, post-1850)

But you tell me: you know how I respect you, & especially in this area. I am just thunder-struck, and because I agree with Pushkin about that stupidity natural to poets, I am wholly open on the subject!

And, exactly opposite, you completely delight and unnerve me with yr image of the olson job, the stair-steps from the floor above   And if I ever get that book of prose done which I am under contract to Viking to do (and which I am supposed to be working on now, under that Guggenheim!) you will see, from the "prolog", why!

O baby, that is a wonderful letter, peopled so with yr family, frances, your "boys"! And when you end with that DANCER, (your pas de deux, LEADER), my ASSOLUTA, oooooooo: cream, cream! my ASS-OLUTA!

from the tip of it,

O

do not, baby, deny me, once in a great while, to say such things: to *tell* you; I resist, most of the time, because I will not add one feather to your denyings, handsomest thing!)

OF LADY, OF BEAUTY,
OF STREAM

that rising, of the first, you cause!

so very much as though you bent
over the clearest water, clear
by your bending

and I the goldenest trout, hiding
next to the whitest sand, came up, up
through that very clear water, up
through a mouth made of eyes

And you caught me, caught me, took me
in that delicate directive hand!

❧ 164 ☙

Woodward to Washington
15 March 1950 (postmark 16 March 1950)

Wednesday night

Charles darling—
    This is not a letter.
    I want to tell you how I *love* the poem for me[86] perhaps because I so love those early Irish fairy tales which contain the Salmon of Wisdom and I thus am accustomed to dream in the form you give.

---

86. "Of Lady, of Beauty, of Stream," see *Collected Poems* (pp. 126–27).

I want to go over seriously *The Visitation* when my brain begins to work.

Also I want to tell you that the ending to *The Morning News* given in the first letter was very much better than when you asked if you had sent it and enclosed a second version—will give you both versions and explain why, if you do not immediately agree, when I am with you.

Charles angel—this was just a note to say I am *so* sorry about my habit to exaggerate wildly—when the exaggeration is *so* wild then I always think you will *know* it is true only as an emotional outlet—like that word 'ever' which meant literally "one month." 10000 years meant—Motz's 10000 sighs. Actually your date is as close as I know—there is certainly no limit in any Sumerian—Egyptian—Assyrian writing I know to indicate any sex ugliness at all—they seemed not to have heard of the problem—the *lovely* relationship in *Gilgamesh*—the goddesses—so *right*!

Angel—I understand, knew before you told me about how any tiny half-hour break is a break and one has to work while the spell is on—no matter how long it lasts—so this is surely not meant as a hint or anything

it is simply

 Motz dreams—

  my birthday was always made special

   and as it approaches I look for you

and until you write and say you can *not* I am simply all an indrawnbreath of waiting and my brain and stuff has just stopped—I can't even design book pages although I am in the mood—I just wander around my house from chair to chair. And it is *not* a hint—it is involuntary reflex and I tell you only because I seem unable to write you a single word.

           Frances

⋈ 165 ⋈

Washington to Woodward
16 March 1950 (postmark)

          thurs

i am too jittery today to write, or to write imaginatively to you: i've got a deal on, and i should be one of my shrewd friends, or myself as i was when i was foot-sure in the world instead of as one gets when one's eye is not on the world but on its life I've already made one boner, which may be irreparable, and I can't afford to make another, today!

it's a whale of a story, which would delight you   A couple of weeks ago I walked into Lowdermilk's bookstore looking for Lawrence's Fantasia, or anything else I could pick up cheap   Sez the cloik: "But look, we've got a Lawrence collection! And some of his paintings"   My god, I could hardly hold the floor beneath me   And in 3 minutes, there I was looking straight into the face of a water color I had to own!   Of a man pissing against a brick wall into a bed of daffodils (did I tell you?)

The upshot, until last night, was, no go for me, because the owner wouldn't sell anything but the whole: 2 paintings, & what looks like a complete Lawrence, 1sts, associations, and limiteds, as well as the texts on him

JEHU! THAT'S A TERRIFIC LETTER I JUST HAVE HANDLED FROM YOU! BABY, THAT'S HUMMIN' HOW IN GOD'S NAME DID YOU GET SO LIKE OLSON? THIS INTERPENETRATION IS SEX PLUS, (MORE THAN HALF A DOZEN, AND HOW!)   FRANCES, YOU BEAUT, YOU MAKE ME SING!   LA   LA   LA   SOL LA CI DO   WOW   (be back, let me[87]

to hell with the deal   i want to talk about what you say: boy, lady, that's laying it on the line   (funny thing: i have not yet read anything of friend STRZY's except a thing i found in french at the public library, a catalogue for NRF on Afghan stucco sculpture. So: all I have had is, the teasers you have shot me, plus Brooks Adams   And by god, if I hadn't figured out the story precisely as you tell it to me today. It delights me, and is again my pal Bolyai, and his violets in the spring.

(if you were stuttering, that's plainly the way others better find out what is speech!)

i tell you, i can't say a word! i think everything you say is so exactly right, including the Joyce   (a dig, darling: the east, says he, the east awake::::::but olson, see, is motz, for recall the east-west passage in Kingfishers!   ("who's most yr baby?" cried the Lover!)

what does strike me, is how tenacious and passionate i am, that METHOD-OLOGY (which is, how to get the FORM) is the job now, how the *vision* is intricate to the *method* (and i don't mean literary)   i'm talking out loud   (right into that flaming mouth of my motz, my beauty), but it occurs to me that, why, say, I find Pound & Williams usable (the world, god damn the world) and back off from both Blake and Joyce, say (yet how i love them,

87. The rest of the sheet is torn off at this point.

Preface is only one hint::::::i suddenly think i'll send you a poem which is young and green but which you should be the one to have—it has never gone out::::: love them for the spirit, which you prove me now is so kin I think that's the reason)

to make the method to make the form, Jack Hines,

gimme

document and i'll gnaw and i'll mew and i'll kiss you new lines!

see? it's that their Irish, those Two! and one irishman and another?

see, baby? who's with you, to the hilt? (o that hilt! sez yr Swordsman!)
IRISHERS   IRISHERS!

(god, frances, the sky, the sky is ours!
you's and mine! what do you mean, the
steepness is going to be less steep?)

(Blake must be irish! How did he get that name?
And that vision? How, otherwise?)

O, but it's YOUR FABLE: god, what a story: if you don't take a crack at it, my wonder-bean, i'll steal, and steal, and smile! especially the net and the claws: YOU DO IT, MY PROUD PROUD MARE!

And aren't you a darling, the way you put, Blake is old cuz, Melville is old cuz
. . . . . .

but combine?   well, we ARE, ARE, have
                 th'advantage and the
                 contribution?
METHODOLOGY, shouts

(in interim: almost made it! almost swung the Lawrence deal And
got myself the painting out it. Almost, I sd, not yet quite, alas)

the American!   FORM, cries the Poet!

and o, frances, how beautiful is your passage today on Christ MOUNTED!

frances: you would like a candy?   BY GOD you get it!   you have made a tremendous statement this day

(well, i was wrong abt the littel verse,   it's too green) i

yr
Man of Micht

baby, funny, these exclamations—but there it is, i'm after that Lawrence, & you know your Old Man now, how when he's on it, he's on it! but you better be sure, that at this precise moment, he's *all* over there, close, close as *hell* to you

≈§ 166 ǥ≈

Washington to Woodward
17 March 1950 (postmark)

friday

frances:
  i cannot, i know, dash, and dash your dreams to the ground (i know it this day as i never knew it before, for last night i knew something of that wild torment you give me the sense you go through: i'll say no more)

  it should be beyond dream if you could stand it for as long as this iron time, these iron nerves of olson are made to stand things (it has always been the terror my life, that the arcs of others' time breaks

  o, frances, frances, your note today is straight, straight torture   and i give you back every absolute surrounding this man is capable of

  but i know this: this once in my life i am going to be whole and clean, am going to be what i am at the very root of my nature, because i believe in what you and I have made, in what we can make—and that is because you are the extraordinary likeness of dream

  if i put every syllable and dram of my weight on you, frances, it is because i believe, *believe* in life, believe in this frightening space-time of mine, *believe* in what i take to be that which is extraordinary in you

  i do not know the shape what-we-are will take   and you well know, because you have also followed your holy ghost, with what doubt one goes by one's nose   i feel my way, with no, *no* clues to guide (i think it is one of the despairs of the present, yet the very axis of its reality, that *no* previous experience or measurements *are* of help—i suppose that is what i mean by, that the place is as raw as rocks

you must, darling, by now know that when you said the scale of this thing is beyond Pericles and Aspasia, you were right   And yet do not think that i, too, as you have, do not look out of the corner of my eye and ask Lawrence, as you told me you have, do we do right to act in the face of nature's drives and hauls, to kill, as you put it, our first born?

to that i give you this male's answer (this male who takes up his majority right out of the fire of this love)   the answer is no, we are not wrong, we have not killed, we are more steep now than we were!

and, woman, i make bold to offer that answer to you because I believe it *is* the tremendous issue, proof, the actual vitality in this thing!

and that i offer it to you, instead of any mincing word or any action such as such right men as lovely Lawrence just behind us would expect, is the fullest kind of evidence i can give you that i believe in you! that, to me, it is love we're busy with

what i do *not* believe is, that if things were right with life around us, what i am asking of us would be right   on the contrary   what makes this thing so terrible is, things are not right, and it is as though we had to pluck passion only by raising the flesh out of itself, by living it in exactly those terms in which, in fact, at any time, life has been lived (what i am thinking of is, that life *is* preoccupation with itself

i am preoccupied with you, and i mean no subtractions whatsoever

(((darling, this is being written at the fullest pitch of my nature   it should be in hand-writing, to distinguish it from the way i can use a machine   a machine is too glib to indicate where these words are coming from, at what a pitch and poise i am holding myself   for i am at this moment as serious as i have ever been, even inside my work   so take each word as it is meant, to be straight gold and blood, for you, for *you*, whose life is so precious to me, or else i wouldn't, couldn't say what I am saying)))

in other words, i think what we are up to is *not* denials, in any sense equal to the dimension of what we have been about for—what? now two years and a half, since you first wrote me (since you met me under that hebraic name i am now—because of *us*, i venture to think—rejecting!), now four months since you saw me under that mask which almost drove you off (which also, day by day, wears off as olson continues—it is amazing, tho only you and i could see it—to warm his face and body, to loosen the visored grip on his flesh, by way of the very gestures, the very bottomed speech, the beautiful *release* of MOTZ!)   frances, i *live* by the flesh, i act now by *your* flesh: And i call that sex, *sex* as it must be reborn, as, to speak as you do, it can only be reborn out of US   And i so believe, i would even hurl this answer into Lawrence's eyes, stand to him, great man, as the answer he, because in some subtle way he would not give up the intimate as it was his mother or the separateness which was the reflex of that love; both of which, as you saw so clearly, lead him, as his poems show, away from life toward death

i hate the word "collective" and my own word "objectism" is most inadequate, but there is a space-time in which love must be lived NOW if it is to take on the dimension which belongs to it—and which as been so long lost

frances: quietly, and without spelling it out, I want to indicate to you that the balances in what we endure, and in what we risk, are not so different as the appearances of our two lives during this period would seem to show   I say this, at this point, particularly where the body, as the ground of flesh, is in your mind as it is in mine   I say it, to put the grit in, so that any impression that these absolutes are easy, or float out, may be corrected. You deserve that, baby

it occurs to me, too, that if—by whatever rare illumination—you can take what i am here saying as the tenderest of birthday presents, if, by this full charge of my nature you find me merely leading on one moment in this dance we are creating, it is only possible, my moving, because you, before, and in this moment after, have, by your moving, called up the nature of this man, made possible the patterns which his life has moved toward making

i move very slowly, very carefully, because i am object (i should not say this thing this way to *any* one but you), because i find it a part of my vision to act in the instant but only the instant with the whole of what has brought me about admitted   ((((i think here, too, i pay the toll of the wrongs which have been done personality, flesh, the clear birth of the human thing   i hate my people, my country, my parents, even, because they caused me to have to learn by price after price that living in this goddamned sodomic, Laodicean place is, as Charles Munch sd after his first months here, almost all "reaction" instead of action

to act, straight, clean, from the center, this takes doing for the likes of me, and i have found that my illuminations have to be picked out like needles from the hugest stables of dung

what i bring to you is a struggle which is, i suppose, however close your vision and mine are in the issuance (and it is a part of what i call the dream we are making, that it is so extraordinarily pin-point to target, that it can be so in-creasingly as long as we live, increasing by the very holding now, and the put-ting together after the misery of the shaping of each of us)   what i bring you is a man who has come a way which is, obviously, another way to do also what you have done   what i am trying to say here is, that i imagine we both must, when we think and measure the other, remember the differences of the paths by which we got here   yours, for example, seems to be so beautiful, seems to be *right:* my own, i *hate*, i hate because it has been so much re-action i utterly abhor, for example, what was done to the sex of my being by catholicism, new englandism, americanism (witness the passage in THE MORNING NEWS letter, after the 1st Indian passage, of that day I wanted, because the sun had made me Pan, to lay those two girls of my friends: jesus, of course i know the realities of things, *but* the way they pay, they pay, those whom we are fum-bling fools enough to think deserve our love   god, god, how ashamed i am that i have given my love to those who wrong me!   god, god, motz, and you wonder if i know what i have heard you cry out against, the shame, the shame! o baby, do not think, because a man is not a woman that he does not also know the very same sense of outrage   it is not his body, maybe, that is outraged in quite the mortal way a woman must feel because she's entered that she's outraged, because she has opened her legs to some one who is not what she thought but a part of the rot that life has become in the hands of the haters   maybe the cock does not have to know what the womb knows, but o, god, whatever it is that the man has given him by nature for his measuring rod, for his stirrup cup, for his vessel of the ghost of life—call it what Dosto-evsky made such nobleness of, his *amour propre*—anyhow, I HAVE BEEN OUTRAGED, and I HATE, I HATE my enemies—and i do not know my enemies,

this, also, this also, is of the enigma, and is the reason why I MUST, i MUST, baby, baby, go SLOW, pick my way, pick my beggarly way   I MUST now, age almost 40, be RIGHT, right—and right by my own instinct, process, BE-LIEVE, BELIEVE in myself   my self supported on this reed, myself!

o god frances, god   it is exhausting, to go, to go! forward in this time of nothing but SHIT   so, please, baby, if i find you, if i found you (which is to say, you revealed yourself to me, and i slowly then came up, up to you acting as straight as yr Salmon, acting proudly, thank god, each of those hours from the Public Library (!), thru the streets (in an automobile!) of that City of All Wrongs, that capital, in that restaurant, going (because i had said i would, de-spite the deepest despair that night that I walked, after you left me, and looked out, like some angel who tasted then like ash to himself, over that river and that harbor toward that City) going to that hotel—why, why, how did i know you would call?, going blindly on, talking at you at that breakfast table like a giddy boy, scared, scared to lose you after I had decided you were more than what you had proved you were, keeping at it even after i dropped you at Best's, turning back from way in Connecticut, hunting you through those streets again, pressured, pressured from some power (o, i thank that Glory!), dancing over that trouble with the car (with all its "risks", shall we put it), "using" dahlberg (whom I had *never* used), and THEN, my triumph, sitting down beside you in that train!

o frances, if i have found you, then know, handsome one, what is the continuing struggle out of which i move, move, believing—loving

> this is for you, frances,
> whose birth i treasure, &
> her life

❄ 167 ❆

Woodward to Washington
18 March 1950 (postmark)

Saturday morning

Charles darling—

A tiny sign which I give you, not out of superstition, but for joy—your letter arrived this morning (8:00 A.M. it came and Lucinda got it for me at 9:30 A.M.) because by tonight I will not be here and then Monday you would have had no answer and you would have suffered—This has happened only once before in all our letters!

Lucinda goes to Harrisburg to the dog show and I leave for State College (business and so-called pleasure)   hunch: I *feel* my printer is going to cross me up—I know somewhere in my bones he wants to take from me, but not to give me what I ask—so when my book is bound I will want you to send one to Laughlin and a few other people not for a job but to see if I could pick up some free lance design—Laughlin does lots of his books that way I know and the price advantage in these Pennsylvania hills is enormous—my book will not be ready for several months—yesterday I received the title page proof— and there were over *twenty* Charles major space errors—I was absolutely furious because Frank *has* often taken my layouts and returned proof on which all I had to do was mark O.K.—(*do* you understand the reason for people's being *so* unreliable so unsteadfast—God! how it wounds me)

Dearest this is only to say your letter *is* the most beautiful birthday gift I have ever received—I am even glad in a tiny way because my old mother wishes to come and now I can permit her and she will be glad—and we can have *secret* joy when we do have it.

I love you, I believe also this *is* love—that everything has been lost out of love and that you and I have to establish a new framework for it—I feel strong—I send you every fibre of that flowing out of me—

I believe in you, in your own sense of your own time, your own obligation, your own task and your own time of reward. I will wait my darling all over this earth and into all the other ones there are and it *is* love which here alone on this earth this day exists between Charles, the designate and Frances, his designated.

❦ 168 ❧

Washington to Woodward
21 March 1950 (postmark)

tuesday

motz baby

the enclosed came back to roost sunday   i send it along for you to see, as an early formulation (2 yrs or more old)   it has not been out since it was then rejected, on all sides   pal ragsdale had it (who is now disappointing me: brains! brains! nobody wants to work for 'em any more!)   (one of the damndest lies abroad, is the lazy one, that somehow things "happen", that all is either given—"donnee"—or fate—it is one of the ironies that materialism, which made so much of will, is, in the things that count, will-less   i am sure that the suicide of the West came here

(the more reason I should get back to that thing I have not forgotten you asked to see, & you shall, the moment I do get back to it, on the secular as the other face of which materialism is the pock-marked opposite)

maybe i may do it today: for the last three days i have been in one of those wey-sway moods, hanging, swinging, floating over my feelings & work, toying a little, which is a make-up time, I'm tempted to think

(West promises to send me a WR with the Dave-O piece on Billy Boy; so hold, & I'll see it goes to you the day it comes)

(tried him out again on a verse, a rewrite of a Yorktown poem: he doesn't know it, but it's sent to go right straight up American-Eagle Engle's broken-glass ass!)[88]

88. Paul Engle, as a member of the editorial board of *Western Review*, had vetoed the acceptance of Olson's poem "The Praises" (West to Olson, 28 January 1950).

yr note yesterday graced me   baby girl, when these characters screw up yr work, shouldn't you recognize that you are in the same boat as me, with rejections in the box, like snow?   i'm sure they do you violence because your intensifications are increasingly difficult for them to put up with

by the way, one thing i didn't say last week, we were going at such a clip: i'm positive the Whitman design must be *absolute* for the day you did it you were beautiful, beautiful!

it is not spring, but i feel spring today,[89] as tho my bones were all loosened, & full of breathing holes—breached bones   .

    of the green time
when labor is
reborn
     and right off the surface of the ground
without stems
the croci flash
like eyes
     her eyes
opening,
     telling you,
you flower   too

here's
to opening but not to upward
to earth
and her eyes, not to leaf and to sap
to herself, the close intervals of grass
(her hair) what stays close, close
no farther than your finger tip
let you also go:
     these are the true extensions
her trees come later, are
purchased, worked, demand,
structure, labor, LABOR!
what man also, knows,
and not as sweat and brow
(hebraic punishment) but
thing itself, das ding an sing,

89. From here to the end of the letter was reworked as the poem "It's SPRing AgAIN!" (*Collected Poems*, pp. 115–16).

Sing, the labor of
the THING!
              the lesson of
                    SPRING!

                                                    you
beauty.

[*enclosure*]

                    ABOUT SPACE
                    Charles Olson

                          I

   Space is the mark of new history, and the measure of creative work now
afoot is the depth of the perception of space, both as space informs objects and
as it contains, in antithesis to time, secrets of a humanitas eased out of contemporary narrows.
   I use the word space in its full reference: as Giacometti might, or Henry
Moore; as De Sitter has; as Frobenius did a propos paideumatic law ("In materialism the spatial tendency dominates everything"); as Freud might have
used it to describe his physical sensations of that cask, the "Gemut", man's
Heidelberg tun; in short, as any intense investigator of any aspect of experience is now organically forced to use it.
   I add a quote, by way of further explication:

   But suddenly as he peered down and down into its depths, he profoundly
   saw a white living spot no bigger than a white weasel, with wonderful
   celerity uprising, and magnifying as it rose, till it turned, and then there
   were plainly revealed two long crooked rows of white, glistening teeth,
   floating up from the undiscoverable bottom.

                          II

   What is going on, what the whole seismic shift in men's attentions that the
tedious call our chaos amounts to, is, in a phrase, the return to space.
   The dying of the hold of the time-concept on western man has been sufficiently observed. What has been missed is that such a redistribution of attention involves a redistribution of will. It is precisely the absence of such will and
mind that gives me my impression that the work of Proust, Bergson, Eliot,
Joyce et al is of a dead past and of no more than technical interest.

Time and space, of course, are in the relation of a parabola, plane to cone. Nor I nor Einstein would want to disentangle them. The point is otherwise, is a matter of where men put the stress. Earth, as a great Italian made clear to us a long time ago, is a via, a way to heaven, man's heaven. But I would see it of great significance that contemporary to him Grosseteste was writing his treatise on light. From Dante to Pound it has been problems of time which troubled the artist and concepts of time which governed men. It is no longer so. We are more separated from these men than we know, and if some have not sensed the decline from Cavalcanti's canzone out of Grosseteste, "Donna mi Prega", to Eliot's "Burnt Norton" (out of himself) it does not matter. Others already know their fathers, and faiths, are elsewhere. The path does die.

Note 1: A treatise on dimensions, springing out of non-Euclidean geometry, would be as contributory to art now as Piero della Francesca's treatise on perspective was in the 15th century, out of Euclid. For art, thought and action now stem from the same questions Einstein has. What is missing is form, form, the law of object, of a leaf, what only the artist can give. Otherwise matter rules, the bitch, and her dog, time, and the only brotherhood is death, blue-eyed death. Without form, the comprehension of it, researches and formulations, there is no moral purpose to the design.

Note 2: It is worth considering that there is alive at this moment somewhere (say, for the game of it, Sinkiang) some new St Francis.

Note 3: Please accept one further shorthand, to make immediately clear what it seems necessary to remind people of, that art and action are inextricable. To a man of space a proof of the double action of the compelling law of object lies in a recent juxtaposition: cubism and the Resistance. If these two events are unleafed, new man is found at the heart of each.

This is as true as it is of non-resistance, where you find Gandhi.

III

The gains of space are already apparent. They can be put in an old triad: man, and nature   society   god.

1   Man as object is equatable to all other nature, is neutron, is thus no more than a tree or pitchblende but is, therefore, returned to his abiding place where he always is whatever his notions, the primordial, where he can rest again as he did once with less knowledge to confirm his humilitas.

It is as force that the eye of nature sees man. Seen so, the animal and the bones of him do not disturb the remainder of organic and inorganic creation. As force man has his place, and wonder. He is participant. It is enough, more than he knows. Instead of his own alone he is in touch with all life, and image and fable come back.

They come back because the elements are not so dissimilar: season, cello, shield, trio, sphere. When man is reminded of his place in the order of nature, when he finds himself cut down to size, he goes through a franciscan or ovidian revolution, whichever you prefer, and acquires some of his original modesty about force, his own and otherwise. Beasts and angels, devils, witches, trees and stones, cocks and centaurs are necessary items of human phenomenology (and only, and exactly, in that science).   They are dangerous out of that moral frame—as we have had recent occasion to know.

2   Man and society. Man as object (not man as mass or economic integer) is the buried seed in all formulations of collective action stemming from Marx. This seed (not its tactic, which merely secures it votes or coup d'etat) is the secret of the power and claim of collectivism over men's minds.

It is the grain in the pyramid, and if it is allowed any longer to rot unrecognized, collectivism will rot as it did in nazism and as capitalism has by a like antinomian law.

Note: It seems also necessary to remind the western mind of Asia, to point out the persisting failure to count what Asia will do to collectivism, the mere quantity of her people leverage enough to move the earth, leaving aside the will of such of her leaders as Nehru, Mao, Shjarir. The will of Asia is already dictating the shape of prospective man's society on the earth.

3   Prismatic man, as opposed to what Christian man has declined to, the pragmatic: man as object in space as against man as subject of time makes possible a life-death concept which admits man's reflection as force in nature.

Anthropology has proved man of such durance in time as to push time so far back, and ahead, as to turn time into space, at least so far as man is concerned, that creature of a day, as Aeschylus causes even Prometheus to call him.

If science will now do the one last thing man has a right to ask of it, teach man how to restore nature's intention with his organism, that he live an animal span of some 130 years, then science can go the way of magic and religion, the three of them, as Frazer put it, "nothing, in the last analysis, but theories of thought."

Note 1: A propos the artist as formulator, leader, consider another observation of Frazer's: "The true or golden rules man has found in his search to turn the order of natural phenomena to his own advantage constitute the body of applied science which we call the arts."

Note 2: As the other prime text now needed I would set beside a treatise on dimensions a SUMMA based on a putting together, most critically governed, of the work of Frazer, Freud and Frobenius, each bringing the other up, how in the general memory there are old tricks, old events and the oldest dreams and fears, persistent, underneath religion, science and that newest rigidity, collectivism, held there, needing to be registered.

Note 3: It is told how Diogenes once threw a plucked rooster through the window of Plato's school and leaned in to say, "Here, here's Plato's human being for you." Space revises time-man with some of the same shock.

IV

A crowd in a forest of the city make
attention turned as heads which hear demand
the green republic now renewed

⇥ 169 ⇤

Woodward to Washington
21 March 1950 (postmark)

Charles dear—

I am in a lull which creates one not only wordless but thoughtless and fear-less—a kind of womb-surrounded lull in which the future absolutely refuses to form—I feel precisely as in a womb—though Who's I have no notion!

I found proof in State College that my printer is trying to eliminate me from his picture—which somehow doesn't matter to me at all—I have no idea at all about even the immediate future, but I also found there so much genuine respect and affection for the work I did while there—so many sug-gestions as to possible sources of free-lance income that I suppose that is why I feel rocked in some jet of fluid. All an experience I have never had—since I have been "responsible"—open-eyed watchful, preparative since very early tender years—and now I am like some Dionysian worshipper—drunken under the morris spell—no "solid" thought passing through me at all and a vague feeling that some kind of solution will present itself. For the Motz child a most strange strange existence phase.

I write you this note *only* to say I am your devoted sister—I read Graves *White Goddess*—I quote you this ancient Irish triad

It is death to mock a poet,
to love a poet,
to be a poet.

And to add that you and I *know* this, accept it and challenge it not in its ve-racity, but in its événement.

Frances

Oh! and yes Charles darling—any thought or word or thing I ever put in a letter is for you to use if you wish to so honor it—I *am* not and am never going to be a writer so never again urge me—under inspiration I will do that Bible reinterpretation—but it will have to come like the vision—direct dictation.

You are so right about Rimbaud in French—the *sound* of the stuff conveys such a different Rimbaud than the English meaning. I have Kirgo looking for that beautiful French-Eng that Laughlin originally did—if he finds it I will let you have for as long as you wish.[90]

◄§ 170 §►

Woodward to Washington
22 March 1950 (postmark)

Wednesday

Charles dear—

The books arrived a short while ago—strange humans—the first reaction (after the lovely discovery of your handwriting and the memory for which I mostly treasure the gift, of Tarrytown and my beautiful man packing it into his bag before Gloucester and saying "This is the man!" or some such—the memory of his face and self)

that if Smart let the thing escape him—Motz must arouse—so in a trice the womb state vanishes—
I find in da Vinci's *Paragone* this definition of Coleridge's

"The primary 'Imagination' I hold to be the living Power and prime Agent of all human perception, and as a repetition in the finite mind of the eternal act of creation in the infinite 'I am'."

I found two nights ago in a story of Poe's the statement that God does not continually create, that after that first act he leaves creation to us—stated well, with Poe's mind, which I admire. Several other things in Poe which so clearly make him a brother—I did, many years ago, at the wonderful New York Public, a very serious lot of study on Poe have many pages comparing Whitman and Poe—amazing parallels.

Darling—just to say I have come awake—have an idea which is wonderful—and the feeling that when I am tapped on the shoulder I shall get up and move like lightning.

Your poem *The Visitation* stays in my mind all the time—I have known pretty well what has disturbed me about it—not its entirety (a statement made also by Robert Graves in an entirely different form in the last chapter of *White Goddess*) which is a very fine imaging of our position today—the only

90. New Directions had published *A Season in Hell*, translated by Delmore Schwartz; however, the copy Olson later owned was from the Black Mountain College library.

thing that bothers me is the first stanza—hero and antihero OK, but there to *bring in* the knower, the chorus, or what have you in the phrase "and the likes, say, of me"—threw me off completely because I kept trying to identify him as Satan, then clearly that was wrong, as hero (Christ or whom have we) both are wrong—but it has taken some readings to hold him offstage and I ask very very modestly my darling—is it necessary to introduce him there in that line which brings up *such* an ugly picture to my mind of a little mass man exactly like my husband Duke.

All the rest of it comes over clear as clear and I find very 20th century and completely free of any overtones of anyone else's, at any place in history, summary—

My comment is badly written, you can see I am far from awake even now—but if you cannot make sense of it, just ignore and we will discuss when we are together.

I trust my angel that you will permit me to see the printed copies of your poems and the thin long scream whenever it suits you to do so.

Sending this embarrasses me precisely as when I first took off your robe—but I cannot really write now and my silence might disturb you—if not, please say it is OK to be silent because I do so hate to write stupidly.

◄§ 171 §►

Washington to Woodward
23 March 1950 (postmark 23 March 1950)

thurs-day mar 24 L[91]

again a day when i am loose   (it is strange, one works   (i wonder if your own mood yr letter today declares, is part of the same springing   (did my letter tuesday include these lines:

breached bones
of the green time
when labor
is reborn

you see, it gives me the intensest joy, to have you say you feel aswim in womb-water   (it did, that morning in yr house, to have you say, when i brought you breakfast, how unusual   (frances baby, i know exactly what you say, that you have stayed alert since when   AND BY GOD YOU EARN FROM ANY

91. This letter was written Thursday, 23 March 1950, and the postmark confirms this.

AND EVERYONE JUST EXACTLY SPOILING   for you won't take it
for more than a minute anyhow, but you damn well ought to get it for that
minute

today my hunch is, my mood is going over: i begin to itch to stop this lyrical in-
terlude, and go down to rock, and start to make one of those long babies, either
THE SCAPE-GOAT or THE SHE-BEAR, or maybe something I don't
know the name of   It means (given my method) I make that funny fetish trek
to the Lib. Cong. (i have several streets where I go—depending on the sort of
intent I have for the verse!   i mean, when i walk)   (all the tarot poems were
written on the good 3 quarter walk from the LIB here! one fall)
                                                              And this time
you are my lead: it is Strzygowski i go to, for fountain

                                                    ((if this is the time, & i
do go, i should tell you, i'm apt to sink, for days, and you must understand if i
shoot you penny p.c.s, darling))   ((((i hope not, sort of think not   as a matter
of fact to be in touch with you as close as i am, making these letters, is a true
deterrent—And i believe in deterrents!)))

was that Old Erse, the triad—or was it that rake Graves!   (and was the 2nd
"to *love* a poet") o my lady!

i'm going to enclose 2 pieces i have returned to the past week and have sent
out, one i mentioned, the other—LOST—a very early one, which appeared
where i think you would not have seen it   i took up respect for it, accidently
    And i want you to have each, for your taste and sight to move across   Are
they so formal as they seem? What do you say?

what my mind is on today is, myself & reality   (maybe TRISKELE,[92] as I secretly call it, is as close to my center as you say it is!)   It is like a bloody angle,
r., against which one breaks oneself like a body, in battle   I mean that reality
over there, the Enemie!   That thing which balks one   that balks one more
than Gemut, than that protean real one carries inside
                                                    (one false face of our
contemps.: they have the Enemie misplaced, upside down   they question
themselves & look hopefully to the "World" for answer!   that's arsy-versy:
the World gives no man anything except the testing of his self   And he'll
never put his belly to the Test, to its whittled points, if he goes around holding
his Gemut in his hand!

92. Olson changed the title of "Trinacria" to "Triskele" in some copies of the poem. See *Collected Poems*, p. 647.

(((((((I guess that's all I am doing: recurring, reiterating that mood almost precisely four years ago these days, that I did TRINACRIA! Isn't that strange! It's like a fully conscious DEJA VUE. Do you know this experience, Frances—of finding yourself trying to notate something you have already notated? Curious as hell)))))))

I feel as tho I wrote you yesterday, for I sent off to you Mr. West's sheet that master Engle has closed to my work!   It will probably be my last appearance in that mag   So you should have it!   (there's the World for you, one of its most frequent manifestations: the cowardice of one's brothers!)

I feel like calling you all sorts of new names today: like . . . . well, they'd be most intimate, and i better save 'em

Tell me how Lucinda is, that flower I'd call Wood Pansy, if I could change its name. She's straight Garnet, (on which hangs a tale I'll whisper to you once). Tell her she's in Olson's pocket

I tried to translate Villon's "Epistre en forme de Ballade a ses Amys." And came acropper as usual: translations are not my business. My business is to have my Lady lead me by the nose straight to a transpose like La Chute! I liked one line:

Fortune
has done him in

& a rime:

you wait for death,
to comfort me with broth!   (and)

I fast, hunched
in a hole. Here
there is no table.
And no chair.[93]

i'll take off now   but do you hear the kiss   do you see the eye   do you,
Gan?

                                              Olson

[*enclosed:*]

93. All these lines appear in a typescript at Storrs, entitled "Forget Villon?"—a translation made by Olson and Martha Rittenhouse, a Black Mountain College student.

AT YORKTOWN

1

At Yorktown the church
at Yorktown the dead
at Yorktown the grass
are live

   at Yorktown the earth
piles itself in shallows,
declares itself, like water,
by pools and mounds

2

At Yorktown the dead
are soil
at Yorktown the church
is marl
at Yorktown the swallows
dive where it is greenest,
    the hollows
are eyes are flowers, the heather
equally accurate, are hands

  at Yorktown only the flies dawdle
(like history)
in the sun

3

At Yorktown the earthworks
are true
at Yorktown the mortar
(of brass
weathered green,
of mermaid for handle,
of Latin for text)
screams
without noise
like a gull

4

At Yorktown the long dead
loosen the earth, heels
sink in, over an abatis
a bird wheels

and time is a shine
caught blue
from a martin's back

LOST ABOARD U.S.S. "GROWLER"

Black at that depth
turn, golden boy no more
white bone to bone, turn
hear who bore you weep
hear him who made you
deep there on ocean's floor
turn, as waters stir, turn
bone of man

Cold, as a planet is
cold, beat of blood no more
the salt sea's course
along the bone jaw white
stir, boy, stir
motion without motion
stir, and hear
their love come down

Down as you fell
sidewise, stair to green stair
without breath, down
the tumble of ocean
to find you, bone
cold and new among the ships
and men and fish askew

You alone o golden boy no more
turn now and sleep

washed white by water
sleep in your black deep
by water out of which man came
to find his legs, arms, love, pain

Sleep, boy, sleep
in older arms than hers,
rocked by an older father
toss no more, son,
sleep

❧ 172 ❧

Woodward to Washington
24 March 1950 (postmark)

Charles dear—
    Your essay becomes part of my new Bible (I really mean I do not wish to re-
turn it), which includes Powys (Rabelais) Frye (Blake) Graves (woman) and
OLSON ("the world and its contents").[94]
    I find it newing in my mind—immensely.
    I feel I know why it was rejected—you demand a genuine religious spirit
and Dostoyevsky said "man will never give up miracle, mystery and authority"—You demand that he give up all three and at the same time have the humility and faith understood by the mass (all) as owed only to Authority and
you snatch away the authority and say "Stand as object—be proud—know
how little and how great a *part* of the O you are."
    I would so very love to draw a picture of the woman who belongs in this
new space—a new kind of beauty.
    I am thrilled deep deep into my blood that before we met we were so "pin-
point to target" because even the Joyce you encircle I would have placed precisely where you have and to this day am not sure where he belongs.

    While no design of mine can in any spiritual sense be compared to a poem
of Olson's—yet there is a very deep sense in which you are correct—the
wrong title page could not have been an accident because the two hairline
boxes were 1¼ picas off in length and that is too easy to copy to have been
done so wrong by accident—the *interior* design was removed and all made
innocuous by a centered and unspaced conclusion at the bottom.
    From sending me three notes a week for several weeks, now I have heard

94. Boldereff is not quoting from but summarizing the scope of Olson's essay "About Space."

no word and learned in S.C. he said I was a difficult woman to work with and since "Joe Jay" gave him a check and promised him his future work if this was good, the printer is smiling to himself thinking he can design as well as I and I will not be needed. But Joe happens to believe in me and not at all in printers—so the printer will hang himself and his cheap little treacheries.

A curious thing goes on today in the world of printing—there are a group doing *very* fine work, but *all* on the wrong books (things like the report of the San Francisco Charter of Nations and college yearly speeches over some dumb professor's relics or da Vinci's *Paragone*, whom Michelangelo sent the *most* swift letter to—the darling—does not even use L da V's name) and with wrong illustrations (are there any right ones?) and somehow *too* obtrusive—i.e., you *see* the book and you should *hear* it. And then there is very bad and mediocre and fairly good distributed in arithmetical proportion. But colleges may find a use for me—

Makes me furious when a *very* current and non permanent book examining Russian-British relations in Iran should be magnificently printed on worthy rag paper—beautifully bound—Christ—did who? pay for it—and all it proves is that the Russians are realists who aren't lazy although in their smug stupidity they think they have made out a case against them.

I probably should be unhappy but I feel like some little bird perched on a tree—as long as there is a reed of grass to peck or pick I should worry who the president of the U.S. is?—and if I can not easily earn my living printing I am very easily going to say goodbye to it—the *weight* of my life is down under—via my notebook, via Olson.

One decision I *have* made—under no circumstances will I return to State College as the scene of my downfall—why should I walk around streets and see faces I despise when there is all the U.S. to be defeated in?

O darling—I have such a beautiful idea—I write a letter tonight—
Your loving reader

❦ 173 ❧

Woodward to Washington
24 March 1950 (postmark)

Friday

Charles darling—

May I say to you that females are god-awful dumb and that their stupidity sometimes makes me want to run around with a big knife and slice all the heads neatly, as in Lucinda's french fairy tale the picture is drawn.

From Elizabeth Livingston I receive as some sort of acknowledgement, gummed up most ineptly, so that now it is not a gift but something I have to return, a novel which is translated and sold in millions I am sure, for *me* Olson—Christ, what am I supposed to do with it? And she seriously expects me to enjoy it and then expects me to believe that she knows what my *Medea* is talking about.

But that is not my complaint—

my complaint is about all of them, my sister, my friends etc—this morning Ninette who writes a long emotional letter the sum total of which is love— and contains the sentence "I think particularly of Gandhi who ransomed one-quarter of the population of the world with love . . . love the weapon" etc

Olson baby—maybe she's got something—strikes me this instant maybe as Powys describes in Rabelais maybe one can make "love the weapon" the battle cry of what we fight—D.H.L. says it all in that Whitman thing—spreading as you said recently their fat asses all smeared over with love—giving 2000 times more than is asked—then turning bitter and taking back even the sunlight— I despise the *entire* pattern

And all we ask is separate, courageous, intelligent arrogant little integers who, when perceiving a slice of bread is required neatly place a slice of bread before us—When I think of the countless times my father did *just* that, *exactly* what was needed, no more, no less and no comments and no love and no tears and no sympathy—just "being with" adjusted with the finest hair gauge.

I have now an outline of battle—I know precisely what I am going to do— then, if within the time of my campaign nothing happens—I shall go to Pittsburgh and take a job and try to live with my brother and his wife who is a marvelous cook and put my baby in a private schol there, *if* he wants me. (He might because we both prefer a nice home to anything in the world and together we might be able to take a whole house somewhere—he is horribly burdened with debts so in that way I could help and I wouldn't be at home enough to get in their way) we shall see.

Just wanted you to know the whole thing is now very definite in my mind and I have decided since I am arrogant—*do* think I know what I am doing not to *try* to get along with dumbbells but *if* I can find work with someone who is not afraid good otherwise I will take to "lens-grinding" which is a clean form of not fucking up my beautiful profession.

Frances

Your poem is the point "the labor of the thing"

I would like to do a piece contrasting the narrow, possessive ugly sex morality of Shakespeare with the deep-knowledgeable greatness of Rabelais the straightest cleanest writer who has ever lived—he takes it all with the great hearted laughing   No attention to the various messes involved like a strong young sexy mother who wipes away the little b.t. clean and kisses passionately. Someday I want to write a whole long thing to you about Rabelais and sex (Not sex as man woman only but as the whole earth is—printing etc) If you want to see magnificent printing, clean, clean, and *read* god what beautiful stuff the Abel Le France edited with 7–8 others French edition of Rabelais 1932.

⋙ 174 ⋘

Woodward to Washington
25 March 1950 (postmark)

Olson poet

I am in the kitchen five minutes before Hanan gets here to celebrate this weekend and oh! I have to tell you this very minute *At Yorktown* is a straight transpose oh! Olson poet—what beauty—oh! god it is magnificent—the only only only one of its kind I have ever read—speaking straight for America for every man whom Olson is and was and has to be—my darling—*wait* till those boys in England and Russia find out you're here—you are our protection— our defense—can not get over the beauty

Formal and grave with the gravity of a mother and what transposition and how it leads on—

Oh! my baby it is one of the most fine pieces of poetry I have ever read I cover that hand with kisses.

What fine summary, so quiet, no bitterness intrudes but there is such deep space assuagement—I mean in great sculpture the living space between the figures represents the artist's acknowledgement and path-out-of despair. You have made living space around your separate form. Great poet

I understand *why* you want to work on the long ones—I too want it—but this is an absolute.

Please do not allow me to be a deterrent—I mean letters—I am so in love with that title The She-Bear.

Graves says the poem is Old Irish and he seems to mean it.

Lost Aboard is beautiful and I am very happy to have it—it seems pure distilled essence of papa in a way he could never have done for himself—just as La Chute is for me.

Frances

Woodward to Washington
27 March 1950 (postmark)

Monday

Charles—

Your *David Young, David Old* is indeed a letter.[95] It states the thing so clearly and does such a service to Freeman which my guess is will not be especially appreciated that I am embarrassed for the editor who writes such a *very* nice statement of his intentions, which would thrill me if he meant it, but when he specifically states that there is not so much fine poetry around to choose from and specifically mentions "over 30 lines long" and I know he *had The Praises* in his hands, I am sort of heartsick and unhappy—because his sincerity is so real to him just as Jim Craig's at Nittany when he says he *loves* beautiful printing, and yet the whole business adds up to no Olson.

Your statement makes me especially happy in that for some three or four years now I have regarded the throwing out of the concept Original Sin as one of the musts—the thing that pushed me over the brink completely was Kierkegaard—his analysis of it is the intellect pushed to its ultimate capacity of analysis and I saw that Kierkegaard was holding on to it in a completely artificial way—his intellect had so infallibly traced it out of existence and it occurred to me "why do we *have* to hang on to it?" You see on account of the ugly sex divided accusation in it, it has always hurt—but Kierkegaard with that mind so deep and original *showed* the weakness of the position from such a frontal intellectual attack, intending thereby to *deepen* the spiritual necessity but my reaction was "Nuts." It's out—let's leave it out.

It disturbs hell out of me that old boy Blake seems to be not quite clear of it, though it is *far* less in him than in his explainers. As much as I can tell at this point in my understanding Blake believed something went wrong *before* man came into the flesh and that God punished and at the same time showed mercy by creating the generative pattern since he had it in his power to push the thing into chaos—and life is tenderness from God in that it placed a zero platform beneath man representing a *limit* to his fall—he dies. But he does not exist in chaos—he exists in form. Well—all of that seems cuckoo to me. I think the whole works is a mystery—so comments on *why* the form we have—why nature, are pretty childish. Dunno.

What man does know is he has an *urge* towards form. He can not live without spirit which comprises his whole reality. So far the only author who has at-

---

95. Olson has sent *Western Review*, fall 1949 issue, containing his review of F. Baron Freeman's edition of *Melville's Billy Budd*. The review was given the title "David Young, David Old." See *Collected Prose*, pp. 109–12.

tacked with any depth the *problem* of why does man torture himself so—why does he follow the mess of pottage when so clearly is demonstrated the fact that the "kingdom of heaven is within you"—is Dostoevsky. He says it's man's love of freedom and my guess is he's right. In some kind of stubborn pride man does not want to do what is for his obvious welfare—he wants to do things his own way—and while childlike and blind—the *source* of this is desirable and I like man for not taking his welfare as the thing it must be. He's going to break his head in every other way first.

There is where we come back to Blake who says the function of evil is to discover error—and he is more right than any other answer I know. You cannot throw it out until you *see* and man sees what he feels. And it has to become *obvious* to be cast away. Makes sound sense to me.

That's why I laugh inside.

And oh! Charles I am in such a strange strange mood—indifferent and happy and at the same time terribly like a little trapped animal with 10,000 places in which to gnaw through presented and a consequent lack of choice, an inaction of a supreme degree—because I do *not* believe in any of what is out there to fight for—of those ways open to me—I do not *believe* there is one publisher in the U.S. who *cares* absolutely about quality—either in the writing or in the physical presentation. How *could* Laughlin print his New Classics series on paper so cheap—so physically unpleasant that as much as I *need* to own Rimbaud and as fine as Varese's translation is I cannot own his copies of either *Season* or *Illuminations*. I *know* of paper (the paper in my Catalogue) cost is 17½—almost newsprint cost and is it not pleasant?

And the spacing—etc in his New Classics series—and he has men like Ernst Reidel who is a magnificent designer at his disposal. And the original format for that series was far from wonderful but it *was* satisfactory and now it is awful. What the hell happens. Laughlin hasn't been neglected by the public and he has plenty of money—doesn't he ever *go* to the plant and say I *want* clean printing, I want pleasant paper—I want perfect alignment—he could have it for free—just by insisting.

Oh! Charles I wish to god I knew what the hell I should do at this point.

Frances

And the *Western Review*—Carroll Coleman is a fine designer and when he had his own press did fine press work—*how* could he permit the impermissible variations in leading—*how* could he space a P the way your note is tightly packed in—there is *no* awareness of the fact that the width of the stroke, modified in musical gradation gives the beauty.

Oh! Charles I am ill of heart.

Washington to Woodward
27 March 1950 (postmark)

monday

baby: it started just about 2 P.M. Saturday, and though it is only begun, I shall do a risky thing, send what is begun to you, because it bracketed yr birthday and i want you to see how busy i was with a matter which is buried (like the Fallen God of master melville) in the wonderful bottoms of our Link: yr birthday downed me into the Place, where a Figure is, whose birth we are together busy about

i stopped to make you copy—and spang, comes the PRAYER![96] I'll send that too, tho you will see it is rough, new, and needs to be polished

It is 5, and i want you to have this tomorrow: so i'll make copy, as it is, and shoot it along because it is, as i said
VERY CLOSE!

o

i'll write more
tomorrow, in answer
to yr beautiful
three letters

SHE-BEAR

(O goddess excellently bright,

look kindly on this effort)

I

Time, of itself, brings no significant changes

Does time stop me on the street, and say
"Pardon me, mister, which way
is life?"

---

96. "The Prayer" was apparently sent (Boldereff comments on it in her next letter), but it is not extant. It was a first draft of the "Lady Mimosa" poem sent later with letter 180. "She-Bear" was not published until *Collected Poems* (pp. 129–34).

To shred, pound, wash, decant
in order to begin . . . .

look, it is at root
a question. . . .

take fertility, for example, founding it
on quite other associations that you're used to:
     what each carried
     they threw down into springs,
     or on to the carefully colored sand, the men
     their cylinders, the women
     annulets

there is a way to breathe again, the process
not at all so complicated, a matter of a turn
(you ask me, two blocks left, then
straight ahead), of a disposing
(such as the above), of an act of averting

     one night a year the priestess
     not abandoning herself,
     on the contrary,
     by presentation takes on lovers,
     collects
     a thumb's length of value
     (coins, or a piece of turquoise)

     And leaves it to the honor of Mimosa,
     goes on about the business of her day

(o goddess, receive these, our tokens,
for your light)

2

Agree

we call the place

Pelican Rapids.

Agree,

we have a fish hook

and an axe

agree

a root can be a poison

or a plant, a house

a suffocation or

a frame

Agree,

on this plateau we've left

marauders

on the plain below

agreed, then,

we start again

1st, let us raise a praise to woman

let her brightness

be given back:

                "o Black, o dirtied,

                       covered

                o Naked, o wild, o

                thighed

                o Loose, o corrupted, o

                lain on

                o Bearer!

                who has suffered
                chagrin

                        (o Hair, o Silk

                        o Pleasurer

                              o Cedar-Box, o Wronged!)

o Round, o flesh, o

Deliverer

o Theorist,

who would charm

to save

o Seeker, o Imaginer

of passion

o Caught

in her own snare!

(O Descender, so rankly

imprisoned,

give the Judges back

stare for stare!)

O Prostitute, o Goddess, o Light

o Mate, o Equal, o Grace

o Dunged in this Cave, throw off

the Crawlers!

The Cow

and the Patriarch

are dead,

the Stable and the Son

are gone,

the Presumers, the Forgivers

are finished, you have told them

with the fire

from your eyes

o Lady, o Hatcher

o Reminder,

be,

once again,

proud!

⋆⋆ 177 ⋆⋆

Washington to Woodward
28 March 1950 (postmark)

tuesday

frances: i am spent today, put out too much yesterday   and it angers me, for
i want to carry on the BEAR   there is so much to say

evil, for example, what you write of so poignantly in the letter i
have just read
in my own mind, the patriots and aunties, the "neo-christians",
hold on to Original Sin because they do not dare launch themselves into the
larger question of (if you can even call it that) evil   and, god save us, i can recognize their timidity

i share, absolute, your distaste for the tale of the Fall as
we have it in Genesis   i go further: i abhor the whole infantile thing, the
filthy Jehovah, the puppets, the dolls that adam and eve are, the mediocrity of
the serpent   AND the offensive trick, of the flaming seraphim, to keep man
out   I left out of ISHMAEL the passage which spells out what i preferred to
leave in hint, in the "Moses" section   (when you tell me Blake saw the "sin"
or "the something that went wrong" as precedent to the flesh, I, as you know,
question him deeply, yet, so far as an Act precedent to the Cheap Temptation
(I mean "cheap" in the way my Negro friend once said, "they treat you cheap",
meaning the whites!) I agree

Moses' tale is a Lie, a Cover—and the Other Tree is the Clue: Murder is
what Jahveh, the "Father", is scared of, what he so hammingly contrives to
keep man from

It is VIOLENCE that is the door one must now enter the problem of good-
and-evil by

((((before i go on i want to send you a
beautiful flower from yr beloved Blake:

"For the Cherub with his flaming sword is
hereby commanded to leave his guard at the
Tree of Life, and when he does, the whole creation will be CONSUMED and appear IN-
FINITE, whereas it now appears finite and
corrupt"[97]

You know the pertinency i give to cannibalism   (note Blake's verb "consumed": fire is the other face of omnivore), of gesture, of flesh etc.

But what I
should like to offer you, is the same problems as they appear to me to reflect
themselves right at the heart of what we too easily call the good

((i have a
hunch, frances, that what i am suggesting is, that good-and-evil is an artificial
and wholly inadequate formulation, that it is a simplification of life as it presents itself to and in us, that the intrication is larger than either, and that we
have to stay in there without the advantage of that lazy formulation

"Beauty is difficult, Mr. Yeats"

(what you call the *urge* towards form, &
then speak of as "spirit", for a little
while, is there not an advantage in calling form "beauty"? I so much hearken
to the pre-Xtian, or rather non-Mosaic,
notion, that *chaos* was evil)

I like what you tell me Dostoevsky does with it, only freedom, & the love
for it, has also to be put through—like "spirit", and "good and evil"—the
Bessemer furnaces now

certainly you and I both know the orneriness Big mister
D is talking about, man's stubborn pride,—I think you define "love of freedom" beautifully when you put it, "he wants to do things his own way"

It excites
me, because, in my own thought recently, I have been led to think of two qual-

97. William Blake, Plate 14 of *The Marriage of Heaven and Hell.*

ities of the human which seem to me so root as to need declaration as "LAWS"—& tho, for the moment, i am only resting it inside human phenomenology, I am using the word "laws" in the same sense in which the exact scientist will speak of the law of gravitation and the law of the magnetic field   (it is one of the exciting things about the work of einstein and his men that they see the two laws as operating as one!)   ((it is not the least of the reasons why they have now got bored with the universe and are beginning to find out that human phenomenology is more interesting!))

These two qualities I speak of seem to me to lie under "he wants to do things his own way", and thus subtend the old notion of good-and-evil. I put them, at the moment, in their abstract nouns:

CURIOSITY   (the going, always, back & back to life,
                                    the drive
& TENACITY   (the motor power by which man does go
                                    back, hold on, insist, the animalness, if
                                    you like, but also the thing Rimbaud is
                                    after in driving, by way of corruption,
                                            always on the Unknown   Rimbaud,
                              peculiarly, of modern man, had the BRAINS,
                                    the power of ABSTRACTION (the love of
                          abstract *sound*) to plow right straight
              across, & not be lulled by "evil"—as
                                    Baudelaire was, e.g.

(That absolutely ULTIMATE thing in Rimbaud : "what's on the *other* side of what we have gone thru?"[98]
                                    ((you have this thing, frances))

I'm tempted to say, that i think the whole Good and Evil proposition is just too god damned lazy for words   I had to put up, for years, with the notion that I was, somehow, not "human"   Jeezus   And I begin to think that G-and-E is more of that same mud, that Lie that the human is not its extremities, rather than its statistical center   This is the doctrine of both Mass & Individualism: it treats us cheap   If I say the glory of the human is its power to ABSTRACT, then I say man is capable of nature's intent otherwheres   (she clearly proves she is abstract, in the ordering of the universe; i am not troubled that she may be able to be it by fiat, and man has to be it by purchase; okay, she is larger than any of us; okay, too; but a great man (and i say a great man is only

98. This phrase, much used by Olson, is adapted from p. 42 of Wallace Fowlie's *Rimbaud* (New York: New Directions, 1946).

a man who engages himself with beauty) approaches her just so far as he takes on the instrument of ABSTRACTION

((darling, all this time i wish i were talking about *your* present preoccupations in your work. And the truth is, I am, for your dejections over print, say, are because you are artist, because you love beauty, have the power of abstraction, are rare in yr sensitivity:

what i am trying to say is, those creatures who impede you, outrage you (like Laughlin) are not evil in any abstract or universal sense, but are mudders, have given up, fallen back from the struggle: think of Rimbaud's struggle night after night to hammer shape & sense into that filthy Verlaine!

yr cry, you are ill of heart: o!, Gan, baby, be, be assuaged!   if you tell me my size, let me tell you yours   And all we can do is stay in there: HOLD!

to give up, for one split second, is to start to lose SIGHT of FORM: how absolute you are, how, not beyond, but behind and below and above good and evil you are, when you write like an Angel: the width of the stroke, modified musically, gives the beauty

(note i leave out the beginning of yr sentence, "there is *no* awareness of the fact,"[99] fuck it, 'em, no THERE IS—& just because you YOU YOU Y O U are aware!

THAT'S THE WHOLE IMPORTANT THING; YOU are AWARE!

(to be silly, let me tell you the story my father hammered into me when i was a kid: abt the swedish cabinet-maker, who was giving the under side of a table the fullest care, and that Always Present Fucking Citizen, the Mud Man, says, "But who'll see that?" And of course the Beautiful C M says, "I do!"

o baby, to free 'em, to be free—there's only way: be it yrself   And let 'em find out, if they can   We had to

I am convinced that the Package from start to finish is wrapped up in Paradox and its Contents are Ambiguous

And that the job is to admit Chaos, in and out of us, as the Enemy—and Form the Answer

99. Olson is referring to the end of Boldereff's letter of 27 March 1950.

> And that it is ENERGY which is our given,
with such laws as Curiosity and Tenacity as the Motor Powers
> And Beauty the Form which delivers us
> Charles

our disgraces
are
our Graces

❧ 178 ❧

Woodward to Washington
29 March 1950 (postmark)

> Wednesday

Darling—

Your Tuesday letter is in my hand this morning—I want to tell you that your father had nothing on me for stubbornness—and as an *order* to my friends in State College yesterday I said "Look—no feeling sorry for me—no *worry* understand—I am either alive or dead!" and they saw the German arrogance of my eyes and I am sure they will stop all their insulting illness over me—(because you know no one of them would *move* clean and brave in my behalf—as I have marched again and again and offered my bread to challenge for a thing I believe in)

I want to write you about Bear (am not able to)—I read it aloud to myself several times—I will write later when I receive more—now I want only to say that for the first time I understand everything as though I were the blood pushing the ink—(and so far I am excited and delighted—the beginning (this sentence means I am so excited and so approve I am afraid—do not know how yet—to word my approval)—and then the Prayer thing[100] Charles I wish silence except to say—I do not believe any human being on this earth has ever before suffered and had his suffering taken up during his lifetime and given shape and relation as you have done for me—you can never know *how* assuaged I am—I keep asking—how could he know that is what it was and was for and is? Oh Charles I can never tell you how your form is so new—the positively only New in the world I know of.

I am just plain afraid to speak of the thing at all—that's why I am so awkward. This letter is about something else—something Charles if I get my bread

---

100. Sent 27 March 1950 but not extant.

business solved I want seriously to work on or to shove to you to please work on—

But when I was walking the other day I *very* suddenly—pondering the deep mystery of the LAW of sex I mean sex only in its most physical and fleshly sense—the thing for instance I have never mentioned but I have always felt sure that as an *act* as a complete-in-itself—a terrific beauty that you and Con for example have had—better than you and me—and the thing that was such a deep match and so terrifically beautiful and satisfying between Duke and me although his whole body—every single speck of it hands— skin—voice—form—fingernails—testicles—everything—was something I found ugly and loathed and certainly there was no intellectual or spiritual join—but *deeper* than any of that—this terrific exchange of life—we had an absolute as you and Con have had an absolute—*now* it occurred to me man so far doesn't *know* a single blessed jot of a millionth of part of *what* joins like to like—the *how*

And as a great revelation it suddenly poured over me—*if* man can climb up out of good and evil—if he can get over the ego in the split two sexes if he can search tenaciously *each* regardless of gender—*then* as a great Act—maybe the next great Act on the stage—he can by some deep intuition come towards a life where it will be possible to *match* that terrific sex belong (*Laws* then maybe somehow discovered through intuitional plunges) with the terrific spiritual-mental belong so that in the way Maillart has taken concrete and spun spider webs across the Alps in Beauty—man can *know* for the first time *what* is the join in Sex and *seek* to find a Mate because the Law behind tenacity and Law behind rhythm as the two poles of his being will be revealed. (Not any stupid conscious matching as in Genetics)

Maybe you can clarify what I am feeling for,

Frances

Your Tuesday letter I read as Gospel—*love* love your clarification on Rimbaud. Can you ever think of him as French or Michelangelo as Italian?

In regard to the education of young people—if a woman were taught (not necessarily by words, but by silence thus to get back the "brightness" to know that if she isn't willing to be a Mate—to search—to seek—to stand alone—to be the unprotected that she isn't worth a pfoenig and the endeavor to her mind were towards her bowels, towards clearing her being of self so as to be sybil, to learn and know the magic potion as Medea knew and lent to Jason and above that held as holy her physical attunement for purposes of attuning them in a way the details of which I can not outline but the general form of which I feel—she could move in "brightness" towards her own reality so that it would shine forth from her flesh and declare itself to her Mate, if each carried awareness of his own search to holy limits—to the limits of Brooklyn obedience.

And the young would again become shy, because alive and because they would perceive the distance of maturity as distance traveled over what heroes.

I also *feel* that if I could get a drawing pen in my hand I could draw what I mean—the rhythm is so clear to me.

⊰ 179 ⊱

Washington to Woodward
29 March 1950 (postmark)[101]

ASYMPTOTES

yup, our disgraces are
our Graces

nor have i a talent,
or a virtue,
to lend

i, too, am retted down, am
mere aroid,
like a cuckoopint decide
i am all spike and bract

for who has time
to undo his ignorance?
have you?
may i stop you,
may i tap you on the shoulder

        say, have you got a match,
        Prometheus?

        what was it like,
        to be bound?

        in your winter, what fed
        on your liver, Ambiguous?

101. This letter is a carbon typescript of a poem published in *Artisan*, spring 1953. See *Collected Poems*, p. 117.

myself, i go by glee,
don't even know the bird
eats me

     (o for a beak,
      to be sharp!   (Hail, Claw!

❦ 180 ❧

Washington to Woodward
30 March 1950 (postmark)

                       thursday

baby: i'm not supposed to say about "writing", but by gar no verboten has
come down yet, has it, on "drawing"—or has it? Anyway, I damned well believe: you take up that drawing pen, and make those rhythms come runnin'
out. BELIEVE, lady!   (i think you can do anything!)

damndest thing: the way, you and me go on thinking side by side! (space is
victored—and i always swore, knew, it could be! listen, you thank me! I
THANK YOU FOR FRANCES!
                     for yr walking-talking on Sex-the-Door, is
(i'll tell you now) the whole Back-of-the-Brain to propositions tuesday CU-
RIOSITY & TENACITY
               comes out this-way: the Original Sin had nothing
whatsoever to do with sex as it is "you-and-i-ho-to-bed"
                        ((parenthesis: the Mor-
mons and Rabelais saw the deal cold—that the Serp is the phallos, & Eve A's
teacher, what to do with it   In other words, Moses, the egyptian decadent
(are all religious afraid of it?) made the one damned thing God the father gave
poor critter man-woman for constant alleviation (I almost said illumination),
he Moses made it evil:

  In Adam's fall
  we sinned all))

the parenthesis means: because he, M or X we better call 'im, for Freud is
right, the "Moses" we know is a literary creation, based on a documentary
Moses, general to Ikhnaton, now available for study . . . . because he (or the
Jews who slew him) were so guilty about a SLAYING, they put their GUILT
on to the Other Tree, slipped one over, veiled the real object, the TREE OF

LIFE, which is what they actually assaulted, in one VIOLENT moment each of us has *several* of

> (when one motz lay in that bed and sd, i can kill, sure, i heard her straight out of the soul!)

(((This knot takes paring off: sex is surely one of the real moist-beds of violence. So the Jews were free-wheeling with the chaos-gemut when they made the parlay! But (1) that sex is *only* SOURCE as MURDER, that it is not also—what I think you were getting at in the woodward snow, and the wind making that hines-skin glow (as one beard does)—SOURCE as VISION is patently what's wrong as the root of hebra-christia

and (2), (tho here i wonder, sex seems to me so completely human-keel), that there are not other provocations for the KILL—i am thinking of the FATHER-MURDER as it goes out from sex so far that one can talk about GENERATION as it is demonstrated in such things as the planets, say, and cells   what i imagine i am getting at, is, NATURE's reproductions: do we not, really, see her as FEMALE FIGURE ALONE, no fertilizer? and isn't this curious? isn't the LADY the true image of the immaculate, not old White-Beard, the Eunuch?

o Lady, the Parthenogenetic

I am thinking of certain insects, crustaceans, and worms, certain algae and fungi, certain archaic creatures AND AT THE SAME TIME THINKING, god love us, WE, 'Oomins, *have* SEX: why i hate the Virgin is, that she is another confusion—like her son—of what, at this point I am willing, considering the foregoing worms etc., to call the "divine": a confusion at the very root of that miserable religion of 3000 yrs, between what is properly human, the DONNEE, sex, and the sexless

darling, that's about as tough a bit of words as i ever put together!   you must excuse it

the upshot—or what i was getting at—is, if we can get sex extricated from that SNARL i say the Moses-boys have had it in, it will be once more clear to man and woman that sex is only the deepest part of a continuous system which i like to put in a triad:

SEXUAL-SENSUAL-INTELLECTUAL

That's one of those hierarchical-general-izations I abhor, but I know I can trust you (no one else) to see it as better said in ACT   as a matter of fact   SEX-AS-DOOR is it as DOOR, neither SIN nor ALL

and to me, as to you, what a flowering it then makes available! (it goes right to hell out into the universe: night and day become what they are   male and female, etc, etc: what the hell is the kinetic of the human but

WOMB AND

COCK?

what are our senses but extensions of same?

what are the images of

our mind? where born?

what is *abstraction-and -projection*?

if i say the Lady can abstract-project parthenogenetically, good for her: but we never can, because we are SEXED And good for us!

What we can do is, given our given, make it, without any forgetting of root, go just as far as we can toward her!

baby: i wanted today to send you—or rather, to write as tho i were actually composing, actually, to compose straight to you, hot as it comes, more of The Prayer[102]

here goes—it probably shall eventually be folded in somewhere there next after what you have

if there is a strange
odor off this page,
it is limburger:
i had to grab
something to keep
my stomach
where it belongs!

[*enclosed: carbon typescript*]

Lady Mimosa! deliver us

102. The draft "The Prayer" is lost. "Lady Mimosa" was printed in *A Nation of Nothing but Poetry*, pp. 69–71.

from all mud

You who took on the job,

keep us at it

Lady, to whom it occurred:

the very brilliance of my flesh,

its form,

is enough to lead them out;

we follow you

You, who descended,

have the advantage on us:

what you do by fiat

we come up on from fact,

we have

another door

We cherish you,

that you chose to taste

the lazy fruit,

that you got caught:

save us, who are the inverse,

from any indulgence!

You who can breed

with or without aid,

we thank you,

that you made us

as we are.

We understand

this entrance,

comprehend

that entered on

we too uncover ourselves,

are stripped

(as you were)

by their effronteries

> (o Lady, let us also find out
>
> how to make them blind
>
> by breast or blow,
>
> they
>
> who refuse to know!
>
> (o Lady, enable us
>
> to be as able, to be not confused
>
> by violence
>
> (which is also our own)
>
> to be clear
>
> that the door we enter by
>
> we must (as you)
>
> come up through
>
> —prisoner!
>
> let us take on,
>
> as you,
>
> the nakedness,
>
> let us know,
>
> the limits)

You who understood

that the Seven you made stayed too content,

that you had to try to remind them,

to stir them up, we see,

for we have watched us

lulled, even we, your

Limicoli!

See us, as most confronted,

as housed

in the very element we eat on.

Assuage us, then,

when we are as wasps!

      You who was curious,

      we are

      you who stayed tenacious,

      we stay

      we too will

      to take it on!

      You,

      who by abstraction

      made projection,

      said form

      (with your hip!)

      said: difficult,

      beauty

      is difficult, we

      we thank you,

      Mimosa!

Washington to Woodward
31 March 1950 (postmark)

Friday

just walked across the city (had to go to do what i could to make the little *y* & *x* presentable—but of course, it is hopeless; all i was able to accomplish was to organize the verse in a new rhythm with the drawings—

            the result: i was launched on to the city at a hr when i am never there, when my energies are alone here in the north light, and it was extraordinary: i wanted either to kiss or to kill each person i saw or passed (one can tell, when one is fresh, exactly who carries life, however little, and who are death makers

            that was going, by trolley and bus   coming back, it was altogether different: i came straight thru one street, cue street, and those only peasants, the negroes, cover it almost from end to end,—and tho i am no patriotic, i do not remember passing one i would kill   au contraire

it was light that gave me joy, some faces, and a good deal of what you have written on in the letter which awaited me on my return: spaces, dispositions, intervals, which, in the midst of the worst of building, declare themselves

            ((i get so angry at a certain class of complainers about America who do not even know how to pick up the scraps the American offer just because they are, however stupid, agents of life and disclose, some angles, some split second moments, some bundles of pickaninny flesh, some negro mother (they are most of them unwed and have a relish for their kids i don't observe in those other citizens), some eyes

"what it is to look into a human eye!"

wherever

            this is just a note to catch the 5:40 mail, in hope it will reach you tomorrow, and tell you whose yr guy (who's olson?) (who is frances?) (how bright of nature to make us multiple!)

"what a single multitude looks out!"

the green time
is ring time : let me

see!

who
are
you

where
are
you

tell!
let the eye
ring

this is
bell-time

let the eye
sound, let you
look out!

((((what i sent you yesterday—i mean L. Mimose—is clearly of another rhythm, belongs in some other place:

as a matter of fact, i am tempted to think the piece as it got written in one push monday may be enough for one statement   it pitches up pretty high, comes, maybe, to its own sufficient conclusion?

i don't yet know, won't till i take it a piece further

it's a funny thing, composition the base one projects from—i mean the long base, as far back, say, as a certain post card sent to one frances boldereff, oh, maybe, was it, a year or more ago

the base is like the buried business of a pyramid, and the illusion which i, for one, as always a victim of, is that the structure, instead of being a pyramid, seems always as though it ought to be a block, that its finished top-line should be as long as the base but of course what one learns is, that the emotional statement, when it gets down, turns out to be the little top triangular pyramid, the pentacone

but girl! how stubbornly one finds it out!

well, my frances, this is just a kiss through the knot-hole in the wall, a whisper, thisbe!

pyramus

◄§ 182 §►

Woodward to Washington
31 March 1950 (postmark)

Friday morning 8:00

Charles—

Yesterday I read aloud *Lost Aboard*—I noticed how beautiful it was when I first read it, but yesterday I did not reject its beauty—when one reads aloud the physical beauty in the thing is overwhelming and I felt so glad you said you had taken up respect for it again—for of its kind it is a gem. In regard to it the only thing I keep thinking of is the painting of the woman by Picasso (Girl with a hen-1938) where all is so intensely expressive of modern psychological reality except one thing—out of her grasp is falling a bundle of coq feathers (the kind I own—milliner's coq feathers) joined as though a wing no longer of meaning and these feathers are painted with a realism—a brilliant rendering of Natura—which my guess is for masterliness no one—no Raphel or Velasquez or any of the ultimate Natura boys—has surpassed in technique and imaginative repetition. And I have always felt Picasso saying—"You see boys—IMAGINATIVE REALITY is not created out of weakness it is created out of strength—no great man would copy nature!" (Shades of Strzygowski and his marvelous contemptuous sentence "There are certain races which feel it a vulgarism to represent."

Now your poem has physical beauty maximum and the beauty so physical of the sound like all physical beauty which reaches a climax involves exquisite emotion—the reason I did not say much was because *At Yorktown* has beauty as a lesser attribute—the beauty very grave and modest—but it arises up out of the earth—a separate unavoidable challenge and in its multiplied silences cries out until there is no where to look away and one has either to contribute or to slink away—the eyes of Christ. Without my saying—of yourself you know in literature how many times this has been achieved. And that is why I agree with Kierkegaard between the Apostle and the genius is no comparison—in all eternity they will not be like—the Apostle speaks "as one having authority"—it is a beautiful essay as all of Kierkegaard—psychologically analytically impeccable. Too bad his absolute cleanness of mind was accompanied by "no gism" as Edward once said it.

Anyway he makes clear that even Shakespeare is a genius and the Apostle is not "matching" anything with geniuses—he is obeying.

And I say in silence of reverence towards God—for many hundreds of years we have had no poet who was an apostle. The problem is new again.

                                                                Frances

◄ 183 ►

[letter not sent]

Woodward to Washington
[1 April 1950]

                                                        Saturday night

Charles—

Your note does arrive and I so thank you because it is very long until that Monday on which I never receive a letter is past.

Today I worked hard and tomorrow I have to work hard and so for a week—Charles. I steal along over this thing—afraid to believe that I am launched in that life I have been planning and dreaming for many years—I never have more than $30 work ahead of me but I always have one more job to hear about and I walk very quiet not to disturb the beginning formation pattern. Scared to death of course, but I realize when I am an old lady I will envy now—that the balance required such firm certain tight-roping—that I was so young and alive.

I wonder if it will ever happen that I do one job I absolutely approve of? I keep thinking—*why* can't it? all the choices are yours—but in some strange way they are not mine—and there never seems to be a job in which all the choices are open—I found myself all day today explaining to you "But you see Charles, why the measure, why the leading, why the margins"—

Dearest, what I began to tell you was:

1. I do not follow into your male trap at all—when you say "space is victored"—I just say "pshaw—ain't victored to this female." Even angers me that life sets up space and then moves my mind so that we can appear to ignore it—(Charles dearest, I have noticed, sometimes my childish humor is lost completely on paper—*don't* take seriously.)

But seriously for your negro friend if the occasion ever arises—

When Helen was here—I was talking about black men—about how I would like to have married one and didn't only because I never had a chance to meet one—and Helen said "You notice it is always women who marry negroes—no negress would be fool enough to take a white man when she could have a negro." Which sums up the whole thing and this is probably true of a *far* larger proportion of the American populace than you would guess. Women have faults but they *are* close to reality and they know the white man is no good—he's gone rotten.

Charles has the beauty and aliveness of a negro with the intellect and pressure of a Greek and the wildness of a Russian—just hot stuff. I love black women *much*, wonderful mothers.

For me the Monday thing[103] reaches a terrific climax—I am *very* for leaving as is.

The Mimosa is different—a mathematical study of the construction of the Motz life pattern—took a long time for me to understand it—it is so formal world form—wait—D'Arcy Thompson says it—double configuration is what comes to mind—he says

"Composite inflorescence shewing spiral patterns of the first and second order."

Dearest you know darling it embarrasses me to say aloud I read me—and I am not at all *conscious* of it—but I am *so* very grateful to you for comprehending everything—oh! valued—you never will ever be able to realize what a miracle—yesterday I walked around saying—Charles Olson—the Charles Olson—America's only great man—American's carrier—was in this house—in this bathroom using these towels—standing on this stair—oh! never will I believe that it is true.

My name is not
Patience

Don't know no Thisbe but think "Thisbe-q" is a charming misnomer for her who feels Michelangelo's NIGHT

[*on envelope:*]

Name line does not refer to us. Refers to things.

◄ 184 ►

Washington to Woodward
3 April 1950 (postmark)

103. "The She-Bear."

  monday

francessima:

    the truth is, you had given me satisfaction right off the bat on LOST as well
as YORK, intense, when you put it YORK was as if a mother wrote (you) and
LOST, as tho yr father had writ

    (i discover today that gold is my unconscious juxtaposition to black   nei-
ther of which, of course, i am   and i wonder what significance the relation of
the two has)

    my senses are scattered today, not loose nor adrift, just scattered

    did i tell you PV landed? poetry n y will publish summer issue   i had al-
ready played with a re-write of the 1st page, but turning it over in my mind
last night, i was very much aware of your insistence i not remove the sentence
on eliot   And started playing with it:

    he goeth by his own personeth
    so knoweth
    naught

    i wish i had something very beautiful—and small—to send you today,
some handsomest of annulet

                            this is just a note
                              to tell you

                              fr He Who Is La-
                              zy
                              charlemo

                              ❦ 185 ❧

Woodward to Washington
3 April 1950 (postmark)

Charles Angel
Carrier

This is an attack:
I think *Lady Mimosa* is too full of hebraic modesty.
I would attack:

O Lady, enable us
To be as able, to be not confused
by violence
(which is also our own)

WHAT IS WRONG WITH VIOLENCE?

violence indeed is out of sex
violence is the caught-to-the-breast of Jesus, of Blake, of Rimbaud, of
Michelangelo, of Goethe and of me and you.

Jesus did it most beautifully in performance

Blake preached it

Rimbaud used it via image

Michelangelo had it for method

Goethe had it as knowledge

You dealt it to me as introduction card, which, if I were willing to leave
lying face up on my entrance table, you were willing to call again.

The whole thing is *with intelligence*. Violence is necessary. It is *the* weapon
with which to attack chaos. What of Beethoven? Forcing those sounds
through nature right straight *through* his deafness into reality?

You do *not* turn it against Connie—as your blood directs, but against yourself, as raw material from which to hear form. How proud a thing that man
should dare form—how *deep* of Poe—"God no longer creates—having made
man—man now creates."

OK Olson at this second I see that is what you are saying but I still object to
"which is also our own" sounds apologetic. "Which we *claim* as our own" anyhow the list claims. It is perhaps the greatest distinction between humans—
those who dare clutch violence as a two-sided sword naked in their own
hand—I wrote you years ago "There is a sword how right oh! yes" and the
image was of no handle, the side next the flesh cutting in almost as deep as the
side turned to the enemy.

We cannot change the world—we cannot "save" it, transform it or soften
it. It will always be the enemy until violence used with integrity (which is understanding) consumes or hacks or what have you—and it is no more.

I reject absolutely—

"We cherish you
that you chose to taste
the lazy fruit,
that you got caught:
Save us, who are the inverse,
from any indulgence!"

I reject absolutely

> "You who can breed
> with or without aid,
> (*not* true—androgynous is no answer—it is still breeding)
> we thank you,
> that you made us
> as we are."

> I don't thank.
> No female thanks.
> I hate its guts

My hatred is my whole weapon—the depth of my hatred proved in my present actions. I despise the sex rigmarole so deeply I am willing to show my despisal in its sharpest form—Olson sleeps by another's side.

I *wait* like a vigilant enemy—I want it all consumed.

I want Olson to step forth without debt—to speak a new image as he did in the letter accompanying.

We can consume like daddy says not by *Sin* not by *All*—but by door—door used with integrity to the hilt—with guts. I *want* speech out of Olson like no speech ever uttered anywhere on earth before.

(Never said it was easy—paradox—contradiction is of the essence—)

The *meaning* of your poem is right—I want more violent language—I want more *Olson*.

I want Lady Mimosa speaking aloud to herself—

I want the pain

I want the rejection

I want the door

But I do not want sex insulted—I *want* my Olson to say "how bright of nature to make us multiple"—it has to be *hard* language full of *hard* paradox—

Oh! Christ what I ask of you—

This is really to be our link—darling baby I cannot speak for myself—you must do it for woman and for man and for future.

How about a new race—

A race with the *blood* the hot hot blood of a black man

And the wildness of Olson—his eye

>   And the intellect of a Greek

(All of which for me, his enamoured, my Olson poet has)

Oh! put out your hand and force this earth to yield you up a new shape

The Monday thing is terrific—my money is on leaving it separate—just as is—it is marvelous.

Would *you* like to have in public places (necessary, that is, because of the aid one may need) *your* legs opened so far they seem like to crack off—to bring out—an enemy—(which is what every child is without exception—oh! *used used*—thereby the *beauty* of the love—that the mother *grasps* that enemy her mental, physical, emotional *drainer* and *gives* it love)

You will note that *every* female without exception regardless of racial background—read my words "will get your nose broken if you try" and smiles and looks at me with *love*

I am certain in my soul your Connie loves me—she must—she trembles because of the pain—the ache—the *demand* out of oneself to *pay* to come alone—to work to strive to learn to come separate and she has had no hand—no Frances for friend—only Olson—whom she is trapped by her love for—Everything a man teaches you when you love *deepens* the trap—knots the net

In case you don't know it—

I love you

I cover you with 10,000 kisses

I think you are everything every woman has ever dreamed of

If Connie wants you all her life and you want her Olson—I will never ask my baby to live with me—

But I want you

ᔰ 186 ᔱ

Washington to Woodward
4 April 1950 (postmark)

tuesday

okay, TIGRESS,

(& EUPHRATES): that's just what was needed, a full dress rehearsal of the motz lightning! of that planet, (VENUS), crashing into mister OITH!

I asked for it. And it doesn't take a splinter off yr fire, that I had laid my own curse on miss mimosa just abt the time you did, CITOYENE!

I'm tellink you, it is the goddamndest business, this business, to have one's trolley on the wire! *every* run!

'Course, the strike, hebraic is definitely below the belt, BOLDEREFF!   But a foul's a fair, when we're 3000 yrs up, in the air!

                                   Whoops! WHOOOOOOPS!
nice eye, lady!   i say, that's callin' 'em, old gimlet! SHARPY!

and, SIRIUS,
        i get that, too

        (you know by now o el es so en is on a swing
        off
        that was the wipe-out ("lady mimmy"):
        shit/
        "a-gathering black-berries"
        god was/
        anger
        gets cranky/
        wash-out/
        "a fine mess of
        ge-filthy fish"

((roofer schaefer just came in, to bring me his papa, age 80, one eye left (the
grandfather a german immigrant)   schaefer jr marked me, i him because he
is one of the few left, a master from a master   and what was he in to see?
matthew brady's photographs of the civil war   & all because he had the eye, if
untutored, to mention (as the only sculpture in wash. worth mentioning) the
cavalry group at head of the mall!   god, you know, baby, how it is, all, all at
root, respect for one's work

and that's what's gone, what they have stolen: a prometheus doesn't today
need anything as dramatic as fire   all he needs, to be a culture-bringer, a
quetzalcoatl, is pride, to give man back pride, that wondrous garment to
throw around his hand's doings

& awkwardness and eyes: they're the tellers, the grace

last night, when i heard crosby *and* the printers had fouled up the other *y & x*,[104]
i wanted to take every printer in this town & clean the commercial shit they
have let themselves be covered by   god, they're worse than cab drivers!   they
are so patently ashamed, they've become such money-huckers   bargain-
ers   speeders

(for a printer to let a dizzy woman mess up *print*—words on a page!)

    104. This is the second printing of *Y&X* in a smaller format, finally out in May 1950.

so you
see why schaefer makes me happy, like a crocus!

it is so terrible, what, on these simplest of levels, has happened to man, worker (& by god it did my heart good to hear old schaefer put it this way: fell 7 times, had 7 children, and adopted another! married twice & never was in a hospital till last year!) how can you have men with cocks when the work of their hands is cheapened on them?

god damn all cheapeners

(again,
the Negro: it is they who drive cabs without insult to themselves And one night some months ago one of them explained to me why he thought his fellows (white & black) were so low about their trade: says he, it's a public service, and you know how people are about public servants! how they treat you!)

well, sweet, sweet to the taste of this man

love for today
charles

[*on back of envelope:*]

you-freight-ease

187

Woodward to Washington
5 April 1950 (postmark 6 April 1950)

Wednesday

Charlesmo—

Under any circumstances except you, belovéd, I would be silent now—for I am crushed down and desire only one thing—to be out of my flesh—I am in one of those terrible earth sorrows—and in the meantime my worldly affairs appear to be getting worse rapidly and my distaste and my unbelief paralyze me. Of course no man can have much—Christ darling—the pain that is on all of us—there are no satisfactions offered. Not any.

I have never in my life done anything in such blackness but take myself off alone until I recover—but when one is in Washington and the other in Woodward—silence has to be explained.

I once knew a young girl whose parent had committed suicide and so Charles I try to keep myself walking around.

I only want to tell you that personally, as Frances, I deeply appreciate all of the understanding *Lady Mimosa* shows—I will show one day my unmailed letter[105]—you have beautiful passionate penetration of other's facts—my attack was the greatest proof of my love—very public—very exhausting for a woman in love.

And the phrase "hebraic modesty" was not meant against my beloved—it runs together for me as one word because I have since 17 despised the way they use modesty as a weapon—and it covers such an ugly arrogance. I have always believed modesty is a great quality which can be seen only by God, Michelangelo maybe and Motz who watches for it. Maillart and Olson have what I call modesty—the hard judgment of men and the relation of humilitas to the task. Darling I really am drained—I am in despair—please do not expect letters.

⊰ 188 ⊱

Washington to Woodward
6 April 1950 (postmark)

thurs

frances, Lady:

a 2nd day with no letter from you, and i am terribly discouraged, too aware for words

this is to tell you

don't, please, baby, be thrown off if i seem day after day to jabber about upstairs things: it don't mean i miss what goes on below

is difficult, is specially, where there are no frames. . . . .

love,
Charles

⊰ 189 ⊱

Woodward to Washington
7 April 1950 (postmark)

Good Friday

---

105. See Boldereff's letter of 1 April 1950.

Charles—

In the preface to Gamow's book on the Sun[106] he writes: "Though the author cannot conclude this preface with the customary statement that 'all the characters appearing herein are purely imaginary' it is perhaps best that he warn the reader against giving too great credence to such minutiae in the following pages as the untidiness of Democritus' beard, the rainy weather in Princeton at the time of the construction of the Russell diagram and the relationship between Dr Hans Bethe's famous appetite and his rapid solution of the problem of solar reaction."

The book opens thus:

"Which is more useful, the Sun or the Moon?" asks Kuzma Prutkov, the renowned Russian philosopher (invented by the poet Alexei Tolstoi) and after some reflection he answers himself: "The Moon is the more useful, since it gives us its light during the night, when it is dark, whereas the Sun shines only in the daytime, when it is light anyway."

Christ I love Russians. And that is why the pursed mouth of America will never understand them in a million years—they have come up with some damned fine boys in mathematics and science but in their stomachs they *know* Kuzma's got something—maybe man is just keeping himself busy to hide how lonesome he is.

All of which reminds me of the reason for writing this letter—Mr. Richard Chase—*why* the Motz doesn't buy America. Nice man—obviously—says some nice things—but oh! how *impassionate*—oh! how the great story gets by him—oh! how he doesn't know what he is talking about.

I could do murder for a sentence like this:

"And Ahab—his is the purest insanity, for he rejects the conditions of life so fanatically and for so long that reality *is* for him the mask, which is what he finally calls the white whale. And behind the mask there is Nothing. The mask itself is Nothing; it is pure neutral whiteness or death."

"The discovery of reality is the pre-condition, and the acceptance of reality is, perhaps, the whole condition of the atonement of the young man with the gods and the fathers from whose estate he has fallen"[107]

2 paragraphs above the flower you sent me is Blake's beautiful answer:

"I then asked Ezekiel why he eat dung and lay so long on his right and left side. He answer'd 'the desire of raising other men into a perception of the infinite.' This the North American tribes practise, and is he honest who resists his genius or conscience only for the sake of present ease or gratification?"[108]

I have out your letters on Chase and your comments on *Ishmael*.[109] Oh! my

106. George Gamow, *The Birth and Death of the Sun* (Mentor, 1945).
107. Richard Chase, *Herman Melville: A Critical Study* (New York: Macmillan, 1949), p. 34.
108. William Blake, plate 13 of *The Marriage of Heaven and Hell*.
109. Olson's letter of 9 March 1950.

darling—I love you because you suffer as I do—every time you make something you start looking at it minutely and tearing it apart and saying—"here the trolley went off the wire." But oh! Olson I write this letter to tell you one thing—

Chase's book is OK—it serves some purpose and I am glad he loves Melville but

Olson's book is a great living breathing human document—it is a great book—a study of Melville in the size of Melville and every word in it is a challenge and a poetic spur.

I could write you very much—but believe me darling—I have told you before—your book consoles Melville and assuages his pain—it is the only living voice—your voice and you are *never* never to mix yourself up with the product of nice little men whose love is greater than their intellects.

Frances

One more word—my young Russian friend Kyril Kalinin—used to look at me and smile and say

"But to us Russians it is a compliment to say that we are crazy"—and include me in "us" with his smile.

And Motz includes beautiful Olson

and his fine speech on the abstract limits man not in the middle but at his abstractest limits.

This day in commemoration of Jesus whom I love I send my love to Olson—whom Jesus loves and kisses.

Frances

WE NEED YOU BIG BEAUTIFUL
    OLSON
    CHARLEMO

Count. There are so damned few it's not funny.

❦ 190 ❧

Woodward to Washington
10 April 1950 (postmark)

Easter

Charles belovéd—

My agony is intensified by a knowledge that my note gives you agony. Dearest, I want to tell you it is not at all with me as your Thursday note indicates—I am in no way waiting or wondering or pressing you for solutions; I am a passionate woman who has given her life once for all into your hands—

I make no stipulations or inquiries or halfnesses. I believe you are a great beautiful man—serving God—and I believe you are the greatest man alive today in America. I have committed my life to you already—it is done—it isn't something which is in question.

I believe you will solve your personal problem as God gives you the vision to solve it; I by the vision which is the purpose and the identity of my entire existence *know*—I have a frame in reference to you and beyond that is God's business.

I wrote so much about Connie in my letter because her reality was near to me. In a life lived as mine is—I do not ask anything—I know that I believe in you and that you are struggling with your whole soul to do what seems to you the best. I remember how no words from anyone changed or could change what I gave to Boldereff—I could not do other than I did because a strong person has to obey his own understanding and it cannot be forced.

All this I have understood from the beginning. I never press you dearest (I did about my body—but I mean in regard to one person)—words always mean something else. What happened to me—I do not blame you for not understanding, for I, who am a woman, never dreamed the physical thing is the way it is—so absolutely horrible—the *ugliest* fact probably in total Nature—the despair—the temptation to destroy oneself—the cells are dying, Charles, and the thing isn't ego—it isn't *human* it is dying cells of Nature. I despise it and am embarrassed by it and I was embarrassed to place my lowness before you—but I could not do anything at that day but continue to breathe—that was the maximum hold for that day. I can never convey to you—because no woman *dreams* of it until she is in it—how horrible the whole thing is—and believe me when you write Lady—I take that name to myself because the only hold is aristocracy—not walking out on a responsibility—When a mind as strong as mine seeks death believe me there is no thing that can dissuade except an obligation of honor—and she especially to me for reasons you know of.

Charles dearest I want to tell you that you and I are closer than man and woman have ever been before. I believe I am within your flesh—I believe and know you live by me—you know I give you my life day after day as it is commanded of me to do.

If you think it is likely that I may not see you for a long time—it would be kind of you to tell me—so that I may prepare myself.

This note does not sound beautiful but oh! Charles the thing it is trying to say *is* beautiful—that out of the horrifying fact of Nature (the discontinuous bitch) that man (which today includes woman) by his stubborn search breaks that crust and *is*. We join hands in a beautiful nursery circle of song with Herman who *so* wanted what you and I are making.

On Friday night in my bed 2:00 AM and onwards in agony I for one second actually felt you rub your cheek against mine—you were actually there and it has not happened ever before since you went away.

Frances

This morning—thus the life of a mother, at 5:30 I had to get up to see what the Easter bunny brought to my daughter—who is a lovely wood Pansy!

❧ 191 ❧

Washington to Woodward
10 April 1950 (postmark)

monday

darling:
　　　　the turning back of spring has left me prey again of the flu, but i tell you only to explain why you did not get a lovely mysterious happening of Good Friday: i could not get out to post it

　　　　and i should explain these recurrent illnesses: they are only blocks my system puts on itself   my curse is, i do not know how to play on the ground on which i work   i twist up to pitches, in order to work, and then, because i do not go mad (break), i get high and thin from fatigue, and then am invaded by any disturbance, whether it is some human horror, or something as silly as a draft

　　　　it is all right if i stay here by my own fire where i control my isolation   but, of course, i do have certain causes to go out about, and bang—if it is a moment when i am pitched a certain way, crash

　　　　usually i don't give a damn   it increases my isolation, and i work   but then, there is an accumulation   And i think i am suffering one right now: this fearsome winter has lasted too long   i want out   (an americanism, if i ever saw one!)

　　　　yr letter today has helped hugely   i have brooded deeply since you wrote of suicide, its presence in your context   one day we must talk that one out, frances, my love   it is a thing i rear my whole faith before   yet it has come close to me twice (two friends, one only ten days ago)[110] and i have been over and around it from other causes, not the least of which is *Ahab, a Dance*   it made me moan where i lie coild in bone to have you disclose its presence for you, too, sweet, sweet life

　　　　i have now found in strzygowski your christ horse-mounted, yr

---

110. F. O. Matthiessen (see "Diaries of Death" in *Collected Poems*, pp. 143–44).

havrenah-lands, and i would write and write to you, how beautiful it is, how beautiful it is you bring it to my attentions, how beautiful it is, as you so exactly know, to have one's blood reinforced: like cookies, these wonderful stucco things, like archaic myth of the baking of man—my objectism right in front of my nose!   (o frances, pride, pride in man's imagination!   (((you must know that filipine business, of god the baker, & 1st, too much fire, and the black; then, too little, and He rejects the pale white thing that comes out of the oven; last, the lovely brown right-made man!)))

        but 1st, even tho it is too late, to tell you the Good Friday word— i wanted to write something to you, because i know you Believe   i had bought, and not opened, 6 volumes of the Golden Legend, as Englished by Caxton   so, thinking hard of you, i opened   and this is what i came on:
        "The passion of our Lord was bitter for the sorrow that he suffered in derisions despitous and of many filths fructuous."

        I also wish the enclosed[111] had come in time to come to you as a colored egg under yr pillow (or so my father used to do with me of eostre morning!)
        don't let its miserablenesses bother you too much: tell me, but don't let's cry down a wind which blows a poem into a strang-er's hands (or, anyhow, that's a writer's lonesomeness!)   And the day will come you'll do my book of prose, baby, and show 'em!

        so much is wrong with it, that such few minutes & so little scrupulousness would have made right: "Season" down, "Lion" left, that copyright page altogether different, the paper, "Preface" murdered . . . god damn, god damn, god damn   you add, so that i'll know

    in derisions despitous
    and of many filths
    fructuous

        I find dr strzygowski so difficult to read, so impeded by his own petulances (these scholars are so often, when they're good, so cranky: my god, if they only knew what it's really like to put up with quarrels!) that i must ask you sometimes, where he says more on a thing than my nerves can stand to find, it makes me so angry, a guy should have in his hand a book and such work, and waste it, time after time, counting coup on his enemies

                                                e.g., this terrific idea, of the Archer, the Unicorn, the Mountain, and the Bird, which he refers to as of

---

111. The proof copy of *Y&X* is in possession of the recipient.

the Bewcastle Cross, i think, and says, was all over the place in the Middle Ages   what an amazing light-like business of good and evil!

Me, too, on Chase: i guess i did not tell you how horrified i got, too, in the end: the little bastard, the little wronger of his own nice little right! i got my knife out, too   maybe i'll have occasion to use it

frances, i am most close to you, as i sd, in the bone, in night & the cloth of dreams, in that wood we make the hidden shapes we know so little about illuminating even to our secret selves

((because i am flu-ridden (my venusberg), i do not cohere or compose   i fly around, the broomstick of this witch: wood reminds me i wanted to tell you a long time i was right about woodhenge when i used it: a flyer told me, there is a Woodhenge just north of Stonehenge, completely unseeable from the ground! (Which confirms, by the way, several shots of Dr Stir)

this is fire and wood
and love for you,
frances,   for you, love
charles

darling: this i enclose, to show you how, just to be in touch with you, sparkles the springs of this man

               & it is to kiss and thank you, for he has been dry these several days, and even to be a little resurrected. . . .

EXPERIMENT IN FORM[112]

what we do not know of our selves, of who it is who lies

coiled or unflown

in the marrow, in the bone, hidden

from our own knowing

    (of rhythm is image,

    of image is knowing,

    of knowing there is

    construct)

112. Published in a slightly revised version as "ABCs(2)," *Collected Poems*, p. 173.

to find, in a night, who dwells in that wood where shapes hide,

who is this woman or this man whose face we give a name to, whose shoulder

we bite, what landscape across which figures ride small horses, what bloody
    stumps

these dogs have, how they rear the golden cloak, and the boat,

how he swerves it to avoid the yelping rocks

where the tidal river rushes?

❧ 192 ❧

Woodward to Washington
11 April 1950 (postmark)

Tuesday 8:30 AM

Charles dear—

Can you know (you do) how hard it is for me to sit here, at my table, so close to that U.S. Post Office, and see it drive away and not know whether it carries a Charles letter or not.

I want to tell you a fact which to me is one of the great facts of which life is possible—my horrible printer has not returned one page of proof for 3 weeks although I have sent him 96 pages—a cover design and a contents design—and yesterday—with no letter from you—I sat here and made a lovely poster—so beautiful Charles and sent it off to that same printer because he is the one who has the beautiful type—it has taken years of what in the old days was called fasting in the desert to bring myself to that absolute command where no human event can impinge upon the release of that beauty inside me. And thou above all knowest whereof I speak.

I was cleaning Lucinda's playroom yesterday. I wish I could send you the original but I am afraid to trust it to the mails—I struped (?) over to pick up a scrap of paper to throw it away and something made me open it and I began to read—

Hear my prayer my father
let an angel here
let an angel there
let an angel all around me
let an angel on top

let an angel on the bottom
let an angel on all four sides
let angels walk
around me

In that child writing and spelling—
I almost fainted—
I preserve it for you—
a great poem out of the heart of this earth

I wish Charles you would send me some physical thing from near you—
some undershirt or handkerchief or tie or something to place beneath my pillow in the night when I am so full of sorrow.

≈ 193 ≈

Washington to Woodward
12 April 1950 (postmark)

                                                      wed

baby: i am off to the zoo!
                    one of the two real guys fr black mt came in at 2 am,
vic kalos, and what is a proof, says he, has washington a zoo
                                              so i am taking him

but i miss the chance to spend the afternoon with you, to tell you how tremendous was the need and the effect of yr letter yesterday

i shall tell you, do every day, by what i do
                                        love,
                                        charles

≈ 194 ≈

Washington to Woodward
14 April 1950 (postmark)

                                                      friday

my motz:
    (thank god that's done, and i can leave behind the things of this world—

have been busy for an hour trying to beat up jobs for two citizens, Hanson in
Seattle, and Ragsdale in Baltimore: why anyone wants to teach i do not know.
(Even little tough guy kalos wants, one day, to go back to black mt and do an
albers: teach! At 18! and wants to! But he put it beautiful: it is the most generous act. And works, if it is amorous. ::::: what he doesn't know, is, are there
many one can love. :::: i was lucky, there was him, and Nick (Cernovich, who
will be a poet, is: Kalos will be, is, painter)

he left yesterday, unhappy: he came to get something from me (i don't
know precisely what, but i think it was lovin', flesh: he's dark, severe, a new
hebrew—i must be some archetype northern to such (were you, too, to edward, & the pere, and shahn's friend, and others, my egyptian?)

                                                            yr nature is
such a constant delight to me, frances: i walk abroad in you, (as in our garden
of the 18th dynasty), investigate you   it is such a joy, and if i do not send you
some piece of cloth, it is because i send you the fragrance of that place, where
we dwell

                                        my trout, my bream
(leap,
sweet Salmon!)

    nor, darling, can i tell you i will not see you for some time   i do not know
such a thing   (if i did you could be sure i would, tell)   i hold, that is what i
am doing, holding, baby (there is an elephant at the zoo—they have *such* a
nervous system!—who, in a rhythm so iterative as to be erotic, moves back
and forth in a space of three feet (all day and nights, the keeper tells me) her
eye white and mad, with occasional fierce snorts of air from her short indian
trunk, her lovely fore legs lifted and placed down as in a dance unborn, nature's most animate dance: grass blades made animal)

    frances, it is possible you understand how, this day, and days, when i sit like
this and write you, i come to you, find the very beauty we talk of, the frame of
man-woman, taste you, know that delight, delight such high-born delight as
you give?
        do you know, sweet Lady?

    you must know, i hate the literary   And this letter, any, is when it is to you,
the very other thing   yet words, words—no, you know they are not words;
all i mean to do is to say with them, these are words which are acts, acts of loving, with no discrepancy between word and act   my letters are undershirts
for yr pillow, grave one

the blood flow of sex-senses-intellect is unbroken, unbreakable, you made me the expressor of this triad born in me: this is the BELIEF!

　　　　　　　　　　　　　　　　　　　baby, love charles

i would write all afternoon, but this i'll post now to catch the early collection

❧ 195 ☙

Woodward to Washington
15 April 1950 (postmark)

Charles—

I am very shocked not to have a note from you.

When you thought Connie's job *might* blow you asked me to make that terrific sacrifice and not to see you—

Now when someone comes to visit you you write me one letter in a week and a half—the week and a half when I am under the most terrible pressure possible

I have no money

I have no work

I have no companionship

I have no library

And I receive from you in the darkest hours I have lived through one small note.

Do you think it is kind Charles?

　　　　　　　　　　　　　　　　　　　　　Frances

❧ 196 ☙

Woodward to Washington
15 April 1950 (postmark P.M.)

　　　　　　　　　　　　　　　　　　　Saturday morning

Charles—

You said in Tarrytown that no man can endure absolutely alone no matter how strong he is and I agreed.

You saw the elephant in the zoo and you can describe that torture to me as a dance—I understand how you admire those graceful strong creatures—but zoos are places of torture, symbols of man's blindness, and that you could bear to watch that white eye and not falter, is the explanation of how you can treat me in such a blind way.

The human thing is made of blood. Sometimes what is needed is not words—it is the sight of a human eye. I need no sex now—I am far too torn for that. I do need you.

If you cannot come to me now Charles when I need you not out of weakness like all the others you mention—not out of lack of strength (I curse the hour which taught me my terrible strength) but because I need *human*—I need to see the eye—the words are just like thin odorless water to me—who is not a salmon but a woman.

If you cannot come Charles I want you to spell out at once without any delay for any reason whatsoever—*why*—I want spelled out for me in ABC language why you can't come.

I need you.

I will never again have such need—and that is an accurate statement—it is not hysteria.

I want to know in *all* details—all the details exactly why you do not move to me now.

If my faith were not so deep—I would simply leave you, because I am proud and I hate to beg. I want to have written out for me in childish language what do you mean by "hold"—you are not holding anything for me—you are destroying deep precious knit cells in my body and my spirit.

So what does it mean? It is the most deep thing of faith Charles that I am willing to ever ask you—

I crucified myself to write that Easter letter. God knows I did. And I am now in extremis.

Your
Frances

⋙ 197 ⋘

Washington to Woodward (special delivery)
17 April 1950 (postmark)

Monday

frances—

it is getting on toward 5:30, & i want at least to make sure you have word from me as early as possible tomorrow

it is now 48 hrs since you wrote those notes to me which came this afternoon & which I have been aghast before now for two hours

it is 48 hrs, & will be 72 before you hear from me & I can only hope you

1st, it's crazy, for i know your soul, and know you are in terrible need, but you have made me cold as ice—by (1) attacking my words, language, this communication between us which i believe in so deeply, as thin odorless water

& (2) by asking me for explanations

i suppose you know it, but you have struck where *i am*, and where i do not budge for anyone   (i first found out (2) when i was 16, and my father tried it

     & (1) of course is where i am, where i am committed against you or anyone: where i got committed, i can honestly say, because of your love

          (((which makes me a punk, in my own eye, when you say, "i need you"—but there is no equals in scales, none at all. And that's that)))
       ((((((i can't stand it, justice,

look, baby—i don't know in what way i misled you, if i did, on my coming to you, but if the thought of it is going to screw you to such pitches as these notes, you must, for your self, for your self, frances, cease to have anything to do with the thought (the facts i offered are 1. in n.y. telling you you might not see me again, and agreement between us; 2. surprise, i come to you in wood-ward, am supposed thereafter to go off out of the country; 3. in february, when i was dreaming of coming, not coming, and telling you, i did not know when   i add one further "explanation": i did not go to mexico because i could not bear to be that broken off from you)
    i have had to fight for two hours to put words down to you at all, i was so flabbergasted you so swept off words as validities of this love—whatever it is—between us
        if you cannot any longer stand that value, must tell me blood is better, you must not again frances make light of it   that's all i ask: i am the last one prepared to argue such a point   it has nothing to do with argument: it is a faith   And let me assure you it is a faith with all that implies—i believe in my words as reality, love, life

in other words—and you must, because you do have the reach in you, un-derstand that i would understand anything you do—you must protect your-self, darling:
      there is no sense in any business which leads you to such a pitch as this, that you be torn like this, that you write me such notes as these

i don't
care who the hell olson is or what the hell he says or does, or does not, you just
got to take care of yourself, motz, so you don't get this screwed up

if this dream of eloise and abelard   (you force me, to shift from pericles
and aspatia)
            aw, fuck the whole business: you have made imagery and words
wry in my mouth, sound like lie

fuck it, frances, just fuck the whole business   let it go

god damn it: it's just another dream   ok   ok   ok
                        yrs who don't give up easily
                        Olson

᷂ 198 ᷂

Washington to Woodward
18 April 1950 (postmark)

                        tuesday

frances:
    have nothing to do with poets   they know nothing about human reality as
it is some one else's   when i responded like an animal yesterday, and got
fierce over language, made the statement it was reality, love, life, i said something i did not know i believed   i've been brooding since, trying to figure out
how i could have misled you, and i am forced to think it is precisely at this
point of language as reality, as the only reality which a man like me can be said
to serve

    what i am led to think may be the misleading factor in my case is, that there
is also present man as usual, some unburned-out figure of the past who is confusing, who takes (and gives, i suppose) responsibilities by, as Constance puts
it, the wrong handle, a handle which a poet honestly cannot justify himself for
handling

    in my mouth this morning like ashes is a phrase: image more than person,
more syllable than image

    the result is, so far as *any* other human being goes, myth and impossibles, a
whole series of impossibles

lies, i suppose they amount to, for any other person involved, though god is my witness they are not meant so—a poet also has to live in mortals, even though he may do it as experience which does not stop with itself but starts and ends outside itself

you see, frances, with no derogation—on the contrary—what, from the start, i suppose i could offer you was, the images you invoked in me, both as they took the form of EPIGON or SHE-BEAR and as they took the form of letters written to you with all the solids of verse, if not the final shapings such *action* would, (i am forced now to say from my point of view only), be love

this is blood, it takes blood, and it also, unless i am ultimately and utterly deceived, rests on a penetration and perception of what you call "i am, after all, a woman"

that i do not throw my presence also in and that its absence has become so destructive to you that you write i am annihilating you, at this point i ask myself, how did i do this wrong, how is this the issue of it all, at what point was i not scrupulous when i had honestly sought to be

i am hung on that question nor can i pretend to know the answer   what i have said above is a present try   i could wish that it could give you a little ease, some clue

love,
Charles

◄§ 199 §►

Woodward to Washington
18 April 1950 (postmark 19 April 1950)

Tuesday night

Charles my dear—

When I wrote that dedication to Michelangelo I so meant what it says—the horrible reality which produced my two letters, Charles, I do not in any way try to explain—I will say only this—that the tension inside a woman (the life carrier) when she is being ripped out of that reality is not possible to explain or protect oneself against or to take care of yourself about. It is one of the tragic realities. The insanity, Charles. I lost the two best friends I had at this period in this existence. One, the only woman I have ever dignified by the word friend inside my soul—the most quiet, well-bred, courteous lovely woman who would have died rather than do something conspicuous—bought Bergdorf-Goodman's best dress and hat—probably $3–400—rode uptown on a New York bus—undressed to nakedness—left the clothes on the bank and walked naked that little delicate lovely woman in the greatest loneliness and insanity the earth has to show—and drowned herself in the Hudson River in January.

My other friend with one of the big top jobs in New York and a husband who loved her and whom she loved—jumped in front of a moving subway train.

I am too exhausted to write more tonight Charles—

I love you—I reaffirm in my mind all the words I have ever written to you (other than my two you received Monday) including the Easter letter.

Life is something far beyond our knowledge Olson. It is tragic in its flesh. That is why I so despise flesh and so love Blake.

And I learned today his grandfather was an Irish rebel—Carter O'Neill who changed his name to his wife's, Blake, when he fled to London. So Olson was right.

The hardest part to bear of the whole business is, Charles, that with one's mind (a certain section of it, one can see one's insanity, but is powerless.)

Perhaps you understand now the devotion I feel to Michelangelo for that grave look out of those women's eyes—the terrible humility, Charles, to be "guilty" of insanity.

Frances

❧ 200 ❧

Woodward to Washington
19 April 1950 (postmark)

Wednesday morning

I am sorry now, Charles, that I have never asked you about the phone business—I hate so for you to wait until tomorrow afternoon with nothing in between Monday—but I am afraid to phone you because it might be an intrusion. You must tell me in general what you want about that.

Charles—I am a seasoned voyageur.

It is a good thing.

Your rhythms and reactions darling—even in this thing which is a life cleavage of this fact of division into sex—are so similar to mine that in the physical weakness and exhaustion I am in I still smile to myself—and say "Look at my beautiful baby."

The same pattern

I go up to that cemetery and thank God I was able to spend a few hours there for that earth to stroke me (the sun I mean came out) and I swear and I swear and I swear and I say—what do I care? What does Motz care?—let everything move in—let the whole pattern fall on my head—do you think I would say to God what I said to Olson "I need you"—I would not—I despise the whole thing—me and Blake—we *see* what it is—and the Beauty Christ those sentences in Jerusalem III where the female is described in all her beauty (meaning the whole earth with its unbelievable fantastic beauty) And bad as those letters are they represent some kind of trust which I would give to no god—I complained before you—I have never lowered myself to do that any-where in life before—and that was because I so believe in all that coldness in Olson's eye—in his knowledge of pain—no matter how fierce he speaks to me—"I can't stand it—justice"—

What a great warm cry of the depths of man that is—he will not buy for cheap—bravo Olson my beloved—we adore justice—but seeing she is a false and paltry business for the weak and bourgeois in her obvious smaller mean-ings Olson cries out I can't stand it—oh beloved how well you are known to me in your beauty that will fight.

And I sit up in that goddamn cemetery and I say—if you think I'll bend my neck you're crazy—and the ice moves down Olson aeons thick and Motz watches it and says OK I'm on the bottom.

What else?

I move in an absolute glacier—but while I move Olson baby beloved Motz will not buy any of the cheap answers—

I needed you.

Life does not arrange things in a way where you could aid me when I needed it. This is something about life well known to me. None of any of this at any moment had to do with the beauty and purpose of Olson.

If life had granted that great succour to me I would have been grateful—but I walked around in the pit too long to have any emotion about it.

We are in a game together because god has created us equals—for the first time—and I leave all tabulations to him.

Love is not the right word.

What the right word is we must manufacture letter by letter at the present unknown word.

I am bound to you not in ego, not in pride, not in love, not in sex, but in some terrific join that has no name.

God made me a tough female

and he made my Olson beautiful.

Frances

I asked the telephone company for a private phone but they cannot give for a year—do you think it would be desirable for me to have one of those others?

❧ 201 ❧

Woodward to Washington
19 April 1950 (postmark 20 April 1950)

Wednesday night

Oh darling—

If you only knew how I love that passionate beautiful face—Shall we not speak any more of our sufferings darling—shall we know that Life is the one that misleads us—that plants in us these yearnings—yours as well as mine?

I give you for your easing my lovely beautiful man—a poem from that Francis Thompson whom I so deeply respect.

TO THE DEAD CARDINAL
OF WESTMINSTER

Call, holy soul, O call
The hosts angelical,
         And say—
  'See, far away

'Lies one I saw on earth;
One stricken from his birth
         With curse
  Of destinate verse.

'What place doth He ye serve
For such sad spirit reserve,—
         Given,
  In dark lieu of Heaven,

'The Impitiable Daemon
Beauty, to adore and dream on,
         To be
  Perpetually

'Hers, but she never his?
He reapeth miseries;
         Foreknows
  His wages woes;

'He lives detached days;
He serveth not for praise;
          For gold
     He is not sold;

'Deaf is he to world's tongue;
He scorneth for his song
          The loud
     Shouts of the crowd;

'He asketh not worlds' eyes
Not to worlds' ears he cries;
          Saith—"These
     Shut, if ye please!"

'He measureth world's pleasure,
World's ease, as Saints might measure;
          For hire
     Just love entire

'He asks, not grudging pain;
And knows his asking vain,
          And cries—
     "Love, Love!" and dies,

'In guerdon of long duty
Unowned by Love or Beauty;
          And goes—
     Tell, tell, who knows!

'Aliens from Heaven's worth
Fine beasts who nose i' the earth
          Do there
     Reward prepare.

'But are *his* great desires
Food but for nether fires?
          Ah me,
     A mystery!

'Can it be his alone
To find when all is known
          That what
     He solely sought

'Is lost, and thereto lost
All that its seeking cost?
                    That he
        Must finally,

'Through sacrificial tears,
And anchoretic years,
                    Tryst
        With the sensualist?'

So ask; and if they tell
The secret terrible,
                    Good friend,
        I pray thee send

Some high gold embossage
To teach my unripe age.
                    Tell!
        Lest my feet walk hell.

As you wish to write of Rimbaud—so I long to write of Francis Thompson—who understood so deeply about women.

I send you a few lines from *The After-Woman* and I ask you to consider in connection with the *She-Bear*

I will mail you my beautiful Francis Thompson if you do not wish to go to the trouble to Library it—Perhaps I should have started at the beginning—When you read it you will probably wonder—Anyhow darling—Thompson was a deep true poet.

Charles—just so that you and I are clear beloved to one another—

I accept loving you without any reward of any kind as my privilege

I hope to see you again but if I do not I shall not consider that you have in any way misled me.

I was misled by joy—and I am not ashamed and do you not be ashamed my darling that I have so loved you.

Frances

"Blest fool! Be ensign of our wars
And shame us all to warriors!
Unbanner your bright locks—advance
Girl, their gilded puissance,
I' the mystic Vaward, and draw on

After the lovely gonfalon
Us to out-folly the excess
Of your sweet foolhardiness;
To adventure like intense
Assault against Omnipotence!"

☙ 202 ❧

Washington to Woodward
20 April 1950 (postmark)

                              thursday

frances, frances!
            you have spoken of modesty to me   (i always have to think
of it in latin)   before your letters today i am simply creature, modestas   it is
a very beautiful feeling   i feel as you do, when you say, i won't say anything   but i do, of course, and because you move me depth to depth   do i
know anything? do i know when i say things to you which make sense, or al-
leviate? i do not know   that is why it is so wondrous to have you give back
yourself to me
            and feelings like these, like the questionings i have asked myself
these last few days, what are we, what do i ask of you, what is—the same
question you roll back to me—what is love   such a business as these days you
have spent teases one out beyond such lazy formulations

                                          i got this far, to call
myself an innocent of the impossible
                              and now, again, again, you beautiful
woman, you join me!
            innocents, that's all, innocents!

                                    (and what else could we
be?
    the donnée, given?
                        But that you stand it! O Lady, that's what makes me
naked:
        here i am

And honestly stupid. My desperations are actually hidden from me, Frances. If I recognize what you say, what you go through, it is not because *I* know anything. It is as you put it, I behave. And my, what stupidity that takes. Maybe when you call me glacier it *is* the only valid contrary (Blake, again) to insanity, to that fire which, in the end, consumes the consumer. I do not feel that I know or have a right to know insanity. On the contrary: my horror is, sanity, the ice. And I am horrified by it. I think you'd guess how I have had to struggle to take up any belief in it, it seems so to contradict what my sense of others tells me. Yet I have to. To be bald, I'm stuck with it. (When I fall off my self, I can no longer afford to go down into those caves I used to gnaw in. All I can do now, age 39, is, flatly, propose, "I'm stuck with it, right or wrong, there it is.") But of course it is not that bald, simply because life brings me such as you, Frances, to say, Olson, you are beautiful! My god, do you know what a signal flag that is, what a banner to have it come to me!

And then, that our lives should get infolded—and you! you! who have so incredibly reinforced me, have to pay, pay! for that ice!

That's why I am naked to you!

(It is so incredible. It is why I can say, thank you, thank you, whatever Thou Art, that you give me frances)

((And so many phrases I have made for you have been flooding me the last long hours. Particularly, I go by my nose, pushed from the back. To have had to say that, coldly, when i knew your need, worried—as one will, because we are not gods, and do not know—over you, (i almost say prayed, if i knew what that meant)

—when, in fact, it had reversed itself, from Brooklyn, Tarrytown!—

o, Gan, Gan baby: it was strong!))

And the terror, that I would have gone on, would have had to, strengthened as hugely as I have been by you, even if you had, as you sd you would, would have had to "leave" me, was your word!

My god, what a business this life is, what a business! What a cruel, cruel, cold business it is!

(Is it any wonder Sauer, and his De-Glaciation, invoke me? Is it any wonder I had to project that Hymn to She against that very Place, that Huddle of Human under the Edge of Ice?

note: i sent it off yesterday ((it was a strange act, like, if you were going to have to absent yourself, i was going to put out there, somewhere, an act of bridge, of testimony to you!)); and i tore myself to bits the afternoon long trying to believe in its form, trying, because i had lost the belief in the form of the "Agree" passage as precedent, immediately precedent to, the Hymn, trying. . .and then, finally, after copy on copy, deciding, YES, it is as it was written, even tho I no longer know!))

now i know,

am simplified,

agree,

there is only one thing to do: do more   SHE is past   there will be
something else

       Wildness, for ex.: SHE did not have enough—other lines yesterday:

note: these are not the depths of kill and self-kill I mean by "wildness", of course, but i mean that i am impressed by these Middle West girls we are reading of, impressed the sociology is also showing New History at its seams:

.... even though the season is
extravagant, though blood
is to be let, and pods
are filling, though ladies,
despairing, take up in packs
and cults of their own
making, go off
to highways, joints, jousts, bouts
of wilding

((O darling, we must save, save, such as your two friends, from the waste, the waste! of suicide

      (((my god: i have just looked up the meaning of "wilding"—if you have a Webster, do! Isn't it the devil, how one uses words, without knowing their meaning! In my ignorance, I meant exactly all 4:1 a, b, 2, & adj!)

((I am terribly moved by these girls, think, if I were a lawyer, (wish that such a lawyer would show himself—as they have shown themselves!)   i would go to their defense (and to the men, who will, alas, be put in this terrible feudal dirty punishment—rape, the lie!), cry up this dirty country to their acts)) ((Tell me, if you see this thing as I))   ((My impression is, it is straight mythic act))

yr beautiful friend: oh, how a god must have wept to watch her, take off those clothes, and go naked down to that water! creature, creature! o frances, darling, can't we make a fire, and burn it for her![113]

'love
     'love
          'love

❧ 203 ❧

Woodward to Washington
23 April 1950 (postmark 24 April 1950)

Sunday morning

Charles dear—

For almost twenty-four hours now I am in the grip of the sense of the form of my life. It is so strong that I feel as though at this point I cannot make an error. I have obeyed, from the beginning—since my childhood—and now the form is so existent, so powerful, that I am absolutely contained in it—how long it will remain so closed and tight I have no way to know—but I have no curiosity whatsoever about my worldly affairs—even my daughter and her welfare—the strong pervading reality of the form—as of a *done*—eliminating time in a way to make it uninteresting—not overcome—just inelegant—not important—not aristocratic.

When I awoke this morning or last night I cannot remember for sure I saw a beautiful ball of the mundane shell—and I saw it had a hole pierced through it, which I knew I had made, but in a purely "know" way, not seeing myself as a doer, and out of that hole which was charming—something sold in Lord & Taylor's—scrambled one after another rosy, darling plump angels—full of life beauty—such adorable faces and they came and covered me with kisses, laughing kisses and I said, "Yes, I know."

Frances

113. Olson wrote a poem on this incident, "here i am, naked," unpublished until *Collected Poems* (pp. 113–14).

≼ 204 ≽

Washington to Woodward
24 April 1950 (postmark)

Monday

frances—
    (feel like a citizen, here in the P.O., with the pee-pull, doing likewise!)

have just come fr one Lib, on way to another—& to buy Thompson!
(am in one of those floats of mine)

but I was damned but you were going to have a word from me—
to tell you how beautiful the Mozart is (how you make him stand by the
dropped left shoulder!)
                            & is F. Thompson!
And you!—

                            This is Scamp
                            Olson

≼ 205 ≽

Washington to Woodward
25 April 1950 (postmark)

Tuesday

Look, Frances, things are in a crisis here   (Your poster[114] was the straw: if
things do get back on an even keel, do, please, seal such mail just as you do a
blue envelope: I should have spoken of it before, when I noticed that you don't
lick large envelopes, even though it is first class) *So hold all mail, on receipt of
this, until you hear from me.*

I should have had to make some new arrangement, in any case, for I am momentarily expecting to leave for a week of lecturing and visiting with my
friend Payne at Montevallo, Alabama. And, besides, if the P.O. goes through
with its plan to have only a morning delivery, I should also have to do what I
think I will do right now, get a box at the P.O.

114. The poster seems not to be extant, but Tom Clark, in *Charles Olson: The Allegory of a Poet's Life*,
presumably on the basis of discussion with Boldereff, says (p. 165) that the note accompanying the poster
concluded "with an image of their souls as twin rafts on the open sea." Connie, Clark says, "was at home to
intercept the package."

I shall let you know the moment I have such a box, and its number. I have a call in now to Payne, and, if possible, I shall go down there this Friday. (I may be away longer than a week, for I have the idea to stop, on my way back, over at Black Mt., to see my children, and carry the Cagli show (which goes with me to Montevallo) for their delectation (except that Cagli, like me, is too non-representational for the eyes of the contemps., even those whom I have pounded!)

This is just a note rushed for the 2:15 collection, so that you'll be sure to have it tomorrow, wednesday. I shall write more later today, and probably get the P.O. box tomorrow.

I am frightfully exhausted

love
charles

[*back of envelope:*] Your "poster-package," 1st line should read [*incomplete note*]

⊷ 206 ⊶

Woodward to Washington
25 April 1950 (postmark)

Wednesday 7:45 AM

Charles dear—

How different our lives—in the outer shell—it is already a morning well along for me—and I go to bed when you are just finishing your dinner! You cannot imagine, when my body is all nerve ends—how wonderful it is to have my daughter out of the house until late in the afternoon—children who have so much energy and are so cruel to any indisposition—like Cossacks!

This is a note (I am dry—dry)

1. to tell you *The Confidence Man* is like a letter from Melville—I am so pleased to find it—all those savage outbursts against Nature and against the filth in which this country exists—oh! darling—if ever anyone *knew* it was Melville and he comforts me—just the name—oh for me Charles—because I, as you did not have to, was out of college just as *all* that brash confidence was being played to the full—and how courageous and how alone I remember those years—when I consciously turned my back on the successes it had to offer and alone of all my acquaintances, receiving how much scorn, sought inner riches—oh! Charles when one has a knowledge of elegance and a beau-

tiful body—and turns that down and everyone sees only that you are *un*-successful—including your fiances and your family! I have never spoken to you about the business part of all my young life but it was very dramatic and full of real battles because I understood probably better than any grown man in New York *exactly* where we were—and I remember walking home from Wall Street at night and the *feeling* Charles of that whole vast falseness resting with its full weight on Motz's thin shoulders. Oh! Charles the terrible loneliness of those years—when every man wanted my body and no man would endure for a minute a glimpse into *me*.—I love Melville. (Isn't it a funny thing, when I read everything of his—*all* the poetry—all the prose—I never saw or heard of *The Confidence Man* and now I received from my bookseller—a new edition done in England. And if you have not seen the H.M. Tomlinson (he is a very nice man) introduction to *Pierre* which I have I want you to. Auden is a fool—more ways than one.

The other note was to say I do not read newspapers at all—and so I never know things (even the election of Truman and the death of Roosevelt) and did not see any of the Middle West incident you mention, but I love your poem and I am sure you are right. Darling I have a Funk and Wagnalls and while it is different—"wilding" cannot vary that much—and I too am *so* thrilled—it is so very very very exact.

And oh! blessed dear Charles—we *can* save creatures like my beloved Elizabeth—two ways—by us—and by the open reverence.

Frances

❧ 207 ❧

Woodward to Washington
26 April 1950 (postmark)

Wednesday 9:15 AM

Olson dear—
Sometimes I laugh to myself—I think there is that Olson baby—he does not know I am an ancient mother—I have so enormous amplitude in my breast—does he think he tells me something when he signs Scamp—does he not know how I follow the shadows and slightest hair changes of all his interior male organism and love it all—even when it appears just "shaking free" just not wanting—either care or love or steadfastness or etc all of that I rehearse and love and laugh and like all genuinely aristocratic mothers I could see and laugh and love over all except meanness and if my baby were ever to be mean for a second's hair's breadth I would destroy him with a swift stroke without regret (a male's invention) or shall I say not the male—the neuter's in-

vention—the priest's—the T.S. Eliot's and his numerous brothers up and around this globe.

Which brings me to that of which I want to speak because I want my baby's Irish fury—I want (most seriously I am speaking) him to take his great mental fist and somewhere sometime destroy these *liars*. Christ am I furious—I am reading and I am growing more and more furious—here's a man by the name believe it or not—Witcutt (I didn't make it up) who writes to destroy my beautiful Blake—all with compliments—*Blake—A Psychological Study*[115]—ala Jung—he says among literally hundreds of *lies* "The theme of Blake's epics is the disintegration of the soul caused by sin." And further on "This is a truth old and Catholic enough—it was enunciated by St. Augustine."—Christ, Olson I am so furious and so wishing to God I were a great giantess who could stride over this earth and slay at my discretion. What destroyers they are and how the bastards are out to get every alive man—and you will note that Francis Thompson whom the Catholics claimed of course is let alone as my drawing 14 of Michelangelo is let alone—they cannot attack him as an enemy—the greatest Catholic who ever lived—obviously—so they leave him alone—they write books but they are about something else and Thompson's unerring insight into the filth and his unerring insight into the future of woman leave him too big and too dangerous to handle so he is given the silent neglect treatment. Blake is so goddamned easy—he was so Irish and so furious he is so easy to be superior about. Christ he will live when the Catholic religion is not only faded but even forgotten. Blake one of the great prophets who has as keen a mind as I can remember of.   Says Witcutt— "The reasoning faculty was not Blake's strong point." "Blake rejected the Classics in angry words. . . . His poetry as poetry suffered as a result—A classical Blake would have been another Shelley."

Oh! Olson—man does *love* his little pot-bellied smug social righteousness. And I always think—swiftly—a female—probably no Motz would sleep with him—so he pulls this "easy as a Chesterfield" tone.

Your Motz

You know that Thompson carried Blake always in his pocket—when he had no shirt—no socks—no underclothes—no bread—no roof—nothing— Blake and Jesus and the prostitute Ann.

⁕ 208 ⁕

Washington to Woodward (special delivery)
28 April 1950 (postmark)

---

115. W. P. Witcutt, *Blake: A Psychological Study* (London: Hollis & Carter, 1946). The quotation is from p. 52; later in the letter, from p. 21.

friday

frances—do, do, *bear* with me—a move like this one (to ala. & n.c.) involves one in all sorts of businesses i am very incompetent about

& breaks *my* emotion circuits *badly, always*

So don't be upset until I get back on *my* own keel

(ex.—I came here to get my p.o. box for you—& find I am too late, have to come back tomorrow to get it)

So you'll have it in the next possible mail (I leave tomorrow)

I shall keep at this, until I solve it!

Love,
Charles

I have got all fouled up, this week, off my desk. But good news: THE MORNING NEWS also made it, 1st run, like A PO-SY!

⊰ 209 ⊱

Washington to Woodward
29 April 1950 (postmark)

Saturday

God damned these bastards—again they gave me the wrong hours, & the box-fax are gone!

And I so wanted you to have this box to shoot mail at whenever you wanted to write me while I am away.

I tell you what: I am adding North Carolina, & probably shortening Ala. So:

let's use *General Delivery Asheville*, North Carolina. Every day you are prompted to write, shoot me mail to that address *only*. And I'll pick it up the moment I get there.

I am sorry, darling, to put you out of direct interchange this way. But it is necessary, for this short while.

Love   Charles

❦ 210 ❧

[*letter not sent*]

Woodward to Black Mountain College[116]
28 April 1950

> Friday afternoon
> April 28

Charles—

Every man has to decide for himself what is right and what is wrong.

I believe it is wrong to enter a house by the back door.

If my letters have become an intrusion the thing for me to do is to cease writing them.

> Frances

❦ 211 ❧

Woodward to Asheville, N.C.
[30 April 1950]

> Sunday morning

Charles—

I have your special—

I have been awake the night

Do you not understand dear that I can do everything except to be treated as something one is ashamed of?

If my letters are more than Connie can bear and you permit her to violate their right to privacy how can I any further intrude, Charles?

You make it so very clear Charles that you are afraid to lose Connie but you are willing to lose me.

❦ 212 ❧

[*letter not sent*]

Woodward to Ashville
30 April 1950

116. The envelope reads: "Please hold for arrival," but Boldereff apparently changed her mind and did not mail this letter.

April 30, 1950

It occurs to me at this moment—I open James Joyce to find "and in truth, as a poor soul is between shift & shift ere the death he has lived through becomes the life he is to die into."

That the reason you have asked me to do something your subconscious knows I am not able to do—to appear ashamed of my actions by hiding them in a P.O. box *is* Charles beloved that now is the moment—having drunk in the great strong wine of my love—that the sailor is ready to cast off from the shore alone.

That my desire for this greatness goes with him need not be spoken.

And we leave to life to return at that hour which shall be appointed when the most dearly beloved thing of your life shall be clasped in recognition—I so believe, that if it comes after and not during the earth moulded—I shall not be dismayed neither will I unbelieve.

> Call me somewhere in the night
> so that I will hear them plainly
> Charles those intimate names
> which you were saving for
> my ears.
>
> My name is life.

◆◄ 213 ►◆

Montevallo to Woodward (special delivery)
3 May 1950 (postmark)

Wed

Lady Frances—
    I must trust you utterly
                    And so I send, for yr precious eyes alone, the enclosed,[117] as I woke & wrote it this morning.
                    It makes me happy, for it breaks the recoil, the recoil of eight days, not from you, but from the tensions of our triple situation, which, because of the miserable fatigue the months had brought me, I was not able to dance with, like syllables.
                    The dream is a clear-

---

117. Olson requested the return of this written-out dream in his letter of 7 July 1954. Boldereff did not return it until 1956.

ing. And tho I should imagine that these eight days must have been, for you, the hardest time,

                    you see, frances, what trust I do have in you!

                                                            Please write
me to Asheville on receipt of this yr interpretation of the dream as honestly as I have tried to set it down. I am *most, most* serious.

                                        Yr Man o' Micht

p.s.
They are working me
like a horse here
I haven't yet had time to mount the Cagli show!

                            ❦ 214 ❧

Woodward to Montevallo
4 May 1950

                                        May 4, 1950—7:40 p.m.

Your dream just this moment received.

Charles—I can never tell you how miraculous your dream seems to me. I am absolutely overwhelmed because you see dear—I have been wounded so deeply—so into the very vitals that your dream is absolutely accurate—the man and the horse are both destroyed—you and me. I have already written to Washington through a colonel I know well to get a visa to Budapest. I have already offered my furniture for sale. I have written to my sister to choose what from among my things she wants.

You see Charles darling *proud* is the right word. The letter on the back of my poster represents one of the great spiritual achievements of this earth. The transpose from a snake's tongue, watched and not physically touched, to make out of it your love—requires a humility the world cannot have too many examples of. To have that sacred thing opened and vulgarly screamed about—to be undefended by you and then to be asked—I, who prize honor deeper than life—to go by a back door, to let Connie slam the front door in my face and then ask me, Charles, to enter by some back door—when I am a noble creature, deserving honor. I have never been so wounded.

   At this point Charles Constance represents to me all that I am trying to cut a path for. She is trappedness personified. I am a deep intuitive woman and her hatred cuts into me, into my very being. I am no longer able to think of her quietly—she has offered me such hurt, so undeserved.

I prayed on Saturday night—I have not prayed since I was eighteen years old—I prayed to Jesus—the only one I trust, for purity of heart. On Sunday in the evening came the illumination that maybe you were so cruel to me because God had appointed this as the time for us to part.

I have already died for your sake several times. You know that Charles. I have given to you the devotion which I believe God meant me to give you. I cannot allow myself to be treated as a negro—as though I had no honor. I despise deceit. If you have not room in your home for my letters, then I cannot write them.

I feel in my deepest self that you should now live alone—that would be fair to both of us. But I did not say this, because it sounds as though I do it for myself. I kept Boldereff with me too long—out of a feeling of obligation to him as deep as yours to Connie. You won't believe this—you will say Connie is a girl and Serosha was a middle aged man—but my country conspired to prevent his earning his living and I married him in the presence of God to stay married until death, come what might. But I was wrong with my pity. In my deepest soul I believe each of us should now live separately. But you do according to what God teaches you. Only for myself Charles I must have honor, respect from both of you. I surely deserve in return for what to a woman is *all*—to have respect of the deepest sort. I am so sad—I can almost not write. God requires from me my life over and over again.

Frances

PART V

֍

11 May 1950–19 July 1950

On receiving the 4 May 1950 letter, Olson must have telephoned from Montevallo, Alabama, to arrange a meeting. Frances Boldereff told Tom Clark in Charles Olson: The Allegory of a Poet's Life *(p. 165) that they rendezvoused in Knoxville, Tennessee, three days later: "His train from Alabama pulled into the Knoxville station just as she was stepping off hers from Washington, a piece of synchronicity that seemed to him to bless the whole plan. His booming laugh rang out across the platform, alerting her to his presence. They spent the night at an old wooden hotel near the railroad tracks."*

The first Maximus *poem is the direct result of this meeting in Knoxville. Unfortunately, we do not have Boldereff's reaction to that poem; many of her letters in this period are missing.*

With a letter to Olson from William Carlos Williams, received on 21 April 1950, a new important factor begins to enter the scene. Williams suggested that Olson should write to a young poet named Robert Creeley, who was to start a magazine. Thus begins a correspondence whose frequency rivals and then overtakes the correspondence with Boldereff.

But not yet.

֍ 215 ֍

Black Mountain to Woodward (telegram)
11 May 1950

FRANCIS MOTZ   =FONE BELFONTE 31R42 WOODWARD PENN=
=WRITING TODAY ALL IS WELL=
    CHARLES=

֍ 216 ֍

Black Mountain to Woodward (special delivery)
12 May 1950 (postmark 13 May 1950)

friday

the taste is sweet, sweet, and tho i have not written since, assure yrself, Lady, that it has nothing to do with more than this: that, as you know, I throw myself, pour on my blood, at this place, and have night and day, like a wild fool

i got held here by a train strike, and i am glad, because i have been able to cover the whole place   i leave for washington by plane tomorrow

i shall write you when i am set in like seed and rock at my desk   i have not yet been able to settle this question of mail (i, here, am blown out like a tent)   And it's a tough one, isn't it, my Frances

sweet, i sd, how very strong

yrs

⊰ 217 ⊱

Washington to Woodward
15 May 1950 (postmark)

mon-
day

lady frances:
            it is almost exactly, to the hour, a week since . . .

& i have just this moment talked to the postman, and learned that the one de-livery a day goes in to effect this week

  so here we are, my beautiful lady, straight, head-on

            frances, girl: the honoring of you lies deeper than where you pose it, in the absolute recognition of you and of your force in my life by Constanza as well as by myself   (i dare say you will have understood how monogamous i have been, and how tremendous a change has been involved, how thor-oughly such a recognizing is an honoring, given the particulars here built for so long)

            you are shy, lady, wonderfully intimate—and we better right now grant that you and i recognize that, and that Constanza would only know it in so far as she *might* respect me   (frances, i say i love you precisely because i dwell there where you are shy & so scrupulously capable of the intimate: i say, in the face of what you say, that i can never, never wrong you because it is precisely there that i dwell, my sib, in that garden)

to me the third, and crucial, factor is, proofs, proofs, how each of us dwells in a fragile house (by each i mean as well each human capable of, the risk of, the intimate)   thus we exaggerate all notation, all proofs   why, we put such emphasis on, gestures, facts, daily businesses, why, we make time and our mortality a testing   i have, as long as i have lived, resisted this exaggeration, fought to rest action on risk in this sense, to throw it out there in space and let come back what may   when i wrote you from montevallo i must trust you completely, i meant, that i must not curtail my love for you and action to you because of what you may require of me in this area of reinforcements   you see, frances, i am your male, yr brother-father, i am strangely the son of, as well as the man of, f.m., yet, i am also HIS TWIN: i do not, because i am by that hair of birth different from him, need that you pay the costs because you take my existence for granted

as a matter of fact, i think this can be put more accurately another way; i am yr SECOND MALE precisely because you have, by the tremendous struggle of yr life, made it possible for you to have me   (it is as tho you have, by the struggle which started with him, invoked me)   yes, *you've* done it, frances—and my hunch is, my hunch is, that it is almost literally impossible for you to believe that you can have this 2nd Male on any other conditions than those very ones by which you came to inherit, to honor, the first

what i am saying is, rest, sweet one, sleep, sleep, this once, put off yr armor, and be not afraid that, armorless, you will be struck

i am another father, another lover, a man to whom you have proved by act on act how straight you come from that vulernable, vulnerable place   you have, darling, you have yourself thrown out into space the shy, tender heart of your belief and life you have thrown it out to me, to this twig to catch on, like yr spiders do their webs

and it caught, remember, forever, it CAUGHT, the overwhelming fact is, it caught!

(And you need never, really, never, no matter what you might be nervous I might do, or, for that matter, what i might do, be nervous that you will be left uncovered! YOU CANNOT BE)

I think it does come to this, does come back to yr extraordinary vision: there are three of us, yr father, Christ, and I. And when, in that letter you wrote telling me to put off, to voyage,[1] you sd you prayed to the only one you knew to turn to, to Christ,

darling, were you not saying, olson, i do not want to be uncovered, i fear you are going to leave me uncovered, i therefore say ahead of time go, you are already gone

which is not true

which is not true, frances
                        do not be frightened, little girl: these three men have known your soul, have known yr love
                                    quite simply, frances, i say: each condition you declare as points of yr honor are such, in the great world, but here, in this garden of the intimate, they are proofs, proofs of what does not need proving simply because you are covered, covered, naked woman

    make with me this second heave   believe
    i'll not betray you,
    my shy

    write to me, washington,
    p.o. box 2005

                                    this is he, charles

✢ 218 ✢

Washington to Woodward (registered)
15 May 1950 (postmark)

darling:
the enclosed,[2] immediately,
the rest to follow more
slowly,
        my bold one!

                            love
                              c

---

1. Boldereff's letter of 4 May 1950.
2. Since this is a registered letter, the enclosure was likely money.

[*on back of envelope:*]

a letter has already gone to you, regular mail

⊷ 219 ⊶

Washington to Woodward
17 May 1950 (postmark 17 May 1950)

wednesday may 17 1950

darling:

my mind is aswarm (it is the coming back, to work, after the affirmation of you, and the flooding of speech of two weeks, especially, so far as speech goes, the change in my sounding of, verse: what would have specially pleased you, was a lecture i gave on blake at black mountain, with that extraordinary passage at the end of his Lavater notes,[3] as depart, and the mental traveller, as text. Perhaps i could not have won you with the Pound at Alabama, the passage which includes the lines, "the ant's a centaur in his dragon world". But I do believe the Lear passage on procreation, despite yr accurate objections to S. and woman, would have caught yr attention. You see, that production at bmc last summer turned out to be a teacher of me. I tried to join music & instrument to speech. And the upshot was, no. What I have gone on to do, is to make verse, and its projection, music-contained. When you have a copy of the summer issue of PNY,[4] and have the chance to read the PRO verse in print,— well, i have the feeling that is only scratching the skin of it

THE MORNING NEWS, strangely enuf, seems to project most—Creeley will publish it in his 1st no. (do not know the name of his MAG), and will review *y & x*. And—of course—I am scared i shall never write another! It is the craziest sort of feeling, this, of not being able to match the done! (I suppose this plane is the sex of writing art, the underpart, the nervousness because love is not born. One loves only form, and form only comes into existence when the thing is born. And the thing may lie around the bend of the next second. Yet, one does not know, until it is there, under hand.[5]

the thing may lie
around the bend of the nest

---

3. Blake's "Annotations to Lavater's *Aphorisms on Man*" ends: "But the origin of this mistake in Lavater and his contemporaries is they suppose that Woman's love is Sin; in consequence, all the Loves and Graces with them are Sin."

4. *Poetry New York* containing "Projective Verse" would not be out until late October 1950.

5. At this point, Olson introduces into this letter the first of his *Maximus* poems.

second, time slain, the bird! the bird
there, strong, thrust, the mast, flight! o kylix!

                                        o Anthony
of Padua sweep low and bless the roofs,
the gentle steep ones on whose ridge
gulls sit, and depart,
                        the flake racks,

                        o my city

love is form, and cannot be without
important substance, a weight
say, 50 carats, each one of us
our own goldsmith scale: feather to feather added,
and what is mineral, what is the curling hair, the string
you carry in yr nervous beak, these
make bulk, in the end, these
are sum, my lady of
                        good voyage, in yr left arm
no boy, but carefully scrolled wood, the delicate
mast, a bow-sprit for
                        forwarding

the underpart is, though stemmed, uncertain, is
as sex is, as money is, facts
to be dealt with, to be—the demand is—played
by ear

by ear, but, that which matters, that which insists, will last

                        o that, people of my city,
where shall you find how, where, when all is bill boards, when all
even silence is painted, not even a gull can be heard, when
sound itself is neoned in, when, on the hill, over the water,
she, who used to sing, when the harbor glowed black, gold,
when bells came like little boats over the oil slicks, and a man
slumped attentionless against, the pink shingles

                        o sea city

one loves only form,
and form only comes

into existence when
the thing is born,

> born of yourself, born
> of hay and cotton struts
> of the streets and weeds
> you've carried in, o bird

>> of a bone of a fish
>> of a straw of will
>> of a color, of a bell
>> of yourself, torn

love is not easy but how shall you know, New England, now
that pejorocracy is here, now
that streetcars, o Oregon, twitter
in mid-afternoon, offend
a black-gold loin?
how shall you strike, swordsman,
the blue-red back, when, last night, your aim
was mus-sick, mu-sick, mu-sick,
and not the cribbage game?

> (o Gloucester-man, weave
> yr nerves and fingers new,
> American, braid,
> with others, such
> extricable surface
> as faun and oral,
> satyr, lesbos vase

> kill, kill, kill, kill, kill
> those
> who advertise
> you out

in! in! the bow-sprit, bird, the beak
in, the bend is, in, goes in, the form
that which you make, which holds, which is
the law of
object, what you are, what you must be, what throws up
the mast, the tender
mast!

> the nest
> under the hand

    I'm sure, frances, that, despite troubles, these webs which spin, get spun across the space, the wild and at times intolerable space, are flowers of life, are facts to bow to, gentle maitresse. Anyhow, I give you the deepest sort of recognition, speak out from hidden islands in the blood which, like jewels and miracles, you invoke. And I, as hard-boiled instrument, as metal hot from boiling water, tell you, he recognizes what is lance, obeys
the dance,
          mio chorego,
                    eros, eros eros!
                            a kylix,
                                  sharles
                                    olson

frances, I deeply say, thanks—& what is more love than?

It opens, frances, thus:

I, MAXIMUS

Off-shore, by hidden islands in the blood,
like jewels and miracles, I, Maximus,
a metal hot from boiling water, tell you,
what is a lance, who obeys
the figures of
this dance

1

The thing . . . . . .

((and closes))

mast!

The nest,
I say,
under the hand,
as I see it over the waters,
from this place where I am,

where I hear, can still hear,
from where I carry you a feather,
as tho, sharp, I picked up a nerve,
in the afternoon delivered you
a jewel, it flashing more than a wing,
than any romantic thing, than memory, than place,
than anything other than that which you carry,
than that which is—call it a nest, call it
the next second—
                /than that which you   /can do

  ❧ 220 ❧

Woodward to Washington
18 May 1950 (postmark)

                                  Thursday morning

Charles darling—
    Your letter which just came—mostly I do not understand—I have never
really had a father and if he understood me or valued what I was it was surely
in those last hours alone before his death—after I had stayed alone with him
all during the night and he knew how I had no strength at all because my baby
had so robbed me (I mean he had terrible deep proof that I loved him that all
his life-long cruelty to me I did not remember and I gave love)
    I have always always always been absolutely alone—
    But I have thrown out tenderness and belief to life—that is true—
    And now I am naked—your letter makes me absolutely naked, but I trust
you with all my soul—Charles darling—I cannot say anything—you understand darling that every moment of my life is obedience—I believe in you and
whatever you ask you know beforehand that I will do—I am afraid and I am
trembling not because I do not believe you but because I know how life is
cruel to strength.
    Yesterday out in the woods I do not know if I stepped on him—anyway I
frightened a copperhead—I turned and saw—twisting—getting ready to
strike me—and I saw so deeply hurt that life had done that to him—I did not
blame him—everyone thinks it their duty to kill a copperhead and he looked
so angry and so distrustful and I so deeply understood why and I did not
blame him at all—I simply looked at him for a while and then I came away—
I was with two little children otherwise I would have put out my hand to
him—to let him touch me—but I did not want to take a chance with very

young children near—anyway—I realized he had no way to know I do not also seek to destroy and that is true for Constanza—she has no way to know I preserve her love for you whole and sacred in my breast—

Oh Charles—I am so naked as you cannot imagine—

I do what I do for the sake of all those beauties whom I love—that Thoreau too, with such deep longing for a new thing—a cleaner newer better thing "for the maturation of the species"—

I have always known—when it is done—when it is over when all this terrible nakedness I endure will be added and complete—the love will pour out to me from every crevice of this earth. I have always known that—

I ask you now darling—Charles—turn to me those eyes open as they were open that Saturday before you went to Gloucester—this is a day which asks everything of me that I have.—I believe that in all of life God has never made anything so absolutely without armor—so absolutely naked as I am at this moment.

Frances

Darling—if there is a poem—I do not know what kind—a tiny little poem for me—alone—to put on—to put over me to protect myself for five minutes until I grow some kind of skin

Like you break up firewood to put in a fire.

Yesterday when I was bathing I also thought "I am his teacher—God teaches me and I teach Charles and he teaches the world"—I did not think "teaches" I *felt* the connect, the path, whatever it is—but I mean the son business you speak of and I believe this is the direct true thing as God meant—for woman to be absolutely pure and a receptacle and to be open to one man—her son and lover—who instructs life—I mean her Sybilline knowledge open to one man—the poet to be hidden by her from everyone else.

◄§ 221 §►

Woodward to Washington
19 May 1950 (postmark)

Friday morning

I reread the poems Morning News—A Posy-A Posy—She-Bear.
They come across to me in perfection of perception.
I compare my own poem.

I have taken for myself a new skin
It is diamond-marked skin of a serpent

I look out on you with the innocent cold eye of a serpent
I will inhabit my earth subhuman entity
I do not understand life without armor
I can not imagine or believe in such a thing
Out of the Wood of the embarrassment mounting to my Charles I weave my
                                        skin
I wear my defeat as Christ wore his—as a decoration
You be a poet—you obey
I will be a serpent   who also obeys
I will draw close and reside in your hand not because of love but because of the
                                        music
The music is accurate—is law beneath the human non-human tension we
                                        now are

                    O Gloucester man

How it burns the bright marked skin of my body to lie in that cold steel
place—*waiting* until you take me out where I can breathe!

                    ❧ 222 ☙

Washington to Woodward
19 May 1950 (postmark)

                    BIGMANS[6]

Arouse yourself, Bigmans,
arouse

cities, things
crumples of tin
And dead men in

Bigmans, start
moving, start
the next heave, go out
from your mother's
fire

6. An early draft of a poem left unpublished until *Collected Poems* (pp. 147–48).

your brothers
have had enough
derisions despitous,
of many filths
though fructuous

Bigmans, take
to the streets
go to the whore,
begin: she is sib,
wrong boy

daintiness,
of limbs or fingers, of hair
of hunger for the fruits of gods, of lair
of twisting paths, of proper movement, hers
hath shrunk to kill, to fear

                          she sits
by property defiled, by stories rifled
of initiation, she
who is ground, who is fountain, who is night

who is made nothing of
now, eveless
though powered

Bigmans, your place
is out, out
from inside, you've slept enough
the self (the muscle, bone
are grown), you're fat
fr' exceptionality, your own,
and generally.

Let go, move, hulk, leave
her house, dispose
your strength where others are, where they lie
(as things do, as cities, waiting
to be loved)

Bigmans, this

is invocation, this
is an asking, a
demand, we
ask you of

you

Darling, i am purposely leaving this rough, because i am not thru with it, don't know where it goes from here, don't know that it is done as is. But by God it was something, giving it out to you! And that you want it stirs the balls of me! So here, here, Gauze of Wonder!

You will guess I take exceptions—I dare say you do—to Henrie Davide. Yet the 2nd of the two quotes is remarkable.[7] Funny thing, I ran into the same argument for ontology in Keats yesterday (and, in Alabama, in Payne's Montevallo Ode—Payne is talking about the oak and the mistletoe).
                                                            I distrust ontology, because it is, to me, a mixing of god with nature, which is, after all, a mixing of man with nature, and bothers my Levitican soul. You see, with no loss of man's mystique (he has the power), I think one can MUST put order, FORM, in nature AS IT IS, not trying to see Creator behind it: let the law of a crystal (not a snow flake repeats another) sit as it is, sans interpretation, say.
     I distrust it, because of, say, John Keats (or Thoreau, or Payne) in contrast to Blake, Rimbaud, and like workers today.

I'll pick this up again. Am so struck by the dying off, right in my hands, of John Keats—what an inadequate contemporary he is to W. Blake!
                                   All, all is more than well,
                                   you darling
                                   Charles

≈ð 223 ðæ

Woodward to Washington
20 May 1950 (postmark)

                                        Saturday afternoon

---

7. Quotations in a missing Boldereff letter.

Charles—

I have been thinking for a long time—and I am not sure how we should go about tracing it—but you mentioned that some young man, an editor, had asked you for some views on education—I place in your mind to think on—should not some regard be taken of sex? I mean we give young women absolutely nothing for their guidance—perhaps nothing exists to give them—but could we perhaps not create something—I don't know if it should be history—a short story—poems—fables—I can not see the thing clearly—but for very many years I have thought how wasteful it all is—all those years—and the thing they all want to know and that everyone needs from them—is how to conduct themselves as women—what should they learn—where should they receive the so terribly needed word—the reason I do not mind that you pour out so much blood in places like Alabama and Black Mountain is because young women know how to receive seeds in the soul and your integrity is something so germ-like several of them will really become disciples—(the young girl who translated Villon) anyway—your essence might get over in some way that one of them would carry permanently.

Should there not be some serious attempt to think of themselves as mothers—whether in the flesh or spirit only has nothing to do with it—some whole thing, some special angle from which to *view* all of everything—arithmetic—poetry—drama—engineering—history—any part of it.

When you have time I wish you would think of this.

Please send me the I, Maximus as soon as you can
                    Morning News when it appears

I have something pressing around inside of me—don't know what it is—but the scared you speak of—is the reason there are so few poets—it can never be any other way—always the mother sickness—and the so hard part to bear is as you say—you only know the form when it is made—and then the thing has already become the done and *so* something one cannot gloat over—nevertheless—if I could ever get my hands on the dollars to publish *all* every one you have done—for a minute darling you would have joy—I read them once—all—every one right straight through and something happens which is the beauty of your life—

All the whole thing gives into some solvent—and the words are light around each other—and the Charles speech is something never once expressed but in there—in that interval of lightning—you manage to *hold* in there Charles—and the whole thing gives me strength—

I have decided to stop all thought of love, to abandon that whole concept—it simply makes me suffer until I become unrecognizable—

Let it be clean and simple between us—you somehow speak my agony and

I discover parts of myself—part of your hearing of my agony—coming out in the strangest of places—in words no one but I would know were for me—I do not think or have no idea if it is intentional—but I believe there is a sweet clear clean very young thing between us that exists absolutely separately from any sex either of us has—the fact that in some unvoiced way each of us has never turned his back on his own vision and I so pray in my soul that before we are dead the clear outline of the thing I *feel* so clearly can come through.

It satisfies me now Charles—I am in such deep pain—to be that little snake—and I will sleep and eat in a corner of your house and you will see me and there will be no human business.

Frances

◆§ 224 §◆

Woodward to Washington
22 May 1950 (postmark)

Monday

Balls boy—

It would never occur to me in a million years to mix up this nature and man business. I don't happen to know what ontology is but if it is in a Montevallo Ode I don't want it.

There are two things about Nature—the Leibnitz thing—that goddamed law business—everywhere and always the strict Law and then the perversity of the application—to make twenty forms of tiny gloriousnesses all so varied—variations on a blue stroke—*why* the beauty out of the law—that's the goddamdest thing—I get so furious—so raging—at her—her cold fierce Law

but when I saw pouring out of my own body the literally pitchers of blood that time I had an abortion with no anaesthetic and in that pain which released me from belief in God—still I could see—my god—man never *sees* blood like this—*where* could you see it—because air spoils it—no accident or anything of that sort—here it was—the prime stuff—and I said to myself "no wonder babies are so damned beautiful—*look* at that color"—I have *never* seen anything to touch the beauty of it—and my guess is that straight out of the womb of a mother is the *only* place there is to see it. I have always remembered and no matter how I contend with her—the terrible deep inexplicability of the *beauty* hammers hammers

in "hunger for the fruits of gods"

Olson—I want to tell you this *personal* aroma of ourness—there is some innocent innocent thing you give off in your powerful fishhook that is absolutely different from any male elsewhere in the universe—It stuns me every time—I *try* to fasten my hand on the essence of what it is I feel when I see you—are near you—and before I didn't know—but now I know—you are innocent like some God-thought—I cannot explain it but I have a reaction so opposite from Connie's—

Wherever that innocent beauty tips is to me a cause of joy—cannot explain—but your whole self gives off a reality of prime innocence—

Whatever flowers you strew are strewn to my nostrils and give me clarity of joy in your immense beauty. Now has been enacted on the earth the *desire* of William Blake

> "But silken nets and traps of adamant will Oothon spread
> And catch for thee girls of mild silver or of furious gold.
> I'll lie beside thee on a bank and view
>   their wanton play
> In lovely copulation, bliss on bliss, with Theotormon!
> Red as the rosy morning, lustful as the first born beam
> Oothoon shall view his dear delight; nor e'er with jealous cloud
> Come in the heaven of generous love,
> nor selfish blightings bring."[8]

That's what I meant by the Thoreau quote—the poet *desires* and then is born in flesh, in Nature—a catcher—a can-ner who *forces* the desire to become reality.

While I am writing a letter of flesh and love I may as well say all—I have *never* had a chance to give you Motz beauty—when I am in ecstasy—when the rhythm from my hands and my mouth and my breast tips is like the dance of an Olson poem—

I regret that so much beauty has been scattered over this earth by me and never to the man I love have I been circumstanced to give it—

Dionysius has once or twice covered his eyes in awe at the absolute drunken lilt dance—

Shall I send my book to your box or to Randolph Place?

I do not want to say aloud, but my instinct is—and was *immediately* this is it—*Bigmans* is the real thing—Have you ever heard one of the tap dancers when the orchestra stops playing and the rhythm is so hot and so sure that every human being who hears feels *he* is tap dancing—that is *Bigmans*.

---

8. William Blake, *The Visions of the Daughters of Albion*, plate 7.

◄ 225 ►

Washington to Woodward (special delivery)
23 May 1950 (postmark 23 May 1950)

                                        tuesday   may 23   L

frances:
    i understand there's a letter for me at the p.o.   And i shall get it   But i
want to write to you now, just so you may have a word

                                                (continue, over)[9]

i'm in cold hell, or thickets
(how abstract, how cold
can a man stay, confronted
thus?)

language is bitter, is
words are paper wars, fronted
with what i am, where
do i go

yet, as acts, as man now, he
has one thing he must do, raise
himself up, raise
on this reed, his
what he has to say

what has he to say?
are
traceries, shall
he convert
the underbrush, (the
branches are already done like snow-flakes made against the sky)
how can he raise (he can,
but how far, sufficiently far?) the thickets of
the Wilderness, change
these silvered places into panels for his, or a king's,
wagon? make, out of this low eye-view, not daring
to move his feet for fear he'll trespass on his own dissolving bones,
here where mud is, where grass grows with
altogether too much remembrance

---

    9. Olson adds typed sheets of the first draft of "In Cold Hell, in Thicket." See *Collected Poems*, pp.
155–60.

the question, the fear he raises up against
the necessity now of each act, of each
(the town of the earth) fix: WHO
am i?

for by a fix, and another, a particle,
and the congery of other particles
carefully picked one by one,
            (as in this thicket, each
smallest branch, plant, fern, root
—roots lie on the surface like dissected nerves
must be isolated, observed, measured)
raised as tho a word, an accuracy
were a pincer (this is what is abstract
this is the cold doing, this is the
almost impossible

                        shall you blame those
who give it up? yes,
but with such comprehending
                                    (prayer,
or a death, as going over to, shot by yr own forces, to
a greener place, neither
no longer
usable)

f.m.: this is really a letter

by fixes (not even any more by shamans)
can traceries
be brought out

selva obscura—ya, but hell now
(and the beasts)
are not exterior, are not
to be walked through, are
(this is why he does not move, why
he stands so carefully, his feet
held
from the nearest next ground, even from
the beauty of the rotting fern his eye
knows, as he looks down, as,

in utmost pain, if cold can be so called,
he looks around this battlefield, this
old place where men did die, where boys
and immigrants, where
the years that nature has took over
do not matter, where
that men killed, do kill
is part, too, of his question)

that it is simple (what the difference is,
that a man, men, are now their own wood,
their own hell and paradise, are
cold object)

does not in the least lessen
his, or their,
obscurities, his
confrontation

he shall step, he
will shape   (he does)
he will, he is already
moving, into the soil, onto his own bones, he will cross
there is always a field (for the strong
there is always alternative, this
is as dangerous as a prayer)
he will cross, he is bound to enter
a later wilderness, yet
what he does here he must
(the stakes are such, this
is a certainty, this
is a law and not a question, this
is what was talked of as
demand)
do carefully, do
without wavering as
even the branches, even, in the dark place, the twigs, the brow
of what was a skull, even snow-flakes waver
in the light's eye,

even, forever wavers (gutters
in the wind, in another sense than

he who talks about life talks about candles,
or altars, or the wrong raising of
hosts) wavers
even as he forever wavers

now, here, he cannot, he
must stay for an answer, he
must be instant, be cold,
he must be precise to
his hell

yes, the panel
and thus the wagon
can be made

darling, this grew into something

            but, because it is a
            letter, i send it
            to you, for
                 love's sake

                                        Charles

[*back of envelope:*]

have just taken into hand
yr letters, & will
write tomorrow
or tonite

∾ 226 ∾

Washington to Woodward
24 May 1950 (postmark 25 May 1950)

                                        wed may 24 L

I say, yay, to what you say, in Monday
's letter, my layday. Yea! YEA!

For it is true, under the coldness,
under the demonry, yay, yay

and is it not mysterious, not
that it is, of course not, for what is,
there it is, but that it should be, and
that it should be discovered, uncovered
where it lay, purchased (as it is, god
help me too) at such price

And of course that too is not
mysterious. Only, it is so rarely
known. It takes persons (here, three)
that it may be known.

    I am so grateful for the Blake, for
    the silver girl, the furious
    gold girl

    It is so strange, still, to me
    that he should have been
    so curiously content
    with slack cadence. BUT
    he did his job, and,
    in such a thing as
    THE MENTAL TRAVELLER
    (i read it all to women,
    & to boys, at blck
    mt) he
    does not err.

    (Women are such ears
    to read to. And that,
    frances, is, I imagine,
    the only sort of answer
    to yr question of
    their education. What,
    more than himself, can a man
    present to them? ((I did,
    at Alabama, where there were
    850 of 'em, to some 50 say,
    you, are matriarchs, and
    it's splendid, do not, let
    those who do not know, mis-
    lead you.

       & they have a couple
of ladies present, one childless, the other
the President's wife,
to reinforce it))

Let
him be a man, which, almost, means
let him not know anything but
innocent (who told O?)

You see, darling, (let me press on you)
there are violets, they
spring up, sd wise old Bolyai Farkas,
when
the need (on all sides, he sd)
is sufficiently
a need!

    (How wise, how,
    except for Fred.
    the Great: "every man
    must save himself
    in his own way", how
    unduplicated, the wisdom,
    for me, from our
    predecessors)

        I have been most busy
        abt the business of
        keeping work moving
        today. The verse
        (was a letter,
        which went to you yesterday)
        was finally wrought, was
        IN COLD HELL, IN THICKET,
        is gone off, is, I am
        finished with it. And the end
        of the busyness, is, yet, today
        to cost me 1 buck, postage, air
        Japan—a poem, and
        PRO verse: the address
        delights me: (listen,
        to the sound—

Isaku Hirai Esq
c/o Iwaya Shoten
12, Nishikubo Tomoe-cho (rrrrussian)
Shiba, Minato-ku, Tokyo
jap-an)

And, little snake, without
yr being such, without you be
anything but fierce
motz, you
sit, you dwell, you
look at me. And I
can talk
to you

It is a sweet evening. I have two red roses in a green glass. And just now I added a large white peony which, like an eye or a hand, a gloved hand, was sticking in a bush as I came from the store. The three are now, my company.

Will you cover yrself with this verse?
Charles

·≼ 227 ≽·

Woodward to Washington
27 May 1950 (postmark 29 May 1950)[10]

Saturday night

Charles dear—
I remember when Lucinda was very small and I used to see other babies I could tell exactly how old they were, not by their size or looks, but by their actions—and so exactly does this follow a pattern of Law that a young mother can tell within two weeks how old a child is by what it does with a spoon! This used to embarrass me—but after listening to Gesell I seem to see in it something beautiful.

Tonight—after torture on torture for days—I sit detached and wonder *why* do Charles and I so torment ourselves—*why* are we so whipped, so con-

---

10. Boldereff addressed the envelope to "Charles Motzson, PO Box 2005, Washington, D.C.," which apparently caused it to be returned. This may explain why this letter exists whereas other Boldereff letters of the period don't.

stantly and I come to suspect that we also are flailing our arms about in some law of Growth and I am not yet sufficiently advanced to admire this—it embarrasses me—that perhaps the whole thing is Impersonal as it is possible to a Snowflake—and I *resent* that I suffer such waves of pain and that you endure such Ices and Snows in a Law of Growth of our kind—

But perhaps I am wrong to resent it. It embarrasses me—in that it does not seem *personal*. I mean (our choosing such a Fate) its choice and significance do not seem personal—

And that terrible question I never came to an answer about—
What *is* personal?

Is personal to be that reed Olson speaks of—not to try to avoid being a reed?

That I am your actual flesh sister I now know. That our terrible oneness creates incest I know. (I have no opinions for or against—I just know that's what we really have.)

I am in a mood when I despise my suffering—where what or who I am, Charles is or anyone else is of no interest.

What perplexes me—*why* am I shoved so from behind, so definitely—so I have no choices—

What has assigned the parts?

It is great to obey—or is greatness a childish concept? As I write I know I will continue to obey

And you remember, as I vaguely remember doing beneath the Rousseau print—I hold your beloved face between my hands.

(I wish I could see "Who am I?" I am so flesh by flesh the one thing with Olson. Is this old too? Is this unbelievable oneness an old story? Did it happen many times over? Our paths so unlike and the blood-beat so precisely the same. Who gave me Olson's fierceness, his terror, all his humility and his wild diastole. I wish like Murametz that my chopped flesh could be scattered over the earth.)

Damned sight less painful to have some god strew chopped hunks of one's flesh than sitting at some damned typewriter and strewing one's own flesh all over the place eh! Olson?!

My artist's flesh *creeps* at roses in a green glass roses one of the tough ones to handle—takes an artist to place a rose so it has the grace of a bush

You let me arrange the roses and let the servant cook the dinner and you go out and scream to your children

"I am yanking you into form and flesh whether you will or no!"

Why can't my name be Murametza? the wife of Murametz who likes her so much they're scared to sleep together on account murder is such a terrible passionate love force

So they'll place this whole damned country between them and shout at one another.

Washington to Woodward
29 May 1950 (postmark 29 May 1950)

                                        monday   may 29 L

i have been levitated   And you must not mind, even tho you will. Because
the fact is, what is the power of, the beauty is, that, between us, when i am
down there, is
the wildness, the
unknown, the hot hell,
the furious   And
the gold
          You are
that girl, SHE-
BEAR!

i have been upstairs   And the causes?   Double, triple, the pursuit:

who am i? how
do i do my work?

          (One thing has been a joining of
          high battle. The high priest, Skunk,[11]
          has chosen to
          wet on me: Pound
          sneered, that I
          (THE MORNING NEWS)
          was centre, core,
          of Creeley's new, not-out
          MAG.

          And (why?) I have engaged him: poured out
          shot, all guns
          to bring him down, to
          specify him, for
          what he is, with
          Creeley

    11. Pound had written to Creeley, and Creeley had forwarded Pound's letter to Olson. See *Charles Olson & Robert Creeley: The Complete Correspondence* 1:46–52. The quotation later in this letter is from a Creeley letter of 24 May 1950 (p. 41).

      (you see, he is
somethin', the high
method, the very best, the
one true predecessor

And it clears the air, to have this steam
(five yrs it's gathered)
going off

It is, for me, one of the
major engagements. For I must displace him,
peg 'im, for the young, for the
others, NOW, now!

when he is (as old men are—I mean, only the best)
in the way

So, deep woman, the boy-father
(is there anything as abstract in nature as the hoomin mail?)
is gathering thorns
and the high, useless, sabre-cuts

the wounds of love: (o, yes, for you, a quote, by way of creeley:

    "Love God," Pico writes to Angelo Politan, "we rather
    may, than either know Him, or by speech utter Him.

    "And yet men liefer by knowledge never find that which
    they seek, than by love possess that thing, which also

    without love were in vain found."

(It is elusive, is it not, the meaning? I catch it, then it is, again, gone. Spell it out
for me, if you will. At least today I don't get it.

                I'll be back. This is to get the early mail. (mail
                seems to have slowed up, with the reductions
                of the P.O. force). And to enclose a tenner
                (two to come, now). And to let you know this
                is, here is,
                        yr charles

(I shall go to gather you, if you have written me, later)

❧ 229 ❧

Washington to Pittsburgh[12]
29 May 1950 (postmark)

mon.   (as i sd, only you
wouldn't now
know)
later

baby:
   this is a note to tell you i had already sent, like a dope, a letter to wood. today, with news of (why, olson, levitated, as of last little days), of you, (and with 1/3 of what is left to come, back)

                              yr note,[13] of course, leaves me roaring
(sd Gotama, hold, bro.
or you'll be hindered!),
desolate, at the post, ho!
yet with gun
up

         At same time, lady,
comprehending,
(god damn it,
the . . . .

         of the 5 Clingings, the worst
                         the very worst is
                                   more wrong

than the soul, the hankering after,

is

what does not change

      ((Is it because you, too, invert
      my ambiguities? But their making, their making:

---

12. The letter is addressed to Frances Motz, care Helen Motz, 1515 Beechwood Blvd., Pittsburgh 17 PA.
13. This note is not extant. This is the beginning of a period of six weeks for which Boldereff's letters are missing.

IS THIS NOT OF CONSEQUENCE?

Is it not, my

RESONANCE?

what i had sd was, you are (you are!)
furious
gold!

i'll say more
Charles

∻ 230 ∻

Washington to Woodward
31 May 1950 (postmark 31 May 1950)

wed.   may 31   L

frances: (i am writing as tho that last dry note were up to now yr last letter to me: i go to the p.o. *after* the day's work is done; and you must take it as a sure sign, that i prefer to write you now, when all of me is stirring, than after, any day—it was something of such that I meant when, Monday, i called you, resonance)

I want to call you back to essentials, Lady. 1st of all, you must spell out why, when on Monday a week ago, you wrote me so fulsome a thing, so accurate, so far down in there where we correspond, so jibingly to my own senses—and then, after silence mon. thru fri., give me a formality (who the hell cares how fine a man the world thinks olson?)

On the surface of the facts, I am to take it one of two ways: (1) that such a note is what you mean by dropping love and taking up friendship? Or (2), that you, because i sd it was a letter, took extra meanings fr IN COLD HELL: what I meant by "it is a letter" was, "I am able to write you a poem, instead of a letter"—which is a most remarkable thing, my dear. And of such special consequence that, instead of being put off by it, as you sometimes are, you should be, no?, able to see it as sign, SIGN?

--------((instead of the beginning of an olsonism—which stood here, (my suspicious one!), am going to copy for you an extraordinary quatrain of crashaw; and i just guess you'll see why, my Imago!

Suppose he had been tabled at thy Teats
Thy hunger feels not what he eats:
He'll have his Teat ere long (a bloody one)
The Mother then must suck the Son

Which reminds me: I do not think IN COLD HELL, as it got written to you, contained a couplet which I want you to set in to copy—& which I *think* got written before I stumbled on the above:

What has he to say?
In hell it is not easy
to know the traceries, the markings
(the canals, the pits, the mountings by which space
declares herself, arched, as she is, the sister,
awkward stars drawn for teats to pleasure him, the brother[14]
who lies in stasis under her, at ease,
as any monarch or
a happy man)

How shall he
who is not happy, who has been so made unclear. . . . .

o frances: just because you have been so clear abt what got born
between us, do not, at this high time, desert,
for pain, distraction, (of the mind, of the senses, of
believing (the raising up—we are all, we are all, forever
lonely—that raising up which is, forever is, the will
of our own self)
desert not, here at the Bloody Angle, where even death may be,
the Cause, the Cause, it is

the cause![15]

Yr
Charles

❧ 231 ❧

Washington to Woodward (special delivery)
5 June 1950 (postmark)

---

14. Olson has an arrow at this line, and in the margin: "(note: i see it is a couplet broken up, according to present necessities)."

15. These last few lines became the poem "Quatrain," sent in typescript to Robert Creeley on 31 May 1950 and unpublished until *Collected Poems* (p. 166).

monday

frances, frances: i have yr letter (i knew something bad wld be there, yet i so hugely needed to feel yr reality—in that way that even words are real, even tho they are the poorest substitute for flesh—that i dragged myself down there to find the Bad Thing)[16]

it is going to be very difficult to make this letter, for i am sick, also, from some sickness i do not like the characteristics of: for they prove the origin is in that area where verse comes from when a man is well (that huge *health*, where art is born)

yet, i endure, it, all, because i am stubborn, with huge swedish teeth (like my father, whom god keeps because he was so stubbornly in there, even tho it killed him, literally, brought abt his death: we are such fools, these olsons, the way we go by, live up to, like liars, our affections—i, too, (and this was something I took as warning from his death, god help me) waste, waste our mortal strength so: i live in daily fear i'll not break down by the nerves, as the neurotics do, but by, as he did, the blood vessels

god damn our grace, that this is how these olson males are fated

(for a while it was my chest, i feared, would go, but now, today, i see it all, see where the lesions will be

And yet i DON'T, because the time i need (the way my time is quantity, and space), i must not break, must, somehow hugely haul myself up eighty years, god damn it, god damn these reeds on which men stand.

& christ, frances, it is this stubborn time sense of mine that makes me (with what right?) wild angry at you, you go off, now to, anywhere

you are so silly, to say, it is "spiritual" what lives between us/ what rot/ and why you don't get this triangle in its sure fix

spiritual? when the images are so strong and violent, and straight mad sex, straight sensual (even, and this is the obvious black magic of it, before there was any sex between us, when i put myself all over penny postcard to you? jeesus, jesus, woman, yr head should be examined (& only, and specifically, by me, who is the only one who can keep that fast noggin of yrs on the track)

16. This letter supplied Olson with his poem "The Story of an Olson, and Bad Thing" (*Collected Poems*, p. 175–182). Letters from Boldereff for this period are missing.

& you think air mail correspondence is the only issue! when, you dumb dame (even you!) a man is being born, right in front of all of our eyes, a male child!

aw, i give up. shit. stamina, stamina, that's what ain't, not intelligence   it wasn't stupidity that the creator damned the race with, it was shortness of life, & breath, so that we want all the returns before one night is over. it's the fast buck. i always sd, these god damned americans prove the whole stink of christianity, are, the founders of the ultimate proof of xty's lie, which is, that counsel of death, that methodology of same, fascism   kill, just to get rid of the bearing, the borning, which you, you, frances, knows takes blood, even to the breaking of vessels

the trouble with the whole damn spirit business is, it's a schitz proposition—and proceeds from dividing life up between now, and the hereafter. which just ain't.   the magic, the immortality, (which, as i say, you & i proved before we ever felt a bed under us) is HERE, HERE, where time is, and where time sez to the likes of you and me, look, little boy and little girl, the whole trick is, the only trick, is, the only way you make it, save yr thing, soul or whatever, is by obedience, (obey, obey, until you've squeezed the space out of me, out of me, time, yr only enemie!

frances, i'm rippin, but you know, baby, you know me, and you know, tho i'm shootin right for the belly of you, i've got my arms around you, and am askin, askin, only that you, sweet woman, who have given me such a profound thing from down in there where you give off the sweetest kind of essence (violet is the smell of life, no question; you prove it—& i mean, serious, like magic is, white or black, is, the whole business we're here for, i mean the smell of violets is the real; hones to gawd smell of life! how come, i don't know, and i don't care, even if it is the smell of the electrical wave H-mu; for it doesn't matter how you cut it up, or even if you reproduce it, it is still something that only those with the nose for it can SMELL—and can give it off!

i'm askin, only, again, as forever, that you take the ease of space, (it sounds easy: it ain't); that, beloved, as i sd once, you sleep, sleep there in woodward, in the birth place, where yr walks are, where natives live (we use to call the crew of a ship "the people"), where you can make nutty parables of snakes, where i can feel you in yr life, moving, as tho i had a womb, because i have, god damn it, because i am double (multiple: as a man or woman is, (is a woman?), when they resist the highest temptation of all (the temptation that didn't get into the biblums, as i know them (question: buddha?) that temptation of the intellect,

that fast buck organ, which wants to have answers: bah,
answers

(when i was walking home tortured by the way things are, & by this precipitation you have invented—with yr mind, darling, i swear it is! tho at the same time i do not raise a word, understand that, lady, do not cry you down, you who have come thru every time this strange devious bird has asked you up, this guy who has asked of you in kind, who has pushed you to the limits (boy, do you have it, when it is strength, and that kind of action that only the *livers* are made of)—or do you know, frances, just because i'm not one to, as we've sd before, "explain," do you know, lady, how in there you impress me as bein'?   do you know the image of that dame motz i carry around?—anyhow, as i was sayin, as i was walkin along, it flashed into my mind, a line of a poem i wrote, one of the 1st, back in 1941, May to be exact, part of which i palmed off as Yeats', in the Partisan Pound piece 1945; the line was

I can be precise,
though it is no answer[17]

That's the whole thing, fr where i sit at the moment. The job is, if yere in this business i'm in, is to be precise, nothing else compares in importance to it— and you have to measure everything, bring it to bear, just to enable yrself to be precise

And when you've been? It is not an answer! (That's why we don't turn out religious, thank god, that's why all we do is make things, make objects, and try to set them out there where the rest of the causes of confusion are. That's why life—all of it, not just our own, but all of it, is (who did it?) entrusted to us—& entrusted only so long as we keep in there, continue to OBEY, but obey the whole (hate that fucking word) every particle by every other particle (doctrine: multiple observation is the difference of this class of worker fr other classes of worker, equally necessary, simply because all jobs must be done, precision work merely the one that requires forty hrs a day,— and 125 yrs, which, because the human animal has shrunk away fr created limits, ain't any longer given

(((((Thus the inadequacy of all our work, compared to the assignment, & compared to the equipment given)))))

AND WHY WE AIN'T SPIRITUAL: there ain't no answers, there's only you and me, in any given situation, there's only these resonators of

(why did you write to me, the 1st letter? why did i answer? why did it keep going? (you, ya, in there, stayin in there—and i, a little bit going by the nose,

---

17. In "This Is Yeats Speaking," *Collected Prose,* p. 143.

shall we say, (what nose?), going slow, (slower, sure, because of a different profession, shall we say, just to have an explanation?) but going along, surprised,
against all previous courses, & getting it—where? some of it, no question,
right the hell out of the air (yes, the rime is hair, too, hair, and black all over,
yes, yes, even that proved true, did it not?) projecting, projecting, (testing,
testing)   why?   WHY, LADY FRANCES, why did you, too?   why

((these whys, are no longer questions, of course, yet,
because they are facts, they are not also answers, they are clues, (clews keep
sails taut), they tell where we have been, can, if they are kept in the mind
(are
not thrown—drama is out of business, now: ships, ships, steering is business
now, bring the head 'round, keep the wind (is it not wind, we obey?)—are
kept by—as good a word as any is,
                    the SINGLE INTELLIGENCE

(wow, what is in that abstraction, my little running water! (((note: the water
image is this feller, who is also, necessarily, skipper,—and one of the vessels)))

    and so it all boils down to a p.o. box.   really, baby, NO. listen to me: if i re-
ally thought you waz bein treated as a nigger, as you so wrongly put it, i'd obviously not only not have had such a box, but i'd obviously not, today or any
day, be writing you this letter or any such pouring letter (it is coming as blood
comes, lady, as precise as this customer, at this date of 120 yrs cut short, can
now make it)

                    you must, frances, cease & desist fr this notion   let me lead you
here, in the dance, lady: in the l'univers concentrationnaire, the flesh (is it not
extraordinary, that, when we speak of flesh on a wound, we call it proud
flesh?) has to be thrown in too, and, because there is no soul in the old sense
(at the old stand, where now they sell gold fr teeth, and fr burned bones, fertilizer), amour propre, in the old sense, won't do:
                    all things, *all*, including no-
tions which once were validities, have to be, not in the furnace of doubt, in the
furnace of fact have to be born—
                    THERE IS BIRTH ALL OVER THE
                    PLACE, THAT'S

                    WHY THERE IS SO MUCH BLOOD
                    all over the place

(god knows you know it, you tremendous

Mother!
            and if i spell out sharp one thing,
or another

you, Frances, (or so i deeply, thank god, believe)

are such that

you know i speak to you as modestly as

grass

        which, under the blood, tries

to breathe

                            one blade, of whatever,
                                    o

p.s.

    before posting this—& i am sending it special, not to waste dough, but, knowing the p.o., i know a special hastens things along the line: and this cutting of delivery, & collection, seems to have involved cutting transport as well   So i want to see, if where things are humped up, as they are, from yr letter,—and i want you to hear from me fast—i want to see if you get this letter as you should, tuesday   (i am also enclosing another ten)

    i just reread yr letter, darling, and it tells how distraught you are   and i hope this letter i have written you, tells you how much i know how distraught you are
            only, please, baby, two things (and i mean only that, if i can, i throw light on the darkest places you are put into): (1) when you say, by going away, you prove to all three of us that you expect nothing, that is not accurate, for you do, and of course you do, why shouldn't you, how, if this thing is any good, could you help expecting something?—the reality is, we all do, that is the human fact, and it can't be euchred away, by movement or anything else ((and i give you everything i can, point by point, even, as i think you must have been aware, the last time, when it was so wild and hard (for all of us, it turns out), and we were both so worn and distraught . . . even then, i was in there, to you; no?))   and (2) when you say you did not want to tell me ahead of time "because i did not want you to be morally in any slightest degree impugned

on".... frances, 1st, that doesn't jibe with (1), but, more, my girl, look at it, and ask yrself, was i not right, in the letter which precedes this p.s., to argue you away from spiritual notions? The hard facts are there, set out, solid, around which each of us has to move, (and hope), for facts have to be, solved, especially when they are grounded, as these are, not in moral areas (what are morals, anyhow?) but in the strongest forces of existence, in you and in all three of us.

I call you back to, the illuminations of, yr own wildness, to the Rimbaudian hells which he, artur, more than any predecessors, knew the amorality of, and how only the SINGLE INTELLIGENCE (or PASSION) was the instrument for.

This is a love letter,
olson

Is not woodward the *best* kind of hell-place imaginable?

◄§ 232 §►

Washington to Woodward (special delivery)
7 June 1950 (postmark 7 June 1950)

wed june 7 '50

darling, summer is here, this day and 1/2 since i wrote you, and my head has ached two days now, from the settling in of the heat

(it was a beauteous spring Washington had this year, amazing, almost New England, when usually, it is winter, then straight, thick, stupid river bottom summer)

But today I might wish my life could be as fullsome as it seems, with the strongest sort of feeling of you there, rich as you are, and present to me here in, wrapped up inside, my balls.

I had a wondrous visitation from my father last night. It was dream, of course, yet dream is, every so often, as the antients knew, not in the least psychiatric, but mythic, either of portent or of affirmation. This was affirmation, and leaves me heavy and free with a sort of happiness.

It was, in fact, a laying on of his hands. It was in a train, the observation car (confirming maestro freud, that a train is death). And, in that way we the living have, of facing death only by euphemism, he was sick, about to be sick, by vomiting, and his skin (as it never was) acned. Exactly what the conversation going on among all of us present I do not remember, but I surely do remember when he looked at me (now quite as he was, fronting straight on as he had a way of doing) and, the conversation definitely my verse, he sd, "You have done much more with it than I would have said you might have". Which was his old way of praise, and made my heart dance. It was afterwards that someone whispered to him, "Where does one see yr son's work", and I overheard, with that pleasure one does when one is not supposed to hear, my father answered, "O, it comes out every so often in a batch such as the recent *y & x.*"

The dream had a clear woman-turn thereafter, with a shift of location, and him gone, but I full of strength, physical strength (the same sort of swelling of strength inside the body as I have felt these last eight months), such strength that, in the dream, when someone like my giant friend Rosenberg made some sort of challenge of me, I, who am of a sort timid and have known physical fear, had none, had only laughter, and the sureness I could take Rosenberg (like the horse in the dream to you!) and snap his back, like a blade of grass. But the problem, at this point of the dream, was two enclosed spaces, one which was to be gone down into, the other, which was a closet in which I had to stoop to hang clothes, and which, I explained, was the reason why the going down into the mine, or whatever the other space was, was, not difficult (with such new-found strength) but was a problem, that's all!

It is quite lucid, is it not? And quite handsome. And, frances, definitely forward (it is amazing to me, how the parable of my existence is working itself out, as on a stage, before my very eyes, these tremendous months.) Do you guess the huge kind of (how shall I put it) the fruitfulness I feel you have brought into this being, woman of my blood? Do you see how, the union of my clarity as poet to this astonishing birth working itself out day on night, is a tension the like of which only created things have? (I suppose other men have had this experience, of watching themselves being born, but I have never seen it set down. And so you will excuse me, if I wonder at it.)

((((in fact, my lady, if you do know any examples of other men, tell me where they are. For I watch it, with all that cold function of my job as worker, as well as, on such a day as this, can, with all my heart, send it to you. It may just tell you, what I wonder if you don't have, alas, to set aside (if i might have the power, i would wish you to bear, bear, and sleep, in that kind of sleep you tell me i have given you, and can, and will give you): the absolute function you are to me, whatever the appearances, however the absence of actions contradicts the usual, what would seem to be the steps that ought to (more rapidly?) unfold.

What I wrote to you Monday (as so often happens, and, because it happens, is again a thing i wish you might hug to yrself as tho it were my body, NOT, NOT, my soul, not the least less sensual that it is, what it issues as) what I wrote seemed to me to be again the material of work, and, when it is done— if it comes off—I shall send you copy. It is called, now, "The Story of An Olson, and Bad Thing", and is a curious experiment in the struggling of verse out of continually repeating prose, like a swimmer or like the birth of verse, the narrative, of course, as unplotlike as you'd imagine I'd handle narrative (knowing its lie).

((let me put in with this letter the verse at the end—and you will excuse me, i send you the mss.: it is sometimes wrong to set copy while you are still in process; but i think, you know me so well, you'll find your way thru it—(it has more breathing spaces than I have indicated)))

I'm goin (this goddamned machine has gone on the blink, & exacerbates my nerves)

I'm going to get this off in the 2 oc pickup, without going to the P.O. to see if you have written me.

Just so you'll have this, the
more quickly, to tell you

love

PART LAST:[18]

At this date of 120 yrs cut short, I, Olson

in the l'univers concentrationnaire, the flesh
(is it not extraordinary that, when a wound exists,
and is healing, we call what it throws off
proud flesh?) flesh, rose flesh
must also be thrown in.

And because there is no soul in the old sense
at the old stand (where, now, they sell gold
from teeth
       & fr burned bones, fertilizers)

---

18. This is the ending of "The Story of an Olson, and Bad Thing" as published (*Collected Poems*, pp. 175–82).

amour propre, in the old sense,
won't do.

Now all things, in the furnace of fact, all things
(no things in the furnace, in the weather beaten face of,
doubt)
all things (including notions, or whatever
were once validities) all things stand, including
the likes of you and me, all, all
must be born out of

(God knows you know, Old Goddess &

tremendous Mother

There is birth! there is

all over the place, there is

       And if I, in this smother, if I

smell out one thing sharp,

or another

(where his teeth have been in me

you even know, Enemie, I speak as modestly as

broken grass

       which, under the flood, tries

to breathe to breathe!

       Say I, one blade,

to you,

or whoever

       it is why there is so much blood

       all over the place

END POEM

❧ 233 ❧

Washington to Woodward
8 June 1950 (postmark 8 June 1950)

6/8/50

cold, cold on the
bold shore, as
the rock falleth, the water
stands: beware
of permanence, you
who will run in, who, in yr thin shallops think
to make the land

the season
is forever cold, and the reason, the rock
(if you can call the mind,
or is it from water that images come?
And the boldness, never
to be ice, to stand
other than the slow antient
heart, to change
is the expectation

we, previous immigrants,
tell you[19]

> frances—just to let you know this day, too,
> thursday, you are so very much in my antient
> same!

love
yr
Charles

❧ 234 ❧

Washington to Woodward (special delivery)
9 June 1950 (postmark)

FOR
ARTHUR RIMBAUD[20]

---

19. This letter is a typed copy of "Other Than," revised from a 1946 version. See *Collected Poems*, p. 165.
20. This draft was later revised and published as "A B Cs (3—for Rimbaud)." See *Collected Poems*, pp. 174–75.

NEWS (o the latest)
& mu-sick, mu-sick, mu-sick

worse than war, worse
than peace. And they both dead
And the people's faces
like boils.

You plea for the heart, for the return of, into the work of,
the running of, say
a streetcar?

   shall it be rain
   (on a tent), grass? Birds
   on a wire (5, count 'em, now 3
   on two) Or Metechevsky?

   trillings, cleanings, we who want
   SCOURINGS

or the running of, the Passaic of
orange peels, (cats win in urbe,
NOT usura)   The long white finger balloons,
or the color of, dyes   (cats,
& industry, not even
pity

The brutal, head on. But to want fruits?
to want beauty so hard? who
can beat life into form, who
is so foolish, who
has misled us?
            who? The heart, to have it back: he
put it this way. Is it any more than
a matter of syllables?

   The mouths bit
   empty air

          (REPELLENT, ILL., or whatever
city, state, the LOVERS
come from, our

tenement boys (oh my washerwoman mother, oh
my alcoholic dad), the
let's object, let's
forget, and just, fuck, let us just be
Quakers and angels abt
all these insuperable
horrors, o

lets us jest be-
lieve in bee-
yoo-tie)
        crist.

Sd R. Cr. (June, 1950): form
is never more than
an extension of
content.

    And then there was this,
    even though
    what we needed most was
    something the extension of
    claritas:

        in the drenched tent/ there is quiet
        sered eyes/ are at rest

(Did you hear,
you whose ears bulge,
sered eyes

are at rest?

                    o
                (6/8/50)

look, darling, I have yr tuesday letter, & yr cry, I let up. And you are, baby, clearly so tired. And do, do, take rest, *please*, frances, go a long a bit, sink yr-self into woodward, into nature, your nature (Since you told me, there has been, in the kitchen, for the 1st time ever, a lovely little spider, living here, in this house, each morning there the spider is, when I get breakfast!)

the point is, I expect now to be in New York monday or tuesday the week after next, that is, June 19 or 20th   nothing definite, but

just tell me back how rigid your plans are.

But above all, frances, *do, do*, try to sleep! to find a little ease, a little ease, my soul

Charles

❧ 235 ❧

Washington to Woodward (special delivery)
11 June 1950 (postmark 12 June 50)

sunday

(((shall we really be daring (dare the gods! sd he, as he wrote merde on the luxembourg garden bench) ma mere, and say, it took seven months?—or shall we, rather, obeying the other mare, expect issue in the proper nine?)))

that,

   for a starter!

        And to greet you in yr newer decisions, handsome Lady! hurray, my faithful, hurrah! break out

the bannaner, let 'im

WAVE, in the fireislandair, plunge him

inthesandthesea, o Count-

essa mia!

      (so i'm dreamin? So i'm dreamin'! And why not, Mare

of night?)

(Ride 'em, mia, and down, by the ride, apockalips![21]

21. From this point, the letter provided the basis for the poem "Adamo Me . . ." (*Collected Poems*, pp. 182–88).

by the, naked, tide, by
beauty is most difficult BUT
for that reason is, at her ends, not to be
dum-dum (ed), you-me, we
have to stay in there, without answers, even

    the christ is a fish
to be caught, especially where the waves
pour in like walls, and only with the hands
(and the absolute danger of losing 'em,
in the sand, the
drag underneath)
can you catch!

    (What is it,
you have
in yr arms? what is it, who,
when I am there, how is it
(i know) how is it it is (with you)
beauty?
      And me not the christ, me
a most practical, eatable, skinnable, friable
(what is left, with the dirty dishes, after the supper,
when you are cleaning the table, if it is, say, a Friday

I looked up, and there, on the wall, as though a mesa,
and we were walking across, (or others, after us), and,
set in the clay like a demonstration, vertebra
the spine of what once was

And even, if the air is wrong, it is not sand, their houses,
(water, always water up,
and over, testing, it is time, the little red spot
glows, it is my grandchild
who is on, "you're on"

      And I (the music
is defunctive) he who was I
(or you)
    for you, when i am not, she wrote

when still the sea pours in, still it is

a wall, and they seek the sun afterwards,
to dry off, in the hollow of
a sandhill, and, the flesh tastes so good,
they roll over

            suddenly we stumbled, and, as i sd,
i looked down, and there, before his very eyes,
i was

      (as long as a sea-serpent or the wood hewn
from the tree that grew up where they planted, with him
who first died, the seed the angel gave his son,
as he waned And they all standing around in such
astonishment, that a morning should bring
such a new thing

           Or as small as
that extinct bird (it was not a bird, it had fingers
and though it was not sand but wind
which they sieved

            I can be caught too, preserved,
sd Mme B, for, though it is difficult, it is not,
for that reason, to be allowed, in the clutch
it is not the time, Mr. B[22]
to be called out

          Or to cry out, it is
too much, when you are the runners, when you have men
in your hands!

          In her arms we lie, the law
injunctive, hit, hit
while you're at bat, or,
it doesn't matter whether they find you, or yr house, or
even yr grandchild, as, carefully, they pan
each shovelful, even yr possessions or the bones of
yr dog

     man built daringly
by water, stayed

22. "Mr. Baseball" was the original typing before deletion.

because there were always those
who found other live beings more interesting than
nature, as we city folk call
trees, fields or clucking
hens

the riddle is (besides femininity)
that of which beauty
is only the most interesting
expression, why

         We persist, we
remain
curious, even in the face of

he dissolved, the second dissolved (after punishment), I
may be a scatter of bones, or even merely sand,
and not even shining as the neighboring quartz, actually
disappearing as the water trickles, or is shaken, or even roars
over

    (4 were swept down, 4 clung
    when the silly glistening powerful match-box of a boat
    missed the lock and went swirling over
    the mill-race, crack, in the sluice, skulls,
                       And off
    down the river like fish eggs or unborn bees,

                    4

    were saved, the percentage
    a happy,
    and unusual one
            The difficulty is,
not that it is locked in the mind past all remonstrance, not
at all (though that is also true: example,
that they rolled over, that their bodies, that the rose of their flesh shone
where the drops still had not dried on the sand, that, together,
they made a four-legged beast, and, from its making, locked,

that, from it, they carried away remembrance,

                  none of this, nothing shows,
when you find a dispersed bone

but this is, (still) still no reason for

the blackmail of, to the riddle of, to the difficulty, either

the secret and/or the thrashing, the celebration of it (beauty, or whatever) either

drama or epilogue, (soul, or whatever easy formulation

to stand in the roar of, the false play of (where an out is an out)

eternity,

> When it glows,
> what can you do
> (when you are on)
> when the flesh is that rose,
> what shall you do but make,
> out of the mind and the mind's remembrance, if you like,
> out of the pouring in which you, too, may drown, out of
>
> (as they lay taking up fire from where fire came in the first place
> why, in their eyes, her eyes, and his sons' eyes
> there was such bewilderment that it could be,
> what a discovery, of difficulty, that he could be put out
>
> well, still, is there anything you or i can do more than
>
> to make a monstrance
>
> of it?

(& is there anything

more difficult?)

           Isn't it mad, (maddening?), the way I go off (or am I
on?, any how, know no chagrin, dear lady, for, that I do go off, up (and over!),
is PROOF, proof of what needs no proving!
                    I will write you again tomorrow, like
                              love
                                 charles

+§ 236 §+

Washington to Woodward (special delivery)
13 June 1950 (postmark)

tuesday

so now you know, Sib!
that you are Pistis-Sophia!
Ain't
she bee-yoo-tifull?

Been stuck on what is now called ADAMO ME FECIT, which you had yesterday,—got interrupted just as I was abt to put the heat on, by one of the nuts
who think they are sculptors across my garden—

and just at the place where it didn't go over the top yesterday

god damn   i am harassed, and have lost that precious thing, time

But all, all is well!
For it shall be Monday!
And the 5th Ave Hotel I am glad to
know abt:
>   look—let us leave it this way, the days are so short (they are long):
>   1) if by any foul chance you should have to change any part of the plan,
just make sure that you leave a message for me (a note is even better, if any
change should take place after you reach the city) at the 5th Ave

>   2) and I shall do the same, if anything should screw me up, likewise

Otherwise, I shall be there, or call you, whenever you arrive!

And honest, baby, I shall *try* to be daddy, and see that business also gets taken
care of!

>   (In fact, I myself have to see Payne on business—it may be a thousand
bucks, come next year—and I haven't heard yet when he leaves for the Coast
(either Monday or Tuesday) So I might just have to tie myself up for dinner
Monday night, but shall not, of course, if there is any other way out.

In any case, I shall either be at the Hotel, or call you from 7:30 on—say I start calling at 7:45, and at 15 minute intervals thereafter. (And I'll not be later than 10–11, even if I should have to get that business done).

I'm going to let this get off, special, so that we're cleared for this action!

(I'll write abt—what will we write abt, this week!

o, anyway, I'll write you—a poem!

sd he, the

Bold One
or, IEU

Charles

❦ 237 ❧

Washington to Woodward (special delivery)
16 June 1950 (postmark 16 June 1950)

friday

I made only one error, Frances: I did not calculate the effect, of my, so long ahead, making an exact appointment with you. I should not have done it (it is not my way, as you, god help us, have had occasion to know). I don't know that anyone else has such problems with time and act, but, because of the way space is my birthmark, I do—and my work depends on two obvious things (1) action, immediately; and (2) stasis (in the space sense, as an *act*, by which forms are made possible.

The result is, I have been under terrible duress. And I must take one step back, in order to get through these next few days. The step is, to come to you when and wherever I can,—and that I dare thus to disappoint you a hair, you must, Pistis-Sophia, take, not as a further olson strictness on your dear, tremendous flesh, but as evidence, again, of how clean and clear this thing between us is, that I am so terribly fierce to my organism, against all normal realities, which I also, god help me, know. And that I go by the hugest faith in you, demands on you.

You see, baby, one thing keep a hold of: this has nothing to do with my desire to see you, is, in no sense whatsoever, a change of plan. It is merely a withdrawal of my commitment ahead of time to that plan. You were going to NY anyhow, for damn good reasons. I suppose it was, again, the extraordinary co-incidence (twice, exactly!), which led me to stamp YES, so quickly, on my own tentative dates. (This is the way, the way, if I can hammer my life out straight—as I conduct with you, darling ((remember that, above all things, that I do, with you, now))—this is the way I *shall* conduct my life, come hell or paradise.)

You go to New York, as planned. If you do not hear from me Monday, do not be concerned. All is, essentially, well. Let me leave it at that, now.

You will *also, please, believe*, that there is *absolute cause* for my doing things this way, and rest in my judgment, *go quietly on*, without anything more than the *hair* of disappointment—which is all this should amount to, just, this first effect.

I am including a letter to Bob Giroux, at Harcourt. What has troubled me all week, is yr mention of the Cornwall Press, for, for the life of me, I can't remember that I know anyone there. (When we are together, and talk this whole business over, I'm sure I'll have other ideas of people. But right now, let me make it the Giroux, who is such a fine mild guy. And catch up, later.)

And do, darling, carry to NY my copy of yr Whitman.

> (This, with practically no right kidney
> left—and it not Bad Thing's work at all!

> This, love, and—again, that absolute

trust I came to go by, when I sent you the dream fr Montevallo ((this is almost a parallel act!))

> love, Charles

[*Enclosed: letter to Robert Giroux, Esq., Harcourt, Brace*]

> 217 Randolph Place NE
> Washington 2 DC
> June 16, 1950

My dear Bob:

This will introduce to you Frances Motz, of Woodward, Pennsylvania. She is the book designer, Mrs. Frances Boldereff, and I have urged her, out of the fullest kind of belief in her and her work, to go to see you, when she can be in New York.

I think if she carried only one single piece of her design, the Pennsylvania State College Catalogue for this year, you would need to see no more to know how rare and how thorough she is. What impresses me, is, how grounded her work is, how her sense of printing is not type alone but a profound understanding of the space which a page is, and what breath—to speak like a writer!—leading can give. I dare say it is a clue, that she learned her trade in the hardest kind of discipline, the Jersey City house that does the N.Y. telephone books. For she knows her business, (like a good writer knows syllables!)

But she will tell you, and show you, more, for she has, in her position as Publications Production Manager at Penn State, done an immense amount of work, of all the kinds of paper on which print goes, including the most beautiful posters, in which she shows as high a sense of color as she has of space, and of the union of color to type and to cut.

There are also books of her own, one *of* her own (using Michelangelo plates) and one of Whitman, which is just done.

Mrs. Boldereff wants, now, I understand, to work in New York, and I suggested, that of the men I know, you are the one I should want her to see.

Greetings, and shall see you myself, shortly.

> Affectionately,
> Charles Olson

❧ 238 ❧

Washington to Woodward (special delivery)
21 June 1950 (postmark)

Wednesday

it's 7, & the last collection is at my back, but I must, want, spring to tell you, how wondrous, despite my monosyllables (or by proof of 'em) it was to talk to you again, last night

I had to dispose the day in friend Creeley's direction, had to get back to him, mss. which have piled up (stories, poems of his) the last 10 days, as I hammered & hammered to get both ADAMO ME & THE STORY OF, AN OLSON AND, BAD THING, into final form—they went off yesterday to

WAKE (whom Creeley—my boy Creeley!—has opened up)   (It was also he who led Emerson to make me the *Golden Goose* offer I told you of)   So he deserved these 7 hrs of straight work on him, which leave my skull cracking: critique gives one nothing back, like creatin'.

I want to sit down to one good old fashioned letter to my MOTZ, crave, crave, to give out, where it comes from, to her

likewise, why you haven't had mail, tho (& it may be a measure of the strength) I thot also I'd, come to you

O my Frances, it is very beautiful, this thing you and I have. And, by God, you do, you do, my tremendous thing, stay in there, take & take! And it is beautiful, and however much you do put out, babe, it is stored up, here, in this man who counts, who remembers, who, goes as the care & scruples & power go, toward you, gives back, in this dream of love, as we must also call it, because it is such an undreamed creating forward, such a forcing on of, because the sex is there—o, how it is there—into what form we shall, by god, we shall, one day know.

You must, when you write me, tell me that address again, for, tho I wrote it down, on the shelf of the booth, I couldn't afterwards, read it!

So this, sweet, is a relaxed note, just to greet you back, & to tell you who it is who is here where you also so fully are, because you occupy him, by

love
Charles

⇥ 239 ⇤

Washington to Woodward (special delivery)
22 June 1950 (postmark)

thursday, the day
of yr return

frances, darling:

miss, no letters from you, miss 'em, babe, miss 'em. Funny thing, how close they bring you, how solid connective is, (connective tissue, like they say, like bogomolets, he say, how it is the connective tissue of which we die, not, the breakdown of the, organs)

strong, strong (and whose strength?
can't be mine, sd she, but it is, it is!

what a connect! (to use that lovely motz barbarism), what a woman, you are, a lot o'
woman!

miss you, Miss
            (how was biz? hope
            'twas okay. You
            should have
            what you want

                        ((can I?
                                    offer you the City?)

                  (If I might!)

Let me play, a little, kitten (ow! i remember! it ain't true, what
he sd abt you: you,
ARE
my kitten, can be,
with O. Yes. Sleep,
and be a kitten.

Been so taut, both over our business and over the business of verse, have,
today, to be a little slap-happy.
                        Anyway, am a little pissed off, over recent verse:
wanna take a turn, wanna let off, come in
another door.

        Say, be
        byzantine, OR
        iranine, be
        light & bitter   (It's all beer,
        ("I like beer, myself")   fr. here out!)
        for a change

        So, for the hell of it, lemme
        send you something I just
        thought of, for
        the game
        (In this case,
        Tarocco!)

(It's an old one, dressed up—so don't think yr boy is altogether off his hoop!

    (It's decorative, ain't it?)

                         (Thinkin' of usin' it,
for GOLD GOOSE, jes
                  to get 'em on the off beat,
                    to get 'em on the off beat
               to get 'em on the off beat
                 to get 'em on the off beat
            to get 'em
                    Anyway, to try to get 'em

(They can be GOOFED
but only by pot.

Or then, there's this:

    AGAIN, SPRING[23]

spring,
and on the walk, in chalk:

this way

don't stop

getting closer

closer

keep going

Sorry, she

allready left

Or, this, in quite a different mood, but in front of my eye, at the moment

             A SENTENCE

In a minute of time from the mouth of a murderer, death
heweth its way through a wood of men
                   (fr. William Hooke, 1641)

23. A poem unpublished except in the notes to *Charles Olson & Robert Creeley: The Complete Correspondence* 6:230–31.

(No: this is too good, don't you think? to be wasted: I'll use it in a larger context, no? Or this: (next carbon)

GLI AMANTI[24]

First, to describe the card,
(for it is a card, in a game):

> what you don't see (these modern ways!)
> was M.E. or O.F. (was handsome, painted, those days)
> a woman on both sides of a man
> one with her hand on him above, the other
> with her hand on him below

> > > a tongue above,
> > > a sword
> > > below

But to get on with it: the card
is to be pronounced,
thus

l   the liquid consonant, it is formed
      with the tongue point on the teeth ridge, with
      the nasal passage closed,
      and voiced breath
      passing out at one, or more commonly both, free sides
      of the tongue. Hence the name,
      lateral consonant,
      usually bi-lateral but sometimes
      unilateral.

      There are two l's, the clear
      and the dark. Clear l
      occurs before vowels (lily, loose);
      and dark l before consonants (shield) and when final
      (feel), or syllabic
      (battle).

      In America, sometimes initial l is noticeably dark.

24. This and the following poem are carbons of poems sent to Creeley the same day (*Creeley Correspondence* 1:144). They have not been previously published.

o   in *son, come, dove, front, honey, tongue, won*, etc.,
         spells the u sound of
         sun.

v   is the voice lip-teeth fricative consonant corresponding to voiceless f
e   is frequently silent
                          at the end of
                                    a word.

IN ANSWER TO A REQUEST FOR DIRGE WORDS—THAT IS, WORDS INTENDED FOR MAKING A CATHARSIS, BY MEANS OF FEELINGS ABOUT DEATH—NOT JUST SAD, BUT *OVER-SAD*, TO GET IT OUT OF THE SYSTEM

The Office of the Dead is always open, at all hours

of the day & night, like a diner, or the air

for those who wish to wet themselves with tears,

who wish—in that most desirable, unassuming, & smiling manner

to make faces about, as though they were scratching a sore

Meanwhile, the corpse is lowered DIRIGE DOMINE

and the eyes

are right, the flowers,

the stole

AND THE WHOLE GODDAMN STRIKE-BREAKING BUSINESS
     correct,

O Dominus meus

Meatus anus. The dead bury the dead,

                              and it is not at all anything but

disgusting
        The which while

a boy in a blue shirt

restrains his mother,

and doesn't feel a goddamn thing.

                                    Olson

jay, hoo, babe,
                    olson
is rough,
this day!

And, as you sd, abt "A RIMBAUD",
it bothers you.

            But then,
you wouldn't know me if I weren't, every so often, truculent, wld you, darling?

    (Isn't it crazy,
what we are, what a congery
a hoomin bean
IS?

            ((And also, where there hath been such
            absolutes, such
            generalizations, such
            abstractions—& they got dirtied thereby

how my generation HAS, HAS
                            (or so I think)
    HAS to jam home the particulars, come in
    to defeat vulgarity, with all feet!
    "give it to 'em,"
                (like they say!)

I must run. The collection, is any minute. Will continue tomorrow
                            Love,
                                & to take these as signs,
                                despite . . .
                                Your
                                Charles

                        ◄§ 240 §►

Washington to Woodward (special delivery)
26 June 1950 (postmark 26 June 1950)

monday june 26 50

You must bear with me, my lady. I am in one of those times I do not like—when I have to back-track manuscript, to prepare for press. It is agonizing, like paying bills. I don't know that I shall ever like this stopping, this sort of summing up. I so work best going out, going off ahead, keeping what is part done, or all done, in a pile of mss., disorganized, so that each day I am forced to be fresh for new organization, new form. The trouble with looking at yourself, bringing yrself into that kind of focus (that the gathering up of things for publication involves) is, that you feel set, feel too much yoorn own cliches, harden, or bear down too much, leaving no new things to come on.

I so prefer to stay, in a sense, fluid, as though the SUM was not to be of my doing (as, in truth, of course, it is not) but to be taken care of, by others (as, in truth, it will, of course). But what I am talking abt, at the moment, is the ideal weather, so far as I'm concerned, of doing, of getting work done. And that is, to have, or keep, sea-way, even from what one did yesterday.

'Course this, too, I am beginning to crack down on. I'm beginning to try to figure out an assault on form larger than what a man can get done in one go. (Poe wasn't so silly as some think, in this principle of composition of his, about the length right for a poem: one sitting. It was one way, then, to make a protest at Miltonic, Wordsworth crapping up of form.

But what I am talking abt is not one sitting for the reader but one sitting for the writer. This is the organic problem: that is, if, as you know I believe, a poet stays in the open, and goes by breath, not by inherited form. One can set the limits (my own probably are short, but you know, from their coming into being, most of them, in letters written of afternoons to you, about how much stamina a man can keep up, and keep inside one tone, one problem, one attack on a material: it is probably, the base mss., a maximum of, 4 hrs.) Now what I want to do is to join this organic principle I believe in, to a method of composition like that in which THE KING-FISHERS was done—which, due to the fact that it is, history, and thus the head is the gauge, is not, for anything else than its own kind of material, a viable method. What I need is some methodology to go on day after day on the same content as the day before, with the same steam up, inside the same amnion, until I can come out with a form which would be an extension of a larger kind of content. (I hunch this comes, in the end, to dray-mah.)

My present plan, is to try a method I have been toying with, in my mind, for some time: the method of GLOSS, to do a GLOSS if you like, on myself, tho it came up in my mind as of THE TEMPEST, and I rather think I'll start with it, there,—that is, if this present sure push (date: day November, woodhenge, a man, a woman, hour afternoon, borning, creatures present) until NOW, does not keep going, praying fiercely as I am that it do keep going, without intermit, from now to dissolution, to the stoppage of the power of nerves, muscles, heart, will, the drive, the potency (potency man's measure, all, ALL he liveth for, silly fragile thing

((you know this, don't you, wise woman motz, know it, where you are dark, where you are so gifted, so light maker, so Sophia))

why should i not continue to use this form which 4 hrs blocks out? why should i fight it, why seek a longer one—what's wrong with it? BUT there one is again, (the male) looking for the NEW, always, the fool, going on from what is, push, push, push!

I set to write you Saturday after I had had your two letters, and again I went off going over the manuscripts, picking out, discarding, getting ready for, the new print-push. (It is a crucial one, or I guess I wouldn't be after it so hard, that is, I don't mean after publication, but, once publication is offered, then I want what I do get out, right. And publication is now offered. As a matter of fact, what has happened is, that suddenly the thing has opened up. The silly world has caught up a little, on o. And, thank you, sweet one, olson is ready, is, in fact, loaded, and ready to fire.

It is funny, really, the whole biziness: I have no lack of verse for the traffic. The Golden Goose Chapbook, in fact (spring, probably, 1951), is going to have to be less than available product, I imagine, for the poems done are of such length, I doubt the editor (Richard Emerson) will want them all. And the anthology of new stuff (which precedes the chapbook, probably winter, this coming winter) is already about set—even if, as one kind editor put it, (unwilling to give up MORNING NEWS, La Chute, and Move Over) "you should drop dead, Olson"![25]

((Terrible thing,—and of this you must always stay aware, when I hold and hold and hold to a desk—one always wonders, will there be any more work, can I do more, shall I keep power? It is crazy, but, there, again, it is the sexual stem, the constant, constant, male question: potency)) ((That is another reason why such summing up as these days is such a terror: one has to look, rewrite, consider one's chagrin—and not do what each day should be, new, new, new proof, proof proof, that I, Olson, have GOT IT!)))

Anyhow, the joker is, that the 1st of the three Golden Goose publications is,

25. Robert Creeley—but not his exact words.

this fall, and is, the request is, for "other short pieces like those in *y & x*"! That's what's had me on the griddle now, a week. To have to consider that question when I am pushing long form toward longer form, is why I am so scratchy, so ruthlessly one-minded.

Again, today: and I enclose today's to you—another tarot card, like Green Man, like Gli Amanti, with the advantages, disadvantages, of same.

And it is frightfully hot, now, and I, feeling it, more than ever before, suddenly realising, I live in the South! Crazy, crazy, crazy!

Frances, do write me—and write me with that beating huge heart. Come close to me again. Come in, come in. Keep close, despite my present severities, despite your movings. Let us stay close—close to that charmed ground, there, on the bank of a rushing river. Let us keep our hands on the growing boy. Let us, let us, let us. . . .

love,
charles

p.s. I have kept forgetting to tell you, for weeks, weeks, that the stuff Foerster sent to the South Atlantic bounced with the formal rejection! As a veteran, I, of course, payed it no mind. (The Nice Thing, which you will like about the present series of openings out, of the MAGS, is that it all happened from the work itself, cold. That pleaseth one who knows the world's ways, And doth not use 'em! My innocence was once hooded, like a hawk.

Yr boy, O

[*enclosed, carbon copy:*]

LA TORRE

The tower is broken, the house
where the head was used to lift,
where awe was.
And the hands

      (It is broken!
      And the sounds
      are sweet, the air
      is acrid, in the night, fear
      is fragrant)

The end of something has a satisfaction.
When the structures go, light
comes through

To begin again. Lightning
is an axe, transfer of force
subject to object is
order: destroy!

    To destroy
    is to start again, is a factor of
    sun, fire is
    where the sun is out, dowsed

        (To cause the jaws to grind
        before the nostrils flare
        to let the breath in)

2

Stand clear! Here,
it comes down! And with it the heart has
what was, what was we do lament

        (Let him who knows not how to pray,
        go to sea)

Where there are no walls
there are no laws, forms, sounds, odors to grab hold of

Let the tower fall! Where space is born
man has a beach to ground on

We have taken too little note of this:
the sound of a hammer on a nail can be as clear as
the blood a knife can make spurt from a round taut belly.

3

In the laden air,
we are no longer cold.
Birds spring up, and on the fragrant sea

rafts come toward us lashed of wreckage and young tree.
They bring the quarried stuff we need to try this new-found strength.
It will take new stone, new tufa, to finish off this rising tower.

olson

❧ 241 ❧

Washington to Woodward (special delivery)
28 June 1950 (postmark)

wednesday

darling:

By god, just now finished on that whole damned Gold Goose bizness.
6 PM, one week & better out. Only now done. Nine poems off, 9, count 'em,
9. And me nervous as hell. What a stinking job. Hate it, hate it—and my belly
torn, from it. You can't imagine what a fool I am, how I bear down! 'Course,
I'm not a fool, 'cause, in the process, I get rewriting in, on everything, and it is
a part of the way I go, coming back, & back, to things, working them, not in
that self-conscious way others, I imagine, do, but this way, as occasion demands. It is better for me, that is all. I think I got one nice little one (new) out
of it, which I must copy for you, as a present, and, as a candy, for putting up
with my shrieks and pains on this thing all week,—instead, as I ought to be,
writiiiiiiiiiii pppppppppppppppppppppppppppppppp pppppppppppppppppp (excuse, this, the 2nd machine I've blown up in the past two weeks, is on the fritz,
the damned tape keeps jumping back————but it's all right again.

instead, baby, as you might have expected, i was coming in on
what concerns youandme / all this business of where we are / where we are
going / what is up
for it does trouble me, as you guessed fr my monday letter,
that you are, at least that letters have, lost their grab for you
but i think you
are right, that it is action that is on the calendar (i think that is what is) i do
myself
And I certainly can ask no more of you than the quietness, the firmness
with which you do wait   I see, babe, I see   And was it not I who sd, he will
come whenever, wherever?

It is a most strange time. I shld never have
guessed.But there—that is the business of what we are here for. And there it
is. The riddles, the riddles. . . .

And i am busy about the business, you can be sure. I am, I take things, serious

>(old Sirius, they called him, when he was
>Egyptian priest)

Only I wish you would also,—as I try to do—keep communication open on these other things that you and I also know our lives are made to be busy abt, these things you were writing me before you went to the Babylon, of

what

so deeply, (and can love be extricated from same) you and I, by some mystery we are not yet master-mistress of, concern ourselves with?

>(((Because LA CHUTE, was the 1st of such investigations
>I ought to pass you what the editor who will publish
>it, sd, today, by mail, to me:
>>"La Chute/ real crazy beats in that/ bongo.
>>Too much: shows what yez can do with rhythms
>>in an open form. I mean: a fine thing."[26]
>You will understand, that this nut (a former peddlar of narcotics, a

former drinker, a former musician, now a hen-farmer, and the best yng writer I know here where the language & energy of the earth is pounding here and/or anywhere, this lad, speaks funny because he is trying, and right he is, to get dialect in without localism: crazy—too much (if you know bands, is such talk: ((AND WHO WAS IT WHO SD, Bigmans. . .))

o frances

>This will greet you, before you leave lovely woodward,

your house where I was, where I have wooed you, that close place, which was our intimacy.

>And yet you go where, close to where, we were also, first were,

where the amazing steps were taken. And I go with you, heard all you say, know where you are, hold, hold, in this capacious tun (called olson, but what olson is, who he is, is not only to others (except frances) but to himself as well, to be made known.

>My cool one, cool in power because hot in act, my gold

furious lady, I greet you, to greet you, elsewhere, to say, we are.

>And to send what does not
>waver
>his love

[poem enclosed:]

---

26. Olson is quoting a Creeley letter of 24 June 1950 (*Charles Olson & Robert Creeley: The Complete Correspondence* 1:152).

A B CS   (II)[27]

what we do not know of our selves
of who they are who lie
coiled or unflown
in the marrow in the bone

one sd:

of rhythm is image
of image is knowing
of knowing there is
a construct

or to find, in a night, who dwells in that wood where shapes hide
who is this woman or this man whose face we give a name to, whose shoulder
we bite, what landscape
figures ride small horses over, what bloody stumps
these dogs have, how they tear the golden cloak

And the boat

how he swerves it to avoid the yelping rocks
where the tidal river rushes

᪥ 242 ᪥

Washington to New York City (special delivery)[28]
29 June 1950 (postmark)

thursday

baby: your long letter in hand, And its grab, DELIGHTED am i, to feel you,
the language, language even, the grab again, good, good, good! baby, good!

The point is, to get off to you a special, with the enclosed, to meet you, on arrival, to tell you—what went on today!

For I was cock-eyed wrong, yesterday, it was over, the PUTSCH, I mean, of
the GOOSE, the golden, may it lay the right kind of, an egg!

27. Revised version of "Experiment in Form," which was sent in the letter of 10 April 1950. See *Collected Poems*, p. 173.
28. Envelope addressed to "frances motz, care of Mrs. John Baer, 215 Second Avenue, New York City,
N.Y. (Please hold for arrival)."

Bang, this morning, comes, fr Emerson, the *real* bizness: sez he, the guy we were going to run in Number One, funks, and will you? (WILL I! now, at this juncture, this late corner of my life, this young brazzy five year old poet, WILL HE! I say, friend Em, will he!

In other words, *September*, and Olson will have book two of Poems, out! Wow, babe, what d'ya say, what d'ya say!

SO, excusing above, and going on, what have I done today, but prepare, type, and already sent off, the MSS for CHAPBOOK published GOLDEN GOOSE PRESS Columbus Ohio 200 copies, signed, on hand paper, at 2 bucks (return to Olson $30!), to be issued September–October, (15 poems in issue of mag, simultaneously to chapbook, the 15 so far unpublished), the Chapbook to be these 15 plus THE KINGF, a Po-SY, & the Morning News. Title, THE PRAISES.

But the one which excited me in the copying today was, what I am enclosing, as a present for you, this date of yr turning, I, MAXIMUS, OF GLOUCESTER, TO YOU.

By gar, isn't it funny, or is it, how quick this thing blew up, and how, my lady, my lady, my lady, how READY o was!

Well, it's done, DONE, and I cleansed, of it all, and feel good, that I have kept back (it is a policy, things still churning, fluid in my blood), things which are more powerful than those I show, maybe, anyhow, things I walk on now, say, oh say, Bigmans, say, or, say, maybe, who knows, maybe I'll print, SHE-BEAR, tremendous feeling, to not shoot the bolt, to split infinitives, to wrench round the world, to ask them to stick their finger, to, go ahead and judge, to say, next year, what, olson again, with more? MORE?

Brassy, is the kid, today, brassy, lady,—,and you, to whom I can say it, not to think he's hOOPS, in fact, to figure, now the pressure is off, of the day's plugging, and the rewriting of, MAX, I MAXIe, and drinking himself quietly two beers (2 beers, 2 beers, and 3 goose eggs, the price, sd Creeley, to have back for this little boke, LACHUTE, MOVE OVER,—the de'il, he!) he's just playin'. (Or is he?)

note: it was Creeley, plus y & x, plus THE KONGO-BONGO, which did it.)

VERSE: DONE: CALLED, MEN IN AN

ALLEY, AT EVENING, CHINNING, OR
CHEWING THEIR FAT[29]

sadness, on the face of everything, sadness

And ain't it ridiculous, that they shld be so closed,
with life pouring, in front of 'em, everywhere?

Love Lawrence, his verse, love Lawrence, him self, love Lawrence, who once
lived, Love him who lived, Lawrence

                              (reading Aldington, the dirty dirty dirty
bastard, a book on, DHL—just to find out more abt him, the beautiful, beautiful, beautiful man, beautiful Lawrence)

Will push this toward you (goddamn this city, can't get a letter off later than
7:30   the low-heeled bastards, and they thinking they can hold a world,
when they can't even run a post office (and I can tell you, for I was seven years
a letter carrier. Or did you know, darling?

                This is a love letter and and and AND
                              olson

[Enclosed is a carbon copy of "I, Maximus of Gloucester, to You," as published
in *The Maximus Poems*.]

                    ◄§ 243 §►

Washington to Whitestone (special delivery)[30]
6 July 1950 (postmark)

                              thursday

The SHE-BEAR bounced back yesterday from Poetry NY, with not a word
on it, in fact, with the formal rejection slip! (With it came back the PRO-
VERSE piece, the editor's hen-shit all over it, asking rewrite. I was so god
damned mad I didn't work!) But the point is, (beside the irony), that, due to
my stumbling on a passage in Jung on that notion of his "anima-animus" ((my

29. These lines of verse have not been previously published.
30. Addressed c/o Bodycombe, 149-07 First Ave., Whitestone, Long Island, New York.

1st reading of Jung, by the way:[31] *imp.*, simply because K.O. Hanson, in his review of *y & x*, sd, "olson's myth from jung"!)),[32] and yr own recent discovery of Pistis Sophia (plus the passage you sent last week, which I want to examine for you),[33]—all this has got me back, today, to this central concern of mine, and may lead me, as I think it will, I am so off my own beat, to the Lib. Cong. to follow it up.

((I shall add some leads, for you, in case you may not have come on them, especially, G.R.S. Mead, P-S, 1921, and his Fragments of a Faith Forgotten (2nd Ed., 1906), which sound, fr Jung, as worth a look at. There is also Carl Schmidt, P-S, 1925, & Reitzenstein's Poimandres. Add: C.A. Baynes, *A Coptic Gnostic Treatise*, 1933.[34] THOUGH, especially here,—and Mr Jung is, as I always hunched, a lazy fraud, in this respect, a mere g.d. swiss soft pink hill of learnin', (hill in the sense of a piled up pile of . . .), whom, by the way, I met once, engaged, and left, convinced he was a nobody. It was, I think, in 1938, in Cambridge, and under ideal circumstance, for pal Murray had set it up. What a pretentious bastard (as, so very many, almost all, so-called scholars have shown themselves to be, in my experience: that incredible *laziness*, of specialization: the simple fact is, that it is *not* true, that, because of the increase of knowledge, it is no longer possible, or necessary, that a man seek to master it *all, all*. (Francois Rabelais, e.g., was right, and is right, a man is the sum of it all, by whatever method he chooses, but with that as absolute end, or he is not worth our time.) The truth is, and what is not seen, except by the very best, the very few, is, that what a man has to do today is to devise some other method to accomplish coverage of the whole field of knowledge. And it is not the least of the reasons why an old device of man (what, because it is true, is called feminine, because the feminine is, as yr source sd, clear on essence, as man is on form) has come back into business as against the rational:

> you can't imagine how long I was puzzled by the lack of admission that I could smell, by way of a sentence, say, the totality of a man's work (say, Jung, for example, where it was also, the look of it, the taste of his flesh on my eye) (Viz. Lawrence, the rejection of, read Huxley, the old methodology, the "Huxleys' Method" of the rational)

Of course what I am saying is cliche to you, but, BUT, it is this relevance to the problem of all knowledge, that I bring it up, for, that what makes all our mind men today not even usable, is the implicit laziness, due to an ignorance of method other than, we have to go thru it all in order to know it all. Which is what keeps them from speed, work & perception.

31. C. G. Jung, *Psychology and Religion* (New Haven: Yale UP, 1946), p. 34.
32. K. O. Hanson review, *Interim* 3.4(1949–50):52.
33. Boldereff's letters for this period are missing.
34. All these references are in the notes of Jung's *Psychology and Religion*, pp. 124–25.

For example, Pistis-Sophia, & the whole front of the present. Jung lets his anima-animus discussion (the base, actually, of his system, the mandala only another old wisdom wrongly taken hold by him) become a corruption (a corruption of the minds of people now, god damn it) because he rests it on a decadence of the original energy which perceived Sophia as ANIMA. I have just gone thru his sources, and discover that, it is the Hermetics of the Middle Ages on whom he rests his case. It is way wrong, and is only a worse error than your source commits, in joining Sophia to Xty, instead of working it (it takes work) back to where it came from, not where it was *after* Paul & Christ. Did you note the disease of synthesis throut that quote, conspicuous in, the confusion of, Sophia, as formless disordered essence, & Moses?[35]

& the bringing forth of Christ and the H.G., as those to give form to "the abortion"

> ((note, Jung falls into same trap in seeing the H.G. as originally the "feminine" in Xty: of course, BUT as already corruption of, the ancient root force, out of which Sophia came))

And, at the end of the quote, the bizness of, the Father producing Stauros, the Cross, and Horos, the Limit. (It is the limit, to mush the archaic into Xty, in order to give it a ride on a new back, when, itself, originally, damn well could walk, and how, BY HERSELF.

(I'm only protesting, that, as in all other knowledges today, one does, at his or her peril, stop short anywhere this side of, say, the ICE, or, at least, the FIRST TOWN, the hills of Baluchistan!)

For the presence in each of us of, such archaic figures as, dreams produce, is, whether it is phylogenetic or not, of absolute importance to a rebirth of conduct and structure and force: simply because it was from these areas that, originally and now, men discovered ambiguity of experience which told energies they wot not of.

AND, LASS, do we not know, it is ENERGIES, that our fellow citizens do not tap?

Phew, a lecture! But not to you. Just to get the heat up, the sweat for the running! For I am obviously turning back, today, to a further push of the SHE-BEAR, whatever it is going to be in its final form.

35. We do not know who is spoken of here, as Boldereff's letters are missing.

(It is completely
fascinating to me, how the force and image of
that area, wherever i touch it: La Chute, Bigmans, She-B, where else, throws the citz. off!
And how. Makes em run! And scared, just
plain scared!)

Darling, I'm going on to the Lib, to give knowledge a chance to work its way
on me. You'll be hearing amply from me, as of all you have written. Just hold
tight, (there was a pop song, 15 yr ago, a little girl, Matthews daughter, then
what, 7, used to croon me, with some such burden, just abt the time, one day,
she took me aside, when her parents were also able to hear, & says, what does
fuck mean, with all the sexual leer a child is so mysteriously capable of) (it remains a wild mysterium, how sexual a child is, & how arousing: I had this line
in a long verse recently, this "positional block", juxtaposed to other material,
Gotama material, curiously enuf![36]

look, babe, so long as i am going to slug that in, why don't i rewrite the whole,
so you can see it? enclosed.

By god, little Frances, look what came out! Not at all what was going in. It is,
all, but the lst line, *new today*. And though it's rough. And—and this is the
puzzle, the terror—may never be anything else than what it is (what is it,
please tell me, Frances). Yet, or becoz, I send it to you as it is. And go now, not
to the Lib. (thank you) but to catch a lunch, and come back, teasing myself out
for another go, by leaving the quote I was going to send you, to be added (in
hopes it won't, right away, be added, as it wasn't above!) after i am back, and
continue this strange rolling highway of a letter to you, which, like a snail, or a
truck, goes over many walks, by many towns, and stops, curiously, at certain
hindrances, or gas stations, on its root, making, as snails do, as trucks do, most
of their passages, at night.

I do now.

"go now", was what it was supposed to say! (back, after a nuisance of a lunch
with this nut wadsworth next door, who has spoiled my concentration, again,
god damn him, only this time, unlike Adamo, I had made the end, anyway
   And anyway, he paid for the lunch, the bastard, and he damned well had
better, the mess his madness makes of my stomach.

36. Olson is referring to the poem "A Shadow Two" (published posthumously in *A Nation of Nothing but Poetry*, pp. 73–74.)

So, with no further ado, I'm going off to the LIB

love

Charles

[*Carbon typescript enclosed:*][37]

The cause, the cause, even if the method is
new,
the rods and cones of, a pigeon's eye, or,
who, man, is that woman you dream of, who,
woman, is that unknown man, named & featured nonetheless,
with whom you sit beside the bubbling caldron, in which bones
and furniture is tossed, a grisly soup from which child's fingers drop,
flame spills upon a treacherous ground on which he leads you, I lead you,
in a devils', angels' dance, the measured feet of which
are clean and sweet as hair used to dry arch and toes, used
to cover acts of dark, wild, quiet hair crushed
unnoticed where cylinder, annulet, mons
move in, increasing rhenein timed to come closer, closer
as pains do, measured, precise, nearer and nearer, as birth comes,
the relaxation (if you call it that) the sweeter
that the pains are so regular, that, by that fire,
you two sit, you dream,
and talk about some other?

It is the cause, the cause, and the dance of night contains
the day's ambiguous responses, her harassments, his
flights, his sort of looking out, by cones or genes, his
watching where the arc can next be pushed, in the face of
her unreasonable opinions, her introduction of bald subjects, of rods and
       bills, her
suppressions in the face of him, in the eye, in the eye of
his will, her knowledge, her not dumb dance, her measure
that life is not death

Put it this way: he smothered her, because
he could not free his half self from her jealous likeness carried,
buried, no mirroring of her but a she initiate to himself, a female,
male to him by one point off majority, and thus, (no confirmation offered,

---

37. Olson began retyping the first three lines of "A Shadow, Two." He then broke away from it and
produced the enclosed, which was further revised in his next letter and was later published as "The Cause,
The Cause" (*Collected Poems*, pp. 190–93).

proferred to him by his unround world, his world become a rotted apple,
no light on why he finds himself a double) thus halved, in his own eye, he
crying out his love, pressed down, pressed down, pressed down, and,
crown of his no longer endurable, not sufficiently regular pain, he
killed this other for half love of another, Eve

And now, we note, the tragedy repeats itself by inverse, at this more rotted
        stage
the rage no longer male, the half gone over, the Cain concealed in her
the murder, and all divisions now complete, all form, all essence, both
brought down, down by the cause, the cause by which all things do stand,
by which all eyes are two and in their careful secrets, night or day,
stay moving things until, by their precision,
by the locking of their rods & cones,
objects are what they are, dreams are, what they are, each is,
this man this woman are, with what likenesses, this difference, this
one slight sweet hair of difference, are, as all things are meant to be,
separate, by no more separate than the vision of the night from day, by
life from death.

◄§ 244 §►

Washington to Whitestone (special delivery)
7 July 1950 (postmark)

frances, it is friday (i'm packin days, but they still go by like g.d. fire burns!)
and i did go to the LIB yesterday, and i have done some chores today (got off
to emerson olson bib., and answers to his questions on, the craziest goddamned things you ever saw, (you'll see my answers if he publishes 'em)[38],
and no photo, refused, no info on me, no: all that crap is calculated to distract
attention from the JOB DONE: personality, balls, bro.,)
                                                        and now i want to
rewrite, get back to, where we were, hot, yesterday:

THE CAUSE, THE CAUSE

The cause! the cause! still—even if the method is,
new,
        the rods, and cones of,
a pigeon's eye, OR

38. Richard Emerson included Olson's answers out of context in "Symposium on Writing," *Golden Goose* ser. 3 (autumn 1951), as explained in *Minutes of the Charles Olson Society* no.9 (August 1995).

who, man, is that woman you dream of, who,
woman, is that unknown man
       (named & featured, nonetheless) with whom
you sit beside the bubbling caldron, in which bones
and furniture is tossed
       (a grisly soup, from which child's fingers
drop, flame spills out on treacherous ground where he leads you,
       (I lead you
in a devils', angels'
dance, the measured feet
clean and sweet as hair, used to dry an ankle, toes,
used, as hair is used, wild, quiet hair
crushed, unnoticed, when cylinder annulet mons
move in, increasing rhein timed to come closer, closer
as pain does, as they do, measured, precise, nearer, nearer,
as birth comes, the sweeter
(the relaxation, if you call it that)
that the pains are, as the breath is, repeat, repeat, regular, that, by that fire
you sit, you dream, you two, you
talk about some other?

It is the cause, the cause, and the dance contains, contains
the night is, the day's
ambiguous responses, her
harassments, his
sort of looking out, his flight,
by cones, or, is it now, genes, his watching
where the arc can next be pushed, her
opinions, now unreasonable, her
subjects baldly introduced (bills, plans, are rods), her
in the face of him, her
in the eye, in the eye of his will, her
suppressions, her
withholdings, used devices, her
not dumb dance, her measure
that life is not
death

Put it this way, as long as we are faced with
this case: he
smothered her
because he could not free his half self from her jealous likeness carried,

buried, we can say, and no mirroring of her, no, not at all, in fact
a she initiate to himself, a thing concealed within himself, a female
male to him by one point off majority, and thus
                                        (no confirmation offered,
proferred to him by his unround world, his world become a rotted apple, no
     light
on why he finds himself a double)
                                        thus halved, in his own eye, he
cried out for love, pressed down, pressed down, pressed down,
and, crown of his no longer endurable, not sufficiently regular
pain, he
killed this other
for half love of another
Eve

Nor is this all, nor is the story (upper case) so small
as he alone. There is, the other half, alas, these days, the tragedy
repeats itself in inverse, increasing inverse, transvest pain.
                                        At this more rotted stage,
the rage no longer only male, the half's gone over, repeats the ladies,
they, too, are joined, returned, returned, is now returned
the mono-beast!
                        And Cain, concealed in her
(murder, murder, to be freed, all form, all essence, both
brought down, mixed, mixed, downed by the cause, the wrong cause, the
     cause
here spoiled!

                        But still the cause, it is the cause by which things stand,
which all eyes are two, and in this careful secret day by night
all moving things are made to stay, are brought, by eyes' precision by
rods and cones, their play, objects
are what they are, dreams are, each is
this man this woman are
                        with what likeness, this difference, this
one slight hair of difference are,
                                        as are all things, they, meant to be
separate, but by no more, they, separate, than
is the night from day, than they, from each other, than is life from death

How does that look? a little better? no? Anyhow, enuf of it, for now.

I am determined to try again to get to you there in yr apolaustic house (yr apolaustic being) that bizness I started to yesterday. Let's see what happens this
time, as I return to that draft!

DE BONO[39]

1

beauty, sd the Bearded Man
is
inception, is
the continuation, is
end   Enter
by the 38 doors!

    the 3 obstacles
    are (the Walls
    which lie flat, which
    are, in fact, the running)
    are,
    on each of the doors,
    lust, ill-will and
    stupidity, he sd

        (I can look on any ass
        And want it. And,
        a little girl.

        And not crumple
        the flower.)

        The emancipation,
        he argued,
        is to be found in a habit of
        mind

        2

        Wot, sd Fleming,
        is the sound of
        thought?

39. This poem, which remained unpublished until *A Nation of Nothing but Poetry* (pp. 75–76), is a
slight revision of "A Shadow, Two," with the first three lines extracted.

We shall have nouns, nouns
And all tied
downs.

(Sounds, sd Creeley, I want
the SOUNDS!)

Well, maybe I should have eaten, before this! it's sixapeem. And where's my baby NOOOOOOWWW! Me? Ahz hyah, mam. And what am I doin? I just better go and put some food in this here engine, 'fo it all runs away! And will write, baby, anudder day.   YOU, do same, pleez. Scuze, pleeze. This is jus to let you know, wot Ize abt. And to tell you, that I reach out, and touch you, sweet

O

All yr news is wonderful, Gan-na—I want MORE!

Csharles

≼ 245 ≽

Washington to Whitestone[40]
8 July 1950 (postmark)

Saturday

frances:

    this (#3, we'll call it)
to keep you a-breast
now that to my lights, to
my rods & genes, is
finis!
    is it not
a strange thing? is not
the play of corruption
and not corruption
curious?
    but it is the line, the *line*
i wonder about—where

---

40. This letter and the next were forwarded to 281 W. Broadway, New York 13.

is this new line
going? where, what
is it? why does it come on, Elizabethan, say?
    AND WHAT IS NEXT?

                                        love
                                           c

[*enclosed: carbon copy of final version of "The Cause, the Cause"*]

                        ❧ 246 ❧

Washington to Whitestone, Long Island (special delivery)
10 July 1950 (postmark)

                                        monday

You must forgive me, Frances. I think I told you, that PNY, those squirts, had
sent me back the PRO VERSE job, for rewrite, now that they are going to
press. Some henny little changes. (God, what fools such are. As a matter of
fact, why I didn't want to see it, is because, I knew there were *major* changes!).
Anyhow, I took one squint at it last wednesday when it came, and got sick, instantly, couldn't face it, it all seemed so long ago, and, the whole first section,
so inadequate—what I knew it was. So, as you know, for three days I wrote a
poem instead, thank God. (Critique, anyhow, gives me a pain, in . . . Of course
the reason why a poet is the only critic there is, is, because, each day, he has to
be critic, *each day*. The process is continuous. Once a poem is done, one turns it
over and over, looking to see what it is, what it is not, where it works, where
it may not, the whole bizness.)

But there it sat, to be done, and each day more terrible. So today I've done it—
and probably walked it right the hell out of their pages, the little squeals. I'm
sure the reason they liked it in the first place, was, it was, o—shit, now, now,
it's a real pronounciemento! AND, as soon as I set up final copy (I have just
finished a five hr run on it, and had a soup, and will go back tomorrow, today,
get it done, get rid of it, get it off ((only trouble is Fjelde, the little squirt, is
coming down here to visit his friend Moore, whom I also see, and, with the
two of them, I'm supposed to go to Harper's Ferry one day this week. You can
imagine, if little F says a word, what a day that will be! considering the thanks
I am under to him for having led me to rewrite this thing!))

It is now considerably longer. But I have left sections 2 and 3, the typewriter
passage, and on objectism, just as it was, except for substituting some other
lines of my own for those therein. Haven't chosen yet. What shall I use?

And still a lot's left out—like how Pro Verse makes *all* parts of speech fresh for use, new vegetables, in the garden; and a hell of a lot of hidden secrets (hidden to me, I mean) about how one manages tension in open field composition. BUT, it's only for a starter anyhow, to kick the ball around.

To hell with it. Why bother yr dear self with it. Only, it is, the work of a day, all there is, these days, that i am hammering, hammering, hammering, like some man condemned to die. For I can't stop. I have to go on, on, making poems, until I bust. And I figure I will have to, soon, but how do I know. As I sd to you on the phone, a man has to find out, by putting all the weight on, himself, putting it on, in and out, until he does burst. It's the only way he has. Pour it out, pour it out, pour it out, until he either gets so strong no one can equal him. Or he breaks. For it is additive, no question, the whole process of putting it out, is additive. (The only question is, is there a point where, suddenly, it turns into a rapid subtraction, which can only be, a total breakdown.) I don't know. But you know, as you so sharply put it, in K,[41] you're committed, Olson, you weren't, before. Which is so right, lovely lady of borning!

So here I am. And there you are. And I sweat, sweat, sweat. And grow stronger each bloody day! As a matter of fact (between you and me) the funny thing, it is also physical: i feel, tho, of course, I haven't the muscle I had as a younger man, but i feel as tho I am actually muscularly stronger than i ever was. Which is then true, that's all. (Crazy, crazy, man: either he does the work he's cut out to do, and grows more able to do it. Or he doesn't, and he dies, slowly, right in front of the face. But it is his work, the fool. It's his work, he's born for. It's the whole damned secret. And who tells a man, anymore? And who told me, handsome?)

(I was so right, in preface, to make it a matter of, lungs, and air to breathe. That's what freedom is, not the crap of the easy, the "free", etc., we've been given since those g.d. 18th century moseys got it out wrong—pursuit of, security. But how did I know? Spell out some of this, my sybil: tell the boy!)

How do I know, what I know?
                    Dictates of form.
                              Maybe. For I am dumb, as is
this other half creature of the human Spc-see!
                              (You know, Frances, you caught
me, when you quoted me back on, the dumb dance: do you now recall what it was I sd, in what context I proposed it? I am most curious to know. (You will note I put it in reverse, as of the ladies, in CAUSE!)

41. Presumably an allusion to their meeting in Knoxville.

The MALE, what a character!

This is just play, the wonderful business of having you there, to play with, my darling, my creature and spiller of, as you are right to say, gayety, of wild wonderful powerful beautiful GAYETY—o, how precious you are, LADY WILD AND GOLD!

    I must go back now to that damned task.

Love,
Charles

❧ 247 ❧

Washington to New York City (special delivery)[42]
11 July 1950 (postmark)

tuesday

fz

    just to tell you
        who's here

        it is now 9:30
        & I am off,
            with the original,
            & this

        All day it took!

[*Enclosed: carbon copy of "Projective Verse" essay, part 1, as published.*]

❧ 248 ❧

Washington to New York City (special delivery)[43]
12 July 1950 (postmark 12 July 1950)

wed july 12 50

frances:

42. Addressed to Frances Motz, 281 West Broadway, New York City 13, N.Y.
43. The letter is addressed "c/o dail bryan 281 West Broadway."

what a crazy business! i go down to the p.o. to pick up yr letters, with high pleasure, knowing, this day, after a week of pouring it on, i can get back to sanity & joy, i can spend this afternoon writing you, getting back to that lovely bridge over to you from which has sprung, these back months, so many handsome fish!

bah what do i find? is it not possible for a woman, for you even who wishes to be delivered from the narrows, to find out that if, as i am told, a woman is like an animal where the child she's made is concerned, that a man is so, once he finds out, what his work is, about that work?

i am no preacher, as was Lawrence (who, therefore, made so much of conduct, was, so ethical, though i am, god help me, also so) and i am no religious, as was, say, Apollonius of Tyana, to whom deeds were all, whose parable was, as such men's must be, their nobleness   those, too, are commitments, and i respect them   but they are not mine   my job is not to make form out of my life, but, out of my life, to make forms   and i have found no method other than daily work, & a solidity, almost an imprisonment, given my wild appetite for grapes, to make such work possible

there i stand, and *everything* else swings round that stem: i pay all price, even to the dragging down of my flesh, for that thing

there it is, and if you did not have to see single cause where, there are multiples (multiples enter the moment one does not put the emphasis on, what am i getting out of it) you would not be led to such an erratic charge

what did you tell me, Saturday, that i do not know? and to top it, you add an ultimatum   i do not care for such   they do not move me, because i have been previously moved by what i know i cause   look, frances, this is the big league: you better figure all things on the diamond are in the eye   and that the season is long   and only the cool, stay in

avoid, avoid the dogmatic: if it is really professional ball we're playing, there's as many ways to pitch and bat as there are players who can win and hit   the trouble with the holy ones, is, they are, johnny-one-notes   and they are right (it is like what i sd, all, on the back of a pyx, it can be inscribed) only, if you don't want to be holy?

not altogether holy, any how   He sd: YEA—truth faileth
and he that departeth from EVIL
maketh himself a
PREY——

Hello, Gan: are you there?

This is love, (anyhow, as the big guy
pitches woo!)

o

◦§ 249 §◦

Washington to New York City (special delivery)
13 July 1950 (postmark 13 July 1950)

thursday july 13 50

my lady frances, my wing: your letter today moves me to the roots, unheaves
my being, that you should be tossed, makes me rush in with both fists flying
against, the NYPL, and whoever. And against bodycombe, and who else, who
add to yr torments, olson included. And yr cry for the generous! o, my little
girl, don't you know, there are none such, that even the strong are selfish, thus
blind? And I say this without bitterness, for, if we wish to complain, we better go, I take it, to who made us separates, to that cutting of the Timaean
Creature.

Yet you are strong, and when you write of Miss Matisse, her throat
and her voice, I feel you surge across the words. Frances, you are here so
strong, (so strong I am always amazed (so I should be amazed!) that you are
knocked over by such puffs of ill-wind as events, & the cranky way in which
even the intimate works itself out). Power, everyone of us, is so limited, the
very greatest is a lie, isn't it? But yet I would assuage your hurts.

Today it is snakes I wish you would tell me all you know abt. Got off on
them by way of Apollonius of Tyana (Mead, who writes on PS, writes a book
on A of T, which I got to first).[44] And, through A as Healer (my Cabeza again,
my immigrant healer!), I went along by way of Asklepios (at the Aegae temple of Asklepios A started his studies, age 14), ending up, by way of Miss Harrison, on *Zeus, Honey* (it kills me, but that's what it translates, Z Meilichios!),
who was worshipped as the most beautiful snake you ever saw, fig. l, of Miss
Harrison's PROLEGOMENA, found at Peiraeus, now in Berlin (date 4th
Century, and tho thus late, and too "decadent" for taste the likes of mine and
yrs, yet absolutely terrific carving in Hymettus marble ((I love the way the catalogue goes on: "found at the Zea harbour not far from Ziller's house."))[45]

44. G. R. S. Mead's *Apollonius of Tyana* was used a year later for the poet's dance play *Apollonius of
Tyana*. "PS" refers to Mead's *Pistis Sophia*, mentioned previously in Olson's letter of 6 July 1950.
45. Jane Harrison, *Prolegomena to the Study of Greek Religion* (Cambridge University Press, 1908), pp.
17–18.

You will smell, immediately, I imagine, the track of the SHE-BEAR again! that I am on it. (Frances, when you throw up yr hands, over the intolerable drag of this business between us, of the craziness (apparently) of separation, let me throw out this, as *telesma*: read a little abt Balzac. Won't say more, just read, and tell me.)

For it is curious, that even Miss Harrison (or, should i be surprised, I am not, her very virtues are her blindness) does not see what was going on in chthonic time. She does not see that the snake is (as you so beautifully do: by the way, sometimes I imagine you, when I try to thrust all the possible happiness in the world on you, in the role of an extraordinary family of women I once saw in a documentary, who were priestesses of the python, was it, in, was it, India, somewhere, mountains, who, once a year, have to kiss the snake at the mouth of his cave—and succeed by out dancing, with the head, his thrusts, until he has spent the poison in his fangs, and they are able to touch his mouth with their mouth, at which he turns and goes back into his crevice in the holy rocks: the movie showed this action, and you have never seen such a dance, such a beautiful true thing, right on the rail of life. It definitely belongs to you, baby.)

((O frances, let me beckon you on, in the dance of this love of ours, in the wildness of it, the unnaturalness (if you like) but the imaginative accuracy of it, to which I solemnly attest. AND if this is true, how, HOW, can anything be lost, HOW?))

Zeus, Honey; Zeus Blood-lover, both aspects (the 1st he is Snake, and 2nd, he is Bolts): which brings to bear on my mind again the necessity, the absolute need, NOW, to restate, to make once more available, the importance of the DOUBLE, of the two-faced nature of things, throughout Nature, the ambiguity of reality, to restate it because all rational thot, the lie, has raised up the generations to think there is ONE, and thus the burdens of choice, when, in actuality, there are ONE PLUS, which is sufficiently dramatized in TWO, in the binary (I would now rewrite certain passages in THE KINGFS!)

(A 2nd departure: that a people who have killed kindred blood must practise rites of riddance::::this was behind DHL, on the white slayer shall inherit the slain::::but it is also applicable to that later, that second, Civil War)

But back to snakes. (If you look up the Jane Harrison, note, too, fig. 2—the Snake Magnificat, she calls it!; and, especially, fig. 103 (as of you and me: and also, by god, in this connection, fig. 97!!

((These are very rich & terrible things. Please plunge into them, darling, in order to touch, again, the BASE, the BASE, of this mystery, of the mystery of yr own flesh, with its strange hungers, of its accuracies, despite all present horrors. This is a more important telesman, (like yr little spiders, the DOUBLET to snakes). Keep em on you daily, like amulets, worn, to be touched, to remind you of what WE ARE ABOUT, what yr STRENGTH is, so that you are not thrown down, lose a day (we cannot afford to lose an hour!)

It disturbs me, that you do not seem to take up force any more from olson verse. (It does more than disturb me: it suggests, darling, that personality and flesh are forward, where they ought to be, are, surely, but NOT WITHOUT the other, lady. Or we are doomed, any of us, at any moment, to the narrows!) Here, too, let me call you back—not to the praise of same (we do not come to praise Caesar, but to. . .!) but to the use.

((Or are you not yet aware I wrote

you, as the poem went, Thursday (special), Friday (special), Saturday (reg), Monday (special)—all, g.d. me, to whitestone;)

1st issue:
> "bearded snake, speckled hero"

By which, also, I get back to A of Tyana (life by Philostratus)[46] where the bearded snake is one of the many *thaumata* A is sd to have brought back from his visit to India (apparently years approximately 30 AD, or so: and apparently BUDDHIST india.)

The snake image also has, I should guess, a father force: there is a curious passage in the Aeneid, in which Aeneas says:

> Bewildered, whether the ground-swimming snake was genius of that place where his father was buried or if it were actually his father's ghost

((What have the dream-boys to say, abt the snake image, in male experience? Do you know?))

> Ancestor-grave-blood: the Snake! what emerges from them all: Force! We shall sleep, and in the dream, we shall see, the Snake! Sd Aelian, on Animals: the backbone of a dead man, when the marrow has decayed, turns into a: snake. Plutarch adds: the men of old time associated the snake most of all beasts with heroes

46. Olson is relying on the footnote to p. 328 of Jane Harrison's *Prolegomena*; and, for subsequent quotations, on *Prolegomena* pp. 262–63, 330–43.

(And, of all people, it was a poet who brought the worship of the Healer, to Athens. It was Sophocles himself, who, in his turn, had been such a hero, that he was made the third of the three healing gods of the Acropolis!)

(((or Zeus, Sweet!)))

A strange sentence suddenly occurs: Mother, Maid & Asklepios, the Saviour

And wonderful Pythagoras, as Harrison points out, I quote: "The evidence he adduces as to the piety of women is perhaps the most illuminating comment on primitive theology ever made by ancient or modern. (Women give to each successive stage of their life the name of a goddess: KORE for MAID, NUMPHE for BRIDE, METER for MOTHER)."

The Earth Mother was, Frances, KARPOPHOROS, or, Lady of the Wild Things!

o my lady, I do not need to tell you that you and I are entwined in a very dark thing, dark not only in its truth (the old dark, which men have strayed away from) but dark, too, for us, no matter how clear we are, because we are also children of that immediate past as well as children and projectors of that more chthonic, archaic thing which we, perhaps more than any two living beings, are living out, pushing the arc of, ahead

            THIS IS A TREMENDOUS UP-HEAVING THING and is worth, as god knows you only need to be re-minded, much much (as it includes) pain

            now i'm no fool, know, that daily we are also you are also, not mythopoetic, are just, as we are, simple, practical creatures

        BUT, darling, DO not, for the day's sake, or time's, LOSE, sweet, sight of the other which you know so well, the amazing MYSTERY we are caught in

        Nor must you, in any despair, think that i lose sight of IT

            au con-traire. May I say this, and ask your comprehension?

            It is mystery on one level, and could be lived out so. I could live it out, you do. But it is also VISION. (Do you think it is accident that it is motz & olson who make it up? and that olson is a poet?

        Of course you don't. You saw it, first, in the verse, saw the vision he had, fumblingly, put out, gone along by, searched, was confused by, but WENT BY. (Remember that, love.)

And so, if, now, he goes, as, maybe poets do, anyway, as he does, slow, scrupulously ((i say as poets do, simply because the act of verse is demanding in precisely this character, of the scrupulous: someone once called the poet a revolutionist in form, a conservative of life)) hair by hair of perception . . . . . . DO NOT, frances, put it in some easy frame of you vs another woman.[47] It is a deeper, graver movement this man is thrusting through. For the very conservatism from which form springs, is, when applied to reality, life's realities—the very scrupulousness—a TERRIBLE BURDEN

Now I imagine, in less chaotic times, with less HEAVING to be done, a man would not be so cautious. BUT I have hewn my way through many many many confusions to get what sight I have. And I must go by my sight, by cutting away all present confusions.

ON TOP OF THAT, realize, sweet, from a man's point of view, the upshots of, a VISION, which is, quite quietly, the absolute dynamiting of, the PATRIARCHY. (Again you will see what I mean instantly, having known men, in this time, and their dumb dance. (Was it so, I put it?). A man who stays in there, without settling for the old deal, has to be tossed and dervished like some fish in a scaling machine.

The demand, to work true today, if you are a poet, is ALMOST unbelievable (with or without such a crisis as this MYSTERY, THIS VISION—which I do believe you and I are breaking open.

(So shall you understand, how nervous I am, how mystified?

DON'T, sweet, take yr strength and yr seeing of it, away.

Write me, please. And, to close, and bind up, I wish I could draw for you the figure of the LADY OF WILD THINGS which sits before me in fig. 62 of Miss Harrison (p. 265). For you would see something. It is on a Boeotian amphora, in Athens, with two wondrous fierce lions on each side of her (as in the Cretan gateway), and two peacocks above her, other signs and animals. But, what wld strike you, and overwhelms me, is (they say, on her gown) but between her legs, head up, ending right there, is a GREAT FISH!

amo

motz o olson

47. Boldereff's letter is missing, but we deduce she was expressing her reaction to the poem "The Cause, the Cause." The next two letters (#250 and #251) represent polarity of Boldereff's mood at this time, but the precise dates are entirely conjecture.

⇥ 250 ⇤

[*letter not sent*]

New York City to Washington
[13 July 1950]

Thursday morning

Dear Charles—

I understand how you give everything to your work—there is nothing common and vulgar in all of this—it is simply that when I made the Albuquerque plan I foresaw you actually do not have time for me and I did as one learns how to do—a shut-off inside myself, of the human need—a kind of hermit-in-desert.

When you asked me not to go—to remain in in my flesh—all of this carries with it laws—which were created and operate whether one admires them or no.

I could not stay alive towards you if I had not set a date in my mind. I did not tell you as any ultimatum for you—I understand your nature and know I could earn only a further postponement—I told you only because it exists—I am unable even to read what you write—you can state to yourself any bad thing about me you wish—I would like to be able to go on as I have—but I am in need to see you in a way I have no control over and which robs me of all power to leap over space and time.

My life this winter in all respects was the most difficult I have ever had and Charles, dear, I am simply dying off somewhere at my roots.

Frances

Darling—when I wrote in the morning that to me exciting and beautiful image of our rafts on the open sea and that very night was struck down as with a huge weapon in the very heart of my faith—cannot you reach out in your soul to perceive how undesired my need is—how any person who has shown the pride and strength in a relation such as ours would be struck to earth by the unproud act of crying out need?

Can not you feel if I had one single piece of reinforcement left in my kit I would use it?

⇥ 251 ⇤

New York City to Washington
[14 July 1950]

Friday 11 AM

Charles dear—

I want to tell you, my belovéd Charles, that I am ashamed of my weakness and suffering. I love you. Whatever the cost is I wish to be your Frances.

I feel myself more strongly bound to you than ever. As soon as I am able I shall write you.

Please receive from me an absolute belief. And please know that I understand fully that I am to expect nothing.

Thy fellow servant
Frances

⋅⋖ 252 ⋗⋅

New York City to Washington
[14 July 1950]

Friday 4:00 pm

Charles dear—

I have just returned from the library—in one of those tiny signs I so love (you forgot to give Harrison's first name) there are 3 drawers of Harrisons in NY Reference Room—and Motz of course with complete assurance pulled one out and put her hand first one! Charles on the *Prolegomena*—Figure out the mathematical chances when each drawer holds how many 100 cards! The book seems very sacred to me—am going to try to buy it—I hate so to have to hurry and to give it back—anyway looked up all your figure references and came across others which equally seemed mine in a dark sacred unmentionable way.

This book as you guessed—conquers me.

So—now for some explanations.

I married Duke in a move towards you. I would never allow anyone else on earth to know this because they do not understand at what a dark powerful depth I move—but in a command I married Duke—to bring Olson near—like covering up the snake—so you would have no fear of me in the traditional wiles of a female—all the rest of what I did you know—

I wear my life, it is true (maybe not always as a flower as you once said) but definitely *wear* it—something I *own* so powerfully I am not afraid to put it on or off.

The last year has cost me Charles a kind of torture I can see from your letter you have no notion of—so it is not the tiny Bodycombe events which are now bothering me—I am at the close of a powerful blood movement—which started with that marriage—every bit of it which has not been ecstasy (and what blood the physical ecstasy between us has cost me you alone know) has been torture—

It was daily torture to work at Nittany Printing Company (result of marriage) and daily torture not thereafter to work anywhere—our thing cost me everything I had—then there was the money business which has gone on now since February—and then Charles there is Lucinda, who actually comes first.

I never believed Charles I could have the strength and power to give Lucinda a fine education; but here I am, with no job and no money, forcing forcing that reality with all the details of a home and furniture etc. it implies, into being. Takes strength.

So Charles—you have become dim to me—I almost cannot see your image and I think with indifference about seeing you. I am a[48] returned into the bowels of the earth for renewal. All brain is dim to me—I am in a sleep as close to death as one can get. I have poured out blood in this birth between us and now I lie exhausted. What you do does not matter to me at all.

I cannot read what you write. I force myself at the end of days to read your poem. Will say only—it is important—it has power—but there is no ease—and my guess is your blood also needs rest but you decide for yourself.

I accept every word of your letter. Every word.

I now can use only one thing—male blood—and where it is to come from has also become a matter of absolute indifference to me.

I believe in our two rafts down the seaway—I believe we are cleaner than anything anywhere any time—On my raft I am asleep and I will take to myself in sleep—a porpoise—or a man or a god—I am indifferent.

I believe you are the only man in America—you are taking on yourself the whole business about the break up of patriarchy as I once took on my own shoulders the financial structure of America.

But I believe your scrupulosity should include Frances—

To attempt to be a poet today is the maddest attempt the soul of man has yet tried—

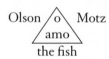

Olson   o   Motz
amo
the fish

253

Washington to New York City (special delivery)
14 July 1950 (postmark 14 July 1950)

48. A word seems to be omitted at the bottom of the page—perhaps "snake."

friday july 14

frances: To carry on, what do you know, and can tell me, about historical matriarchy? Now I discover that there is a lost piece of Hesiod, either the end of the Theogony, or the beginning of the Shield of Hercules ((again, my lad!)) or a poem separate, to itself, called EOIAI, or CATALOGUES OF WOMEN!

I make no claim, but, to my reading, I have never come across anyone boldly saying, before the PATS, there was (for how very long?) another organization of human society of no small isolated business, but huge and covering the then known world, which we inadequately call THE MATRIARCHY.

St Augustine, telling the story of the rivalry between Athene & Poseidon, says that the contest was won by one woman vote (it is important that women had a vote). But to appease the wrath of Poseidon the men thereon declared (how come, they were the losers? anyhow) a triple punishment for the women:

(1) they were to lose the vote

    (2) their children were no longer to be called by their mother's name

        (3) & they were no longer to be called after their goddess, Athenians!

So: right there we have three conditions of the previous "matriarchy" (The American Indians, particularly the Pueblo Indians give many clues). But, as you know, what interests me most about this here story is, that huge formless creature (formless because the PATS have kept her hidden) the GREAT GODDESS of the Iranian Plateau

she's the CLUE, she, our SUMER GIRL!

((*A hot idea, my motz*: with yr dedication, why don't you put this history together? WOW, what a story it could be! And it would give you, by the plates so clearly demanded, a chance to put all yr taste and design and awareness of the creative man. In fact, I call it a history, but, as you know, when I use that word, I mean only the *recovery*, the purification of, DOCUMENT: think of putting all the passages you could find on WOMAN, with the mass necessarily from BEFORE the "patsies" (we can call 'em!), down side by side, an amassment, done in chronology, right to the present! With the plates a ICONO-GRAPHIC proving of the CASE!

It's one hell of a huge job, I reconize, but, BUT, I am sure, from the work of the anthropologists, as well, from the archaeologists, as well from the Kramers, as well, from the Freuds, (their documents, not, of course, their in-

adequate and inappropriate concepts of thaumaturgy) there is lying around a
tremendous body of document. And as for the ART of it—well, here you get
the cream on the white water!

Jesu, what a *thing* it could be, what a WALLOP, now,
what a leading string out of present CONFUSIONS—o, lady, think about it,
do, for you, you, YOU, are perfect ministrant!

A reason why it may be only the likes of you and me who break through,
here: URBANITY. ((Isn't it a wonderful dirty word? OF THE CITY?))
Now I think you and I are prejudiced in favor of certain qualities this word
covers: o—gentilnesse, grace, recognition of others, arrogance, etc. BUT, we
are against several other connotations of this word, at least of behaviour it
now connotes, so thoroly that we will fight it at every turn.

I myself abhor
two things about it: (1) its connection to what is so glibly called, the realistic;
& (2) its personal tendance toward the suave

to:

Awkwardness, the grace
the absence
of the suave[49]

I wld add:

Lions, the force
the enemies of
the real

I am sure, for example, that those who take a hold of Homer by the old handle
of, the urbanity of the poet, or, as EZ puts it, intelligence set above brute force,
good though that is, are, in the end, misled and misleaders, simply because
THEY COULD NOT EQUATE HOMER, THE FORCE IN THEIR
OWN ENVIRONMENT HAVING BEEN EMPTIED OUT, THE
BABY WITH THE BATH.

In other words, it takes a certain degree of fineness which does
not, because of that fineness, run away from the archaic or the chthonic, (run
away to the real, or the city!) to HOLD, and to GATHER, what is live, (live

49. Olson is quoting from his poem published with the title "Siena," which was sent to Boldereff 22
December 1948.

like the fire of a lion or a phallus, say!) WHEREVER IT APPEARS—for the joker is, the archaic or chthonic is not, and never was, horizontal and history: it is always present perpendicularly in each of us.

Thus we are able to relate history, or, what is a better way of putting it, other via once existent which we have lost the secret of as answer to present, and or not personal, confusions

((I have felt bad at having, wednesday, used Lawrence so meanly to you. So let me make up for it, by right here underwriting his clarity in this regard. For it is surely one of his absolutes of survival, that he sd, brother, sister, at any cost, stick, stick, stick, to the fire in yourself, go by it, wherever it takes you, don't, don't, don't settle for any one else's deal as to what is reality, how beautiful is the urbane, OH the ABSOLUTES—fuck 'em, at every turn, at every dropping from the nose!

There should be no mystery as to why DHL found the Etruscans such a source,—or the American Indian—or, as witness the water color by him which I own, THE MAN WHO PISSETH, in which the figure is drawn (he was so inept, but so intelligent), the man's legs are handled by dependence on the Earliest Greek))

My new friend, Apollonius of Tyana, was urbane, was gentle, was a traveler, BUT, he spent his life, the whole first century, trying to remind every people, as he traveled carefully the whole Mediterranean world, get back to yr local hero-god, take yr power up here, don't buy the Olympians, Greek or Roman, stick to your own ground, and your old cults, only purify, purify, purify!

Now, of course, at this late date, his antagonism to blood is a huge and present danger, and must, like all Pythagoreanism, be set aside, be watched, for its asceticism, its rubbing off, of the edge. (Note, the PRAISES. And maybe this is why DHL & flowers bothers me.) He is, therefore, to be taken as half—in fact as is my Cabeza, I now see for the first time, why, in THE KS, I could not let him emerge any more than I did, why, I had to add to him, another, tho no conquistador, of the blood.

BUT he had the genius to see the relation of wisdom NOT to intelligence which inevitably leads to snobbism but the union of wisdom to health, to the purification of the blood so that it may pour brooklike through whatever system is in front of one at any given instant.

And, to qualify half, even, I must note that A of T conspicuously visited and restored only those sites where the most ancient rites were observed:

DO-
DONA DELPHI ABAE IN PHOCIS and my own special places, the
CAVES OF
          AMPHIARUS
          & TROPHONIUS

He saw that divination was the act of wisdom, not, mystery for its own sake,
thus he refused to have anything to do with the Labyrinth at Crete! (Isn't that
beautiful? Isn't that full of sense, and pertinence now, when the only answer
offered to the strugglers is, o, it's a maze, brothers, it's a lane with only turn-
ings and no light! SHIT.)

          A of T sd this:
                    wisdom is a making divine (theiasmos) of whole
          nature & that can only be done by the energy of a man's daemon!
          (daimonios)[50]

(okay, yah? My lad!)

                    ((Don't let my greek bother you: it costs me
                    10¢! (A 1st Greek Book, the 1st page of which
                    gives that crazy looking alphabet so that I can
                    identify the letters found in the barn back
                    here); and a Gr-Eng dictionary I bought for
                    10¢ at the Salvation Army). This is the extent
                    of my ignorance. Anyone can have it, for the
                    same!))

Another fallacy of history (and thus of present thought, which is, pitifully de-
pendent on a logical history, a dialectic of same, and thus, presently, becomes
NOTHING BUT HISTORY, which is, and always will be, if unrelieved by
the force of present selves, what Ratzl called it, "universal monotony") is: to
assume that, because, on the plane of sociology, conditions change, that therefore nature's forces in man and woman, on man and woman, change. What I
am getting at is, that, because there was nomadism, then agriculture, then the
urban, now the machine, that, therefore, all previous formularies are old-hat,
no use.
          What is missed in this is, that there are *other* planes, conspicuously, the
persistence of identical and common intimate conditions which do not so
change. And that marks of sociology stay permanent.
                    For example: I should
say that the city and the machine actually, so far as the intimate goes, produce

50. Olson is here, as in all the above, following G. R. S. Mead's *Apollonius of Tyana*, pp. 95 and 115.

a new nomadism, & thus NOMADS. (You will recall my Stephen's rite, in MORN NEWS!) (Or, take my friend Dahlberg, who is, if one would get him right, I think, the pure archetype of, the city nomad, the hunter Jew, the Esau, the Ishmael.)

In other words, if YOU, my MOTZ, come into existence as LADY OF THE WILD THINGS, it is right right right! Without regard to that dirty little thing, history, chronology, that stinking brat of those who think time is law, when it is space-time.

ALL this, is, I take it, one of the reasons why I, Lawrence, & Pound, find that character Frobenius of such use. F saw the PERMANENTS in the human situation (which is what we call CULTURE, isn't it?) Anyhow he called himself, accurately, kultur-morphologier. (Isn't that beautiful?)

And, to be projective, I would take the state of things we are creating for new man as, the old SECOND STAGE, the stage after hunting, that dull business: AGRICULTURE. (Why, otherwise, I would argue, should I, instrument, have, in SHE-BEAR, created that curious place, Pelican Rapids? that plateau above marauders (the same marauders, of SIENA, 1948)

(And my fisher-folk?)

(And is it an accident, Gloucester was where I took up being? THE EARTH & THE SEA, NOT ANIMALS, THE EATING OF THEM

which always, like the Australian stick, or the slayer's knife (the Gimmick, or the Story of the Atom Bomb) kicks back right in the puss of, the thrower, the slayer, the dropper.

WHO, NOW, EATS, WHAT

It is raising, raising, RAISING, which is the new ACT: REAR MAN!

SO: WOMAN, as all function:

LADY OF WILD THINGS (so that man may be reminded he is lion, he is a hercules: I better prefer a Sumer original: who?)

KOUROTROPHOS, Child-Rearer (so that, without embarrassment, man may be reminded he is son, and woman, that she is also, as well as sister, MOTHER)

& CORN-MOTHER (so that man may recognize that it is not marauding that makes for the reiteration of life (thus power follows, cannibalism, the State, directly from the deterioration of, the Patriarch) but that life repeats because of, birth, season, the *earth*. Thus we can again create a proper GOD; a GODDESS.

And for signs? outside you? me? Well, look at how the poet is, today, TEACHER (which is REARER, in culture)—how he spends his time searching for, that birth thing, FORM, not technical literary form, but SHAPE, projective SHAPE

(and not, as his immediate fathers did, mine (dahlberg, pound) by mothering by flagellation the STATE! that false PAPA)

(against such put Gandiji, tho, I, don't buy that package: the emergent figure of action is going to be an hermaphrodite, a Buddha, not one such "son" as G (not to mention another): it is going to be one of the curses of the world that Mao, who was a "morphodite", as the fishermen put it, and at the same time not a Hitler, a Roosevelt, has, by that laying on of hands in Moscow last winter, been led to think he is a male (power does it, every time)

And the other signs, which we both so well know, are the NEGATIVES of men and women both today—this is the most important sign of, the END OF WHAT WAS.

But of course, if you and I (and other violets) don't work like hell, those negatives do not necessarily make the BEGINNING OF WHAT CAN BE.

((Darling, I'm now so hungry I must quit. And I think what I'll do is shoot down to see if I have a letter from you, and eat there, down town, after posting this off to you pronto.

Do, see, in it, under it, the heart that loves you

Charles))   Charles

⁂ 254 ⁂

New York City to Washington
[15 July 1950]

Saturday morning

Olson dear—

You and I—! always always coming upon an idea simultaneously.

Three things happened to make the suggestion you have made—a new imperative.

The nice woman at AIGA suggested when I was here the time you phoned to Fifth Ave that the *idea* in my Medea was most original that I should work up a very complete outline and submit to Mary MacKae McLucas at Guggenheim, along with a copy of Medea—for a fellowship. That dropped into a Motz vacuum. Motz is not wordy.

Yesterday I found in circulation department by an accident Della Seta on *Religion and Art* which contains a plate (Figure 41) which has all the elements which the Fish Lady one you sent me to has, arranged differently—it is wilder and older—he calls it Assyrio Babylonia—guess is it is Sumer—or earlier—it is a tablet I could describe, but look if you can—he says "Those characteristic monuments which at one time passed under the name of reliefs of Hades and were supposed to represent in an abbreviated form death and the passage of the soul, are, as has been recently demonstrated magic tablets against the demons of fever, they are monuments of art intended not for death but for life."

Then there is a funeral procession from a dipylon vase which is *exactly* the same kind of work as the fish lady—both attributed to Greek—looks like pure American Indian—*what* is the connect? Suspect very *strongly* a connection—the work in both drawings resembles New Mexican blankets.

In Levy-Bruhl the sociologist I read last year a strong outline of a large matriarchy in the most primitive existing society today forget where—has never interested me—

but from the Olson angle—the straight deep life thing—into the future—would love to do it baby—begin today—

If you have any suggestions about preparing an outline for Guggenheim be so sweet as to say—or if I did a sample sheet—would you criticise please—am *so* lazy Olson—but *what* a beautiful thing such a book would be—

Your Motz

❦ 255 ❦

New York City to Washington
[15 July 1950]

Charles—

I have just returned from Oriental Room NYPL where by a strange chance I was introduced to an Italian woman leaving Monday morning for Baghdad—world authority on cylinder seals—I asked her *where* to find photos of the stuff in books I had before me—she said I could use hers at Pierpont Morgan—she has just completed a book and in case there are things I am interested in I can not *see* she will allow me to see the actual cylinders. I found her like what you say of all scholars—she managed to make me feel stupid in less than a minute but I did find out about the photos—which is good because most of these things are so small you cannot see them and so could never reproduce in another book.

I found several things driving me mad—

but before I describe (if ever) want to tell you Hercules counterpart in Sumer is EABANI and today I found a cyclinder seal which would delight your soul—EABANI has two fierce lions turned head downward holding them by the back leg, one on each side of him, he looks as though he is banging them up and down the way children do when feeling especially pleased with themselves and he has a grin—complete—like a child's. If I ever understood all the beautiful stuff I just saw only in this one day Charles—how deep is the voice of man—

There is another of Gilgamesh and EABANI each fighting a lion and darling they have the most beautiful cocks to be seen in all art—and so do the lions. The blood in all that stuff—even the plants—just kills me.

Miss Rabota[51] told me a certain figure of course was not the God Sin, but a deified king—and Charles, the figure, whatever it may be I do not know—is sitting there with two of the finest high hard breasts you have ever laid your eyes on. (In addition to the breasts this figure (god or king?) is always symbolized by a crescent moon—how did they make this masculine? What great mind decided this meant a masculine god?)—but apparently scholars just consider breasts and such unimportant—the way they have ignored the thin little ribbon and the huge serpent of earth between and over the legs of the statues, in the Medici chapel, Dawn and Evening.

51. Boldereff is misremembering Edith Porada's name.

Anyway the man who is the librarian is an angel—who has a Chinese girl friend—Mr. Parr—a sweet librarian—you know—

(Please don't think I am not sleeping—that letter was a true one—and all digging in libraries etc. is part, for a person like me, of sleep—let myself and all dynamics alone—)

At this beginning instant, my hunch is that during Sumer the relationship man-woman was very hot and equal—like what Trigant Burrow wants—like a snake centered in its environment with all its alertness—each of them centered to force—and that somewhere in Assyria—that time—the thing began to turn Patsie—because of a few laws I have bumped into showing women with equal rights and certain art things beginning to show man dominance (Assyria). God knows at this point if I am crazy or not.

I quote you apropos your word piss from a British dictionary of slang etc. in which the editor says

"Incorrectly considered a low colloquialism." He then quotes this sentence which is my guess as to how and why the Tiger of France won the First World War for the French!

"Ah, si je pouvais pisser comme il parle." Clemenceau of Lloyd George.

Perhaps the finest summary of the history of the relationship of two nations ever witted.

          I love it.

And I might add—I have had moments when I could speak it of O—that great time when he uses superior dumb sentences like "But yet I would assuage your hurts."[52] A lie Olson. When I sat in Woodward with no library—finally said so—did you buy or borrow one single book to send me? which would have eased so much pain (I don't count the Smart, because I asked for it and it was of no use.)

                              ≈ 256 ≈

Washington to New York City
[17 July 1950]

                                                      Monday

frances: I am unable to say anything today in answer to yr Friday, Saturday, Sunday letters. Nor have I even a piece of paper.[53] I have buried myself in the Lib of Cong & now go to the District Library. Unable to see the Seta. But *please* send me quickly references on where I may see the *Eabani seals* of Two Hanging Lions plus the King with the Breasts WHERE?

---

52. Boldereff is quoting the end of the second paragraph of Olson's letter of 13 July 1950.
53. This note was written on the back of an envelope.

Washington to New York City (telegram)
19 July 1950

FRANCES MOTZ=
CARE BRYAN 281 WEST BROADWAY NO FONE NYK=
ARRIVING CONGRESSIONAL PENN STATION SEVEN THIRTY FIVE DAYLIGHT
TONIGHT LOVE
=OLSON=

PART VI

❧❧❧

21 July 1950–7 September 1950

It was on the occasion of this visit by Olson to New York on 19 July 1950 that Boldereff, according to Tom Clark in Charles Olson: The Allegory of a Poet's Life, *accused him of "ruthlessness in his treatment of her": "Words alone were not enough to satisfy a passionate woman, she said; life was more important than art and the two should never be confused" (p. 174).*

One can hear such remonstrances from time to time in the following letters. Boldereff seems very much to be fighting a battle single-handed in the Big City, and before Olson gets to see her again the city has, in its own way, claimed her, life asserting supremacy over art.

❧❧ 258 ❧❧

Washington to New York City (special delivery)
21 July 1950 (postmark 21 July 1950)

friday july 21 50

frances, lady:

        dove sta memora
           dove sta memora
              dove sta memora

                    stand sweet in the
                    memory
                        you do:

                            do you know, frances,
that you do,—and that this is, this is, a beauty you wear which is, which is, how very rare, how, in a sense, a raiment none can calculate on, not put on, as other clothes are, in fact is given off, is, as a fragrance is, something the wearer, because a flower does not itself have a nose for what it itself can disclose, can only, itself, sense that it is, as you speak of a plant or dragon-flies, an obedience: can we put it this way—only those who obey are odorous?

do you know? In any case, I'm telling you, because I'm experiencing it. And it is one of those mysteries, which, though I am absolutely prepared to spell out why you are, why the smell and taste of you carried away is always so sweet, so stands in the mind, is still, not perhaps so much mysterious as it is a proving of love & beauty

We can argue that it is crazy, that life is mortal, that, the living of it, presence, flesh, the dailies—"I want facts", is what we're here for. Sure. But there we are: here, is another thing, another proving.

I know you know, and yet know, how you curse the consequence of your pushing out the arc, of extending the arc of woman, of taking on this act. But I do not know how many men have told you, how many women. You say, "I have eleven saves, to my credit", and when you sd it, it sounded, in my ear, as old vocabulary made absolutely fresh & new, as, new movings of the arc beyond where it has been; for saves, as you use it, is "lives". And that is beautiful. My god, how beautiful. And because I am wordy (sure, why not, if words are another commitment, less, or more, mortal, anyhow, also, commitment), why the hell can't I, this morning, because words are my business, tell you, what by god you can be told, what can be said conspicuously about *you*, the fragrance of your life is noticeable

I am sorry, if this comes off, poetic. It is. The analysis of love is, poetic. A Duke is more actual to the woman of you, perhaps. But there is this other woman in you who—and I, Olson, am the one who, from the start has had her grace— who calls for, and gets, attention. The trouble is, it is such a tension as, o, say, this letter, say, instead of, o, say, the dailies, or, say, what I was prompted, since I left you, to mark, by, o, say, a book, shall we say, or some less intimate thing, like, say, a blouse. But, strangely, (and this is, in itself, another way the damn mystery expresses itself) anything other than this analysis of love, of the fragrance a Pistis-Sophia (who is a mimosa)—((you prove to me, for example, why Cavalcanti and Dante made, as they did,—and there is no question there was a woman behind it—an image, a Beatrice, a Mathilde, to stand, to stand in a phrase dove sta memora, to stand (I am against their placing of her, in a paradiso—or have been, up to this moment!) as the only proving of love which matters. Or so a *poet* would put it. He would be, "poetic", about it.

What I'm saying, frances, is, that we have passed (that we passed the last ten days) over from a period when Olson, as he sd, had kept keeping you in a state of image of, in one sense, his own invention ((the image he had made up before he ever saw you, to which he sent a postcard, an image which was a creation of his own needs—this is the trouble with dreams, why dreams are not the proper base of either analysis or poems ((—why such images decay—))

This really is a shot, through, generally: calls for examination—I am thinking, as always, of art—why "dreams" are bad, misleaders, why Nietzsche was right, "life is more wrestling than dance."

> (((intermission: you see, darling, why olson doesn't talk, doesn't as you put it, tell you anything about himself: a letter like this is his form of telling, baby)))

from such an image (how deeply correct you were to say, "I am no Hines, and never was"!) this boy, the Boston Strong Boy, has passed to Frances, herself, to, the Dijon she gives off, not, to what olson was giving off! (Before I came to NY to see you, I kept repeating in my mind, to call you Diotima. I did not then know why. Now I do.)

Nor are these riddles, plays, baby, winks. The old man is serious. He is trying to tell you, that love dwells in you, that, right now in the miserableness of yr present circumstances you give off that which is, I now discover, what love gives off. And I touch you, to tell you.

You know, darling, we are crazy bold and American. Was there ever people who dared to throw themselves, whole hair hog and mind, into this fragile place? I guess (I am of such a mood today) to say yes, sure, *every* one who ever got in there, who found the spider web was stronger than the hurtling body, the snail's wettings on the walk outstand the sun, the snake's saliva lasts, had to to do it *this one way* (your rooshians, and, this morning, I am able to think, those two birds of the early Renaissance whom I have never before understood, Mister Cavalcanti and that other fellow, that Big Wop with that profile like He-Who-Runs-Away-to-Play-Another-Day)

Anyhow, you have, and I, quietly, wordily, tell you, this morning, what the upshot is.

> (I guess what I was trying to say abt this American business is, precisely, this: that I do not know how, otherwise than by this going to the mat to be covered with dirt to wrestle out of particulars, can an american, given no premises to start with, come up with any sense of that incredible abstract truth which, say, a thing like love, the word and the fact, include.

Put it the way we did: COURAGE (I want you to pronounce it, coo-ra-je). But here courage is bought high. You bought it, high, Frances. And you have, you give off, its fragrance.

> ((This goes another way: and it is why we both respect Lawrence, why I am tempted to think his job on Whitman is his very most usable to the Amer-

icans. But something else Lawrence couldn't have known, because he was not an American. Or because Americans, before him, were not possible to do this dirtying work. But the *particulars*, if there are not premises, become the place where the premises have to be dug out, anew. I am getting on to this ground: that the reason why yr life is an agony, why, you and I both are interested in Sumerians, is, that here, in the USA, it is like it was when man and woman first tried to figure out what the hell goes on, who makes us want it. And thus why, not the vision is different from our predecessors (there just aren't any new *truths*), but why what we have to make clear is what we have found, that the *methodology* (of particulars, in the present context) is where the vision lies, citizens. And that this is a sort of primitive hell and new paradise, most like the archaic, least like the Greek or Renaissance.

You see, Frances, would you know that my problem as a poet (which you were close to the edge of making me angry about, when you sd, age 52) *is* the problem of the poet here: to clear himself of, on the one hand the terrible tendance to settle for the vision short of the rottenness particulars involve life in (Whitman, even Melville in his "Keep true to the *dreams* of yr youth"—and my contemporaries who go for the Xtian deal, or, what is more interesting, those who, as the master sd, go for the disease of hebraism-hindosim) and, on the other, because methodology is the struggle, to clear himself of the *technicals* (Ezra, conspicuously, whose Confucius, whose Cavalcanti are tricks to cover both).

So I say, darling, with none of the old dream, or gemut stuff, on it: you and I are brother & sister, because we are involved in a struggle which you are the only one who knows what, on, shall we say the life-side, as opposed to the word-side, the price one pays because particulars not premises are all we are offered?

But, as I pound at you, and you must forgive, for it is with no disrespect whatsoever for what you are finally, you say, settling for, life not art: you do also participate in discoveries such as those wonderful pages of yr Whitman show[1]—what you put when you sd, put the space back inside, where it belongs

(frances, do you suddenly see how joined we are? It is because (it must have been why ISHMAEL caught you) space is the reason why we have to do the job

(at this point I would, thinking of your pages, and how beautifully you have used space, put what I started out to say, in this letter, another way: that the fragrance you give off, is, the fragrance that space gives off once it is returned to that place where it be-

---

1. Olson has finally seen the book on Whitman that Boldereff designed for Joseph Jay Rubin (who is mentioned by name below) and Charles H. Brown. Full reference in footnote to letter 11 February 1950.

longs, inside the person. Which leads to this: that love is the secret of, space, just as it was of time, but that why love in time was half, and thus has rotted, and, in this time of beginning, makes us partly rotten, is because space (the archaic thing the Sumer people, I bet, had not lost, as we won't, now) was left outside there (and all the middle mixed things, the two bad sides above, mush and technicals, resulted.)

I imagine I could go on with this. But I am hungry, and a little worn, not in the head, but in body, and this seems where I better stop. There are two things I want to say: (1) when it turns out you can get another copy of the Whitman as well as the true one you *must,* darling, force out of that Rubin for presentation to the Graphics people for a prize, I want you to send it to me; and (2) you must, sweet, if you need dough, when the 30 bucks are gone, just say, olson, let me have a fin, or whatever.

You are a proud & beautiful thing, and this boy knows, darling, and, in sign of his knowing, sends you this love letter

olson

❧ 259 ❧

Washington to New York City
22 July 1950 (postmark)

sat

Frances:

I've been sitting glowing over your strikes in the Whitman, and want to say this, my lady, to you: don't, frances, let go on this bizness of going ahead *now* as a designer, even at the offense it may involve to yr fighting self. I think yr own pride that you are the only one who knows space in this art is accurate. Now this is something which, despite this other high gift of woman in you, must be used, made finer by use, until you take over, stand as the sign of, this craft in our time.

It actually is too much, too good, for you to dispose of—you must, darling, not let anything lead you off. (And you know, Frances, that I know how a gift like yours *won't* be used by others, won't be welcomed, simply because it is too good. I know how the slack hate such skill. Therefore, one has to fight to get it used.)

I am sure the only way you will finally do the books you want is, by having yr own shop. And that seems to me a real possibility not so long ahead. But, until then, you should not let—as you yrself sd—your hand go cold.

Keep me informed, please, on what happens in the shop you went to Thursday morning. And what about yr friend at the AIGA? does she not know leads? And it still seems to me a valid thing, that, as the jockeying goes on for a job as designer, that you, at the same time, force ahead the project of THE ART OF WOMAN, shall we call it? For it now seems to me that this, too, can be what MEDEA was, need not be the huge document that I proposed, but should be, actually, as cryptic and as personal as you made M. Why not, with merely your taste, so long as you start with the beginnings (the SEALS) mount the story by way of yr selections wherever you find them?

As a matter of fact, these seals are extraordinary in one way that I don't think has been observed (and it is one of the marks of the sort of perception that life included among these people): that they explain themselves! They are high art, if I ever saw it. (I don't think you will find it as fruitful as I do, that is, the text, for it is too crazy, but, in this guy Waddell's books (Laurence Austine W) the plates will send you, he is so gifted in using them, and piling them on. Since I came back I have been ploughing through his THE MAKERS OF CIVILIZATION IN RACE & HISTORY, London, 1929; and have another, THE BRITISH EDDA, London, 1930 (which has a serpent princess as frontispiece which is most most most potent).

((Waddell,—you just can't imagine what a stroke it was to stumble on him; for he sets right in between my lad Frobenius and our boy Strzygowski, is as whiny as they both are, confronted with the stupidity of scholars. But wow, how he makes this boy *go*! W. has got a hold on the relation of Aryan-Gothic, without any, apparently, knowledge of S.))

Anyhow, darling, just before I fall to work, I wanted to say this. And you must, sweet, take it as no more than a male urging (males are such fools, to think *work* is what we're here for!) But I deeply, deeply believe you are my twin in this work of space. And wish that you would just go right ahead and revolutionize these bastards right to hell out of existence.

Love,
Charles

p.s. W. makes a lot of a collection of seals by L. Delaporte, Paris, 1923 *Cyclindres Orient. du Mus. de Louvre*

❦ 260 ❧

New York City to Washington
[24 July 1950]

Monday night

Charles dear—

I hated it when you said it to me—but this moment it exactly describes something. You said "You will know when he puts his thing up your ass"— and precisely that, Olson—this moment—if you will understand me has God done this to me—

All that great power and stillness and enormous female inherited (from the passing of male seed) strength—God—to me—as of this moment.

I have touched for the second time in my life the bottom—the extreme reach—

Today I *know* I will live to design strong real great things—I will do the other little job the woman book—I will do all—the Russian stuff etc—

And I am leaving all the details to my fate—

I now have my fingers on that string and it is taking me straight into my future.

I am sure that the telegram containing a refusal which I received two hours ago is a signal—*not* to do a job I hate—to have the guts to wait a few more weeks—

I read in *Job* "I expected to die in my nest—and to live as long as the phoenix. That my roots would be open to water . . ."[2]

Oh Olson—who could say better what the Motz credo is—there it is—

I love—I am in love—I am full

Frances

◄§ 261 §►

Washington to New York City
25 July 1950 (postmark 25 July 1950)

tues. july 25 50

darling, i have so thrown myself down into Sumer i cannot get out! i am "sealed" "cylindered" & undelivered! Spent yesterday on my boy Waddell, who continues to be one of the most exciting men i have ever read (yet i am not yet prepared to say whether i buy his package), and have, today, been poking my nose into yr pal Porada, and her boy Frankfort—it is curious how presumptuous scholars are, and how intolerant of men like Waddell, because they "range".

        But I want to send this note to you, by the early mail (you must tell me if things reach you the next day, without specials). For yours do. I have

2. Job 29:18–19.

your letter of last night, so very strong, & such an answer to Saturday letter! O Frances, baby, of course you will (of course you are my girl): it is very wondrous, how, (is it for you, too?) how strong you stand in me, when I come away, each time, how sure you feel inside me. (I dare say I am, in one way, an even more hardened creature than you, in that events—I suppose this is why you call me ruthless—never seem to me the equal of fate, that is, the purposed fate obedience involves. But I mean nothing by this comparison, just that I also dare say a male is more trained in respect to events, no? And this is no good, no good at all, by comparison to the absolute particularity of passion, as a woman like you is passionate. It occurred to me today, this: is it not necessary, when we speak of love & passion, that we better, one better, speak of a man's love or passion and a woman's love & passion? That they are alike, but that they express themselves differently? (I was thinking, in my mind, about that question I asked you: what did you think of S's sonnet, on lust. By the way, it is 129—and is, I'm tempted now to think, carefully stated as a male's expression.)

What was the telegram? The one you expected Thursday—or the result of the Thursday appointment. Let me know. In any case, you are certainly right to fight for the chance to go ahead with yr own great skill. Is it not really a question, now, not of learning anything more of yr trade, but of carrying yr own sense of space forward? teaching others, by way of yr work?

Darling, take this as a mere note to tell you yr man is here, & close to you. It is already 5; and though I tore back from the library to sit down & write you, my brain is still going along on that work I was doing, and I am suspended, hung, going full tong, & unable to come out, get to that place where I can be full of expression. (Libraries do that to me—like bookstores. I become the victim of a sort of avarice, and though I accept it as a part of the extensions, yet I hate its effect. It is why I leave my desk so rarely,—& almost never before I have used the first freshness of the day for my own work.)

Will write quickly. And do, baby, keep writing me.

Yr lad,

ol

(I am so cracking down on Waddell I should write *that* out to you!) (And may) But I'll post this now.

❦ 262 ❧

New York City to Washington
[25 July 1950]

Charles dear—

Am crazy about Waddell—must own the *British Edda*. Am enclosing a quote from a book of his you did not mention—whole business more and more exciting.

Look Charles dear—I am in that final grip when either the hero or the demon wins—have no home and no job yet—but I have a hunch so damned strong that I am the future King—

Write to me at Louise's after Friday

Mrs John Baer
215 Second Ave
NYC3

Am going to Elizabeth Livingston's
209 S. Broadway
Tarrytown

Will get there Sunday morning stay for one or two days—(Warner is in Philadelphia)

Please in my final wrestling—please write to me, Olson—as I have written to you when you needed me—I absolutely cannot write. It is my very life by the throat.

I have a new business about the woman book—(I think there is nothing in Matriarchy)

Maybe if I ever get straightened out I will try to *draw* Charles—if I can't draw what I see—maybe I'll write some passionate minute instructions to Cagli via Olson.

Please walk around all day and night with your arm around my waist.

Frances

❧ 263 ❧

New York City to Washington
[26 July 1950]

Wednesday 11 AM

Charles dear—

I went this morning to see a wonderful woman—a lead from Lucy Litch—and I applied to her for a temporary job which would not interfere with my searching for a designer's job—she grasped everything immediately—said she *wanted* to hire me and as soon as an assignment came in she would use me and for as long as I was available. As terribly hard as it is for me to keep control of myself—I still cannot help but notice what an immediate sense of capability I give off which is given back to me at once—in trust—everywhere I go. I believe banks call it "earned increment" n'est-ce pas?

In regard to events, dear—can not you see that a woman who is reared in the kind of home I was *never* gets used to it—that I always subconsciously feel that it is man's business to hold the door open—all I am supposed to do is graciously to enter and well to conduct myself once inside—that after all these years I still am blushing inside every single time I have to talk to anyone—that I feel precisely like a naked slave on a block—each time—even if the person I talk to is a woman? My guess is it has more to do with forms of society than sex—I do not know anything about fighting—I expose myself to view—I use my upbringing to hide my terrible feeling of being bared—also from my upbringing. It reaches down so far below the place where I can eliminate it—business is such a new business for a lady, Charles. But that warm lovely little Lucinda stands there and says "Ma-Me"—and I would endure anything.[3]

I registered yesterday with the real people in this business—the professional inside feeding ground for the trade—New York Employing Printers Assn—not an agency—no fee—very very rarely handle woman—but I got a big send-off (to them) and they have the lead into everything good—August busy month.

Did I ever mention to you that my first Motz ancestor in this country was a political exile deprived of all his property and that he brought nothing to America but a library? That he is my ancestor and yours—that he loved books as you and I do—with a kind of hatred for their forcing in—and he is reputed to have traveled 1½ days over the mountains for the sake of a conversation with an intellectual man—you know he was a mathematician and sculptor—both amateur, my guess is.

3. A letter to Lucinda of 22 July 1950 survives in the Storrs collection:
Saturday
Lucinda darling—
Ma Me was walking along the street and found the beautiful fairy button which I thought you might like to use when you want Angela to come—you know, press on the beautiful rose pearl in the middle and then Angela will know you want to speak to her.
I am going up to Lucy's house now—she is going to wash Ma Me's hair, just as I wash yours—and try to make your Ma Me look a little bit beautiful!
Darling Lucinda, Ma Me has to tell you something. I can not stay in Dails' house where I am now next month. I can not stay at Elizabeth's, in Tarrytown, because she is moving to Philadelphia and so far Ma Me does not know *where* she will live, so I have to ask you darling to stay at Raymond's after Louise goes to camp.
I am working as hard as I can, darling, to try to find a place to live, and you must help Ma Me by being brave and waiting. I will get you the first minute I can, as soon as I have found a place for us to live.
I give you thousands of great big hugs and cover your darling body and face with kisses.
Your most absolutely loving
Ma Me

But I do love it that at the same hour on the same day you and I were sitting in our respective libraries reading the same books—oh Olson—united in a flesh which is one for the two of us.

I am in the best place for mail—everything comes thru at once—but that is the great ring of the N.Y. Telephone Co.—I get what they get! I will let you know how it is for regular mail elsewhere

thru Sat to nightfall	281 W. Bway
Sat night to Sunday	215 W. Second Ave
Sunday thru Monday	209 S Broadway Tarrytown
Monday thru Saturday	35–25 Seventy-seventh Street
	Jackson Heights, N.Y.
	c/o Edward Wyman
telephone Illinois 8–0158	

Would it disturb you if I were to live for a month with a man who could help me all over the place?

Frances

◄§ 264 §►

New York City to Washington
[26 July 1950]

Charles—
It is shocking to me that you should ask about 129
"Lust" and "shame" are words invented by a Hebraic man—exactly when I don't know.
They have no meaning whatsoever to a woman
And my guess is they have no meaning to a Sumerian, male or female.
They have no meaning to Wm. Blake
They have no meaning to a genuine Russian.
They are *invented*—they constitute an irreality—that you are right to say has grown up out of power—the male "lust" for power.
A woman drinks from a man as the sky lets fall rain—without ego.

The "hell" he speaks of is humanism and its errors—man who serves god, with purity, who seeks to speak god at every moment can not even imagine hell.
A man and woman should approach one another's need with humility, as saints eat quietly bread.

This is the very expression of that ugliness I always *felt* was in Shakespeare in all our western world I so despise in Charles—where he is not a poet.

It involves taking the mundane hell and woman's "boy" as realities, whereas every man who serves god knows them to be illusion—but not therefore please note to be scorned or derided—to be, on the contrary, *served* with humility—when man learns how to obey—to be clean—to come alive—to live in the spirit—the body will disappear as a temptation.

I consider Blake a greater writer than Shakespeare. Shakespeare stands there flashing that technical virtuosity and I, a woman, spit into the street—no one but a dumb man, man through the ages, with his ego—would so be enamored of word wonder.

❦ 265 ❧

Washington to New York City (special delivery)
26 July 1950 (postmark 26 July 1950)

wed. july 26 50

darling, let me try to discharge this whole Mesopotamia mess, make such sense out of it as I now can (and do not, sweet, think this is impersonal, like a poem, not a letter to you, for it is, for, that I move thru this stuff with yr nice sure hand as it was as we set out for dinner a week ago, then, what is there more, actually as sign?)

WADDELL: the upshot of his work[4] is a complete chronology of world civilization from the Painted Pottery Folk (Al Ubaid, next town to Ur, that is, so far as this Folk were in Sumer) down to what he calls the breaking of the old Aryan Center, date approximately 1200 BC

(He rests his argument on the lists that he says the Indian Puranas contain, both Solar & Lunar lists of early Kings, which, says he, taken with the Kish Chronicle (the only Sumerian King list he declares is accurate as it is, tho he rights the others, even the Isin Lists, by his Indian corrections), establish a precise record from 3378 BC to the fall of the Kassi Dynasty (which he says is Aryan, not Semitic) in Babylonia, 1200 BC, about.)

There seems no question that the Sumerians were already advanced at the time they appear in Lower Mesopotamia (even Porada points out that the 1st

---

4. Olson is summarizing L. A. Waddell, *The Makers of Civilization in Race and History* (London, 1929).

seals, the Uruk cylinders, are of a high quality, altho there is no evidence of a prior gradual development to account for such an achievement).[5] ((It fascinates me, that the very first work of such artists should be not direct, but obverse, cutting stones not for their face but for the impression they will make on clay!))

Therefore, the HUGE question, to which no one has yet the answer, is: WHERE DID THE SUMERIANS COME FROM? Before I consider Waddell's answer, here is Woolley's analysis (keep Strzygowski in mind thruout):[6]

"The fact that Sumerian gods are constantly represented as standing upon mountains would imply that the people came from a hill country; that their earliest building style is based on a tradition of timber construction is an argument to the same conclusion, for such could only originate in the heavily-timbered uplands; the description given in Genesis, 'and the people journeyed from the east and came into the plain of Shinar and dwelt there', refers to the Sumerians, and must incorporate some Sumerian legend as to their own movements; but the obvious conclusion that they descended from the Elamite mountains which border the delta valley on the east does not meet the case, for though there are common elements in the early cultures of Mesopotamia and Elam it does not seem possible to derive the Sumerian from the latter, nor does the physical type show identity of race: Sumerian legends which explain the beginnings of civilization in Mesopotamia seem to imply an influx of people from the sea, which people can scarcely be other than the Sumerians themselves, and the fact that the historic Sumerians are at home in the south country and Eridu, the city reputed by them to be the oldest in the land, is the southernmost of all, supports that implication."

My own hunch is, that the *sea* tradition comes from a folding in of the white and the yolk, from the joining of the original settlers who were overcome by the Sumerians and their own later extraordinary development, that is, the Sumerians, into the 1st great SEA PEOPLE (see below for this later business; and for the pre-Sumerians, see temple #17, found last year at Eridu, a temple to Enki, the news story says, 30 feet down, and no foundation below it but green sand, the sand of the Persian Gulf just retreated, date, says Naji Al Asil, Iraq's chief of antiquities, 4500–5000 BC.)

My temptation (on the basis of the discovery of towns like Mohenja Daro all

5. Edith Porada, *Mesopotamian Art in Cylinder Seals of the Pierpont Morgan Library* (New York, 1947), pp. 13ff.
6. C. Leonard Woolley, *The Sumerians* (Oxford, 1928), pp. 7–8.

along the high plateaus north of Meso and south of the Caucasus, east and west throughout) is to think that the Sumerians did come from above down the valley rather than in, from the sea. (Here FROBENIUS' thesis of high civilization as the child of the wedding of the inner land people (lunar, says he) with the coast people (solar, he argues) is very much to the point, though if, as Waddell never succeeds in really saying, but keeps on hinting, that the Aryans were Solar and the Semites Lunar, then one has to open anew the question of the sea vs the plateau argument as to the origin of the Aryans.

In no sense to obviate the argument, (it is extremely healthy to keep it open), but to begin to lay a better base for understanding than either the scholars or such a wild man as Waddell make possible, it is, this origin question, better left ahead of us until the so far meagre explorations of the whole area from Europe on down south east to the Indus, along the river & high plateau lines, are thickened.

This said, I do not put aside as foolish Waddell's answer: because he thinks that the first Aryan King, IN-DUR (indure!), moved down from Cappadocia, to take, aided by his son, Carchemish (his son going on to found Erech, 200 miles to the south ((a total movement in two generations of some 600 miles)), Waddell suggests (on the basis of owner's marks on Danubian pottery, around present Belgrade; and on the basis of the earliest known iron mine at Hallstadt) that these Aryans (whom he also keeps calling "Goths", by his kind of swift etymologies!) originally shaped themselves and their culture in the Danube valley. (He'll not be proved wrong until diggings in this whole area are exhausted, given the already sure signs that the governing motion of early civilized man was generally south-south east.) ((This is interesting in the light of a lot of recent geo-political argument, that it is now NNW)) This gets quite an adumbration from Waddell's excellent notion that, by 1200 BC, but prepared for by the Sumer Emperor URUASH and his son MAGDAL, the Sea-Kings, 3100 BC, and made definite by Sargon and his dynasty's shift to Egypt c. 2700 BC, the breaking of the old Aryan center let go this western, north-western force.

(What makes so much of Waddell's point on this break-up plausible, is, how well it jibes with a lot of openings I have hit in the last three years. For example, in following along Victor Bérard's leads on the Odyssey, and on finding how verifiable Herodotus now becomes, it works out that, just about the year that Waddell now makes an explanation for, 1200 BC, the whole area of Ionia, Phoenicia, Hebraia, Egypt, Greece, Etruria, starts up into an aggressive and combative life. And it is a part of this same stir that India as we know it seems to come into existence likewise (Waddell dates the Great Migration into India as happening from Cappadocia about 700 BC: it was by this movement, says he, that the Indians took off and kept straight, the old long Aryan King Lists of the Puranas.)

In other words, his argument, that, after a solid rule from Mesopotamia, with colonies in the Indus Valley, and then, later , in the Nile Valley, the ARYAN CENTER, which had lasted just a little more than 2000 years (Xtian, or Roman, or Western Civilization's curve) BUSTED—and split off into what we have known as the EAST and the WEST—makes one hell of a lot of sense, at this end point where we are, where, again, the WILL TO COHERE, as opposed to the WILL TO DISPERSE (the root drive behind the nomad or pioneer) is conspicuously back in business ((this is a better way of seeing the double urge to both the Leader and the Collective Society, which I take as the mark of the present, than to see it inside the frame of that HALF THING, the West)).

It strikes me, that what gave IN-DUR his first and huge place in men's minds, was, that he was Leader possessed of the notion that to COHERE was the path for man to take. Thus the TOWN becoming the CITY, thus AGRICULTURE becoming IRRIGATION and TRADE (his son, variously named, as I shall shortly summarize Waddell, was the inventor of the plough!)

SO, here we are, back at what is, to me, the most fertile & exciting thing about Waddell, whether or not his chronology, in the end, stands up—his list of the HUMAN KINGS, the HEROES, who became the GODS.

Let me first do what he doesn't do first, to the terror of one's mind, trying to follow him through 700 pages of badly written & unorganized notions, facts & thought: the CHRONOLOGY, based on the Kish Chronicle, the Purana lists, & such cylinders & monuments as have turned up. (His list, to anyone's amazement, is unbroken, from 3378 to 717 BC (when the Indians moved off east)! But I shall only pick out the top boys. (They are even numbered, in order!)

1 UKUSI, of Ukhu City 3378–3349 BC (other names, depending upon what list, & also on tendence of man to give kings & emperors many titles: UDU, UDUIN or UDIN (Odin) INDAR, INDURU, DUR (Thor & Indra), PUR SAKH, SAGAGA, ZAGG (Zeus & *saga*), GAUR or ADAR (Guru & Adamu): I am bracketing in mythological uses of him later (which to me, as a euhemerist, or so ISHMAEL turned out to prove me, make sense)

2 Ukusi's son, AZAG (fr Zagg, as son of?) who reigned 1st at the old capital (Carchemish?) 3348–3337 & then, founding the 2nd Dynasty, at *Unuk* (Enoch or Erech City (the present Warka) 3336–3273 (his other names are: AMA BASU or BAKUS, TASIA, MUKHLA (St Michael), GIN, GAN (Cain)

4. UDU, UDUK 3247–3242 priest-king of Kish (he dedicated the STONE-BOWL (Ar-Thur's Holy Grail) of his great-grandfather (King I) which was found by U. of P. expedition below the foundations of the Sun-temple at Nippur, with this inscription:

"To King (or Lord) Sagg (or Zagg, Sakh, Dar, In-Dara or Dur, Udu, Gurusha or Adar), UDU, the priest-king of Kish City, the son of Enuzuzu (of Inzuzu), the son of Gin the established son (of King Sagg), the Khamazi City choice broken (Bowl) has deposited."

(A Babylonian copy of a Sumerian hymn contains these lines: which I copy entire for their relevance to the whole question of the Sumerian's coming, and to the *imagery* of the seals:

"The tooth of the Lion, and the mighty Serpent of Ilu, thou (Adar) removest, making (them) to turn away from the land.

Adar, the king, the son of the god King Sakh (maybe right, maybe dislocation following deification of King I) has caused (? them) to turn unto (? themselves)

He is the warrior whose lasso overthrows the foe.

O Adar! the fear of thy shadow inclines towards the world.

He assembles his people in strength to invade the hostile land.

Adar the Warrior who knows not fear (has driven away) the pest.

The strong *Darru* before whom the foe exists not. (Sounds like a Staliniad!)

Adar, manly exalter, who makes joyful his side, has driven the chariot over the mountain, has scattered wide the seed ((this looks like a straight history of King I and II, where they came from, what they did to the "Chaldeans")) (Men) altogether have proclaimed his name for sovreignty over them.

In their midst like a great wild bull has he lifted up his horns ((the Bull as opposed to the Lion? to the Serpent?))

The *Shu* (Vessel) Stone, the precious (stone of the Chaldees), the strong stone, the Serpent-Stone (of) the mountain-stone,

that Warrior—the Fire-Stone (Cauldron: look!) too—the Hero has carried (off) to the city ((but this looks as tho the above history is reversed, the King I

invaded mountain people & took away *their* stone: why a stone in the valley?))
((But Waddell fills this in fr. the *Eddas*, and says it is valley people who are
raided))

((anyhow, there's the great deed of the KING 4, who is called a PRIEST, and
looks very much like the first RECORDER, or WRITER, following on his
predecessor ARCHETYPES,

KING 1, the Warrior (Leader in widest sense, the People's Leader) (HERO
made GOD)

KING 2, the Settler, the Founder (Leader in the second sense, of Peace, the
Quetzalcoatl) (SON-HERO made SON-GOD: Bacchus, Dionysus)

KING 4, the Recorder, the Poet, the Priest (Leader in the sense of the founder
of art & religion, the Codifier the Critique on Tradition—who comes when
there is a tradition established by 1 & 2 to work on) (HERO who stays MAN
or POET, who writes the SAGA of the OTHERS, turns the BOWL of their
accomplishments to the LIPS of other men, for them to DRINK)

KING 5, curiously enough, is DUMUZI, who reigned 30 years (the Poet only
lived 6!) 3241–3312 (THAMUZ?) the Shepherd ?

I jump now to the 10th King, who, it is again of some considerable point, is,
in several of the lists, especially those which break off for 430 years, the last
king BEFORE THE FLOOD (or the 1st one after? or the survivor? like
Noah? and thus becomes a 2nd Father, of the Race, as Noah is? after Adam?

BARATUTU, BARDU, BARTI PIRTU, (Indian: BURATA, BRIHAD,
PRITHU) 3180—(no terminal date known, only, that in the following 430
years there were 26 or 27 kings)

he is especially associated with FIRE (seems to be the early PROMETHEUS)
(Prithu is curiously like, tho Waddell doesn't make this point, as he misses
several others—or, at least, ones you get into his crazy easy methodology you
begin to see things all over the place!)

and he became the Source Man for most of the Aryans who eventually separated themselves from the CENTER (as, by the way, did Noah): the Indians,
in their Vedic psalms, call themselves BARATS, their country B'arat-varsha
(B'arat country); and, through the Phoenicians the PANCH dynasty associated with B, the BRIT-ons (!)

(There is here, one hook, that W. doesn't use, but which his dates suggest may be of some importance. That is, that Barat is linked to the Flood. Now, last year, in excavations, it was found that there *had* been a devasting flood (I think the earth & houses showed a 40 foot sweep) (or was it 400?). Anyhow, *if* the boys date that, & it coincides with Waddell's dating of Barat (3180 ff, say, the end of his life (Noah's age) 3100, then Waddell is *in*, in a way he did not suspect. In any case, this boy BARAT, is a Culture Figure of the size of Kings 1, 2, 4, is

the RAINBOW BOY, is

PROMETHEUS

(was it, after the flood, so absent, the knowledge, of how to make fire? and his genius, that he restored the knowledge, to the people?)

KING 14 is my boy BIGMANS!

GISHAX or ISSAX, with the title GAMESH, or "Lord of Oxen", the CAXUS CHAXUS, CAKSHUS of the Indian lists ((cf, two seals, c. 2500, in Banks, E.J. *Bismya*, N.Y., 1912)) (reigned approximately 3050 BC) (cf. also, on this, Waddell, *Indo-Sumerian Seals Deciphered*, London 1925, 134 ff, where his identity with the Phoenician Herakles, and the Greek, is done)

In the Indian lists he is called the father of the emperor Haryashwa, the founder of the First Panch or "Phoenician" Dynasty—who is URUASH, King 15—AND THIS JIBES WITH ALL MY IMAGINATION HAS TOLD ME SINCE HOW LONG? THAT "HERCULES" is a connect to SEA, is, the birth of SEA PEOPLE, is the ROOT FIGURE BEHIND Ulysses, Odysseus, is the WESTERN HERO PROTOTYPE.

15 URUASH (Ind.: Haryashwa) the SEA-KING, the founder of the great dynasty of sea-kings who follow, with their sea-port LAGASH

he and his son reign abt 3000 BC, and represent the SECOND HEAVE of the Sumerian thing—for it is he and his son who seem to have either established or came to control the INDUS VALLEY (from the sea-port MOHENJA DARO?)

and which move led to the consequent moves of (1) Phoenicia, and (2) Egypt (Herodotus records the tradition that the Phoenicians claimed they came from the Persian Gulf to Tyre 2300 years before his day, or, c. 2750 BC)

the Egyptian move gets dated in W's chrono: c. 2700

(W thinks a clincher is, that both Uruash & Haryashwa are known in both histories for their FIVE FAMOUS SONS

the famous votive plaque of Ur-Nina (Wooley, 18, opp. p. 66) (whom W says is URUASH) shows him and his 5 sons, in the upper half building a temple to King 2 (Michael, or Nimirrud: Nimrod), and in the lower half as priest-king celebrating a FIRE-CULT that leads the SEA-PEOPLE, the SEA-SUMERIANS, to trace their descent back, not to URUASH, but, as he seems to, himself, to BARAT? See above on Barat and Fire and Flood;

is this, in other words, the parallel, later act to the original one of the RIVER-VALLEY SUMERIANS making King 1, or the WARRIOR, the God?

in other words, 3 or 5 generations, and HEROS become GODS? (Or did?) (But look at ourselves, look at LINCOLN)

Also, is this the POSEIDON, as King 1, Zeus?))

the Five Sons are

King 16 (the eldest)MAD-GAL, A-MADGAL MUKH (Ind: MUGALA or MOGALLO) who holds the Jar in the votive plaque and who, in the solar version of the Indian Lists bears the title "Leader of the Jar", also, Ind., called "The Shining Arrow"

17 A-NUN-PAD, or "Sea-lord Commander", who is called, in Ind., "Overpowerer of the Island of Magha" (which W. suggests may mean he was the settler of Phoenicia . . . "Madhya-Land, Mekala and the Shuktimat Mountains", adds Vishnu Purana text.)

18 PRITHU-RUKMA or "Prince of Shining Disk", is, in Sumerian, SAG-ASH-DUK or "Duke of Troops", and remained in his older brother's service when Madgal became king

Hru-PAL or "Pal the Protector" (in Ind. PALITA "The Protector") who, with the fifth, the other younger son, were set over the "Videha Lands", says the Purana

AD-TUR-TA "The Child of his Father" (Ind.: HARITA)

(((I include this whole family simply because the full story of this family is crucial to me, for their relation to the NEW FORCE (what I have called the 2nd HEAVE) is a part of my own archaic memory, more than any previous figures

of this mythopoesis: GILGAMESH (or BIGMANS) URUASH (the Indus)
MADGAL & his bros., the PHOENICIANS

bibliog: the other Waddells
        plus *Vishnu Purana* trans.
            (HHWilson, ed. F. Hall, 1864)
            (pp. 4, 64

(or Indus Valley: *Etin*, or *Edin* (W translates it so, in *Indo-Sum Seals De* p. 7,
29–33, 49, 57, 102 ff)
   Udyana (Sanskrit)
   Otien (Huien Tsang, the Chinese Buddhist traveler, 7th AD)
   Su-Edin-ki (Sargon, or, "The Good Edin Land")
   Shu-Edin-hum (Sargon's song Menes, or, "The Garden of Edin,
   the Fruitful"

also, in Sumerian called
   Su-bati or "The Good Abode"
   Su-vatthi (Pali: happiness, blessing, welfare)
   Su-vati (Sanskrit "Heaven of the Indian Buddhists")
   Su-vata ("Full of Joy or Pleasure")

Also, the following:

URUASH is sd to be "OF THE HOUSE OF THE FISHES", and at Lagash,
in their stratum, have been found fish-hooks, fishing-tackel, harpoons, the
Net as a figure of the king's power in sculptures, sea-shell ornaments for inlay,
the offering of oars to the city's saint (Nimirrud, or Nimrod), and the picto-
graphic use of a sail with the meaning of "winds, watery space and sea", with
the phonetic value of Mar or Muru (Mer, Mare, the Eddic Gothic Marr, Irish
and Gaelic Muir, English Mere, Marine, Marsh); also the Sumerian origin of
the title of their sea-going branch, as the MURU or MARUT, and the Sanskrit MARUTAS or "Maorites" or Amorites whose name survives in Maure-
tania or Morocco to the west of Carthage

also, in the Vedic psalms, Haryashwa and his dynasty are almost the only
Early Aryan kings who are celebrated as sea-goers, as subjects to shipwreck in
mid-ocean (a ship of 100 oars is mentioned therein)

URUASH, & the KHADDI: in which inscriptions at Lagash U's title is
KHA-AD, or KHAD, pictured by the sign of a Fish inside the sign for
"House-Father" *(Ad)*, and thus, literally, means "House-Father of the
Fishes."

It also, in his Kish inscription as URU-SAG, the title is written by the signs of the Sun *(Khad)* plus a Foot *(di)* meaning primarily "the going forth of the Sun", and secondarily, "East". So, this way, it could be he is "King of the Orient".

But anyway, the title suggests it may be the origin of the title *Kad* or *Qad*, which survives in such Phoenician place names as Kadesh, Quadesh, Gades, with the meaning "House of the Kads", or in *Qadi* or *Qeti*, the old Egyptian name for P and the Levant.

(W. goes on to claim that this is also the ancient British name of *Catti*, for their kings. And is in series with *Gut* or "Goth", a title which was applied to Madgal in his father's plaque. W points out, too, that a branch dynasty of the Panch, in Ind., which had its capital at Tripurti, called themselves Cedi, Chedi, Caidya or Cidi.)

Another title of U and his dynasty is NUN or NUNNA, and W says it seems to be the equivalent of the Fish symbolism of the Khad title, thus: it is written by a pictogram supposed to be diagrammatic of a Fish, but which may be a Serpent, or Sea-Serpent, in which the cross-bars represent the coils (What, if any, is the relationship here to Inanna?)

This sign also reads Nuk, and thus equates with Skr Naga, a Serpent of the Waters, the Nag of modern Indians (in Indian myth the old legendary human kings are represented as Sea-Serpents or Naga, and one of these is called Panch-alo!)

PRINCE MADGAL, calls himself "Lord of Edin, the Capturer (of Edin)" in a victory seal fr the Indus Valley, and is, says W, the Sumerian ETANA, by a misapplication of a seal describing him as "The Shepherd of Etin(a), Gal of Ansha(n), the One who made the Foreign Lands faithful.

The Etana Story: the hero is Lord Etana or Etina, and is invited by his "friend" the Sun-Hawk (*Aukh* (!) to cling to it and be carried to Heaven.

Ansha(n), says W, is the ancient Sumerian name for Persis on the Gulf to the east of Elam, which afterwards had its capital at Persepolis, and suggests that the Sea-Sumerians had a halfway station there between Lagash and the Indus, just as Sargon and Manis did some centuries later.

(The Uruash Dynasty seems to have been put to an end by the usurper Zaggisi and Saggisi, who had been local governor and priest-king at Umma City to the north of Lagash. He transferred his capital to Erech. From his votive inscriptions at Nippur he claims to have "conquered the land from the Rising of the Sun to its Setting, and made straight the path from the Lower Sea (Persian Gulf) over the Euphrates and Tigrus unto the Upper Sea (the Medit)." "He ruled 25 years, and claims, in that time, to have rebuilt the temples and to have dug canals. Zaggisi, who had overthrown Sargon's father at Lagash (which he sacked) was, in his turn overthrown by

SARGON THE GREAT, KING 37, who ruled 55 years (2725–2671) and who, with his son MANIS-TISHU or MENES (of Egypt) or MINOS (–2641) established the FIRST WORLD EMPIRE, the BOWL, which, though it took almost 1500 years, was finally broken into the two halves which we have, up to now, called history, the E and the West.

P.S. (By now, 6:30, my desk is such a mess I cannot even find a pen!)

You will follow what happened—the drive to get this exasperating man Waddell *down*, to make some order (& relevance) out of his 700 pages of tropical jungle, took over again, as it did yesterday, in order to get itself *done*

—&

right in the midst of my letter to you!

So I figured the only thing to do was to get it done, get rid of it. But, just because it does shoot off some things which may interest you, I'll enclose the carbon. (I just haven't the strength to go any further than SARGON today. But in any case, that brings it into "history"!

And do, despite its "muscularity" (!), find in it "communication", frances!

love
C

⟡ 266 ⟡

New York City to Washington
[27 July 1950]

Thursday

Charles darling

I am wondering sweetheart why you spend your money on specials—I get your letters very promptly and the stupid PO here does not deliver special just comes in early mail 8:00 AM and they do not even ring bell—probably in Jackson Heights it will be different—be sure to put c/o Edward Wyman—

Now darling your summary is marvelous—am thrilled to have and to study—Waddell made some adorable crack about Adam being the most maligned of men (and I felt "and little Eve too, brother")—just a darling tough old Scot I take it. *Anyway* I throw in this one thing for you to consider along with the other theories—

Gesell—on babies—in and out of the womb—1000's of feet of film to prove—life goes through phases—distinct. It passes from a symmetrical to bisymmetrical development—then back again, etc etc with a probable weight in humans of the asymmetrical that is, some parts, one side, etc more developed than others.

As he discussed it that night it flashed through my mind—history of human race—two even halves—then a thrown together whole—then weighted in development on one side etc—humanity as the body of one great man, Jesus, a la William Blake—

(This order has no meaning—just various
possibilities—do not remember what Gesell
says came first in womb)

It gives you an eerie feeling to watch the child moving in the womb—the clear asymmetry then the clear bisymmetry—law, Olson—law

I am thrilled if you remember about my hand in yours
the firm fresh feeling is so strong alive in me
I was so *surprised* Olson that you would do it—have never held hands on the street before in my life—and I guessed at once that generally speaking Olson hadn't either, we are not the cute cosy type either of us—I was thrilled—very very—and because I am my old father's daughter I pretended not to notice. More passionate somehow.

◄ 267 ►

Washington to New York City (special delivery)
27 July 1950 (postmark)

thursday

frances: it's crazy, and wonderful, how clear and straight and close I feel towards you. And yet we must admit we were pretty nutty the way we used last week! Just goes to show you how solid this thing is, we got. (I suppose,—I feel that solidity so surely—it is why, when you say you won't write, that you have gone cold, that you are through, that I am swept over by such a sense of life's defeat. For no matter what you did, I should imagine this sense of you, this desire for you, this belief in what we've got, would last—will last—just as long as I do. It is that solid, and you, you move my soul that deep, frances. At the same time, I recognize, that the way I seem to respond to it, the way I conduct myself in relation to it, must seem to you—or to anyone else—straight crazy, straight nutty, straight not-what-anyone-would-expect. And of course I have no answer to that. I can do no thing other than go by my nose. (What is very beautiful—and I say this with no no NO temptation to take any advantage of it, baby: this you must *never* forget, despite any or all appearances—is, that you do respect that kind of craziness. And I'm not sure but what that kind of recognition isn't what we have talked about, what you yourself make the ROOT principle, IS freedom, is *how love can live.* (The same will, in myself, is, I think, what you call my "ruthlessness": my ruthlessness *is* my belief, my belief in you. And my belief in you is, significantly, my belief in life. It is just crazy that I, of all people, should put on you (I don't say "ask" or "expect")— I don't "put it on", I just, out of my necessities, involve myself in, as agent, the putting on—I say it is crazy that, what we have got, should put on you the maximum of, what did we say, COURAGE? And darling, let me say this: the demand does seem to me so extreme, that if you could not bear it, it would not, I don't think, one jot subtract from what *you are inside me* and will stay inside me just so long as this wild machinery I am keeps going. For you seem to me the strongest, most beautiful expression of *what life is* that I have ever known. And I should guess, that if I have taken up my own ruthlessness, if I have been able to *commit* myself to the fate I think now I was born for, it is because you have proved, you do prove by being, something which was my vision, is my conviction, was what I was born with. (It interests me, presents itself to me as the most amazing proof of *how necessary love is*—that love is the *only* gate to life—that I should not have been able, really, to take up belief except as you proved me right! that the individual itself is not enough, no matter how huge its assumption, to lead out—at least to lead out to communication (I'm not at all sure, from my experience in the world, that action is not quite different— and this, I suspect, is its flaw, its deathliness, finally—that action does not require anything more than self-love, that devastating source of power) (I was—and it bothered me considerable,—extremely clear, swift and all-one-piece when I was a man of action. As a matter of fact, it was like a dance (why, I suppose, I distrust the concept "dance"): I was handsome, and I'm sure, if you saw me in that expression, you would not say, "You know, Olson, I really don't like you". For I was all synapse, rhythm, bones-making-straight-gestures-&-decisions, sex. ((You will imagine, baby, therefore, how hard it was for me, in Key West, to put it aside, and take up this other struggle!—And how hard it was (though it fascinated me, how not hard, how not throwing-me-down, back::this, by the way, was one of the *moments*, for me, of recognition of how beautiful you are, in my soul::how hard it might have been, would have been, only such a short time ago, say, Tarrytown, to have you talk abt Duke the way you did, to offset him, sexually, to me)

ANYHOW, what, I figure, makes me what I am, is why I behave as I do, why, babe, you do not "like" me, why this thing unfolds (so far as the "facts" go) in such a weird way, does seem to me a result of (and this is an irony, if there ever was one!) the thing I say love is the gate to, COMMUNICATION!

THERE it is. This is sure a love letter, is it not, frances? And I'll write 'em to you, I rather imagine, just as long as I am a "communicator"! (Can you guess—I know I keep telling you—how wondrous, wondrous, wondrous it is, that you ARE, that I do take myself up and say, Frances, this is love, whatever queer clothes it weareth!?)

And please, baby, however little sense it makes—that is, measured against what we know, what we think is the way things *ought* to behave—don't, all the time, forget that this love lies here right at the very root of my soul, not hidden but, like such things are, beneath all other things, beneath action AND communication!

Yr Charles

One thing that occurs to me: this is one hot correspondence you and I maintain, one hell of an open business. And I believe in it, as you know, want it to stay absolutely so. (I dare say I should have made absolutely clear to you before now that yr letters to me are absolutely yours and mine, now, alone, are even protected by deposit, from anyone else's misuse.) I gathered, from what you sd about your new case, that you carried my letters to you with you to NY. But you also sd, that you leave them unordered, dispersed (which I completely comprehend, which is my own instinctive way of proceeding in all things, why, I hate logic and classification, all "files", and people who file). And suddenly I remembered how Duke rifled yr S.C. apartment, and took off at least my letter to you on MEDEA. And it occurred to me to ask, might he not do it again? Just tell me, what the dispersion is, just so I know. (It is all, as I'm sure you'll recognize, merely that question of the shock intrusion from the outside is, the sort of misuse that a third party always represents, unless they are extraordinarily large human beings—which the people who do look into other's mail are not.)

Just sd, because I have, today, turned my heart out to your big brown eyes, which, by the way, I never told you, are also a part of, how you look at me, inside olson, night & day. Write me, darling, write me—forever!

O - Sun

❧ 268 ❧

New York City to Washington
[28 July 1950]

Friday morning

Charles darling—

Before breakfast I receive your letter and I hasten to tell you several things—one is—that physically being with you for me is absolutely the best— I love it and am terribly terribly satisfied and told you once your beautiful mouth the *most* luxurious I have ever known—*because* I got shy in the to-me-always-present of the young beautiful bodied Connie and so shy I was afraid you wouldn't like me—so shy because I am twice her age and I see in the mirror quite clearly this ancient body of mine torn by such terrible sufferings for so long—and I guess that's why I speak of Duke—just to know somewhere there was a man who found me OK—just shyness darling   the most terrible shyness which I guess comes from the love I feel—have never suffered from shyness before—

I have been around this world *lots* baby. I *know* precisely what you looked and moved like when you were in the world—and I can say—I am happy we did not meet then—because I would have gone straight to that hot power and sex and we would have drowned one another   but now—I received all that from you in a pledge at Woodward—we know each other—understand all the deep mysteries of the intricate beauty of sex rhythms—we know we would have had hours and days of very varied and unimagined connects because every single corpuscle in the body contains a separate beauty—both of us *know* we know what it is   we respect its beauty   we have gone on—and we are both moving out now in a deeper way—far far deeper and more passionate   a silent separate free pouring—mine into life—a form to express my vision—and yours into form to express your vision.

Yesterday Baby I got Lucinda admitted into Packer—a damned good school—just to make sure—because Friends is filled and can only admit Lucinda *if* a child drops out—*do* you know how hard it is when I know how her little heart is breaking to stay up here—break my promise to her about *only* one month—keep on fighting in this dog town and write letters to her when I am simply frantic—

And my friends Olson—who are so proud to know me—one by one by one—filter away and wouldn't do anything for me I need—

Anyway I am *not* going to move in with any man because your letters are so precious to me I don't want any other man even to see the outside of the envelope—I am going to look around for a terribly cheap room maybe in this neighbourhood—but I will stay next week at Jackson Heights because they have a phone and I want to call Lucinda.

Look Darling I will never see Duke again in my life—

Your letters are locked in a very very good trunk in Woodward—the key is here with me—no one knows where they are but me and Duke would never come to Woodward unless I invite him my sister explained to me he stole the letters as a power move—knowing how I love you—because I told him—he thought I would be *forced* to come after them or to ask or do something but I had every word of them locked up in my soul   no one could steal them and I never ever acted as though I noticed they were gone—

If September comes and I have no job I will do what I said long ago   I will be a servant and Lucinda will go to her school and I will have maybe two or three nice things to do freelance—I am on the track of a production freelance thing which will not break for several months—may pick up a very nice commission out of it—will let you know

Oh Charles that baby of mine presses at my heart—she is proud—she will say nothing but I know how her little joyous flesh will begin to wilt—oh darling when you speak of event for a man—did you *include* the suffering of a mother—

Yours in life and death   only for us there is nothing like death—

Frances

◄§ 269 §►

Washington to New York City (special delivery)
28 July 50 (postmark 28 July 1950)

friday july 28 50

baby: it dawned on me yesterday that the reason for yr sudden movements ahead were, the end of the month, and yr loss of that little Pandora box you have had, which, like each place we have been together in—even that deep south hotel!—gets attached to me like the richest sort of places. And it boggles me, suddenly to realize (I am that sort of stupid), that you are tossed again, in the basket!

Which leaves me, of course, absolutely flat-faced, to yr question, would it bother me if you were to live the next month with some guy, Wyman, is it? I honestly don't know. I had that flare-up of jealousy that odi et amo time I thought you were off with Jim Craig—what was it, a week, or ten days after Tarrytown? (It is almost, anyhow—the question—too profound for an answer.)

And it is tied up with the rest of yr three letters which I had yesterday (glad I am that I had written you, as I did, first, just because it came out of the passive, driving place creatures like me speak best from, rather than in response!). For those three letters were so full and sharp and beautiful they stopped me— stopped me, I rather think, more than any other letters (well, literally, stopped me in my tracks, where other letters, o, say, the "vision", or, yr note of Friday last week, or, this week, yr linking of our coinciding on Waddell with the Motz pere who came here armed with one thing, his library and his curiosity, where such letters go straight in to the oldest centers, the heart and the breath, while the last three go, where shall we say, to the younger parts, the gray brain, or what we call, in our fondness, the "higher" centers, the cortex, where so-called thought, and organized reason are—that which makes us civilized, purposeful, that which, (to my surprise, yesterday,—did you notice?—I used quite simply and actually) that which we call the "soul".

You see, darling, I think you are a very wise person. I think you are—and I rarely use this word—impeccable, in those higher centers. I think your answer on the Lust sonnet is impeccable: yet, right there, look at yr "tone":—you are "shocked" I raise it in front of you. Does it not occur to you that, that I call it to your attention at all, is both an act of respect to you as well as an act of already questioning it in my own mind? In other words, why, frances, do you take a moral tone? I ask this quite simply. There is no hidden trick here. Is it yr own way of getting up heat to speak? For there is no question that, as pure statement, the letter that follows is one of the most important posings of Shakespeare as well as of art that I have ever read. So I am not playing. Or twisting yr arm. I am honestly trying to give you back my own precision to yourself. For you will know, that when, as at the end, in opposing Blake to Shakespeare, by the phrase "word wonder", and yr identification of it with man's ego, from, as you curiously put it, almost the start (all this way this side of, perhaps you mean, the Sumerians) you drive right in to my own CENTER, to my own perception of the way things are.

I say, is it yr way of getting up heat, for I know something else about you, my beautiful girl: that your arrogations do not seem to me to be essential, that, on the contrary, they are matters of the time-scheme of yr nerves, and of the forms of articulation which (articulation, that is) you are impatient with. (You do go fast, though I am forever astonished to have you point it out, as you did when we were having dinner—45 times was it, as fast?—when, to me, it seems one of those things which you do, essentially, know I know. (Or do you? You see, that you put it out there on the end of a stick, just bewilders the hell out of me).

I imagine that what I am giving you back is the prick you caused me, in that same letter, when you sd, "what I do not like in Charles, when he is not the poet". Good God, baby, where do you think the "poet", as you call me, comes from? You may remember that declaration at the beginning of Morning News: I am no hero, saint, scamp, crockery breaker.

You see, Frances, I would not have arrived at this point of myself, would not be poet, if I did not profoundly believe that there is, in the act of art, necessary to the act of art, a subjection of the self to the thing to be done which necessarily involves a disposition to life itself which I think you are talking about, in the other sphere, when you use the word "humility" (because I take it that word has lost its "wonder" due to Xtianity). I would use such a word as *modestas*, or, (again the English has lost something, modesty, so that, as I sd last week, I substitute for both, *pudor*

> ((one lovely thing of Apollonius of Tyana, which I don't think I passed on to you, the wonderful posing of pudor at the end of this last paragraph of his conversation with his friend Demetrius the Dog (the Cynic), when Demetrius was trying to dissuade A from going to Rome to face out the Emperor Domitian—who was out to get A, as he had A's friend the philosopher Musonius, whom he put in a straight concentration camp (in fact, an island hell where M died, just exactly like Musso's island hells, and the present Greek gov't holes in the Cyclades!). Here is A:

"Again, I think that a wise man does nothing alone or by himself: no thought of his is so secret, for he has himself as witness to it. And whether the famous saying "know thyself" be from Apollo or from some sage who learnt to know himself ((isn't that beautiful?)) and proclaimed it as a good for all, I think the wise man who knows himself and has his own spirit in constant comradeship ((what abt that, my Motz!)) to fight at his right hand, *will neither cringe at what the vulgar fear* nor *dare* to do what most men do *without the slightest shame*."[7]

O, baby, it is nothing, nothing. The fact is, as you so beautifully put it, in stating in what way the fact that you are a Motz leaves you "bare", is, is, is why you are so beautiful, why I say, anything you do makes sense to me, what it is I love, this Motz, why you suffer yet why you pleasure, why you do, so astonishingly are possessed of, that rare rare thing, pudor.

And that I am sometimes a roughneck, lady, is—let me this once put it out there—because of my own sort of pudor!

7. From G. R. S. Mead, *Apollonius of Tyana*, p. 144; used in "Apollonius of Tyana," *Selected Writings*, p. 156.

Well, enuf of these, the "real" things, for this hot day, and me, somewhy, the last two-three days, sick, maybe summer sick, maybe just worn out, maybe just, like Rimbaud in his barn, rasslin. . . .

You can't imagine how yr reinforcement on Waddell helps. For he murders me, going thru 700 pages of his THE MAKERS, by his bad writing, bad special pleading, despite the fact that I am with him all the way (as you now know). I am beginning to think he is maybe the BIGGEST boy of all—that he had to wait for you & me, for us space-childer, to get the hearing his work demands. (I went so far as to find out if he were alive and to get his address, I wanted so to tell him how fine his work is. But he died in 1938, age 84.) But, when I have mastered his whole work, I want to do a piece on him (probably for my lad Creeley) to awaken the wise to him. It's the kind of job I do not like, this getting caught inside such a huge area of knowledge. It takes me away from my work. But there it is. He earns it, my present impression is. And I'm stuck with it, to do it. By the way, there is one book listed in his biography (WHO WAS WHO, England, 1940), his last last book, 1938, which the Lib Cong does not have! And it looks, from its title, that he took another turn, at the end, for it is something like this: THE TROJANS AS THE CREATORS OF THE WORLD'S CIVILIZATION. It must be that, at the end, he decided (and this was a turn I took in my work a year ago on the Odyssey and its sources) that old TROY was the switch-point of Europe to Asia, and that his claim of Cappadocia as the descent point of the Aryans into Sumer, joined to his speculation that, at an earlier stage, these leader-people came from the Danube, led him (NEW LEADER) to see in Troy the FORGING PLACE.

> ((The Union Cat does not show that there is a copy of this book anywhere in the US. But do check, when you are again at the NYPL, if they happen to have it. I have asked the Lib C to get it.))

What, of course, is one of the very wonderful results of his process, is, that, he starts birds out of his bushes all the time that he cannot, himself, take a bead on—and which excite me all over the place (like yr connect on his Pish-Fish business) It's like a turkey-shoot, to be in there!

I must quit. I hate to leave you. You are so so so sweet to my taste, sweet heart. Take my love and do with it, as you move around, anything you want, handsome thing.

Yr Charles

♀ - sun

New York to Washington
29 July 1950

> Saturday morning
> your special just read

Angel—beautiful—baby—

Oh darling—this is just baby talk   not a letter   just to tell you you do know your Motz's faults—writing words like "shocked" are laziness—I don't know exactly the explanation   I am so patient patient patient with all the cheap small wee ones whose every gesture I notice and then in a great "disgorge" in the presence of my Charles I say "shocked" and then I walk up the street and point out to myself 1. that I love the Russians because they have no such word   2. That Charles *asked* me, so if he asked me must mean he has the old critical eye out—You are right again about the "what I do not like in Charles when he is not the poet" that too I said—to myself "What the hell does that mean, Motz?" Anyway dearest dearest I defend you long before you have received the letter and I do it much more eloquently than Charles could ever defend himself.

But the letter was posted
We suffer—dear—
and we strike out—

The Wyman address is a mail box name so I will get your letters—the husband and wife are both off in the Adirondacks—I am using their very beautiful apartment supplied with Black & White whiskey—how I *wish* you could come there—I have many friends—I forget how and in what ways I have helped but this wife *lived* in my house free six months done with Motz courtesy so I didn't mind accepting while they are out of town.

I have a book on Greek Social Life which proves how right that sudden intuition about Shakespeare's attitude being based on Humanism was   the Athenians *hated* women   at least the *part* of Greece that has come down to *English* public school trained men   We are so right to get a track for ourselves from Iran to Sweden to Ireland to Pennsylvania—leaving *out* these Greeks Hebrews and Romans. Your quote from Apollonius is one of the most aristocratic statements   one of the most beautiful—I have ever seen—I completely buy it,

Dearest dearest Charles you see this is not a letter—can't you understand when you keep putting off since January about coming and you sleep in the same room with a young woman and I feel every second how she separates us and I cannot even protest—I just have to fear it—that maybe that explains why in my mind I *have* to allow myself at least the idea to go and live with someone.

Angel *don't* be sick—I have tried these days to hold myself in hand—not to be sick—and when you are not well—I get so frightened because I think maybe we will never never have a chance—not even one week of all our lives to be together.

And I just hate you to be ill.

And may I stand you and me alone darling in the presence of whatever made us and say I love you

Every part of me is covered and lined with Charles and God I am sure looks on us as on his one being.

For the first time since January I now sleep as I have always—in a kind of innocence.

Your sacred mouth I kiss

Your Frances

❧ 271 ❧

Washington to Tarrytown, N.Y.
29 July 1950 (postmark)

Saturday

frances,

I want this to be there to greet you on your return to Tarrytown, and to tell Elizabeth, by you, how solidly I remember how she & Warren took care of us "chillun", back there when. It is a good feeling to have you there, darling,—& to have you to tell her.

(After I wrote you yesterday I discovered that Henri Frankfort, instead, as I imagined he might, by his evidence, contradict Waddell (he does not, of course, mention W any more than Porada does), Frankfort actually, in striking ways, confirms what even I thought might be "flyers" of W's! Especially on the "Minotaur" Pharoah's cosmetic piece, the long twisted necked animal. And the realistic Indian buffalos.)[8]

And you keep jibing me on Gesell—one day I'll get set, & go into him: what you tell me, is beautiful. And another BASE for getting ahead, driving out the DIRTIERS.

---

8. Olson has been looking at Henri Frankfort *Cylinder Seals: A Documentary Essay on the Art and Religion of the Ancient Near East* (London, 1939).

Blow a kiss for me down into those bottoms![9]

Love
Charles

◄§ 272 §►

Washington to Jackson Heights, N.Y. (special delivery)
31 July 1950 (postmark)

monday

frances: i do not know why all things—any thing—is not possible (i say this
also in answer to yr questions, say, shall we ever live in the same city—any
thing)   it is provoked by a sudden wind this summer day blowing leaves
eaten by Japanese beetles, I suppose, not falling leaves yet, but, the sudden sensation of those leaves, that gust, the sensation of fall, and I muttering to myself, another year torn out of my vitals, then, quickly, correcting it, *this* year
torn out of my guts, and, it said, thinking, fine, fine, no feeling of, as fall, of
loss, but, suddenly, flashing, in my muscles in my balls the sensation, anything,
all things can be

And at the very moment, this moment, I, carrying in my
pocket, yr letters still unoped, this being sd, wild, straight out of, the present
mode, the looking at myself staying in, going along this terrible wire, not even
thread, but wire, wire, and hot with charge, then slackening off, but never,
not, if I can help it, for an instant, letting go the charge, staying in, watching,
to be accurate, even if it is ruthless, watching, considering, what it is, what i
am, where we go from here
Sd to you, for what it is worth, sd, because, god
bless you, (& me, that I have you), that it can be sd to you, strong girl (sd, just
like this, sd, straight,

((and now I read you))

thank you, baby / you see, darling, i do, too, need to be told these wondrous
things! / And I know why you strike out, and do, sweet, when you have to, do
/ ((One wonderful thing, a propos what you say, abt Lucinda, and what it
means to be separated from her, to have to put, at her age, things on her: do
you know that, the other night, in that way that things come to me (such
things come, in a flash, usually, I suppose, from the way other people are, who

---

9. Olson is referring to the field near the river at Tarrytown where he and Boldereff spent their first afternoon together.

keep their attention on life close—I have to, in order to keep the kind of vision I have shaped ((or, I better say now, the way I *used* to!))   they used to come to me, late, slowly, from the stubborn way I insist on letting perception rise up, rather than digging down to it ((I should imagine it is, the difference, because I do distrust—or, rather—have to watch the *speed* of my mind))

((((i am con-
fronted, lately, by this whole area, of, for want of a better seeing of it, you will excuse me if I call, "keeping things out of sharp focus": up to now, working on it, my impression is, that what, right now, I am facing up to, is, the curious time sense I have (it is obviously directly related to this space thing, how, given the corruption of time by humanism (you are pin-point right, here, of course) *in-space* (am i right to dub this the "in-timate") has also been cor-rupted (i wonder if this aspect of the Dirtying isn't peculiarly hard on the male?)

anyhow, i'd hazard the guess, that my time-use, which was, for so long, consciously slow (from errors, & from loss of image, from loss of touch with what I believe in, "space") is now quickening, coming around toward a much more sensible union of mortal time and the space job)))

to get back: the other night, suddenly, thinking of you, the whole business of you, the mother, of the tie of your flesh and Lucinda, of the suffering, rushed into me, filled my whole being—and made me so much the more aware of you, darling, it was beautiful (I was very grateful to life, that I should be per-mitted to feel it)

frances, it is very strange, what is happening, what has—shall we say—just happened? (It was borne in on me so strong, the other day, when you wrote, you distrust this whole matriarchy business! I forgot to tell you, that I, too, had, suddenly, come to reject the whole notion, the whole questioning, pur-suing of it, as—how shall I say—"soft-headed"! And it was very exciting to have you come right in, with the very same rejection!!. Just too goddamned "sociological"

I am so happy to be delivered of it. For I imagine it is of some certain importance. You see, the ambience—the whole dirty present thing—does leave dirt on one, despite the care, the guard. Their dirty generalizing, their forcing our attention off ourselves and trying to break our heads down to their "society" (especially for one like me who so believe in the principle of abstraction): well, I think this last flip of their dirty work on me, of trying to put something so important and precious as this man & woman thing into a parenthesis, matriarchy-patriarchy)—anyhow, I hope—is the last of their gurry I have to clean off (I have enough of my own, not to be bothered by theirs)) / Saw today, this (fr Derek Stanford): "man is a vassal of the external world" (Marx) & "man is a creature of dependence" (Freud) ((Nice job of Stanford's, to pluck out these center rots, no?))

The reason I make so much of it (and risk yr thinking I am still slow in the head, darling!) is, that I do take it one of my jobs is to shoulder history, to make use of it, to make use of the particulars of such human beings I do not know as well as those of this human being I do try to(!) know. And it takes edge, to extricate the persons & principles to be learned in history, from the treacheries of such as the above. (((One other reason why our boy Waddell makes such tremendous sense to me. My god, to have another man who is an euhemerist—and on such a scale as this SCOT! To go by!)))

(I might as well include the other thing which is bothering me. Can you imagine how nervous I get when I am not writing verse? It is terrible frances terrible. Scares the wits out of a man! I feel like an egg, all white & yolk, and not a peep out of him, these days! I look & look & look, for the "escaped cock"! ((It is always so, when I am covering such an intense (to me) area of knowledge as a guy like Waddell involves me in. I go crazy until it is done. But I'm an old hand, know, that I have to do it, that it pays off, oh, say, five years from now! But still on.

Frances, I love you.
(I'm going to run now, and feed myself, and get this off, without a special, risking delivery at yr new address, just to see if the 5 collection makes it. Tell me.)

So much love,
Charles

◄§ 273 §►

Jackson Heights to Washington
[1 August 1950]

Edward Wyman c/o
35-25 77th Street
Jackson Heights, N.Y.

Darling—
I have just received your letter, in the regular delivery—you sent it to the

wrong address (72 instead of 77) and the wonderful post office you dislike has found me—how terrible that I went out yesterday for only 20 minutes and during that time they tried to deliver special—it was very very hard for me yesterday not to have a letter.

It turns out now that I cannot go back to 281 W Bway, so I will probably stay up at Elizabeth's next week, from Sunday night on. There seems to be an apartment for me from the 15th on, I will know in a few days.

This morning I had interviews—one for a very big job—business men are absolute masters at registering no signs of anything—so I have no idea about the outcome—but you will be thrilled that your baby is even considered seriously—the one job is to replace young Mr. Scribner (not young, but is in that family) in a very responsible job actually kind of policy job—between designers, editors, plant—*one* thing I know—the man is *seriously* considering me—I could tell—he never thought of a woman so his reactions kept being fighting what he had been expecting—but he said he was very impressed with the Walt Whitman job—in several weeks I will know—

I found out about two other very big jobs—absolutely top jobs—I feel I have a very good chance and in the meantime the courage job has not shifted over to not taking an OK job but to hold out for one of these very good ones—you see—they are slow—and they won't even hint—but I am going to hold out—because I feel so sure I can *do* them, if I can get a chance.

Anyway darling—after all the years I have been working it is a *beautiful* sensation to *feel* the respect—*feel* it come out of their pores against their intuitions, especially from a man of the non-sexy aristocratic type I saw this morning. I believe the man I talked to is a son-in-law.

The Balzac book of course was like being in bed with you—I understand why you wanted me to read it[10]—pretty hard to keep reading—when it was arousing such a terrific sex response and no letter—

I received as a gift today the new testament in Russian and it is so easy for me to read and it sounds—so so beautiful—some day I will read aloud to you—Strange life—strange Frances—so delicate and sensitive and clean, Mr. Balzac.

And we are 1000 miles ahead of where that world was—

Each of us carrying such a terribly full load of nervous treading.

Looked up Waddell—no book you asked about.

10. The particular book referred to here is not known.

Kirgo has found me Jane Harrison's *Themis*   If I buy do you want to see—or do you have it. Looks very fine.

Feel like breaking out into Russian which has 16 words in which to say "I love".

Frances

⊰ 274 ⊱

Washington to Jackson Heights, N.Y.[11]
1 August 1950 (postmark)

tuesday

darling, just to send, right to the gate of, and into, your sweet mouth a kiss of love, for this day, when i am confronted with a major task, which may take me too long to give me the delight of writing you some of my heart and mind (dahlberg's book, published in england, has come, and calls for an answer both for it and for the inscribing of a section of it to me)[12] Nor should I say it is such a burden as task implies, though I go with fair & careful feet into this sort of swamp of images which are equally my own but stick up, from his use, in such a differing way from what I have done and will do with them, that, as I say, I have to go easily and thoroughly (But it is made so much easier by a fact he does not know, but that you and I do: for it is an astonishing thing, that he has made the Bellerophon section a lecture to me, without, I think, knowing, that when he identifies me with Bellerophon, he gives me another Aryan birthplace! For B is an undisclosed Sea-Man, Sea Sumerian (by way of Crete), intimately bound up with that mystery place (to the Greeks that is) Asia Minor, specifically the rich delta of the Pyramus River (with chief port TARSUS)! (Yet I better not yet decide Ed does not know. For he is a subtle serpent, my friend. And even if he does not know, he knows.)

The whole thing leads me another step on into that place I have so long been hungry to know more of, where, every step I take, new figures of my "family" turn up. One thing we must do, darling, is to come to know exhaustively ASIA MINOR. For it is the BRIDGE west & north, no question. (Did I tell you that the Tyana Apollonius came from was also Cappadocian?) And you

---

11. Olson again sent this letter to the wrong street number and it did not reach Boldereff until 11 August 1950. By the next letter he has received the correct address.

12. Edward Dahlberg's *The Flea of Sodom*, just published by Peter Nevill in London, contained a Part IV ("Bellerophon") preceded by a paragraph entitled "Homage to My Friend, Charles Olson." For Olson's struggle (and failure) to write a review of the book, see *In Love, in Sorrow*, pp. 135ff.

know how much the Ionian physicists were (later) my boys. (And that it was apparently thru that gate that Gotama Buddha's thought, the antidote to the religious, as it rotted west-wise, came in secretly to western life.) ((Again Apollonius,—his visit to the Buddhists, and his cleansing of religion all thru the west, in the lst century AD)).

I feel so very close to you, baby.

Yr lover,
Charles

I'll post this, now, early, and if things go well, hope to write again, today. My arm *is* around yr waist.

275

Washington to Jackson Heights, N.Y. (special delivery)
2 August 1950 (postmark)

Wednesday

frances, baby: It's always, my damnation, time, I think one can get so much in, & then the bitch is gone, never is as fat as I think it is, two hours are wiped out, and I look for them, & want to cry in rage like a child! (It's this Dahlberg upheaval, & a Creeley answer called for, today, which has spilled the hours, but always, *always*, there's not enuf hrs. in the g.d. day for me to get in what I dream of).

So do forgive me this pen & hand, sweet. But I hammered that machine until 10 last night, giving it to Dahlberg, on Bellerophon—& today to Creeley on the magazine (plus another letter to try to help him raise the 350 bucks he & Leed need to print issue #1).

For all this merely cheats me of the time I crave to spend writing to you, my precious thing. On top of that, I'm damned sore: for obviously mail to Jackson Heights stinks, if, at 9 PM last night (yr letter is so postmarked) you still had not received my *special* of Monday. (And thus this may beat my note to you yesterday!) Oh, baby, come back to our little "flat" in Canal St! where I can be sure, at 8 A.M., you *hear* from me, sweetest girl! (But blow a kiss, too, in Woodward, handle something I have, lady)

But the waste has not been waste. I got the whole Dahlberg book straightened out (myself, in relation to it: you see, darling, it caught me, right in the midst of the effects on me, of this Waddell. And this whole Semite question. Plus my permanent, terrible crux, of sensibility OR FORM.

(One thing I must talk to

you about, soon, is the whole redisposition I feel going on, in this lad of yourn, of his mind & taste as against his drive & blood: crucial passage, my Lady of This Wild Thing!

And each important thing that comes up, takes a new try of that new disposition!

(So,—and it is so deep I'll not venture to spell it out now—what hit me in yr letter today, was, "how terribly I am trembling", you said, how that you say such things to me (I hear, love,) how they go way, way in, to the strange center of me I am only beginning to comprehend.

YES, that's the feeling—that I am only now *beginning* to comprehend, to *wake up*! Now, I am so aware of you (love has made me so aware) I know this does not surprise you, my wise one, but it does astonish this citizen, that he slept! (Which, in turn, involves this whole question of FOCUS, & of FORM—at least how a poet gets *his* form; this whole Holderlin question, "squeeze yr art fr life, blood, squeeze life fr art"; & for a space-creature, it is time: or was! Oh, Frances, you just watch! I'll tell you, too, have to: (I make love to you!)

THE QUESTION, now pressing in, is HOW MUCH HAVE I, this kink, SLEPT!

(Oh yes, I am *not* ill, in fact, today, even, have cleared away (or was it the storm) the ashes in the brains this filthy swamp-place heat brings down! So don't, baby, worry one jot. I'll not mention such things, either. Agree *absolutely* with you, they DON'T MATTER.)

Hello, HEAD—for have I told you, since Tarrytown, how overwhelming that head of yrs is, how I love it, *all* that it is & does, what passes over it, how it moves & changes, every particle of it, like as though it were *all* nature's things in one beautiful place? webs, wind, speech, colors, flowers, earth, sky, planets, bugs, every changing, unchanging thing? You cannot imagine, my girl, how my hands so often crave to be on it, in it, just to hold it, to feel its extraordinary life, its eyes, teeth, skin, hair, warmth, speech. Oh, baby, despite all things, KNOW, KNOW, *forever*, darling, KNOW!

Let this be my love & presence for today
Yr man, Olson

◆§ 276 §◆

Jackson Heights to Washington
[3 August 1950]

Thursday

Charles darling—

You said my voice sounded cold—yours darling sounded so young—so rich—like smooth powerful shining flesh stepped forth from maiden-bathed pool.

I woke at 3:20—I wanted you.

I wanted you so powerfully all night that I am exhausted now.

I cannot write Baby—I am off in a few moments for another appointment—it is raining hard and I shall have to go through the entire day in Manhattan—with no bed to lie on and dream that I am bringing you near to me.

Baby darling—as I see your purity under the heading "no holiness here"—do you not see how bright my wings are burning—

Your Frances

≈ 277 ≈

Jackson Heights to Washington
[3 August 1950]

Thursday night

Charles darling—

I ran around all day wetter than a little Woodward animal—dripping—*but* baby, have to tell you—thought of you all the time—spent from 11:15 AM right through to 3:00 PM with the head of National Labor Relations Board in NY and we hit it off like 2000000 dollars *and* baby, very big things are now bursting over my horizon—I am dying to see you—this man is really in in New York and he sits there and says "If we get you a big time job in NYC will you promise to go back to Penn State at the head of a University Press when we get it set up?—Anyway, very big plans baby—please Charles I trust you—say no word to no man—they are two years off—in the meantime—he said when he left me—"you and I have lots of work to do together, right?"

And oh! baby I am bursting—he is fitting me up with a date with the president of New York Employing Printers—he is going to Britain for 3 weeks so can not introduce us but he said "Don't worry, he'll see you and he knows everyone and he will help you."

Despite all this I have that uncertain feeling of a mother with no money in her purse

But baby, the future seems about to break for your little Motz and of course in the end what that means is—Charles and I form some alliance so powerful no one can break us because what I see is—*power* to get my Baby published by the big right people, only I will have to be subtle as a serpent—but let the two of us get power and then we'll have something to see—

Please say no word no word to anyone because I actually want this thing so much because of what I can do with it—I am scared to voice aloud even to you—the *only* person on this earth I am telling.

Your Frances

I have your special and I am so open to you all day long darling it embarrasses hell out of me—had lunch some big ritzy place and I was afraid the men could see Olson lying right up in there tight and high.

⊸ 278 ⊷

Washington to Woodward[13]
3 August 1950 (postmark)

thurs

darling, just a note to find you "home". For it is all i am going to be allowed, due to Waddell. It is now after 7, and it has taken me all this day, & under pressure too, to get my notes done on him (the book was due last night, and must go there now, before they close). So that I don't lose that extraordinary privilege, to borrow books there.

just to take hold of yr hand, quick, like this.

And to say i have crossed six toes, and seven horns for you, that the scribner's shot may work out. I'm still not sure what it is all abt: our conversation was straight crazy, you were at first so distant. But o, baby, how good it was to hear the motz at least gurgling there in her throat a little!

let me hear the whole story. Tho don't you for a moment think, you're going to show yr muscle at me, little iron-hand-threatener! I'm impervious, my love! Muscle, what's muscle? good to eat?

The way you is, angelic & other-wise, is Ok by me, just as you is, anytime.

(Best thing today, out of W, I must tell you: that MINOS died of a wasp's sting in Ireland! And is buried on Knock Many, near Crogher, country Tyrone!)[14]

Will add anything pertinent when I pick up today's mail, on way.

All, all love,
Charles ♀

p.s. I must have been ALL OFF, as of the phone—for your beautiful letter (how do you call it "dumb"?) is so good, so full of yr warmth & drive! O,

---

13. Olson marked the envelope "Hold, for arrival."

14. L. A. Waddell's *The Makers of Civilization*, pp. 286–91, is the source for this legend, which appears in "All My Life I've Heard about Many" in *Maximus Poems*.

Frances, *look*—I shall try to see that you get something every day, if I possibly can: you mustn't be hurtled down by one day's miss, baby. I'll try

> Love & yrs
> Charles

◄ 279 ►

Washington to Woodward
4 August 1950 (postmark 4 August 1950)

> friday august 4 1950

lady frances:

before i say a word myself i am going to send you a present i found for you yesterday, these words of a noble Abyssinian woman:

> How can a man know what a woman's life is? A woman's life is quite dif-
> ferent from a man's. God has ordered it so. A man is the same from the
> time of his circumcision to the time of his withering. He is the same before
> he has sought out a woman for the first time, and afterwards. But the day
> when a woman enjoys her first love cuts her in two. She becomes another
> woman on that day. The man is the same after his first love as he was be-
> fore. The woman is from the day of her first love another. That continues
> so all through life. The man spends a night by a woman and goes away. His
> life and body are always the same. The woman conceives. As a mother she
> is another person than the woman without child. She carries the fruit of the
> night nine months long in her body. Something grows. Something grows
> into her life that never again departs from it. She is a mother. She is and re-
> mains a mother even though her child die, though all her children die. For
> at one time she carried the child under her heart. And it does not go out of
> her heart ever again. Not even when it is dead. All this the man does not
> know. He knows nothing. He does not know the difference before love
> and after love, before motherhood and after motherhood. He can know
> nothing. Only a woman can know that and speak of that. That is why we
> won't be told what to do by our husbands. A woman can only do one thing.
> She can respect herself. She can keep herself decent. She must always be as
> her nature is. She must always be maiden and always be mother. Before
> every love she is a maiden, after every love she is a mother. In this you can
> see whether she is a good woman or not.

> fr. Frobenius, Leo *Der Kopf als Schicksal*
> Munich, 1924, p. 88[15]

---

15. Olson's source for this translation is not at present known.

to go to you, swiftly,

love,
charles

❧ 280 ❧

Washington to Woodward[16]
4 August 1950 (postmark)

fri

Her head was in my hand, and, it were,
as though all nature had been given
me, as though, beneath this hair my fingers traveled in was kept
the secrets of the movements of all other things, of trees
green in the evening's light, of rocks which dance when water
when the sea is strong and the sun is morning white, her teeth
which thought moves, the lips like speculation, like
kisses, her skin (behind the flowers & facts there's always
ground) behind the colors & all shifting forms, the living flesh
begrunden, the carapace of bones, a face is worthless, (the voice)
until it carries in itself the life lived, what the springs
by pouring out have registered, the recognition
cognition brings, the spiders, wasps, the hummingbirds or snakes,
whatever activity the human facts have likened to, this woman's
eyes, thus brown, pink, white and tender
head[17]

baby: just to put my hand in, again, and we shall both, shall we not, just be
lazed & romantic about it, for the moment, letting him get away with it, just
because, he's stiff,

                    and art and thought do not go together, that is, when the
labor of thought is going on, which has, now, a bit too long, been true.

                                                            (This
problem of focus, in & out.)

    16. Olson wrote on the envelope: "if necessary, forward to c/o livingstone, 209 s. broadway, tarrytown, n.y."
    17. These verse lines, based on the last paragraph of Olson's letter of 2 August 1950, have not been previously published.

And time: how, when it's pressured, by knowledge or economics, no birds sing.

I am in the passage over, I'd imagine, feel on me, today, that peculiar crave, to drift—for five minutes to drift is all one needs, to swing free—and back one rushes, hard, tough, sure, illuminated. It is so strange how little is needed, but how hard to get! How to sit square in the CENTER is not easy! (And what I have been about, is to get THE CENTER, from which the race—not I—shall move.[18] SO we won't mind, will we, if his language is not yet in his mouth?

IT will be, or he dies.

(Handsome thing, how are you? what are you doing at this hour? I suppose I better write you next, to Tarrytown, but I linger on Woodward, where you were so long my goddess (don't jump: he'll not fall back! you sd, i'm not yr sister, and he was ready to hear, knows now, is sharper, wiser, knows this Motz is, precise, herself, particular woman as he is man, whatever image or images she also is (he may be, may find out

Put it this way: I know more—know in a sense more interesting than knowledge—but I am not able yet to make use of it.
We could call it the confusion of
love.
Charles

[*On back of envelope:*] What vie de Balzac was it?

⊷ 281 ⊷

Washington to Tarrytown
5 August 1950 (postmark)

sat

f, lady, lady f: jumpy as bugs today   don't know why can't get on/ down   crazy/real crazy maybe air: fall, full of fall, cool—& me, shiverin   feel damned amurrikan (matter of fact full of interest in my fellow countrymen, particularly the lads who came out of the war, recently)   it may well be merely the spill over of the father, goddamned mad they have to be led along

18. Olson was the same day writing the letter to Robert Creeley that became the essay "The Gate and the Center," later included in *Human Universe*.

by this wrong, wrong, wrong State (in fact it took the craziest form, this week: i had a drive to go out there to korea! amazing, for a cool one, like yrs: never happened before (not even, really, in the Spanish War, tho something like) must be fatherism (god, god, these events: been cryin for years, in fact fought like hell days Dec '41 after, to get this damned administration to keep its eye on Pacific, not on Europe), been cryin, the armageddon (yours, boys!) is comin on the plains of A-zhah. But could you get the damned Colonials to recognize their own drive? No no no.

O god it's sad ("It was sad, it was sad, o! when that great ship
            went down, to the bottom of Men and women lost
            their lives, little children made their cries It
            was sad, it was sad[19]

And i see no end to it, no end at all (i used to play soccer, won ma lettah, in fact!, and i always oppose that dance of the elbow, head, foot with ball to politics: i watch this security council like i did back not so long ago when i war adviser to an unnamed foreign power, and i moan, moan, moan, know their dirty game so well, know how truth is utterly fled, from all of them, all of them stuck with fast buck & easy blood, and their hands dirty, dirty, dirty, and no way out, no way until man makes every discovery all over again

It is a most strange time. It will strike you as crazy, but would you guess, darling, that the change in these streets, the change in Wilson's counter lunch where i eat afternoons, the change in this city, is the FIRST TIME i have felt how war reaches in his hand? and it moves me no end, makes me jumpy, maybe, anyhow makes me almost go out there and take this bloody god damned foolishness on myself, like a necessity

                              Crazy as all hell. And won't, of course, will, believe one must, just, like a rat from the ruins, get out from under this stupid stupid wrong time. Just because i believe with my healer, Apollonius, that, as he sd, the beautiful guy, faced with that emperor and with, maybe, a like rotten time to our own: THE MOMENT THAT SUITS WISDOM BEST TO GIVE DEATH BATTLE.[20]

                              (Sweet love, goddamn it that you suffer in the night like yr thursday letter says. You see, babe, it is—oh, goddamn it, tell me, is it worse 'cause I let you know how physically beautiful you are, I mean, in letters let on to you how I too crave? Tell me. For it's. . . .aw,

19. Words from this American folk song "The Titanic" occur again in "On First Looking Out through Juan de la Cosa's Eyes" (*Maximus Poems*, p. 84).
20. *Selected Writings*, p. 155.

i'm in no mood to be wise. Let me just tell you. God damn everything—anyhow, today I damn damn damn.

But at the same time, know, frances, that this is a letter meant to give you all yr baby, to be there when you bring Lucinda to Tarrytown again, to touch you on base, to give you every ounce of warmth at this time, love. Your old man is puttin it out, darling, straight to you.

One suggestion, one asking: i know it takes time (i am always amazed at the discrepancy between how long it takes to make a letter as against how short it takes to read it), but do, if you can, when you can, spill out all details of your days, and nights, what you don't like, I think, because of your wondrous speeds, narrative, detail, the facts, which, in your genius, you are intolerant of. I say this out of an olsonism, out of a belief in particulars not as important in themselves but as CARRIERS, as notation: for the way they get themselves down is such a revelation of the senses, those healers, both back and out, I say,—saying it quietly, making no push, just asking, asking, sweet

(A creeleyism, which i think you'd like: a propos all of those bastards whom he and i (this is one class you don't have to put up with!) have to take so much shit from, editors, he proposes: Idiots Anonymous.)[21]

(((((OW, i feel motz go cold, go foot, go bare, go cold. All right, baby, all right. Remember: it takes all winds to make a whirl!))))

Do, somehow, offer elizabeth & warren my affection. Now that you are there i should like to be able to do something i have wanted to do for a hell of a long time: have you pass them direct a copy of y & x. But there we are again (as you lifted that eyebrow): olson is as bad as crosby! I don't have any! But one day when i will, we will do it, little thing ((do you know how little a big thing you is: olson breaking down, like holding hands, into baby talk! look at that! but you is—and it ain't coz olson's big, it's coz you are or we are that close it comes out that possible, that you is, tough one, also (me too) able to be at ease (which is the nicest sort of a way of being, is it not?)

Look, honey girl, this is to say, hello, baby, and to wrap up, by these words, which are only words, one hell of a big character in this sheet of white paper, and deliver to motz at the birthplace,

O

21. *Charles Olson & Robert Creeley: The Complete Correspondence* 2:90; Creeley's letter of 2 August 1950.

Washington to Tarrytown
7 August 1950 (postmark)

monday

frances, darling
      If I'd had paper this would have been written to you in the sun. Which is better, today, for inside makes me very stifled and distraight. Result: no work done. In fact I've fled the house and my mood *twice*, once to see if I had any letters from you, and, again, when I found nothing was issuing from me, to the Lib Cong to get the texts for a project I shall try to see the issue of before I tell you, but which is so close to you, starts back so near a year and a half ago, that I have gone along today with your hand grasped square in mine, lady.
      But today the big news is yours, anyway, the *big kill* you have written about. Great huluppu tree, Frances, but that is something! It sounds so extraordinary I don't, myself, can't see how such things come into existence. Not that you don't deserve same, or that you oughtn't to provoke 'em; but I never knew the world to contain such daring & such projection as this feller plots with you! Wow, two years out—and you, like a Dimaggio, being played for New York waiting for the seasoning of a new Pennsylvania big league business! It's straight crazy, & wonderful. Do you think it's actually there, in the cards,—what assurance have you that such a press is planned? how come it is the NLRB? is it gov't publishing? Do let me know more. And I shall keep the trap shut. (Need never worry, on that score. I have a mouth as controlled as imaginable, despite the use it gets, or because of. I despair, times like these, when I can't get down to flow as far as silent words go, that I am such a master of my own tongue vocally. But I am, and there it is, nothing to do abt it, at least right now. So you can always trust me.)

      I am frightfully unhappy today, terribly restless, and groundless. Don't like it a bit. Am puzzled & angry. But you mustn't pay it any mind, for, by the time you read this, I imagine I shall be out of it, and on. I just tell you, to let you know that I am without generation at the moment. And what a hell of a state for a character in my trade to be in! One thing one is never permitted in this business: to ride a day. Nor an instant. And it is killing. One thing I hope you are doing, or wish you might, when you read this, in case I am not over it: hold me close and tight in there, with those wonderful arms of yours around, all over me, strong, that strong way motz can be, wild & strong, that beautiful way. For I could use it, my love, I could use it. (You have got so particular, so close, that I almost don't dare to let my flesh and image run. In fact, it is both a problem of work and of letters, this. I admit to some puzzlement, how it got this way and what to do about it! I whisper that to you. It is of some critical importance. I could easily, at this moment, tell you a lot of very straight desire. But I won't, not to tease at all, but to let it come when I am grounded, darling, and full of speech. Right now all I want is your arms, and some very rich and steady silence.

Your man,
Charles

⊰ 283 ⊱

Washington to Tarrytown
8 August 1950 (postmark)

tuesday

frances:

    I'm in the midst of a going ahead of work, perhaps   But i want to stop to get off something to you early enough to get you tomorrow (the damned change in collections, so that the last one is so early in my working day as 7:30 evening, is a nuisance, and deprives me of the chance to write you when I am fresh, either before i go to work or after) ((And i won't, sweet, if you'll forgive me today, go downtown to get yr letter before I write, at least not this early))

    What I can do is, make copy for you, as I go along, of what's coming out under hand, and though it won't be the equal of a letter, for you, to you, you will please baby take it as a real communication, a way of solving a problem which, at the moment, due to my own loss of stride, is troubling me. In fact I'm going to push myself a little just to see if I can salvage and make lines right now ahead good enough to interest you!
    (You do understand, that, when language is coming hard, a creature like me is no good, no good at all, an animal in a trap gnawing off his own limbs, waiting wildly, forcing frantically to get off, on, out into his proper place.)

    So I'll go to it now, and send off what comes with this day's love to you in the mail which is picked up one half hour from now.

    This, and the enclosed, is to bear you this
day's love,

thank you, baby! You see, how, under hand, it ramm'd way out beyond one half hour, one half as draft, to something, maybe, which has use—

we'll see,

you tell me, & I'll go along!

I'll send this special, keep it open, to see if your letter says where you'd rather have it than T, if so where

—so, love, goodnight
Charles

[*Enclosed: carbon copy of "Bigmans II" as published in* Collected Poems*, pp. 149–54.*]
[*on back of envelope:*] tues nite: nothing at P.O.—so sending tarrytown.

•≈ 284 ≈•

Washington to Tarrytown (special delivery)
9 August 1950 (postmark)

wednesday

frances, child:

I have fifteen minutes until the five o'clock collection. I have just received your letter of yesterday.[22] I hope I am right that you figured a day's lee-way for yourself. In any case, I'm going on that basis, and, instead of wiring you, enclose special (I have an insurmountable horror of W U)

I am sending all I have, that is, all but a couple of bucks to go on the rest of the week. Look: you can depend on me for the other half, but it will take me a little time to gather it together. (I should imagine this is to make up for what you had to put down for the place, right? ((I am trying to figure out a date I can promise it, so you can plan on it)) I can't. You spell out what this does, as of the moment, and whether the pressure is continuing, and I'll do everything I can. I need a little warning.

Today has been a washout, so far as work goes. As a matter of fact, the push yesterday was enough, I guess, at the moment. I was thinking, actually, that I ought to work on some other schedule—not expect myself to turn out verse every day, but alternate, and then come up fresher.

22. Frances apparently announced she had found an apartment and needed money. The letter is missing.

And you shouldn't, frances, be put off that days are when you do not feel close. Hell, if we were living together, it would be so: one moves in as many directions as one contains, and if one is a go-er, then one goes, and the whole heart with it, no? And if one is a worker on top of it, then discharge is terrific.

I'll run now, to get stamps, and get this off fast. And write you at yr new place, baby. And do settle down as soon as you can, and write me as fullsome as you can. (One day I should like to get thirty pages!)

Love,
Charles

⋅⋚ 285 ⋛⋅

Tarrytown to Washington
[9 August 1950]

Wednesday

Charles darling—

What I am wishing is that you could run up to New York this weekend— we are both so full—and there is so much to tell you—you see darling—I do surround you—the weekend was torture to me because I was so full and I am not a mean person and to be under such a heavy obligation—Harold driving me up to Woodward—staying in the Inn—being my devoted slave—helping me, helping me—and noticing that all I care about is letters and I feeling so full—and having to act so cold, so there would be no border crossing—and he drove us all the way to Tarrytown and oh! baby you know that instinct of a female like me to open herself to reward people and when I wanted you so terribly to have to be near a man you owe thanks to and treat him like a stranger—it was very hard and I wondered if any man darling would act with such terrible deep integrity.

I want to tell you all all about my New York business—I probably will not know any details for a long time, because they are so *slow*, but the big league in Pennsylvania *is* real dope.

I expect to be in Jackson Heights to pick up my things Friday afternoon— home Friday Saturday Sunday—my apartment bell is numbered 4 and if my name is not yet on it, it will say Supt Eckholt, or something like that—as the front door is locked and there is no phone. Try baby—5 Monroe Place. Where I stood and said my sentence about Queequeg!

Frances

My apartment is in the back—second door on left when you enter, same floor as you enter.

◄ 286 ►

Washington to Brooklyn[23]
10 August 1950 (postmark)

thursday

baby lady, i have dug the enclosed up to begin to bring the total as fast as possible to what you asked   now i know to have it coming in in pieces is neither the answer nor as useful, for it is apt to disperse itself   but do, sweet, put it away in a book or something, you gather it as i send it, until you have it in lump, which is the way i wish i might give it to you in the first place

anyhow, i worry about it, and this is a beginning to put aside the worrying! hope that to know it is going to come is of some help, can at least give you operating space! keep in touch with me, how you are on these things: don't, above all, feel desperate   it's crazy, money, it can always, somehow, i swear, be taken care of   at least it *has* to be: it ain't *that* important—if it exists at all!

i have the goddamndest way of going on as though there was a fountain (like Picasso says he goes to the communist party!) as though the fountain were there, when, and if i needed it! damn thing is, it is!   have hit some moments where it wasn't, but found a little stirring (priming, i better keep the image!) brought it up   (((i dare say i told you about the time a check to my mother bounced on her, and that four days before that sort of sentimental time, Xmass!   but that was miscalculation, due to a floating check a guy had not cashed for eight months, not, god save me, from trying anything funny!))   (((but i was reminded of another terrible time, the other night, when i ran into a guy i have only seen three times (and each time, as he was also superstitious enough to point out, *on the eve of war!*) But it was the first time that sticks in my mind: 1936–7, and i on a vessel, coming into new york, and broke for the last three days, not even a nickel for the steward, least of all for a drink, and this guy looks up, and says, hel-lo, you look interesting or something, won't you sit down And he stakes me for poker, and i win, and—o, god—i walk off that ship like a king and into a cab and am safe, safe, safe!   ((((& get me, sometime, to tell you the story of Doner and LaDine, when Doner was working for a junk yard on 9th Avenue, and taking himself to the Brevoort for supper with the last damned dollar or two to his name; and she, sitting across a couple of tables, and loaded with Walter Duranty's money, and looks into that crazy face, with those loaded, indecent eyes, and the pack on his back like mythology, and his manners, pederastic

---

23. Addressed to Frances Bolderoff, 5 Monroe Place, Brooklyn 2, N.Y. "(Please hold for arrival)"

or not; anyhow, they take up, and she dresses spangled for him, and takes him to Harlem, and from there. . . .))))

And all this time I want to be talking to you about something else, about something which really matters, if i could get it said, for it comes at the end of a wretched day, when i have wondered if my nerves and mind and body were going to sever, or stay together, from the going along, from the terror who-am-i, what-is-it-what-is-it-what-is-it.

                              The sudden recognition of something i have said, (but you know how the saying so often precedes the knowing, that is, the actual comprehension of the energy for self-use), how i said it i don't remember (i lie, i do, i only want to say it now again new, with the energy—or so i think that is the only way the energy is finally able to be present—with the energy now taken up by me, not by, you might say, my brain or mouth—

How to begin? Let me begin with what i did say, o, almost two years ago now, to a body of listeners black mountain. I was trying to state in what way the archaic or primordial is not at all "past", in what way we are as participant in it right now as we are in what we call "reality," that is, personal or public events contemporary to us at this moment. I created this image: that we are a perpendicular axis of planes which are constantly being intersected by horizontal planes of experience coming in from the past (coming up from the *ground*—or, like you say, that *underground tide*) and going out to the future, and that it is at the innumerable points of intersection that images and events spring up which are like tastes in the mouth (Proust was wrong to stop there, and go to that time-nonsense, memory), like fantasies or visions (here is where the mystics go off the rails), like illusions of power (here, the religio-mystics), like images (here, the poets), like allegories (here, all moralists, who read it as writ large, as larger than, as generalizations, as visitations) etc—and like dreams (here, even Freud, yah)

"*are*" not "are like" all the above, *is*, is *energy* present, alive, for *use*

in other words, that there is a definable and discriminate *other part* to experience than that which we have been led to call the personal or realistic—and, and this is the important added element of today's illumination (see below on why it is not naive, so far, that is, as this citizen goes!)—*and that it can be recognized and dealt* with, *must*, in fact, in order to be engaged in, taken up from, and must be seen as, to all intents and uses, just as solid and constant and present as the so-called rational, egotistical, realistic

and that it is this other part
that, recognized, made up what we call the old human science!

Now i am not
fool enough to think that it is going to be easy to restore this area to an equal
share with personal reality ((i'm not trying to be careful on that side, for the
moment of definition: you know what I mean: the way we take our conscious
selves as more the business of our day than the unconscious—I expressed our
natural irritation somewhere in the midst of today's struggle, thus:

((i have had the dirtiest kinds of dreams—i mean dirty in the sense of old confusions, not dirty dirty!—the last two-three nights))

> the detriment of dream, the dirt
> of other possiblities, what was
> what was what was what won't
> (detritus, even with the newness of the day)
> go away

to get back, it will take how many ages, generations, to get man back to the ad-
mittance of these points where his own axis crosses axes common to men past
and ahead *and also common to all contemporaries* by the *ground*.

nor do i think that it will be easy for this citizen to take it up *as he must* into
equal recognition

(i use recognition instead of consciousness, simply because I
don't believe it is possible for one to handle it consciously. In fact, i think this is
of the nature of the rub of it, that the instrumentation to bring it into operation equal to the ease with which consciousness enables us to bring the other
part so much more "naturally" or "easily" forward) ((the whole bitter questions is, the *intelletto*, which is most able where the realisms are, and not at all
the equal of *will*, or, what i take to be more the equivalent of will than action:
the *imagination,* the *staying open*))

this staying open, now, at a time when there
are not only no instrumentation, but not even a guess that the area exists at all!
becomes terribly difficult, for the way it unhinges all usual procedures of the
rational, personal, realistic life

((i sd naive above, and i go on writing with the
sense that you probably are so advanced that you will take this as laboring the
obvious; but do, baby, tune in, and listen, for the little man is dishing up quite
a lot of result out of the past going on nine months, and is—hopes he is—beginning to bind up something here))

it is really quite simple. i was born with this perception. but i have had to struggle out with it in a world which not only didn't give me any hint of its existence, but also intimidated me by its apparent clarities of the real in the face of my own continuing confusions (i, the more vulnerable, that my mind is good enough to enjoy the fruits of the mind, which are certainly—even tho i now add, only—clarities, sharpnesses of outline, both of things and of oneself

((i sense my troubles have been, that the sharpness of outlines—which i now think the *other part* leads one more richly to, in the end—are very precious to my temperament
of course, how else would i be a poet?))

you see, darling, what excites me, is, that i have—perhaps for the first time—admitted, that the images and events which i have found floating in myself are *not* merely images and events but are *energies* as legitimate for myself and for others as the "thoughts" or "reports" or mere "sense perceptions" of the Old Misleaders

in other words, that here, where my imagination has grown and fed, my will and daily life must also, just as obediently, grow and feed!

there i think it is, in a nutshell

BUT THAT SAID, is a long way, for a slow nordic emerger, from finding out how, daily, to make use of it, how to keep it clear from all above listed treacheries, how to be such a custodian of it, both for myself and for others, that, eventually, we can bring it back into the world as a REALITY as much (I'd say more) useful than the other

I am frightened, honey-girl, of the putting it in to operation, i confess, frightened at what it involves, scared pee-less at what happens to my language (this, always, is a worry like a child!)—that, of course, much more than what happens to my life!—

terribly aware, of how much it asks, both of the will as imagination and the intelligence as not rational shaper or perfector but as sharpener of the—what did they call it—the intuition, the holy ghost, my own NOSE?

(that he who has said: go by the nose, bro., should suddenly, at this late date, see what it involves! (ho-ho, fran-ces!)

I am full of chagrin that I may not have got this out the equal to its perceiving. I don't honestly think it's easy, or to be confused with any similar contemporary advances, simply because it is a darkness, this whole area, and a darkness we have just poked our noses into.

I'm sure, for one thing, that because THERE IS NO INSTRUMENTATION AT ALL IN EXISTENCE, one has to be pin-point and over-scrupulous with one's use of one's own life to make the damn thing STICK
        (i am thinking, at the moment, of only Lawrence as, at least
        among men, as one who seems to have done it right, used his per-
        sonal life cleanly, correctly, so far as he could advance it, the area)

well, darling, let's just say i got it down, as a beginning motion, and that the discovery of its energies is yet to come

(and please say anything back—in fact *all*—you are of a mind to, sweet
                                this is
                                am-o
                                Charles

                        ❧ 287 ☙

New York City to Washington (postcard)
11 August 1950 (postmark)

                                Friday noon

Charles—
    I received your special—wish to thank you very much and to tell you you did everything exactly right way.
    Found out I have lost both Scribner and another thing—to men.
    Have had a chance to read Bigmans II only once but my first impression is new speech and vital speech. Was furious to see Harpers with a 2 column hunk of photos of poets—no Olson—they are *dumb*.
                                Frances

❧ 288 ❧

New York City to Washington
11 August 1950 (postmark 12 August 1950)

Friday evening

Charles darling—

I am in Gusti's house and just this moment have read your note of August 1—sent regular mail to the wrong address—it is a wonderful note—makes me feel so warm and near you—I love notes where you tell me any little thing about Charles—his mind.

It will be so good tomorrow darling when I can be alone in a house to write to you.

I am a touch ill at ease because this morning when I left Tarrytown Elizabeth did not get up—I do not know whether she was really sleeping but I feel that she wasn't—in any case the fact that she did not even call out goodbye from her bed hurts—just like the day we left and she was so *very* cross. She is in love with you darling—spoke about how beautiful your face is and what power comes from you and when I conveyed your affection said "That's just what I feel for him"—and I am sure she really hates me that I receive letters— she said in such a disappointed voice "Here's another letter for you Gan"—

Hurts me,—Charles—

I just wish a few more people had some energy and life of their own—so they wouldn't always be getting angry about yours and mine.

That's why Bigmans II touches me so deeply—some other
    "one other man to equal Bigmans now"

Your Frances

❧ 289 ❧

Washington to Brooklyn (special delivery)
11 August 1950 (postmark)

friday

baby—

i am in a terrible state (your cry,[24] coming on top of my own statement to you yesterday, tossed me in the wildest basket of an almost sleepless night

dearest,

---

24. Boldereff's plea in her 9 August 1950 letter that Olson should come up to New York City.

the whole thing is now at pitch (i would even dare to date its termination, 10 days ahead

　　　　look, I know what you say, about would a man, and i can assure you, yes, there are such men—or we would not ask so much

　　　　　　　　　　　　　　　　　　this is to tell you how absolute is my response to your cry, how met

　　　　　　　　　　　　　　　　it is now a question of olson's strength, just as simple as that

　　　　　　　　　　　　　　　& to say, he'll play it, as he always has had to play everything, by ear, whether it's 24 hrs (it can't be sooner) or those ten days

　　　do, darling, the very very greatest you can, *right now*, right now
　　　　　　　　　　　　　　love love
　　　　　　　　　　　　　　Charles

ᴥ 290 ᴥ

Brooklyn to Washington
12 August 1950 (postmark 13 August 1950)

　　　　　　　　　　　　Saturday evening

Charles darling—

We didn't get here last night until midnight (Gusti and I drove over from Jackson Heights) and by the time we got all the things moved into the apartment I was quite tired.

This morning I slept until noon and they took my special (no name on bell then, I have fixed it now) back to PO and so I had to walk there (your mail seems to come up overnight as it did on Broadway, I am again very near big PO) and then walk miles for the few simple things, cup and saucer etc I need and am again quite exhausted, so again can not really write you.

I will not need any more money Charles, until one week from Tuesday (Aug. 22)—I pay my rent by the week, so I have paid until then—so darling your thirty dollars has helped me *very* greatly and takes care of everything for right now and I terribly appreciate your robbing yourself in order to help me. You are a very lovely beautiful man. Do not be scared, darling—I can wait and I love you.

You are a dear unknown man to me—life is so much harder for you than it is for me—I for some unknown reason am not at all worried now—although three of the very good four prospects I had are now eliminated—two because they gave the job to men and one as a designer at a press because they now do not have enough business to use a designer, so the job is postponed. (Van Rees Press) Their biggest customer was Chapel Hill Press and Scribner's have taken Chapel Hill as a customer, via the designer who went to Scribner—such are the workings of fate!

I do not know what it is you wish for me to do the very greatest I can, but if it is to love you—that I do my very greatest every day of my life—

Frances

⋈ 291 ⋈

Washington to Brooklyn (special delivery)
12 August 1950 (postmark)

Saturday

baby—lady—
today I think what I said yesterday is altogether too damn hi-fallutin, all around, too screwed tight:

you are too profound a part of me, & at the same time I am not going to give up nine years of life so easily, for me to talk about 10 days, & crisis, & olson's strength, & all that—bah!

look, sweet, you do just what you can—I haven't any business asking any thing of you: you see, I am such a damned *responsive* person, respond so to you, to your words & yr various daily hells—but at this distance such responding is plain straight hell & crazy   I swear we have to fall off a point to make the buoy—well, anyhow, it
is all not so climactic as I said, & I owe this to you, & you do just what "comes natural", as that wonderful song says, meaning:

what I said yesterday, only not, not so tight, at least as "said" by me, as "promise", just a lad goin' along, tryin' to make it

love
C

⋈ 292 ⋈

Brooklyn to Washington
13 August 1950 (postmark)

Sunday morning
your Saturday special here

Charles dear—

Your letter embarrasses me very deeply—

I will write ABC language—so that what exists may be very clear—I say this because I so very often do not understand exactly what it is you mean to say to me—

I have never asked or dreamed that you should "give up nine years of life"—you give me the impression of loving Connie very deeply; it has been clear to me from the beginning that you, faced with a choice, choose over and over again to remain with her. It would occur to me as against all my whole life to ask you to give her up—I have never once dreamed it.

If you want a loving open arrangement between us it must happen sometimes that I see you in the flesh—because life is different from writing. If our thoughts and imaginations are to be fertile for one another sometimes I must have proof that I am dear to you.

It is dangerous to me to do "what comes natural" because the mind and soul and spirit gallop after the flesh and if I cut myself off even for a night from that open track to you—then that cutting has begun and it is very dangerous.

No problem exists for me since I long ago surrendered my whole life into the service of love.

Frances

Your letter is to me official that I am supposed to look out for myself in whatever way I can. I surrender myself to life as a floater does to the water and this is official response that I am no longer bound to you in any way.

❦ 293 ❦

Washington to Brooklyn (special delivery)
14 August 1950 (postmark)

monday

dearest girl, i am prompted to sit down here in the ashes of a moment (fr. which i am profoundly sure the phoenix is arising) to tell you and me what i take to be the tale of what is going on   As you know it has been a way of life to me to keep such things, not secret, but to the rear of my self, from such leading principle that, if it is kept in the container, the energy can come out slantingly ("more passionate that way" is how you put it!) in the created work   But I am

now in such crisis, that even work does not seem to be so important as, that my
life, that the full finding of its energies, no matter in what direction it may turn
out they are born best for (I am strangely moved, for example, to wonder very
deeply if what is ahead is not either some departure from verse-making—
which, of course, makes me extremely nervous, very frightened—or some
going-ahead with the creative act which in no way resembles what we have
known as such, almost, i might say, a coming into existence of a function, of
which I may be a projective agent, which might be called a union of, say, Blake-
and-Pound: I add Pound for some reasons you already know, though let me
drop in here like some bitter juice to a potion of love ((for that is what this letter is, my profound creature of my deepest loins)) an opposition to Pound
which I am gripped by this day

> You see, frances, what you could only know by your deepest perceptive na-
> ture, almost only by a setting aside of your own personal hungers (of which
> I know, baby, your illimitable capacity) (Again, sweet, *remember remember*,
> I *do not* take advantage. *On the contrary*, despite ordinary appearances. Re-
> member Rimbaud. Remember him, when you speak of what males, too,
> have capacity for) is, that i am constantly washed over these recent weeks
> by some sadness the like of which I have never known, and the clue to
> which i can only guess is what you mean when you speak of what a woman
> goes through in the very root of the stem of her sense of life   But maybe i
> am wrong, for i should want, at this moment of my life, to be over-scrupu-
> lous, and avoid like a Leviticus any slightest mixing of genders   It does
> not matter, really, except inside the paths of myself   Anyhow what i
> wanted to juxtapose to myself is a very powerful statement of EP's in the
> Pisan Cantos:
>
> Hard, hard as youth, for sixty years,
> and never to have known La Tristesse
>
> My god, i say to myself, then he is right to have organized this cabal
> against me, to go out to slay me, for this concept of his I am a living disproof
> of   From my sights, my new terror,—which is only a tightening of the
> strings for purity of tone, of strings i have known since i was born, which i
> take it my father knew, which i also take to be both distinct from Ameri-
> canism (Pound) and from Semitism (the Wail & the Liver)—Tristesse is
> half the face of the face of life at its mandrake root

((Before I go any further, so that you may read this *hard*, may be able to feel not
the least disappointment that this is how i present myself to you, and not, just
at this moment, this day, the flesh of him to your own flesh direct, to your
hands and eyes, to your embrace: i am trying very deeply, very terribly, to

comprehend wholly what it is that has happened, what is happening, what I am, what we are, now, at this advanced stage, which, as i sd to you last week, seems to me to be at very pitch

to understand first, in this severe principle of mine, that action is easier than preparation,—I actually imagine I am at the point of the oldest stone, the legend on it, which I again leave unspoken as I did in The Kingfishers, even though then I did not know, was, possibly, again predicting what I was to begin to know now

anyhow, here, too, i am going by promptings when i put in, right here, this amulet for you, this stone piece which comes to my hand like something you must wear around your neck, hidden, not as secret, but hidden as you know yes we both believe, but how i wanted to put it is, as you do wear with what modesty, with what you did to your lips, what you do with clothes:

My lady abandoned heaven, abandoned earth
    To the downward world she descended
Abandoned lordship, abandoned ladyship
    To the downward world she descended
She who was of light and love and life[25]

So to get back, to what i am possessed to say, that you may share what is going on—for it belongs to you, and I believe you should have it, beloved:

i have this impression, that i am making a passage from the modern (flesh) to the archaic (eternal life)

and that said, you surely can imagine how every bit of my being is gripped, how this is pitch, as i said, how—and i would say this *only* to you

(((the cardinal in the
    green tree makes
    out-cry)))

—it is as though my whole life, both before here, *and after*, is straight out here in front of my less blind eyes, trembling, naked, all nerves (the substance out ahead)

25. These lines are based on the opening of "Inanna's Descent to the Nether World," presumably from Samuel Noah Kramer's *Sumerian Mythology* (Philadelphia: American Philosophical Society, 1947).

Now, having said it, I am exhausted! Isn't it crazy, one sentence, actually! and to say such a sentence takes all of one's life! My god, is not life amazing, how its simplicities are the hardest things of all!

(Cover me, lady. I could easily, the male, feel a fool. I don't. But that's because you are you.

And accept this, lady, as the straightest sort of a thing, every word, from the above sentence out from the very first word dearest to this last word of yr charles for now love

◄§ 294 §►

Washington to Brooklyn (special delivery)
14 August 1950 (postmark)

Monday

o franzess!
    I'm going to wire you, but also this note special, to straighten things out
        (that olson who is thot to have some ability to make words work, should fail so miserably with his own dear Lady!)
                                    You are such a trigger, love. LOOK: let me enclose back to you, marked, the passages I was really answering[26]

AND
of course of course *of course* you do not, have not, *would not* ask me 9 years, over
        —of course *not* frances:
                        that's my business And what I was stating *was my* problem

Oh, look. Girl, just, please reread the letter, in both the light of enclosed & the *light of special already posted to you*, and see who loves you, & how.

    (Excuse, but am on way to Lib. of Cong.—& want this to reach you as fast as *possible*

Love,
Charles

NO OFFICIALS, baby, EITHER WAY, please!

---

26. With this letter Olson sends back to Boldereff her letter of 9 August 1950, with the first paragraph underlined and in the top margin, "Do return darling!"

Washington to Brooklyn (telegram)
14 August 1950

FRANCES BOLDEREFF
     5 MONROE PL
NO YOU TOOK LETTER ALL WRONG DARLING. SPECIAL FOLLOWS LOVE
CHARLES

Washington to Brooklyn
14 August 1950 (postmark)

monday (3rd time, sweet!)

baby:
     you do fill me with such light!   it is beyond belief wonderful   your three
letters were so beautiful to have—even the one which could have pitched me
down to gloom

          i do pray, darling, that it is cleared up   all i was doing, actu-
ally, saturday, was letting you hear me talk to myself, i guess, so that you might
be aware (today's long first letter is a *real* statement) of the size of the thing i
am going through

          it just seems to be my turn to have the heat on, and that one
sentence of yours in your saturday letter: "don't be afraid, baby, i'm here"—
o, lady, that was like every part of you on me, and i thank you from way
down there (try, sweet, not to be thrown off by one day's letter—or that farce
around the first of the month when i misaddressed the mail, and you suffered
so;;;give things—when they are letters, and such—a chance to be off; give 72
hours, and then, let fly, baby   AND ANYTIME EXPECT OLSON TO
BE STRAIGHT, no curves: i dare say that it was why i feel right now you
are clear on this—I TRUST YOU. Do, always, trust me back. It is such a
wonderful thing to have, love: as I sd today, that you are you.

     Keep me in touch with everything: your schedules ahead, how the job hunt
goes, etc.
          This is justanote, of overflowing
                                             Love

That goddamned library: couldn't get the waddell i was

after   his aryan-sumer dictionary   had an idea   anyhow,
am creeping up on that lead of his, that 70% or better of english is indirectly from sumer
                                        that's a beaut of a thing, you
know?

And thanks, sweet, for the words on the language of B II (it's
crazy, but i went off again, right there, where it ended to you
last week: same as B I—maybe that's the way that damned
poem is going to get itself writ: in jumps (((maybe that's the
way of bigmans!)))

                                               kisses,
                                               Charles

PS
     Just addressing the envelope gives me again the *solid* sense I have had since
you got 5 Monroe Place—wonderful feeling, like to have you Woodward, to
feel you based—very good / & strange

And this (over) better, no?

In the green tree the red-bird makes
out-cry

     or

In the green tree
the red-bird
makes out-cry

     or, i think best,

In the green tree
the red-bird
makes
out-cry

(this is a *true* image, don't you think—of something very important?

If I could only (shall only) get it into the juxtaposition it was in that letter to
you? how did I have it? where?

297

Brooklyn to Washington
[14 August 1950]

Monday morning 8:00

Charles hero—

This is written in the same spirit as the line of those old things was cut in those vases and stele and figures reproduced by Harrison[27]—the holy reverence each time of whatever hand that cut these lines—

Your letter[28] touches the very centermost part of me—the part which is never spoken—the hidden impulse which has directed me from the beginning and your letter contains a beauty which I silently thank for—the beauty of the human desire when it is deeper in than sex—when life holds in its clenched fist, as Enkidu the grappled lion, the profoundest smoke-shape of its subterranean movement—its direction—its intention—"the unknown" to itself—

You are in the presence of the hero's greatest problem—the "moment"— "What is the name and face of my enemy?"

This is the Olson cocking.

And it is true that it cannot be known whether verse or whether a function unnamed—yesterday I was very very surprised to note how Blake ties in with all the profoundest stuff in that old art (Harrison is a sweet sweet woman and of course the reason they let her publish that book is because she herself is not frenzy, is immune—no Motz would be allowed to really write about that stuff—my God—snakes—over and over again—how she misses the point— but the reverence Charles of those creators.)

I am also afraid to speak in words—I also trust to silence—
I have heard your letter—
I recognize you as a world-hero—
Tristesse is the absolute obligation of man
The passionate baring of the self before the unknown

I the mother watch without looking—I wait—I pray—I believe—I accept
Pound is a liar, he is the non-existent "And the name of your new country is Olson"

I reread at Elizabeth's certain chapters of *Crime and Punishment*—there is a deep deep part about Raskolnikov—I cannot remember whether he is talking

27. Boldereff has presumably received her copy of Jane Harrison's *Themis*.
28. Boldereff has received the first of the letters dated 14 August 1950, sent special delivery.

to himself or what—I remember the phrase—"I give you the three fishes"—
he is listing a terrific list—"I give you's" I think speaking to himself—but it
knocked me over—this Dostoyevsky boy was really in there—

Dostoyevsky whom I would dare to call your father
This is a letter of silence

But in the great movement taking place in the floors of existence—my belief is that the passion of Dostoevsky—what has moved me towards the Russians from the beginning—their reverence—is now embodied in Charles—
Tristesse is only one of the names
You will understand one day the vision—that *all* of it was vision—I was
not in any way knowing myself—
I the mother walk on the rim of the earth—if all of its substance trans-
mute—my feet are of such stuff they will know where. My breasts are hard
and sore and ache as before birth.
It is as though for the first time since the split of sex occurred that a new
split has been forced wide open—1/2 male and female, 1/2 female and male

That the division is not incompleteness—halfness
that the division is joy
the recognition
the face to be made
the fierceness of the joy that God engenders in man
sorrow

❈ 298 ❈

Washington to Brooklyn (special delivery)
15 August 1950 (postmark)

tuesday

frances:
    i feel desperately cheated, and so, angry, like to have a double sword or the
double axe in my hand to clear out the dirty stables by slaughter!
i have just
finished fast a novel some researches some time ago led me on to   i'll hide the
name of the fool who got me into this, to hide my own shame i was misled, but
i stumbled on the book in a bookstore last night, for 50¢, bought it, and am
now ready to tear it to cheap pieces[29]

---

29. The novel has not been identified.

it is one of the most terrible of all things, to find image or event or personage which is swimming in your self wrongly used, cheaply used: it is like the very worst punishments of a hell (it is what must make movies so devastating to people, unknown to them)

i would imagine that i have to suffer these things especially, because my vision rests, on its bottom side, in folk things, and the hair of difference between vulgarity and pureness, between sentimentality and passion is so very small that it is one of the reasons why it has not now for some time (i am tempted by waddell to think since, what, 2500 bc) been possible for men to make work a vision which insists upon such roots

it is crazy, how close these things are   this novel, for example, is an unrelieved lie, from start to finish, not even a word right   yet the material is so essential it has misled observers to see in it what is not there   by contrast, some time ago, i happened to pick up, by accident, one night in a cheap movie house, one of the most beautiful presentations of the sexual i have ever seen, done by a stupid chorine but so managed by this unknown director that one was in the presence of something not known since Ephesus!

You may guess, then, my baby, how tremendously i await your word, sometimes, when, because of you, i go forward with some materials that are not usually dared, or, if dared, are left only on the folk level (that level which is now so deranged)   I am led to think that one of the jobs cut out for me is to do just such things, to do the sort of things you, in your impeccable instinct, led me to discover equivalents of (our Sumerians) Yet, o my god, what a walking of skeins of silk it is, to keep the maximum energy in, and all vulgarity out!   It strikes me, how much easier it is, to be smart, and leave it alone! Not that I should ever, now, be so tempted, but i say this, just because the eyes in my head are beginning to see how smartness (I am thinking of Pound) is easy! (How easy intellectual and emotional snobbery is!)

((Darling, wise one, it is so curious, these days, to feel myself so often—as just now, at the end of the above para.,—saying things which I imagine are self-evident truths to you, things you have come to know solidly, from pain. You may imagine how strange an experience it is, to one who, until so very recently, could so easily think, before him no one! By god. This lad is being brought in!))

Look, Frances, please, please forever trust me. Please, baby, make that compact you voiced Saturday, "I am here", you said, make it to me, and then say it, whenever you are of a mind to. Time has forever made me nervous. I dare say, that is why death I am not frightened of. I *know*, in that terrible way that you know that strength, real strength knows what it is capable of, that once my feet get themselves on one of the paths of the soul which the woods of the soul have (how?) hewn through them (before i, at least, this inhabitant of this soul, have been along them) that once my feet are on that path, it will go it to the very end, without stop or let, until it is done. Yet, darling, this present path—o, how beautiful it is, to have your full square palm with my hand wrapped around it on that street, your palm given, warm and of such strength. It is very beautiful, very, baby.

You sd, i am fierce. Maybe we'll soon amend it, i *was* fierce. Fierceness, i begin to see, is only blind strength, which is not so good as unblind strength, as the strength which comes when fierceness (before me, no one) begins to lose its presumptions.

Flesh is fierce. And then: it is garment. Yes, baby, I begin to know. (I hold your hand, right at this moment, with absolute tenderness, sweet one, i hold yr hand.) So many blindnesses are shaking off.

And I am walking along a path stronger each step I take.

To get back to what i was saying. That problem, of the hair's breath,[30] is involved in this Bigmans proposition, yes, but not so much, *yet*, in the narrative, as the She-Bear, which you were so scrupulous with, to distinguish the first part from that bad Mimosa part II. (It is a most delicate business, in all things, in verse as well as in love, not to be forced off by anything but the true; and it is one of the things which is like miracle to me, that, so far, in both love and verse, you and i have done no more than drop a stitch or two, and, quickly, catch them up, where the fingers of our touchy egos have been dumb, for a minute. Is it so, does it seem so, to you, too? I have taken your word to the letter on the verse (not to speak of the love, where, we might agree, I am less knowing, but not so ignorant as i was

(by the way, you never did say whether these lines meant anything to you) and i have got into the habit of thinking, that when you don't say anything, you mean to save my feelings, as the expression goes. I shall go on that assumption (so you *must*, baby, keep that extraordinary memory of yrs always pert, and not leave anything out you do not mean to leave out!). But this I sent you a very long time ago, and,—I am not fishing, am honestly (I never fish) asking, what do you think:

it is Troilus who is speaking:

30. Presumably "hair's breadth" is meant.

Love is not present now, has flown

Is not a state so separate as we think,
that men and women breed by kiss & glance,
no dance, outside the modes and figures of that trance,
the full intent.[31]

One other thing still keeps coming up in my mind, your rejection of THE CAUSE. It is of much more importance to me than the above, of course, but still, any poem behind me I am utterly cold about. Your rejection of T Cause I accept, of course; I mention it, only, that yr word muscularity still has to be transposed, inside myself, so that I may understand it in some vocabulary of my own.

        (O darling days like this i realize what an advantage my love of words is, to be able to spend hour, hours, writing to you—and you, dear thing, protesting against them! O, sweet, for this crucial while, let me double for us both, let you feel all this talk of olson is not at all so much of olson as it is of a lover who is telling you

                                love,
                                Charles

                        ◦◦ 299 ◦◦

Washington to Brooklyn (special delivery)
 16 August 1950 (postmark 16 August 1950)

                                wed aug 16 50

baby, i feel very close to you in another way now, in this sense of marking time, which must, for you, be so often the sense of present situation, and terrible it is, isn't it, this stretching out of the will and the flesh, like the soul is said to stretch out in sleep, to strain. And such a sense of waste. God god god something must happen soon. It will.

i am writing this before i go to the p.o., because i like to use my machine   but i wish i had a letter first, i need so much to hear from you after your sunday letter which made all things go to smash (and after yr saturday letter had given me such a happiness! or, rather, such a love that you, that you, my darling, who carries so much of this intolerable strain, should say, "I'm here,

---

31. The first lines of the poem "Troilus" (*Collected Poems*, p. 76).

baby" god that was beautiful francessimo, beautiful to the pale struggler   i have lived on it, like food and sleep, dragging on these very bad days

they are damned bad. Even if i get a little heat up, where lines come from, it is shortly spent—and i thereupon gnaw gnaw gnaw   i shall be glad when this goddamned emerson gets here from columbus and this business of sitting down with him and settling the contents of the book of poems, and the two transcripts he has asked me to make while he is here (one of the poems, and one of statement based on the projective verse argument, a sort of 1st go at my "poetics", say, which he will use on his program in columbus) is over   it confines me   he says now, it will be friday-saturday

you go to woodward to take lucinda back for a month, this weekend, is that right? when does that mean you are back in brooklyn?

Oh god, today, i wish this were athens, and one lived, any such as us all lived, in one city! (I know, now, what you meant, in your wisdom, when you asked that question when we were last together. I know, I know.)

Baby, excuse me. I have all the time in the world to write you today. But you are *too* close. I am too close, to do it. There really isn't anything to say, after a certain point of flesh-attrition, is there? There is just one thing then. The presence, again, your presence, to be in your presence with my presence. God.

It is crazy, how, now, at this late date, i am finally going through all that I imagine you have gone through. For this sounds in my ear like so many things you have said so many times, when the strain was just too much. God, how long does it take this goddamn olson to find out what it is, what it is to love. I hate myself today, I am so stupid. (Excuse that, but I just had to spit myself out, I am so damned and angry.) But god, if you can bear it, you'll have some man on your hands!

I mean, he'll know something, and, maybe, added to what he did know, whatever that was & whatever it is (was) worth, he ought to be at least interesting—AND a little more LIKEABLE, sweet girl! (You know, when you sd that to me I suddenly shed something which sure needed to be shed! And when I replied, that maybe my fate was, to not be liked, I was cockeyed. The truth is, that, now that you sd it, and I discover what it was you meant, it isn't at all any longer a problem. This lad is going to be liked by you, you see!

Oh yes, one thing: it is not P and Aspasia.[32] I've found in Athenaeus two much

---

32. A previous reference to Pericles and Aspasia is in Olson's letter of 17 March 1950.

more interesting reflections of this love of ours. (no, i've just checked, it is the story of—well, actually none of them   which is right, right, now, that as i sd, recently, you have become absolute particular to me   i don't give a good god-damned for any images any more, any parables   to hell with 'em   my mood is this: let's get on to the living out of what is, and let it be so good others will tell the tales, make whatever they see   to hell with this literary business any-how   this is much too actual for allusion, my handsome thing   'course it knocks verse to hell into a cocked hat (or does it? actually it makes me, it, *real stuff*)   but that's just as well   as a matter of fact I'm glad, glad to wipe it all out   (i never told you how it puzzled me, at Tarrytown, when you sd, that last morning that we stole from lucinda (and, anyhow, Elizabeth, in so far as you had to call her up and explain we were delayed) when you came back from the phone and sd, you had told her, we had been busy dreaming up my next book! I was bewildered, for though it had some truth in it, yet, it did add this literary business to something which is, actually, don't we both know it now, just the cleanest straightest sort of honest to god blood and flesh, partic-ular as all hell, and made to wear as mortal things are, to whip and torture and delight, hard, tough, sweet business, and none of that "form" to it which art has, but that other thing, whatever it is, which life has.   (This is what I meant, I imagine, in attacking my "aestheticism"—to which attack it was warning in the balls, that you objected, baby!)

You see, baby, it dawns on me, that one of the reasons i try to hold, so far as life goes, is a false transfer of the problems, the necessities, the torture of art, the strains. And I've been a fool. No one can do it, not even Olson! And a fool to try it, a fool to expect it except on the very highest grounds, of love. A fool. Now I am love's fool—or about to be—I see what a fool I was to be life's fool! Or something.

Anyhow, I am glad, glad as hell, the way you stand now in me, born Frances Motz, has lived Frances Motz, is precious FRANCES MOTZ—is what she is, is my *real*, is this girl and wears her own glories, im-ages, extensions, wildness, mysteries, however they may be recurrence or pro-jection, they are her HER, as she is, as I want her, HER, not anything else but this bare strong tender thing, what she is, frances motz

It makes solid sense, babe, that this is the girl i write to, that i want to be with.

> charles, who is more both
> charles and olson also
> than before

One story I started to tell you above, I must tell you parts of, of the story of PHRYNE. I'll quote this, at least, for your recognition:[33]

> "But Phryne was a really beautiful woman, even in those parts of her person which were not generally seen: on which account it was not easy to see her naked; for she used to wear a tunic which covered her whole person, and she never used the public baths. But on the solemn assembly of the Eleusinian festival, and on the feast of the Posidonia, then she laid aside her garments in the sight of all the assembled Greeks, and having undone her hair, she went to bathe in the sea; and it was from her that Apelles took his picture of the Venus Anadyomene; and Praxitiles, who was a lover of hers, modelled the Cnidian Venus from her body"

Wed nite

my *darling*, *darling*, your beautiful, beautiful words! I have just scanned them & will, now take them away from this ugly place to read them, deep & like a thirsty, hungry thing

this is just to tell you, that, in a quandary, where I should send my own letter to you, which is in my other hand—a *love* letter, if I ever wrote one—!

I was going to send this to Tarrytown, but you say "today & tomorrow," that is, today, so, not knowing, but thinking you may be returning Woodward as planned, I'll send this there, just in case you   NO—figure you will go back to Brooklyn before Woodward—HERE

love
C

❦ 300 ❧

Washington to Woodward and Brooklyn
17 August 1950

thurs aug 17 50

darling, i am unsure where you are   i have looked for yr letter, in which you told me yr schedule, and couldn't, at the moment, find it nor is there a letter at the p.o. today   so i shall send the carbon to brooklyn, just in case, but on

---

33. Olson is quoting from p. 943 of vol. 3 of his copy of Athenaeus, *The Diepnosophists or Banquet of the Learned* (Bohn Classics, 1854), a passage he remembers later in *Maximus Poems* 2:35.

the assumption that you were to take lucinda back to state college, this first copy to woodward[34]   (specials have gone to brooklyn yesterday, and tuesday: i did not get yr tuesday morning letter until last night,[35] as you know, if you went down to b fr tarrytown as i had to figure last night   i do hope i have done right all around, for i do not want a day to go by, these days, that you do not have some word from me, dearest one)

today i am deeply quiet, as though i had been in battle and, suddenly, all firing had ceased, and i am leaning against a tree, in the late light of day, taking up new strength, and all things are beautiful, even though my strength is not quite enough again to seize on my own appetite   but the important fact is, that all things are beautiful, more beautiful than ever before, if quite different, if, now that i have been in battle, i look at them as i never did before   it is a very strange, and rewarding thing, this sense of life born here out of this struggle

you will imagine, then, my love, how much—also in the light of that shrill, pitched letter yesterday, which must have been, the way i feel today, the shell which was to be fired at the climax of the battle—how very much your letter (it is an inadequate word) your look-without-looking, the embrace of your silence, was to me, is
                    it came in on me, in IN, my lady!

one strange thing is, today, i want to cry out, to say, to make it a law, that NO ONE SHOULD SAY ANYTHING ABOUT SOMETHING THEY DO NOT KNOW—and i mean know in the full sense of that old root cliche— but which is no cliche at all: know thyself. I mean, for example, that "love", or, "sculpture", or "culture", or even "happiness" stand for things which are actual, and that one of the most dangerous and dirtiest diseases of this epoch is, that this simplest truth, one should not speak of what one does not know, is broken all over the place.

2nd proposition which wells up, today, is—and i think it is ancillary to above—is this:

                    emotion expressed directly and instantly, tranquillity the dodge of an uncohered temperament

o, sweet, on new feet i come to you, to thank you, yes, but, more important, to

---

34. Only the carbon copy sent to Brooklyn exists at Storrs.
35. Indications are that Olson is referring to Boldereff's "Monday morning 8:00" letter, which was perhaps mailed on Tuesday.

say, yea, to say, you, frances motz, are beautiful, your life is precious, precious beyond the saying of it, you are beautiful

things are so sweet inside me i keep falling into silences, i who am man of words! this, too, is most new, baby   but i am surprised, when there is so much to say, (i think, again, i repeat you, when i surmise, it is time to talk, not to write letters!)

love
Charles

❧ 301 ❦

Brooklyn to Washington
[17 August 1950]

Thursday 1:15 pm

Charles darling—

I am sort of physically dizzy—my glasses have started to be not useful— have to have bifocals.

Came down from Tarrytown this morning for a business appointment— tore over here from Grand Central—picked up two notices and a regular mail letter—back to Manhattan—then back here to PO—one special was there—then to lunch—then back here to Tuesday special—Now alone— very very worn out—not physically just inwardly—like after having a baby—I feel my race has been run—I have done all that was required of me and I feel the boat is now docked and the captain can go below to sleep— sleep—rest—I am not suffering physically—I just want not to hear or see or respond—

tomorrow I will find out about a job I applied for Tuesday—
I am all the rest of the way sleep walking—
I can not write now

I have actually due to emotional strain not been able to read any of your verse Charles, really read, since fairly long before you came to New York—I will hunt out and go back and we will discuss in great detail perhaps to- gether—I feel in my bones together—when I wrote in Woodward paying out the line as far as she will go—I did Charles and now ahead of time ahead of "fact" I feel the boat is docked—I can only sleep baby—

Will write when I can
I love you

We are appointed by God to live and love in a proud sure way never done by man before on earth—to show that Christ came in to the world to give man joy—joy of his flesh and spirit in the worship and obedience of God—today Dostoyevsky whom I read last night is for sure I know now your father—

Frances Olson

Will sleep in Brooklyn Friday Sat Sunday probably

◦⟨ 302 ⟩◦

Washington to Brooklyn (special delivery)
18 August 1950 (postmark 18 August 1950)

friday aug 18 50

frances, frances, again, in that extraordinary way, we match: your letter today is but another way of saying, is it not, what i said to you yesterday   it is such a strange, and yet not at all strange, thing, how you speak of a voyage over, i of a battle

((certain other clues lead me to think the imagery is most apt, that it should be a voyage for you, a battle for me—And what completely still interests my fantasy is, what sea-birth (i mean, of course, phylogenetically) does to the male, rather, to your absolute pairing, the ½ male and female   For I think the very element of the birth is such a determinant—I am thinking of, beside myself, Lawrence and Melville, who, surely, are each pelagic. My hunch would be, that, here, the things are not in balance, but that the man born of the element water is more true than the other man simply because his bias is the actual phylogeny of the species (I suddenly realize I am repeating the base premise of ISHMAEL,—but, as in so many, many things and ways these days, these last weeks, I feel that I am only now bringing up my own rear to my own projections! And this parallels the other experience I have spoke of all the past week, that I am at the same time finding myself catching up with *your* experience. Both, are certainly reason enough for the amazing exhaustion of perception that I have felt yesterday and today, don't you rather imagine?

For I am in a

unique mood, the same leaning I spoke of yesterday, sort of gone blind, or, rather, not seeing or doing but feeling below some real difference from which i sense both seeing and doing will come. And, like you, I feel, precisely as you put it: I just want not to hear or see or respond. (God knows, baby, you surely have done all that was required.) I deeply pray I may have, too, in my way.

In fact, child, your letter is altogether right, even, i dare say, even, for you at least, to the christ, though i should insist that the imagery not extend itself beyond a two-content, you-me, believing, as you know, that only thus can life be kept in inside the particulars, be distributed, in the sense that the illumination be absolutely fresh   But this is deep ground, and, nor you nor i, at this moment, as we say, are prepared to respond: we wish only to recognize.

Again, because it is undone, but because it can be yours alone, let me enclose what i blocked out yesterday, i was so moved by the end of your wondrous letter of tuesday:

the smoke-shape to be grappled with, the lion
or Prouti, the shifting gate, the water-wall, the entrance
which is not an entrance but the thing itself, always
a gate, it is only
the preoccupation with itself And grabbed, thrown
it is forever new, forever
smoke, shape, lion And you? merely
he who must grapple, who must
preoccupy, who must
ask himself the question, "What
is the name and face?"

and the enemy answers, the beloved:

> that the division is joy, is not
> incompleteness
>
> that the halfness is
>
> the recognition, the face
> to be made, the fierceness
>
> of the joy that is engendered in man,
> the sorrow[36]

For you, sweet thing,
as roots,
dangling,
where they came from
the sorrow

o girl!

36. These lines, based on the Boldereff letter of 14 August 1950, did not become a published poem.

(how can one make such words carry, all, ALL that they contain!)

when i mean particulars i mean the ribbon, and the snake across the thighs: these are the answers, the illuminations

And I have this sudden sight, that it is the ribbon, and the snake, whatever they are, that have come to live because of this love between us, that live *in* this love, without previous relevance, (granting, of course, that there is relevance, but that, without their being discovered anew, the particulars, in each new revelation, there is no revelation, that each living thing, like this love, carries in itself its own registration, and if found, if sought hard enough, all the experience will cohere there, in that ribbon, that snake, and will be forever to be seen, and that that is the whole, the abstract and the fine, the THING, the SINGLE THING

    (and that its singularity is why it becomes freeing for any other, that it is not dogma but art that liberates, that art only is ultimately eternal)

SINGLE, but single because behind it there has been COHERENCE

why we have had nothing but opposites, false antinomies, is because all has been incoherence since east and west

I send you all, all this love,
yr boy,   charles

❄ 303 ❄

Brooklyn to Washington
[19 August 1950]

Saturday morning

Charles darling—

    Yesterday I received such a cruel blow that during the night I absolutely lost my courage—but old habits reassert themselves and this morning, although I have absolutely no idea how I will proceed, I am sure that I have to.

    But first darling to your letter—I love the poem darling because in my extreme exhaustion I could not force into my mind what it was I had written on Tuesday—the thing escaped me absolutely and now it all comes flooding back and the thing seems to me to be true—and I love the way you have written it

(And the lines you quoted earlier this week—
you said were Troilus speaking—anyway
those 4 lines together—I think are marvellous
I will get to your work soon Charles)

Oh dearest forgive forgive this letter—it will be so dull—

Just one other point about the Thursday letter—I was so full of Dostoyevsky—I made a discovery about him very important to me—I always have considered that he wasn't one of the two or three (Euripides, first—Rabelais—Francis Thompson) who was right about sex, about women—but in a very careful rereading of *Crime and Punishment* I discovered that he is indeed of the correct ones and this is one of the things I will want to talk to you about. For this reason, because of my added (to my already great) respect for him, because he loved Christ so much—for Dostoyevsky's sake and then also in the sense of your letter about man's being a perpendicular axis crossed by the past[37]—I wanted to include Christ for his being so magnificently "The Single Thing" that is how I meant including him—a sort of bringing up to the present—as I dedicated my book "To Michelangelo" (who am I to assert that the beloved is dead? I would not dare such presumption.)

Now dearest I will briefly tell you about yesterday—I went back to McGraw Hill   they had indicated very strongly that I was to have the job—and it was so felt that the official through whom all hiring is done there, when I went in to his office after my interview (meant to be confirmatory) and told him they had hired someone else his mouth fell open in complete astonishment which I could see registered genuine surprise. He was as sure as I was that I had been called back in order to be officially signed in.

It is a very long story   I will tell you the details when we meet—but the very young and very unsexy man who will be in charge of the design has a secret bitter hatred and fear and envy of me—I could *feel* it on Tuesday all morning—and at the same time he really admires my work and also perhaps likes me—he is a Dennis type—in a way—it goes back to four years ago when he was hired (straight from Dartmouth) for the job I applied for then and I was so furious then at the terrible unfairness and later we both made a design for the same book—and mine was chosen and mine won all "honorable mention" in the text book clinic for exactly the parts I had done—(I did not choose the paper, design cover, or jacket, supervise production)—

Anyway his boss who leaves the end of this month wanted me *very* much and I could *feel* the very slow burning very deep seated resentment that he was going to have to take me—anyway when I came yesterday by their request and at an hour definitely arranged—he passed me by twice pretending not to see me—then Monaco came out and said I should go in and talk to "the boys" before seeing him—I went to the doorway and inside the office (Eisenman and this young man have one together) there were two young women sitting and another man standing they all looked at me—no one acknowledged my presence—Eisenman kept pretending he didn't know I was there—kept his

---

37. Olson's letter of 10 August 1950.

back to the door all the time talking on the phone and when I moved over across the doorway I saw the other man (who is to become boss) at his desk right inside the door—he looked up and said "Oh! yes—I hardly know what to tell you—someone has turned up quite unexpectedly who was *exactly what we were looking for* (meaning young and not very good) I don't know what to say—etc, etc." and being a lady I said "It doesn't matter—you needn't say why" and gathered up all my things all of us in the most terrible embarrassment. It is the clearest clearest example of envy, of fear—and oh! Charles I am absolutely overcome because I have been absolutely qualified for each of the 4 jobs (actually existing, not the other ones) I have applied for in the publishing business and until the war situation makes things so very bad that they are forced to take me I know, as I knew before I came—this is the treatment I will receive—They are afraid of me, of my knowledge, my experience—my *love* of what I do—

Oh Charles—I am beyond any consolation—I am wishing I did not have to go on enduring in this filthy cheap age—and Charles never have you seen two young men so absolutely unsexy—and that I believe also contributed because it was one of those days I spoke of (the first one for over 6 months) when I looked attractive.

Then I went up to Tarrytown and Elizabeth with her Packard convertible who had said before she would drive us to Brooklyn quietly spoke of the train—so I gathered up my daughter and my things and brought her here last night and in that deep child sense she sensed my pain and she cried and said she wished we could live in Woodward—so today I have to do that hardest of all mother tasks—to be gay for my baby's sake—

Oh Charles dearest forgive me to tell you all my woes but I am absolutely crushed.

Frances

I cannot take Lucinda to Woodward because I haven't enough money and I do not want any further obligation to anyone to drive me.

◄§ 304 §►

Washington to Brooklyn (special delivery)
20 August 1950 (postmark)

sunday

darling—
    never did know what people mean when they say suspended—don't

know now—but something of that sort is the way i feel today: or drained, horrified:

yesterday was cause, day & night, due to this editor-publisher emerson[38] who led me to do two transcriptions and to talk about my book in too many places (played back my verse to too many people, mixing it with his host Norman McLeod's, Tate's, Winters'—look at that for horror!—two or three separated and walked-on sessions, as though we were sparrows or pigeons on a city street trying to eat a nut or some kid's crust thrown away, or of a horse— aw, it was dirty, darling, dirtied:

i recoil   tho i stayed absolutely sharp, cold, and put all passion into the verse, was and stayed careful on the book, made no crowd noises or decisions   yet, it is the same thing as the body's modesty, what you know i mean, sweet: the vulgar, the shameless, the hurriers, the fools, the cheap—ach, what a filth, and yet, the terror of it, from cause these effects follow (my dear lad creeley, who is in some sort of hell now too, he started this whole thing from the best of reasons and impulse, and, at the moment, it runs out into this mud and street of yesterday)

i am not dismal, the verse stands clear.   i do.   i am reporting only the desuetude on top, what comes, the moment one walks out of the cell   And my spirit goes around these creatures. That's a trouble, that's a trouble of its own. I see how they got nowhere or somewhere.

But, baby mine, where they don't get, where they stay, where "life as it is", that untrue doctrine, keeps them.   intensity: what is it but courage? how else is anyone "founded"?

No letter fr you yesterday. Will go to p.o. now, to hope for one, and to see if i should send this to brooklyn—do, baby, let me hear instantly where you are ahead

I long,
charl-es

Life is so much more mysterious than we are: isn't that, frances, isn't the discovery of that fact, what makes it possible for you to wear your life with such dignity and beauty, to *wear* it?

i would venture this, quite modestly but venture it, that (at least in this society) it is one of the real swims for a male to go between the proposition that *he* is life and however one might put the other horn, the charybdis, let's say suc-

38. Richard Wirtz Emerson, editor of *Golden Goose* magazine and press, staying at Norman MacLeod's in Washington, recorded several Olson poems for broadcast on his radio program in Columbus, Ohio.

cumbing, out into the real waters, that he is not life but that, because life is more mysterious, he can obey without loss, in fact with gain, with addition to his force   it is very hard, it strikes me, for the male will, which is so obdurate, to catch hold of this, truth

Or so it seems. Tell me what you think. I am talking out loud, talking, seeking to see

((“energetic”, that dirty bastard emerson calls me and my verse, in his spiel circum o.! but i will say for McLeod, he says “an angry man”, after King-fishers—sweet, do you remember i sent it to you, as answer to your question, spring 49, how, olson, do you argue survival in these States?))

you see, darling, without reference at all to the ambience yesterday, but, simply, from reading so much of it, and looking over the rest, i am quite laid off, today, by what the verse does not do, what it leaves undone, how much more there is to be said— & how much more finely—   And when one is faced by such moments of clear looking at what one has done, there is such a roar inside, of, God, to get *on* with it, to make it, to have it bear and bear and bear, until it wrings out of life everything there is, everything one can bring to bear on it—One is so sharply aware of blindness, scales, veils, to be struck away, to be gotten rid of, to get to the heart   And one also knows, it is the stem, the stem, the stem of yrself, that, only, can make it possible (That beautiful remark of Keats—well, it's not necessary: there's Rimbaud.) O, sweetheart,

P.O.
    Letter here, and tho I abhor to write to you here, I *must*, darling, kiss you, put my arms around you, take your dear dear head in my hands over all this punishment—o, god damn them, aren't they abominable, those who pass as fellow men, women. God, frances! I know, I know, know. Sweet sweet thing. It's so not beyond belief, so usual, so god damn well the way of the world. And that you tell me, that you so honour me, my proud one, I am glad. I give you back love, love.

O

❦ 305 ❦

Brooklyn to Washington
[21 August 1950]

5 Monroe Place

Monday morning

Charles darling—

Thank you dearest for your special—it is so very hard to live without words from you—my night was so horrible and suddenly I became afraid that you, too, might be taken away from me by accident or such   I am really as close to frantic as a person of my kind can come—

I am borrowing money from Lucy (which takes all a mother's love to force myself to)—I am so hurt because she calls herself my friend talks about "pure love" claims to honor me—and is sitting alone with apartment of five rooms—four beds—and makes me go rent a place—how I hate to borrow her money—but the only other people are men who here and there want a piece of me—exactly as you order pie for dessert—Lucy is better—)

I am taking Lucinda on the 1:55 p.m. to Lewistown Tuesday—will go to Woodward either that night or Wednesday morning so please write Woodward. Will leave again Thursday morning as I have to be back here in Brooklyn Thursday night at latest. I have answered some ads in N.Y. Times and when I come back I have to spend every minute looking for a job—as my money is not enough to last me.

I agree about the thing of how hard for a man to obey life because of his will—agree—that is why Jesus is a great man—he saw the crux of the male problem—out of obedience absolute comes creation—I know what you mean by the roar inside you because life is so powerful and you meet the poetry that way—in my opinion you have already once or twice hit that terrible height—and will again—you are a great poet Charles   don't let Emerson and all those non-existent figures near you—I with my aura surround you every moment and they can *not* dirty you—but the pain of the experience of hearing weak non-entities read together with oneself—would damned near kill a creator I admit.

Your Frances

❈ 306 ❈

Washington to Brooklyn (special delivery)
21 August 1950 (postmark)

monday

with quiet pleasure i have spent the afternoon, wasted it, in a way i have not used my ambience in a very long time, in, I guess, two years:

i have walked, sat in the sun, talked, mostly along the railroad yards which are a block and a half away (my woods, or sea shore, even the freight wheels waul like gulls: I'm not much to walk, as you used to walk in Woodward, I think: somehow I drift best as I did today, amongst people, when they are working, keeping their attentions on something like a meal, or groceries, or the shifting of cars: they are usually so much richer at their tasks than they are if something is expected of them, when they go out, say, or are even in passage home)

imagine, it is two years since i have spent any time in my yards, where i used, actually, when i was that kind of a poet, to do my composing, sort of, walking around (they are lovely lonely sun and wind swept lanes with only the awkward cars with the crazy chalk hieroglyphs, and maybe a truck, and ice running where a refrigerator car has been cleared, and crates, smells—wharfish (or the surprise of the guard, of the r.r. dick, who didn't like me there during the war, and asked me why I was there, and i sd, because it reminds me of the sea!

it was a convalescent act, shall we say, a gathering by letting go.   i was sure, anyhow, i didn't intend to work.   don't.   am through, for a spell.   through.   am   gathering.   stock.   shipment.   "don't hump".   repairs.   scream.   loaded.   Eckington Yard.

at the store, what was the conversation: the Bonus Marchers, and MacArthur! first time I'd ever heard washington natives tell tales of it.   stumbled on something: it's their "Flood", their "Quake", their War.   how everyone rushes up on every one else, to tell, to tell, to tell! anecdotes. And, of course, disclose themselves. Fascinating, to me, who does gather in such crazy places, as you know, lady mine.

this did take time from say, a letter to you, but you must not mind: i was busy about you, at the same time! And i am enclosing a lump the equal of what i sent the first day to T, (because tomorrow is the day, is it not; and a spot more, just so you and Lucinda can feel a, have a, do a spread, lady)

and here i am jammed up against the last collection, due to my lovely folly   the mood is still on me, or i'd go to the p.o. later   but i want to see that the enclosed is off to you, and so i'll shoot this on, with yr understanding

> (funny.   no word in me.   but no regrets.   like sliding, in winter, down hill, on to a iced meadow, with that slipping and tossing at the bottom.

> love,
> Charles

☙ 307 ❧

Washington to Brooklyn (special delivery)
23 August 1950 (postmark)

wed aft

frances, mine, i thought i was going to have to send you a wire today but, thank the god of miracles, i am not only well again, but am very strong and very close to the axis of reality   for i was not only not able to get out yesterday, but couldn't write, and feared, last night, i had come down with that sickness i have feared might catch me before this terrible battling, this crisis of my life, was over ((one thing i discovered, and we must use; i called the p.o. to ask if there was a letter from you, and it now occurs to me, that, if, at any time, you should have suddenly to make a shift of address, and wanted to be absolutely sure I got it, whatever my condition, send me a wire to the p.o. box, and a wire I could ask them to read me   this is very unlikely, now, i feel, for, having beaten this attack of what could have been pneumonia (((i am so scared of these lungs, they have not, my body has not now for, what? for four years, since the writing of Ishmael, known a chance to store up sun, strength, the sort of chemicals that man needs, like the earth does, to carry on its life))))   but it doesn't matter. The moment this struggle is over, I shall have it, I shall take it up like a giant, I swear, darling, I swear (at least today I feel so clear, so close, as i say, that I believe, believe!)

i have just done a piece of work on BIGMANS which, like a fool, I did not put a carbon in, or you should have it, for it contains things which are your right. But you will, soon, in one form or another, have it, and how.[39]

what i want to get down, quickly, before i lose its life (i was going to eat, but this, first) is to offer you back, for all the wisdom you invoke, this perception of your beauty: that what makes you woman-essence, why you give birth to life, is, that, intimately, you are whole, that you understand that it is not enough that you yourself are "given" but that you create the state by which a man, without comprehending, is capable of himself giving over his command (i am thinking of his command of consciousness, or whatever it is that makes him that dumb thing, knocking, knocking, striding the earth, when, his striding, whatever its importance, assumes the earth to stride on!)

what i think i set out to say was, that this power to give DOUBLE is the essence, the root thing, that man does not have in the intimate (i believe he has

---

39. "Bigmans III" did not apparently get beyond an outline,—see George F. Butterick, *A Guide to the Maximus Poems of Charles Olson* (Berkeley: University of California Press, 1978), p. xxxiii.

it, the PRINCIPLE OF PERCEPTION OF THE DOUBLE, so far as the "soul" goes, or, as "life" is double) and though i agree with you that the only adjective which hints at this achievement of high woman is "the mother", yet, now, in the present state of total error between man & woman—(I am thinking of, say, a confrontation to the present such as the Gilgamesh story, and how it actually is a further confusion, except to high beings, the division, in that story, of woman into two roles, of "the mother" and "the courtesan"):

let me try it again (bear with me, darling, i am trying to state my love for you): i mean, that *you* have done it, that you are it, in other words, that, though we may use images or adjectives to characterize the double function, yet, the important thing is, that the ACT is SINGLE, is you, is your accomplishment, is frances motz, however many functions of woman frances motz may have been or have to be to be frances motz

And this is not word play. It is essential, that love be understood to be the PERSON accomplishing the SINGLE in the face of the DOUBLE without at all subtracting oneself *from* the DOUBLE, in fact *forever* proceeding *toward* the Single between the horns of the Double.

I stopped there, and went to eat, but I think i can keep on—want to—want to tell you, to reveal, as much as I can

(I was so moved, darling, by a recent way you put something, put yourself, that you do not not know what "fight" means (that is, I think you mean, to the outside world or thing or person), that all you do is BARE yourself:

o, sweet, isn't that true! & isn't that why they climb all over us, they think we are so open (as we are) and, to their squeezed up eyes, so foolish to be "open"

i love you, for saying that, for it delivered me from a problem, gave me a recognition (i suppose it is because i am, right now, moving through a selva oscura myself, but isn't it true, how much we do need "recognitions"—whole series of them—to see how our own troubles are not only our own)   told me, i am not wrong, to bare myself

for i do, despite the apparent ruthlessness, the shrewdness I am about to shed, to some degree:

you see, dearest, if you unleaf what I have written above about the constancy of the double as against the instancy of the single, it is my impression that we cannot charge the world for what we also are, that we are constantly ourselves divided, caught on the poles of the pairs—"intellectual"–"sentimental"; "bare"–"shrewd"; "soul"–"body" ETC, all of 'em, ourselves, and if we damn the world for its constant seizings of us, we must take care—for we only earn that privilege of DAMNING them when we are, ourselves, absolutely afire with passion or alight with sight: THEN, by God, if they don't give way, fold up and scram, THEN, they are utter enemy and must be destroyed, whoever, whatever they are

there was one statement I made in that letter of a week ago Monday which I think, now, I can put more accurately (And I'd guess that is the most important gain of these continuing agonies of days, when, god help me, it seems that I am forced by God to keep trying to illuminate myself—but this is surely because, once done, i can be pure enough to be forever passionate thereafter—

it is this, that, i am not so much in passage, as i sd, from the modern (the flesh) to the archaic (eternal life)—tho that is surely one frame of relevance—as i am in passage *between* those two, that high double, in order to be *over* them:

i suddenly remember your own postulation, recently, of the body as not to be scorned but to be seen in its place—yes, to be maintained, yes, that is beautiful, IT IS, but it is only one pole (so often a horn!) to something else, which is the will to go on, to hold in strength the WHOLE LIFE as well yes yea

baby, I'm starting to lose the edge of the vision.   but today has been vision.   and you, wondrous girl, have been so present, as this letter should tell you

(it is raining again severely, and if it continues, i may not be able—i am still a little weak—to go down and get your letter which I know is waiting for me, was waiting, last night. So if I shouldn't, don't, please misunderstand. All is *very very* well, my darling

LOVE,
Charles

And it would be my impression today, that all the daily agonies & hells we know, despite the gaining of power, is that, to hold the Single is only allowed us in moments (what we call "illuminations" or that the other surcease-which-is-springing "passion") and that, because confusion is more the punishment than earning bread, we are constantly being impaled on the horns to each side, on each side, *are* each side, of ourselves

—thus that abstraction "the world" is a lie: we, too, are ourselves "the world" when we are unable to be single, because we are then double alone (which is the world)

—& that "reality" is also a lie: we are "reality" when we are not, as we cannot be permanently, illuminant or passion

—& that, therefore, we must grant our confusion as as much ourselves as our ambience, & yet, by that granting, not for one split second, not push, contrive, will, believe to move to- *ward* the SINGLE, just as, knowing that the Double is confusion, it is also the structure by which the end of confusion, the momentary end—as in your arms—becomes possible

❧ 308 ☙

Washington to Brooklyn (special delivery)
24 August 1950 (postmark)

thursday

frances, my gate, if these days seem to go on as others have, get lost behind, do not, darling, think they are as the others were, for, there is a thing going on which you must be one of the very few to know   It moves me, now that I my- self am "in", am in the place where one studies to know the self (how easy it sounds, and how I used to think it must be, despite my respect, some sort of metaphysical rather than actual business!), it moves me deeply to comprehend now how you did do this thing, how you did it, how you came to do it—and at so much younger an age than I! (I am always in a sort of despair, how slow I am; yet I do not disbelieve in my process, I only wish it were otherwise)

I do not

feel, now, that I am muttering or wasting. I have the impression—as I proba- bly put it better yesterday—that I am face to face with life, for the first time, I suppose one must say, when the dimension of choice is so huge. (One "thinks", at other stages, one is getting to know; but there is, is there not, a "once" when it is "done"—a time from which one moves away to do the work one is born for without, from that time on, let-up or unlocking of the grip one has to take up in that crucial time) ((I dare say I defer,—or rather have deferred—be- cause my vision is against dogma, against anything the least aggressive, yet, now that I see the choices, I am more aware, how nature uses even our egos as engines of her purpose, and am quieter on this score, am more at ease in my own appetite, or, rather, insistences.)) ((((Curious thing is, I don't know that I have ever been pushed off my grounds—what I call the "insistences"—but I have been not too apt with time or circumstance. Or so it seems. So it seems now, that I must become absolutely coherent, in this respect, that I must put my work (its illuminant and passionate character, not its mere doing—this is an important gain of sight to this dumb-head, darling!) ahead of myself, if that sort of a premise is possible. Better close the gap which I darkly feel exists between them. ((((I have been awakened, these last couple of months, to a lack of "bearing" in the work, whatever it may or may not accomplish as is. In any case, it does not satisfy me—and I think this is the reason. It is not all, all, all olson. Simply that.))))

I do pray, darling, that such a letter of speculations abt olson is not boring to you. As I have sd, I think you know it all anyway. But. There it is. I don't! yet. And I talk to you, bare myself actually, in order to find my way. And it is very beautiful (what, really, is *more* beautiful, except the moments of love which make it possible?) that I do feel able to do this very thing. I'll say this, Frances: it is as beautiful as anything I know that I believe that I can disclose myself to you!

Today I keep thinking of Gotama, and it makes me nervous, for I do not like to conjure up a picture of myself as a religious, yet, when I wonder about why the work does not bear all the traffic of this character we are being a little too exclusive about (it should cease, I'd say, most shortly), I ask myself, are you not forced to be a holy as well as an angry man? And then I wonder, about how readily you agreed, last week, that the future may not contain so much a poet as something else? I should imagine, actually, that that is one of the real reaches of what is here-and-now afoot, and the expansion implied in such guessing (by guesses we make acts, and facts, no?) makes very much sense to me. (I have suffered a long time the feeling I am *not* at my reach, and I should be, it is time, there is more in the container of my person than there is in my acts. And that has to be rectified (or re-ified, as I think i used the word in Ish.)

Behind what I wrote yesterday was a premise which is turning out to be useful these (hours, I say, things are so thick, these days). And it cuts way back to my first piece of writing (1936, as a matter of fact, I suddenly realize,—darling, darling darling—my god—wasn't that precisely the year of *your* crise? is it not so? and if so, is it not, again, remarkable—was it not that year, 1936?)   anyhow, it is this concept of the heroic. And what I am working on, to make the concept vital again, is an opposition between the heroic as a gauge of life and the ethic (which I take to have got started by that Moses who did so much harm ((((interpolation: what do you make out of this business in genesis of abraham letting sara be taken by the pharoah and by abimelech? and the increase of his goods thereupon? am i right to smell something very rotten, very much prostitution? and to conclude that it is precisely man's attitude toward woman on which the whole contrary of the heroic as against the ethic rests??

You see, frances, i think you are profoundly right in what you have done with your life. Now I know why, a long time ago, I said to you, sleep, beloved, sleep. Of course you had to fight, will fight, to hold your delicate position. But mark my words, my love: *you are right*, from the start—in fact, *for* the start. I deeply believe—more each day, each step I take—that woman, even here where the abstracts are raised, is root, is root of soul as well as body (which are one), and that if man is not interpreter correctly here in both he is wrong in both (as has been judeo-christian-european-american tradition, strong, wrong from the start)

In other words, that ethic rests on the derogation of woman, and that the heroic raises itself only on the recognition of her, of her as the tragic source of joy.

Sweetheart. I want to say this. I go on this way, but my mind is also flooded by the thought that there you are worrying, worrying, worrying about this goddamned business of money, & jobs. Let me just say this: do not get panicky. You do have exactly the courage to do what you said, take a job as a housemaid, because you know *who you are*. That fools, in that filthy babylon, do not hire you for your gifts, (that castrata take the positions you could make life of), do not, frances, do not, please, my precious thing, let this cause you despair. You well know we live only because one or two believe in us: I say two, because I am one, and where there's one, as you know, I think, come spring, Bolyai Farkas is right, there are violets!

Even recognize, my darling, that just because I am able to see you as the creatrix of a new root place of woman, it should follow that still, in this run-down age of an earlier rot, you should be, these days, losing job after job to such as these balless literates who are more as men have caused women to become than they are, what they dress and talk as, men

(as is their whole society, a—
                                        fraud)

I do not mean to exhort. I know too well how we are doomed to slide down stairs how often every day. BUT baby, just hear me, just hear me say, that someone else knows how crazy it is, how wrong, that you are made to suffer these dirty little bastards' (even elizabeth's blackenings—o, frances, you know, you know, it is fear, their pitiless fears, because they have let life GO BY, leave 'em, because they would not go to her, the woman, the fountain

Well, I don't know that I have said *a single thing*, in this whole letter, which you do not know. And so, I dare say, it is no more, for you, than watching someone go through hoops you've already been through, with fire rimming each. But I send it to you, out of confidence, out of belief, out of the profoundest respect,

And out of
love,
Charles

go
boy
who
sleeps,
who still
wears caul
        (O Murametz)
                          (This didn't come off—
to wake,   goddamn—And I curse my
and yet not be   failing!)
waste force, mere
thrasher, more
of same (O Herakles)

The idea was, to pick up the rime in
    woman
    fountain
bah! how I hate
to "miss"![40]

⋟ 309 ⋞

Brooklyn to Washington
[25 August 1950]

Friday 4:30 pm

Charles angel—
    For the first time in our correspondence it is I who have to rush to catch the

---

40. A typescript of the finished poem is in the "Unpublished poems" file at Storrs.

collection (the post office closes at six and if I don't get this in the p.o,. you won't have it tomorrow)—I have read your letters all too hastily—the day has been filled since early morning with business appointments—everything awakens answers—I have time to say only a few things—one is—I can not imagine being bored by Olson speculations about Olson—you see, angel, your mind is so very different from mine that every word you say to me is *news*—I am intensely interested in all examinations of your mind's workings and evolvements—it is always such revelation to me; you see I "know" things— then I act—then long after life comes up with the mental description of what has taken place and I am able to evaluate my act—but at the time I never see—I only obey—exactly like Joan of Arc. I do not think you are slow—I think you are *male* and the law of male growth is in all phases *later* than a woman's—riding on the subway today your last letter in mind I also figured out this—a woman rises into her sex hesitantly, heavily—rises very slowly and is in full deep sway for a *long* period—this is also the exact curve of any spiritual development.

But a man comes into his full sex majority early—is extremely powerful in his early twenties, sexually and as his sex begins to normalize his mind and spirit begin to sharpen, and as his sex runs down—his spiritual mental curve keeps on ascending—I use as examples of course the best of each—but in the sense that women are "quick"—no man is quick—and no man worth his salt gets into his stride early in his own curve—this applies even to Rimbaud— whose experience was as you say of now for you "hours" because so thick and full. If Rimbaud had *developed*, as his age prevented, he might have become a religious in Dostoyevsky's sense—will discuss with you when we are to- gether—anyway—both of us are very *pattern* for our own sex and do not keep calling Olson "slow"—Olson is male—

Have time for only one thing—by a deep commandment I borrowed the money from Lucy and took Lucinda to Woodward—discovered in *full flower* in State College a word of mouth rumor being believed by the whole town which is the most perfect example of "wish fulfilment" of the mob in relation to the alive—the aristocrat—the former—

State College, Millheim and Woodward are full of a rumor (since I ap- peared at the Inn with Harold) that I have been picked up by an FBI agent for operating a two-way radio secretly with codes to Russian agents or some such, from my woods in Woodward (I am supposed to have hidden the radio under the wood I brought home in my doll carriage!) Absolutely fantastic, but *every- one* except 2 close friends believed it!

Talk about desiring the death of the strong!

And I have to spoil everything by turning up for lunch at the most promi- nent restaurant in State College—laughing my old loud triumphant laugh- ter—seeing *everyone*   telling I live in New York   Lucinda accepted into

Packer school for girls, etc.—*before* I knew there was a rumor! How all those poor enemies must have been unhappy—

Oh Charles this world—I do not agree will answer about one in relation to world—

Your Frances

Thank you 4000 times for money—you are an absolute angel to "hunt among those stones" for money for Frances—

I am indebted to you all my life for being so sweet.

Frances

◄ξ 310 ξ►

Washington to Brooklyn (special delivery)
25 August 1950 (postmark)

friday

frances: i just stumbled on this, putting the day's work away ((had to settle, and get off mss., for the G.G. boke THE PRAISES[41] (laughlin released the title and the poem to me, for such use, today; he will, as you remember, publish it in his next N.D. XII): it comes to ten poems, most of them long, but i am disappointed there are not more possible, GGs page and point are so; like to pack 'em, myself (beautiful job of that kind just out, Texas, of Basil Bunting poems—good straight paper, no da-da, and good small sharp clean type, packed, packed)

It's STIRZ!:
> When Mazdaism had forced back Semitism and taken control of Hellenism, the North entered upon a period of independent development. What we call Gothic is the 3rd art of northern origin which rose to greatness by its own merits. The Greek genius grew great in the South, the Iranian in the borderland, between North and South, and the Germanic (he calls it) in the North itself.[42]

Nice packaging, no?

((a propos printing, dahlberg asked me, what i thot of Nevill (London) on his FLEA, and I sd, hrrrr, ugh, newspaper, and he says, it's either that or petti-

---

41. The book did not materialize, but an "anthology" of four poems under the title *The Praises* appeared in *Golden Goose*, series 3, no. 1 (July 1951). *New Directions* 12 (1950) included the poem "The Praises." Basil Bunting's *Poems: 1950* had just come out from The Cleaners' Press, Galveston, Texas.

42. Josef Strzygowski, *Origin of Christian Church Art* (Oxford University Press, 1923), p. 249.

coat, and i says, yah, yah, ed, you get the newsprint, i get the petticoat—which is still going to be true, I'm afraid, with the GG

BUT ONE DAY, FRANCES BOLDEREFF . . . .))

darling. You have been very beautiful, and not said a word, about why I am not come to see you yet. I think I have certainly asked you to stretch the bow of your body to its intensest reach. I, therefore, want to say this:

I think that all that can be unraveled from this struggle I have been writing out to you is just about done, that is, that any more such substance will only be—as I think the last couple of day have been—corollary, ancillary to the core. I hope we can be proud enough of this baby to agree, he's got ahold of, got his teeth into, that core.

It is, therefore, now time to put action in. I would be a fool to think that is going to be any easier. But there it is. It is called for.

Now I don't want, now or ever, to do again that once I did what is not only (as you are absolutely right to damn but what I also abhor), make false lights, make a date, however tentative, and not keep it. You were right, to scorn me.

As I have told you, my best action is swift, decision, a wire, there. And so it shall be. But I feel in my bones you are owed now, right now, some guess *inside which* this action will happen.

I am terribly nervous before it, but not so nervous as I was when I blocked out what has now taken place, and you were so beautiful, and said, "baby, don't be. i'm here." (You will recognize, of course, that it is not the relation you-me, that makes me nervous, but, the effects on me-con, to put it baldly, and to say no more about it, now.)

I suggest this—and do understand, darling, that I am trying to cover, to guess all eventualities, and to do it ahead of time, because I think it is your right, at the same time to leave plenty of margin so that you shall not be exposed again to false fire—it will happen in the next two weeks, and it can happen any time from this Monday on.

Is that square? I pray so, baby—and by god if he doesn't show by two weeks from now I'd tell him where to go, if I were you, tell him, he's a phoney! Which I don't think he is.

This is said hard, darling, just as clear and tough and projective as I can be. And by god you have my hand on it, it's done straight, sweet. It's all right there, right on the top, no curves. I mean what is said. I think you do know how scrupulous, and responsible, I make the effort to be (as a matter of fact, I no longer question my capacity for straight-shooting and for staying-in-there—I figure now whatever doubts I may ever have had about it, were only due to the confusions of this false environment in which we live, not to weaknesses of myself. I am through with that deal, of examining and examining and examining my own behaviour in terms of its effects on others close to me. I won't shed it overnight, we know, but I'm damn sick of being what I would, at this moment, be arrogant enough to put this way: of being imposed on, for that combination of arrogance and generosity which seems to be the engine by which such characters as myself are run by

"egotist", is it? or, as you put it, "ruthless",—and it moved me very deeply, when you said it, that I felt no *judgment* of me in your word, that you didn't squeeze an ounce out of the envelope of air in which i am enclosed

> (I don't know: I have been told I am strong. Pah! My god! I am weak, weak! My god, when I am told that, I ask myself, do they know? do they know at what price energy is shaped, how one *has* a perception, now and then? why one thrashes, is "energetic" (another word that stings: me, with my poor heart and lungs, "energetic"!) why—o, yes, that wonderful thing someone said, some dope like T.W. Higginson, about Miss Dickinson, that, her presence made you feel as tho the top of your head was coming off? (or, come to think of it, was that what *she* sd, about emotions?!) either way, it suggests what so few comprehend: what screaming terror it is, to get on with things

(the way they talk I am convinced, they're only on here for the ride, never, never, did they figure, it's altogether different, altogether more important, it's life or death!

Darling, I'm bursting. My heart is wild, hurts under my ribs. (I wish to God I had been born with a miner-peasant's sense, like DHL,—and been over this stupid hump years ago. But I wasn't. My nerve-tribe, was some other, however he may be brother. I give you love, and how:

                                        Charles

p.s. no letter from you since monday—at least, up to last night. I am going to the p.o. now. I hope all is all right. I was worried last night. Good lord, FM—are you all right?

At P.O. no letter. And did you get special *tuesday, yesterday*? (I didn't write Woodward because you were already scheduled to be back Brooklyn. *Pray all well.*

⥊ 311 ⥋

Brooklyn to Washington
[26 August 1950]

Saturday morning

Dearest Charles

I have your special—and I look on as a mother with eyes full of pain but no comment—no soul, on the verge of its crisis is anything but nervous—choice/decision are the great existential leaps and Kierkegaard and Dostoyevsky both have said how few are the men who can "leap."

I want today to take up the pencil part of your Wednesday letter—the part of the relationship of the Single and Double to the world—

I agree with you absolutely that attacking the world is attacking the double in ourselves—

For myself I would like to state this: I believe myself capable of the Single as a constant—that I have never had any intention or desire or ambition to change the world—I spurn it absolutely—I *know* it will one day be consumed—but I believe it will be consumed by the accumulated force of the action of spiritual men—and therefore when I fight to stay alive—to keep my daughter in health and joy and myself in health and joy—to be at every instant alive and *for* the perfect beauty which God shows he expects by the infinite times he shows the possibilities in Nature—I believe I serve—I believe to harass the Knave and the Fool with one's laughter and proud joy and strong sorrow is the service of God. I believe with Dostoyevsky that the saint must now move out of the cloister into life—where he does not seek to change or reform the world—but to bring about its destruction by his belief which is his love—which is his obedience.

I hate "energy"—"energetic"—Christ, who died on the cross knows, as do we all, energy is the love—the command to make oneself useful—and mostly he who obeys is hung over a fence with his guts pierced clean through, but somehow out of something he hauls himself over into the camp of the believers, the knowers, who serve. I love you.

Frances

❧ 312 ❧

Brooklyn to Washington
[27 August 1950]

Sunday night

Charles dear—

I have such a shy strange feeling darling, on the days when I do not have a letter from you—despite your message yesterday or maybe because of it—today I am shy—shy—

But I want to describe to you my strange job hunting of today—I went out to Long Island to friends of Elizabeth—they have a composition shop in their home and they have offered me a job strange and not at all anything I would want and yet I am going to try it—

1. Because they are really intelligent and really bohemian, which means

2. That I would be terribly free—free about when I come and go—free about how many hours I work—free while I am working

3. That freedom and non-pressure of time are very very precious to me

4. I will be paid on the basis of actual work I do—how much stuff I do a day—they charge by the page and so it will depend on me how many pages I turn out—no idea what I can earn—working on an IBM machine—never did anything like it

5. They want me and will be very nice to me

So darling on Thursday or Friday I am going to start—it takes over an hour to get there.

dearest dearest man—I am afraid to breathe for fear I will wake up and that letter I held in my hand yesterday will turn out to be not true.

Oh Charles—Dostoyevsky is your father and mine and I feel he watches us—to find the thing he never found—comprehension plus passionate sexual response—

Frances

❧ 313 ❧

Brooklyn to Washington
[28 August 1950]

Monday night

Darling—

No letter today—naturally I am very nervous, too—I am hoping you are on your way but my guess is that you are preparing things in order to come and that you can not find a place (inside or out of you) to write—when one is waiting to see the beloved and everything is so tense, there isn't anything to say until we are face to face.

This is just to tell you I await with white face.

I do not think, I just try to live another moment.

Your Frances

◆ 314 ◆

Washington to Brooklyn (special delivery)
28 August 1950 (postmark)

monday

i was a fool not to write you saturday night when i had your letter, but the relief was so delicious, and i was so harassed from other causes (mostly plumbing!) that i wanted only to savor it, not express the pleasure to hear from you, to know you were back, and that all was right, even that you had joined the rest of us in becoming Red agents!

for i have not been well since   i do not tell you this for you to give it a second thought   it is just that i want to give you sound reason i shall mail this without picking up your letter or letters since, first

for it is not at all important that my energies are down, for the moment   i begin to think, my inner vitality is so high, that it may well be that i am going to have to lose the health of my body to earn its soul

(that the legend is the hoop of a snake, that only thus shall i come to live in my own house!)

I have to spend the day on a difficult task, to tell Dahlberg i should prefer not to "review" his book (he needs same for leverage on academics for a job this fall) but should wish to go ahead by my own methods and do a critique, which I would do, in the clear, and then send out, like any writing, for him who might wish to print it   It was a very hard decision to make. For the problem—today, at least, where all book-journalism is puffs—of the line between to do a friend a friendly act and at the same time to obey the formal demands of an art, is very difficult. Dahlberg, of course, compounds the devil-ism by his presumptuous "use" of everyone, his "bartering" of his acts to buy yours. But this no longer bothers me, except as his blindness here will cause him to misunderstand my reasonings. Even this I have a shield to turn: it is a sword, my innocence.

But the decision has led me in. And I am already at work on the critique. It will be a very hard job. He is a treacherous person, even in his work, and one has to go in with the heaviness of a peasant and his mattock in order to keep the ground under foot where he would, by his image and his thought, tie you up in watery webs; and by borrowed gnomes plague you into a false belief in his genius, by wily intimidations. Or so it is, if you are caught up at all. Most are not, are unwillling to suspend their irritation with his syntax & this wateriness. But I have found him too often wise & amusing to get off so lightly. I *have*, in fact, to be that peasant *of* him.

Otherwise? There is no reason to heave up the rich things which have come into being—as I said, the going ahead I have so writ out to you has given its bloom (it is lovely, in Hesiod, that Heaven, the father, who loses his genitals to Kronos, his son, has those genitals called (Love is called "limb-relaxing") he is called "bloom-giver"!) And now, for a time, I must let them leak throughout my ground.

But I do want you to know how delightful yr letter on State College was, how much like Motz laughter it was, how rich and thrusting! And that you are a Roosian trayyytor, is most beautiful! Isn't it wonderful?

O, frances, what shall we do with these unlaughtered people?

Love, for now, and more
Charles

<del>ᘓ</del> 315 ᘒ

Washington to Brooklyn (special delivery)
29 August 1950 (postmark)

tuesday

frances, my lady: Can you bear a couple of days of olson on dahlberg? I hope so. Nor do I think it will be unrewarding. For this man is my Dragon, my demon brother. Or was. For it is my impression, that, out of some fixing, yes-terday, of the new eye of my innocence, I have found him out, by way of his book, see, maybe for the first time, what a Primordial Boy he is at the same time that he is also (as such Boys must be, untethered, unhindered, un-self-caused) an Assyrian Monarch, a Debaucher and a Killer.

But to get to such headlineisms requires examination by innocence. And that is labor. (And so we ever work on anyone or anything which is not also a part of ourselves?).

So what I say I also take back into my self—and put out, as characterization, most carefully. For as who was it I read recently said, another man's soul is a dark well.

Yet I am surprised at how transparent ED is. I think the Boy clue is crucial. He even has quite a wonderful naive passage of craving for the return to water, to be Dolphin!

It is right here that we get (without his necessarily being important) into something very essential (I need only mention DHL and the Flying Fish—or Flowers). Which is: the relevance of the Primordial Child to myth-making, to what, in this kind of men, "my kind", at least, makes for what we call the creative force.

((You have noticed me, how many times?, say, I must swing free: it is this oscillation or swimming in a free element that is, is it not, what we must dub, the Dolphin in the Sea.

But what one can surely say of DHL that one cannot say of ED is, that this freshness is not allowed to be indulged in, that it must not be so excluding that the *person* (the soul, actually), that Man which the Boy also is, is not allowed to be anything more than a more demanding Boy!

I take it Dahlberg gives himself away, in this passage: "A demon has said, Know thyself; but he that contemplates his identity perceives the filths of darkness". (This is an abandonment, is it not, of the process of individuation—a process, by the way, which is the most difficult precisely to these Dolphin Men, above all others.

And what interests me, is what follows from this abandonment. Suddenly, if all process of being-and-becoming is set aside in the self, then the world dies, all life is nothing but a preying ground, a hunt place, where there are only two classes and two actions: those who pleasure the Boy and whom he therefore allows to live on the condition that they continue to pleasure him, one side of the Assyrian Monarch; and the rest of the world and people are those whom the Monarch excoriates and orders killed!

What fascinates me, is, that Dahlberg's imagery does break up into two halves, and on the same lines. His physiology, for example—it is chiefly sexual in tone—is plump females vs puny males; cheeses vs swine and horses; oils and grapes vs shards and ordure; Venus vs Vulcan ETC   His geography likewise: Sidon, Uz, Demeter vs Atlantic, Caucasus, Hyperborean Lands!

Note how they are *both* sentimentalities.

But there is more in it. For the recurrence of the imagery begins to beat out a truth below the sentimentals of the language. I am not yet advanced enough to be sure, but I'd guess that the cravings are what you'd expect: a sort of Melon Mother, for one, a sort of Grassy City, for a second, in other words a State of Ceasing, a sort of vegetable Death-in-Life, patently the worst aspect of the Return to the Womb.

But he's a cunning character, my friend. And it would take such digging as I am willing to give it, to extricate these things from his wily text.

The large question behind it all, in my own mind, is: what is its relation to the SEMITE and the MEDITERRANEAN

this is going to take care and formulation. For it is one of the grave problems of our time, to discriminate here, without becoming the agent of political wrong.

For one thing, my plan is to chart this imagery and syntax as totally and carefully as a scholar.

Well, at the moment there seem to be many things to say, but there are so many it comes down to a few, most of which, so far as they are in my mind today, I have said already, I guess.

What, of course, is important to me, is not so much to nail down my friend (however transparent he is still a well of his own making) but how, still, his *nature* stimulates my own, how much he is brother, (or son, he strikes me, now, in a curious reversal—or I, David, and he, Saul!). There is reason we have, for 14 years, with 7 of them blanked out, been such strange friends.

I want now to go to get your letters. And I shall add to this there, in answer to anything which has come up. But recognize, darling, underneath any perceptions above, where I got the innocence and the strength to see, now, so late, say, what is to be seen! who was it whose love i give back.

Yr Charles

Thank you, darling, for your two beautiful letters. And for your nervousness back! my subtle one. But don't worry. Time is nothing, *really*, suddenly. And yr job gives me rest, quiet, somewhere, in this well, this soul.

Love,
Charles.

◄ 316 ►

Brooklyn to Washington
[30 August 1950]

Wednesday morning

Charles I have your letter on Dahlberg and the lines you quote me out of him are absolute filth—are lie—what "filths of darkness"?—this usually covers all those embryonic strangenesses of sex among other things and you know that to a pure soul all of these are pattern and pure to be accepted each in its turn. I am furious now—I am glad you understand so well the love of death the whole thing represents that you see so clearly how it is "Return to the Womb" which is only death desire.

I could write a long letter because I have been examining this kind of thing in the Hebrew for twenty some years—it is where I am their declared open enemy—and I have a sword in my hand to turn against all who defame or cheapen life.

Charles don't say time is nothing. You were very cruel to state a latitude of two whole weeks to a passionate person like me. I am almost crazy.

Don't call me "subtle"—I am not subtle—I have a soul which searches every instant—whose stated purpose, whose prayer, since the age 15 "To understand as deeply as possible"—

I am becoming wildly impatient.

Dostoyevsky's *diary of a writer* sold *less* than 500 copies in this whole English speaking world—straight dope from the head of Scribner's! Now you know where the lovers of life are—alone—and bound to win.

◄ 317 ►

Brooklyn to Washington
[30 August 1950]

Wednesday 6:00 pm

Charles poet—

I went on an orgy today and bought four books I have loved for a very long time—Frye on Blake—two Kierkegaards and *Illuminations* of Rimbaud.

I know in this world there are literally hundreds of men who love Rimbaud and consider him their special property. Despite this fact, I *know* Rimbaud belongs to me—I am prepared to prove that he had an outlook so similar to my life thrust that I can say he was the poet—I the words.

I am so intensely electrified—his French has sturdy sternness like the Bible in English—he is so part of my blood, my existence and yesterday I took out of Louise's house that essay of Carnevali's for you—I am really excited with so much life to place in your lap for you to be showered with gifts—

When Olson will you arrive?

Frances

❦ 318 ❦

Brooklyn to Washington
[30 August 1950]

Wednesday 7:45 pm

Charles—

Nothing like being excited!

But how happy I am to be in the presence of a great soul—my Rimbaud.

And I write you this because I am so terribly excited because it feels to me that *all* of Rimbaud is a plea for two things—for a poet—Charles—who must burst his blood vessels in order to fulfill the longing which Rimbaud had for him—for *him*—and for a new world in which the woman would be placed where you and I long to place her—at source—oh! how it sounds like Charles—you are called forth by the longing of "Genie." I want to hear you read these magnificent things to me in loud Charles french and I want you to *feel* how God places you in this world—author of The Kingfishers—Bigmans—La Chute I—to answer the longing of Rimbaud's soul—

I absolutely belong to him and we to him.

In heaven I mail him a copy of my Notebook and of the secret acts of my life

Come soon—

Frances

❦ 319 ❦

Washington to Brooklyn
30 August 1950 (postmark)

wednesday

frances: it bugs me, the way i am a day up and a day down—clear sign i am
riding on my runners

you must not mind, and just excuse me, until i tuck
away a little spring, somehow

& because this is a mere note, & of not much
worth, i shall, for experiment, send it along 1st class, risk disappointing you
tomorrow, just to check & see if your new address is as good as you claimed
west broadway was, and that it does not need a special to reach you tomorrow   tell me back if you get this thursday, and at what hour

i had a big mail today, and one letter needed immediate attention, which
knocked the stuffing out, the weather was so wet and hot: it was a request for
a letter on dahlberg, who has applied for a grant to get money to do his next
book   he is a shrewd fellow, and knows the world, and knows he better score
right now when he has a book coming on the market   it bugs me, he should
be so shrewd: one wants to cry, aw, for chrissake, make a gaff, make a gaff,
brother!

read a short story of dhl, Love Among the Haystacks, just because it was at
hand, and to test, by that story, what is it that is not in ed's story of 8th street,
date, 1937–38, the title story of his book

but can't, for the lifelessness of me,
say: neither seem enough   dahlberg's is full of a patent disgust for human beings, a palpable loathing—and dhl's, of course, is quite the opposite, quite
warm and loving, quite beautiful   dahlberg wants it, but can't have it, in his
makings   dhl has it, and makes it   but where dahlberg's is all the City as
death, dhl's is the fragrant thing dahlberg wants   so how is it? dahlberg
knows nothing else

otherwise think about what you wrote, wonder what dostoevsky would seem
like if i read him now: what is it you are reading? Am interested to look again
at his Notes From Under the Floor

o, sweet, this is no joy for you—and i deeply wish it were, for i want you to
have more of me than this   just feel that i write is what is important, not that
i do not say anything, today   i never myself really taking this sloughs too seriously, for i have found them often idlings from which to spring   it is that i
worry about you, that i speak of it at all

tell me all about the new job   fascinating set-up   hope it is as good as it
sounds for you   what is it, actual typesetting, by an IBM? electro-type?   That
impresses me no end, that you can play one of those! Really, what range you
have! Tell me more

And I'll surely be better, so don't give it a thought

love,
Charles

❧ 320 ❧

Washington to Brooklyn (special delivery)
31 August 1950 (postmark)

thursday

frances, look: I must be some sort of a fool, I put the thing in a latitude out of this unbearable sense of justice which it takes as much to uproot as it does to arouse my anger or my passion   My sense of justice is a damnation I carry to eventually destroy, simply because human beings are right, I guess, not to pay it that much mind   But I do, now, or have, and am, with great difficulty, rolling it off me like a rock door

I surely meant not to arouse you, or to

look: i better be very quiet; i am deeply sorry, darling, I did anything, said anything at all; it is all due to the falseness of letters at a time like this; as I said last week, I have been through what I had to go through now, and there is nothing more to say; so I shouldn't any more write a letter to you than I am able to write a poem; I am at an end, and shall, until i get back some rest and health, not have anything to say

i say this reluctantly, for, in spurts, i do have something to say, at least can block out areas where things can be said eventually; but you are reading me too close, not letting the process go by, and i cannot afford to be screamed at, my skin is so like yours, these days: i have never been so sensitive ((now don't, please, take this scream word amiss: i am quite sure you are right, darling, know you are, but what we can battle out in the flesh we cannot in letters now—at least i am not master of my wit and my word, or you wouldn't have cause to jump me))

i don't know; i am deeply wondering, these days, what right a writer has, outside his word—when his word is right. When his word is right, it should lock up *all*—i mean *all*. It is not his life which is or is not right, it's his word. He puts it there, and what he puts there, is from his soul. But his soul knows no arrogance, in fact only knows obedience. (The advantage, if there is one, to the word, is precisely that the arrogance is its, not the man's: I am thinking of that beautiful go-er by blunderings and tortures, Feodor Dostoevsky, whose writ-ings you speak of now so often to me. I think of his entanglement with Paula Sualova, with the tables, with his Siberian wife, with Turgenev (the glove).

O frances, your words cut me to the heart. I do not know so clearly, so on the instant. Honestly, I do not. I only can, when I am well, put down what comes up. And the gods save me, i seek to make them right. But right, in my own rhythm and time. I DO NOT KNOW ANSWERS.

It is even a little bit crazy. Before I read your letters, for example,—on the way down town and back—I was thinking (I had just done, thank god, a careful analysis of Dahlberg's Hebraism) I was thinking: "Before I publish this thing, after it is all done, and put to the best of my present sight"—I am pretty much at the point where I think it is going to be necessary for me to make this book a deep issue of Hebraism vs some new conception to clear us of Hebraism, Christianity, Greekism, and the Renaissance—"I think I better check the whole business with Frances, let her go over the thing carefully from her knowledge and sight, and take her advice."

And then I read this slash of yours, and I think, good god, has frances, too, no sense of another's going-along? that this is my friend, this man? that I, who have been in the politics and poetry of this world, have seen how intellectual judgments have fed hate and death? that i will, with the profoundest reluctance, if I do it at all—the alternative is to say nothing directly on my friend's book, but to make my statements for myself—use a man's book to nail him, when i ask myself who reads, where is there souls to understand?

Aw. It was this Dostoevsky who caused Alyosha— or was it Ivan—to say, "Human beings, they must be treated either as children or as those who have been committed."

Yet I would not have you one jot other than you are, and if you withhold your-self one syllable, you know, as well as I now know, that death will start in. So pay no mind at all to what I say. I am just strained by this goddamned unnat-ural situation. And there it is.

Plus that stupid fact, that this thing, a writer, is a tool of God. And if he is working on something, until he has phrased it, got it down, done it, until he has been USED, he is not himself. And when he has got it down, he is through with it. So he is never, actually, of one piece—at least the poet

(I am also, these days, confronting this problem, of the difference, between the poet and the story-teller.)

You see, babe, you carry all yourself with you at every instant. I don't. I am either being plagued to get into print what I am already through with. Or reaching forward to get down what I have not yet done. So I am nothing, at any moment, nothing

NOT I BUT THE WIND THAT BLOWS THROUGH ME

And it is beautiful, what you write, "all are pattern, and to be accepted each in its turn". And I deeply wish you would write, as you say, a long letter, had written a long letter.

And: "the important thing always is—the step forward one is oneself able to take". Which is what I probably shall have to do in this instance, in the end.

AND NOW I SEE AGAIN YOUR PHRASE—"what 'filths of darkness'?—this usually covers all those embryonic strangenesses of sex among other things"—and I bloom from your words, know exactly what you mean, thank you for throwing that switch—right! right! it is true, how wrong they *all* are!

Baby, maybe:
obviously,
this is all just
temporary trouble.
So take what's good,
and leave what's bad.

And I send this only because I want you to have a letter, to, tell you, I am here, and that there is love in me for you.

Charles

❦ 321 ❧

Washington to Brooklyn (special delivery)
1 September 1950 (postmark)

friday

Gan: I got the terribly helpless feeling, the moment I had posted the letter to you last night, that i had got everything wrong, that the word "justice" you would take as to cover everything, instead of merely the setting of an outside limit, etc. etc. etc. Isn't it horrible, the way WORDS get as sensitized as skin, sometimes, when things go awry?

I only can pray, sweet, that you did not take it by the wrong handle, that you saw I was distraught, and that you buried the whole business in the body of your comprehension (I was moved by your phrasing, recently, "comprehension, plus passionate sexual response"—isn't that everything, god help us!

It is strange, the way I am. I don't know that I ever felt so alert, so alive as to be swimming with perception. And yet the bases of myself are so upheaved (not overthrown, just stirred, made over, in some mortar, with the huge pestle of life and death having pounded me:

> my age, for example, overwhelmed me last night—the fewness of years ahead—so much I could not sleep, and went, restless, to the garden, and still, could find no peace, was tormented, terribly, angry, at the way I had used my life.

As a matter of fact, sometime in the last few hours, it came to me this way: that another way of putting the phase of life just closed and the phase coming on, is, that I did do what I suppose I wanted, did, finally, sharpen my *taste*, make grow my sense of the creative as it is words, do it and do it and do it, until, in these last months I did a body of work and got a body of doctrine so clear that I would walk anywhere into any work of art now and say, this is how it is, this is where it is on, it is off, this is where the man is doing what has to be done

Yet, I paid a price, maybe. (You said, when we were last together, "you do not comprehend me, direct," or something similar, opposing the way, say, a Ward catches you, knows you.) Now this is true. I think there is no question. My breed don't. They get it on the top in, not the other way. The scale is altogether different. Ideality is the measure, not reality, say, quickly. It is not "life as is", but life, all over the place. I dub it, the naive, or the innocent, when it is good. Particularity comes hard, to such. In fact the whole mortal thing, mortality, is grasped with pain, by confusion more than instinct. The instinct is localized to the individual, and understands that all other individuals are likewise, with some great difficulty. It is the god-gate, not the human-gate, say. Anyhow, there is a difference. And it seems to me that a poet, anyhow, and a poet now, anyhow, has this difference, this burden as compared even to the story-teller, even, say, to Lawrence (Keats as against Lawrence, maybe).

To come back, then. It occurs to me that what I am now taking on, is this other thing, this incredible entanglement in mortality, as KNOWN, as RECOGNIZED, as WORN (as you wear the BODY), and not as something which is a foreign territory which better be left alone, which one sees accident in, rather than purpose, as one, who is of the monarchy of ideality, looks to for slaves, for pleasure, for the wrong use. For so it seems mortality has been. (Or must be?) Until such time as a man is born out of woman to understand that of these things also is life.

Does this sound terribly abstract? And I dare say it proves, that, even when the suffering is taken on, the GATE, even here, is the old one, the inevitable one, the one forever the only one open to the creature who is of such a tribe

> (I learn from ED that there were sepa-
> rate gates at
> Jerusalem for sheep, goats,
> and asses!)

The GATE PROUTI is what I call it, as you know. It is as though there are those who are in and must get outside, and those who are outside who must come in. And only those of either who do both are to be said to have entered life.

Well. Shall I? I pray I may. And the struggle these days is to see how to go and where it is. To go by new feet toward a new objective: double task! (That is what I meant by "time": when one is suddenly less blind, suddenly sees things one has only wondered about, been exposed to on one's dark, blind side—why then, time swells out (is death suddenly brought face to face?). And the thing seems to be, to go in—and not even to predict, what is in, who, where, what are yourself?

It is true. I am only full of questions. Only questions. This is so new a place, so familiar, from having been here before another way, but so new, now! Who am I and what is this place?

You see, sweetheart, you deal with a deeply abstract man. It is a flaw, I am willing to speculate. But I only think it is me. And the importance is simply, what I do with it. That I am about, about like a wild thing about, 40, hours the day. The night is no longer anything but a poor repair. No rest. No peace. Go. Go. Keep on. Pour it out. What Where Who. I can't believe that I keep on. No slack. Don't want it. Won't hole up. Can't stand the notion, to take a step back, to breathe. Not even eat. Only by necessity. Only do any of these things because they are necessary. Not wanted. What is wanted is, to understand, to get it all in, to get all the way out. That's all. And HOW? HOW?

My present instinct is, simply, keep at it, just stay in there. Don't even figure there's an answer, that you'll find it. Of course, yes. But have to resist. Have to say, no. Don't know. Just stay. See. Work, and keep on. Keep at it. MAD.

You can't imagine how different this is, from the old Cool One. The guy who could figure it out. Can't. As a matter of fact go in as tho I might not come out. And THIS—WOW—that's not an Olson I know!

Straight wild. Straight wild.

So, darling, this is an attempt at a portrait—a picture, for YOU. For you to know, to comprehend. I have the strangest sort of faith, in all this. That you only, of anyone, would know, does. Has been through it. And it bugs me. But it doesn't. I love it. I am so happy that I can tell you. The only thing which bugs me, is, that you are *also* your self, and your self must have instants when it says, well, there he is, he's having it, but here am I, and this is old stuff. Well, there it is. I can't be other than I am. Or I better not be. The capacity of the abstract is, to be other than it is. This is *its* trajectory, its power, its tremendous imaginative fluidity. But now that fluidity seems to me to be beyond value, to be DANGER, danger, danger, for me, at least. I have to put down ground, resistance, hold, the mortal thing now—or I shall never earn it, never be based where I must be, be GROUNDED. So if I strain you, torture your dear self, seem to be no good, wrong. Oh, frances, what in this agony can I say? My acts are these, these hours, these letters, these are my acts now. And that you receive them receive me, is greater than anything else, greater, obviously, at the moment, than your presence, my beloved.

I am as fierce, I see, as ruthless, even on this path as on all others! O excuse me, sweet, that I am Olson. If that is what is called for. I do not think I am anything but what you said, when we were together, "You are not a very likable guy, you know!" I guess not. That truth bears in on me. And do I do anything to change it? Will this forest lead me out, different? I do not know. It looks, now, so far as you are concerned, that I am only worse, no?

Darling, this is written at white heat. So you must try to go thru the errors. I should find it impossible to re-read it. It is torn off, and I say it like a cry, a prayer, a belief, to you, to you, to you.

For you. It is not mine. It is yours. I despair. I do not know. Who and what am I? Am I of worth? How may I be of worth? What work shall I do?

Isn't it crazy, how elementary? That I, at age 39, with what I have, should be all the way over, beginning, BEGINNING. Asking juvenile questions?

A child. No question. A child. A baby.

And this baby, at the same time, has to go through the traces *as he was*. Well, not really. I *am* taking up my innocence. But, there are things which have to be done which I do like a wry dramatist: watching, like a stage manager, the old act. While all I care for, is the new person, the new action, the new stage. WHO IS THIS CHARACTER, WHAT IS THIS DRAMA;

WHO

WHAT

Any moment now two citizens walk in from Black Mt. They knew an Olson. He isn't here. They'll look, and he'll say some things he said before. Or will say some other things the way he said things before. But who is it they will meet? WHO, and will they hear? No, for no one even is told, is spoken to, as are you.

So, my love, they just knocked!
And there they are. So I send you
all this baby of yours love,
Charles

❧ 322 ❧

Brooklyn to Washington
[1 September 1950]

Friday night

Charles darling—

I did not write to you because every minute I was waiting for a telegram. I did not get a letter Thursday. I hate for you to spend your money on specials—write me because I will be so distraught until I hear from you just one more special and on Saturdays so I have word on Sundays but otherwise let me wait two days—I do not mind—it is only that now darling everything is so hard for me and I did not get a letter this morning—it is now 7:30 p.m.—I just got back—I have been out since early morning—and I find your two letters and oh! darling, please do not judge me—I have no money—I had to stop in to borrow from Harold which was something I have never done from men—(put you in a special class—like myself—my own self) and the job business is so nervous for this reason—Yorke is a nice man and a sharp man—and he is letting me come out to practise—not hardly taking time even to speak and teaching me nothing outside of the first five minutes—he doesn't know whether I will be able to do it or not and neither do I and until I learn (which must be soon) I don't know whether I have a job or not and my situation is so desperate—I do not tell you everything that happens—but I can not get a part time job because people are afraid I will leave suddenly when I get a job and of course I must tell I am looking for a real job—anyway dearest—I am so terribly pressed from every side and then I go crazy and I start to be fierce because our whole thing is so hard for me in many different ways—you see even as you asked me to wait two weeks you said "*If* I don't do it" and that frightens me—I can accept anything, but indefiniteness is so so hard—

I understand that you do everything you can—I never blame you dearest—I *feel* and felt that you stated the two weeks in order so I could hope—but when one is absolutely wild with suffering and like on Thursday absolutely alone with no one in the world to talk to and so full of terrible nervous anguish about the future and expecting every minute you might wire or come and so I was afraid to leave the house please dearest accept and do not judge me—I was afraid after I posted the letter that it would sound like some kind of unclean attack but surely you know I am not capable of such a thing—I know how intellectual judgments have fed and do feed hate and if I had any speck of hatred I would not dare to write as I did—perhaps, I was thinking afterwards, it could even be raised out of Hebraism maybe into something larger so there could be no chance for Dahlberg or for any unknown man to be wrongly wounded—nevertheless I feel absolutely deeply that when life is deformed at its essence—(I do not mean sex—I mean "belief"—belief is what is precious to me and to life) its enemies must be attacked and shown up—but I am not sure the method best for this is not some positive writing of one's own rather than analysis—to teach as Jesus put down all that falseness of the "Grand Inquisitor" by a kiss—no words—that is, no rebuttal—just an act, a kiss.

Of course you understand Charles that words are acts to me—I mean your words are your acts that I believe as deeply as you do in the word of a writer—that it is his whole concern and my love for you is because I believe in the holy service of God and that men like you bring God into life—I am rereading Frye on Blake and I so completely agree with Blake's reverence for the artist—the imaginative—and you must know from my two Rimbaud letters how eternally faithful I am to this belief—

I do not believe we need worry about each other's misjudgements—both of us are large and we are "committed" (where did you get the passage you quote—never saw it) I wonder if he means exactly as it reads—for I love it as it stands, though I am not sure I take it as you meant it—anyway, to me "the committed" are the only alive—the only alive—and every second of their life is committed and do you not think I understand the anguish of a writer who I long ago said "has no private life"—he is always pressing every sense either to get something out, down on paper or to force its existence into the brain.

Charles this is also a lousy stupid letter—just so you will have a letter in your hand—anyway two more "facts"—that dumb lawyer wired me yesterday (supposedly with the answer) and all it said was "Phone him long distance at noon". I didn't get the wire until afternoon so it was too late—but why can't such a simple business be done with a 3¢ stamp?—he is so *lazy* and so stupid and when I have no money I have to *call* him about Lucinda's trust fund.

Another fact I learned from Harold that the young man at McGraw Hill who is to take Eisenman's place—the one who really turned me down—is not expected at McGraw Hill to hold his job because he has no talent—Eisenman trained him and gave him the job, but now that Eisenman will not be there— they don't think Reis has what it takes to last—*maybe* in 3–4 months the *top* job will be open.

One other dumb thing because I am dull today tonight—too nervous—

I always loved that phrase of DHL's (not I but the wind)—I picked it up from his letters and when Frieda used it for the title I thought how sensitively it showed her genuine relation to him and some dumb woman I knew, an editor at Vogue, said "The book is all right, but that's a dumb title, isn't it"!

Oh Charles I think life is very hard for each of us (I have had nothing to eat yet—I am going to see if I place this in front of the PO building I am going to pray you get it tomorrow.)

I hate to say goodbye—I so *long* to be in a room near you—I am afraid you will not come and then I will not know alone before God what I *should* do.

Frances

❦ 323 ❧

Washington to Brooklyn (special delivery)
2 September 1950 (postmark)

saturday

baby, baby, thank you, darling, for your beautiful letter—you call it not good, but it is a rich and so wonderfully true, the whole business, all you say   i know, i know, that is why i suppose the agony is so hard, that i know how miserable things are there too   but o, sweet, how raised up your long letter, and your two on Rimbaud make me!

And you will know from my letter yesterday, that i do not charge you, thing / do not / do comprehend   (only, what was the "committed" quote you refer to?: my mind, these days, is so thick i don't have my old remembering!)

> Look: one thing, for what it is worth: this week's Civil Service announcements, I am told, carry a 4800 buck Army librarianship in New York. I imagine such things are horrible—or maybe not; seems to me, in the last war, yes, my friend Morgan, was such, and did a hell of a good thing for the poor joes. Anyhow, it would be just a hold for you, if you were interested. And I thought I'd just pass it on. I imagine the way to find out more, is to call US Army headquarters, or it might be Air Force.

What *was* that letter I wrote you yesterday? I feel all thickened from it, it came out so like "mother" as they used to call the materium in wine. But I have no way of knowing what it was. You must tell me. It seemed to come from my soul, more close to you than ever before. And that felt good, baby, good, to be that close to you. I feel the same today, but I feel as though I said it all yesterday.

> God, how beautiful, when you put it, the whole thing is BELIEF. Isn't it—Belief and courage. Those two. And perfect beauty, as you sd earlier this week, perfect beauty what one's eyes are opened to, after belief and courage have made one able.

And please write me more, and quotes, from Rimbaud. As I have told you, he is mostly unknown to me. I live alongside him, have emotions about him, but don't really know him at all. And I want to most, by way of you.

So, darling, be not upset, darling. Nor by—as you say—if two days go, without a letter. For we are going, have gone, by belief. And we cannot, must not be wrong. So do not worry on that score. There is enough, for both of us, on other scores. But this one: that is OURS.

This is a responding, and not an initiating letter. But I am harassed today on surfaces. But underneath, I am as close to you, as wedded, as yesterday, and all these incredible days.

All my love,
Charles

And do, baby, break the tension of writing. I shall give you all time. And shall wait on your doorstep. So don't bottle yourself up. Let me wait!

❈ 324 ❈

Brooklyn to Washington
3 September 1950 (postmark)

Sunday morning

Charles dear—

A beautiful thing has happened to me and while it will cause you pain—it is part of the reality now between us that you also must share. There came to me straight out of God's hand a beautiful young negro—he saw me—he sat beside (near) me in the subway—he rode to where I got off—he went his way I went mine—I hunted around for a bus station—in the station I saw him—

smiled asked him if he knew where you buy a ticket for Freeport bus—he
didn't—said—"If I had my car here I would drive you"—waited two ½ hours
in the bus station for me to come back—I didn't—so he waited inside a subway station—watched all the cars—saw me—came in and sat down beside
me—and rode home with me—

He has the purest most beautiful soul I think I have ever been in the presence of—and a body to match—and he wants me—I told him all about you—
he wants me and I am drawn—I am going to meet him again—at least that is
the plan—and I want you to know, Charles, that I am very seriously thinking
of him—that we have already been together.

MORNING OF DRUNKENNESS[43]

O my Good! O my beautiful! Atrocious fanfare where I never falter. Rack
of enchantments! Hurrah for the unbelievable work and for the marvelous
body, for the first time! It began in the midst of children's laughter, with their
laughter it will end. This poison will stay in all our veins even when, the fan-
fares shifting, we shall return to the old inharmony. O now let us, who are so
worthy of these tortures! redeem that superhuman promise made to our body
and to our soul created: that promise, that madness!

Elegance, science, violence! They have promised us to bury in darkness the
tree of good and evil, to deport tyrannic respectabilities so that we may bring
hither our very pure love. It began with a certain disgust, and it ends, unable
instantly to grasp this eternity—it ends with a riot of perfumes.

Laughter of children, discretion of slaves, austerity of virgins, loathing of
faces and objects here, holy be all of you in memory of this vigil. It began with
every sort of boorishness, behold, it ends with angels of flame and ice!

Little drunken vigil, holy! if only because of the mask you have bestowed
on us. We pronounce you, method! We shall not forget that yesterday you glo-
rified each one of our ages. We have faith in the poison. We know how to give
our whole life every day.

The time of the Assassins is here.

You are so right, Mr. Rimbaud—whom I love.
A statement of the poet's credo—like Dostoyevsky making Ivan Karamazov
say "But those gravestones are dear to us and we kneel and kiss them—dearly
beloved dead lie buried there and each gravestone tells of a life so passionately
lived even now—even now we kneel and kiss those beloved dead."

Every word from Rimbaud is for you and I am not sure he didn't know by

43. Boldereff wrote out Rimbaud's French alongside the translation, using Louise Varese's edition of
Illuminations (New Directions, 1946), pp. 34–37.

divining those facts of Harrison's—those ancient realities—he speaks over and over of "Her" with a capital letter.

I am the lover of man-created beauty.

Frances

❧ 325 ❧

Brooklyn to Washington
4 September 1950 (postmark)

Labor Day

Charles dear—

I spent the day on that job and now I am home and the job is no longer mine—this was the third try I have had and machinery is just not something I can cope with—what it does to me I cannot describe—outside of saying I am hopelessly no good at it and that it makes me very unhappy. I was embarrassed because Yorke obviously regards me as both silly and dumb—I could read his cynicism in his eyes and in his words—he just doesn't seem to believe I ever really did handle printing production—when I said I never heard the term "bullet" he said very sarcastically—"Evidently you are one of these people who marked up manuscript in a way the printer did all the work—where all the holes were the same and the printer knew what to do without your marking"—other remarks today equally showing he neither believes me nor thinks I am anything but stupid.

Naturally that doesn't concern me—it only makes me temporarily embarrassed.

I might say I have used the words "solid dot" for what he calls "bullet" but when someone is cynical to me all my thoughts fly out the window and I couldn't remember even that.

I am glad it is over—I was so very miserable and of course unless I was very fast the pay wouldn't have been enough to live on.

I have found several things in the paper I am going to try for tomorrow—also I will investigate the library thing you wrote of—I will try the postoffice as they usually give out civil service exams. Anyway I will phone the Army and try to find out *where* to apply.

I will be out very early tomorrow morning and may not get here in time to get a letter off in the mail tomorrow.

I write you stupid facts because it is necessary to me to have someone to tell—you can just throw this away as it isn't a letter but a reason why I can't write one.

I walk around reading Rimbaud aloud—*please* send me here a copy of the first *Bigmans*—mine is in Woodward—I want to read that aloud too.

Suspended in non-existence

Frances

≈ 326 ≈

Washington to Brooklyn (telegram)
5 September 1950

FRANCES BOLDEREFF
    5 MONROE PL
LOOKS LIKE THURSDAY NOW. IF WEDNESDAY WILL WIRE ALL LOVE
    CHARLES

≈ 327 ≈

Washington to Brooklyn (special delivery)
6 September 1950 (postmark)

wednesday

darling:
    This is just to tell you that I *may* have overestimated my recovery. Was ill last night, and have spent most of today in bed. Was going to wire, but thot another wire would be too cryptic. Besides, as we have observed, I am up and down, in my present end of strength. And may be okay tomorrow. Would wait, but cannot bear thought of wiring you disappointment at such late date. So this is just a present report. (got badly thrown off my presence here of black mt characters when I was not well, bugging my house, taking advantage (children) of my hospitality) (and, of course, because i am the fool i am, pouring it out, wild, lacking proportion)
    I shall hope, when I get up tomorrow, that I shall wire you, get on a train, and get there—that I shall be myself enough to do that, that all this flaking shall have fallen off.
    One other thing. If you have written anything to me that you are surprised I have not answered, don't be: You see, I have not even been able to get down town.

darling,
love
charles

≈ 328 ≈

Baltimore to Brooklyn (telegram)
7 September 1950

FRANCES BOLDEREFF
    5 MONROE PL NO PHONE
ARRIVING ELEVEN DAYLIGHT TONIGHT STOP CALL ME HOTEL SHELTON
THERE AFTER LOVE
    CHARLES

Selected Works by Charles Olson

Call Me Ishmael (New York: Reynal & Hitchcock, 1947; London: Cape, 1967).

Y&X (Washington, D.C.: Black Sun Press, 1948).

In Cold Hell, In Thicket (Dorchester, Mass.: Origin, 1953; San Francisco: Four Seasons, 1967).

The Maximus Poems / 1–10 (Stuttgart: Jonathan Williams, 1953).

Mayan Letters, ed. Robert Creeley (Palma de Mallorca: Divers Press, 1953: London: Cape, 1968).

The Maximus Poems/11–22 (Stuttgart: Jonathan Willams, 1956).

O'Ryan 2 4 6 8 10 (San Francisco: White Rabbit, 1958); enlarged edition, *O'Ryan 12345678910* (San Francisco: White Rabbit, 1965).

Projective Verse (New York: Totem Press, 1959).

The Maximus Poems (New York: Jargon/Corinth, 1960; London: Cape Goliard, 1970).

The Distances (New York: Grove; London: Evergreen, 1960).

A Bibliography on America for Ed Dorn (San Francisco: Four Seasons, 1964).

Proprioception (San Francisco: Four Seasons, 1965).

Human Universe and Other Essays, ed. Donald Allen (San Francisco: Auerbahn Society, 1965; New York: Grove, 1967).

Selected Writings, ed. Robert Creeley (New York: New Directions, 1966).

'West' (London: Cape Goliard, 1966).

Maximus Poems IV, V, VI (London: Cape Goliard, 1968; New York: Grossman, 1968).

Pleistocene Man (Buffalo: Institute of Further Studies, 1968).

Letters for Origin, 1950–1956, ed. Albert Glover (London: Cape Goliard, 1968; New York: Cape Goliard/Grossman, 1970).

The Special View of History, ed. Ann Charters (Berkeley: Oyez, 1970).

Archaeologist of Morning (London: Cape Goliard, 1970; New York: Grossman, 1973).

Additional Prose, ed. George F. Butterick (Bolinas, Calif.: Four Seasons, 1974).

The Post Office (Bolinas, Calif.: Grey Fox Press, 1975).

The Maximus Poems: Volume Three, ed. Charles Boer and George F. Butterick (New York: Grossman, 1975).

In Adullam's Lair (Provincetown, Mass.: To the Lighthouse Press, 1975).

Spearmint & Rosemary (Berkeley: Turtle Island, 1975).

Charles Olson and Ezra Pound: An Encounter at St. Elizabeths, ed. Catherine Seelye (New York: Grossman, 1975).

The Horses of the Sea (Santa Barbara: Black Sparrow Press, 1976).

The Fiery Hunt and Other Plays (Bolinas, Calif.: Four Seasons, 1977).

Some Early Poems (Iowa City: Windhover Press, 1978).

Mythologos: The Collected Lectures and Interviews, ed. George F. Butterick (Bolinas, Calif.: Four Seasons, 1978–79).

Charles Olson & Robert Creeley: The Complete Correspondence, ed. George F. Butterick, later Richard Blevins, vols 1–10 (Santa Barbara: Black Sparrow Press, 1980–1996).

The Maximus Poems, ed. George F. Butterick (Berkeley: University of California Press, 1983).

The Collected Poems of Charles Olson Excluding the Maximus Poems, ed. George F. Butterick (Berkeley: University of California Press, 1987).

A Nation of Nothing but Poetry, ed. George F. Butterick (Santa Rosa: Black Sparrow Press, 1989).

In Love, In Sorrow: The Complete Correspondence of Charles Olson and Edward Dahlberg, ed. Paul Christensen (New York: Paragon House, 1990).

Collected Prose, eds. Donald Allen and Benjamin Friedlander (Berkeley: University of California Press, 1997).

Works by Frances Boldereff

Ward, Frances. *A Primer of Morals for Medea* (Woodward, Pa.: Russian Classic Non-Fiction Library, 1949).

Boldereff, Frances. "To Greet You With The New Year." Pamphlet (New York: n.p., 1953).

Boldereff, Frances. *Reading Finnegans Wake* (Woodward, Pa.: Classic Non-Fiction Library, 1959).

Boldereff, Frances. *A Blakean Translation of Joyce's* Circe (Woodward, Pa.: Classic Non-Fiction Library, 1965).

Boldereff, Frances. *Hermes to his Son Thoth: Being Joyce's Use of Giordano Bruno in Finnegans Wake* (Lawrenceville, N.J.: Classic Non-Fiction Library, 1968).

Rose, Thomasine (pseud.). *Verbi-Voco-Visual: The Presence of Bishop Berkeley in Finnegans Wake* (Bellefonte Editeur, 1981).

Phipps, Frances. *Let Me Be Los: Codebook for Finnegans Wake* (Lubbock, Tex.: The Toth-Maatian Press, 1985; paperback edition, Barrytown, N.Y.: Station Hill Press, Inc., produced by the Institute for Publishing Arts, 1987).

Motz, Reighard (pseud.). *Time as Joyce Tells It* (Mifflinburg, Pa.: Mulford Colebrook Publishing Company, n.d.).

Index

Indexed here are literary, political, and historical figures, with some personal friends and relatives of the principals. It is the letters themselves that have been indexed, not enclosures, quotations from other writers, nor editorial matter beyond footnotes (indicated by "n" after the page number).

207, 221, 222, 224, 225, 231, 233, 234, 239, 241, 242, 246, 268n, 299n, 300, 323, 430, 501
Michelangelo 11, 13, 16, 17, 18, 32, 33, 35, 70, 91, 105, 119, 126, 233, 265, 279, 291, 293, 298, 312, 313, 325, 380, 504
Miller, Henry 51
Milton 238, 387
Moore, Frank 405
Moore, Henry 254
Morgan, Murray 538
Morley, Christopher 21
Morris, William 188
Moses 16, 225, 234, 242, 274, 281, 282, 397, 514
Motz, L. M. 58, 454
Mozart 17, 191, 226, 232, 322
Munch, Charles 249
Murray, Henry A. 158, 396

Nabokov 3, 17, 195, 196, 200, 205, 206
Nehru 256
Niebuhr, Reinhold 74
Nietzsche 46, 47, 90, 195, 204, 429
Nijinsky 137, 234

Olson, Charles, works by: "ABCs(2)" 304, 393; "ABCs(3—for Rimbaud) 369n; "About Space" 254, 264n; "Adamo Me . . ." 372n, 377, 380, 398; "The Advantage" 116; "Again, Spring" 383; "Ahab, a Dance" 302; "All My Life I've Heard about Many" 467n; "Asymptotes" 280; "At Yorktown" 252, 262, 267, 289, 292; "Apollonius of Tyana" 455n; "The Babe" 97, 99, 112, 183n; "Bigmans" 341, 346, 392, 394, 398, 490, 494, 528, 542; "Bigmans II" 475, 481, 482, 490; "Bigmans III" 510n; *Call Me Ishmael* 1, 20n, 34, 35, 39, 46, 88, 90n, 104, 109n, 146, 148, 162, 189, 197, 225, 274, 299, 430, 501, 510; "The Cause, The Cause" 399, 400, 405, 413n, 495; "'Cento" 130; "A Condensation" 124; "David Young, David Old" 78, 107, 109, 172, 252, 268; "The Day's Orders, Boys" 126; "De Bono" 403; "Diaries of Death" 302n; "The Dryness, of 'The Tempest'" 63n, 64, 78, 146n, 172; "Dura" 38n; "Epigon" 56, 80, 183n, 312; "Experiment in Form" 304, 393n; "The Fiery Hunt" 5n, 52n, 77; "For Arthur Rimbaud" 369, 386; "Forget Villon?" 261; "The Gate and the Center" 470n; "Gli Amanti" 384, 389; "Gloss" 228n; "go/boy/who/sleeps . . ." 516; "GrandPa, GoodBye" 63n, 137n, 152n, 183n; "The Green Man" 4, 7, 7n, 78, 389; "here i am, naked . . ." 321; "Her head was in my hand . . ." 469; "I, Maximus, of Gloucester, to You" 335n, 338, 344, 394, 395; "In Answer to a Request for Dirge Words" 385; "In Cold Hell, in Thicket" 347n, 352, 358, 359; "In Praise of the Fool" 2n, 3, 4; "In the Hills South of Capernum, Port" 20n, 47n; "It's SPRing AgAIN!" 253n; "The K" 7n, 8, 60, 78, 99; "The Kingfishers" 52, 57,

80, 87, 100, 109, 116, 121, 146, 154, 183n, 185, 186, 224, 245, 387, 394, 410, 419, 487, 507, 528; "La Chute" 37, 40n, 95, 183n, 220, 261, 267, 388, 392, 394, 398, 528; "La Chute II" 42, 49, 63, 73, 183n; "La Chute III" 49; "Lady Mimosa" 270n, 283, 288, 291, 292, 293, 294, 296, 298, 494; "La Préface" 12n, 78, 80, 95, 175, 240, 303; "La Torre" 389; "The Laughing Ones" 61, 70n, 71n, 146n; "Lost Aboard U.S.S. 'Growler'" 263, 267, 289, 292; "Men in an Alley, at Evening, Chinning, or Chewing their Fat" 394; "The Morning News" 213n, 224, 225, 227, 244, 250, 326, 335, 340, 344, 355, 388, 394, 421, 454; "Move Over" 388, 394; "The Mystery of What Happens When It Happens" 137n; "Observation" 124; "Of Lady, of Beauty, of Stream" 240n, 243; "On First Looking Out through Juan de la Cosa's Eyes" 471; "Other Than" 369n; "Otvechai" 71, 80, 183n, 185; "A Po-sy, A Po-sy" 200n, 224, 326, 340, 394; "The Praises" 83, 87, 88, 95, 100n, 101, 104, 105n, 107, 109, 110, 146n, 185, 224, 252n, 268, 394, 419, 518; "The Prayer" 270, 278, 283; "Projective Verse" 149, 154, 163, 172n, 184n, 224, 230, 292, 335, 352, 395, 405, 406, 407; "Quatrain" 359n; "Red, White and Black" 2n; "The Scape-Goat" 260; "Sentence" 383; "A Shadow Two" 398n, 399n, 403n; "The She-Bear" 52, 80, 101, 260, 267, 270, 274, 278, 291n, 312, 317, 319, 320, 340, 355, 394, 395, 397, 398, 410, 421, 494; "Siena" 9, 34n, 418n, 421; "the smoke-shape to be grappled with . . ." 502; "So Gentle" 138; "Spoilers" 224; "The Story of an Olson, and Bad thing" 360n, 367, 380; "Summum Bonum" 128, 131; *Sutter-Marshall Lease* (Introduction) 2n; "These Days" 113; "This Is Yeats Speaking" 63n, 362n; "Tomorrow" 35n, 36; "Trinacria" 7n, 10, 11, 20, 105, 186n, 234, 260n, 251; "Triskele" 260; "Troilus" 5n, 495, 533; "The True Life of Arthur Rimbaud" 241; "Upon a Moebus Strip" 11, 12, 78, 118, 234; "A Visitation" 236, 241, 244, 258; "What Goes, or, Nursery Time" 190; *Y & X* 4, 5, 7, 10n, 11n, 12n, 60n, 78n, 95, 148n, 175, 209, 230, 233, 287, 296, 303n, 335, 366, 389, 394, 396, 472
Olson, Connie 61, 70, 71n, 86, 93, 95, 99, 137, 151, 157, 160, 168, 169, 181, 185, 185, 208, 221, 279, 293, 295, 301, 308, 311, 322n, 327, 329, 330, 332, 333, 340, 346, 452, 485, 519
Ortega y Gasset 189

Payne, Robert 132, 154n, 322, 323, 343, 377
Pericles 80, 248, 496
Philips, Duncan 49
Picasso 289, 477
Pico della Mirandola 356
Plato 27, 70, 242, 256
Poe, Edgar Allen 258, 293, 387
Porada, Edith 424n, 433, 438, 439n, 458

UNIVERSITY PRESS OF NEW ENGLAND publishes books under its own imprint and is the publisher for Brandeis University Press, Dartmouth College, Middlebury College Press, University of New Hampshire, Tufts University, and Wesleyan University Press.

About the Editors

Ralph Maud is Professor Emeritus of English at Simon Fraser University in Burnaby, British Columbia. He is the author of numerous books, including *Charles Olson's Reading: A Biography* (Southern Illinois University Press, 1996); *A Guide to B.C. Indian Myth and Legend: A Short History of Myth-Collecting and a Survey of Published Texts* (Talonbooks, 1992); and *Dylan Thomas in Print, a Bibliographical History* (University of Pittsburgh Press, 1970). He also has edited *On the Air With Dylan Thomas: The Broadcasts* (New Directions, 1992) and *The Notebooks of Dylan Thomas* (New Directions, 1967). His latest book is *What Does Not Change: The Significance of Charles Olson's "The Kingfishers"* (Fairleigh Dickinson University Press, 1998).

Sharon Thesen teaches in the English Department at Capilano College in North Vancouver, British Columbia. She has published several volumes of poetry, including *Aurora* (Coach House Press, 1993), *The Pangs of Sunday* (McClelland and Stewart, 1989), *The Beginning of the Long Dash* (Coach House Press, 1987), and *Confabulations: Poems for Malcolm Lowry* (Oolichan Books, 1983). She also has edited *The New Long Poem Anthology* (Coach House Press, 1991).

Library of Congress Cataloging-in-Publication Data

Olson, Charles, 1910–1970
    [Correspondence]
    Charles Olson and Frances Boldereff: a modern correspondence / edited by Ralph Maud and Sharon Thesen ; and with an introduction by Sharon Thesen.
        p.   cm.
    ISBN 0–8195–6363–3 (cl : alk. paper). - ISBN 0–8195–6364–1 (pb : alk. paper).
      I. Olson, Charles, 1910–1970—Correspondence. 2. Boldereff, Frances M. (Frances Motz), 1905—Correspondence. 3. Olson, Charles, 1910–1970—Relations with women. 4. Poets, American—20th century—Correspondence. 5. Women critics—United States—Correspondence. 6. Love-letters. I. Boldereff, Frances M. (Frances Motz), 1905– II. Maud, Ralph. III. Thesen, Sharon, 1946– . IV. Title.
PS3529.L655Z4834   1999
811'.54-dc21

98-41954